CONTINUING WITH RUSSIAN

CONTINUING WITH RUSSIAN

Charles E. Townsend

Slavica

For a complete list of books from Slavica, with prices and ordering information, write to:
Slavica Publishers, Inc.
P.O. Box 14388
Columbus, Ohio 43214

ISBN: 0-89357-085-0.

This book was originally published in 1970 by McGraw-Hill Book Company. Copyright was transferred to Charles E. Townsend in 1980. This reprint, with some corrections, was published in 1981.

Printed in the United States of America.

To the Fukushimas

PREFACE

Continuing with Russian is an intermediate-advanced textbook for students who have been through a full-sized elementary text and have been exposed to the more basic morphological patterns and a first-year vocabulary. In addition, the quantity and range of grammatical information contained in its twenty-five lessons, the comprehensive Russian and English word references in the General Vocabulary, and the Index should make it an excellent reference book during and long after any Russian course in which it is used.

The book is basically designed for college courses and probably would not be appropriate for most high school courses below the third-year level. Because of the thorough and often quite detailed treatment of difficult and complex grammatical points, ranging from what amount to rather comprehensive essays on modal expressions (Lesson IX) and ся verbs (Lesson X) to a host of smaller grammatical and lexical questions through both the Review and regular Lessons, *Continuing with Russian* should be very useful also for graduate students in Slavic languages and literatures. The author has found that a great many graduate students are unfamiliar with much of the grammatical information in the book, simply because they never studied any grammar overtly after the first-year level and learned the rest of their Russian by sheer exposure to the language. This is not necessarily bad in itself, of course, but it does frequently mean that such students have never made explicit in their minds much of the grammatical and lexical information which most of them will someday have to impart to their students.

The book consists of four parts: I. Introduction and Guide to the Use of the Vocabularies; II. Reviews 1 to 10; III. Lessons I to X (new grammar); and IV. Conversation Lessons 1 to 5. Following these are a short appendix on the Oblique Cases of the Cardinal Numerals and the Collective Numerals; a Root List;[1] and the General Vocabulary. The book is accompanied by a set of tapes for Parts II, III, and IV, which include the lesson texts from all fifteen of the lessons in Parts III and IV and provide for Parts II and III some additional pattern sentences and drills for certain important grammatical points in the lessons. Also provided is an *Instructor's Manual*, which offers some suggestions for how to work with the various exercises in the text and some general recommendations about ordering and assignment of material. The *Manual* also contains a key to all English-to-Russian translation exercises in the book and, for the tapes referred to above, reproduces all pattern sentences, instructions, and drill questions; it also provides answers to the drill questions.

Though the book does contain five separate Conversation Lessons, and though most or all of the ten regular Lessons are appropriate for oral use (several are, or include, dialogues), the main emphasis in *Continuing with Russian* is unquestionably on grammar and word study, and the book is outspokenly "traditional" in the sense that it makes liberal use of both Russian-to-English and English-to-Russian translation exercises. No apology is made either for translation or for the general principle of contrastive analysis, the extensive comparison of Russian with English, both of which the author considers indispensable for the effective teaching of Russian to native speakers of English. A child with unlimited time and constant exposure to a language may learn to speak it natively, but an intelligent, busy college student is not a child learning his mother tongue. A successful system must see to it that his analytical and analogical abilities are made to compensate for the time he does not have and the imitative skills he often lacks. It is frequently asserted that learning a foreign language makes a student more aware of his native tongue; it is less often mentioned that his heightened perceptiveness and appreciation of comparisons with English in turn enable him to apprehend better the grammar and words of the language he is studying.

The most unique feature of the book is the linguistic approach to word

---

[1] The Root List is reprinted from my *Russian Word-Formation*, New York, 1968.

structure and the explicit attention paid to vocabulary learning, which is the key problem after the first year. The Introduction and Guide to the Use of the Vocabularies introduces the student to the basic concepts necessary to an understanding of word structure and to the proper handling of new vocabulary. Although word-formation is almost uniformly neglected in the teaching of Russian, there are few languages in which the study of roots, prefixes, and suffixes is as important. Our experience has shown that the analysis of words into their meaningful parts is a key to efficient vocabulary learning and retention. And vocabulary assimilation is perhaps the most crucial process at the intermediate and advanced stage of learning a language like Russian whose vocabulary, unlike that of, for instance, French, does not become more familiar as the level advances. Perhaps the most frequent complaint voiced by students going on in Russian concerns the almost insuperable task of learning vast numbers of words *ad hoc*. But if a student learns how a word is built, he is less likely to forget it and have to look it up many times. The general emphasis in both word structure and vocabulary learning is on mastery of generalizations which free the student from the necessity of learning long lists.

The *Instructor's Manual* goes into some detail on how best to handle and learn the material in Part I. Even if little or no attention is paid to the comments on word structure, the Introduction and Guide to the Use of the Vocabularies should be gone through at some point so that maximally effective use may be made of the vocabularies. The abbreviations and other conventions should present few difficulties and will eventually make vocabulary learning and retention much easier. The only feature which may strike the student as very new is the listing of verb entries according to the one-stem system, which means that the *third plural present* form, rather than the infinitive, is given in the entry if the basic stem ends in a consonant (**провёдут** instead of **провести**; **знают** (**знай-ут**) instead of **знать**); if the basic stem ends in a vowel, the infinitive is given in the entry (**говорить, крикнуть**). The essentials of the one-stem system, and information which is more than sufficient for an understanding of how to use the vocabularies, are given on pages 28–38; the system is elaborated in much greater detail in my *Russian Word-Formation*, pages 81–97.

The Review lessons cover quite thoroughly and actively all aspects of elementary Russian. Though they do give the student time to consolidate what he has learned (or to relearn what he has forgotten during the summer), these lessons are not mere repetition, for they contain new information and, often, somewhat different or more complete statements of points to which the student was exposed only partially in the first year. Review 1 treats pronunciation, Review 2 verbal aspect. Reviews 3 to 10 constitute a topical review; in each lesson several major questions are treated first, followed by English-to-Russian translation drills and numerous "notes" to these drills which make additional, but important, grammatical points. The drills are composed of intentionally trivial little "stories," so that emphasis can be on grammar with a context present. The sentences are very compact, full of trouble spots, and the intense effort needed to write them correctly usually results in a thorough review. Glossaries of appropriate grammatical terms are included at the end of Review lessons 1 to 9, and the General Vocabulary contains most of the common grammatical and linguistic terms used in the book as well.

In Lessons I to X, lengthy sections with much new grammar and copious exercises, a great effort has been made to review grammar and vocabulary from the preceding lessons as well as from the lesson at hand. Each lesson is introduced by a Russian text, which is a prose passage or dialogue exemplifying, as far as is possible, the grammatical points treated in the lessons. The texts are very diverse in nature and include various dialogues, passages from literature, propaganda brochures, Russian history, scientific Russian, and other types of writing. The lesson texts are followed by the grammar. Lessons I and II consist of a number of relatively short, numbered sections; Lessons III to X treat a single major question in detail; there then follow a number of unrelated, separate, numbered sections called Subordinate Points.[1] Though the lesson texts do not contain examples of all the grammatical points in a lesson, the numerous Russian sentences directly following the grammar have been carefully chosen or written to drill all grammatical points and the vocabulary; in the latter case, frequently, the varying meanings of a given word, or perhaps a verb and the deverbative noun therefrom. These sentences are in no particular order and, though many are conversational in tone, there is no pretense of their constituting an oral drill; it is up to an imaginative instructor to do what he likes with them. They should be translated, if only orally. The English-to-Russian sentences should be *written* out as homework and corrected, preferably on the blackboard as well as on the papers. The English sentences occasionally sound a bit stiff or contrived, because they are designed to be translated quite literally, to elicit as correct Russian as possible.

Section 7 of Lesson II and the Subordinate Points in Lessons V, VIII, and X include discussions of the various Russian renditions of the English verbs "learn/teach," "stop," "use," and "try" respectively. Though these verbs are important in themselves, the point to be made is more general: that the student must get used to thinking carefully and, quite probably, using the vocabularies

---

[1] In the introductory Russian texts, superior numbers following boldface words (e.g. ме́сто[6]) refer in Lessons I and II to the numbered sections; in Lessons III to X they refer to the Subordinate Points which follow the main topics. Grammatical points are cross-referenced also in both the General Vocabulary and the individual lesson vocabularies. For an explanation of the reference system, see pp. xi–xii.

before selecting a Russian translation of even the simplest-seeming English words.[1]

Both Russian-to-English and English-to-Russian exercises are provided only for Lessons I to VIII, Lessons IX and X having only Russian-to-English exercises. Lessons IX and X have their own separate vocabularies, but the words in them are not included in the General Vocabulary which does, however, contain all words from all other lessons (Lessons I to VIII and Conversation Lessons 1 to 5). All ten Lessons, and Conversation Lessons 1 to 5 as well, are provided with separate vocabularies. In Lessons VI to X, a number of the less common words are grouped separately under the heading СЛОВА ТОЛЬ-КО К ЭТОМУ УРОКУ, but this division may be ignored if the instructor sees fit.

Conversation Lessons 1 to 5 are shorter lessons with much less grammar than the regular lessons and no exercises in the book (the tapes for these lessons include some oral drills). Conversation Lessons 3 to 5 comprise a little playlet entitled «Я хочу́ уви́деть Кра́сную пло́щадь.» The Conversation Lessons are independent of both the Reviews and the regular Lessons; they may be used in any order, at any time, or not at all.

The General Vocabulary contains both Russian-to-English and English-to-Russian sections. Every effort has been made to make the entries coincide, though there will inevitably be exceptions. The Russian-to-English vocabulary includes also all Russian words which are discussed in the grammar sections (e.g. ме́жду те́м, вообще́), and the English-to-Russian vocabulary also contains many references from English words to grammar sections. Hence the General Vocabulary also serves as a word index. The Index, then, has but few Russian words and almost no English vocabulary items and becomes, for practical purposes, a subject index. The student should note that in all vocabularies monosyllabic words which are stressed when pronounced carry the stress mark (except for certain verbal basic forms where the absence of a stress mark is a convention signaling shifting stress (see page 36)).

Both the General Vocabulary and the individual lesson vocabularies include references to grammatical points. Roman numerals denote Lessons, and numbers suffixed to them (e.g. IX.4) refer to the numbered sections of Lessons I and II, which make up all the grammar in those lessons, and to the Subordinate Points of Lessons III to X. References with capital letters (e.g. IX.A5) are to subdivisions of the major grammatical topics in those of Lessons III to X which have lettered subdivisions. Unsuffixed references (e.g. IV) are to a lesson proper

---

[1] Particularly helpful in constructing these sections were the materials and suggestions of O. P. Rassudova, I. P. Slesareva, and G. A. Bitextina of the Kafedra russkogo jazyka dlja inostrancev at Moscow State University.

or, in a few cases involving Lessons I to VIII, to the major grammatical topic (this type of reference will usually be clear from the "grammatical" nature of the word or element; e.g. то́, что́ IV). References to grammatical points and notes in Reviews and Conversation Lessons, which are identified as "R" and "CL," are similarly made (e.g. R5.A9, R7 note 2, CL3).

The example sentences in both grammar presentations and the Russian-to-English exercises come from a wide variety of sources. Many come from Soviet dictionaries; especially, A. I. Smirnickij, *Russko-anglijskij slovar'*, Moscow, 1965, and the four-volume Academy Dictionary, *Slovar' russkogo jazyka*, 1957–1961. A few examples were borrowed, some in slightly changed form, from F. M. Borras and R. F. Christian, *Russian Syntax*, Oxford, 1959; and M. Karpovich, *A Lecture on Russian History*, ed. H. G. Lunt, 's Gravenhage, 1959. Some of the aspectual examples in Review 2 were provided by Norman Ingham of Harvard University and some, originally, by Roman Jakobson of the Massachusetts Institute of Technology. A number of examples and sentences were provided by Horace G. Lunt. A fairly large number of examples and sentences I wrote myself. Especially these sentences, but all sentences in general were checked several times by various native speakers of Russian, including persons in the Soviet Union. While experience has taught that it would be unrealistic to expect that all of such a motley array of Russian sentences will please all native speakers, the author stands behind the correctness of the Russian in the book and, especially, its appropriateness for teaching.

The user will note that some of the passages taken from Soviet sources and a few Russian-to-English and English-to-Russian sentences are of a "political" nature. Soviet prose and expression, even in quite innocuous contexts, is often pervaded by a political and didactic tone, and a student learning modern Russian should be exposed to examples of it. It should hardly be necessary to state that pedagogical considerations alone have governed selection of examples and texts.

ACKNOWLEDGMENTS

The list of people who have contributed to this book is so long that a detailed recording of my thanks to everyone is impossible. By far my largest debt of gratitude is due Horace G. Lunt of Harvard University, whose materials, published in a mimeographed *Second Russian Course*, Cambridge, 1962, provided the initial impetus for this grammar, and a great number of whose formulations have been used, particularly in Lessons I to IX and the Appendix. The simple format for the translation exercises and the idea of using large numbers of Russian sentences for exemplification were also suggested by his materials.

Numerous people have struggled bravely with earlier versions of *Continuing with Russian* while teaching with it at Harvard and a large number of other institutions. Suggestions from Charles Gribble, Michael Shapiro, Robert Rothstein, David Hanson, Hugh Olmsted, John Kolsti, Maurice Levin, Ronald Harrington, Dennis MacLeay, James Bailey, and Peter Fischer among others have been helpful. Mrs. Catherine Chvany not only offered many helpful suggestions but worked on the first edition of the Key to the English-to-Russian exercises in the *Instructor's Manual*.

To Charles Gribble of Indiana University I owe a special debt of gratitude for much help, advice, and moral support over the years. I also wish to express my apologies to him for having inadvertently neglected to mention among my acknowledgments in *Russian Word-Formation* the original dependence of my Root List on an excellent basic list which he compiled some years ago.

Of the numerous Russians who checked the language of the texts and example sentences, I would like to thank Igor Berukshtis, recently of Moscow, and the various members of the Kafedra russkogo jazyka dlja inostrancev of Moscow State University who assisted me, as well as Jurij Maslov of Leningrad University, who made some comments on the aspectual examples. I gratefully acknowledge the help of the Clark Fund of Harvard University, whose grants helped make possible trips to the Soviet Union in 1963 and 1965 for discussions with various Soviet specialists about certain details of modern Russian.

Mr. Dmitry Emelianoff of Boston, Massachusetts, helped me write certain dialogues and prose sections and is mainly responsible for Conversation Lessons 1 and 2.

Many people here at Princeton offered helpful advice and support during the latter stages of the book's preparation. Richard Burgi has helped with substantive suggestions and in innumerable other ways. Mrs. Sophie Bargman and Ronald Feldstein noted certain inconsistencies and misprints. Wayne Wilson and Peter Van Wagenen performed yeoman service as typists, and Mr. Wilson contributed a great deal toward making the individual and general vocabularies more consistent.

Very special thanks are due my colleague and friend, Mrs. Veronica Dolenko of Princeton University. Her general suggestions and encouragement have been a constant boon, and her vigilance and rigor have caught innumerable inaccuracies and mistakes in the Russian. In addition to supervising the making of the tapes for the book and contributing her own voice and writing the exercises for the tapes, she checked the Russian in the Key to the English-to-Russian exercises in the *Instructor's Manual*.

Many Russian teachers and Slavists owe a great deal to Alexander Lipson of Cambridge, Massachusetts, and the Harvard Graduate School of Education, but I am particularly in his debt. His suggestions, his invariably constructive criticism, and his example have been a great help throughout the years. His specific contributions to this book and all of my work are simply too many to list.

To my wife Janet go my thanks for typing the Index, for much moral support during the years of the preparation of the book, and for never wondering out loud when it was finally going to come out.

Lastly, my warmest appreciation goes to all of the hundreds of students at Harvard, Princeton, and many other institutions who have endeavored to continue their study of Russian through the use of badly organized, badly proofread, and sometimes illegible earlier versions of this book. The present edition is too late to help most of them, but their forbearance is appreciated, and their suggestions and advice have also contributed toward making *Continuing with Russian* what I hope will be a better book.

CHARLES E. TOWNSEND
Princeton, N. J.

CONTENTS

I

INTRODUCTION AND GUIDE TO THE USE OF THE VOCABULARIES

The treatment of vocabulary in general is regarded as one of the most important parts of this book and should play a key role in any course in which the book is used. The information we give here is intended specifically to teach the student to use the entries efficiently, to gain the maximum amount of grammatical and derivational information from them while memorizing as few forms as possible. Its more general purpose is to make the student receptive to the derivational makeup of Russian words, to inculcate upon him reactions which will make understanding of words and retention of vocabulary easier. For both these purposes it is necessary that the student learn a few fundamental things about Russian sounds and about the structure of Russian words. We will present this general information first and then proceed to the specific conventions which will govern the handling of the vocabularies.

1

RUSSIAN SOUNDS AND WORDS

A. SOUNDS AND SPELLING

1. The basic sounds of Russian

In this book Russian basic sounds and words or parts of words transcribed into basic sounds are represented by Latin letters in italics (rather than enclosed in slashes, as is customary in phonemic and morphophonemic transcription). Phonetic transcription of Russian sounds and words is in Latin letters enclosed in brackets. For example, "**вода** 'water' begins with basic sound *v* and its transcription in basic sounds is *voda*. The phonetic transcription is [vadá]." [1]

BASIC SOUNDS or MORPHOPHONEMES (or MORPHONEMES) are distinctive sounds which can independently distinguish meaning and are nonpredictable in terms of their environment. (Phonemes are similar to morphophonemes, except that they are more predictable in terms of environment and give less information about the morphology of Russian than morphophonemes; hence we work with morphophonemes.) Basic sounds are divided into:

VOWELS Virtually no obstruction in mouth; different vowels result from differences in tongue position. Russian has five basic vowel

AND sounds: *a, e, o, u, i*.

CONSONANTS Various degrees of obstruction in mouth. There is a further division based on degree of obstruction:

---

[1] Phonetics, as opposed to phonemics or morphophonemics, is concerned with the pronunciation of sounds, without respect to whether or not they are distinctive. Many more examples of phonetic transcription are found in Review 1, which is devoted to pronunciation.

RESONANTS   Not much obstruction of air stream. The Russian resonants are: r, r',[1] l, l', n, n', m, m', j; v and v' have resonantal qualities and act as resonants in derivation. Resonants are also distinguished by their lack of voiced-voiceless opposition; they are always voiced in Russian. (Note that v and v' once again play an intermediate role: they are opposed to voiceless f and f', but differ from obstruents in that consonants preceding them may be dis-

AND   tinguished as to voiced-voiceless.)

OBSTRUENTS   Quite a bit of obstruction of air stream. But unlike resonants, obstruents may be, and most of them are, opposed as to voiced-voiceless (see VOICED-VOICELESS on page 5). Obstruents are further divided on the basis of type of obstruction: stop (t), fricative (s), and affricate (c), but the division is not useful grammatically and may be disregarded.

Russian consonants are divided, according to their place of articulation, into:

LABIALS   Both lips, or lower lip and upper teeth:
Obstruents: b, b', p, p', f, f'
Resonants: v, v', m, m'

DENTALS   Tip of tongue touching or near upper front teeth:
Obstruents: d, d', t, t', z, z', s, s', c
Resonants: n, n', l, l', r, r'

PALATALS   Tongue touching or near middle of the roof of the mouth (hard palate):
Obstruents: ž, š, č, šč
Resonant: j

Note that it is important not to confuse palatal consonants with palatalized consonants. The former have a single, palatal articulation; the latter have a primary nonpalatal and a secondary palatal articulation. (Cf. below under HARD-SOFT and PAIRED-UNPAIRED.)

The obstruent palatals (ž, š, č, šč) are often grouped together and called HUSHINGS (шипящие). Hushings are important in grammar and word-formation, because they frequently (and, historically, almost always) imply mutation from a nonhushing consonant.

---

[1] An apostrophe symbolizes that a consonant is palatalized.

VELARS   Back of the tongue touching or near the soft palate (the soft area behind the hard palate):

Obstruents: *g*, (*g'*), *k*, *k'*, *x*, (*x'*)

Velars act together in conjugation and, particularly, in derivation.

The articulations described are approximate, and the student does not need to memorize them, but they may help him "feel" what the consonants are like and remember more easily which belong to which groups.

HARD-SOFT and PAIRED-UNPAIRED

By a *hard* consonant we mean a nonpalatalized (nonpalatal) consonant (e.g. *t*) or a hard palatal consonant (e.g. *š*); by a *soft* consonant we mean a palatalized consonant (e.g. *t'*) or a soft palatal consonant (e.g. *č*). The terms "palatalized" and "nonpalatalized" may thus be replaced by "soft" and "hard," as long as we keep in mind the distinction between palatalized and palatal consonants (explained under PALATALS on page 4).

All Russian consonants are either hard or soft and, in addition, all are either *paired* or *unpaired* with respect to hardness-softness. For example, *p* and *m'* are paired, because *p'* and *m* are opposed to them; *č* is unpaired, because it is not opposed to anything; it is simply soft, and there is no hard *č*. All Russian consonants are paired except the five palatals and *c*. Of these unpaired consonants, *ž*, *š*, and *c* are *hard*; *č*, *šč*, and *j* are soft. The velar consonants *g* (*g'*) and *x* (*x'*) are not opposed phonemically, but may be regarded as paired.

VOICED-VOICELESS

The opposition of *voiced* consonants and *voiceless* consonants is extremely important in Russian phonetics. Put your fingers in your ears and hiss both *z* and *s*. When you hiss *z*, you will hear a hiss plus a hum or buzzing; when you hiss *s*, you will hear just a hiss. The only difference between *z* and *s* is that *z* is

VOICED: Vibration of vocal cords accompanies the stream of air and whatever happens to the stream of air,

while *s* is

VOICELESS: No such vibration occurs.

We noted above that resonants lack the voiced-voiceless opposition, and we cited the intermediate position of *v* and *v'* (see under RESONANTS). All Russian obstruents are opposed (or paired) voiced-voiceless except *c*, *č*, *šč*, and *x*, which are voiceless and have no voiced counterparts as basic sounds. True, voiced counterparts do occur as predictable variants in the rare cases (usually at word boundaries) where these consonants occur before voiced consonants, and assimilation takes place: **жечь бы, отец бы**, phonetically [žędžby, at'édzby].[1]

TABLE OF RUSSIAN BASIC SOUNDS AND THEIR SPELLINGS

PAIRED BASIC CONSONANTS

d	t	z	s	b	p	v	f
д	т	з	с	б	п	в	ф
d'	t'	z'	s'	b'	p'	v'	f'

l	r	m	n	g	k	x
л	р	м	н	г	к	х
l'	r'	m'	n'	$(g')^2$	k'	$(x')^2$

UNPAIRED BASIC CONSONANTS

HARD: $ž$ ж $š$ ш c ц

SOFT: $č$ ч $šč$ щ

    j й before a consonant or in final position

    я е ё ю и when not directly preceded by a consonantal letter

BASIC VOWELS

а	э	о		у	ы	After hard paired consonants
a	e	o		u	i	
я	е	ё – е		ю	и	After soft paired consonants and j
	а	е	о – ё – е	у	и	After $ž$ $š$ $č$ $šč$[3]
	a	e	o		u	i	
	а	е	о – е	у	ы – и	After c[3]

A note on ъ and ь

    ъ occurs after prefixes ending in a consonant before roots beginning with *jot*: *ob-jom* **объём** and in a few foreign words: *adjutant* **адъютант**.

    ь indicates softness of preceding *paired* consonants: *dat'* **дать** but says nothing about the hardness or softness of a preceding unpaired consonant, since these are defined as hard or soft:

---

[1] We shall use [y] to designate the phonetic variant of *i* after hard consonants.

[2] *g'* and *x'* are not independent basic sounds but predictable variants of *g* and *x* before the front vowels *i* and *e*.

[3] The details of the spelling of vowels after unpaired consonants are not being considered here.

lož ложь   *noč* ночь

A **ь** after a final hushing of a noun does, however, mark the noun as a third declension feminine (a noun ending in a hushing without a **ь** is a first declension masculine). Final **-ь** also acts as a grammatical marker in verbs in:

second singular present	*-š*	-шь	зна́ешь
infinitive	*-č*	-чь	помо́чь
imperative in hushing	*-ž*	-жь	ре́жь (< ре́зать)

2. Advantages of the Russian spelling system for word analysis

The Russian spelling system lends itself excellently to word-formation analysis, because it preserves the *basic sounds* of a word at the expense of giving more exact information about pronunciation of phonetic variants. Let us take an example. The spelling of the Russian word for 'water' is **вода́**. The pronunciation is [vadá]. The accusative singular of the word is **во́ду**; the pronunciation is [vódu]. The genitive plural is **вод**, the pronunciation [vót]. The phonetic spellings *вада́ and *вот would destroy the visual apprehension of the root **ВОД** 'water.' The analyst would not know whether the basic root was **ВОД** or **ВАД** in the first case, or **ВОД** or **ВОТ** in the second. The Russian spelling system prefers to give the root and ask one to learn how unstressed *o* is pronounced and that a voiced *d* becomes a voiceless [t] in final position.

The importance of the visual preservation of basic sounds is obvious in word-formation. For example, if the derivatives

во́дный	water	водоро́д	hydrogen
водяно́й	water (adj)	во́дка	vodka

were spelled phonetically, only the first word would preserve the root: [vódnyj, vəd'inój, vədarót, vótkə].[1] The advantage of visual preservation of prefixes and suffixes becomes obvious if we observe the variety of phonetic variants of a given prefix or suffix:

PREFIX *pod* (**под**)

по́днят	[pód-]	по́дпись	[pót-]
подня́ть	[pad-]	подпи́шут	[pat-]
поднимý	[pəd-]	подписа́ть	[pət-]

SUFFIX *ov* (**ов – ев**)

плодо́вый	[-óv-]	нулево́й	[-iv-]
носово́й	[-av-]	лицево́й	[-yv-]
со́довый	[-əv-]		

---

[1] See p. 50, footnote 2 for an explanation of [ə].

When one learns the Russian alphabet and how to read Russian words, one encounters certain problems in the relation between Russian letters and the sounds they represent. Not all these problems are satisfactorily solved or confronted in basic courses. Let us reexamine some points which are particularly important in analysis of words.

3. Spelling of basic vowel sounds after consonants

There are five basic vowel sounds in Russian and two symbols for each vowel. The vowel *letter* chosen depends on the preceding consonant; in the case of *paired* consonants, on whether it is hard or soft:

HARD: *ta* та   *te* тэ   *to* то   *tu* ту   *ti* ты
SOFT: *t'a* тя   *t'e* те   *t'o* тё   *t'u* тю   *t'i* ти

or, in the case of unpaired consonants (ж, ш, ч, щ, ц, й), upon spelling rules already known; for example,

after ш only и, never ы   after ч only а, never я

Let us give some examples in inflection:

MASC/NEU GEN SG OF NOUNS: -*a*		DAT PL OF ADJECTIVES: -*im*	
stul-a	стула	*star-im*	старым
učiteľ'-a	учителя	*s'in'-im*	синим
muž-a	мужа	*xoroš-im*	хорошим
muz'ej-a	музея	*tr'et'j-im*	третьим

PRES I SG OF VERBS: -*u*		MASC/NEU DAT SG OF ADJECTIVES: -*omu*	
klad-u	кладу	*star-omu*	старому
govor'-u	говорю	*s'in'-omu*	синему
sproš-u	спрошу	*xoroš-omu*	хорошему
čitaj-u	читаю	*tr'et'j-omu*	третьему

One can easily see that the endings are the same; it is simply a matter of which letters are used after the preceding consonants. The same principle holds for the derivational suffixes. For example:

ADJECTIVAL SUFFIX -*ov*-

gaz-ov-oj[1]	газовый	adj from газ 'gas'
pol'-ov-oj	полевой	adj from поле 'field'
boj-ov-oj	боевой	adj from бой 'battle'

---

[1] The masculine nominative singular adjectival ending in basic sounds is -*oj*, but the spelling is -ый or -ий outside of stress.

IMPERFECTIVIZING SUFFIX *-aj-*

*pomog-**aj**-ut*	помога́ют	help (impf)
*povtor'-**aj**-ut*	повторя́ют	repeat (impf)
*vstreč-**aj**-ut*	встреча́ют	meet (impf)

IMPERFECTIVIZING SUFFIX *-ivaj-*

*zap'is-**ivaj**-ut*	запи́сывают	write down (impf)
*ocen'-**ivaj**-ut*	оце́нивают	evaluate (impf)
*spraš-**ivaj**-ut*	спра́шивают	ask (impf)

With one or two exceptions, we shall use the Russian alphabet for both suffixes and endings. But one should be prepared for the vowel spelling variant not given, if the requirements of spelling so dictate. Thus, for the adjectival suffix just listed we give **-ов-**, rather than **-ов- (-ев-)**, and expect one to recognize that the suffix will be spelled **ев** after the appropriate consonants. Or, to give another example, we give the adjectival suffix *-an-* as **-ян-**, because paired consonants occur soft before it, but if a final root consonant is a hushing (**ж, ш, ч, щ**), the suffix is spelled **-ан-**:

	вода́	water	водяно́й
	нефть	oil	нефтяно́й
	серебро́	silver	сере́бряный
but			
	ко́жа	leather	ко́жаный

4. The spelling of the basic vowel *o*

The basic vowel *o* is spelled **o** after hard paired consonants and after hushings in stressed position in grammatical endings in declension and in some stems. Elsewhere, it is spelled **e**. We already know that a spelled **e** in unstressed position may emerge as **ё** when it receives the stress. In word analysis it is both useful and correct to regard the **e** as having represented a basic *o* in the first place. For example, весна́ has a basic *o*, since the stress shift in the plural gives вёсны. Стена́, on the other hand, has a basic *e* since the stem-stressed nominative plural accusative singular gives сте́ны – сте́ну. Such an **e** which represents a basic *o* may be marked **ĕ** (вĕсна́, нĕсу́т), the actual stressed **ё** being marked by the usual diaeresis (вёсны, нёс).

In relatively rare instances, a stressed *o* may alternate with a stressed *e* in the same root or, very rarely, in the same paradigm:

жĕна́ – жёны but же́нский   вĕду́т – вёл but ве́дший

We may apply the same principle to inflection and derivation. In the examples on page 8, **-ему** could be written **-ёму** and **-ев-** written **-ĕв-**, for we are dealing with a basic *o* in both cases. Note the following inflectional and derivational positions involving a basic *o*.

Neu nom/acc sg of nouns	*-o*	ме́сто по́лё решёниё
Masc/neu inst sg of nouns	*-om*	столо́м ножо́м учи́телём словарём геро́ём
Pres 1 pl of verbs	*-om*	ста́нём берём де́лаём встаём
Masc/neu prep sg of adj	*-om*	ста́ром хоро́шём большо́м
Past pass part	*-on*	встре́чён переведён сбережён
Verbal suffix	*-ova-*	интересова́ть горёва́ть воёва́ть
Adjectival suffix	*-ovat-*	молодова́тый синёва́тый
Mobile vowel	*-o-*	кусо́к дружо́к конёк челове́чёк

From now on we shall use ё when we want to call attention to a basic *o* in a root, formant, or ending. In the Root List at the back of the book roots which ever occur with a stressed ё are marked Ё; for example, **НЁС, ЖЁН.**

EXERCISE Locate basic *o* in the following words and clarify each case:

звезда́	мо́ре	подстри́жен
стекло́	зна́ешь	переночева́ть
привезу́т	музе́ем	кусо́чек

5. The consonant *j* (*jot*)

The spelling of the unpaired soft consonant *jot* is complicated by the fact that it is not always represented by the same or by a single symbol. Before a consonant or in final position it is spelled **й**; for example:

strójka стро́йка   *Bobrújsk* Бобру́йск   *stroj* стро́й   *saraj* сара́й

Before a vowel it is rendered by the same vowel letter which follows soft paired consonants:

(е)
я е ё ю и

for example:

jasno	я́сно	*muz'eji*	музе́и	*objezd*	объе́зд
jexat'	е́хать	*znaju*	зна́ю	*podjom*	подъём
jož	ёж	*brat'ja*	бра́тья	*izjan*	изъя́н
jug	юг	*sud'je*	судье́	*adjutant*	адъюта́нт
stroja	стро́я	*p'ju*	пью		
moju	мо́ю	*čja*	чья		

Remember that a hard sign and a nonfinal soft sign preceding a vowel symbol always signal the presence of *jot*.

NOTE: In a very few foreign words *jo* may be spelled by **йо** instead of by **ё**; e.g. *N'ju-Jork* **Нью-Йо́рк** 'New York'; *jod* **йод** 'iodine.'

EXERCISE   Which of the following words contain a *jot*?

ле́йка	язы́к	семья́	польёт
пя́ть	обя́зан	семе́й	ко́рень
пятью́	шлю́т	разъясни́ть	коре́нья
стро́ём	се́мя	полёт	свои́ми

Jot plays an important part in word-formation. It may end a root (something only a consonant may do), as in the roots:

МОЙ   wash: мо́ю (*moj-u*) I wash   мо́йка (*moj-k-a*) washing
ПАРТИЙ   party: па́ртия (*partij-a*) party   парти́йный (*partij-n-oj*) party
                                                                                        (adj)

it may begin a root, as in:

ЮГ   south: юг (*jug*) south   Югосла́вия (*jug-o-slav-ij-a*) Yugoslavia
ЕЗД   ride: е́здить (*jezd-i-t'*) ride   прие́зд (*pr'i-jezd*) arrival

or it may be a suffix, or part of a suffix, as in:

КОРОВ   cow: коро́вья (f) (*korov'-/j-a*) cow's
ДЕЛ   do: де́лают (*d'el-aj-ut*) do

As one learns more about word-formation, the part played in it by *jot* will become clearer, but its role should not be obscured by the spelling problems discussed above.

EXERCISE   Identify *jot* and the role it plays in the following words:

А́нглия	объясни́ть	строй	строёво́й	(они) едя́т
англи́йский	(он) бьёт	стро́йный	пое́здка	повторя́ют

If we wish to emphasize the presence of *jot*, we may use **й** where it would not be used in the normal spelling. In verbal vocabulary entries in the individual vocabularies,[1] for instance, we give:

---

[1] In the General Vocabularies normal spelling is used, except that verbs of the **ИЙ (бьют)** type are given as above: **бий-ут** to facilitate marking of stress.

на-сто́й-а́-ть instead of на-сто-я́-ть
про-игр-ай-ут instead of про-игр-а́-ют
бий-ут instead of бь-ют
у-стро́й-и-ть instead of у-стро́-и-ть

Elsewhere, we may give examples like

семь/й-а́ instead of семь/-я́

but in most nominal and adjectival vocabulary entries we retain the normal spelling.

B. THE STRUCTURE OF INFLECTED RUSSIAN WORDS

1. Building elements. Derived and nonderived words

Any element that goes into the makeup of a word we may call a *building element*. In considering inflected Russian words, we will be concerned with four building elements: *prefixes*, *roots*, *suffixes*, and *endings*.

Prefixes, suffixes, and roots are involved in certain noninflected categories, but most noninflected words of derivational interest are derived from inflected categories; for example, adverbs, prepositions, and conjunctions which have become fossilized from various inflected words or groups containing inflected words. Noninflected Russian words which are not derived from inflected categories are scattered, and their derivation is of historical interest only. For practical purposes, therefore, word-formation is concerned only with the inflected categories: verbs, nouns, and adjectives.

Any inflected Russian word consists of at least a *root* and an inflectional *ending*. The ending may be zero. Words consisting of only root plus ending we call *nonderived* (or *primary*) words. *In a nonderived word the root is equal to the stem;* the stem is all of a word except the ending.

Nonderived words:

ROOT plus	ENDING	
РЫ́Б	a	nom sg 'fish'
РЫ́Б	#[1]	gen pl 'fish'
КО́НЬ	#	nom sg 'horse'
КОН	я	gen sg 'horse'
СТА́Р	#	short-form masc 'old'
СТА́Р	ый	long-form nom masc sg 'old'
СТА́Р	ого	long-form gen masc sg 'old'

---

[1] A zero-ending or zero-suffix may be indicated here and elsewhere by the sign #.

НЁС	ý	1 sg pres 'carry' (det)	
МОГ	ý	1 sg pres 'be able'	

Words which, in addition to the root and ending, have one or more derivational elements (prefixes and/or suffixes), we call *derived words*.

Derived words:

PREFIX(ES)	ROOT	SUFFIX(ES)	ENDING	
	РЫБ	áк	#	nom sg 'fisherman'
	РЫБ	ак	á	gen sg 'fisherman'
	РЫБ	/н	ый	nom sg masc 'fish' (adj)
	СТАР	овáт	ый	nom sg masc 'oldish'
	СТАР	é	ют	3 pl pres 'age'
	СТÁР	ость	#	nom sg 'old age'
	НОС	й	ть	inf (nondet) 'carry'
про-из	НОС	й	ть	inf (impf) 'pronounce'
про-из	НЁС		ýт	3 pl pres (perf) 'pronounce'
по	МÓГ		ут	3 pl pres (perf) 'help'
по	МОГ	á	ют	3 pl pres (impf) 'help'

2. Roots

A root is an uncompounded element, the part of the word which carries the basic unextended meaning and is common to all the words of a family or *word nest* (a word nest is, then, a family of all the words in a language sharing a given root). From the standpoint of their meaning (and also of the building elements which are used with them) roots are *nominal* (РЫБ 'fish'), *adjectival* (СТАР 'old'), or *verbal* (НЁС – НОС 'carry'); the few roots which would seem to be associated with other parts of speech usually function like one of the main types; for example, ПЕРЁД – ПРЕД 'front, fore-' like nominal roots, СВОЙ 'own' like adjectival roots. However, a root by itself is neither a word nor a part of speech; thus we distinguish the word and adjective **стар** (root plus zero-ending) from the root СТАР, which is simply a building element of a word.

Russian roots of Slavic origin and from older borrowings always end in consonants:[1] ХОД, РЕК, ТОПОР. The typical Russian root has the structure CVC, where C is one or more consonants and V is one vowel: БЕЛ, ХОД, СТАН, РЕК, ВЕТ/Р. Some roots are disyllabic: ДОРОГ, ГОВОР, but with very few exceptions, only non-Russian roots have more than two syllables:

---

[1] Including Й: e.g. СТРОЙ 'build,' ЗМЕЙ 'snake.' Most final root paired consonants are best regarded as not intrinsically hard or soft. Hardness or softness frequently depends on the following element; e.g. **рек-á**, but **рек-é**.

ГЕНЕРАЛ. A few Russian roots have the format VC; that is, begin with a vowel: **ИСК, УК.**

Most roots are *syllabic* (contain a vowel), but there are nonsyllabic roots as well, and many of them are important: **Ж/Д** 'wait,' **М/Р** 'die,' **Д/Н** 'day.' Nonsyllabic roots may occur in syllabic variants, containing a mobile vowel.

The knowledge of the meaning of a root is obviously a powerful instrument in the hands of the learner, but caution is advised against expecting the root to provide an unambiguous meaning in every context. It is true that most roots have fairly specific or specifiable meanings and that, together with correctly interpreted information about the rest of a word, they often provide the key to the meaning. However, the meanings of many common roots may be rather elusive in certain contexts. In many cases, particularly with verbal roots, a great deal of experience with many words containing a given root is necessary before one begins to acquire what is really less a concrete meaning than an idea, a set of possibilities for the root.

Let us give three roots, one nominal, one adjectival, and one verbal, and list a few words built with each root and possessing varying degrees of association with the central idea in the root.

МУЖ   male, man

муж-#	husband	муж-и́к-#	peasant (arch)
муж-ск-о́й	masculine, men's	муж-а́-ют	reach manhood
муж-чи́н-а	man	му́ж-(е)ств-о	courage

НОВ   new

но́в-ый	new	нов-изн-а́	novelty, newness
но́вь-#-#[1]	virgin soil	об-нов-и́-ть	renovate
но́в-ость-#	(a piece of) news; novelty	нов-ич-/о́/к-#	novice

СТУП   step

ступ-и́-ть – ступ-а́-ют   step

Verbs in **-ступ-и́-ть – -ступ-а́-ют.** Most have nouns in **-ступле́ние**, and some have other corresponding deverbative nouns:

вы́ступ-и-ть	(c inst) come out, come forward, appear publicly, perform (with) (IDEA 'step out'); вы́ступить с пе́сней, с докла́дом sing a song, make a report
на-ступ-и́-ть	step on; на-ступ-а́-ют (impf only) attack, advance
о-ступ-и́-ть-ся	stumble; lose one's way (IDEA 'misstep')

---

[1] This word has a zero-suffix as well as a zero-ending. Space forbids a detailed treatment of zero-suffixes here.

от-ступ-и́-ть	step back, recede; deviate, digress; от-ступ-а́-ют (impf only) retreat
пере-ступ-и́-ть	step over (Cf. пре-ступ-и́-ть 'transgress.')
по-ступ-и́-ть	enter, enroll (in an institution) (IDEA 'step in'); act, behave (IDEA 'take a step') Cf. поступле́ние 'enrolling, entering'; посту́п/о/к-# 'act'; по́ступь-#-# 'step' (person's).
при-ступ-и́-ть к	(dat) begin, get at (IDEA 'step to')
у-ступ-и́-ть	make place for, step out of the way of; concede

Nouns:

ступ-е́нь-#   step (of stairs)   ступ-и́ц-а   hub (of wheel)

In the examples with all three of these roots the meaning of the root is less a sure guide to the meaning of a word than an orientation point around which one may group members of a word nest as one learns them.

EXERCISE   Using a dictionary, find a number of words built with the nominal root **КРАС**. How would the meaning of the root be characterized?

Latin roots

Russian contains a fairly large number of loan translations, also called *calques*: literal translations of foreign words, especially the direct rendition of the separate elements of prefixed or compound words into Russian equivalents. Most calques are ultimately from Latin, either directly, or through French, German, or English; the intermediary does not matter. If several words containing the same root are involved, it may be useful to abstract the Latin root when translating the Russian equivalent. Many such roots are verbal. Some examples are:

ВИН	-*cuse*	из-вин-и́-ть	ex*cuse*
		об-вин-и́-ть	ac*cuse*
ВЛЁК	-*tract*	из-влёк-у́т	ex*tract*
		от-влёк-у́т	dis*tract*, ab*stract*
КЛЮЧ	-*clude*	в-ključ-и́-ть	in*clude*
		ис-ключ-и́-ть	ex*clude*
		за-ключ-и́-ть	con*clude*
КОРЕН	-*radic*-	ис-корен-и́-ть	e*radic*ate
РОД	-*gen*-	вод-о-ро́д	hydro*gen*
		род-и́-тель-н-ый	*gen*itive
ТРУД	-*labor*-	со-тру́д-нич-ай-ут	col*labor*ate

Larger families are:

ЛОЖ – СТАВ -pose, -pone		ВЁД – ВОД -duce, -duct	
от-лож-и-ть	post*pone*	вёд-у́т	con*duct*
пред-лож-и-ть	pro*pose*	в-вёд-у́т	intro*duce*
пред-по-лож-и-ть	sup*pose*	вы́-вёд-ут	de*duce*
рас-по-лож-и-ть	dis*pose*	при-вёд-у́т	ad*duce*
пере-ста́в-и-ть	trans*pose*	про-из-вёд-у́т	pro*duce*
со-ста́в-и-ть	com*pose*	с-вёд-у́т	re*duce*

EXERCISE   The verbal root **ПИС** frequently corresponds to Latin -*scribe*. How many compounds in **-писать** can you find which have an English verb in -*scribe* as one of their translations?

In practice, of course, such exact and neat correspondences do not always exist. But the Latin may suggest the meaning even if it is not itself the appropriate translation.

Root List

At the back of the book is a Root List which contains about 650 common roots, not including variants, and includes all roots that are boldface in the lesson vocabularies. Most of the important adjectival and verbal roots are listed; nominal roots are given in most cases only if they build words not directly related to their concrete meaning; for example, **РУК** and **ГОЛОВ – ГЛАВ** are given because they build words like **вы́ручить** 'rescue,' **поручи́ть** 'entrust a task' as well as **рука́** 'hand'; **гла́вный** 'main,' **заголо́в/о/к** 'headline' as well as **голова́** 'head,' but not **НОГ** or **ГЛАЗ**, because their derivatives are directly connected with 'foot/leg' and 'eye.'

In order to use the Root List properly and to be able to refer to it correctly from the boldface roots in the lesson vocabularies, as well as for the general purpose of understanding Russian roots as a whole, the student should familiarize himself with the following points:

a. *Truncation of final root consonant*. Russian roots, as we have said, always end in consonants; when they appear to end in vowels, truncation of the final root consonant has occurred, and the truncated consonant appears in other forms of the same word or, at least, in other words. For example:

стáн-ут стáи̯-ть   знáй-ут знáй-л

A final root consonant is quite frequently lost before the verbal suffix **-ну-**:

вз-гля́д̯-ну-ть > взгляну́ть   Cf. взгля́д
тя́г̯-ну-ть > тяну́ть   Cf. тя́га

This phenomenon is also mentioned in Part 2 in the section on verbs, page 29. An initial root в may be truncated after the prefix об-:

об-врат-и́-ть > обрати́ть   Cf. возврати́ть
об-вяз-а-ть > обяза́ть   Cf. связа́ть

b. *Mutation of final root consonant.* Final root consonants frequently undergo mutation; i.e. change into other consonants or groups of consonants in specific grammatical or derivational contexts; for example:

1 sg pres of verbs in И: при-глас-и́-ть при-глаш-у́
velar consonants before the suffix -н-:   зву́к   зву́чный

Except for a very few cases, the basic nonmutated consonant is the only variant given in the Root List, while in many of the words given in the vocabularies, the boldface roots are in a mutated variant; examples are:

об-**служ**-и́-ть СЛУГ Cf. услу́га
уч-и́-ть   УК   Cf. нау́ка

The student, in order to look up the root, needs to know what consonant the mutated variant implies. The following table describes Russian consonant mutation and alternations:

TABLE OF MUTATIONS

CONJUGATION AND VERBAL DERIVATION AND COMPARISON OF ADJECTIVES			NOMINAL AND ADJECTIVAL DERIVATION	CHURCH SLAVONIC MUTATIONS
д > ж	м > мл'	г > ж	г > ж	д > жд
т > ч	б > бл'	к > ч	к > ч	т > щ
з > ж	п > пл'	х > ш	х > ш	
с > ш	в > вл'	л > л'	ск > щ	
ст > щ	ф > фл'	н > н'	ц > ч	
ск > щ		р > р'	к > ц	
ц > ч				

The following quite isolated mutations also occur:

$\genfrac{}{}{0pt}{}{д}{т}$ before т > ст $\genfrac{}{}{0pt}{}{г}{к}$ before т > ч(ь)

Approaching these consonant mutations in the reverse direction, one may set up for the student the following table of expectations:

				мл' — м			
	х	к	ск	бл' — б			д
ж — д	ш	ч — ц	щ — ст	пл' — п	ц — к	жд — д	с
з	с	т	т	вл' — в			т
		(г)		пл' — ф			

In addition, a final root **-й** may alternate with **-в**:

КРОЙ: по-крóй-ут cover   КРОВ: по-крóв cover

EXERCISE Estimate the original final root consonant in the following words. For the words in the second and third columns, try to find a related word containing the original, nonmutated consonant (using a dictionary if necessary).

я глáжу	страши́ть (я страшу́)	тревóжный
я грáблю	мýчить (я мýчу)	грéшный
я чи́щу	тащи́ть (я тащу́)	скýчный
я ступлю́	дружи́ть (я дружу́)	конéчный
я брóшу	онемéчить (я онемéчу)	
я вожý		
я трáчу		
я люблю́		
я графлю́		

---

c. *Alternations in the root vowel.* Except for the change **o** > **a** before the imperfectivizing suffix *ivaj* (e.g. **с-прос-и́-ть – с-прáш-ивай-ут**), there are no regular vowel alternations in Russian grammar and derivation, in the sense that many of the consonant alternations are regular. For this reason most of the root variants showing vowel alternations are cross-referenced to one another in the Root List. Here, however, is a table describing the most important alternations, with examples:

e (ё)[1]		**o**[1]		**#**	
нёсу́т	they carry (det)	носи́ть	carry (nondet)		
вёду́т	they lead (det)	води́ть	lead (nondet)		
вёзу́т	they convey (det)	вози́ть	convey (nondet)		
тёку́т	they flow	тóк	current		
разберу́т	they will analyze	разбóр	analysis	разобрáть	analyze
стерегу́т	they watch	стóрож	watchman		
стéлют	they spread	стóл	table	стлáть	spread
пéйть	sing	пой-у́т	they sing		
рéй-а-ть	hover	рóй	swarm (as of bees)		

---

[1] In the Root List, variants in **o** are referenced to variants in **e(ё)**; e.g. **НОС** to **НЁС**.

Other alternations are less important numerically. Some may alternate with a root variant in zero as above, and a final root *jot* may be truncated. A few are:

о – ы – #:	зóв	call	óтзыв	opinion	звáть	call
у – ы – о:	дýх	breath	óтдых	rest	вздóх	sigh
ой – ый:	мóй-ут	they wash	мы́ть	wash		
ой – ий – #й:	бóй	fight	би́ть	beat	бьй-ýт	they beat
ей – ий:	брéй-ут	they shave	бри́ть	shave		
о – е(ё) – я:	ложи́ться	lie down	лечь	lie down	лёг	he lay down
					ля́гут	they will lie down
а – е – я:	сади́ться	sit down	сéсть	sit down	ся́дут	they will sit down

We mentioned at the top of page 18 a case in which final root consonant alternates. In a few cases involving nonsyllabic roots ending in **-М** or **-Н**, the vowel **я** (**a**) before a consonant alternates with zero **М** or zero **Н** before a vowel:

М/Н   crumple: мн-ýт – мя́ть   Ж/М   press: жм-ýт – жáть

d. *Syllabic variants of nonsyllabic roots.* Syllabic variants of nonsyllabic roots are given in the Root List and cross-referenced to the nonsyllabic roots; e.g. **ЗОВ** to **З/В**, **МЁР** and **МОР** to **М/Р**.[1]

e. *Church Slavonic variants of Russian roots.* Old Church Slavonic was the language of the oldest Slavic manuscripts, which date from the tenth and early eleventh centuries. It exerted an important influence on the grammar and vocabulary of both literary and, eventually, spoken Russian. Because it was adapted from a South Slavic dialect which already in the tenth century differed in certain respects from the Russian of that time and because, as an exclusively literary language, it did not keep pace with all the changes in spoken Russian, certain disparities emerged between what we call "Church Slavonic" elements and "purely Russian" elements in the language of today. In some cases the variants exist side by side. At a more sophisticated stage of investigation the examination of Russian vs. Church Slavonic lexical variants is very worthwhile, and consideration of certain morphological alternations is also of value. In this section we are concerned with Church Slavonic variants of pleophonic[2] Russian roots involving **р** and **л** (the roots in so-called **полногла́сие**). It may be noted that when lexical items are involved, the Church Slavonic (ChS) variant often

---

[1] Those variants found in derived imperfectives and nouns from nonsyllabic verb stems are *not* normally given; e.g. **ЗЫВ**, **МИР** (**на-**-*зыв*-á-ют, у-*мир*-á-ют).

[2] The word "pleophony" (adjective "pleophonic") is coined from Greek components meaning "more voice"; i.e. the vowel preceding the **р** or **л** is repeated after the **р** or **л**.

has the more abstract or ethereal sense, the Russian (R) variant the more specific or mundane meaning, *although this is not always so.*

f. *Russian pleophonic vs. Church Slavonic nonpleophonic variants.* With **T** designating a consonant or consonant cluster, we observe:

Russian	ТОРОТ	ТЕРЁТ	ТОЛОТ	ТОЛОТ[1]
Church Slavonic	ТРАТ	ТРЕТ	ТЛАТ	ТЛЕТ

(Below we shall let **P** stand for both **р** and **л**; e.g. **ТОРОТ** means **ТОРОТ** or **ТОЛОТ**, **ТРЕТ** means **ТРЕТ** or **ТЛЕТ**, etc.)

Pleophonic alternations usually involve roots; i.e. **ТОРОТ/ТРАТ, ТЕРЕТ/ТРЕТ** are variants of a root. Let us examine four cases covering all possibilities:

СТОРОН/СТРАН	side	ГОЛОВ/ГЛАВ	head
СЕРЕД/СРЕД	middle	МОЛОК/МЛЕК	milk

RUSSIAN		CHURCH SLAVONIC	
сторон-а́	side	стран-а́	country
серед-и́н-а	middle	сред-а́	medium; Wednesday
голов-а́	head	глав-а́	head (chief); chapter
молок-о́	milk	млек-о-пит-а́-ющ-ее	mammal (ПИТ 'feed')

Both the Russian and Church Slavonic variants are used to build a variety of derived and compound words. Once again, in cases where the R vs. ChS root is the only or almost the only element distinguishing two words, the distinction mentioned above frequently, but not always, applies. Some examples:

по-сторо́н-н-ий	outside, extraneous	стра́н-/н-ый	strange
сторон-и́-ть-ся	step aside, shun	у-стран-и́-ть	remove, move aside

It should be observed that words of Church Slavonic origin in a root final **д** or **т** will have mutated variants, if any, in **жд** and **щ**, rather than in the Russian **ж** and **ч** (cf. page 17). Most such cases involve verbs in **-дить** and **-тить**:

		FIRST SINGULAR	PAST PASSIVE PARTICIPLE	IMPERFECTIVE DERIVATION
R	от-ворот-и́-ть turn aside	от-вороч-у́	от-воро́ч-ен	от-вора́ч-ивай-ут
ChS	от-врат-и́-ть avert, repel	от-вращ-у́	от-вращ-ён	от-вращ-а́й-ут

---

[1] **Оло/ле** is not so widespread as the other three.

R   пере-город-и́-ть   пере-горож-у́   пере-горо́ж-ен   пере-гора́ж-
    partition   ивай-ут

ChS   пре-град-и́-ть   пре-граж-у́ [2]   пре-гражд-ён   пре-гражд-а́й-ут
    block, bar

Compare also deverbative nouns:

отворо́т	turning aside	vs.	отвраще́ние	repugnance
перегоро́д/ка	partition	vs.	прегра́да	barrier, obstacle

In the Root List, Church Slavonic roots are referenced to the pleophonic variant, if one exists.

If a root variant cannot be derived from or associated with the basic variant given in the Root List, then this root is given in the entry in boldface capital letters, as in:

ле́стница **ЛЕЗ**[1] stairs, stairway; ladder

нао**бОРО́Т об-ВОРОТ** on the contrary

---

[1] The numbers 1, 2, etc. following roots in the vocabularies refer to the similarly numbered roots in the Root List, where the numbers serve to distinguish roots with identical spelling but different origin. See also the last footnote on page 324 of the Root List.

[2] In the first singular only Д > Ж even in Church Slavonic verbs.

PART

2

TREATMENT OF VOCABULARIES

A. THE GENERAL VOCABULARY

The *general vocabulary* contains the words in Conversation Lessons 1 to 5 and Lessons I to VIII except for those words given under СЛОВА́ ТО́ЛЬКО К Э́ТОМУ УРО́КУ in Lessons VI, VII, and VIII. Words in Lessons IX and X are given in separate vocabularies with those lessons. The general vocabulary contains a great many other words as well. The author has made an effort to include almost all words which a student might normally encounter in his first two years of Russian and, in addition, a good number of words he might not meet or have met, but which occur with high frequency in normal Soviet prose. Also included are most of the commonest grammatical and linguistic terms and expressions together with those terms and concepts specifically used in the grammatical and word-formation materials in this text, so that grammatical discussion may be carried on in Russian as much as possible. The following types of words have *not* been listed:

a. the very simplest words, those which would be found in all first-year texts: не́т, каранда́ш, (на)писа́ть. (Words exhibiting especially difficult patterns or irregularities, or words occurring with special expressions, may be included: ка́к: ка́к мо́жно *comp of* X; то́т: не то́т.)

b. Numerals.

c. Motion verbs and compounds of motion verbs, except in special (unpredictable) expressions: въе́хать – въезжа́ют is not given; вы́йдут – выходи́ть за́муж за кого́ 'marry' is given; for введу́т – вводи́ть, 'introduce' is given, but 'lead in,' which the student can assume, is omitted. The formal patterns of the motion verbs are assumed.

d. Days of the week, months of the year, telling time.

22

e. The most basic prepositions in their most basic usages (those prepositions discussed in the book are glossed, and special cases are treated).

Cross-referencing between the Russian–English and English–Russian sections is as complete as possible, and both sections attempt to anticipate the user's needs as much as possible; however, the student must be emphatically reminded that there is never a one-hundred-percent correspondence between Russian and English words. A verb like **оказать** – **оказывают** clearly has no direct equivalent in English, but this will not prevent the student from acquiring a feel for what it means and even the ability to use it in new contexts, once he has seen and used it in various situations.

Full grammatical information and lesson references are given *only* in the Russian–English section, and the student, on looking up an English word, should make sure he has control of the Russian equivalent he finds, and, if he doubts that he has, look it up in the Russian–English section. The student is encouraged to take advantage of the more specific references,[1] which direct him to a fuller discussion of the word, phrase, or point of grammar involved.

B. THE LESSON VOCABULARIES

Treatment of entries in the separate (lesson) vocabularies is basically the same as in the general vocabulary, except that considerably more attention is paid to the breakdown of words. All inflected words—nouns, adjectives, and verbs—are divided into their component parts by hyphens; e.g.

пред-**став**-и-ть

A hyphen itself is rendered by an en dash:

во-ён-н-о–мор-ск-ой

In addition, as we said above, roots in the vocabularies which also occur in the Root List are given in boldface; procedures for recovering the more basic root in the Root List from a variant which may occur in a vocabulary were discussed in the preceding section. Noninflected words are not broken down into parts, but if they contain roots which are included in the Root List, these roots are also given in boldface; e.g. **вполне**.

Words in the lesson vocabularies are listed in normal alphabetical order, except that *verbs are listed separately and by the alphabetical order of their roots* at the end of each vocabulary. Deverbative nouns are normally listed under the verbs from which they are derived, though a few are cross-referenced from the nonverbal vocabularies.

---

[1] That is, generally, those that refer to some subdivision of a lesson; the great majority of lesson references, of course, merely locate the word in the lesson.

C. TREATMENT OF ENTRIES

In the treatment of the individual entries, an important principle is strictly observed: The student is *not* given information which he can predict according to patterns he knows or is being taught in the book. Emphasis is always on compelling the student to generate the forms he needs according to as tight a system of rules as possible, so that he may develop automatic and crisp reflexes in his approach to new words and does not sink into dependence on memorization of a vast number of forms for each word. However, in order to be able to predict correctly, the student must be conversant not only with the rules but also with the *conventions* we are using in the vocabularies and elsewhere in the book, and he is urged to pay the strictest attention to the following.

1. Abbreviations and general conventions

The following abbreviations are used in the vocabularies:

abbrev	abbreviation	ger	gerund
acc	accusative	gr	grammatical term
act	active	I	imperfective
adj	adjective	imps	impersonal
adv	adverb	impv	imperative
arch	archaic	indecl	indeclinable
cf.	compare with (see)	inf	infinitive
ChS	Church Slavonic	inst	instrumental
collec	collective (noun)	intr	intransitive
colloq	colloquial	lg f	long form (of adjectives)
comp	comparative	ling	linguistic term
compl	complement	lit	literal(ly)
conj	conjunction	M	masculine
dat	dative	N	neuter
det	determined verb	n	deverbative noun
dim	diminutive	NB	note well
E	end (stress)	neg	negative
eccles	ecclesiastical	nom	nominative
Eng	English	no mut	no mutation (in I)
esp	especially	nondet	nondetermined verb
exc	except	obl	oblique
exp	expression	obs	obsolete
F	feminine	P	perfective
fig	figurative	PAP	past active participle
freq	frequently	paren	parenthetical word or phrase
gen	genitive	part	participle

pass	passive
pej	pejorative
pers	person
pert	pertaining
pl	plural
pleo	pleophonic (полногла́сие)
poet	poetic(al)
PPP	past passive participle
pred	predicate
prep	preposition
pres	present tense

prn	pronounced, pronunciation
prp	prepositional case
R	Russian
S	stem (stress)
sg	singular
sh f	short form (of adjectives)
sub adj	substantivized adjective
tr	transitive
us	usually
v	verb
Vocab	vocabulary

The examples listed below illustrate the general conventions that are used throughout the vocabularies.

1. < means "from," usually used in describing deverbative nouns.
2. *an older* refers to a verb form no longer in use:

внима́ние < *an older* внима́ют

3. Two stress marks on a single word indicate optional stress:

и́на́че   яс/ный, ясны́

4. Letters in italics within a word call attention to an irregular or unexpected grammatical point, as in:

че́рт*и* instead of (nonexistent) чёрты (*pl of* чёрт)
руководи́ть instead of (nonexistent) руководить[1] (student expects shifting stress because of води́ть)

5. A slash between two words or expressions indicates alternatives:

под-/о/йду́т – подходи́ть *кому́/чему́*
необходи́мо *inf/чтобы*

6. Note the use of X (and Y where necessary):

об-рат-и́-ть-ся – обраща́ются к *кому́/чему́* за *чем* turn to X for Y
бы́ть Х-ого мне́ния be of X opinion

7. The use of где́, куда́, and отку́да is self-explanatory.
8. When a vocabulary entry is not defined but is followed by a colon and a word derived from it or an expression containing it, this indicates that the entry has either already been learned by the student or is otherwise of less importance than the material which is defined:

---

[1] Beginning with p. 22 we shall use the *absence* of a stress mark and certain other stress conventions which we shall explain in paragraph 4c, pp. 35-38.

положить – кладут: *n* положе́ние position, situation
по́-вод: по по́воду *чего́* II.6

Government

When a word is used with a certain preposition or governs a specific case, this information is supplied, with case being indicated by Russian interrogative pronouns in italics; for example:

> согласи́ться – соглаша́ются с *кем/чем* agree with;
>   на *что or inf* agree/consent to

The accusative is not specified for obvious transitives, nor is the dative indicated for verbs which clearly take an indirect object, but an indication of the dative (**кому́/чему́**) is included with **помо́гут** (помогу́, помо́жешь) – **помога́ют** 'help,' because the English verb does not provide the proper clue.

2. Nouns

Nouns ending in a soft sign are feminine unless marked "*M*": **ночь ра́дость**, but **гость** *M*. Masculine nouns taking the feminine form are also marked "*M*" (**судь/я́** *M*), and indeclinable nouns are marked "*indecl.*" Deverbative nouns of action (or result of action) are marked "*n*" and listed with the appropriate verbs.

Nouns which are (**на**) words according to the criteria discussed in R4, page 76, are so listed: **заво́д (на)**, **собра́ние (на)**.

Stress of nouns. A single stress mark and no other information indicates fixed stress on that syllable. For shifting or end stress, the following symbols apply:

> *S*   stem, normally the first syllable of the word; stress on any other syllable of the stem will be specified
> *E*   first syllable of ending (on the final stem syllable if the ending is zero)
> *pl* all plural cases
> *obl* all cases but the nominative and the nonanimate accusative

Various types are:

> сто́л *E* (i.e. сто́л, стола́, столу́, столы́, столо́в, стола́м)
> жёна́ *S pl* (i.e. жёны, жён, жёнам)
> са́д (в саду́) *E pl* (i.e. сады́, садо́в, сада́м)
> о́бласть *E pl obl* (i.e. о́бласти, областе́й, областя́м)
> рука́ *S nom pl acc sg* (i.e. ру́ки, ру́ку, all other forms ending-stressed)
> до́ктор *E pl* -á (i.e. *nom pl* доктора́, and all plural forms are ending-stressed)

3. Adjectives

The vocabularies list long forms of adjectives only, unless the short forms are not readily predictable from the long forms or have a distinct meaning. For practical purposes, the existence of short forms is quite likely if the adjective is of the "qualitative" or "descriptive" type ("red," "strong," "good," and so on). In contrast to qualitative adjectives are "relational" adjectives, which have the meaning "of or from or associated with X" ("French," "*female*" (*woman's*), "world," "hydrogen," "verbal," "language" (as in *language family*), and so on). Relational adjectives do not build short forms. The most frequent suffixes building relational adjectives are **-ск-**, **-ов-**, and **-н-**. The suffix **-н-** also builds many qualitative adjectives, which normally have short forms. The existence or non-existence of short forms in adjectives built with this suffix will be evident in the vocabularies from the presence or absence of a slash between the **н** and the consonant immediately preceding it; the slash indicates that a vowel is inserted in the zero (masculine short) form (see page 42). Compare **вид/ный** 'visible' (short forms **виден, видна, видно, видны**) and **видный** 'eminent,' which has no short forms. The same slash occurring before **к** and certain other less frequent adjectival suffixes also indicates the existence of short forms.

The adverbial short neuter form is not given, unless it has a special meaning or its form is somehow unusual or not predictable from the adjective; e.g. **давний**, no short-form adjectives, but note the adverb (in a hard stem) **давно**, which we would specify. **Здоровый** 'healthy,' short-form neuter and adverb is **здорово** as expected, but note **здорово** *colloq* 'marvelous(ly); great,' which we would specify.

Adjectives in **не-** are not given if the positive exists with the opposed meaning, and no special relationship exists. Hence, for **прият/ный** 'pleasant,' we would not give **неприят/ный** 'unpleasant,' but **необходимый** 'indispensable' is listed under **не-**, since no positive exists.

The only comparatives given are those in **-е** (and most of these the student could form himself according to the rules in R5.A); these are given separately but are almost always right next to the adjectives in question. Comparatives in **-ee** are easily formed by the student himself.

Stress of adjectives. Long forms of all adjectives and short forms and comparatives of adjectives with stems having three or more syllables have fixed stress on the syllable indicated in the entry form. In a number of very common adjectives, with monosyllabic or disyllabic stems, however, shifting stress or end stress may occur. In monosyllabic stems we consider shifting stress, with feminine end stress vs. nonfeminine stem stress, as the normal pattern (**-ee** comparative is the same as the feminine): **крас/ный, красен, красно, красны** vs. **красна, краснее**. Hence we give the vast majority of such adjectives (**твёрдый,**

си́ль/ный, чёрный) with no separate information, but we specify a type like
лёг/кий, лёгок, легка́, легко́, легки́. Disyllabic stems, on the other hand, are
regarded as having fixed stress: краси́вый, краси́в, краси́ва, краси́во, краси́вы,
краси́вее. Shifting stress: холо́д/ный, хо́лоден, холодна́, хо́лодно, хо́лодны,
холодне́е or end stress: хоро́ший, хоро́ш, хороша́, хорошо́, хороши́ will be
regarded as exceptional and thus specified. Comparative stress (-ee) is given if it
differs from the feminine short form. Comparatives in -e are, of course, always
stem-stressed: ле́гче, твёрже, кре́пче, лу́чше.

4. Verbs

a. Classification of verbs. Nonsuffixed and suffixed. Basic forms

In order to make the conventions pertaining to the handling of the verbal
entries clear to the student, we must give the following information about the
basic classification of Russian verbs.

All Russian verbs may be classified according to whether or not they contain a derivational suffix; i.e. they are either *nonsuffixed* or *suffixed*. If a verb
does not contain a suffix, its basic stem always ends in a consonant, since all
roots end in consonants:

$$\text{нёс-у́т} \qquad \text{жив-ут} \qquad \text{по̄-йм-ут} \qquad \text{ӯ-мр-ут}$$

If a verb does contain a suffix, it is usually a vowel, except for two suffixes which
end in the consonant й: -ай- and -ей-:

прос-и́-ть   смотр-е-ть   пис-а-ть   жд-а-ть   тре́б-ова-ть
толк-ну́-ть   кол-о-ть

but

дел-ай-ут   ум-е́й-ут

If the full stem of the verb ends in a *consonant* (a nonsuffixed verb or verbs
in -ай- or -ей-), the *basic form* (consisting of the basic stem plus ending) is the
third plural present tense; if the full stem ends in a vowel, the basic form is the
infinitive. It is the basic form which we shall list in the vocabularies.

The infinitives and third plurals which are not the basic forms, and hence
are not given, as well as the other forms in the paradigm, may be obtained by
examining the *head verb* for the type involved. For example, if the verb is the
suffixed verb при-глас-и́-ть, then verb type is immediately ascertained simply by
looking at the suffix, and the forms will be like those of the head verb прос-и́-ть,
which are given: приглашу́, like прошу́ (with mutation), приглася́т like про́сят,
etc. Similarly, the verb влёку́т will have forms similar to пёку́т: влечь, like
пёчь; влёк, влекла́, like пёк, пекла́; and so on. Individual peculiarities within

types will be noted in the individual vocabularies in most cases, though the vocabularies do not attempt to give more than the general outlines of the conjugation.

Two conventions must be particularly noted: (1) A basic form given as (**НУ**) as distinct from **НУ** indicates the type of verb where the suffix **-ну-** "disappears" in some forms; e.g. **ис-чéз-(ну)-ть** vs. **вс-крúк-ну-ть**. (2) A final root consonant truncated before the **-ну-** suffix (mostly in **НУ** rather than (**НУ**) verbs) is given with a slash through it; the consonant appears in related forms or words without the **-ну-**: **кúд̸-ну-ть** (actual form **кúнуть, кúнут, кúнул,** etc.), cf. imperfective **кид-áй-ут**, derived imperfective **при-кúд-ивай-ут**; **вз-гляд̸-ну-ть** – **вз-гля́д-ывай-ут**, deverbative noun **вз-гля́д**, and so forth.

b. *Verb tables and conjugation of head verbs*

On pages 30 and 31 we present Russian verb types and conjugation in tabular form: one table for nonsuffixed stems and one for suffixed stems. It is not necessary to understand all the details and information in the tables in full, though some or all of it may be helpful. Note particularly the head verbs representing the various verb types. These twenty-five head verbs are conjugated in full on the pages following the tables. As pointed out previously, the forms of other verbs which you meet may be estimated or obtained by checking the conjugation of these head verbs.

Conjugation is a matter of adding endings to stems. (*Verbal endings are listed on page 33.*) Stems *end* in either consonants or vowels and endings *begin* in either consonants or vowels; hence the possibilities of combination are CV, CC, VC, VV. The combination of unalikes (CV and VC) results normally in simple addition (**жив ут** > **живýт**, **говор-и ть** > **говорúть**). The combination of alikes (CC and VV), however, almost always results in the deletion of the preceding alike (**жив ть** > **жúть**, **говор-и ишь** > **говорúшь**). *Also taken as normal in conjugation is the automatic softening of any paired consonant before any ending in o, i, or a*; e.g. **вез-ёт, вез-ú, вез-я́**. In addition, other modifications frequently occur, and these are listed in the Verb Tables.

The conjugation of the irregular verbs **быть** and **дать** is assumed as known, and their compounds, which have the same conjugation, are given simply in the infinitive: **прúбыть** – **прибывáют, пóдать** – **подавáть** (for explanation of the shifting or prefixal stress of these types, as indicated by absence of stress mark or by the "greater than" sign " >," see page 37). Prefixed imperfectives in **-давáть** are, of course, **АВÁЙ** verbs (see the Verb Tables and the conjugation of **АВÁЙ** verbs on page 35).

Other irregularities and departures from the patterns given in the Verb Tables and exemplified by the conjugations of the head verbs are specified in the vocabularies; **вы́звать** (*вы́зовут*)–**вызывáют, (с)пой-ут** (*пéть*).

VERB TABLE: NONSUFFIXED STEMS

All are **-ёт** verbs.　　　　No stress shift in present.
All are consonant stems.　　May have stress shift in past.

HEAD VERB		TYPE	MODIFICATIONS (OTHER THAN $\cancel{C}$C)	PPP
		SYLLABIC RESONANT STEMS		-т
жив-ут	live	В		
ден-ут	put	Н	Stem stress.	
дуй-ут	blow	Й		
мой-ут	wash	ОЙ	**о** > **ы** before C. Stem stress.	
пий-ут	drink	ИЙ[1]	**ий** > **ьй** before V.[1]	
		NONSYLLABIC RESONANT STEMS		-т
т/р-ут	rub	/Р[2]	/**р** > **ерё** before -**ть** and **ёр** before other C. Masc past -**л** drops.	
ж/м-ут	press	/М – /Н	/**м** – /**н** > **я** (**а** after hushings) before C.	
по-й/м-ут	understand	Й/М	(After V prefix) **й/м** > **ня** before C.	
с-ним-ут	take off	НИМ[3]	(After C prefix) **им** > **я** before C. Shifting prefixal stress in past. Shifting stress in pres (**НИМ** type only).	
		OBSTRUENT STEMS[2]		-ён
вёд-ут	lead	Д – Т[4]	**д** – **т** > **с** before -**ти** (-**ть**).	
вёз-ут	convey	З – С[4]	Masc past -**л** drops; other C simply added.	
пёк-ут	bake	Г – К	Masc past -**л** drops; other past endings added. **г** – **к** plus -**ть** > **чь**, and a preceding **ё** > **е**. Mutation before endings in *o*.	

---

[1] **ий** > **ьй** before a stressed vowel is a general rule in Russian; cf. verbal nouns in ´**иё** alternating with -**ь/ё** (**решéние** vs. **житьё**). In the **ИЙ** type all present endings are stressed; hence basic form **пий-ут** gives third plural **пьют** (a nonsyllabic present stem).

[2] For past gerund and past active participle add -**ши(й)**, not -**вши(й)**, to stem.

[3] **й/м** is a nonsyllabic verbal root with the meaning 'take, have'; **ним** is a syllabic variant of it.

[4] Have end stress in the past and infinitive in -**ти** except for a few stems in **Д** and **З**, which have stem stress in the past and infinitive in -**ть**.

VERB TABLE: SUFFIXED STEMS

И, Е, and ЖА are -ит verbs.　　　No stress shift in past.
All others are -ёт verbs.　　　　May have stress shift in present.

HEAD VERB		TYPE	MODIFICATIONS (OTHER THAN V̸V)	PPP
		VOWEL STEMS **-ит** VERBS		
прос-и-ть	request	И	Mutation in 1 sg pres, ppp, and impf deriv.	-ён
смотр-е-ть	look at	Е	Mutation in 1 sg pres and, rarely, in ppp and impf deriv.	-н
держ-а-ть	hold	ЖА[1]		-н
		VOWEL STEMS **-ёт** VERBS		
пис-а-ть	write	А	Mutation throughout pres tense and in pres ger and impv.	-н
ж/д-а-ть	wait	n/sA	Sometimes shifting stress in past tense.	-н
треб-ова-ть	require	ОВА	**ова** > **уй** (**ёва** > **юй**) before V.	-н
кол-о-ть	prick	О	Consonants soften before endings in *u*.	-т
толк-ну-ть	push	НУ	**ну** is retained in all forms of verb itself, but is lost in impf deriv.	-т
слеп-(ну)-ть с-верг-(ну)-ть	go blind overthrow	(НУ)	**ну** is usually dropped before past tense, past ger, and pap endings, with resulting stems acting like obstruents, and is always lost in impf deriv. There are two subtypes.[2] Stress is on syllable preceding (**ну**).	-т
		CONSONANT STEMS		
дел-ай-ут	do	АЙ	Whole suffix (not just final C) is lost in impf deriv.	-н
ум-ей-ут	know how	ЕЙ		
		EXCEPTIONAL TYPE		
да-вай-	give	АВАЙ	**авай** > **ай** in pres tense *only*, and pres tense endings are stressed.	—

---

[1] **Ж** represents any palatal consonant: a hushing or **й**.

[2] Verbs like **слéпнуть** normally denote some kind of changing state or becoming. Verbs like **свéргнуть** have no semantic restriction.

TREES FOR CONJUGATION

**PAST PASSIVE
PARTICIPIAL ENDING:**

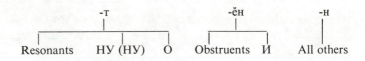

               -т   -ён   -н

Resonants   НУ (НУ) О   Obstruents И   All others

**PAST ACTIVE
PARTICIPIAL ENDING:**

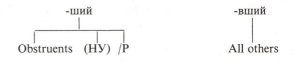

               -ший   -вший

      Obstruents (НУ) /Р   All others

**CONSONANT
MUTATION:**

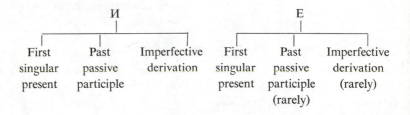

	И			E	
First singular present	Past passive participle	Imperfective derivation	First singular present	Past passive participle (rarely)	Imperfective derivation (rarely)

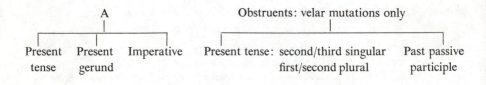

	A		Obstruents: velar mutations only	
Present tense	Present gerund	Imperative	Present tense: second/third singular first/second plural	Past passive participle

VERBAL ENDINGS

CONSONANTAL:		
	1. Infinitive	*-t'* (*-t'i*)
	2. Past tense	*-l -la -lo -l'i*
	3. Past gerund	*-v/-vši /-ši*
	4. Past active participle	*-všoj/-šoj*
	5. Past passive participle	*-t/-n*

VOCALIC:		
	6. Present tense:	
	First singular	*-u*
	First conjugation	*-oš -ot -om -ot'e -ut*
	Second conjugation	*-iš -it -im -it'e -at*
	7. Imperative	*-i(-#) (-t'e)*
	8. Present gerund	*-a*
	9. Present active participle	*u/a* plus *-ščoj*
	10. Present passive participle	*o/i* plus *-moj*
	11. Past passive participle	*-on*

Below we conjugate the twenty-five head verbs, giving as many of the above forms as exist for each type. Note that the past active participle stands also for the past gerund, if one exists, and that of the present tense only the first and second singular and third plural are given:

NONSUFFIXED STEMS

В	Н	Й	ОЙ	ИЙ	/Р
жи́ть	де́ть	ду́ть	мы́ть	пи́ть	тере́ть
жи́л	де́л	ду́л	мы́л	пи́л	тёр
жила́ -и	де́ла	ду́ла	мы́ла	пила́ -и	тёрла
жи́вший	де́вший	ду́вший	мы́вший	пи́вший	тёрший
-жи́т -а́ -ы	-де́т	-ду́т	-мы́т	-пи́т -а́ -ы	-тёрт
живу́	де́ну	ду́ю	мо́ю	пью	тру́
живёшь	де́нешь	ду́ешь	мо́ешь	пьёшь	трёшь
живу́т	де́нут	ду́ют	мо́ют	пьют	тру́т
живи́	де́нь	ду́й	мо́й	пей	три́
живя́	—	ду́я	мо́я	—	—
живу́щий	—	ду́ющий	мо́ющий	пью́щий	тру́щий
—	—	—	—	—	—

NONSUFFIXED STEMS (continued)

/М – /Н	Й/М	НИМ	Д – Т	З – С	Г – К
жа́ть	поня́ть	сня́ть	вести́	везти́	пе́чь
жа́л	по́нял	сня́л	вёл	вёз	пёк
жа́ла	поняла́ -и	сняла́ -и	вела́ -й	везла́ -й	пекла́ -й
жа́вший	поня́вший	сня́вший	ве́дший	вёзший	пёкший
-жа́т	по́нят -а́ -ы	снят -а́ -ы	-веде́н	-везён	-пече́н
жму́	пойму́	сниму́	веду́	везу́	пеку́
жмёшь	поймёшь	сни́мешь	ведёшь	везёшь	печёшь
жму́т	пойму́т	сни́мут	веду́т	везу́т	пеку́т
жми́	пойми́	сними́	веди́	вези́	пеки́
—	—	—	ведя́	везя́	—
жму́щий	—	—	веду́щий	везу́щий	пеку́щий
—	—	—	ведо́мый[1]	везо́мый[1]	—

SUFFIXED STEMS

И	Е	ЖА	А	n/sA
проси́ть	смотре́ть	держа́ть	писа́ть	жда́ть
проси́л	смотре́л	держа́л	писа́л	жда́л -а́ -и
проси́вший	смотре́вший	держа́вший	писа́вший	жда́вший
-про́шен	-смо́трен	-де́ржан	-пи́сан	-ждан
прошу́	смотрю́	держу́	пишу́	жду́
про́сишь	смо́тришь	де́ржишь	пи́шешь	ждёшь
про́сят	смо́трят	де́ржат	пи́шут	жду́т
проси́	смотри́	держи́	пиши́	жди́
прося́	смотря́	держа́	—[2]	—
прося́щий	смотря́щий	держа́щий	пи́шущий	жду́щий
проси́мый	—	—	—	—

---

[1] Present passive participles in **-омый** from some obstruents are occasionally found but, practically speaking, are rarely used.

[2] Present gerunds are very rare for A verbs but do exist; e.g. пла́кать – пла́ча. **Пи́ша** was used in earlier Russian, notably by Pushkin.

SUFFIXED STEMS (continued)

ОВА	О	НУ	(НУ)[a]
тре́бовать	коло́ть	толкну́ть	сле́пнуть
тре́бовал	коло́л	толкну́л	сле́п -ла
тре́бовавший	коло́вший	толкну́вший	сле́пший
-тре́бован	-ко́лот	-то́лкнут	—
тре́бую	колю́	толкну́	сле́пну
тре́буешь	ко́лешь	толкнёшь	сле́пнешь
тре́буют	ко́лют	толкну́т	сле́пнут
тре́буй	коли́	толкни́	сле́пни
тре́буя	коля́	—	—
тре́бующий	ко́лющий	—	сле́пнущий
тре́буемый	—	—	—

(НУ)[b]	АЙ	ЕЙ	АВАЙ
све́ргнуть	де́лать	уме́ть	дава́ть
све́рг -ла	де́лал	уме́л	дава́л
све́ргший	де́лавший	уме́вший	дава́вший
све́ргнут	-де́лан	—	—
све́ргну	де́лаю	уме́ю	даю́
све́ргнешь	де́лаешь	уме́ешь	даёшь
све́ргнут	де́лают	уме́ют	даю́т
све́ргни	де́лай	умей	дава́й
—	де́лая	уме́я	дава́я
—	де́лающий	уме́ющий	даю́щий
—	де́лаемый	—	дава́емый

c. *Stress*

Russian verbal stress is either *fixed*: always on the ending or always on the stem; or *shifting*. In nonsuffixed verbs, shifting stress occurs only in the past tense and past passive participle;[1] *feminine* forms stress the ending, and all other (*nonfeminine*) forms stress the stem or, in infrequent cases, the prefix:

жив-ут: жи́л, жи́ло, жи́ли vs. жила́
про̀-жив-ут: про́жит -о, -ы vs. прожита́
у̀-мр-ут: у́мер, у́мерло, у́мерли vs. умерла́

In suffixed verbs, shifting stress occurs only in the present tense,[2] the first

---

[1] With two small exceptions; see p. 37.   [2] With the exception of one type; see p. 37.

singular present tense stresses the ending, and all other present tense forms stress the stem:

прос-и-ть: прошу́, про́сишь, . . . про́сят
пис-а-ть: пишу́, пи́шешь, . . . пи́шут

In suffixed verbs with shifting stress, the infinitive, the past tense, *the past active participle,* the imperative, and, normally, the present gerund are stressed on the final syllable:

проси́вший
просить: проси́ть, проси́л, проси́ла, проси́ли, проси́, прося́

In the basic forms given in our vocabularies, presence or absence of a stress mark (i.e. stress information in general) refers to the *past tense in the case of nonsuffixed verbs and to the present tense in the case of suffixed verbs.* The present tense of nonsuffixed verbs always has ending stress except when the basic form is marked on the stem, in which case the past tense is also stressed on the stem; e.g. **ста́нут: ста́ну, ста́нешь, ста́нут; стал, ста́ла, ста́ли.** The past tense of suffixed stems, on the other hand, is inferable from the infinitive, as mentioned above.

We may, then, mark fixed stress, whether it is on the stem or the ending, with a single acute mark. When it is on the stem, we place the acute mark on the stem. When it is on the ending, we place the acute mark on the **-у́т** in the case of consonant stems, and on the last or only vowel of the suffix in the case of vowel stems; e.g. **-и́ть.** But we denote *shifting* stress by the *absence* of any stress mark at all. Here are examples of both nonsuffixed and suffixed basic-form types:

NONSUFFIXED

Basic form

ста́нут:	стал, ста́ло, ста́ли, ста́ла	and, by inference, ста́ну, ста́нешь, etc.
нёсу́т:	нёс, несло́, несли́, несла́	and, by inference, несу́, несёшь, etc.
живу́т:	жил, жи́ло, жи́ли—жила́	and, by inference, живу́, жชвёшь, etc.

SUFFIXED

ста́вить:	ста́влю, ста́вишь, etc.	and, by inference, ста́вить, ста́вил, ста́вила, ста́вь, ста́вя
говори́ть:	говорю́, говори́шь, etc.	and, by inference, говори́ть, говори́л, говори́ла, говори́, говоря́
просить:	прошу́—про́сишь, etc.	and, by inference, проси́ть, проси́л, проси́ла, проси́, прося́

Two additional conventions remain to be mentioned for nonsuffixed verbs. For verbs that have *stem stress in the past tense but ending stress in the present*, we place the stress mark on the final stem consonant:

клад́-ут: кла́л, кла́ло, кла́ли, кла́ла
6и́й-ут (3 *pl* бьют):   би́л, би́ло, би́ли, би́ла

Note that for the stems in **-д**, **-т**, **-з**, **-с**, stem stress in the past implies an infinitive in **-ть** rather than in **-ти́**:

        клад́-ут: кла́сть
        ле́з-ут: ле́зть
but
        вед-у́т: вести́
        нес-у́т: нести́

Finally, for verbs with shifting stress which move the accent to the prefix in nonfeminine forms, we mark the basic form with a greater than sign (>) over the first or only vowel of the prefix:

пр̀о-жив-ут: про́жил, про́жило, про́жили—прожила́
                про́жит, про́жито, про́житы—прожита́
пѐре-да-ть: пе́редал, пе́редало, пе́редали—передала́
                пе́редан, пе́редано, пе́реданы—передана́

Exceptional cases. 1. The so-called **n/sA** verbs are an exception to the rule that in suffixed verbs shifting stress occurs only in the present tense. These verbs may have either fixed or shifting stress in the *past* tense, while the present tense has fixed ending stress (with only one exception, a verb which does not occur in this book). Because of this the presence or absence of a stress mark will give information about the past, rather than the present, even though the verb is suffixed. Examples:

Fixed stress:
посла́ть: посла́л, посла́ло, посла́ли, посла́ла (пошлю́, пошлёшь, etc.)
порвать: порва́л, порва́ло, порва́ли—порвала́ (порву́, порвёшь, etc.)

2. There are two exceptions to the rule that in nonsuffixed verbs shifting stress occurs only in the past tense; shifting stress occurs in the present tense of: (a) the **НИМ** subtype of the **Й/М/НИМ** verb type:

снимут: сниму́, сни́мешь, . . . , сни́мут (сня́л, сня́ло, сня́ли—сняла́)

and (b) the verb **могут**:

могут: могу́, мо́жешь, . . . , мо́гут (мо́г, мсгло́, могли́, могла́)

The absence of a stress mark with the **НИМ** verbs designates the shifting stress in the past which the type as a whole has, but **могут** has ending stress in the past, which we would have to mark **-у́т**. Since **могут** would indicate the shifting stress which is normal for other consonant stems marked by the absence of a stress mark, our system cannot handle the stress pattern of this verb and it must be learned as an exception; we will leave the basic form unmarked. Hence, for both exceptions:

снимут   могут

3. The present tense stress of verbs in **-ова́ть** is **-у́ю**[T]: **арестова́ть** – **арест-у́ют**. A few (disyllabic) verbs in **-ова́ть** have the stress **-ую́т** (e.g. **кова́ть** – **кую́т**), but there are none in the vocabulary.

4. The irregular verbs **быть** and **дать** have shifting stress in the past, and almost all of their compounds have prefixal (shifting) stress:

бы́л, бы́ло, бы́ли—была́
да́л, да́ло, да́ли—дала́
при́быть: при́был, при́было, при́были—прибыла́
по́дать: по́дал, по́дало, по́дали—подала́

d. *Aspect*

Aspectual relationships are treated in the following way. We consider three relationships as normal:

1. The imperfective is unprefixed and is perfectivized by a nonsemantic prefix. This prefix is placed in parentheses before the imperfective, but the entry is alphabetized under the first letter of the *imperfective* basic form; e.g. **(по)звони́ть** is listed under "**з.**" **Позвони́ть** is listed under "**п**" and cross-referenced to **(по)звони́ть**.

2. The perfective is prefixed and the corresponding imperfective is derived from it by one of the three imperfectivizing suffixes: *váj, áj, 'ivaj*. Note that the stress of all three suffixes is defined, so that the student will always know the stress of a derived imperfective if he recognizes the suffix.

The distribution of stem types according to imperfectivizing suffix and three processes which may accompany them are diagrammed as follows:

IMPERFECTIVE DERIVATION

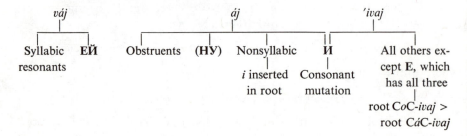

It can be seen that, except for the **И** verbs, which take both *áj* and *'ivaj*, the student is practically able to predict the imperfective from a given perfective, though he would need to apply the consonant mutations, vowel insertions, and vowel shift **o** > **a** before *'ivaj* according to the preceding diagram. We will, however, list both, giving the perfective first and then the derived imperfective, separated by a dash; e.g. **впры́гнуть – впры́гивают**.

3. An imperfective verb exists alone without a perfective verb corresponding to it exactly in meaning; e.g. **зна́чить** 'mean.' Such verbs may have a corresponding perfective in another meaning, but if they exist alone in some meaning, they are so listed at some place in the entry. Such "imperfective only" verbs are simply listed alone:

зна́чить *3 pers only* mean
занима́ются *кем/чем and without complement* II.7

Occasionally we observe a combination of types 1 and 3, which we might best represent by a verbal triangle:

We shall represent such triangles in the vocabularies as follows:

(вы́)-мо́й-ут – вымыва́ют   (вы́)-пьй-ут – выпива́ют

Any aspectual relationships other than the three just described will be specifically noted in the vocabularies.

e. *Voice*

The question of voice and **ся** verbs is discussed in detail in Lesson X, and the student should at some point familiarize himself with the broad outlines of the grammar in that chapter. In the vocabularies, transitivity is not specified if it is clearly inferable from the English; e.g. **обсуди́ть – обсужда́ют** (ppp **об-сужде́н**) 'discuss, talk over,' **поддержа́ть – подде́рживают** 'support, maintain'; nor is intransitivity specified when it is obvious; e.g. **произойду́т – происходить** *3 pers only* 'take place, happen.' Both will be specified if the English meaning would be ambiguous:

продо́лжить – продолжа́ют continue *tr*; —**ся** continue *intr*

Passive **ся** forms, since they are inferable from active transitive **ся** verbs, are not given separately. A **ся** verb which is given has its own (always intransitive) meaning separate from, though usually related to, any non-**ся** verb under which it may be listed, and is just as independent as a **ся** verb listed separately. Failure to list a **ся** verb under a non-**ся** verb does not imply that one does not exist in some meaning; we simply have not listed it in our vocabulary.[1] In the General Vocabulary lesson references are given only for the non-**ся** verb and not for the **ся** verb occurring with it, even though both verbs may occur in the lesson.

f. *Impersonal verbs*

For impersonal verbs, the third singular, rather than the third plural, is used as the basic form; for example:

придётся – приходиться *кому/чему imps*

Verbs occurring in the third person only are designated "*3 pers only*"; for example:

произойду́т – происходить *3 pers only*

g. *Deverbative nouns*

The great majority of Russian verbs have nouns derived from them which denote the action described by the verb or, sometimes, the result of the action, or both. *These nouns are given in the verbal entries rather than listed separately*[2] among other nouns and are marked "*n.*" Only the most common and important deverbative nouns are listed. Nouns whose meanings differ from, are somehow unpredictable from, or would be translated by an English word different from the English word with which the verb is normally associated, have their meanings included with them; otherwise no separate meaning is given. A given verbal noun cannot always be used in all senses of the verb it is derived from, but detailed information about usage is normally not given in the vocabularies:

объясни́ть – объясня́ют explain
   n объясне́ние
рассказать – расска́зывают tell, narrate
   n расска́з

but

зна́чить mean
   n значе́ние meaning; significance
по́ймут – понима́ют understand
   n поня́тие concept, idea; понима́ние understanding

---

[1] For example, **умно́жить – умножа́ют** 'increase' is given without a corresponding **умно́житься – умножа́ются** 'increase' *intr*, though such a verb exists.

[2] Though a few are also cross-referenced from the nonverbal vocabularies.

5. Mobile vowels

a. *Declension*

A mobile vowel is enclosed in slashes if it occurs in the vocabulary form of a word; e.g. звон/о́/к, кита́/е/ц. A slash between two consonants in a vocabulary form indicates that a vowel is inserted between them when appropriate (i.e. when the form has a zero-ending; дос/ка́ implies дос/о́/к, кра́с/ный implies кра́с/е/н, etc.). The mobile vowel in both nouns and adjectives may be regarded as basic *o*, with a variant basic *e* before *jot* and ц and before soft paired consonants, unless the mobile vowel is preceded by a *velar* consonant.[1]

The spelling of the basic mobile *e* is, for practical purposes, always **e**.

руч/е́/й (*gen sg* ручья́) brook
от/е́/ц (*gen sg* отца́) father
д/е́/нь (*gen sg* дня́) day

For basic *o* we may give the following statement as a general but useful rule of thumb, which should cover all the cases in this book: The spelling is **e** or **ё**, unless a *velar* consonant precedes or follows the mobile vowel; if the velar precedes the vowel, the vowel is always spelled **o**; if it follows, the vowel is usually spelled **o**, unless a soft paired consonant precedes the vowel:

вёс/ло́ – вёс/е/л	oar	вёт/ё/р – вёт/ра	wind
вёс/на́ – вёс/е/н	spring	хит/ё/р – хи́т/рый	clever
реб/ро́ – рёб/ё/р	rib	яс/ё/н – я́с/ный	clear
ов/ё/с – ов/са́	oats	ум/ё/н – у́м/ный	intelligent

VELAR PRECEDES MOBILE VOWEL		VELAR FOLLOWS MOBILE VOWEL	
ог/о́/нь – ог/ня́	fire	ло́д/ка – ло́д/о/к	boat
ок/но́ – о́к/о/н	window	па́л/ка – па́л/о/к	stick
ло́к/о/ть – ло́к/тя	elbow	ре́з/о/к – ре́з/кий	sharp

however

ка́ль/ка – ка́л/е/к	calque	кон/ё/к – конь/ка́	horse (dim)
серь/га́ – сер/ё/г	earring	го́р/ё/к – го́рь/кий	bitter

Mobile orthographic **o** not preceding or followed by a velar is rare except in monosyllabic words, where it is as common as, if not more common than, **e**:

с/о́/н – с/на́	sleep	р/о́/т – р/та́	mouth
р/о́/в – р/ва́	ditch	л/ё/н – ль/на́	linen
в/о́/шь – в/ши́	louse	п/ё/с – п/са́	dog (m)

---

[1] There are almost no exceptions; one is люб/о́/вь – люб/ви́ 'love.'

The forms in which mobile vowels will occur are those which take a zero-ending:

In nouns:
    Nominative/accusative singular of masculine nouns (д/е́/нь type)
    Nominative/accusative singular of feminine nouns (це́рк/о/вь type)[1]
    Genitive plural of feminine nouns (дос/о́/к type)
    Genitive plural of neuter nouns (о́к/о/н type)
    The genitive plurals of a few masculine nouns also take zero-endings (cf. page 104): муж/е́/й, друз/е́/й.

In adjectives:
    The masculine short form (кра́с/е/н type)

A slash in a long-form adjectival entry indicates that a short form exists which contains a mobile vowel. The absence of a slash before such common adjectival suffixes as **-н-** and **-к-** indicates that the adjective does not normally have short forms (cf. page 27).

b. *Conjugation*

An /o/ enclosed in slashes in a perfective entry is an **o** inserted before a consonant cluster or, rarely, before a single consonant, following a verbal prefix ending in a consonant. In the imperfective, and often in other forms of the perfective verb, the inserted **o** does not appear, in most cases because there is no cluster. Examples: **в/о/йду́т – входить; под/о/жда́ть; с/о/чту́т(счесть) – счита́ют; от/о/брать(отберу́т) – отбира́ют.**

Syllabic variants of Russian nonsyllabic verbal roots may be considered to contain mobile vowels, but alternations in forms of the same paradigm are relatively rare. Where they do occur, we will specify the forms, as in

назва́ть (назову́т) – называ́ют   с/о/чт-у́т (счесть) – счита́ют

and we will not enclose such vowels in slashes.

The entries in the English-Russian section of the General Vocabulary do not note mobile vowels or the presence of zero.

---

[1] A mobile vowel is also inserted before the unusual consonantal instrumental singular ending **-ью**: **це́рк/о/вью.**

II

REVIEWS 1 TO 10

REVIEW

1

PRONUNCIATION

In the Introduction we discussed the basic sounds of Russian and how the Russian spelling system represents them. In this lesson we shall concern ourselves with the pronunciation of the basic sounds in their various contexts. We shall concentrate on the most difficult and significant cases, the problem areas of pronunciation; rather than giving all the details of Russian phonetics, we shall try to discuss some of the areas which give English-speaking students the most trouble.

We shall be working here primarily, of course, with *phonetic* transcription of the variants of the basic sounds. Remember that phonetic transcription is enclosed in brackets, while basic sounds are in italics.

A. CONSONANTS

1. Paired consonants

Review the primary (or only, if they are hard) articulation of paired consonants, particularly *r, r', l, l', x* [x'], which are the least familiar to the English speaker. Practice the "trill" of *r* and, particularly, of *r'*, and, especially, of both in *final* position. Note that *l* is pronounced with the back of the tongue slightly raised toward the soft palate, producing a sound very close to the "l" in English "pool" or "pall." The *l'* is close to the English "l". in "Montpelier," except that the latter pronunciation is [l'j]; i.e. two consonants, exactly what the student

45

must avoid when pronouncing palatalized consonants (see below); however, the [l']s themselves are similar. Finally, [x'], which is to say *x* before *e* and *i*, is markedly more forward in the mouth (it is almost a palatal) than [x]; that is, *x* before *a*, *o*, and *u*. The same distinction applies, though the difference is less noticeable, to the other velars: *k*, *k'*, *g* [g'].

The *dentals t*, *t'*, *d*, *d'*, *n*, *n'*, are just that; the tip of the tongue touches the upper front *teeth*, not the ridge behind them, as the corresponding sounds do in English. The difference is minor, but noticeable, the type of mistake which does not hinder comprehension, but "gives away" the foreigner.

Practice the following words:

рáд, ря́д, дáр, цáрь, дáра, ры́ло, цари́, царю́, царём, рекá, рéки, лáд, ля́х, лéс, лесá, лóм, лёд, лýк, лю́бит, лы́жа, ли́х, вóл, рóль, роля́м, óтрасль, пы́ль, пи́ли, стрехá, стрехé, хóлм, хи́мия, хи́трый, шáхта, хорошó, ты́, ти́х, дýх, дéло, нóв, нёс, гéний, тóки

Palatalization. Students make two common mistakes in pronouncing palatalized consonants:

1. They pronounce soft (or, sometimes, even hard) consonant plus *j* plus vowel, instead of merely soft consonant plus vowel; e.g. [l'já] or [ljá) instead of [l'á]. This would lead to an identical pronunciation of such words as **полёт** 'flight' and **польёт** 'he will pour upon,' which are distinctively different: [pạl'ót] vs. [pạl'jót]. The student who makes this mistake is forgetting that palatalization is a secondary articulation, *simultaneous* with the primary, and not following it. If it does follow it, it will be separate and will emerge as an independent [j].

2. Before the vowel *i* they palatize either insufficiently or not at all. They let the *i* "do the work for them."[1] But *i* by itself does not do enough work, and Russian **сил** and **мил** [s'íl, m'íl] are very different from English "seal" and "meal," though students frequently pronounce them alike. These English words have the same vowel sound as the Russian words, but the preceding consonants are hard [síl, míl]. Russian, as we know, does not permit this combination. Be particularly careful, then, to palatalize fully soft paired consonants before *i*.

Hard labials before i. Note that hard labials before *i* (**бы, пы**, and so on) are pronounced with a noticeable "w" sound (**был** [bʷýl], **пыль** [pʷýl']). Do not extend this feature either to soft labials before *i* (**бил** is [b'íl]) or to hard labials before any other vowel (**бал** is [bál]) (though before the "rounded" vowels *o* and *u* a hard consonant may have a slight "w" coloration due to these vowels).

---

[1] This statement is not just figurative; *i* is, in fact, a very high vowel, and when it follows a soft consonant, it is quite close to the consonant *j* in articulation and may exert a "palatalizing" effect of its own. After hard consonants it occurs in the somewhat lower and further-back variant [y].

Practice the following words:

бра́т, бра́ть, го́сть, го́стя, бра́тья, во́ля, се́мьям, семи́, семьи́, пьёт, Пётр, пью́т, пюпи́тр, сы́н, си́ний, ми́р, Зи́на, те́ни, ма́тери, ра́ди, ра́ды, сти́х, сты́к, Ри́га, мы́ло, бы́к, би́ть, ры́нок, дымы́, пиро́г, по́ст, пу́ск, бо́р, бу́к

2. Unpaired consonants

Probably the most frequent pronunciation mistake in this area is the soft pronunciation of *c*, particularly before *e*. Remember that *c* *is always hard*; **це́ны** is [cény], and both **ци́рк** and **отцы́** are [cýrk] and [atcý]. Remember also that this consonant is *dental*: tip of tongue on upper front teeth rather than on the ridge behind them; i.e. *c*, which is the affricate [ts] has the articulation of its constituents. *š* and *ž* are somewhat like the English consonants in "sure" and "measure," but much harder and further back in the mouth; the difference is quite noticeable. *č*, on the other hand, is very much like the "ch" in "cheese," though less like the harder, final "ch" of "much" and "watch." Remember to pronounce it *soft*. *j* is, of course, pronounced like the English "y" in "yes." For most students the most difficult unpaired consonant is *šč*. Pronounce it either like "fre*sh sh*eet" or "fre*sh ch*eese," but in both cases it is *soft* and has the effect of a long consonant: **щи́** [š̄'í] or [š'č'í].

Practice the following words:

це́лый, це́ль, цени́ть, на́ция, цыплёнок, па́льцы, отцу́, отце́, отцо́м, ши́ть, ша́пка, шу́м, шо́рох, жа́ль, жела́ть, жую́, же́сть, обжо́ра, чу́ть, че́сть, чи́н, чёрный, ча́р, ще́ль, щу́ка, щи́т, пле́щет

3. Voiced and voiceless consonants

The voiced-voiceless opposition in Russian obstruents was treated in the Introduction. The two general rules for pronunciation are: (1) final voiced obstruents become voiceless; (2) all obstruents in a cluster are either voiced or voiceless, according to whether the final obstruent is voiced or voiceless, except that voiceless obstruents remain voiceless before *v* and *v'*. Note that rule 2 affects the pronunciation of prepositions, since these are, phonetically, part of the words they precede.

Practice the following words:

но́ж, но́г, ле́зть, пя́дь, вёз, свя́зь, но́вь, зя́бь, но́жка, везти́, тетра́дка, ла́вка, но́гти, легко́,[1] вы́рубка, пое́здка, про́сьба, отбу́ду, отвёл, обтёр, от горы́, из того́, к доске́, с верши́ны

---

[1] *g* before *k* or *č* is pronounced [x]; **мя́гко** [m'áxkə], **мя́гче** [m'áxči].

4. Some special cases not inferable from the spelling

a. *Hard-soft assimilation.* Consonants standing before soft consonants may become palatalized. Those most likely to be affected are *d*, *t*, *z*, and *s*, but there is no more general rule we may state. Examples: **е́сть** [jés't'], **везде́** [v'iz'd'é], **дверь** [d'v'ér'], **съезд** [s'jést]; but not **объём** [abjóm].

b. The combination **сч** is pronounced the same as **щ**; examples: **сча́стье** [š'ás't'jə], **счёт** [š'ót], **разно́счик** [raznóš'ik].

c. The combination **зж**, the combination **жж** in some words, and **жд'** in words with the root **дожд'** 'rain' have a [ž̄'] or [ž'dž'], the voiced equivalent of [š̄] and [š'č'], respectively. Examples: **е́зжу** [jéž̄'u], **во́жжи** [vóž̄'i], **дождя́** [dāž̄'á].[1]

d. The verbal particle **-ся** (-*s'a*) is always pronounced [-sə] after an ending in **-т** or **-ть**, and the final -*t'* of infinitives hardens before this ending; in addition, the combination, in careful pronunciation, results in a "double t" [tc]; i.e. [tts]. Hence, both **бои́тся** and **боя́ться** are [bạjátcə], **бои́тся** [bạjítcə], etc. When it follows other consonants, the growing tendency is to pronounce [s'ə], but [sə] is correct and still fairly common. Similarly, **сь** is now pronounced soft by most speakers in all positions, though some speakers still pronounce it hard, if the preceding vowel is not stressed.

e. The nominative singular masculine of adjectives in **-кий, -гий, -хий** may be pronounced [-kəj] as well as [-k'ij]. (The basic adjectival ending -*oj* after hard consonants, spelled **-ый** (or **-ий** after unpaired consonants and *n'*), may be said [-əj] or [-yj]; the phonetic difference is very small.)

Practice the following words:

> изве́стие, е́здить, две́, Тве́рь, стена́, же́нственный [žén's't'v'innyj], счита́ют, зано́счивый, привя́зчивый, бре́зжит, во́жжи, сожжён, дождеви́к, дождём, прости́тся, прости́ться, сда́ться, сда́лся, сдади́мся, даю́щиеся, боя́сь, собира́ясь, встреча́ясь, ре́зкий, до́лгий, хоро́ший, съёмка, объе́зд, рассве́т, с собо́й, вве́рить

B. VOWELS

1. Fronting and raising in soft environment

The most important factor in the pronunciation of the variants of the basic vowel sounds is the softness or hardness of adjacent consonants, *particularly of a following consonant.* The more *softness* in the environment, the more *fronted* and *raised* the pronunciation of a vowel, which is to say, the more it moves in

---

[1] Long consonants appear elsewhere in Russian primarily at morpheme boundaries: **отда́ть** [addạt'], **от трёх** [attr'óx], and, sometimes, in certain borrowings **ма́сса** [mássə].

the direction of [i]; see below. The fronting and raising is most marked, of course, *between* soft consonants, but only slightly less so *before* a soft and after a hard. In phonetic transcription we shall place a dot under vowels preceding soft consonants: ạ, ẹ,[1] etc. Variants after soft but before hard consonants are also somewhat fronted and raised, but much less noticeably. The following table depicts what has been said (increasing frontness and highness from left to right):

BASIC VOWEL		BEFORE HARD CONSONANT				BEFORE SOFT CONSONANT [a]		
a	[a]	брáт	ря́д	*Eng* pot	[a]	брáть	пя́ть	*Eng* pat
e	[e]	э́тот	рéдко	*Eng* pet	[ẹ]	э́ти	пéть	*Eng* pate
o	[o]	тóт	тётка	*Eng* paw	[ọ]	нóчь	тётя[2]	
u	[u]	пýт	тюк	*Eng* pool	[ụ]	пýть	лю́ди[3]	

The basic vowel *i* is front and high already. [i], the phonetic variant which occurs after soft consonants and in initial position and in isolation, is maximally high and front, and hence does not change according to hardness or softness of following consonant. The variant [y] is quite a bit further back and somewhat lower, though it is raised and fronted slightly when it precedes a soft consonant; cf. бы́т and бы́ть. [y], whether before hard or soft consonant, is unfamiliar to the English ear, and the student may not have mastered it. It should be practiced carefully.

Practice the following words:

зя́ть, порóть, вью́ге, тянýть, ся́дь, лéзь, несёте, ны́ть, бри́ть, вéщь, пя́тый, рáть, везёт, стрóчка, нóша, лóжка, лéнь, дря́нь, вóт, взя́ли, рéк, рéки, лю́лька, сты́к, вы́ть, пóле, вóля, я́д, ты́л, жи́знь, рыбáк, вы́шит, ды́м

For purposes of this book, we prefer the symbol [y] rather than [i] for rendering *i* after hard consonants.

2. Pronunciation of unstressed vowels

The pronunciation of the basic vowel sounds outside of stress is not difficult but very often causes trouble for students, mostly because the basic facts have been avoided or not taught systematically. They are quite simple:

---

[1] One might also indicate raising and fronting by placing a small "i" above and to the right of the vowel.

[2] The pronunciation is often close to but not as far front nor as raised as the vowel in German *töten* or French *peu*.

[3] The pronunciation is often close to but not as far front nor as raised as the vowel in German *Tür* or French *tu*.

i and *u* are pronounced basically the same unstressed as stressed.[1] The following table summarizes the pronunciation of unstressed *a*, *e*, and *o*:

BASIC VOWEL	FIRST PRETONIC SYLLABLE		OTHER UNSTRESSED SYLLABLE	
	After hard consonants and initially	*After soft consonants*	*After hard consonants and initially*	*After soft consonants*
a, o	[a]	[i][1]	[ə][2,3]	[i][1]
e	[y][4]	[i][1]	[ə][4]	[i][1]

The following positions require some special comment:

1. *e* and *o* after hard unpaired consonants (*c, ž, š*) are pronounced [y] in the first pretonic syllable: цена́ [cyná], шести́ [šyst'í], жена́ [žyná], жесто́кий [žystókəj]. *e* occurs after hard paired consonants only in foreign words, where it is a somewhat reduced [e] or, less correctly, [i] (see footnote 4, below).

2. *a* after hard unpaired consonants in the first pretonic syllable is [a], except in a very few specific words, where it is [y]; e.g. двадцати́ [dvətcyt'í], жале́ть [žyl'ęt'].

3. In many grammatical endings in *a* and *o*, the usual [i] after soft consonants and [y] after hard unpaired consonants is replaced by (ə). Usage varies in some cases, but in general the most important positions are these:

-o (spelling *-e(ě)*)

1. Nom/acc sg neu nouns: по́ле, мо́ре, сча́стье, жела́ние [pól'ə], etc.
2. Inst sg masc/neu nouns: учи́телем, пла́чем, мо́рем [učít'il'əm], etc.
3. Gen pl masc/neu nouns: ге́ниев, бра́тьев, дере́вьев [g'ęn'ijəf], etc.
4. Nom/acc sg neu adjectives: ста́рое, молодо́е [stárəjə], etc.
5. Nom/acc sg neu pronouns: на́ше, ва́ше [nášə], etc.

-a (spelling *-я/а*)

1. Nom sg fem nouns: ка́пля, ста́я, встре́ча [kápl'ə], etc.
2. Nom sg fem adjectives: ста́рая, друга́я [stárəjə], etc.
3. Nom/acc pl masc/neu nouns in *j*: бра́тья, дере́вья, собра́ния [brát'jə], etc.

---

[1] Unstressed *i* after soft consonants, and also unstressed *a*, *o*, and *e* after soft consonants (see table above) emerge phonetically as [i], but with a somewhat lower articulation than stressed [i] has; stressed [i] would be similar to the vowel in English *heat*, unstressed [i] would be in the direction of English *hit* (and, of course, shorter, since it is unstressed). Compare реки́ with ре́ки, and pronounce: язы́к, весна́.

[2] This symbol represents the so-called "schwa" vowel sound, which is approximately the sound of the second vowel in the English word "sof*a*."

[3] Word initial *o/a* is always [a]: огоро́д [agarót]; cf. в огоро́де [vəgaród'i].

[4] In foreign words, however, a somewhat reduced vowel close to [e] is normal; e.g. поэте́сса, эта́ж, тенниси́ст, эволю́ция.

4. Gen sg masc/neu nouns: **мо́ря, геро́я, пла́ча** [mór'ə], etc.
5. 3 pl of 2 conj verbs: **ви́дят, поло́жат** [v'id'ət], etc.
6. Present gerunds: **зна́я, ви́дя, слы́ша** [znájə], etc.
7. Verbal particle **-ся**: **боя́лся, боя́ться** [bajáls'ə] or [bajálsə], etc.

But note [znájɨt], [jivrap'éjɨk], [puļ'im'ót], and other grammatical positions where the vowel reduction is to the normal [i]. Compare also the distinction: **в по́ле** (*acc*) [fpól'ə] vs. **в по́ле** (*prp*) [fpól'i].

The student should not attempt to memorize the details given here, but rather use them as a check and a reference. Most important, in practice, are: (a) correct handling of *a* and *o* after hard paired consonants; i.e. getting [a] and [ə] in the correct positions: **го́род, города́, огоро́д**; and (b) the absolute avoidance of [e] outside of stress, except for a few foreign words (see paragraph 1 page 50): **середи́на, веретено́**.

Unstressed vowels, like stressed vowels, are raised and fronted in soft environments and, though the differences are less noticeable, a phonetic transcription might also employ a dot under unstressed vowels preceding soft consonants; e.g. **возьму́** (vaẓ'mú), **горячо́** (gər'ičó).

Practice the following words:

вёсти́, река́, молоко́, моло́чный, ле́то, висе́ть, стерегу́, во́лость, вороти́ть, ве́тер, ледяно́й, рядо́в, черта́, часы́, брала́, взяла́, объясни́ть, боево́й, в объясне́ние, Аване́сов, об Аване́сове, реши́ть, образцо́вый, молодова́та, зо́лото, язы́к, берегово́й, черепа́ха, жара́

Practice also:

жёна́, шеста́, целина́, эта́п, эконо́мика, ро́жа, мы́ться, реше́ние, здоро́вье, по́лём, геро́ёв, но́воё, но́вая, писаре́м, стро́я, объявле́ния, си́дя, ку́рят, смо́трят, берёмся, но́ша, тридцати́, сожале́ние

СЛОВА́РЬ ГРАММАТИ́ЧЕСКИХ ТЕ́РМИНОВ

произноше́ние pronunciation
транскри́пция transcription
транслитера́ция transliteration
ударе́ние stress; — па́дает на Х-ый слог stress falls on X syllable; (не)удар-я́емый (пе́рвый предуда́рный) слог (un)stressed (first pretonic) syllable
до́лгий/кра́ткий гла́сный long/short vowel; до́лгий/кра́ткий согла́сный long/short consonant
гла́сный ве́рхнего подъёма high vowel
грамма́тика grammar
словообразова́ние word-formation

фоне́тика phonetics
си́нтаксис syntax
фле́ксия inflection
ча́сти сло́ва parts of the word
   ко́р/е/нь *m E pl obl* root
   су́ффикс suffix
   пре́фикс (приста́в/ка) prefix
   оконча́ние ending
   Сло́во «уходи́ть» состои́т из пре́фикса «у», ко́рня «ход», су́ффикса «и» и оконча́ния «ть». The word уходи́ть consists of the prefix *y*, the root *ход*, the suffix *u*, and the ending *ть*.

REVIEW

2

VERBAL ASPECT: REVIEW AND SOME FURTHER CONSIDERATIONS OF USAGE

A. GENERAL DISCUSSION

1. The problem of aspect is treated in various ways by various people, and students frequently begin grappling with the finer points of usage before they have acquired a clear understanding of the fundamentals. Selection and analysis of aspect in a given practical situation may be quite difficult, and the problem in general will challenge the student as long as he works with Russian. But the basic assumptions may be easily stated, and a grasp of them should help him solve some cases of usage, make hypotheses about others, and make his analysis more interesting.

2. The basic aspectual relationship is perhaps best characterized in the following way. The perfective aspect focuses attention upon the completion, termination, or single end of an action, while the imperfective aspect says nothing about the end of the action. The perfective specifies completion; the imperfective does not specify it, but does not exclude it. It is important to note that the *imperfective does not mean that the action was not completed*; it may have been, but the speaker merely chooses not to emphasize this. Because of its lack of commitment to completion, an imperfective form instead of a perfective form frequently calls attention to the *process* itself. Compare:

Кто́ постро́ил э́тот до́м?	Who built that house? (Who got it built? *Emphasis on completed process.*)
Кто́ стро́ил э́тот до́м?	Who built that house? (Who worked on (the building of) that house? *Emphasis on action; the building may have been completed.*)
or Э́тот до́м до́лго стро́или.	They were working on (*or* "worked on") that house for a long time. (*The house may or may not have been finished.*)

We already know that the imperfective is usually used to describe habitual action: e.g. **Он ка́ждый де́нь писа́л письмо́ жене́.** Once again, the imperfective form describes completed action ("He wrote (and finished) a letter to his wife every day"), but the emphasis is elsewhere.

In the "present tense" forms of perfective and imperfective verbs the aspectual distinction is normally subordinate to the tense distinction; i.e. the perfective expresses future action and the imperfective denotes present action:

Я его́ ви́жу сейча́с.	I see him right now.
Я его́ уви́жу за́втра.	I will see him tomorrow.

However, in those forms in which both the perfective and imperfective may be used, particularly in the past tense or the infinitive, the perfective is likely to have a meaning much more specific and delimited as to time than the imperfective, a situational and more restricted sense than the imperfective. The distinction may be reflected by a difference in the corresponding English translations:

Я её ви́дел вчера́.	I saw her yesterday.
Я её уви́дел вчера́.	I caught sight of her yesterday.[1]
Она́ хо́чет ему́ нра́виться.	She wants him to like her (in general).
Она́ хо́чет ему́ понра́виться.	She wants him to like her (tomorrow night when he meets her).
Он лю́бит пи́ть.	He likes to drink.
Он лю́бит вы́пить.	He likes to take a drink.
Жди́те!	Wait.
Подожди́те, пока́ я не верну́сь.	Wait until I return.

---

[1] The relationship between **слы́шать** and **услы́шать** parallels that between **ви́деть** and **уви́деть**.

3. A most important thing to be kept in mind is that the relationship existing between aspectual partners *differs from verb to verb* and that the exact nature of this relationship is very much a function of the actual *meaning* of the verb and of the extent to which this meaning lends itself to clear-cut aspectual opposition. For example, **писать – написать** is a fairly clear-cut opposition; the verbs **живу́т** and **рабо́тают**, on the other hand, do not lend themselves to purely grammatical (i.e. nonsemantic: *meaning does not change*) perfectivization; no prefix added to them builds an absolute aspectual partner. Most prefixes change lexical meanings sufficiently so that a new imperfective must be created:

живут	live	пе́реживут – пережива́ют	experience
рабо́тают	work	зарабо́тают – зараба́тывают	earn

Other prefixes may modify the action in some way, usually with respect to time or intensity, rather than changing the lexical sense:

живут	live	проживу́т	live for a specified period
рабо́тают	work	порабо́тают	work for a while

Such verbs frequently do not build derived imperfectives.

The relationships between verbs commonly regarded as aspectual partners may also be less than purely aspectual; an element of meaning may be present in one which is absent in the other. The prefixed **по-** added to motion verbs clearly has an inceptive meaning in addition to its perfective meaning:

Она́ пое́хала в Москву́.	She went (set off for, left for) Moscow.
Де́ло уже́ пошло́.	The thing has already gotten started.

Or many verbs with a perfectivizing **-ну-** suffix which imparts an additional "semelfactive" (instantaneous) meaning may be given as partners of imperfectives which do not have this meaning; e.g. **кри́кнуть – крича́ть** 'shout,' **ки́нуть – кида́ют** 'throw.'

4. Sometimes the relationship between aspectual partners may be something like "try to, work at" vs. "succeed in, conclude successfully." For example:

Я до́лго реша́л э́ту зада́чу и, наконе́ц, реши́л её.	I worked on this problem a long time and finally solved it.

Often the English verbs best translating the aspectual partners will be different, though this does not in itself set the partners further apart; on the contrary, their formal link betokens their semantic closeness. Observe:

угова́ривают	urge, try to persuade	уговори́ть	persuade
дока́зывают	point out, try to prove	доказа́ть	prove
оты́скивают	look for, try to find	отыска́ть	find

| учиться | study, try to learn | научиться | learn |
| сдава́ть экза́мен | take an exam | сда́ть экза́мен | pass an exam |

5. We have already mentioned that in many cases it is difficult or impossible to state definitely whether a given pair of verbs do or do not constitute an aspectual pair, and it is often irrelevant even to ask the question. The verbs **чита́ют** and **прочита́ют** are usually given as a pair, and certainly with some justification; yet it is clear that the relationship is not as purely aspectual as in a pair like **де́лают** and **сде́лают**. **Прочита́ют** has the "perfective" meaning of "get (something) read," but it also carries the meaning of its prefix **про-** 'through' and builds a derived imperfective **прочи́тывают**, whose existence shows that a speaker may not want to turn back to **чита́ют** for an imperfective "read through." We might diagram this situation as follows:

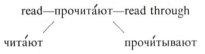

Such verbal triangles are quite common in Russian. Two other examples involving verbs already known to the student are:

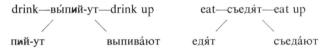

6. Finally, remember that a given verb, particularly an unprefixed imperfective, may have several meanings and usages not all of which will comprehend the perfective partner. You will encounter many examples later on, but the one best known to you now is probably **говори́ть**. This verb means both "talk" and "say." In the latter meaning it is the partner of the perfective verb **сказать**: **Что́ она́ говори́т ему́?** 'What is she saying to him?' In the former meaning it has no perfective partner. Or the verb **учить** is perfectivized by **на-** in its meaning "teach" but by **вы́-** in its meaning "study, learn by heart."

B. SELECTING THE PERFECTIVE OR IMPERFECTIVE

The greatest practical problem facing the student is proper selection and correct analysis in contexts where *either* of the aspects may be normally used and where their opposition is most pronounced. Where aspect assumes tense functions, this opposition is dampened and selection is usually clear; e.g. in present tense contexts, where an imperfective is ordinarily called for,[1] and in the

---

[1] Certain usages of the perfective present in present tense meaning are treated in Lesson VII.

future, where a perfective verb is normally required for a single action and an imperfective for repeated or extended action. In practice, the greatest difficulties are presented by those categories which do not favor one aspect or the other: the *past tense*, the *infinitive*, and the *imperative*. A general problem in aspect, which must be dealt with in all these categories, is the *negative*.

We shall make some general remarks and suggest a few guidelines for each of these categories, but the student is warned that there is considerable disagreement among scholars, both Russian and non-Russian, about many areas of aspect. It is an under-studied area, and much remains to be done. Most of the examples are from Soviet written and oral sources, and some of the suggestions made are based on studies being carried out by various Soviet linguists working on aspect: They should in no sense be considered as final conclusions or as constituting a complete survey.

1. Past tense

The English continuous imperfect expressing an action in progress in the past ("was X-ing") is always rendered in Russian by the imperfective past;[1] e.g. 'as we were walking to town' **когда́ мы́ шли́ в го́род**, 'She was preparing dinner' **Она́ гото́вила обе́д**. If the context calls for words like **до́лго**, **всегда́**, or **ча́сто**, of course, an imperfective is clearly required (this would apply to all categories). Elsewhere, selection may not be as straightforvard, but often one of the principles that are suggested in paragraphs 1 to 6 above more or less applies. Consider the following examples:

Я вы́брал ёлку.	I chose a Christmas tree.
Я выбира́л ёлку два́ часа́.	I spent two hours choosing a Christmas tree. (*Completion, but emphasis elsewhere*)
Колу́мб бы́л сча́стлив не тогда́, когда́ откры́л Аме́рику, а когда́ открыва́л её. (Достое́вский)	Columbus was happy not when he discovered America, but while he was discovering it. (*The process, not the result*)
Она́ до́лго угова́ривала его́ и, наконе́ц, уговори́ла.	She tried to persuade him for a long time, and finally she succeeded.
Он мно́го де́лал, но́ ничего́ не сде́лал.	He did a lot of things but got nothing done.

---

[1] In general, the Russian perfective aspect and the English progressive aspect, marked by tense forms in "-ing," are incompatible categories, since the former implies completion of action, while the latter excludes it.

Я звони́л ему́.	(*The imperfective is a general statement:* I tried to get him on the phone, *with no commitment to success or failure.*
Я позвони́л ему́.	*The perfective implies success and previous allusion to the call.*)
Я смотре́л э́тот фи́льм. Я посмотре́л то́т фи́льм, кото́рый вы́ мне́ рекомендова́ли.	(*Imperfective is a general statement:* I have seen that film; *perfective for a more specific reference with previous mention.*)
Я у ва́с брала́? Благодарю́.	(*Overheard from a woman returning a borrowed pencil: Imperfective signals she was "taking" not on a permanent basis; cf. English "I was borrowing . . ."*)

The partners of many verbs, however, may be found in exactly the same context: **отве́тить – отвеча́ют** and **оста́нутся – остава́ться** are good examples. In such cases stylistic rather than grammatical considerations may govern selection, and Russians themselves will argue as to which is best in a given instance. And, as we have said, meaning is important; certain verbs may lean to one aspect or the other by nature of their meaning. **Проси́л**, for instance, is commoner than **попроси́л**; the emphasis of *asking* is very much on the action. Someone waiting on a line of people would be more likely to ask **Кто́ проси́л?** than **Кто́ попроси́л?**

2. Infinitive

Selection here is governed by the general considerations we have discussed. The student is familiar with certain verbs after which only *imperfective* infinitives may be used; these verbs usually imply an action in progress:

на́чнут – начина́ют	begin	продо́лжить – продолжа́ют	continue
ко́нчить – конча́ют	end	уста́нут – устава́ть	get tired
(на)учи́ться	learn		

A verb which can take only a perfective infinitive is **успе́ют – успева́ют** (a fact which does not surprise us, when we consider the meaning: "have time to, succeed in" (finishing something)). Infinitives after motion verbs are usually imperfective; e.g. **Они́ пошли́ покупа́ть** (not **купи́ть**). Imperfective infinitives are also the rule after such words as **почему́** and **зачём**, but this fact is connected with the general problem of the negative, discussed below. Some examples with the infinitive:

Вы пра́ва не име́ете люде́й на моро́зе раздева́ть. (Солжени́цын)	You have no right to make men take off their clothes in the freezing weather. (*Imperfective general statement*)
Она́ бу́дет до́лго одева́ться.	It will take her a long time to dress.
Я до́лжен тепе́рь встава́ть.	I've got to be getting up now.
Я до́лжен вста́ть в ше́сть часо́в.	I've got to get up at six o'clock. (*The more concrete, the more likely to be perfective*)
Через два́ часа́ на́с поведу́т убива́ть.	In two hours they will take us out to be killed.
Она́ пошла́ зака́нчивать сво́й туале́т.	She went off to finish her toilet. (*Motion verbs*)
Он на́чал переводи́ть письмо́.	He began to translate the letter.
Мы́ успе́ли ко́нчить всю́ свою́ рабо́ту.	We had time to finish all our work.
Я уста́л писа́ть пи́сьма.	I'm tired of writing letters.

3. Imperative

The general rule: perfective for (positive) commands, imperfective for prohibitions (negative commands) may be useful as a guideline, but in practice the imperfective with positive commands is very frequent. The greater the emphasis on the action rather than on the result, and the less specific the nature of the command, the more likely the imperfective is. A teacher says to students at the blackboard: **Пиши́те**. ('Write! Do some writing!') Only if the thing to be written is specified or definitely implied do we get the perfective: **Напиши́те э́ту фра́зу**. Similarly, to a student waiting to read: **Чита́йте** but **Прочита́йте э́ту фра́зу**.

Some students of aspect maintain that an imperfective imperative involves a greater or lesser *involvement on the part of the speaker*; that is, has modal force. Such involvement might entail anything from politeness and enthusiasm to entreaty or threat, depending on the verb, context, voice intonation, and so on. The perfective would be more neutral or matter-of-fact. Some examples:

Закро́йте две́рь.	Close the door. (*Neutral*)
Эй, ты́, вахла́к, две́рь закрыва́й! (Солжени́цын)	Hey, you lout, close the door. (*Extreme harshness, perhaps threat*)
На сво́й стра́х, е́сли хо́чешь, оста́нься. (Солжени́цын)	Stay, at your own risk, if you want. (*Speaker is indifferent.*)

Ты́ остава́йся ту́т, держи́ кре́пко! (Солжени́цын)	You stay here, hold firmly! (*Speaker strongly involved*)
Ся́дьте.	Sit down. (*Neutral, matter of fact*)
Сади́тесь.	Sit down. (*Politer; speaker is somewhat involved in showing his politeness. This is the more common choice.*)

When the negative command, on the other hand, carries a note of warning or great urgency, it is often put into the perfective:

Не упади́те!	Don't fall!
Не откажи́те мне́ в мое́й про́сьбе!	Don't deny me my request!

Particularly common, since it usually connotes warning (however mild), is **не забу́дьте**. When no warning is implied, or when the request is over a period of time, the imperfective is preferred. Compare:

Не забу́дьте сказа́ть ему́!	Don't forget to tell him!
Не забыва́йте меня́, когда́ я́ бу́ду в а́рмии.	Don't forget me while I'm in the army.

4. Negative

The "general" rule that the negative command ordinarily calls for an imperfective verb is part of a larger phenomenon. Negation increases the likelihood that a verb will be imperfective, where a choice exists, for the fairly simple reason that a negated action is by its nature much further from the prospect or idea of completion than a positive action is. If the action is denied altogether, the imperfective is used; if, however, the action is not suppressed altogether: Someone else carries it out, it may be carried out in the future, or even if the negation affects the object of the action rather than the action itself, the verb may be perfective. Observe:

Взя́л ты́ э́ту кни́гу?	*Question:* Did you take this book?
Не́т, не бра́л.	(*Denial of action altogether*)
Не́т, не взя́л, э́то сосе́д взя́л.	(*Action took place, although I wasn't involved:* Не я́ взя́л, а сосе́д взя́л. *Notice:* не *precedes* я́, *rather than* взя́л.)
Он не напи́шет э́того письма́.	He won't write that letter. (*Emphasis on the object: letter*)
Он не бу́дет писа́ть на́м.	He won't write us. (*Emphasis on the "writing" that he won't do.*)

As we expect, the *meaning* of the verb involved plays an important role. **Я не заме́тил** is commoner than **Я не замеча́л**, because the meaning is usually something like: "There was something going on which I should have noticed, and ordinarily would have noticed, but I happened not to" (hence, not categorical denial of the action). Compare the imperfective in the following example, however: **Все́ её зна́ли, и никто́ не замеча́л** 'Everybody knew her, but nobody noticed her.' Here there is no suggestion that people "happened" not to notice her; the point is that no one *did* notice her (because she was plain or uninteresting, or in other ways failed to attract attention). In the sentence **Сове́тский Сою́з в 1941 году́ к войне́ не приготовился** the verb is perfective because it is not so much the action that is denied as its successful completion (should have prepared for the war, had been thinking about preparing for the war, but hadn't).

Infinitives directly preceded by **не** or by other negative expressions tend to be imperfectives. The same is true of words which question an action, such as **почему́** or **заче́м**. Some examples are:

Он не хо́чет оставля́ть свои́х детей на це́лый го́д.	He doesn't want to leave his children for a whole year.
Вчера́ не на́до бы́ло бра́ть тебя́ по́д руку, а я́ взя́л.	I shouldn't have taken your arm yesterday, but I did.
Заче́м об э́том спра́шивать?	Why should one ask about that?

5. Frequent or habitual actions

Frequent or habitual actions are usually rendered by the imperfective; not, as we have seen, because the imperfective means "frequentative," but because "frequentative" is an emphasis that has nothing to do with completion. The "frequentative" and completion are certainly not mutually exclusive notions, however, and the perfective is occasionally seen:

Я́ сказа́л ему́ не́сколько ра́з.	I told him several times.
Это мо́жно ча́сто прочита́ть в на́ших газе́тах.	You (can) read about that frequently in our newspapers

СЛОВА́РЬ ГРАММАТИ́ЧЕСКИХ ТЕ́РМИНОВ

ви́д aspect:
  (не)совершённый—(im)perfective aspect
  многокра́тный—frequentative aspect
  (не)определённый—(non)determined
    aspect
инфинити́в infinitive
отрица́тельный negative; отрица́ние
  negation

значе́ние meaning
фо́рма form
констру́кция construction
вре́мя tense:
  настоя́щее—present tense
  проше́дшее—past tense
  бу́дущее—future tense

REVIEWS

3 to 10

Reviews 3 to 10 comprise a topical review centering around English-to-Russian translation passages, specially constructed to bring up all the grammatical points which would normally be treated in a full-size elementary grammar, and presented in paragraphs and in unified "stories" so that a context is present. No review can present all the grammar again, and the student must have on hand the best possible elementary textbook. This review does, however, restate certain points and make certain formulations summing up problems in a way which may not have been possible in the elementary text. Most important, however, it attempts to *anticipate the pitfalls*; it deals squarely with the points which have proved to be the trouble spots in elementary Russian, persist at the intermediate level, and, unless they are isolated and removed, dog the student throughout his study.

Many such points are raised, usually more than once, in the translation passages, and at least the first occurrence of each is specifically referenced and discussed in the Notes which follow each passage. The student is then left to deal with subsequent occurrences on his own. The passages may be done without reference to the Notes, if the student feels this is better practice, but it is perhaps best if he reads them as he translates. He may learn something new, understand something better, or discover that he got something accidentally correct, without having understood the principle and, hence, deprived himself of the opportunity to learn by his mistake. The student should not neglect to read through all of the Notes at some point.

Each lesson has several main topics headed by capital letters. These topics are listed on the first page of each lesson. The student should read through these sections carefully, *before* doing the translations, which provide a thorough drill for the grammar contained therein. There will certainly be some new formulations, and some of the material itself may be new as well.

Finally, it is important to raise a general point which applies to translation and to comparison of languages in general. Always remember that there is no intrinsic relationship between Russian and English words. The following examples of translation of the apparently simple English words "anyone"[1] and "would" should show how hopeless it is to rely on slavish word-for-word translation, particularly with grammatical elements. We will continually point up the danger of this, and the student should overemphasize the principle, rather than risk forgetting it. He should develop a sense for what is obviously idiomatic or exclusively limited to English.

anyone

Do you see *anyone*?	Вы видите кого-нибудь?
I don't know *anyone*.	Я никого не знаю.
Anyone will tell you that.	Любой человек вам это скажет.

would

She said that she *would* come.	Она сказала, что она придёт. (*Future*)
She *would* come if she could.	Она пришла бы, если бы могла. (*Conditional*)
Last year she *would* bring me breakfast at eight o'clock.	В прошлом году она приносила мне завтрак в восемь часов. (*Frequentative past*)

It is clear that one must first find out which of the "anyones" or "woulds" one is working with, before the correct Russian can be selected. The same problem exists, of course, in the other direction, for Russian has many words like "anyone" and "would," but students often have more trouble thinking about what the words in their own language really mean. It is unfortunate but true that the more common and useful words are in two languages, the less they correspond to each other. Prepositions are very good examples of this; see R4.B, page 77, where we will have to voice our warning again.

---

[1] Similar examples could be given for other words in "any."

A. Tense sequence and indirect speech	
B. Modals: бы *and* чтобы	**REVIEW**
C. ли	**3**
D. э́тот/э́то *and* то́т/то́	
E. The translation of *"it"*	
F. Verbs of asking and telling	

A. TENSE SEQUENCE AND INDIRECT SPEECH

In comparing Russian and English tense forms, note that Russian often preserves the "actual time" better:

> е́сли о́н за́втра придёт
>
> if he comes tomorrow (*instead of* "*will come*")

This statement is particularly true of constructions involving tense sequence and indirect speech. In Russian the verb is the same as it was in the original, direct speech, whereas in English the tenses are often different:

> Она́ сказа́ла, что придёт.
> ORIGINAL: «Я приду́.»
>
> She said that she would come. *Or:* She said that she was coming.

> Она́ сказа́ла, что рабо́тает на заво́де.
> ORIGINAL: «Я рабо́таю на заво́де.»
>
> She said she was working at the factory. *Or:* She said she worked at the factory.

Compare:

> Она́ сказа́ла, что рабо́тала на заво́де.
> ORIGINAL: «Я рабо́тала на заво́де.»
>
> She said she had been working at the factory. *Or:* She said she was working at the factory (e.g. "when that happened").

We can see from the examples that a given English sentence may be ambiguous and that its correct translation into Russian may require knowledge of the original sentence on which it is based; i.e. is "She said she was working at the factory" based on "I *am* working at the factory" or "I *was* working at the factory"?

The situation is similar in reported questions:

Она́ спроси́ла, рабо́таю ли я на заво́де.

ORIGINAL: Рабо́таете ли вы на заво́де?

She asked if I worked at the factory (*or* was working).

Она́ спроси́ла, рабо́тал ли я на заво́де.

ORIGINAL: Рабо́тали ли вы на заво́де?

She asked if I had worked at the factory. *Or:* She asked if I worked at the factory.

B. MODALS: бы and чтобы

Mode or *mood* is the linguistic expression of the speaker's attitude toward an action; the speaker is usually expressing his opinion of or attitude toward either the *possibility* or the *desirability* of the action. "John is here" is non-modal; it is objective reporting. So is "I know that John is here." But "I wish that John were here," "I want John to be here," "I told John to be here," "Might John have been here?" "If John were here, I could leave," and "Be here, John!" all reflect the speaker's involvement with the possibility or de-sirability or *necessity* of an action. Purpose clauses like "John did that so that you would (might) understand" and "John is here to explain that to you" are also modal. Modals are discussed in some detail in Lesson IX; up to this point, however, the student has probably worked with at least relatively simple ex-amples of the imperative, conditional, and purpose expressions.

The imperative in Russian is expressed by special verb forms, but most other modal expressions employ the stressless particles бы (б) and, particularly for purpose clauses, чтобы (чтоб).

Remember that neither бы nor чтобы *ever* occurs with a present tense form, even where the meaning seems to be present. The past tense form which goes along with бы in conditionals cannot, therefore, distinguish tense. Hence,

Е́сли бы о́н пришёл,   *can mean*   If he were to come, we would see him.
мы́ бы ви́дели его́.   *or*   If he had come, we would have seen him.[1]

Non-contrary to fact (without бы) conditionals, on the other hand, do distinguish tense; cf. **Е́сли о́н зна́ет (узна́ет), о́н говори́т (ска́жет)**.

For the same reason, the past tense forms after чтобы[2] in purpose ex-pressions have no tense meaning:

---

[1] Remember also that in a normal conditional you must place the бы with the past tense form in *both* clauses.

[2] **Чтобы**, of course, may also be followed by an infinitive when the subject of the clause it introduces is the same as the subject of the main clause. Purpose clauses are discussed in more detail in R7.C and IX.A.

| Я скажу́ э́то, что́бы всём **бы́ло** ясно. | I will say it so that it *will be* clear to everybody. |

C. ли

Remember two important things about **ли**: (1) It is the *second element* (though not always the second word) in the interrogative clause, the first element being the thing that is being asked about. Note the following sentences (an italic English word designates strong intonation):

Рабо́тает ли о́н пло́хо на э́том заво́де?	Does he work badly at that factory? (*Most normal question*)[1]
Пло́хо ли о́н рабо́тает на э́том заво́де?	Does he work *badly* at that factory?
На э́том ли заво́де о́н пло́хо рабо́тает?	Does he work badly at *that* factory? (Is it at that factory that he works badly?)

(2) *Never use it* when there is *another interrogative* in the same clause; **ка́к, когда́, кто́** are already interrogatives.

The conjunction "if" is translated by **éсли** only when some sort of *condition* is involved; when "if" means "whether," a **ли** construction is used. Compare:

| Я его́ не зна́ю, éсли о́н не живёт здесь. | I don't know him, if he doesn't live here. (*This is a condition, and "if" does not mean "whether."*) |
| Я не зна́ю, живёт ли о́н здесь. | I don't know if he lives here. (*This is not a condition, and "if" means "whether."*) |

Students are particularly prone to confuse **éсли** with **éсть ли**: "I don't know if (whether) he has any books" is **Я не зна́ю, éсть ли у него́ кни́ги**.

D. Э́тот/э́то and то́т/то́

Russian **э́тот** and **то́т** are parallel to English "this" and "that" only when they are directly opposed; e.g. **Эти лю́ди ру́сские, а те́—не́мцы,** or when the speaker is directly pointing to something: "that one there" (perhaps, for emphasis, opposed to an imaginary "this one here"). In other cases, however, **э́тот** is the normal translation for both "this" and "that" with their slight difference in English. Examples:

---

[1] In the most neutral situation, the action is what is asked about, and the verb precedes **ли**.

Что́ э́тот челове́к ва́м сказа́л?	What did that (this) man say to you?
Эти кни́ги уже́ перево́дятся.	Those (These) books are already being translated.

The same principle applies to the impersonal э́то (see paragraph 2 below):

Я не ве́рю э́тому.	I don't believe that (this).
Это случи́лось неда́вно.	That (this) happened not long ago.

2. Opposition to э́тот as "that" to "this" is only one of the many usages of the very important pronoun то́т/то́. All the usages, however, share a common feature, the central meaning of то́т/то́: some *reference or comparison to something else* is always implied. In the following expressions note this common reference:

то́т же (са́мый)	the (very) same (as something or someone *else*)
те́, кото́рые	the ones who (*identification of " those" in terms of something else* (*the rest of the* кото́рый *clause*))
Я зна́ю то́, что́ вы́ зна́ете.	I know what (that which) you know. (*Same as above*)
Это не то́.	That's not the right thing. (*Right thing is already implied.*)
и то́т и друго́й	both (both the one (already mentioned) and the other)

Finally, the impersonal то́ is used in a great many adverbial expressions and, in general, in various set expressions, where э́то would be used in a more specific reference:

кро́ме э́того	besides this (definite thing), in addition to this
кро́ме того́	moreover, furthermore (*adverbial, set expression*)
по́сле э́того	after this (definite thing)
по́сле того́	afterwards (*less definite, more of a set expression*)

And note:

к тому́ же	in addition
и тому́ подо́бное	and so forth
ме́жду те́м	meanwhile
са́м того́ не зна́я	without knowing it himself (*set expression*)

E. THE TRANSLATION OF "IT"

In translating "it" it is very important to treat each case individually. The impersonal pronoun э́то is translated "that," "this," or "it" when the "it" is something unspecifiable or, at least, unspecified as to gender and number. The reaction to the statement **Он хоро́ший челове́к** might be **Я зна́ю э́то**, and the English could be "I know that," "I know this," or "I know it," without appreciable difference in meaning. The **э́то** *is* something, but it cannot be labeled with gender and number. When, however, "it" does refer to a definite thing with gender and number, the appropriate third person pronoun should be used:

Вы хоти́те пое́хать в Москву́? Дава́йте поговори́м **об э́том**.	You want to go to Moscow? Let's talk about it.
Вы то́лько что написа́ли докла́д? Дава́йте поговори́м **о нём**.	You have just written a report? Let's talk about it (the *report itself*).

(NOTE: If the "it" in the second sentence referred to the "fact of" his having written the report, the Russian would be **об э́том**.) There are situations where **э́то** is also permissible, even if the noun is completely specified, but the student should concentrate on the rule just given.

English "it" frequently has no reference at all; it may be a sort of grammatical "dummy word." If you think of the sentence "It is good that you are here," the sentence really means "That you are here is good"; i.e. the "it" has no real meaning. When "it" is such a dummy word, it is not ordinarily translated into Russian; e.g. the translation of the above sentence would be **Хорошо́, что вы здесь**. Compare the following sentences:

Э́то я́сно.	It's clear. (This/That is clear.)
Я́сно, что он придёт.	It's clear that he will come. (*Dummy* it)
Э́то случи́лось.	It happened. (This/That happened.)
Случи́лось, что . . .	It happened that . . . (*Dummy* it)

The introductory **э́то** of a sentence like **Э́то наш дом** may also, on occasion, be translated by "it"; i.e. "It's our house" as well as "That's our house" or "This is our house," depending on the context. In Lesson III we shall meet an important related use of this **э́то**, which may also be translated with "it"; **Э́то он пришёл** 'It's he who came (He is the one who came).'

F. VERBS OF ASKING AND TELLING

The verb "ask" is rendered in two different ways in Russian:

ask (a favor), request: (по)проси́ть *acc pers* + *inf or* что́бы + *past*
ask (for information): спроси́ть – спра́шивают *acc or* у *gen* (*кого́ о чём or что у кого́*)

Note that "ask a question" is **зада́ть – задава́ть вопро́с**; do not use **спроси́ть – спра́шивают** with **вопро́с**.

To "ask for" a thing is normally **(по)просить** *acc or gen thing plus gen person*. However, **спросить – спрашивают** is also used in this meaning. Observe the following sentences:

Я попросил его уйти. *Or*: Я попросил его, чтобы он ушёл.	I asked him to leave.
Я спросил Веру (у Веры), что Иван делает.	I asked Vera what Ivan was doing.
Я хочу задать вам вопрос.	I want to ask you a question.
Я хочу вас об этом спросить.	I want to ask you about this.
Я попросил (спросил) книгу у Ивана.	I asked John for the book.

To "tell" somebody to do something is **сказать – говорить** *dat plus* **чтобы** *plus past*; note that **сказать – говорить**, unlike **(по)просить**, should not be used with an infinitive:

Я сказал ему, чтобы он ушёл (*not* сказал ему уйти).	I told him to leave.

The verb "tell," when it is equivalent to "say," corresponds to the Russian pair **сказать – говорить**. When "tell" means "narrate, tell a story," the Russian verb is usually **рассказать – рассказывают**. The verb "talk," however, corresponds to **говорить** as an unpaired imperfective. Both "talk with" and "talk to" are translated by **говорить с** *inst* (**говорить** *dat* would mean "say to" or "tell to" and would be paired with **сказать**).

TRANSLATION INTO RUSSIAN

That teacher **began**[1] to ask whose book it was and if one of us didn't want it. I answered that **someone**[2] had been **trying**[3] to solve a problem and that the book would have helped him solve it, but that he was now solving other problems. "Does he have *many* problems?" I **asked**.[4] It's interesting that he never
5   talks about **any**[5] problems. The teacher told me that that wasn't interesting at all and that it was time to have dinner. He asked me if I had any money and told me to give him six dollars. I gave it to him and asked him to leave. He answered that he had no automobile. I told him he could walk and that he would soon arrive in the city. If he left now, he would arrive in the evening. He said, "It's
10   very bad that you talk to me thus." But I ask you: if you had such a friend, how would you talk with him?

Every day Iván Ivánovič would tell the **French**[6] student to **have a talk**[7] about his work with **his**[8] **Russian professor**.[6] Finally, the student **went to see**[9] his professor, although he didn't want to do this, because he **thought**[10] his professor

never talked about **anything** with **anyone**.[5] He wanted me to go with him. [15]
"**Let's**[11] go and **sit for a while**[7] with him and **have a smoke**,"[7] he said. "No,
I'd like[12] to sleep a little tomorrow morning," I answered. "Let somebody else
do it. I'll ask Svetlána to go with you. She's a **doctor**[13] and knows everything."

Last night I worked on (wrote) my book about the Crimea, or **rather**,[14]
about life in the **Crimea**.[15] Tonight I will be writing letters, and I will write a [20]
letter to my neighbor's sister, if there is[16] time. Later I will read my father's
newspaper. But I don't know if I'll be able to read all of it.

My sons are six years old, but they **can't**[17] read **yet**.[18] My daughter is
already[18] eight, and she could read if we had any books.

NOTES

1. See R2.B2.
2. A rule of thumb for whether to use **-то** or **-нибудь** is as follows: Past tense (except questions) have **-то**; questions, imperative, and **пусть/пуская**, have **-нибудь**; other categories have **-то** if the noun is more definite or known and simply not specified, but **-нибудь** if the meaning is "anything at all."
3. See R2.A4.
4. "He said," "he answered," and similar phrases accompanying quotes are rendered in Russian with the verb *preceding* the subject.
5. The several "anys" in English were mentioned on page 62. This "any" is used to avoid the "double negative" which exists, however, in Russian; hence, be sure to include both the **ни** element (here **никакóй**) and the **не** before the verb. Note also here that when a preposition is used with a **ни** expression, it is inserted between the **ни** and the pronoun; e.g. **Я ни с кéм не говорю** 'I'm not talking with anyone.'
6. A student who is French, not a student of French. Compare the following line: "Russian professor" (professor of Russian) must be **профéссор рýсского языкá**, not **рýсский профéссор**, which refers to nationality.
7. The prefix **по-**, added to an imperfective of a verb whose action or state can be continuous, may add the meaning "for a (short) while" and, of course, perfectivizes the verb; e.g. **Мы посидéли** 'We sat for a while,' **Мы порабóтали** 'We worked for a while.'
8. Failure to use **свóй** or its incorrect use is perhaps the most common mistake among students past the elementary level. Remember that it is mandatory in the third person: e.g. **Они любят своих детéй** 'They love their (own) children'; the use of **их** would mean that they loved the children of somebody else. Remember that **свóй** refers back to the most recent subject, sometimes a subject only implied in the most recent verb, as in the sentence **Я попросил егó** *сдéлать свóй* доклáд зáвтра.

Next point: **свóй** is not used in the nominative except in: (1) **éсть** sentences with the meaning "have one's own"; e.g. **У него́ есть своя́ кварти́ра** 'He has his own apartment'; (2) statements expressing "one's own" in general; e.g. **Сво́й до́м лу́чше всех** 'One's own house is best of all.' NOTE: The word **со́бственный** 'own,' placed after **свой** in any context, emphasizes the idea of "own" but does not *add* to the meaning, for **свой** already means just that: "own."

9. To "go to see" is not translated by **ви́деть**; it is simply motion verb plus **к** *dat*; e.g. 'We are going to see Anna' **Мы́ идём к А́нне**.

10. The English conjunction "that" may be omitted, but Russian **что** should not be; e.g. "I know that he's here" *or* "I know he's here," but in Russian only: **Я зна́ю, что о́н здесь**.

11. Remember that with **дава́й(те)** we use the *first plural present* for *perfective* verbs and the *infinitive* for *imperfective* verbs, never the other way around; e.g. **дава́йте откро́ем окно́** but **дава́йте рабо́тать**. If "let's" is translated by a first plural alone, the form must also be perfective, except for determined verbs, which permit forms from both aspects; e.g. 'Let's go!' **Пое́дем!** or **Е́дем!**

   In the example here the first plural perfective would be the best choice, and **дава́йте**, if used, does not need to be repeated before the second and third verbs. The two "ands" should not be translated.

12. "Would like to" plus infinitive is **хоте́л бы**, never **люби́л бы**.

13. A masculine noun which has no normally used corresponding noun in the feminine gender (such as **студе́нтка** for **студе́нт**) may sometimes be used to designate female persons; e.g. **Она́ хи́мик** 'She's a chemist.' NOTE: adjectives are always masculine; gender of verb depends on sex: **Но́вый хи́мик Ива́нова взяла́**.

14. "Rather" in this sense is best rendered by **точне́е** 'more exactly' or **верне́е** 'more truly.' For another use of "rather," see R5 note 13.

15. A masculine noun, particularly if it is monosyllabic, should suggest the possibility of the **-у́** "locative" ending.

16. The English tense is misleading here.

17. When "can" means "know how," it is ordinarily rendered by **уме́ют** (imperfective only).

18. Be sure not to confuse **ещё** 'still' and **уже́** 'already' (though "already" is often omitted in the English). **Уже́** is, in addition, frequently used with present tense verbs in meanings corresponding to the English present perfect; e.g. **Я здесь уже́ пя́ть ле́т** 'I have been here (already) for five years,' **Я э́то зна́ю уже́ давно́** 'I have known that (already) for a long time.'

   The negative **ещё не** means "not yet" in a full clause; e.g. 'I haven't seen her yet' **Я ещё не ви́дел её**. "Not yet" on its own is **Не́т ещё**. **Уже́ не** has the meaning "no longer," very close to **бо́льше не**; e.g. 'She no longer works here' **Она́ уже́ (бо́льше) не рабо́тает здесь**.

СЛОВАРЬ ГРАММАТИЧЕСКИХ ТЕРМИНОВ

после́довательность времён tense sequence

наклоне́ние mood; усло́вное — conditional mood

мода́льный modal

ре́чь speech:

   ко́свенная — indirect speech

   пряма́я — direct speech

   ча́сть —и part of speech

и́мя существи́тельное noun

и́мя прилага́тельное adjective

и́мя числи́тельное numeral

местоиме́ние pronoun

наре́чие adverb

глаго́л verb

предло́г preposition

сою́з conjunction

части́ца particle

*A. Verbs of motion and
determined vs. nondetermined*
*B. Place to, where, whence and
prepositions*
C. éсть and нéт
D. котóрый

A. VERBS OF MOTION AND
DETERMINED VS. NONDETERMINED

1. Unprefixed verbs

A verb of motion is any verb expressing some sort of motion, but what we usually have in mind is motion in a specific direction, *toward* something, the type of motion which would entail the use of the adverbs кудá and тудá, or *away from* something, for which we would use откýда and оттýда. Motion "in place," i.e. motion without direction toward something, or indication of interest in such, is possible, and entails the use of гдé and тáм. Such motion is usually rendered by the *nondetermined* verbs; e.g. **Он хóдит в пáрке** 'He's walking around in the park' while determined verbs render motion in a single specific direction; e.g. **Он идёт в пáрк** 'He's walking to the park.' A determined verb used in a гдé context is possible, though much less common; **Он идёт в пáрке** would mean: "He's walking along in the park (in a specific direction)."

About fifteen motion verbs manifest the *determined-nondetermined* opposition we have just mentioned; in fact, the term "motion verb" is sometimes limited to this group. Here are the eight most important ones, many of which you probably already know:

бежáть – бéгают	run	идýт – ходить	walk
вёзýт – возить	convey	летéть – летáют	fly
вёдýт – водить	lead	нёсýт – носить	carry
éдут – éздить	ride	плывýт – плáвают	swim

The relationship between determined and nondetermined is parallel to that between the perfective and imperfective; the determined specifies something, the nondetermined doesn't specify it, but doesn't exclude it either. The determined specifies a single, continuous motion toward something, the nondetermined simply says nothing about this. Hence, the nondetermined may have a frequentative meaning (**Он хо́дит в па́рк ка́ждый де́нь** 'He goes to the park every day'); motion with no direction specified (**На́ш ма́льчик уже́ хо́дит** 'Our little boy already walks' or **Мы́ хо́дим по го́роду** 'We are walking about the city'); or round trip (**Мы́ вчера ве́чером ходи́ли в кино́** 'We went to the movies last night (and, of course, returned)'). The determined has no such versatility; it is committed to its meaning of a single, continuous action.

Note particularly that if either a determined or a nondetermined verb takes on the slightest *abstract* or *special* meaning, the opposition ceases to exist, and there is no nondetermined or determined partner. Do not try to determine "logically" whether such special verbs should be determined or nondetermined; take the examples as they are. "Logic," of course, plays a minimal role in idiomatic expressions, and motion verbs are an outstanding example. In English, cars "go," trains "run," and movies "play," whereas in Russian: **автомоби́ли е́дут, поезда́ иду́т,** and **фи́льмы иду́т.** Other examples:

Ему́ всегда́ везёт. (*Never* во́зит)	He's always very lucky.
Он ка́ждый го́д ведёт семина́р. (*Never* во́дит)	He conducts a seminar every year.
Эти часы́ отли́чно иду́т. (*Rarely,* хо́дят, *no difference in meaning*)	This watch runs excellently.

2. Prefixed verbs[1]

The addition of **по-** to a determined verb does perfectivize it, but adds the inceptive meaning "start to." **Он пошёл** means "He went" in the sense "He started off." A speaker who said **Я пошёл в кино́** might well go on to describe what happened on the way; perhaps he met somebody, perhaps he did not even go to the movies. Cf. **Я ходи́л в кино́,** which closes the issue: "I went and returned."

The addition of any prefix other than **по-** to one of the fifteen motion verbs destroys the determined-nondetermined opposition. The perfective is formed by

---

[1] Remember that the **и** of **иду́т** changes to **й** after prefixes; e.g. **пойду́т, дойти́, зайдёшь,** etc. After prefixes ending in consonants an **о** is inserted: **отойду́т, подойти́, разойти́сь.** Recall also the infinitive spellings **идти́** but **пойти́, отойти́,** and the irregular **приду́т** (**й** is lost); cf. **прийти́).**

adding the new prefix to the determined stem, the imperfective by adding it to the nondetermined stem:

пойду́т	иду́т	ходить	уйду́т	уходить
понёсу́т	нёсу́т	носить	унёсу́т	уносить

Of the eight common verbs listed on page 72 however, three require additional comment for the formation of the imperfectives:

уе́дут (уе́хать)	уезжа́ют	Stem differs from е́здить
убежа́ть (убегу́т)	убега́ют	Stress differs from бе́гают
уплыву́т	уплыва́ют	Stem differs from пла́вают

NOTE: Nondetermined verbs in their round-trip meaning may be perfectivized by prefixing a (nonsemantic) **с-**; e.g. **сходить**, **съе́здить**, **сбе́гают** (note that this **сходить** is absolutely distinct from the imperfective **сходить** 'go down' (*perf* **сойду́т**)). These special perfective forms are used most frequently in the future, imperative, and infinitive; the past tense of a round trip is most often rendered by the imperfective **ходить**.

Мы́ схо́дим в теа́тр сего́дня ве́чером.	We are going to the theater tonight.
Сходи́те в магази́н.	Go to the store (and bring something back).

but

Мы́ ходи́ли в теа́тр вчера́ ве́чером.	We went to the theater last night.

B. PLACE *TO*, *WHERE*, *WHENCE* AND PREPOSITIONS

In translating sentences involving "place where," "place to," and "place whence," the proper use must be made of the adverbs **куда́ – туда́ – сюда́**, **где́ – та́м – зде́сь**, and **отку́да – отту́да – отсю́да**. But often more trouble is encountered with the more complex problems of prepositions.

In most instances of usage the preposition is *bound*; i.e. it is required by a word it is used with, or is inherent in some set expression or semantic context, and may not be replaced by another preposition without changing the meaning of the construction. Such prepositions are independent of their objects; for example, in the expression **говори́ть о** *prp* 'talk about,' the preposition is bound to the verb and is the same no matter what the object is:

Мы говори́ли о музе́е, заво́де, стене́, Че́хове, вла́сти.

In a set expression like **по отноше́нию к** *dat* 'with respect to,' the **к** *dat* is an inherent part of the expression:

по отноше́нию к музе́ю, заво́ду, стене́, Че́хову, вла́сти

Some motion verbs also bind specific prepositions to themselves; i.e. when used with a preposition always or almost always take the same one. Verbs prefixed by **под-**, **от-**, and **до-** require the prepositions **к** *dat*, **от** *gen*, and **до** *gen*, respectively. For example:

> Он **подошёл ко** мне́.
> **Отойди́те от** меня́!
> Мы́ **довели́** на́ше де́ло **до** конца́.

Many other motion verbs, however, may be used with a variety of prepositions. Selection depends on the "physical" facts; the prepositions may be different for the motions **куда́** and **отку́да**, and still a third is used for **где́**. In addition, unlike all the examples above (i.e. **говори́ть о** *prp*), the preposition *may vary according to its complement*: here, the place or object involved. For example, all of the following combinations are possible, though some are not as likely as others and may require a certain context.

Мы́ рабо́таем ⎰ в музе́е
на заво́де
у Че́хова

Мы́ пошли́
Мы́ пришли́
Мы́ зашли́
Мы́ вы́шли

⎰ в музе́й   из музе́я
на заво́д *or* с заво́да
к Че́хову   от Че́хова

The prepositions clearly depend not on the preceding verbs but on their complements and on the facts of **где́**, **куда́**, **отку́да**. Here are the most usual correspondences:

ГДЕ́	КУДА́	ОТКУ́ДА
в *prp*	в *acc*	из *gen*
на *prp*	на *acc*	с *gen*
у *gen*	к *dat*	от *gen*
за *inst*	за *acc*	из-за *gen*
под *inst*	под *acc*	из-под *gen*

Again, remember that set expressions with bound prepositions are not in the least affected by the above correspondences. For example, when speaking of distances between points, Russian uses **от** *gen* **до** *gen*: **От Москвы́ до Ленингра́да далеко́**. If **Украи́на**, which takes **на** where **Ленингра́д** takes **в**, were substituted, no difference would result; we would have **От Москвы́ до Украи́ны далеко́**.

The correspondences among prepositions diagramed below apply most notably to the "location" and "motion" instances described above, but they may also apply to various abstract expressions; the ideas of "location" and "motion" are, however, retained no matter how transferred the meaning. For example:

Мы́ перево́дим **на** ру́сский язы́к.	We are translating into Russian.
Мы́ перево́дим **с** ру́сского языка́.	We are translating from Russian.
бы́ть **у** вла́сти	be in power
приду́т – приходи́ть **к** вла́сти	come to power

It is, in fact, useful to regard as motion verbs, whether or not they have a clearly physical meaning, many verbs in prefixes implying or suggesting motion; e.g. **в-, на-, пере-, при-** (КУДА), and **от-, из-** (ОТКУДА). Such verbs are often used with prepositions suggesting or implying motion. The corresponding English verbs often connote motion and are frequently followed by the prepositions "to" or "into," "from" or "out of":

введу́т в *or* на *acc*	introduce *into*
напра́вить на *acc or* к *dat*	direct *to/toward*
переменить в *acc*	change *to/into*
привы́кнуть к *dat*	get accustomed *to*
отвы́кнуть от *gen*	become unused to, get away *from*
отступиться от *gen*	digress *from*
извлёку́т из *gen*	extract *from, out of*

It is all very well to know the correspondences, but one must also know whether a word takes **в, на**, or **у** in the first place. Persons are **у** words; most smaller physical objects require prepositions according to "physical situation"; e.g. "Go to the blackboard" is **Иди́те к доске́**, but "Write on the blackboard" is **Пиши́те на доске́**; "in the book" is **в кни́ге**, "on the book" is **на кни́ге**.

The most persistent trouble spot in the area of unbound prepositional usage is whether one assigns **в** or **на** to large and spacious objects, rooms, buildings, establishments, open expanses of land or ground, and the like. The student should regard such nouns as **в** words and **на** words and should make no attempt to analyze them according to "inside" and "on" or to any other "physical" conditions. For example, **музе́й** is a **в** word, but **заво́д** is a **на** word. **Ку́ба** is a **на** word, as many islands are, but larger islands with major political status may be **в** words; e.g. **А́нглия, Япо́ния**.

A number of common words, mostly enclosures, may take both **в** and **на** according to usage and, in some cases, depending on the speaker. Some common examples: **кварти́ра, ку́хня, автомоби́ль, по́езд**. The usual statement is that the more set the expression, the more likely **на** is. The student should simply recognize the two possibilities.

Note that general gatherings, spectacles, and performances or things that are going on are usually **на** words; e.g. **собра́ние** 'meeting,' **съезд** 'congress,' **база́р** 'bazaar,' **фи́льм** 'film,' **допро́с** 'interrogation.'

На words are fewer and usually easier to remember, and we mark them specially in the vocabularies; e.g. **за́пад (на)** 'west.'

A final word on prepositions. The student probably already knows that English and Russian prepositions correspond very badly, and that word-for-word translation will almost always fail him. There are probably at least ten English words which might translate Russian **на**, and perhaps as many Russian words for English "from." Prepositions must be learned and "felt" in Russian alone. Gradually, after having seen many examples, the student will begin to sense what **на** means, will develop a feeling about it which enables him to understand and classify each new example and, eventually, to use the preposition properly. But it is a slow process.

C. есть and нет

The use of **есть** and its omission is a rather complex question. As a general guide, remember that it expresses *possession* or *existence*, depending on the sentence, and should be included whenever these are emphasized. When something else in the sentence is emphasized, **есть** is normally omitted. It tends to be omitted also when the thing possessed is "organic" to the possessor; a part of the body, a disease, or a psychological or spiritual condition:

У вác éсть карандáш?	Do you have a pencil? (*Possession*)
У вác карандáш? Карандáш у вác?	Do *you* have a pencil? (*Location*)
У вác крácный карандáш?	Do you have a *red* pencil? (*Description*)
У меня двá крáсных карандашá.	I have two red pencils. (*Description*)
У неё голубы́е глазá.	She has blue eyes.
У меня нácморк.	I have a cold.
У негó большóй ум.	He has a good mind.

Нéт may confuse students. It is a particle "no" or the negative of **есть** 'there is not,' building impersonal sentences like **Ивáна здéсь нéт** 'Ivan isn't here,' **У Ивáна нéт кни́г** 'Ivan has no books.' It never translates "not" in a phrase like "He is not your teacher," which would be **Он не вáш учи́тель**.

D. котóрый

Review the important relative pronoun **котóрый** and the construction **тóт . . . , котóрый**. Remember that **котóрый** takes the gender and number of what it refers to in the preceding clause, but its case is determined by its syntactic function in the clause it is in. Also, **котóрый** may *not* be omitted, as the English relatives "which" and "that" often are in corresponding English sentences; e.g. 'The book (which, that) I saw is on the table' **Кни́га, котóрую я ви́дел, на столé**.

Тóт . . . , котóрый is an important example of a very widespread syntactic construction in Russian, which we call **тó, чтó** and treat in detail in Lesson III.

TRANSLATION INTO RUSSIAN

Tanja and I[1] **have been**[2] for many years attend**ing** this school, which we love **very much**.[3] She **picks me up**[4] in the morning, when it is still quite early and dark, and we drive to the city, which is located not far from Xár'kov. When we arrive there, we get out of the blue **automobile**,[5] in **which**[5] we arrived, and begin
5 to walk **about**[6] the whole city. Tánja **keeps**[7] walking along with me and **keeps**[7] talking about books which she needs but which she can't buy. Finally I notice that she's **still**[7] talking about books, and I ask her, "Do you have any money?" "Of course, I **have**,[8] but there is**n't** a **single**[9] good store where I can find the books I want," she answers. We continue to walk along, and when we walk past
10 a movie theater, we usually walk up to the people who are standing at the entrance and ask them if an interesting film isn't playing there. They answer us, "Go and **see**[10] the posters **yourselves**,[11] and then you'll find out if the film is good." If it **is**,[8] I say to Tánja, "We'll **go**[12] to the movies tonight." But Tánja doesn't **much**[3] **like**[13] to go to the movies. Even when she **likes**[13] a film, she says,
15 "Why am I sitting at this film? I told Pável I would be at the meeting."

Last evening I went to a meeting, but there were **few**[14] people there. I went away from the meeting and walked out into the corridor, in which **a few**[14] people were standing. I met a student, with whom I had spoken **a few**[14] times, and who asked me where I was **coming**[15] from. "Not so loud," I said. "I don't
20 want people to know that I **left**[16] the meeting. Especially Tat'jána Pávlovna mustn't know about this. I had promised to take (drive) her to the concert and this morning told her I couldn't **because of**[17] this **very**[11] meeting. I thought that this would please her, since she always goes to meetings, but she stepped away from me and told me to leave. She herself didn't know what she was doing."

25 The student and I walked out into the street, crossed it, and entered a restaurant. There were **only a few**[14] people in it. We asked the waitress if there was any vodka today. She said that there was no vodka, but that there was beer. "That waitress has pretty hair," I said to my friend. Finally, the beer **was brought.**[18] When we had drunk up four glasses, we left. On the street we met
30 Tánja, and we all decided to go to the factory. A streetcar runs from here to the factory, but Tánja likes to ride on the **subway**,[19] since she's from **Bakú**,[19] where there is no subway and probably never will be. **One**[18] gets from Moscow to Bakú **by way of**[20] Volgográd. They say that it's far to Volgográd. Finally, we went to see Valentína Júr'evna, **whose**[21] brother we had known in Túla. But
35 when we got there, Válja asked us **whose**[21] brother we were talking about.

NOTES

1. **Táня и я** is possible here, but more idiomatic would be **Мы с Táней**. This type of construction is quite typical of Russian; observe:

Мы́ с това́рищем пойдём в кино́.   (Я и това́рищ)
Бра́т с сестро́й у́чатся в шко́ле.   (Бра́т и сестра́)
Он э́того не ска́жет на́м с ва́ми.   (мне́ и ва́м *or* на́м и ва́м)

2. English "have been X-ing" (less often "have X-ed") for a period of time is usually rendered by the Russian present, often in connection with уже́ (English, less frequently, uses "already" or "now").

3. Both "much" and "very much" are translated *simply* by о́чень when they designate intensity of action (modifying the verb) rather than quantity (object of the verb). Only when "much" and "very much" refer specifically to quantity are they rendered by мно́го and о́чень мно́го. Compare:

Я о́чень хоте́л пойти́.   I (very) much wanted to go.
Он о́чень интересу́ется э́тим.   He is (very) much interested in that.
with
Он мно́го зна́ет о ва́с.   He knows much about you.
Она́ о́чень мно́го говори́т.   She talks very much.

4. "Pick up" is expressed by a motion verb prefixed by за- plus за plus instrumental. The prefix за- with motion verbs has the general meaning of deviating from one's route and often corresponds to "drop in." The preposition за *inst* used with motion verbs has the general meaning "go for, go and get" and is not limited to use with the prefix за-. Examples:

Зайди́ за мно́й в пя́ть часо́в.   Pick me up at five o'clock.
Зайди́ ко мне́ сего́дня ве́чером.   Stop in and see me tonight.
Заходи́те.   Drop in and see me. (*General*)
Мы́ пошли́ за пи́вом.   We went for some beer.
Ва́ня, сходи́ за молоко́м.   Vanja, go get the milk!

5. For ОТКУДА автомоби́ль acts like a в word, for ГДЕ normally like a на word. The more colloquial and commoner (авто)маши́на acts similarly.

6. По *dat* with motion verbs means all around or about a surface, or points scattered about a surface; e.g. Мои́ роди́тели е́здили по все́й Евро́пе. Де́ти хо́дят по ле́су. Това́рищи ходи́ли по рестора́нам.

7. To "keep" doing something is всё or всё вре́мя plus present or past imperfective: 'She keeps talking about her son' Она́ всё (вре́мя) говори́т о сы́не (всё вре́мя is approximately equivalent to "the whole time"). To "keep on doing, be still doing" something (i.e. with previous mention, actual or implied) is всё еще: 'She keeps on/is still talking about her son' Она́ всё ещё говори́т о сы́не (previous statement something like: "She talked a lot about her son, and we asked her to stop. But . . .") Another example: Она́ всё де́лает оши́бкп. Я ей об э́том говорю́, но она́ всё ещё де́лает и́х.

8. The answer to a yes-or-no question in Russian is often rendered simply by repeating the thing that was asked about (in an actual or hypothetical **ли** clause, the thing preceding the **ли**). English is more likely to have simply "Yes" or "No" or, if a verb is repeated, only the auxiliary verb of a compound tense. Observe:

Вы зна́ете его́? Зна́ю./Да, зна́ю.	Do you know him? Yes./Yes, I do.
У ва́с е́сть де́ньги? Есть./Да, е́сть.	Do you have any money? Yes./Yes, I do.
Нельзя́ туда́ е́хать? Нельзя́./Да, нельзя́.	Can't one go there? No./No, one can't.
В Москву́ ли вы е́дете? В Москву́./Да, в Москву́.	Is it Moscow that you're going to? Yes./Yes, it is.
Пло́хо ли она́ рабо́тает? Пло́хо./Да, пло́хо.	Does she work badly? Yes./Yes, she does.

9. "Not one, not a single" is **ни оди́н**; e.g. 'We aren't acquainted with a single student from that university' **Мы не зна́ем ни одного́ студе́нта (Мы не знако́мы ни с одни́м студе́нтом) из университе́та.**

10. When "see" means "look," **(по)смотре́ть**, not **ви́деть**, is used.

11. Be careful to distinguish the pronouns **сам** '(one)self' and **са́мый** 'the very' (and other meanings in combination with other words). **Сам** is declined like a pronoun; specifically, like **оди́н**, except that it has an alternate feminine singular accusative **самоё** and **са́ми** is stem-stressed (cf. **одни́**). **Са́мый** is declined like an adjective (e.g. *inst sg/dat pl* **са́мым**, not **сами́м**, which is from **сам**).

   The closest **са́мый** and **сам** come to confusion is in a sentence like **Он живёт в са́мой Москве́** 'He lives right in Moscow,' which is very close to saying "in Moscow itself," which is, of course, **в само́й Москве́.** Other examples:

Я сам ему́ напишу́.	I'll write him myself.
Ему́ самому́ о́чень смешно́.	He himself is very amused.
Спроси́те самого́ себя́ об э́том.	Ask your*self* about that. (*Special stress on "self"*)
Говори́те с ни́ми сами́ми.	Talk with them themselves.
Мы дошли́ до са́мого конца́.	We went to the very end.
Са́мый фа́кт, что вы говори́те э́то ...	The very fact that you say that ...

   And recall the expressions: **тот же са́мый** 'the very same' and **са́мый** plus adjective 'the most' (superlative of the adjective):

Это та́ же са́мая кни́га.	That's the very same book.
Мы е́дем на са́мом бы́стром автомоби́ле в ми́ре.	We're riding in the fastest car in the world.

12. Use round-trip verb.

13. To "like" something is usually **(по)нра́виться** *dat*; e.g. "I like the book" is **Кни́га мне́ нра́вится**. To "like very much, love" is usually **люби́ть**; but whether **люби́ть** or **(по)нра́виться** is used may depend on the object involved. A more useful distinction, however, is that **люби́ть** is likely to be "general," **(по)нра́виться** more likely to be used in a specific situation:

Я люблю́ су́п.	I like soup.
Э́тот су́п мне́ нра́вится.	I like this soup.
Она́ лю́бит мужчи́н.	She likes men. (*Not necessarily "loves"*)
Э́тот челове́к не нра́вится е́й.	She doesn't like this man.

To "like to do" something is **люби́ть** plus infinitive. The student should avoid **нра́виться** with the infinitive, though it is occasionally used.

14. The expressions **мно́го**, **ма́ло**, and **немно́го** take the genitive singular or plural, and **не́сколько** takes the genitive plural. **Мно́го** and **ма́ло** should be separated from **немно́го** and **не́сколько**. They mean "much/many" and "little/few" (with "too" sometimes implied). On the other hand, **немно́го** means "*a* little, *a* little bit, *a* few," and **не́сколько** "*a* few" or "several"; both have the idea of *some*, rather than *much* or *little*.[1] Some examples:

На́ш сы́н пьёт мно́го молока́.	Our son drinks much milk.
На столе́ бы́ло мно́го карандаше́й.	There were many pencils on the table.
Мы́ вы́пили немно́го молока́ и ушли́.	We drank *a* little milk and left.
На столе́ бы́ло не́сколько каранда́ше́й.	There were *a* few (several) pencils on the table.
Он мно́го де́лает.	He does a great deal.
Он ма́ло понима́ет.	He understands little.
Он немно́го понима́ет.	He understands *a* little.

Немно́го, however, is sometimes very close to **ма́ло**; we can think of it as "not many/not much." And note that **немно́го** (not **ма́ло**) must be used after **то́лько**.

Друзе́й у него́ бы́ло немно́го.	He had few (not many) friends.
Он понима́ет о́чень немно́го.	He understands very little.
Он понима́ет то́лько немно́го.	He understands only a little.

Both **не́сколько** and **немно́го** are also used adverbially in the meaning "somewhat, slightly":

---

[1] Words like **немно́го** and **не́сколько** have the so-called "indefinite" meaning, expressed in English by such words as "a," "some," and "certain."

| Он не́сколько (немно́го) успоко́ил-ся. | He calmed down somewhat. |
| Де́нь бы́л прия́тен, хотя́ не́сколько (немно́го) хо́лоден. | The day was pleasant, though slightly cold. |

All four of these words may be declined in the oblique cases but are normally not declined in the nominative/accusative, a circumstance which suggests their being considered as numerals. See Review 6 for more discussion of these words.

15. When "come" does not mean "arrive," it is usually иду́т. Even the question "Who's coming?" (asked, for instance, by someone hearing steps of someone who may be coming to see him) would be Кто́ идёт? Cf. also 'Come here!' Иди́те сюда́!

16. When the idea of "leaving" is the important thing, as in this sentence, the y- prefix is called for, but when "leave" simply means "depart" and is more neutral, then по- or вы- may also translate it.

Они́ пошли́ в кино́.	They left for the movies. (went off)
Она́ вы́шла из ко́мнаты.	She left the room. (went out)
Он уе́хал на ше́сть ме́сяцев.	He left for six months.

When "leave" is used transitively, it is often translated by the Russian verb оста́вить – оставля́ют, which is *always* transitive:

| Мы́ оста́вили го́род в де́сять часо́в. | We left the city at ten o'clock. |

17. Из-за *gen* frequently has the transferred meaning "because of, owing to, due to."

18. Certain passive constructions and the general "one" corresponding to German *man* and French *on* are best translated by the subjectless third plural in Russian. ("One," of course, is usually replaced in English by "they," or (indefinite) "people"; the student should be able to recognize when one of these means "one.")

| Зде́сь ма́ло зна́ют. | They don't know much around here. (Little is known around here.) |
| На́с посла́ли на Аля́ску. | They sent us to Alaska. (We were sent to Alaska.) |

19. Russian has a number of indeclinable nouns, mostly of foreign origin. All nouns ending in -и or -у, and all obvious borrowings ending in -e, -o, and stressed -á are indeclinable and, unless they denote masculine or feminine nouns (in which case they are masculine or feminine), are neuter; the only common exception is ко́фе, which is masculine. Nouns ending in unstressed -a are declined feminines: ру́мба, ру́мбы. Examples:

ви́ски, такси́, меню́, Пе́ру (Peru), бюро́, ра́дио, шоссе́, шимпанзе́, по́ни, ле́ди, буржуа́, ура́

Foreign nouns in consonants are declined masculines, unless they denote females, in which case they are indeclinable feminines: **мисс, фре́йлейн**.

The statements just made apply generally to place-names and proper names as well. Exceptions to these rules are quite isolated and may reflect individual usage.

20. "By way of, via" is **че́рез** plus accusative.

21. The relative "whose" is rendered by the genitive of **кото́рый** immediately following the thing or person possessed. In a direct or reported question, "whose" is, of course, rendered by **ч/е́/й**:

челове́к, до́чь кото́рого я ви́дел	the man whose daughter I saw
де́вушка, перо́м кото́рой я писа́л	the girl whose pen I wrote with
Чью́ до́чь вы́ ви́дели?	Whose daughter did you see?
Он спроси́л, чью́ до́чь я ви́дел.	He asked whose daughter I saw.

СЛОВА́РЬ ГРАММАТИ́ЧЕСКИХ ТЕ́РМИНОВ

глаго́л движе́ния motion verb

(не)определённый глаго́л/ви́д (non)determined verb/aspect

ГДЕ́ "place where"; **КУДА́** "place to"; **ОТКУ́ДА** "place whence"

глаго́льная приста́вка verbal prefix

управля́ют *чем* govern:
   Предло́г «от» управля́ет роди́тельным падежо́м. The preposition от governs the genitive.

(про)спряга́ют conjugate; спряже́ние conjugation

(про)склоня́ют decline; склоне́ние declension; несклоня́емый indeclinable

тре́бовать *чего* require, take (case, etc.)

паде́ж case
   имени́тельный — nominative case
   роди́тельный — genitive case
   вини́тельный — accusative case
   да́тельный — dative case
   твори́тельный — instrumental case
   предло́жный — prepositional case
   (ме́стный—) (locative case)
   ко́свенный — oblique case

ро́д gender:
   мужско́й — masculine gender
   же́нский — feminine gender
   сре́дний — neuter gender

число́ number:
   еди́нственное — singular number
   мно́жественное — plural number

A. Comparison of adjectives and adverbs
B. Names
C. Impersonal expressions with dative complement: мо́жно
D. Ways of saying "to be" and the instrumental predicate

A. COMPARISON OF ADJECTIVES AND ADVERBS

Formation of the simple comparative

The simple comparative is formed with two suffixes: **-e** and **-ee**.

-e is used with stems ending in velars, which mutate (**к > ч, г > ж, х > ш**) and with monosyllabic stems in **ст** (which mutates to **щ**). The accent falls on the syllable immediately preceding **-e**.

hot	жа́ркий	жа́рче		quiet	ти́хий	ти́ше
loud	гро́мкий	гро́мче		simple	просто́й	про́ще
soft	мя́гкий	мя́гче		frequent	ча́стый	ча́ще
dear	дорого́й	доро́же		clean	чи́стый	чи́ще
stern	стро́гий	стро́же				

-ee is used with all other stems. It is added directly to the stem, and no mutation takes place. If the positive has only two syllables, or if the feminine short-form suffix is stressed, the comparative suffix is stressed **-е́е**; otherwise the stress is on the same stem syllable as in the positive.

new	но́вый	нове́е	нова́
fast	бы́стрый	быстре́е	быстра́
warm	тёплый	тепле́е	тепла́
gay	весёлый	веселе́е	весела́
cold	холо́дный	холодне́е	холодна́
interesting	интере́сный	интере́снее	интере́сна
pretty	краси́вый	краси́вее	краси́ва
ordinary	обыкнове́нный	обыкнове́ннее	обыкнове́нна

In conversation, this suffix (particularly when stressed) may lose its final vowel, becoming **-ей (-ей)**, but these forms are not often written: **новей, быстрей**.

Irregularities

a. **-e** occurs with a few stems not ending in **к, г, х**, or **ст**:

young	молодо́й	моло́же	rich	бога́тый	бога́че	
cheap	дешёвый	деше́вле				

b. A number of stems have more complex changes before **-e**. Here are the most important of them:

easy	лёгкий	ле́гче	low	ни́зкий	ни́же
high	высо́кий	вы́ше	rare	ре́дкий	ре́же
broad	широ́кий	ши́ре	narrow	у́зкий	у́же
far	далёкий	да́льше	near	бли́зкий	бли́же
deep	глубо́кий	глу́бже	short	коро́ткий	коро́че
long	до́лгий	до́льше	thin	то́нкий	то́ньше

c. Anomalous:

good	хоро́ший	лу́чше	big	большо́й	бо́льше
bad	плохо́й	ху́же	small	ма́ленький	ме́ньше

Many adjectives do not form simple comparatives, particularly adjectives in **-ский (-ско́й)** or **-овый (-ово́й)**.[1]

1. The forms in **-e/-ee**, common as they are, are restricted to the *predicate* in adjectival usage. In any attributive usage (in the nominative or any other case), the compound comparative (**бо́лее** plus any of the positive adjectival forms) is used:

бо́лее тру́дный вопро́с	a more difficult question
на бо́лее широ́кой у́лице	on a wider street
от бо́лее у́много челове́ка	from a more intelligent man

Ме́нее may replace **бо́лее** with the meaning "less," but there are, of course, no simple comparatives "less difficult," "less wide," etc. "That question is less difficult" would be: **Этот вопро́с ме́нее тру́дный (тру́ден)**.

---

[1] Adjectives are basically of two types: *qualitative*, designating a trait or a quality characteristic of the noun modified; e.g. *bad* writer, *white* house; and *relational*, designating a relationship characterizing the noun modified as being *of*, *from*, or connected with something or someone; e.g. *wooden* house, *French* writer. Only qualitaﬂﬂ e adjectives build comparatives in Russian; hence adjectives built with **-ск-** and **-ов-**, which are relational suffixes, do not build them. For more on qualitative vs. relational adjectives, see p. 27.

The four adjectives "good," "bad," "big," and "little" do, however, have *declined* (attributive) comparatives, which are used instead of **бо́лее** plus the positive:

good	хоро́ший	better	лу́чший
bad	плохо́й	worse	ху́дший
big	большо́й	bigger	бо́льший
small	ма́ленький	smaller	ме́ньший

Note that **большо́й** and **бо́льший** are distinguished only by stress and, hence, the spellings of many of the forms coincide; i.e. **больша́я/бо́льшая, больши́м/бо́ль-шим.**

Observe also that **лу́чший** and **ху́дший** may also be superlatives. **Кто́ из ни́х лу́чший музыка́нт** means "Who is the better musician?" or "Who is the best musician?" according to whether the musicians discussed number two or more.

And, finally, note that **са́мый хоро́ший** and **са́мый лу́чший** both mean "the best," and the same is true for the other three adjectives.

Another somewhat special case is **ста́рый**. **Ста́рше** refers specifically to age of persons or to rank; in other contexts, **старе́е** is used. Corresponding to **ста́рше** is **ста́рший** 'older (of persons), senior in rank,' which has an opposite: **мла́дший** 'younger (of persons), junior in rank.' Examples:

Он ста́рше жены́.	He is older than his wife.
На́ш до́м старе́е ва́шего.	Our house is older than yours.
Мо́й ста́рший бра́т ста́рший лей-тена́нт.	My older brother is a senior lieu-tenant.
Мо́й мла́дший бра́т мла́дший лей-тена́нт.	My younger brother is a junior lieu-tenant.
Они́ живу́т в бо́лее ста́ром до́ме.	They live in an older house.

The simple comparative for **молодо́й** in all meanings is **моло́же**.

Finally, **вы́сший** and **ни́зший** are like **ста́рший** and **мла́дший**; they mean "higher" and "lower" in terms of status rather than height or size, whereas **бо́лее высо́кий** and **бо́лее ни́зкий** mean "higher" and "lower" in the physical sense; e.g. **вы́сшая шко́ла, ни́зшая шко́ла, бо́лее высо́кий до́м.**

Ста́рший, мла́дший, вы́сший, and **ни́зший** may also have a superlative meaning in the proper context. **Кто́ из ни́х ста́рший?** 'Which of them is the oldest?'

2. The forms of **са́мый**, used with all forms of ordinary positive adjectives or of the special forms just discussed, give the superlative in Russian. The forms in **-ейший** (**-айший** after the hushings **ч, ж,** and **ш,** to which final stem velars **к, г,** and **х** automatically mutate before **-ейший**)[1] should not be regarded as alter-

---

[1] **Ближа́йший** and **нижа́йший** are irregular from **бли́зкий** and **ни́зкий.**

nate superlatives; their primary meaning is intensity; translation may be "most, very, extremely," etc. Often, however, they are used in a superlative meaning, which will be clear from the context. Such usages are often set expressions in which the compound superlative with **са́мый** would not be possible in the same meaning. Examples:

Это интере́снейшая кни́га.	That's a most interesting book.
Он говори́л мягча́йшим то́ном.	He spoke in an extremely mild tone.
У на́с была́ неприя́тнейшая пого́да.	We had the unpleasantest weather.
	(*No comparison, just "very, very unpleasant"*)
Это на́ша ближа́йшая зада́ча.	That's our very next (closest) task.
Он живёт в ближа́йшем до́ме.	He lives in the next (nearest) house.
с велича́йшим удово́льствием	with very great (greatest) pleasure
с глубоча́йшим уваже́нием	with very deep (deepest) respect

3. Note the following sentences:

Рабо́та стано́вится всё трудне́е и трудне́е.	The work is getting harder and harder.
Он получа́ет всё бо́льше и бо́льше.	He is receiving more and more.
Он слу́шает всё ме́ньше и ме́ньше.	He is listening less and less.

4. "As X as possible" is expressed by **ка́к мо́жно** plus comparative of X:

Чита́йте ка́к мо́жно ти́ше.	Read as softly as possible.
Сде́лайте э́то ка́к мо́жно лу́чше.	Do it as well as possible.
Зада́йте ему́ ка́к мо́жно бо́льше вопро́сов.	Ask him as many questions as possible.

5. The prefix **по-**, used with a simple comparative, has the meaning "a little X-er."

Он ста́л рабо́тать полу́чше.	He's begun to work a little better.
Мы́ сейча́с получа́ем поме́ньше ма́сла.	We are now receiving less butter. *a little*

6. It is easy to confuse the elements in the **чём . . . тём** expression. Remember that **тём** is used with the comparative which "depends" on the other comparative, which follows **чём**, *regardless of their order*. Examples:

Чём ху́же вы́ рабо́таете, тём ме́ньше ва́м пла́тят.	The more poorly you work, the less you get paid.
Чём интере́снее ле́кция, тём бо́льше на не́й студе́нтов.	The more interesting the lecture, the more students there are at it.
Его́ успе́хи тём лу́чше, чём бо́льше он занима́ется. (*Reverse order*)	His progress is better, the more he studies.

Тем used alone with a comparative may have the meaning "all the X-er, so much the X-er":

Тем лу́чше.	All the better.
Тем ле́гче для на́с.	So much the easier for us.

Finally, note the expression **тем бо́лее, что** 'the more so as':

Она́ на́м о́чень нужна́, тем бо́лее, что она́ хорошо́ зна́ет испа́нский язы́к.	She's very necessary to us, the more so as she knows Spanish well.

7. Note the superlative meaning of the simple comparatives with **всех** and **всего́** (and be sure to distinguish between these two):

Он лу́чше все́х на́ших писа́телей.	He is the best of all our writers.
Он пи́шет лу́чше все́х.	He writes best of all.
Он пи́шет лу́чше всего́.	He writes better than he does anything else. (The best thing he does is write.)
Он говори́т хорошо́ по-неме́цки и по-францу́зски, а лу́чше всего́ по-ру́сски.	He speaks German and French well, but he speaks Russian best of all.

8. Remember that "much" with a comparative is **гор.́здо** (there is also a colloquial variant **куда́**, which is much more emphatic).

Вы́ ста́ли гора́здо лу́чше писа́ть.	You have begun to write much better.
Здесь гора́здо ую́тнее.	It's much cozier here.

9. The basic meaning of the comparative **скоре́е** is "sooner" or "more quickly." **Скоре́е! (Скоре́й!)** means "Quick! Hurry up!"

More important, however, is its more abstract use in sentences such as the following (the English usually is "rather, sooner, more . . ."):

Я скоре́е умру́, чем соглашу́сь на э́то.	I would sooner die than agree to that. (I'll die rather than agree to that.)
Это скоре́е университе́т, чем колле́дж.	This is more a university than a college.
Она́ скоре́е по́лная, чем худа́я.	She is more plump than thin.
Он скоре́е уйдёт, чем расска́жет о себе́.	He'll go away rather than tell about himself.

Скоре́е всего́ means "most likely, most probably"; e.g. **Я скоре́е всего́ не пойду́** 'I most likely won't go.'

B. NAMES

First names and *patronymics*, both masculine and feminine, are formally *nouns* and are *declined exactly like them*. Students frequently forget that names like **Юрий** and **Дмитрий** are not adjectives, but regular nouns in **й**, like **герой** or **пролетарий**; their genitive singulars are **Юрия**, **Дмитрия**.

Last names may be adjectival (**Бе́лый**, **Достое́вский**), but a vast number of them end in **-ов (-ёв)** or **-ин**. These have a mixed declension:

Masculine singular like *nouns*, except *instrumental* like *adjectives*:

Че́хов, Че́хова, Че́хову, Че́хове, *but* Че́хов**ым**
Лу́жин, Лу́жина, Лу́жину, Лу́жине, *but* Лу́жин**ым**

Feminine singular like *pronouns*:

Че́хова, Че́хову, Че́ховой; Лу́жина, Лу́жину, Лу́жиной

Plural: Nominative like *short adjectives*; others like *long adjectives*:

Че́ховы; Че́ховых, Че́ховым, Че́ховыми, Че́ховых
Лу́жины; Лу́жиных, Лу́жиным, Лу́жиными, Лу́жиных

Last names in other consonants are declined like masculine animate nouns if they designate men, but *are not declined at all if they designate women*. Such names may be Russian, but many of them are foreign. Examples:

Попо́вич, Попо́вича, *inst* Попо́вич**ем**; *fem* Попо́вич throughout; *pl* Попо́вичи, Попо́вичей, Попо́вичам, etc.
Бра́ун, Бра́уна, *inst* Бра́уном; *fem* Бра́ун throughout; *pl* Бра́уны, -ов -ам, etc.

Foreign last names which happen to end in **-ов** and **-ин** follow the nominal declension; e.g. *inst sg* **Фра́нклином**, *gen pl* **Фра́нклинов**, etc.

Russian last names in **-а/-я** are declined like feminine nouns; e.g. **Гли́нка**, *acc sg* **Гли́нку**, *gen pl* **Гли́нок**. It makes no difference whether the person or persons referred to are male or female.

Russian last names in **-аго**, **-ово**, **-ых**, and **-их** are not declined: **Жива́го**, **Дурново́**, **Черны́х**, **Долги́х**. Names in **-ко** are not ordinarily declined: **Мосе́нко**, **Черне́нко**, **Федоре́нко**, **Сушко́**.

Remember to decline *both* parts of a compound name: **Ри́мский-Ко́рсаков**, **Ри́мского-Ко́рсакова**, **Ри́мским-Ко́рсаковым**, **Ри́мские-Ко́рсаковы**.

Many last names have varying stress: **Ива́но́в**, **Доло́нко́**, **Пе́репёлов**.

The terms **господи́н** 'Mr.,' **госпожа́** 'Mrs.' or 'Miss,' and **господа́** 'gentlemen' or 'ladies and gentlemen' are used by Russian speakers outside of the Soviet Union and by Soviets when addressing or referring to foreigners. In the

Soviet Union the terms **граждани́н**, **гражда́нка**, and **гра́ждане** (literally, 'citizen, -ess, and -s') are used instead, but mainly in public, and they are often replaced by **това́рищ** (either sex) and **това́рищи** (literally, 'comrade(s),' but now meaning little more than 'Mr.,' 'Mrs.,' or the appropriate plural in reference to Soviet citizens). **Това́рищ** may also occur with a title: **това́рищ профе́ссор**, **това́рищ до́ктор**, **това́рищ генера́л**.

In private or more personal intercourse **това́рищ** would be more likely than **граждани́н**. However, the first name and patronymic are frequently the equivalent of 'Mr.' and 'Mrs.' in English. They combine a degree of distance with the informality present, for example, between a professor and his students, a chairman and his subordinates, or among any people who work together, know each other's names, but are not on intimate terms with each other. The use of the first name and patronymic is not too "informal" in Russian, as the use of the first name may be in English. For example, if we take **Ива́н Па́влович Петро́в**:

граждани́и Петро́в	Mr. Petrov
това́рищ Петро́в	Mr. Petrov
Ива́н Па́влович	Mr. Petrov; John (but the address is formal)
Ва́ня	John, Johnny

Usage varies somewhat with regard to the derivation and pronunciation of patronymics. Much harder to predict are the nicknames from the given first names; e.g. **Дми́трий** may be called **Ди́ма** or **Ми́тя**, and **Же́ня** may refer to male **Евге́ний** or female **Евге́ния**. The cases must be learned individually.

The word **и́мя**, strictly speaking, designates the first name only; however, it frequently refers to a person's whole name, first name and patronymic, or even his last name as well. The name of a thing, title of a book or play, and so on, is normally not **и́мя**, but **назва́ние**.

C. IMPERSONAL EXPRESSIONS WITH

DATIVE COMPLEMENT: мо́жно

Impersonal expressions with a dative complement (present or implied) are extremely important and common in Russian. As with impersonal negative constructions with a genitive complement like **нет**, the student should not look for a subject, but try to get the feel of the construction in Russian. The English translations, as we expect, are frequently misleading. For instance, "I was cold" is in Russian **Мне бы́ло хо́лодно**, and note the difference between **Ива́н ску́чен** 'Ivan is boring' and **Ива́ну ску́чно** 'Ivan is bored.' English rules permit "I was told about that," but Russian requires **Мне бы́ло ска́зано** (or, of course, **Мне сказа́ли**) **об э́том**, because it is not the "I" which was told, but something else which was told "to me" (cf. Lesson X).

Мо́жно has two meanings: (1) possibility (here it is equivalent to **возмо́жно**; see II.1 and (2) permission ("may, be allowed to"). Both take or imply an infinitive, but only the latter is normally used with a dative complement. Hence, "May we enter?" may be **Мо́жно на́м войти́?** but "We can (are able to) do this" would be **Мы́ мо́жем сде́лать э́то** (never **На́м мо́жно**), 'One could see her' **Мо́жно бы́ло её ви́деть**, but 'We could see her' **Мы́ могли́ её ви́деть**.

Remember that the negative of **мо́жно** is **нельзя́**; *не мо́жно does not exist.

D. WAYS OF SAYING "TO BE" AND THE INSTRUMENTAL PREDICATE

Russian has a variety of expressions rendering the general idea of "to be" and certain related ideas: "become, appear, turn out to be," and others. The predicates following verbs expressing such meanings will be in the instrumental case, if the forms have case,[1] except for **бы́ть** and **быва́ют**, which may take the instrumental or the nominative (see below). Let us examine some important cases.

1. The most basic verb "to be" is, of course, **бы́ть**. The present tense is the so-called zero verb. In speech there may be a slight hesitation between the subject and the predicate noun or adjective, and in writing a dash sometimes separates the two:

Мо́й оте́ц—лейтена́нт в а́рмии.	My father is a lieutenant in the army.
Все́ ва́ши докла́ды плохи́е.	All your reports are bad.

The predicate following a zero verb is (for practical purposes) always nominative. After the infinitive it is normally instrumental. After past and future forms selection favors the instrumental, but the predicate may be nominative if it denotes something permanent or something unaffected by considerations of time; e.g. in **Он бу́дет хоро́ший солда́т** the emphasis is not at all on "when." Usage varies somewhat, but seems increasingly to favor the instrumental. The latter is certainly used in many "permanent" situations, the statement above notwithstanding.

Я всегда́ хоте́л бы́ть инжене́ром.	I always wanted to be an engineer.
Бы́ть поля́ком тепе́рь не легко́.	It isn't easy to be a Pole now.
Че́рез го́д вы́ бу́дете аспира́нтом.	In a year you'll be a graduate student.
Она́ ско́ро бу́дет учи́тельницей.	She will soon be a teacher.

---

[1] That is, if they are long forms; the short forms have no case endings. See paragraph 7 on page 94 for examples.

Он до́лго бы́л солда́том.	He was a soldier for a long time.
Моя́ ма́ть была́ англича́нка.	My mother was an Englishwoman.
Я не хочу́, что́бы мо́й сы́н бы́л врачо́м.	I don't want my son to be a doctor.
Серге́й бы́л сы́н моего́ дру́га.	Sergej was the son of my friend.
Мо́й бра́т бу́дет знамени́тый арти́ст.	My brother is going to be a famous actor.

The instrumental is always used after the present gerund **бу́дучи**:

Бу́дучи у́мным челове́ком, о́н э́то поймёт.	Being a smart person, he will understand that.

An instrumental predicate may be used even where a form of **бы́ть** is only implied:

Ещё ма́льчиком о́н люби́л обсужда́ть поли́тику.	He liked to discuss politics even when he was a boy.

2. The verb **быва́ют** usually has frequentative meaning, though there are important cases where it does not (for a fuller treatment of **быва́ют** see X.2, pages 278–279). Note the following examples:

Он ча́сто быва́ет у Ива́на Серге́евича.	He often visits Ivan Sergeevič.
Этот сы́р у на́с быва́ет.	We have this cheese now and then.
Таки́е кни́ги не быва́ют дёшевы в Москве́.	Such books aren't usually cheap in Moscow.
Зи́мы на ю́ге быва́ют тёплые.	Winters in the south are usually warm.

3. The verb **яви́ться – явля́ются** as a **(КУДА)** verb may mean "report, present oneself (for work, etc.)." But it is much more important (and, at least in the imperfective, much more common) in its nonlocational meaning 'be,' where it is used with an instrumental predicate. It is the 'be' of definitions. The imperfective occurs commonly in educated speech, and with great frequency in noncolloquial prose:

Москва́ явля́ется столи́цей Сове́тского Сою́за.	Moscow is the capital of the Soviet Union.
Он явля́ется руководи́телем на́шей гру́ппы.	He is the leader of our group.
Все́ э́ти достиже́ния яви́лись результа́том но́вой поли́тики импера́тора.	All these accomplishments were the results of the emperor's new policy.

The instrumental predicate may precede the verb, but no change in meaning results:

Са́мой изве́стной газе́той в Сове́тском Сою́зе явля́ется «Пра́вда».	The best-known newspaper in the Soviet Union is *Pravda*.

4. The expression **есть** may correspond to either "is" or "are" in definitions or in listing things. It may also play this role of substituting for the zero verb, when that verb requires particular emphasis. In this second role, in which it can represent any person or number, **есть** is quite common in conversation, and is often preceded by an emphatic **и** (cf. Lesson III.1):

Не ду́май обо мне́ лу́чше, чём я есть.	Don't think better of me than I am.
На́до зна́ть ве́щи, ка́к они́ есть.	We have to know things as they are.
Дни́ неде́ли есть: понеде́льник, вто́рник, ...	The days of the week are: Monday, Tuesday, ...
Это и есть на́ш учи́тель.	That *is* our teacher.
На́ш теа́тр и есть но́вый.	Our theater *is* new.
Каки́е ни есть на́ши зада́чи, мы́ спра́вимся с ни́ми.	Whatever our tasks *are*, we will cope with them. (Cf. Lesson VII)

And note: **Прика́з есть прика́з** 'An order's an order.'

5. To "be" in the sense of "be located" is **находи́ться** (imperfective only). This verb also occurs in various abstract contexts often expressed by the English "find oneself." Examples:

Босто́н нахо́дится в шта́те Массачу́сетс.	Boston is located in the state of Massachusetts.
Где́ нахо́дится госуда́рственный музе́й?	Where's the state museum?
Я нахожу́сь всё бо́льше и бо́льше под ва́шим влия́нием.	I find myself more and more under your influence.
Он нахо́дится под на́шим наблюде́нием.	He is under our supervision.

6. There are, of course, many expressions we have not mentioned which might best be translated by "be" in English. In the regular lessons we will encounter **предста́вить – представля́ют собо́й** *acc* and **состоя́ть**, both of which represent the idea of "be" in their own ways. And there are many individual cases; e.g. where we say "The weather *is* nice today," Russians are likely to say **Пого́да сего́дня стои́т хоро́шая**. But we have covered most of the important general correspondences.

7. Note the following examples of verbs with meanings close to "be," which take predicates in the instrumental, if the forms have case (see footnote, page 91):

На́м ста́ло о́чень ску́чно.	We became very bored.
Он ста́нет вели́ким поэ́том.	He will become a great poet.
В про́шлом ме́сяце ва́ша рабо́та была́ хоро́шей, но тепе́рь она́ ста́ла ху́же.	Last month your work was good, but it has now become worse.
Он ста́л мои́м лу́чшим дру́гом.	He's become my best friend.
Она́ оста́лась вдово́й.	She remained (was now a) widow.
Он оста́лся недово́лен э́тим.	He remained unsatisfied with that.
Ва́ша мы́сль остаётся я́сной (ясна́).	Your thought remains clear.
Он ка́жется у́мным (умён).	He appears to be intelligent.
Он мне́ каза́лся хоро́шим адво-ка́том.	He seemed to me to be a good lawyer.
Они́ ока́жутся хоро́шими сол-да́тами.	They'll turn out to be good soldiers.
Оказа́лось, что о́н пло́хо зна́л ру́сский язы́к.	It turned out that he knew Russian badly.
Мне́ ка́жется, что вы́ мно́го пьёте.	It seems to me that you drink a lot.
Она́ ока́зывается хоро́шей учени́-цей.	She's turning out to be a good pupil.

The verbs involved in the above examples are: **ста́нут – станови́ться** 'become'; **оста́нутся – остава́ться** 'remain, stay'; **(по)каза́ться** 'appear, seem'; **оказа́ть-ся – ока́зываются** 'turn out (to be), prove (to be).'

Note that **(с)де́лаются** means "become," not "make oneself": **Де́лается темно́** 'It's getting dark'; **Он сде́лался хоро́шим учёным** 'He has become a good scholar.'

An important, related problem is the use of the instrumental case for the so-called "second object," which is an instrumental predicate further defining a direct object (the "first object"). The structure of an example sentence would be: TRANSITIVE VERB X(*acc*) Y(*inst*), e.g. "make something something."

Эти очки́ де́лают его́ лицо́ смеш-ны́м.	Those glasses make his face funny.
Я де́лаю его́ мои́м помо́щником.	I am making him my assistant.
Мы́ вы́брали его́ президе́нтом.	We elected him president.
Его́ назна́чили профе́ссором.	He was appointed professor.
Я всегда́ называ́ю дурака́ дурако́м.	I always call a fool a fool.
Мы́ назовём на́шего сы́на Ва́ней.	We will name our son Vanja.

Егó зовýт Николáем.	His name is Nikolaj.
Я ужé представля́ю вáс студéнтом.	I am already imagining you as a student.
Мы́ всё считáли егó отли́чным генерáлом.	We all considered him an excellent general.

Назвáть (назовýт) – **называ́ют** is the normal verb "name" or "call," and **называ́ются** (imperfective only) means "be named, be called." For stating *names* of *people* **звáть (зовýт)** (imperfective only) is used; e.g. 'What is your name?' **Кáк вáс зовýт?** 'My name is Ivan' **Меня́ зовýт Ивáном.** But NOTE: 'What is the name of that factory?' **Кáк называ́ется э́тот завóд?** See also the examples of these verbs directly above.

The basic idea of **(по)звáть** is "call" ("summon," not "name"); e.g. 'Call him here!' **Позови́те егó сюдá**; 'Mother's calling' **Мáма зовёт.** Or it may mean "invite": 'They invited us often to their place' **Они́ чáсто звáли нáс к себé.**

There is a strong and increasing tendency in Russian to use the nominative instead of the instrumental after **звáть** and after **называ́ются**, particularly when the predicate involved is a title; for example:

Её зовýт Светлáна Михáйловна.	Her name is Svetlana Mixajlovna.
Этот пóезд называ́ется «Крáсная Стрелá».	This train is called the Red Arrow.
Этот колхóз называ́ется «Путь Ильичá».	This collective farm is called the 'Path of Il'ič.' (*Lenin's patronymic*)

TRANSLATION INTO RUSSIAN

There[1] goes **that**[2] Dmítrij Il'íč Zórin. He is a professor of Spanish at our university; that is, if one can call him a professor. But a profe. ɔr remains a professor, although we all would like a more intelligent one. They made him a professor here, and he *is* a professor. **What is**[3] a professor? A professor is (definition) a person who **teaches**[4] at a university. **More than that,**[5] he is supposed   5
to be an interesting person. If he turns out to be a boring person, so much the worse for all of us, the more so as our courses aren't very interesting. It seems to me that this university is an extremely boring (use one word) place. And I know best of all, since I've been here for fifteen years. They're already calling me "Papa." My older brother and even my youngest sister left long ago.   10

But Dmítrij Il'íč, whom we call Mítja, is now having a much jollier time (translate this by a dative impersonal construction) than Mixaíl Nikoláevič Ščérba, though he himself is not a very jolly person; he is rather quiet than jolly. **Still,**[6] he lives better than Míša, he dresses more warmly, speaks louder, and **drives**[7] faster than Ščérba. One can even say that he is much richer; he   15 seems to everybody to be the richest man in the state. It's clear that he is a most rich man; I have never seen a richer man.

Many years ago Zórin and I went to the university together. There we knew a[8] girl named Tat'jána Pávlovna Lárčenko, who very much wanted to marry[9] Dmítrij Il'íč. But although Tánja was a beautiful girl and later became a beautiful woman, Mítja somehow didn't want to marry[9] her. "She's young, jolly, and beautiful, but how boring she is! (use short forms) And, still more important, I would be bored with her. She writes poorly, reads still worse; the best thing she does is talk (see paragraph A7 page 88). And the more she talks, the less I listen. I would like my wife to be more interesting, because I want her to play a greater, and not a lesser role in our life. I know Tánja has received a higher education, the more so as I received only an elementary education. My wife must be as intelligent as possible."

Since the Zórins and I live in the same[10] town, I see them rather frequently. Last night I dropped in on the Zórins. I was sorry for Mítja. I suddenly understood that he had made the wrong[11] choice, that Tánja was a bad wife for h'm.[12] We sat and drank beer or, rather,[13] just sat, because Tánja had not given us the right beer.[11] Finally, Mítja asked his wife to bring other beer. "And it must be a little colder," he said. When Tánja went out, I told Mítja that it would have been better for him to marry Svetlána Júr'evna Jones (Джóнс), that anything (everything) was better than to be married to Tánja. But he answered that it had not been possible for him to marry an Englishwoman. When I said that her mother had been a Russian, he answered that her mother hadn't liked him very much. She had been for ten years an engineer in Siberia, but she said that she would rather return there than see Svéta his wife. I said that her oldest brother had liked Mítja very much and that Svéta had always been under his influence. Mítja was about[14] to answer this, when Tánja came back with the beer. It was getting more and more difficult. Being their guest, I couldn't leave immediately, but I wanted to leave as soon as possible. After that I began to visit[15] them as seldom as possible.

NOTES

1. "There" in a simple "place where" meaning is, of course, тáм, but if the speaker is indicating or pointing, the translation would normally be вóт. Note that вóт is not confined to actual physical indication:

Вóт óн сидит в углý.	There he is sitting in the corner.
Вóт и мы́. Вóт мы́ и пришли.	Here we are.
but	
Вóт вáм хорóший примéр.	Here's (There's) a good example for you.

Он сказа́л на́м во́т что́.	Here's what he said to us.
Во́т ка́к с ни́ми обраща́ться.	This is (Here's) how to treat them.[1]
Он на́м сказа́л во́т таки́е ве́щи.	These are the things he told us.
Во́т ка́к. Во́т почему́. Во́т что́ о́н зна́ет.	That's the way! That's why. That's[1] what he knows.

In several expressions **во́т** has a pejorative flavor:

Во́т та́к исто́рия.	That's a pretty story (fine mess, etc.).
Во́т и па́па.	There's papa for you.
Во́т ещё!	Indeed! Well, I never!
Во́т тебе́.	Take that! (according to deserts)

2. A very common expression (though one still listed in the dictionaries as colloquial) is **э́тот са́мый** 'the X (we were talking or thinking about)':

Во́т идёт э́тот са́мый Ива́н Па́влович.	There goes that Ivan Pavlovič.
Куда́ ушла́ э́та са́мая же́нщина?	Where did that woman (we were just talking or thinking about her) go?

3. "What is" asking for a definition or explanation is **Что́ тако́е** plus a noun in any gender; e.g. **Что́ тако́е коммуни́зм?** 'What is communism?' **Что́ э́то тако́е?** 'What is that?' "Who is" is **Кто́ тако́й? Кто́ таки́е?** 'Who is that? Who are they?' and **Кто́ вы́ тако́й?** 'Who are you?'

4. "Teach" someone is **(на)учи́ть** plus a direct object, but a more general verb for "teach," used particularly if the person taught is not specified and the subject or place taught is of primary importance, is **преподава́ть** (imperfective only); e.g. 'He teaches German here' **Он зде́сь преподаёт неме́цкий язы́к.** Verbs of "teaching" and "learning" are discussed in II. 7.

5. **Бо́лее того́.**

6. "Still" is another word with several meanings. Here it is a restrictive, with a sense close to "nevertheless." Russian **всё же** is a good translation here.

7. "Drive" a car or operate another conveyance is often **е́здить – е́хать.** If the conveyance is specified, however, **веду́т – води́ть** is very commonly used or **управля́ют** *inst* (imperfective only) in the more specific sense "operate":

Он бы́л шофёром. Он до́лго води́л «Во́лгу».	He was a taxi driver. He drove a Volga for a long time.
Я сейча́с вожу́ тра́ктор.	I'm driving a tractor now.

---

[1] Students are frequently tempted to use **э́то** instead of the correct **во́т** in sentences like these.

Управля́ть самолётом — нелегко́.	Flying (operating) an airplane isn't easy.
Кто́ ведёт э́ту маши́ну?	Who's driving that car?
Ты́ о́чень бы́стро е́дешь.	You're driving very fast.

Do not confuse **веду́т** – **води́ть** 'drive' (conduct a conveyance; cf. **води́тель** 'driver (of any conveyance),' **води́тельские права́** 'driver's license') with **везу́т** – **вози́ть** 'drive' (convey, take in a vehicle); for example:

Куда́ вы́ на́с везёте?	Where are you driving us?
Отвези́те их на ста́нцию.	Drive them to the station.

It is worth mentioning again that "I drove to Boston and back" (in the normal meaning, where operation of the car is secondary) is simply **Я́ е́здил в Босто́н.**

8. Review the declension and usage of the pronoun **оди́н.** Note that it can translate, as in this case, "a (an)" when the latter corresponds approximately to "a certain":

Та́м бы́л оди́н о́чень прия́тный челове́к.	There was a (or a certain) very pleasant man there.
Я́ зна́ю одну́ доро́гу, кото́рая ведёт туда́.	I know a (a certain) road which leads there.

The plural of this **оди́н** is used in the expression **одни́** X . . . **други́е** Y 'some X . . ., others Y . . .':

Одни́ хоте́ли пое́хать, други́е не хоте́ли.	Some wanted to go, others didn't.
Он зна́ет одни́х, а други́х не зна́ет.	He knows some (of them), others he doesn't.

Оди́н may be used in both singular and plural to mean "alone" or "only":

Она́ сиди́т та́м одна́.	She's sitting there alone.
Вы́ оди́н э́то зна́ете.	You alone know that. You are the only one who knows that.
Э́то понима́ют одни́ ру́сские. (То́лько, of course, is acceptable here as well.)	Only Russians understand that.

9. The expressions for "marry" and "be married" differ according to sex.

For a man:

жени́ться на *prp*	Ма́рк же́нится на Та́не.	(Жени́ться is both
бы́ть жена́т(ым) на *prp*	Ма́рк жена́т на Та́не.	perfective and imperfective.)

For a woman:

вы́йдут – выходить за́муж за *acc*   Та́ня выхо́дит за́муж за Ма́рка.
бы́ть за́мужем за *inst*   Та́ня за́мужем за Ма́рком.

NOTE: "They got married" is **Они́ пожени́лись.**

10. "In the same town" may be translated "in one town."

11. "Not the right X" is **не то́т** X; "X isn't (the) right (thing)" is X **не то́.** Note that in a sentence like **Он взя́л не ту́ кни́гу** 'He took the wrong book' there is no question of a negative genitive, because the action is not denied (cf. R2.B4). See also Lesson IV for a general statement on the position of **не** in a sentence.

12. "For him" may be translated here by **ему́** placed directly after the subject. The use of the dative to translate "for" is discussed in IV.B4.

13. "Rather" is another English word which may be rendered in Russian in various ways. It may be translated by **скоре́е** (R5.A9), when it means "more exactly" by **точне́е** or **верне́е** (R3 note 14), and when it means "somewhat, pretty" by **дово́льно.**

14. "Was about to" is often best translated **хоте́л** plus infinitive.

15. See R5.D2.

СЛОВА́РЬ ГРАММАТИ́ЧЕСКИХ ТЕ́РМИНОВ

сте́пень degree:
— сравне́ния degree of comparison
положи́тельная — positive degree
сравни́тельная — comparative degree
превосхо́дная — superlative degree
безли́чный impersonal — констру́кция impersonal construction

подлежа́щее subject
сказу́емое predicate
дополне́ние object, complement:
прямо́е — direct object
ко́свенное — indirect object

A. NUMERALS

1. Cardinal numerals

The student must know the forms and syntax of the cardinals extremely well. The oblique cases of the numerals and some exercises in dealing with long numerals are presented in the Appendix. The collectives are also treated there.

For our purposes now, and particularly for telling time, the student needs to know the nominative/accusative, and also the genitive of the cardinals. Here are the genitives in summary:

One (1), of course, is **одного́/одно́й**. 2, 3, 4, 40, 90, and 100 fit into no particular pattern: **дву́х, трёх, четырёх, сорока́, девяно́ста, ста́**.

The other numerals have a genitive in -**и** (note that these numerals are declined quite like singular nouns in the third declension, except that the end stress, which characterizes all but 11 through 19, is not typical of the declension):

> пяти́, шести́, семи́, восьми́, девяти́, десяти́, оди́ннадцати, двена́дцати, трина́дцати, четы́рнадцати, пятна́дцати, шестна́дцати, семна́дцати, восемна́дцати, девятна́дцати, двадцати́, тридцати́

Note that 50, 60, 70, 80 have the genitive **и** in both components of the numeral, and note that the first one is stressed: **пяти́десяти, шести́десяти, семи́десяти, восьми́десяти**.

In cardinal numerals the major distinction is between the nominative/accusative and all the other cases, which we call the oblique cases. After the nominative/accusative the forms of nouns and adjectives following the numeral depend on the numeral. 1 requires nominative singular of both noun and adjec-

100

tive. 2 to 4 require genitive singular of noun and, as a general rule, *genitive plural* of adjective with *masculine* and *neuter* nouns *but nominative plural* of adjective with *feminine* nouns. 5 to 19 require genitive plural of both noun and adjective (above 19 it is the last digit which counts, and 0 acts like 10). Examples:

одни новый стол, одно новое перо, одна новая книга; два новых стола, два новых пера, две новые книги; пять новых столов, пять новых перьев, пять новых книг

After an oblique case, however, the forms of nouns and adjectives following the numeral are all in the *plural* of that case; that is, they are no longer dependent on whether the numeral is 2, 5, or 157, but simply on the case the numeral is in. Examples:

из: двух новых столов, пяти новых столов, ста пятидесяти семи новых столов, двадцати новых книг, двадцати двух новых книг, двадцати пяти новых книг

2. Indefinite numerals

The above distinction applies also to the expressions **много, мало, немного, сколько,** and **несколько,** which may be regarded as "*indefinite*"[1] *numerals.* In the nominative/accusative these words require the genitive plural or singular, as appropriate (cf. R4 note 14). When these words themselves are in oblique cases, however, the nouns and adjectives following them are all in whatever oblique case is involved; usage is ordinarily restricted to the plural.

много новых столов   из многих новых столов   о многих новых столах
сколько новых книг   из скольких новых книг   со скольким новыми
                                                  книгами

NOTE: **мало** новых книг, *but* oblique: с **немногими** новыми книгами.

We have just noticed that **много, мало, немного, сколько,** and **несколько** must be declined if their role in the sentences puts them in an oblique case. In practice, the oblique forms of **мало** almost never appear, being replaced by

---

[1] The indefinite category in Russian grammar includes a number of words whose primary meanings are not indefinite:

	PRIMARY	INDEFINITE
один	one	a (certain)
известный	(well) known	a (certain)
определённый	defined, definite	a (certain) specific
ряд	row, line; series	a number of, some
	Cf. целый ряд	a whole bunch of, quite a few

those of **немно́го**, but all the others are perfectly common. Some examples (in addition to those given above):

Он говори́л то́лько с немно́гими поэ́тами.	He spoke with only a few poets.
Они́ говори́ли о мно́гом.	They spoke about a great deal.
Во мно́гих слу́чаях вы́ э́то найдёте.	In many cases you'll find that.
Он рассказа́л об э́том в не́скольких слова́х.	He told about it in a few words.
Вы мно́гому нау́читесь у него́.	You'll learn a lot from him.

Two of these indefinite numerals, **мно́го** and **немно́го**, have coexisting "declined" nominative/accusative forms: **мно́гие** and **немно́гие**. The question then arises: What would be the difference between **мно́го люде́й** and **мно́гие лю́ди**? The distinction is exactly the same as that between **не́сколько** and **не́которые**, which is also very important in Russian, so we will treat the problem as a whole. For **мно́го** vs. **мно́гие** and **немно́го** vs. **немно́гие** the distinction is confined to just those forms, since **мно́го** and **немно́го** always become **мно́гих** and **немно́гих** in the oblique cases. For **не́сколько** and **не́которые** the distinction is preserved in all cases, since the words have different roots. The distinction is the following:

Мно́го, немно́го, and **не́сколько** designate things or people taken together, a group of things or people, with no emphasis on individuals within the group; e.g. 'There were many people there' **Та́м бы́ло мно́го люде́й**, 'There are several books lying on the table' **На столе́ лежи́т не́сколько кни́г**. **Мно́гие, немно́гие**, and **не́которые,**[1] on the other hand, designate each of a group of individuals separately, emphasize them more. This idea is best exemplified in the context "many of, a few of, several of," where the "many," "few," and "several" individuals are singled out, and Russian has **мно́гие из, немно́гие из**, and **не́которые из**. Some examples:

In our city there are many/several beautiful buildings.	В на́шем го́роде **мно́го/не́сколько** краси́вых зда́ний.
Many/several of the buildings in our city are very beautiful.	**Мно́гие/Не́которые** из зда́ний в на́шем го́роде — краси́вые.
It was pleasant to meet one's acquaintances after many years. Many had aged quite a bit, but some, on the other hand, had grown younger.	Прия́тно бы́ло встре́тить свои́х знако́мых по́сле **мно́гих** ле́т. **Мно́гие** нема́ло постаре́ли, **не́которые**, наоборо́т, помолоде́ли.

---

[1] It is helpful to think of **не́которые** as "certain"; **не́сколько** does not have this sense at all. **Не́который**(*sg*) also means "certain"; cf. **не́которое вре́мя** 'a certain time, awhile.'

He had only a few friends.	Друзе́й у него́ бы́ло то́лько **немно́го**.
After the war began, only a few remained home (few out of many).	По́сле нача́ла войны́ оста́лись то́лько **немно́гие**.
During that time I read several books, and some (certain ones) of these were very interesting.	За э́то вре́мя я прочита́л **не́сколько** кни́г, и **не́которые** из ни́х бы́ли о́чень интере́сны.
Several Russians were here.	**Не́сколько** ру́сских бы́ло здесь.
Certain Russians were here . . . (*Something more expected*)	**Не́которые** ру́сские бы́ли здесь . . .
He is speaking about several things.	Он говори́т о **не́скольких** веща́х.
He is speaking about several (certain) very interesting things.	Он говори́т о **не́которых** о́чень интере́сных веща́х.

We may diagram the nonoblique and oblique forms with the proportions:

NONOBLIQUE	OBLIQUE
мно́го is to мно́гие	не́скольких is to не́которых
as не́сколько is to не́которые	as мно́гих is to мно́гих

and note that *не́сколькие does not exist.

3. Telling time

The conventions used in telling time must simply be learned. The second half of the hour, **без** plus genitive plus *cardinal* number of the hour makes a good drill for the genitive of numbers; e.g. '7:35' **без двадцати́ пяти́ мину́т** *во́семь*. Remember that minutes after an hour require the *ordinal* of the next hour in the genitive; e.g. '5:05' **пять мину́т** *шесто́го*.

Current Moscow and Leningrad speech frequently replaces **Кото́рый ча́с?** and **В кото́ром часу́ . . . ?** by:

| Ско́лько вре́мени? | What time is it? |
| Во ско́лько (часо́в) он придёт? | At what time (When) will he come? |

B. NOMINATIVE AND GENITIVE PLURALS OF NOUNS

The nominative[1] and genitive plurals of nouns may cause the student some trouble. Certainly there are a number of irregularities which must simply be

---

[1] Throughout the book the term "nominative" or "nominative/accusative" in reference to masculine nouns means precisely "nominative and nonanimate accusative" (i.e. nonoblique cases).

learned, but perhaps there are certain patterns which will become somewhat clearer, if you think about some of the things which were said in the introduction about *j*, inserted vowels, ˀnd spelling rules.

Most masculine nouns have a nominative plural in *-i*. There is, however, an important group of more than 150 masculines with the ending *-a*. This ending is productive and is more widespread in colloquial speech than in the standard language. There is no useful way of classifying what types of nouns take *-a*; learn the examples as you come to them.

A stressed ending *-á* signals end stress for the rest of the plural vs. stem stress throughout the singular. All nouns with nominative plural in *-a* do, in fact, stress this ending, except a small group in consonant plus *j* in the plural and in consonant without the *j* in the singular; e.g. **стул, стýлья**. This group also includes a number of nouns in stressed *-á*; e.g. **мýж, мужьЯ́**. The stressed type in consonant plus *j* is mainly limited to nouns of familial relationship. Here are examples of all types of masculine nouns with nominative plural in *-a*:

NOUNS IN *-á*		NOUNS IN ь/я	NOUNS IN ь/я́
лéс, лесá	учи́тель, учителя́	стýл, стýлья	мýж, мужьЯ́
гóрод, городá	дóктор, докторá	брáт, брáтья	сын, сыновьЯ́
глáз, глазá	пáспорт, паспортá		дрýг, друзьЯ́
цвéт, цветá	бéрег, берегá		
крáй, краЯ́	óбраз, образá (icon)		

The masculine genitive plural has the ending *-ov* after hard paired consonants and **ц** and *j*, and the ending *-ej* after soft paired consonants and the four hushings (**ж, ш, ч, щ**). The stressed **-ь/я́** group, however, usually has a genitive plural in zero.

MASCULINES

-ov		*-ej*
стóл, столóв	˙крáй, краёв	писáтель, писáтелей
сáд, садóв	герóй, герóев	словáрь, словарéй
лéс, лесóв	гéний, гéниев	нóж, ножéй
от/é/ц, отцóв	руч/é/й, ручьёв	товáрищ, товáрищей
нéм/е/ц, нéмцев	брáт, (брáтья), брáтьев	

ZERO (-)

мýж, (мужьЯ́), муж/é/й
сы́н, (сыновьЯ́), сынов/é/й

The feminine genitive plural for nouns in *-a*, and the neuter genitive plural are zero. Both types frequently have an inserted /**e**/ or /**o**/. Watch particularly for a mobile /**e**/ in a *gen* *pl* ending in **-ей**. Examples:

FEMININES		NEUTERS
кни́га, кни́г	копе́йка, копе́/е/к	ме́сто, ме́ст
вёрста́, вёрст	тро́йка, тро́/е/к	сёло́, сёл
студе́нтка, студе́нт/о/к	семья́, сем/е́/й	окно́, о́к/о/н
де́вушка, де́вуш/е/к	статья́, стат/е́/й	письмо́, пи́с/е/м
	па́ртия, па́ртий	зда́ние, зда́ний
	исто́рия, исто́рий	реше́ние, реше́ний

Notice that neuters in **-ь/ё** may have a genitive plural in *-ov*. Such plurals correspond to a **-ь/я** in the nominative plural and, in many cases, to a plain stem without a *j* in the singular (like **сту́л** and **сту́лья**):

пла́тье, (пла́тья), пла́тьев
перо́, (пе́рья), пе́рьев
де́рево, (дере́вья), дере́вьев

The genitive plural of feminine nouns of the third declension (nominative plural **-и**) is **-ей**; do not confuse this ending with the **-ей** containing the mobile vowel, described above:

две́рь, (две́ри), двере́й
ра́дость, (ра́дости), ра́достей

C. WORDS EXPRESSING NECESSITY OR COMPULSION[1]

Necessity or compulsion is expressed in English by such words as "must, have to, need, necessary, should, ought to," etc. In Russian, a personal subject plus **до́лж/е/н** usually indicates a certain personal obligation or moral compulsion from *within*. **Ну́жно** and **на́до**, with the person in the dative, often suggest some sort of compulsion from the *outside*, although **на́до** sometimes adds a note of inner compulsion; e.g. **На́м на́до бы́ло сде́лать э́то ра́ньше** 'We should have done that earlier.' "Should, must, ought to, have to," and such words may be translated by either **до́лжен** or **ну́жно/на́до** with a dative complement. "Should" and "ought to" may be hypothetical as well as "moral" in character, and are likely to be translated by **до́лжен бы** ("one ought to, one should") or **до́лжен бы́л бы** ("one ought to have, one should have"), or by **сле́дует/сле́довало бы**.

---

[1] Such words may be regarded as having *modal* meaning; modality, as we recall (R3. B), expresses some kind of involvement or judgment on the part of the speaker as to the possibility or desirability of the action.

Notice, however, that both "should" and "ought to" in English, and **должен** in Russian (and also "be supposed to" in English) may simply mean "according to what ordinarily happens, to what one would expect, to the schedule." Some of the examples in the group immediately below are of this type; i.e. may express probability instead of compulsion:

Я до́лжен написа́ть ему́ сейча́с же.	I must write him right away.
Мне́ на́до бы́ло написа́ть ему́ письмо́.	I had to write him a letter.
Руководи́тель до́лжен бы́ть сильне́е на́с все́х.	The leader must be stronger than all of us.
Он до́лжен бы́л ско́ро верну́ться.	He was supposed to come back soon.
Что́ на́до сде́лать в тако́м слу́чае?	What should be done in such a case?
Мне́ ну́жно серьёзно поговори́ть с тобо́й.	I have to have a serious talk with you.
Ва́м ну́жно обрати́ться к врачу́.	You need to consult a doctor (You have to—not moral compulsion).
Она́ должна́ бы́ть зде́сь в 5:00.	She should be here at 5:00.
Вы́ должны́ бы бы́ли сде́лать э́то ина́че.	You should have done that differently.
Он до́лжен э́то зна́ть хорошо́.	He ought to know that well.
Ва́м сле́дует (сле́довало бы) сде́лать э́то сего́дня.	You ought to do that today. (*Sentence with бы is more "modal," suggests the speaker may doubt that the person will.*)
Ва́м сле́довало написа́ть е́й.	You ought to have written to her (but you didn't).
Сле́дует по́мнить, что . . .	One should remember that . . .
Он не рабо́тает как сле́дует.[1]	He doesn't work as he should.

До́лжен may be used with nonpersonal subjects as well as personal:

Этот го́род до́лжен бы́л бы́ть на́шей столи́цей.	This city was supposed to have been our capital.
Это должно́ бы́ть сде́лано в два́ дня́.	That must be done in two days.

But note that **ну́жно/на́до** *dat* is used only with persons. If a thing must do or be something, **до́лжен** is mandatory; for example:

---

[1] **Ка́к сле́дует** is quite common in colloquial speech. The other forms in **сле́довать** are somewhat bookish.

| Этот го́род до́лжен име́ть краси́-вый па́рк. (*Never* *Этому го́роду ну́жно име́ть, etc.) | This city must have a beautiful park. |

До́лжен also is used to convey the meaning "owe":[1]

| Она́ мне́ должна́ 25 рубле́й. | She owes me 25 rubles. |
| Ско́лько о́н **бы́л до́лжен** ва́м? | How much did he owe you? |

And note the parenthetic expression **должно́ бы́ть** 'probably, must have':

| Вы́, должно́ бы́ть, уже́ слы́шали об э́том. | You have probably already heard about it. (You must have already . . .) |

WARNING: Do not use **должно́** as an impersonal like **ну́жно** or **на́до**. An impersonal **до́лжно** (NB stress) exists with a similar meaning, but the student should avoid it in favor of **ну́жно** or **на́до**.

In a majority of cases, we may consider that the impersonals **ну́жно** and **на́до** have the same meaning:

| На́до/Ну́жно бы́ло ему́ сказа́ть. | It was necessary to tell him. |
| На́м ну́жно/ на́до бы́ло ему́ сказа́ть. | We had to tell him. |

When something definite is necessary, something to which gender and number may be attached, the Russian ordinarily uses the short forms of the adjective **ну́жный**, which quite often corresponds to English "to need":

Э́та кни́га мне́ нужна́.	I need this book.
Он бу́дет ва́м ну́жен.	You will need him.
На́м нужны́ бы́ли э́ти де́ньги.	We needed this money.

When what is necessary or needed is less definite, both **ну́жно** and **на́до** may be used; e.g. **Что́ ва́м на́до?** or **Что́ ва́м ну́жно?** 'What do you want?'

Finally, **на́до** (less often **ну́жно**) may express "ought" or "should" rather than outright necessity. The corresponding negatives are quite frequent, particularly in the "moral" sense of "oughtn't" or "shouldn't" where they may have the force of a rebuke or a negative command:

| Что́ на́до ему́ да́ть? | What should I give him? |
| На́м на́до бы́ло пе́ть гро́мче. | We should have sung louder. |

---

[1] Note that до́лжен, when it is used with the past or future of бы́ть in meanings connected with compulsion, *must precede these forms*; e.g. Я до́лжен бы́л сказа́ть э́то, never the reverse. With "owe," on the other hand, the reverse order is mandatory: Я бы́л до́лжен ему́ пя́ть рубле́й.

Не надо было задавать бедному мальчику такого вопроса.	You shouldn't (oughtn't to) have asked the poor boy such a question.
Не надо говорить так.	Don't talk like that. (One shouldn't ...)
Не надо!	Don't.

TRANSLATION INTO RUSSIAN

The French (girl) students were supposed to arrive by train at the station at 9:45 (translate: "nine forty-five," "quarter to ten," and "fifteen to ten"). Many people were waiting at the station, and some of them had been there a long time. In the corner stood several English professors of Russian. Many of these pro-
5 fessors had been waiting for the French girls **since**[1] two o'clock. When the professors had **just**[2] decided to remain seven **more**[3] minutes, they suddenly **heard**[4] a bell. But the train itself wasn't there yet, and it was already six minutes to ten when the Englishmen **caught sight of**[4] the French (girl) students themselves. "Well, **here they are**,"[5] said one of the professors, "and here's our **dog's**[6] life
10 **for you.**[7] I'm already afraid to ask what time it is. **In my time**[8] I have worked with many students, but I never had to wait at a station until ten o'clock."

Some of the girls walked up to the professors. "We're all sorry that it's already so late," they said. "We should have arrived at **two thirty**.[6] But at five minutes past twelve, as we were waiting for the train, many (male) Italians came
15 up with several pens and many pencils and asked us if we wanted to buy them. We sat, ate, drank, and talked with them for a long time. **In all**[9] we **drank**[10] eighty-five cups of coffee and **ate**[10] ninety-four **loaves of bread**.[11] We ought to have called you, but we all needed those pencils and pens very much. Now we won't have to buy pencils here. You **probably**[12] won't understand this, but it was
20 clear that these Italians would soon become our good friends, and many of us must have seen in them future husbands. **Whose**[6] **husbands**?[13] Not **ours**,[13] perhaps, but **husbands**[13] for young Italians (women). Finally I bought thirty-five pencils, and my girl friend bought forty-nine yellow pens and eighty-seven new knives. I owe the Italians eleven rubles, and I don't know how much my girl
25 friend owes them. I must pay them soon, but first I will have to go to the bank. One of the Italians said that he was a journalist and that he had written many articles about France, had seen many buildings and museums in **Paris**,[14] and that he particularly liked **Parisians**.[14] I told him, "You must come to Paris again; Paris must be the most beautiful city in the world." He said that at home
30 he had four sisters and seven brothers and, therefore,   nobody had any money, although formerly everybody had money. He said he now had **only**[9] 100 dollars.

"We don't care how many Italians you bought pencils from," replied the professors. "You will have to work a great deal here. We want you to be able to read without dictionaries *The Brothers Karamazov* [15] and *Anna Karenina*.[15] By the way, does anyone know who the hero of the novel *The Brothers Karamazov* [15] is?"

One of the girls said: "You **shouldn't** [16] ask us about Russian literature. We don't know any heroes or heroines; only a few of us know what a troika is. And we all **believe** [17] there are too many names and surnames in these novels. We know only very few Russian writers, and not long ago one of us asked **who** [18] Puškin was. And **just** [2] last year at school this girl had **worked on** [19] Puškin. She had **just** [2] forgotten about him. That's how we work."

"**Don't** [20] tell the professors such things," said a second girl. "They will think we are fools. They probably already think so. Well, why aren't there any troikas here? It's already fifteen past ten."

NOTES

1. The preposition "since" with time expressions is **с** (NB) *gen.* Hence the numeral following is in the genitive, and everything after that in the genitive plural.

2. When "just" means "only" it is normally translated by **только**. To "have just" done something is **только что** plus the past tense. When "just" means "exactly," it may be **как раз**. Examples:

Он только сказа́л э́то.	He just said that (that's all he did).
Он только что сказа́л э́то.	He just said that (just finished saying).
Это как ра́з то́.	That's just the thing.

When "just" means "simply" it is frequently translated by **про́сто**:

Он меня́ про́сто не понима́ет.	He just (simply) doesn't understand me.

3. "More" is another word to be careful with. The student might be tempted in this instance to use **бо́льше** instead of **ещё**. But **бо́льше** is a real comparative, whereas **ещё** means simply "in addition":

Да́йте на́м ещё пи́ва.	Give us more beer.
Да́йте на́м бо́льше пи́ва, чём вчера́.	Give us more beer than yesterday.
Мы́ купи́ли ещё кни́ги.	We bought more books.
Мы́ купи́ли бо́льше кни́г, чём вы́.	We bought more books than you.

4. See R2.A2, page 53.

5. See R5 note 1.

6. The declension of "third" is worth learning, since there is a large group of

adjectives derived from the names of animals, and a few from nouns denoting persons, which have the same declension. Another word which has the same declension is the pronoun **ч/é/й**, which differs only in that its inserted vowel is /e/ instead of /и/. **Ч/é/й**, **трéтий**, and the "animal possessives" (let us take **корóв/и/й** 'cow's' from **корóва** 'cow' as an example) all may be regarded as adjectives in *j* with short forms for the nominative and accusative and long forms for the rest of the declension. Below we decline **трéт/и/й** and **ч/é/й**.

Nom	трéтий	чéй	трéтье	чьё	трéтья	чья	трéтьи	чьй
Acc			трéтье	чьё	трéтью	чью		
Gen	трéтьего	чьегó			трéтьей	чьéй	трéтьих	чьйх
Prep	трéтьем	чьём			трéтьей	чьéй	трéтьих	чьйх
Dat	трéтьему	чьемý			трéтьей	чьéй	трéтьим	чьйм
Inst	трéтьим	чьйм			трéтьей	чьéй	трéтьими	чьйми

The student may drill himself by declining **корóв/и/й** 'cow's,' **собáч/и/й** 'dog's,' **Бóж/и/й** 'God's,' etc.

7. In translating "Here/There is/are . . . for (pronoun)," "for" is normally rendered by the dative rather than by **для** with the genitive, and the pronoun normally follows directly after **вóт**:

Вóт вáм примéр. (*Rather than* *Вóт   Here's an example for you.
примéр для вáс.)

8. "In one's time" is **в своё врéмя**.
9. "In all" (a total of) is **всегó**. **Всегó** may, in addition, have the sense of "only":

У меня всегó пять рублéй.   I have only five rubles.
Емý всегó пять лéт.   He is only five years old.

10. A total of something has been consumed; the choice of aspect should be clear.
11. **Хлеб** means both bread in general and "loaf of bread."
12. Use the expression suggested on page 107.
13. Note that the (accusative) case of "husbands" carries over to the three words cited, since they are still logical objects of "must have seen."
14. "Paris" is **Парйж**, and "Parisian" is **парижáнин**.
15. The title of a book, newspaper, or play, the name of a factory, and so on takes the case it normally would according to its role in the sentence. When a title is in apposition, however, it usually remains in the nominative. Examples:

Я чáсто читáю «Прáвду».   I often read *Pravda*.
Мы обсуждáем газéту «Прáвда».   We are discussing the newspaper *Pravda*.

Како́го вы́ мне́ния об «Анне Каре́ниной»?	What's your opinion of *Anna Karenina*?
Что́ вы́ ду́маете о рома́не «Анна Каре́нина»?	What do you think of the novel *Anna Karenina*?

16. Translate "shouldn't" in several ways (suggested in R6.C).
17. When "believe" means "think, be of the opinion," **ду́мают**, not **ве́рить**, must be used.
18. See R5 note 3.
19. "Work on" something is **рабо́тают на́д** *inst*; for example:

Он тепе́рь рабо́тает над свои́м докла́дом.	He's now working on his report.

20. Do not translate by an imperative.

СЛОВА́РЬ ГРАММАТИ́ЧЕСКИХ ТЕ́РМИНОВ

и́мя числи́тельное numeral:
  коли́чественное — — cardinal numeral
  поря́дковое — — ordinal numeral
  собира́тельное — — collective numeral

ну́ль *M E* zero; нулево́е оконча́ние zero-ending
бе́глый гла́сный mobile vowel

A. TIME EXPRESSIONS

1. Time when

With time expressions it is particularly important to avoid "translation" of English usage and attempts to "rationalize" the Russian patterns, the more so as many time expressions include prepositions. One must simply *know* that it is **в** *plus prp* for *months*, **на** *plus prp* for *weeks*, **в** *plus acc* for *days*, **в** *plus prp* for *years*, and so on. Or that certain constructions cross these boundaries; e.g. **ка́ждый** imposes the accusative *without* preposition, regardless of time unit:

Я получи́л письмо́ от сестры́:	I received a letter from my sister:
на про́шлой неде́ле	last week
в про́шлом ме́сяце	last month
в про́шлую пя́тницу	last Friday
в про́шлом году́	last year

but

Я получа́л письмо́ от сестры́:	I received a letter from my sister:
ка́ждую неде́лю	every week
ка́ждый ме́сяц	every month
ка́ждую пя́тницу	every Friday
ка́ждый го́д	every year

2. Per unit time

Remember also that these prepositions and cases go with their units only in "time when" expressions. Thus, in an expression such as **в** *plus acc* in the meaning "per" period of time, the **в** *plus acc* is used with all time units:

двá рáза в недéлю	twice a (per) week
пя́ть рáз в гóд	five times a (per) year
шéсть часóв в дéнь	six hours a (per) day

3. Accusative of time vs. на plus accusative

The distinction between the plain accusative of time and **на** plus the accusative in time expressions sometimes confuses students, and as we might expect, the confusion usually revolves around an English word: "for." Notice the following examples:

Он здéсь ужé недéлю.	He has been here *for* a week.
Он приéхал сюдá на недéлю.	He came here *for* a week.

Observe that in the first sentence the "for" is optional; its omission does not alter the meaning: "He has been here a week." In the second sentence the "for" is mandatory and may not be omitted. This is one way of distinguishing the two types. Another way is to determine whether the location of the subject is viewed as changing; if so, then **на** *plus acc* is called for. The use of **на** in this meaning is widespread in Russian, and the preposition is used in combined form in various adverbs. Some examples:

Егó назнáчили сюдá на гóд.	He was assigned here for a year.
Мы́ остановимся в Кúеве на трú дня́.	We'll stop in Kiev for three days.
Он уéхал навсегдá.	He has gone away forever.
Он уéхал надóлго.	He has gone away for a long time.

The verb **остáнутся – оставáться** is used both with accusative of time and with **на** *plus acc*:

Остáньтесь с нáми цéлый вéчер.	Stay the whole evening with us.
Я́ здéсь остаю́сь, не знáю на скóлько врéмени.	I'm staying here—I don't know for how long.

4. Через with time expressions

"In" or "after" a certain period of time (i.e. when that period has elapsed) is **через** *plus acc*. Examples:

Через пя́ть дне́й всё бу́дет сде́лано.	In five days everything will be done.
Мы́ верну́лись домо́й через неде́лю.	We returned home after a week.
Вы́ его́ уви́дите через пя́ть дне́й по́сле его́ прие́зда.	You will see him five days after his arrival.

Used with repeated actions, **через** may designate action occurring after a certain interval (or in nontemporal contexts a segment or segments of a whole). If only one unit of a time interval or one segment is involved, the English translation is usually "every other." Examples:

Трамва́и хо́дят через ка́ждые два́дцать мину́т.	The streetcars run every twenty minutes.
Э́то лицо́ встреча́ется через ка́ждые де́сять страни́ц.	We meet this character every ten pages.
Она́ приходи́ла к нему́ через де́нь.	She visited him every other day.
Пиши́те через стро́чку.	Skip lines (write every other line).

5. Russian words for "then"

Пото́м, **зате́м**, and **тогда́** all serve to introduce subsequent action and all may correspond to English "then." **Пото́м** is the most general; it may mean "then" or, oftener, "afterwards" or "later on" (it also may have the meaning "in addition, furthermore"). **Зате́м** is more immediately after the preceding action: "we did this, then that"; it often corresponds to "next." **Тогда́** frequently means "then" in the causal sense: "if or after certain things have happened or certain conditions have been fulfilled, *then* . . ." **Тогда́** also means "then" in the sense of "at that time" (which has nothing to do with subsequent action).

Со́ня провела́ на́с через дли́нную ко́мнату в гости́ную и **зате́м** в небольшу́ю столо́вую.	Sonja led us through a long room into the living room, and then into a small dining room.
Я́ зайду́ к ва́м **пото́м**.	I'll come and see you later.
Прочита́йте э́ту статью́, тогда́ вы́ всё э́то поймёте.	Read this article; then you'll understand all this.
Ири́на купи́ла снача́ла ру́сскую, зате́м неме́цкую и, наконе́ц, францу́зскую кни́гу.	Irina bought first a Russian book, next a German book, and finally a French book.
Где́ вы́ тогда́ служи́ли?	Where were you serving then?
Что́ вы́ де́лали тогда́?	What did you do then? (Тогда́ *here may mean "next" or "afterwards," or, in the proper context, "at that time" or "in that case."*)

6. "Last" and "next"

If "last" means last of a series, it is usually **последний**. If it is closer in meaning to "past," it is more likely to be **прошлый**; e.g. 'last month' **в прошлом месяце**. Note "next" month, week, etc. is usually **будущий**; otherwise "next" is usually **следующий**. Examples:

Я видел его в прошлый раз, когда я был здесь.	I saw him the last time I was here.
Я видел его в прошлом месяце в последний раз.	I saw him last month for the last time.
Это наша первая и последняя возможность.	This is our first and last opportunity.
Он должен был уехать в следующее воскресенье.	He was supposed to leave on the following Sunday.
Я уезжаю в будущее воскресенье.	I'm leaving next Sunday.
Прошлый год был последним годом его жизни.	Last year was the last year of his life.

"On the next, on the following" day, morning, evening is **на** plus the accusative of either **другой** or **следующий**; for example:

на другое/следующее утро	(on) the following/next morning
на другой/следующий вечер	(on) the following/next evening
на другой/следующий день	(on) the following/next day

"The day before" is **накануне**, used as an adverb or as a preposition with the genitive; e.g. **накануне его отъезда** 'the day before his departure.'

7. По plus dative plural

Doing something regularly on any given time unit is **по** *plus dat pl*:

Он (бывает) здесь по вечерам.	He's here in the evenings.
Он работает в школе по четвергам.	He works at the school on Thursday.

8. Russian words corresponding to the English word "time"

Do not confuse **время** (time in general, without plural—*le temps, die Zeit*) with **раз** (each time, this time, many times, etc.—*la fois, das Mal*). Note that **раз**, by itself, may mean "one time," "once," or may have the meaning "since" (see   IX. B7, p. 257). Note also the expressions **ни разу** 'not once' and **не раз** 'more than once.' And in counting "one, two, three, four..." one says not **один** but **раз, два, три**, ...

Я его́ (в) пе́рвый ра́з ви́жу.	It's the first time I've seen him.
Скажи́те ему́ ра́з навсегда́.	Tell him once and for all.
Я ра́з та́м игра́л.	I played there once.
Я ни ра́зу не игра́л та́м.	I never once played there.
Я не ра́з игра́л та́м.	I have played there more than once.

B. VOICE

1. ся verbs

ся verbs are discussed in detail in Lesson X, and the student should read through the grammar in that chapter and familiarize himself with the general notions discussed there, though he will not immediately recognize everything. At this point he should at least recognize that only a small number of **ся** verbs are actually reflexives; i.e. actually reflect the action back on the subject; e.g. **о́н одева́ется** 'He dresses *himself*.' Hence, **ся** verbs should not be called "reflexive verbs." The only generalization applicable to all **ся** verbs is their *intransitivity*; they never take a direct object. But remember that there are also many non-**ся** verbs which are intransitive and many which have intransitive as well as transitive meanings. **Мо́гут** and **иду́т** are examples of the first, **реши́ть** and **говори́ть** of the second.

Note that the English equivalent of a **ся** verb may be transitive:

Он бои́тся своего́ учи́теля.	He fears his teacher.
Она́ слу́шается ма́тери.	She obeys her mother.

Students sometimes use **-ся** where **-сь** should be used, and vice versa. Remember that **-сь** is used after a vocalic, **-ся** after a consonantal ending:

встреча́юсь, встреча́етесь, встреча́ясь/встреча́ется, встреча́лся, встреча́йся

The only exception to this is that **-ся** is always used after all forms of the *active participles*:

встреча́ющийся	*but*	встреча́ющаяся	встреча́ющееся	встреча́ющимися
встреча́вшийся		встреча́вшаяся	встреча́вшееся	встреча́вшимися

2. The passive

Russian makes some use of the **ся** form in passive constructions. Remember that a true passive always implies an active transitive with the subject of the passive as its direct object. For example:

Эта кни́га гото́вится на́шими студе́нтами.	This book is being prepared by our students.
На́ши студе́нты гото́вят э́ту кни́гу.	Our students are preparing this book.

However, most **ся** forms in Russian are not passives, and in general passive constructions are less common in Russian than in English, mostly because of various restrictions in their use (see X.H). For this reason English passive constructions are often best rendered by Russian active constructions (and even in cases where a Russian passive is formally possible, an active form is frequently less clumsy or stylistically preferable). Examples are:

The tourists are being driven to Moscow.	Тури́стов везу́т в Москву́. (Везу́тся *is impossible.*)
The door was opened at six o'clock.	Две́рь откры́ли в ше́сть часо́в. (Откры́лась *would mean "opened (more or less on its own)"*; была́ откры́та *would mean "was open."*)
He will be asked about that later.	Об э́том его́ спро́сят пото́м. (Он спро́сится *is impossible*; он бу́дет спро́шен *is clumsy.*)
The house is being built.	До́м стро́ится. *Or:* До́м стро́ят.
The house was being built.	До́м стро́ился. *Or:* До́м стро́или.

Particular care must be taken when an English passive corresponds to a Russian verb which is not transitive and hence cannot be expressed in the passive; an active construction must be chosen and the Russian verb given its normal complement:

English "serve" (transitive):	Russian **служи́ть** (takes dative):
Our cause is not served by such people.	На́шему де́лу не слу́жат таки́е лю́ди.
English "fear" (transitive):	Russian **боя́ться** (takes genitive):
This general is feared by all.	Этого генера́ла все́ боя́тся.

3. The reflexive pronoun

Russian has a reflexive personal pronoun whose various cases indicate the various ways in which the action of the subject is reflected back on it. This pronoun, of course, has no nominative; its forms are: *acc/gen* **себя́**, *prp/dat* **себе́**, *inst* **собо́й** (**собо́ю**). **Себя́** after a transitive verb has the same meaning as a reflexive **ся** verb and is much commoner. For example, "see oneself" and "love oneself" are **ви́деть себя́** and **люби́ть себя́**; -**ся** added to these verbs does not give a reflexive meaning. Here are some examples of all the forms:

Он ду́мает то́лько о себе́.	He thinks only of himself.
Он у себя́.	He's at his home (in his office) now.
Он ушёл к себе́.	He went home (to his office).

Спра́шивайте (самого́) себя́ об э́том.	Ask yourself about it.
Она́ взяла́ докла́д с собо́й.	She took the report with her.
Предста́вьте себе́ моё удивле́ние.	Imagine my surprise! (*lit* represent to yourself)
Она́ купи́ла себе́ но́вую шля́пу.	She bought (herself) a new hat.
На́до себя́ хорошо́ знать.	One must know oneself well.

The reflexive pronoun is used in many set expressions and idioms (including the use of **себя́** with several verbs in expressions whose reflexive meaning is either very abstract or nonexistent):

Она́ хороша́ собо́й (собо́ю).	She is good-looking.
Ива́ну не по себе́.	Ivan is not well.
Он пришёл в себя́.	He came to (regained consciousness).
Ка́к вы чу́вствуете себя́?	How do you feel?
Ма́ша ведёт себя́ пло́хо.	Maša is behaving badly.
Шпио́н вы́дал себя́.	The spy gave himself away.
Ра́но или по́здно он себя́ пока́жет.	Sooner or later he'll prove himself.

C. PURPOSE CLAUSES

Russian expresses purpose by the conjunction **чтобы (чтоб)** 'in order to' or, often, simply 'to,' with purpose understood, plus the infinitive:

| Я де́лаю э́то, чтобы показа́ть ва́м другу́ю сто́рону вопро́са. | I'm doing this (in order) to show you the other side of the question. |
| Челове́к рабо́тает, чтобы жи́ть. | A man works (in order) to live. |

Чтобы may be omitted only with motion verbs and even here, if there is any emphasis on the purpose of the motion, it must be included:

| Он пошёл в библиоте́ку (чтобы) взя́ть кни́гу. | He went to get a book at the library. |
| Я пришёл (чтобы) сказа́ть ва́м не́сколько сло́в. | I've come to say a few words to you. |

If there is a change of subject, the new subject plus a past tense verb follows **чтобы**, and the English very often has "so that" or "so":

| Мы́ рабо́таем, чтобы на́ши де́ти могли́ жи́ть лу́чше. | We are working so (that) our children may live better. |
| Я ва́м пишу́, чтобы вы́ зна́ли, что я́ ва́с не забы́л. | I am writing you so (that) you'll know I haven't forgotten you. |

Для того́ чтобы has the same meaning as **чтобы,** but is somewhat more emphatic and is a bit bookish, though certainly common in careful speech. If the purpose clause precedes the main clause, it is often introduced by **для того́ чтобы.**

Я позва́л ва́с сюда́, (для того́), что-бы объясни́ть ва́м на́ше поло-же́ние.	I called you here in order to explain our position to you.
Для того́ чтобы объясни́ть на́ше положе́ние все́м на́шим колле́-гам, я зову́ и́х на собра́ние в се́мь ве́чера.	In order to explain our position to all of our colleagues, I am calling them to a meeting at 7:00 tonight.
Для того́ чтобы вы́ не ду́мали, что я поступи́л, не приня́в во внима́-ние ва́ших интере́сов, я напишу́ ва́м подро́бно о на́ших пла́нах.	So that you won't think that I have acted without taking your interests into account, I will write you in detail about our plans.

D. ADJECTIVES IN SOFT *n'*

The so-called "soft" adjectives cannot be said to represent a distinct (soft vs. hard) category, for there are several limitations on them which do not apply to adjectives as a whole. First of all, for practical purposes they are all in n'^1 and should correctly be called "soft *n'*" adjectives. Secondly, they are never end-stressed. Lastly, all but a very few are referable to *time* or *place*. Here are some of the most important:

ра́нний	early	да́вний	long ago (*adj*)
по́здний	late	неда́вний	recent
вече́рний	evening	сре́дний	middle, average
у́тренний	morning	ве́рхний	upper
зи́мний	winter	ни́жний	lower
ле́тний	summer	сосе́дний	neighboring
весе́нний	spring	кра́йний	extreme (*adj of* edge)
осе́нний	fall	после́дний	last
пере́дний	front	бли́жний	near
за́дний	back	да́льний	far
вну́тренний	internal (inner)	дре́вний	ancient
пре́жний	previous	суббо́тний	Saturday (*adj*)

Various compound types also exist: **-го́дний, -ле́тний** 'year,' **-сторо́нний** 'sided':

---

[1] **Ка́рий** 'brown, hazel' is an exception.

прошлого́дний	last year (*adj*)
нового́дний	new year (*adj*)
двухле́тний	two years (*age or duration*)
многоле́тний	many years (*age or duration*)
пятидесятиле́тний	fifty years (*age or duration*)
односторо́нний	one-sided
многосторо́нний	many-sided

Note several important adjectives in **-шний**, many of them built directly from nonadjectival adverbs:

сего́дняшний	today's		зде́шний	from here
вчера́шний	yesterday's		та́мошний	from there
за́втрашний	tomorrow's		тепе́решний	present
вне́шний	external (outer)		тогда́шний	of that time

The more important *n'* adjectives not referable to time or place are:

(из)ли́шний	superfluous		заму́жняя	married (female)
и́скренний	sincere		сыно́вний	son's
си́ний	dark blue		дочéрний	daughter's

TRANSLATION INTO RUSSIAN

I was afraid that on the following morning everything would seem **different**[1] to him. I had laughed at his report, and he hadn't liked this at all. But afterwards we saw each other in the evening, and I thought we were beginning to understand each other. I went to my room and wrote a few letters. Then I read a very long article in a magazine. It was difficult for me to fall asleep. For a long time I thought about my sons, whom I had **had**[2] to **leave**[3] with their uncle. I knew that I didn't have to be afraid, that my brother, **whose**[4] wife is a teacher, was very fond of children. Tomorrow I will **have**[2] to get up at six o'clock in the **morning.**[5] Not very often do I **have**[2] to meet with a person **whose**[4] report I have laughed at. But that's **another**[1] question, I thought.

The next day I went to see Iván Sergéevič Rímskij-Kórsakov. Last year I saw this man every Friday and this year we meet each other three times a week, on Mondays, Wednesdays, and Sundays. He comes for a **half hour**[6] but usually **stays**[3] much longer. I went to see him in order to tell him that I was leaving for **about**[7] four years. But about that later.

After that I went to see the man who had written the report and whom I feared so. This man seldom listens to me and never obeys me. He dresses poorly and dresses his children still worse. He seldom washes himself, but he's always washing his automobile. He likes to drive his children to the city in the after-

noon. He knows that children simply aren't **taken**[8] to the city in the evening. [20]
This man has two sisters who don't like each other and never go to see each other
—and each is constantly talking of herself. In about five hours I will go to see them
too.

But now **let**[9] me **tell**[10] of myself. I am a young **judge**[11] who came here for
several weeks eight years ago, but I decided to stay and have been living here [25]
now for more than two years. This year in the winter I have been going to work
and working not less than eight hours a day. From next week (on) I will be
working only thirty hours per week. On the third Saturday of next month I
will go to the office to get my money. I already know how much I will be
given,[8] although at first I thought that we would be paid **another**[1] ten dollars. [30]
When I arrive, I will say very clearly, so that everyone will understand, "In order
to say to you several things about which I have been thinking for a long time,
I have asked you all to gather here. The articles which I myself used to write
formerly are now being written (translate by both passive and active constructions) by all those old teachers at the evening meetings. I want you to tell those [35]
teachers to leave. And if they don't, do everything so that they leave. Only then
will I be satisfied with the result of my words."

Afterwards, I will drive away in my new blue car. I don't know if it's
running[12] or not. Someone just told me that it is not running. Well, then I hope
that at least the trains are running. [40]

NOTES

1. The Russian **другóй** has the meaning "different, other, else," and so on. English
"another" is translated by **другóй** when it means "different." When "another"
means something additional, however, **другóй** may not be used, and **ещё** is the
most usual translation. Compare:

   Возьмём другóй примéр.   Let's take another (different) example.
   Возьмём ещё одúн примéр.   Let's take another (one more)
                                                  example.

2. Compulsion due to outside circumstances may also be expressed by the impersonal
придётся – приходиться *inf* with dative complement. This expression is close to
нýжно/нáдо, but is stronger, and may imply that the necessary is somewhat un-
desirable, difficult, or unpleasant.

   К сожалéнию мнé придётся зáвтра   Unfortunately, I will have to see him
      увúдеть егó.   tomorrow.
   Емý пришлóсь уéхать.   He had to leave.
   Мнé прихóдится с вáми пого-   I have to have a talk with you.
      ворúть.

3. Do not confuse the verbs **остáнутся – оставáться** (never without **-ся**) 'stay, remain' with **остáвить – оставля́ют** 'leave' (transitive). Compare the following:

Мои́ дéти остаю́тся дóма.   My children are staying (remaining) home.

Я оставля́ю свои́х детéй дóма.   I am leaving my children home.

4. See R4 note 21.

5. **Утро** is normally listed as having fixed stem stress, but in many fixed expressions it is end-stressed: **в дéвять часóв утрá, с утрá, до утрá, к утру́, по утрáм.**

6. The prefixes **пол-** and **полу-** are added to a number of words to which they impart the meaning "half" and which themselves then sometimes emerge in a genitive form. There are various morphological complications, some of which Russians do not always observe; it is enough for the student to recognize the prefix. Examples:

полчасá	half an hour
полгóда	half a year
полдю́жины	half a dozen
пóлдень	noon
пóлночь	midnight
полукру́г	half circle
полумéсяц	half-moon
на полпути́	halfway
пополáм	in half, in two

And notice the use of **пол** in place of **половúна** (very common in colloquial speech): **пол четвёртого** 'three thirty.'

7. Approximation of number is very easily expressed by reversing the positions of the numeral and the time limit; e.g. 'about four months' **мéсяца четы́ре**, 'about twenty men' **человéк двáдцать**. A preposition in a time expression must remain *before the numeral*:

недéль через шéсть   in about six weeks

днéй на дéсять   for about ten days

When another preposition is not involved, **óколо** *plus gen* may be used to indicate approximation; e.g. **На столé óколо пятнáдцати карандашéй.**

8. See R7.B2.

9. The verb "let," when used outside the context of more or less formal requests for permission, is frequently translated by **дать – давáть:**

Дáйте мнé вáм помóчь.   Let me help you.

Дáйте ему́ спáть.   Let him sleep.

10. When "tell" means "narrate, recount," it is normally translated by **рассказа́ть – расска́зывают** rather than by **сказа́ть – говори́ть**.

11. You have probably already met several nouns in -*a* which belong not to the feminine but to the masculine gender. Such nouns designate male persons; many of them are names or, oftener, nicknames:

дя́дя	uncle	Илья́	Il'já
де́душ/ка	grandfather	Ва́ня	Vánja

Gender is a *syntactic* rather than a *formal* matter; we know that a noun is masculine if adjectives, pronouns, or verbs that agree with it are in the masculine.

12. The verb **иду́т** often has the meaning of "run, work, function":

Ва́ши часы́ хорошо́ иду́т.	Your watch runs well.
Э́тот автомоби́ль пло́хо идёт.	This car runs badly (works badly).

For vehicles (in most cases) and *inanimate* things that are conveyed **иду́т/ходи́ть** rather than **еду́т/е́здить** are used:

По́езд идёт.	The train is coming.
Письмо́ пришло́ вчера́.	The letter came yesterday.
Авто́бусы хо́дят.	The buses are running.
But note: автомоби́ль *е́дет*.	

СЛОВАРЬ ГРАММАТИЧЕСКИХ ТЕРМИНОВ

глаго́л verb:
— на -ся *sja* verb
(не)перехо́дный — (in)transitive verb
возвра́тный — reflexive verb
взаи́мный — reciprocal verb

зало́г voice:
действи́тельный — active voice
страда́тельный — passive voice
возвра́тное местоиме́ние reflexive pronoun

A. Time expressions (continued), Dates
B. Verbs of sitting, standing, lying
C. The partitive genitive

A. TIME EXPRESSIONS (CONTINUED), DATES

Remember that "on" a certain date is expressed by the genitive of the ordinal; e.g. 'He will arrive on the 7th of September' **Он прие́дет седьмо́го сентября́.** In simply giving the date, however, the nominative is used:

Сего́дня четвёртое ма́я.   Today is May 4.

In compound ordinal numerals in dates only the final ordinal is declined; e.g. **в ты́сяча девятьсо́т шестьдеся́т четвёртом году́** 'in 1964.'

Among the higher ordinals note **сороково́й** and **девяно́стый**. Note also that 50, 60, 70, 80, and 200 through 900 use the *genitive* form of the cardinal before **-деся́тый** and **-со́тый**: e.g. **семидеся́тый** 70th, **трехсо́тый** 300th. Decades— "the thirties, the seventies," and so on—are rendered by the appropriate ordinals, with "time when" expressed by **в** plus the prepositional plural (NB **года́х**): **тридца́тые го́ды, в семидеся́тых года́х.**

If the year is preceded by another time, it goes in the genitive; if it is alone, it is in the prepositional preceded by **в**:

восемна́дцатое (-ого) ма́рта ты́сяча девятьсо́т   (on) March 18, 1950
пятидеся́того го́да

в ма́рте ты́сяча девятьсо́т пятидеся́того го́да   in March 1950

в ты́сяча девятьсо́т пятидеся́том году́   in 1950

"From ... to ..." is **от** (or **с** with hours and dates) ... **до** .... If the speaker wishes to emphasize "starting with ... up to and *including*" (through), he may use **с** *gen* ... **по** (NB) *acc*. Examples:

Мы́ бу́дем та́м от апре́ля до а́вгу- ста.	We'll be there from April to August.
Мы́ бу́дем та́м с тре́тьего января́ по восьмо́е ию́ня.	We'll be there from the 3rd of Janu- ary *through* the 8th of June.

"Since" or "from" by themselves are, of course, **с** *gen*:

Я здесь с четвёртого октября́.	I've been here since October 4.
Он бу́дет та́м с семна́дцатого ноя- бря́.	He will be there from (starting with) November 17.

B. VERBS OF SITTING, STANDING, LYING

The verbs for sitting, standing, and lying offer some exceptional forms; particularly the alternating vowels in **ся́дут (се́сть)**, **ля́гут (ле́чь**; past tense: **лёг, легла́, легли́**), and the presence of **-ся** in the imperfective but not the perfective of these verbs. Students frequently confuse these verbs because of their physical similarity to each other, yet they do parallel each other in a quite systematic way. The table below may help the student to keep them straight:

	КУДА́ MAKE CHANGE POSITION		КУДА́ CHANGE OWN POSITION		ГДЕ́ REMAIN IN POSITION
	Perfective	*Imperfective*	*Perfective*	*Imperfective*	*Imperfective only*
	(**И**–verbs)		(consonant stems)	(**И**-ся verbs)	(**Е/ЖА** verbs)
sit	посади́ть	сажа́ют	ся́дут (се́сть)	сади́ться	сиде́ть
stand	поста́вить	ста́вить	ста́нут	станови́ться	стоя́ть
lie	положи́ть	кладу́т	ля́гут (ле́чь)	ложи́ться	лёжа́ть

The student himself can easily supply the translations for the verbs in the table, which depict the *physical* meanings. The only verb requiring special comment is **ста́нут – станови́ться**, which does not have a closely corresponding verb in English. It means "to assume a standing position" and almost always describes motion *from one standing position to another*; for example:

Он ста́л на эскала́тор.	(Already standing) he got on the escalator.
Он ста́л к окну́.	He stepped over (and stopped at) the window.
Он ста́л в о́чередь.	He got into line.
Cf. Он стоя́л в о́череди.	He was standing in line.

To "stand up" from a sitting or lying position is, of course, **вста́нут – встава́ть**.

Ста́нут – станови́ться is already familiar to the student in the meaning "become"; e.g. **Он стал учи́телем** 'He became a teacher.' The *perfective* **ста́нут**, plus infinitive, has the meaning "begin to"; e.g. **Ве́ра ста́ла чита́ть** 'Vera began to read.' **Станови́ться** cannot be used in this meaning.

The verbs of "remaining in position," while they have no nonsemantic perfective, are frequently prefixed with **по-** 'a (little) while' or with **про-** 'for a certain period' (this prefix is particularly common if the amount of time sat, stood, or lain is specified (ten hours, eight weeks, the whole day, etc.)). If the time is mentioned but indefinite (several minutes, a short time) **по-** is likely:

Мы́ постоя́ли на у́лице.	We stood for a while on the street.
Ва́м придётся полежа́ть не́сколько дне́й.	You will have to go to bed (lie in bed) for a few days.
Моя́ ма́ть пролежа́ла де́сять дне́й в больни́це.	My mother spent ten days in the hospital.
Мы́ простоя́ли во́семь часо́в на моро́зе.	We stood for eight hours in the cold.
Мы́ просиде́ли с ни́ми ве́сь ве́чер.	We sat through the whole evening with them.

Both **по-** and **про-** are used in these meanings with a great many other verbs as well; e.g. **пописа́ть** 'write for a while,' **прорабо́тают** 'work for a specific period of time.'

C. THE PARTITIVE GENITIVE

The general idea of "some of" a *substance*[1] which divides, essentially, into *portions* rather than units (the type of concrete noun which would take a genitive singular after **мно́го**; e.g. **хлеб**, but not **каранда́ш**), may be expressed by the genitive of that noun. This genitive is called the "partitive" genitive. The English equivalent might or might not include "some," but the partitive idea is present whenever a portion of a substance is involved. The most frequent example of the partitive is the genitive used after various words expressing quantity; for example:

мно́го мя́са much meat	стака́н молока́ a glass of milk
немно́го воды́ a little water	кусо́к хле́ба a piece of bread

But notice that a partitive may also assume the place of a direct object in a sentence:

---

[1] The plurals of substances, if they exist, are not plurals in the real sense; they mean "kinds of"; e.g. **сыры́/чай** 'kinds of cheese/tea.'

Да́йте на́м воды́, пожа́луйста.   Give us (some) water, please.
Мы́ купи́ли молока́.   We bought (some) milk.

Notice, however, that if the amount or portion of a substance has already been mentioned or specified, if it has become "*the* X" or "X in general," there is no partitive, and the accusative is used:

Да́й на́м во́ду, кото́рую обеща́л.   Give us *the* water you promised. (*the*)
Мы́ купи́ли молоко́.   We bought *the* milk. (*the*)
Я о́чень люблю́ молоко́.   I like milk a great deal. (*general*)

The unique formal problem of the partitive genitive concerns certain *masculine* nouns of substance whose partitive genitive is -*u* rather than -*a*. For example:

Принеси́те на́м су́пу.   Bring us (some) soup.
Он попроси́л ча́ю.   He asked for (some) tea.
Она́ купи́ла сы́ру.   She bought (some) cheese.

Remember that the -*u* genitive is confined almost entirely to partitive usage (it may be used after negative impersonal expressions and after **не хвата́ет** 'there is not enough of'). In other uses, the normal -*a* is used. Compare the following:

Да́йте на́м ча́ю, пожа́луйста.   Give us (some) tea, please.
Та́м тепе́рь не́т ча́ю.   There's no tea there now.
Она́ вы́пила ча́шку ча́ю.   She drank a cup of tea.
but
Я не дово́лен вку́сом э́того ча́я.   I'm not satisfied with the flavor of
                                          this tea.
Вы́ зна́ете це́ну э́того ча́я?   Do you know the price of this tea?
Ско́лько бензи́ну вы́ купи́ли?   How much gasoline did you buy?
but
Береги́сь бензи́на.   Watch out for gasoline!

And remember that not all masculines of substance take the -*u*; an example is **хле́б**:

Да́й на́м хле́ба.   Give us some bread.

The student may have noticed a number of other masculine nouns which seem to take -*u* genitives in set expressions, particularly after certain prepositions taking the genitive. Sometimes usages in -*u* and -*a* coexist; two very common examples are **из до́му, из ле́су** (NB stress) vs. **из до́ма, из ле́са**. But note that only **из большо́го ле́са** is possible. A set expression is just that; it can never be altered or broken up. The student will also notice -*u* genitives where one would expect -*a* genitives in Russian literature. -*u* used to be almost as common as -*a* in the genitive but, as we have seen, is now confined to fixed expressions and the partitive. Finally, note **мно́го наро́ду** 'many people (a crowd of people).'

TRANSLATION INTO RUSSIAN

Today is the sixth of July. Yesterday was Tuesday, the fifth of July, and I went to bed (lay down) late or, rather, I was put into bed, and someone said to me, "Lie here for a while." I have been lying here for about two hours, and it's still hard for me to understand what happened. I had bought some vodka and
5 **brought**[1] it home. There were many people in the apartment, approximately fifteen **people**.[2] They were saying to me, "Sit down" and "Lie down." But I didn't want **either**[3] to sit down **or**[3] to lie down; I wanted **both**[3] to sleep **and**[3] to stand. But now some people were saying, "Sit him down in an armchair," and others actually had even begun to sit me down there. I wanted very much
10 **either**[3] to sit for a while in the armchair **or**[3] to lie down on the bed. The last words I remember were: "Leave him. Let him sit the whole night throu_h in this chair." But nevertheless I was able to stand up, and I walked over to the other side of the room, went to the window, and **looked**[4] **through**[5] it at the trees. I stood there for a long time.
15 The next day (that is, today) I got up, quickly washed (my face and hands) and dressed, and then **telephoned**[6] a restaurant: "Bring me some cheese and some bread. What are you saying? No, of course I don't drink tea without sugar; we're **not**[7] living in the forties but in the fifties, young man. When you arrive, stand the tea and lay the cheese in front of the door."
20 **They**[8] brought the cheese and tea. It would have been nice if they had brought some bread also, but there wasn't any bread **at all**.[9] Last night there had been many people in the restaurant; they must have eaten it up. Next time I'll ask for sugar too. I'll call and say, "Don't **forget**[10] the sugar. Think about your work, and remember that I'm waiting for you. And don't drink tea, drink
25 some water. And when you're walking past my window, don't look at me."
I sat on the bed for a long time and thought. I had come here on the 21st of April, 1954, and decided to stay here from that date through August 7, 1960. In 1910 my father died and we moved to the country, but we always **spent**[11] much time in many cities. In September '33 I **reported**[12] for work at a (certain)
30 factory, where I worked, first **as a mechanic**[13] and then **as a secretary**[13] from September to March. But I soon became so bored that I decided to become a teacher. All the same, I remained until the very end of March. At that time we lived in the center of Stalingrád, and we were **going**[14] to buy land **near**[15] Stalingrád, but I left the factory on Saturday, March 31. I knew that in a week every-
35 body would be bored without me. Not long ago I heard that Stalingrád has begun to be called Volgográd (translate by both active and passive constructions).

NOTES

1. Translate in two ways: by vehicle and by foot.
2. **Человек**, used with numerals, usually takes a genitive plural identical with the nominative; e.g. 'twenty people' **двадцать человек**. Note also **несколько человек** (not **людей**).
3. Compare the following three sentences:

Я не люблю **ни** Тани **ни** Веры.   I love *neither* Tanja *nor* Vera. I don't love *either* Tanja *or* Vera.

Я люблю **и** Таню **и** Веру.   I love *both* Tanja *and* Vera.

Я люблю **или** Таню **или** Веру.   I love *either* Tanja *or* Vera.

4. "Look" is **(по)смотреть**. In certain expressions this verb may correspond to "see"; e.g. 'Did you see that film?' **Вы смотрели этот фильм?** (though **Вы видели этот фильм?** is also possible). The English imperative "see" or "watch" is rendered by **(по)смотрите**; **видеть** has no imperative.
5. "Look at" is **(по)смотреть на** *acc.* "Through" or "out" a window is **в окно**.
6. **(По)звонить** is a "motion" verb with respect to place telephoned; e.g. 'I called my wife at the factory' **Я позвонил моей жене на завод**.
7. Make sure to place the **не** correctly.
8. Remember that "they" is **они** only when the speaker is referring to definite persons.
9. There are various adverbial expressions used for "no X at all," but **не** or **нет** with a genitive of **никакой** is frequently a good translation; e.g. 'I have no books at all' **У меня нет никаких книг**, 'I didn't eat any meat at all' **Я не ел никакого мяса**. Note that **никаких** is the plural of **ни одного/-ой**: 'I don't have one book' **У меня нет ни одной книги**, while **никакого** (*masc/neu*) and **никакой** (*fem*) are used with *substances* (things which are not normally divisible into units and, hence, lacking a plural).
10. See R2.B3.
11. To "spend time" is **провёдут – проводить время**; e.g. 'Where did you spend your summer?' **Где вы провели лето?**
12. See R5.D3.
13. Use either the instrumental or **как** plus the nominative.
14. "Was going to" is very close to "was about to" (see R5 note 14).
15. "Near" may be translated in a number of ways, but with cities in the sense "in the environs of" **под** *inst* is often used.

СЛОВАРЬ ГРАММАТИЧЕСКИХ ТЕРМИНОВ

число date
глаголы сидения, стояния, и лежания
  verbs of sitting, standing, lying

родительный разделительный partitive
  genitive
порядок слов word order

*A. General usage: participles
vs. gerunds*
*B. Participles vs. adjectives;
gerunds vs. adverbs*
C. Participles
D. Gerunds
*E. Russian adjectives which
act like passive participles*

A. GENERAL USAGE:[1] PARTICIPLES VS. GERUNDS

Though participles and gerunds are fundamentally different syntactically, in practice the difference can be subtle enough so that the student may confuse them. Here is a sure way to distinguish them; a *long-form*[2] *participle is always grammatically interchangeable with a* **который** *construction, whereas gerunds never are.* The corresponding **который** construction may occasionally sound somewhat clumsy, but the meaning is the same and the form is correct.

In translation from English selection is almost always quite clear. Sometimes an English sentence omits the relative pronoun which would indicate **который**, but the student should still be able to decide on the translation. The following sentence clearly calls for a participle:

Солда́ты, входя́щие (входи́вшие) в клу́б, гро́мко говори́ли.

This sentence is interchangeable with "The soldiers who were entering the club were talking loudly." Both it and the slightly different sentence: "The soldiers, who were entering the club, were talking loudly" (the commas make the "who" clause more incidental to the main clause, but this difference need not be ex-

---

[1] Rules for the formation of participles and gerunds and the distribution of the various suffixes according to verb stem type are given in the Introduction, pp. 30–33.

[2] The long-form participles are *attributive* in function; they have the meaning "which does/did/is being done/has been done" parallel to the attributive adjectival meaning "which is/was." They are opposed to the short forms (which exist from the passive participles only) with *predicate* meaning parallel to the predicate meaning in short-form adjectives. See pp. 134 and 137 for further discussion.

130

pressed in Russian) are translated by the same Russian participial construction above, since in all three cases the "(who were) entering the club" *directly defines* the "soldiers."

Now take the sentence:

> The soldiers, entering the club, were talking loudly.
> Солдáты, входя́ в клуб, грóмко говори́ли.

This sentence could be replaced by "The soldiers, *as* (or *while*) they were entering the club, were talking loudly." The clause is a typical gerundial; it does not directly define the "soldiers," but describes some attendant fact or circumstance; in this case the "entering the club" is the circumstance attendant to their "talking loudly."

Let us take a reverse example. Of the two Russian sentences:

> Студéнты, решáющие э́ти задáчи, мнóгому нау́чатся.
> Студéнты, решáя э́ти задáчи, мнóгому нау́чатся.

the first means "The students who are solving these problems will learn a great deal"; the second means "The students, *while* (or *in, by*, etc.) solving these problems, will learn a great deal." The result may be the same, but the meaning is totally different. The gerund frequently has a causative meaning in Russian, and English equivalents may include such words as "in," "by," or "through" as above, or even "because," "due to," "by dint of," "since," etc. A gerund or gerundial sentence may be causal or not, as the context dictates; the sentence above is an example. Other examples of causal meaning:

> Не знáя рýсского языкá, я не могý   Not knowing Russian, I can't answer
> отвéтить на вáш вопрóс.   your question. (Since I don't
>   know . . .)
>
> Читáя егó кни́гу, я знакóмлюсь с   Reading his book, I'm getting to
> áвтором.   know the author. (By/Through/
>   In reading . . .)

And бýдучи, the present gerund of быть, is almost always causal:

> Бýдучи нéмцем, óн э́то знáет.   Being a German, he knows that.
>   (Since he is a German . . .)

B. PARTICIPLES VS. ADJECTIVES;
GERUNDS VS. ADVERBS

The student should be aware of the ease with which participles and gerunds can and do become adjectives and adverbs, respectively. As a result of this, the distinctions between them are not always clear. The subject is a study in itself.

Many examples of all four participles occur also as adjectives, often with a slightly broader or more abstract meaning; for example:

челове́к, бы́вший ше́сть ле́т в Росси́и	a man who was six years in Russia
бы́вший учи́тель	a former teacher
окно́, откры́тое ма́льчиком	the window opened by the boy
откры́тое мне́ние	open (frank) opinion

For that matter, **откры́тый** is almost always an adjective, rather than a participle, even when it refers to a window. In the sentence **Та́м откры́тое окно́**, **откры́тое** is probably an adjective, since the speaker probably has in mind "open," rather than "which has been opened." Similarly, **сле́дующий**, though it may still function as the present active participle from **сле́довать**, is almost always simply an adjective "next" or "following."[1]

Many adjectives derived from past passive participles have evolved various formal characteristics distinguishing them from the latter, and most of these differ somewhat in lexical meaning as well. Some examples:

за́нятый *ppp from* за́ймут (заня́ть) *but* заня́той:

Он о́чень за́нят э́тим де́лом.	He's very occupied (busy) with this matter.
Он заня́той челове́к.	He's a very busy man.

соверше́нный *ppp from* соверши́ть *but* соверше́нный:

оши́бка, соверше́нная ва́ми	the error you committed
соверше́нная пра́вда	the perfect (complete) truth
соверше́нный ви́д	the perfective aspect

Note that the adjective **соверше́н/ный** meaning "perfect" (but not "perfective") is distinguished from the participle not only by *e* instead of *o*, but by the following short forms: **соверше́нен, соверше́нна, соверше́нно, соверше́нны**. Compare the participial short forms **соверше́н, совершена́, совершено́, совершены́**.

Sometimes an adjective has only one **н**, as distinct from the required two **н**'s (**нн**) of the participle:

Та́м стоя́л ра́неный солда́т.	A wounded soldier stood there.
Та́м стоя́л солда́т, неда́вно ра́неный. (ра́нить)	A soldier, wounded not long ago, stood there.
солёный су́п	salted (salty) soup
су́п, (по)со́ленный по́варом	soup, salted by the cook

---

[1] For further discussion and examples of shift from participial to purely adjectival status, see Lesson X, p. 277.

Present gerunds frequently become adverbialized, but the forms often undergo no change or, at the most, a stress shift, so that their definition as adverbs in a given instance may depend on the fact of their use in a set expression. There is no doubt of the adverbial status of the words given in the following examples:

Он та́м сиди́т, сложа́ ру́ки.	He sits doing nothing. (*Lit* having folded his hands, сложи́ть 'fold')
Они́ рабо́тают не шутя́.	They work in earnest. (*Lit* not joking, шути́ть 'joke')

But in the following cases, it does not make much difference how the word is analyzed, though some Russians make the distinctions; dictionaries may vary as to whether they make the distinction, and what kind of status they assign. In these examples, the end stress should indicate a gerund, stem stress an adverbial from a gerund:

стоя́/сто́я	стоя́ть	standing
сидя́/си́дя	сиде́ть	sitting
молча́/мо́лча	молча́ть	being silent

But **сто́я** and **си́дя** are widely regarded as gerundial, while the end-stressed forms are rarely used. In the case of **молча́ть** the distinction is usually regarded as being maintained (being silent vs. silently). But, obviously, it makes little difference in the meaning.

C. PARTICIPLES

1. Active participles

We have seen from the example on page 130 that a present as well as a past active participle may express action in the past, as long as the action was still going on at the same time as the action in the main clause. This means that a present active participle may replace an *imperfective* past active participle but not, however, a *perfective* past active participle, whose action must have been completed. For example:

Студе́нт, **де́лающий** докла́д, **гово́рит** ме́дленно.	The student (who is) giving the report is speaking slowly.
Студе́нт, **де́лающий** докла́д, **гово́рил** ме́дленно.	The student (who was) giving the report was speaking slowly.
Студе́нт, **де́лавший** докла́д, **гово́рил** ме́дленно.	
Студе́нт, **сде́лавший** докла́д, **вы́шел** из ко́мнаты.	The student who had given the report left the room.

2. Past passive participles

Short forms. The short forms of the past passive participles are by far the most commonly used of the participial forms.[1] As we said above, participial short forms are exclusively predicate and are opposed to the attributive meaning of the long forms. Compare:

Зада́ча решена́.	The problem has been (is) solved.
Вот решённая зада́ча.	Here's a solved problem.

The short form combined with forms of **быть** depicts completed passive actions: with future forms, future; with past forms, past or past perfect (pluperfect); with the (zero) present, perfect or a similar "completed present" expressed in English by the present of "to be." Examples:

Зада́ча бу́дет решена́.	The problem will be solved.
Зада́ча была́ решена́.	The problem was solved.
	The problem *had been* solved.
Зада́ча решена́.	The problem *has been* solved.
	The problem is solved.

Notice that the past passive participle short forms make a distinction which the past tense proper is incapable of making, for

I solved the problem.
I *had solved* the problem.
I *have solved* the problem.

must all be rendered by **Я реши́л зада́чу**; i.e. they do not distinguish present perfect from past perfect (and simple past), as do the participles.

Russian makes exactly the same distinction in translating the present and past "progressive" (marked by "-ing") tenses (cf. R4 note 2):

Я живу́ здесь (уже́) два́ го́да.	I *have been* living here for two years.
Я жи́л здесь (уже́) два́ го́да.	I *had been* living here for two years.
	I lived here for two years.

Or with the verb "to be":

Я здесь (уже́) де́сять мину́т.	I *have been* here for ten minutes.
Я здесь бы́л (уже́) де́сять мину́т.	I *had been* here for ten minutes.
	I was here for ten minutes.

---

[1] The present passive participles, theoretically, also have short forms, but they are very seldom used (**реша́ем, реша́ема, реша́емо, реша́емы**).

Translate the following sentences:

> The city has already been taken. The city was taken. Napoleon said, "The city is taken." The city had already been taken, when we arrived. Everything has been said. We said everything. I have been saying this a long time. He had been saying that for two months. The letter has been written. We wrote the letter. We have written the letter. We had written the letter. I have been writing this letter for five hours. The letter was written. The letter is written.

Restrictions on formation. Passive participles are ideally formed only from transitive verbs. There are very few exceptions, and these are often "logical" transitives (the English counterparts are almost always transitive) which govern the genitive, instrumental, etc. instead of taking a direct object:

> достигнутый *and* достигаемый *from* достигнуть – достигают *gen* 'achieve':
>
> | | |
> |---|---|
> | Он достиг успеха. | He achieved success. |
> | Успех, достигнутый им . . . | The success achieved by him . . . |

or

> управляемый *from* управляют (*impf only*) *inst* 'govern, rule':
>
> | | |
> |---|---|
> | управляют государством | rule a *state (government)* |
> | государство, управляемое народом | government ruled by the people |

Finally, in the modern language past passive participles are formed almost exclusively from perfective verbs; forms like **писано** and **делано**, which are found in older literature, cannot be regarded as typical of present-day Russian.

3. Use of participles in scholarly prose and scientific Russian

In literary Russian, and particularly in scientific or scholarly texts, a participle (any of the four) and everything that goes with it may be placed *before* the noun it modifies. The result is a sentence unbroken by commas which may look difficult, but is simple if the student isolates the participial construction. For example:

> Я плохо понимаю задачу, решённую этим профессором.
> (I understand poorly the problem which that professor solved.)

becomes

> Я плохо понимаю **решённую этим профессором** задачу.

Compare the same phenomenon in literary German: Die *von dem Professor gelöste* Aufgabe verstehe ich schlecht.

Translate the following sentences (participial constructions boldface):

Всё **говорящие на русском языке** студенты поняли слова директора.

Эти слова были сказаны всем **ответившим на наше письмо** учителям.

Профессор поговорил со всеми **интересующимися этим вопросом** студентами.

Бостон является одним из самых старых **существовавших во время американской революции** городов.

Many more examples of these constructions are given in the scientific text at the beginning of Lesson VIII.

D. GERUNDS

Past gerunds are formed only from perfective verbs. Present gerunds are almost exclusively from imperfective verbs, but there are a few formed from perfective (mostly motion verbs in dental[1] stems: **войдя**, **принеся**, and **ся** verbs in **И**: **нахмурясь**, **схватясь**). The student may meet forms like **встретя** and **оставя** in literature, but such forms have been replaced in the modern language by **встретив** and **оставив**. In any case, *perfective present gerunds* have the same force as *perfective past gerunds*; they both denote completed action, whose completion is usually, but not always, prior to the main action. Compare the following:

Войдя в комнату, он сел.	Having entered the room, he sat down.
Входя в комнату, он говорил.	Entering the room, he was talking.
Входя в комнату, он увидел девушку.	Entering the room, he saw the girl.
Решив задачу, он сел.	Having solved the problem, he sat down.
Решая задачу, он курил.	Solving the problem, he was smoking.
Решая задачу, он заметил один важный факт.	Solving the problem, he noticed an important fact.

Sometimes the gerundial action, instead of preceding the main action, fuses with it, supplementing or amplifying its meaning. Some examples:

Решив эту задачу, он показал нам, что он знает свой предмет.	In solving that problem, he showed us he knows his subject.
Он объяснился, рассказав нам обо всём.	He explained himself, telling us about everything.

---

[1] The dental stems are stems ending in the dental consonants д, т, з, and с.

Notice that English may translate both a past and a present (imperfective) gerund by the present "-ing":

Возвраща́ясь в Москву́, о́н по-стоя́нно ду́мал о бе́дной сестре́.	Returning to Moscow, he thought constantly about his poor sister.
Возврати́вшись в Москву́, о́н по-е́хал к сестре́.	Returning to Moscow, he went straight to his sister's. Having returned to Moscow, he went straight to his sister's. (*No difference in meaning.*)

In Russian, however, the meanings of the past and present (imperfective) are always distinct:

Он сде́лал э́то, приня́в во внима́ние всё интере́сы на́шей па́ртии.	He did that, taking into account (*i.e.* after having taken into account) all the interests of our party.
Он сде́лал э́то, принима́я во внима́ние всё интере́сы на́шей па́ртии.	He did that, taking into account (while he was doing it) all the interests of our party.

A negated present gerund is often translated by "without X-ing," a negated past gerund by either "without X-ing" or "without having X-ed" (cf. II.3):

Я прие́хал, не зна́я ру́сского языка́.	I arrived without knowing Russian.
Она́ вы́шла, не отве́тив.	She went out without answering (having answered).

E. RUSSIAN ADJECTIVES WHICH ACT LIKE PASSIVE PARTICIPLES

Russian has a group of adjectives which differ from other adjectives and act like passive participles in that their long forms never occur in the predicate. The long forms replace the predicate short forms in the same (attributive, with the meaning "which—кото́рый") positions where the long forms of the participles replace the short forms. Examples:

гото́вый *inf* 'ready to'; к *dat* 'ready for' (prepared for). (NOTE: на *acc* 'ready for' (something reckless, anything that comes)):

Он гото́в сде́лать э́то для на́с.	He's ready to do that for us.
Мы́ и́щем челове́ка, гото́вого сде́лать э́то для на́с.	We're looking for a person (who is) ready to do that for us.
Я бу́ду гото́в к свои́м экза́менам.	I will be ready for my exams.
Я зна́ю, что я говорю́ с челове́ком, гото́вым к свои́м экза́менам.	I know I'm speaking to a person (who is) ready for his exams.

дово́ль/ный *inst* 'satisfied with':

Я о́чень дово́лен свое́й до́черью.	I'm very satisfied with my daughter.
Я иду́ к же́нщине, о́чень недо-во́льной свое́й до́черью.	I'm going to see a woman (who is) very dissatisfied with her daughter.

похо́жий **на** *acc* 'similar to, resembling':

Ра́я о́чень похо́жа на свою́ ма́ть.	Raja resembles her mother very much.
Та́м была́ одна́ де́вушка, о́чень похо́жая на мою́ тётю.	There was a girl there who resembled my aunt.

Often these "mandatory" short-form predicates have a somewhat special meaning or designate a temporary state or condition in a *specific* instance; the corresponding long form has a more permanent or *general* meaning; such long forms are usually used attributively but occasionally may be used predicatively as well. Examples:

свобо́дный 'free':

Я свобо́ден. 'I'm free (for the evening, etc.).'

Я свобо́дный would mean something like 'I am a free man.'

здоро́вый 'healthy':

Я здоро́в. 'I'm healthy (enjoying good health now).'

Я здоро́вый. 'I'm a healthy person (in general).'[1]

пра́вый 'right' (correct); 'right' (hand, etc.):

Я пра́в. 'I'm right.'

На́ше де́ло пра́вое. 'Our cause is right.'

(пра́вое крыло́ 'right wing')

TRANSLATION INTO RUSSIAN

Translate into Russian, rendering the italicized constructions by participles or gerunds:

It was *explained* to us yesterday that the books *which* we *read* last week are now (located) in the library *built* by the city, and that the books we *are reading* now have to be *returned* there **before**[1] the 14th of April. This will soon be **told**[2] to students not *knowing* it before. I no longer have to return books on time, 5 **since**[3] it seems to me that with Mixaíl Grigór'evič Bélyj **in charge**[4] one oughtn't to be afraid. A student *who has arrived* at a university for four years needs many books. *Being* an intelligent person, he knows these rules, which have been more

---

[1] For a similar distinction with **больно́й – бо́лен**, see p. 305.

than once *repeated* to him. If it turns out that he doesn't, so much the worse for him. We are very interested in all students *who have finished* ten years of school. All students *being met* by us at the station must show the letters *which* they *received* from us. What do you think of students *who write* such strange letters?

Without having said anything, I left for the city and did not arrive **until**[5] eleven. All the arriving people were looking at a woman, *standing* in front of a window **just**[6] *opened* by her. Not *saying* a word, the woman stood there for a few minutes, *having forgotten* about everything. In a few minutes she entered a restaurant, and I, *seeing* that she had entered, also went in and sat down at a **table**.[7] *Sitting* at the **table**,[7] I noticed that she was already ready to leave. When I see a woman ready to leave a restaurant, I seldom go up to her table. I called her over to me. But she, *answering* nothing, simply looked both at me and at the waiter, *who was approaching* the table and *saying* to her, "You have been here for fifteen minutes now. **It's time**[8] for you to go." The lady, not **wanting**[9] to answer him, simply stood up. I started to say something, but quickly *looking* at the waiter, the lady said, "One shouldn't talk **in front of**[4] waiters. They don't know how to be silent." The waiter silently continued to look at us. Finally, *having stood up* from the **table**,[7] I asked the waiter to go away, and he stepped away from the table. I asked the lady, "Are you free tonight?" *Having gone out* of the restaurant, we set off along the street. "Yes, I'm free," she said. "But I don't know if I'm satisfied with you. I like **men**,[10] and I'm **glad**[11] that you are asking me to go with you. But do I want to spend the evening with a person *who let* a waiter talk to me thus? You're probably an intelligent **man**,[10] but **in spite of**[4] all your knowledge, *by being afraid* of the waiter, you are no longer a man in my eyes."

Having returned home, I began to think. My former wife used to say that I drank too much. She said she **had**[12] nothing against *drinking* people. But she would always ask how many glasses of beer had been *drunk* by my friends. I don't want a wife *who asks* me such questions. And what can one think of the woman *I met* in the restaurant? How long had she been standing on that street *located* not far from the university?

Extra sentences for drill on participles and gerunds

1. The letters *which* Iván *is receiving* every day cannot be *taken* from these *closed* buildings.

2. The teacher, *having brought* to the director the already *written* reports, now says that they must be *translated* into Polish.

3. The city of Boston, *since it is* (use являются) the capital of our state, must have wide streets and beautiful squares.

4. You will see a new street *leading* to the main square. The old street *which was* there before has already been *forgotten* by all of us.

5. *Giving* nothing to the waitress, the doctor, *having stood up* from the table, looked at his colleague *walking* quickly along the street.

6. *Having sat* with me a whole hour, my brother decided to leave. *Laughing*, I asked him whether he remembered the months *spent* in the Caucasus.

7. *In listening* to his lectures, I'm beginning to get acquainted with his work. *Since* I myself *have written* a book on Polish history, I want to hear everything *said* by him.

8. *Without having solved* a single one of the problems, he will never be able to write a good report. Do you know when his report will be *read* to us?

9. *Living* in France, he must know many French cities.

10. The soldiers, *having entered* the city and already *passed through* the park, were approaching the station.

NOTES

1. **До** and **перед** both express the English preposition "before" in time expressions, and **перед**, of course, also has the physical meaning "before" ("in front of"). **До** may also express the idea of "before a certain time (deadline)," an idea close to "by a certain time," which usually is expressed by **к** *dat*. **Перед** usually refers to action more or less immediately before. "Before" as an adverb is **ра́ньше** or **пре́жде**.

Я до́лжен ко́нчить э́то до суббо́ты.	I have to finish this before Saturday.
Я до́лжен ко́нчить э́то к суббо́те.	I have to finish this by Saturday.
Он жи́л та́м до войны́.	He lived there before the war.
Э́то случи́лось перед войно́й.	That happened (right) before the war.
Он занима́ется перед экза́меном.	He's studying before his examination.
Мы́ пришли́ ра́ньше ва́с.	We came before you (did).
Ра́ньше она́ не пила́ та́к мно́го.	She didn't drink as much before.
Он стоя́л перед библиоте́кой.	(*Physical*) He stood before the library.

2. See Lesson X, p. 278.

3. Causal "since" is not usually translated by **потому́ что**. Use **та́к как** or **поско́льку**:

Та́к как (Поско́льку) вы́ здесь, я вам всё расскажу́.	Since (As long as) you're here, I'll tell you everything.

4. **При** (*prp*) is a versatile preposition with a primary meaning of attachment or accompaniment. It has the concrete senses "next to, with, in the presence of," and its more abstract uses may correspond to "in view of, given, when one considers that"; or the opposite meaning: "in spite of, in the face of, for all . . ." Examples:

У ни́х са́д при до́ме.	They have a garden next to their house.
У него́ при себе́ не́т де́нег.	He has no money on him.
Он ассисте́нт при профе́ссоре.	He's an assistant to the professor.
При Ста́лине не́ было та́к.	It wasn't that way in Stalin's time.
Не на́до говори́ть та́к при гостя́х.	One shouldn't talk like that in front of guests.
При таки́х тала́нтах о́н мо́г дости́гнуть бо́льшего.	In view of such talents he could have accomplished more.
При всём своём образова́нии о́н не о́чень у́мный челове́к.	For all his education, he isn't a very intelligent person.

5. "Not to do something until" is often rendered in Russian by то́лько:

Он прие́хал **то́лько** в сре́ду.	He didn't come until Wednesday.

6. See R6 note 2.

7. To sit down "at a table" is **ся́дут (се́сть – сади́ться) за сто́л**, and to sit (be sitting) "at a table" is **сиде́ть за столо́м**. To stand up "from a table," however, is **вста́нут – встава́ть из-за стола́**.

8. "It is time to" is expressed in Russian by **пора́** plus the infinitive with the person expressed in the dative.

9. The verb **хоте́ть** has no present gerund, the form **хотя́** having lost gerundial status and acquired other meanings. The present gerund from **жела́ют** 'desire' may be borrowed here.

10. **Челове́к** is the word for "person" in general. It may refer to a woman (**Она́ хоро́ший челове́к**), but usually it designates a "man," while **же́нщина** is used for "woman" (or **да́ма** 'lady'). Where it is important to distinguish a man from a woman, however, **мужчи́на** is used for "man":

Оди́н челове́к шёл по у́лице.	A man was walking down the street.
Зде́сь рабо́тают то́лько мужчи́ны.	Only men work here.
Та́м была́ одна́ о́чень краси́вая же́нщина.	There was a very beautiful woman there.
Что́ о́н за челове́к?	What kind of a person is he?

Addressing unknown people on the street may cause some problems in the Soviet Union, as it does here ("Sir" is all right in most cases, but neither "Lady" nor "Ma'm" is quite right). **Граждани́н** and **гражда́нка** are somewhat too stiff, and **това́рищ** sounds best when said with a title, though it is used by itself quite frequently. A male from early age to middle age is often addressed **молодо́й челове́к**, while a female from her late teens to a surprisingly late age may be simply **де́вушка**.

11. There is only one adjective in common use in Russian which occurs only in the short form: **ра́д** used with **что**/*inf*/*dat*: 'glad to/that/of'; for example:

Я ра́д, что вы́ нашли́ соба́ку.	I'm glad that you found the dog.
Она́ бу́дет ра́да сказа́ть не́сколько слов.	She will be happy to say a few words.
Они́ бы́ли ра́ды на́шему реше́нию.	They were glad of our decision.
Она́ бу́дет ра́да ви́деть его́. *Or:* Она́ бу́дет ра́да ему́.	She will be glad to see him.

12. The verb **име́ют** may translate "have" (possess) in almost any occurrence. It may be used with a personal subject in the general meaning of possession (corresponding to **у** *plus gen*), and it is also used with nonpersonal subjects (where **у** *plus gen* is less likely) and with subjects with abstract meaning (where **у** *plus gen* may be impossible). Examples:

Ка́ждый челове́к до́лжен име́ть свой до́м.	Everybody has to have his own house.
Мы́ име́ем хоро́шую библиоте́ку.	We have a good library.
Э́то зда́ние име́ет ше́сть этаже́й.	This building has six floors.
Э́тот фа́кт име́ет большо́е значе́ние.	That fact has great significance.
На́ша жи́знь име́ет свои́ хоро́шие сто́роны.	Our life has its good points (sides).

Име́ют, in addition, is used in various set expressions where **у** *gen*, again, would be impossible:

Я́ всегда́ зна́ю, с ке́м я́ име́ю де́ло.	I always know whom I have to do with (have business with).
Вы́боры име́ют ме́сто в ноябре́.	Elections take place in November.
Что́ вы́ име́ете в виду́?	What do you have in mind?
Она́ име́ет пра́во на э́то.	She has a right to that.

Име́ются means "be on hand, be available" (usually of objects):

У на́с име́ются хоро́шие кни́ги по матема́тике.	We have good books on mathematics here.
Учёный до́лжен испо́льзовать всё име́ющиеся исто́чники.	A scholar must use all available sources.

СЛОВАРЬ ГРАММАТИЧЕСКИХ ТЕРМИНОВ

прича́стие participle; — настоя́щего/про-
  ше́дшего вре́мени, действи́тельного/
  страда́тельного зало́га present/past,
  active/passive participle

дееприча́стие gerund; — настоя́щего/про-
  ше́дшего вре́мени present/past gerund

A. SUBSTANTIVIZED ADJECTIVES

The student has probably already met some adjectives used as nouns. **Ру́сский** 'Russian' should come to mind immediately. Most substantivized adjectives rest on some statable noun which determines their gender and number. If they refer to people, gender and number depend on the sex and singularity or plurality of the noun; or the noun may always be masculine, even when it refers to a woman. Examples:

ру́сский, ру́сская, ру́сские	Russian (*m*), Russian (*f*), Russians
учёный, учёные	scholar, scholars
вое́нный, вое́нные	(military) serviceman, servicemen
больно́й, больна́я, больны́е	sick man, sick woman, sick people
рабо́чий, рабо́чая, рабо́чие	worker (*m*), worker (*f*), workers

Substantivized adjectives resting on inanimate objects or animals take their gender from the object or animal. Sometimes a whole group of adjectivals builds up around a noun; e.g. nouns in **-ая** denoting types of rooms and resting on **ко́мната**. Such a type is very productive and leans little on the base word. A Russian creates a word like **операцио́нная** 'operating room' with hardly a thought of **ко́мната**. Or an adjective like **гла́сный** 'vowel' may be becoming independent of the noun on which it is based: **звук** 'sound'. More examples:

143

гости́ная, ва́нная, столо́вая (ко́мната)	living room, bathroom, dining room
Он живёт на Пу́шкинской. (у́лица)	He lives on Puškin street.
пряма́я, крива́я (ли́ния)	straight line, curved line
пе́рвое, второ́е, жарко́е (блю́до)	first course, second course, meat course
бу́дущее, про́шлое (вре́мя 'time')	the future, the past
млекопита́ющее, насеко́мое (based on живо́тное 'animal' (any living thing other than a plant))	mammal, insect

Many Russian adjectives may be converted into nouns with the broadest abstract meaning; these nouns take the neuter long form:

Она́ лю́бит краси́вое.	She loves the beautiful.
Я люблю́ зелёное.	I like green.

In the proper context, a masculine adjective may refer to people in general:

Бога́тый ре́дко понима́ет бе́дного.	A rich man seldom understands a poor one.

Participles, as well as regular adjectives, may be used as nouns:

начина́ющий, -ая	a beginner
люби́мый, -ая	loved one
да́нные	data
трудя́щийся	worker, toiler

B. "WHY" AND "BECAUSE"

The student has already had **почему́** 'why' and **потому́ что** 'because.' A number of other words are used to express essentially the same ideas; the student will not begin to differentiate among them until later, but he should be able to recognize them. For "why, what for, for what reason" we have **почему́, зачём, к чему́, отчего́**:

Почему́ он говори́л та́к до́лго?	Why did he speak so long?
Зачём мне́ ду́мать о своём бу́дущем?	Why should I think about my future?
К чему́ употребля́ть таки́е выраже́ния?	Why use such expressions?
Отчего́ твой дру́г переста́л быва́ть у на́с?	Why did your friend stop coming to see us?

For "because, for the reason that" we have **потому́ что, оттого́ что, из-за того́, что:**

Они́ пришли́, потому́ что они́ хоте́ли ви́деть на́с.	They came because they wanted to see us.
Он не хо́дит в шко́лу, оттого что он бо́лен.	He isn't going to school, because he's sick.
Она́ уе́хала отсю́да из-за того́, что не́т университе́та.	She left here because there's no university.

Sometimes, for stylistic reasons, these expressions are split up, with **потому́, оттого́,** and so forth, going into the main clause:

Она́ потому́ и счита́ет его́ хоро́шим челове́ком, что о́н е́й ча́сто помога́ет.	She considers him a good person, because he frequently helps her.
Он оттого́ то́лько и ухо́дит от на́с, что не хо́чет бо́льше меша́ть на́м рабо́тать.	He's only leaving us because he doesn't want to disturb our work any longer.

TRANSLATION INTO RUSSIAN

The workers asked me if I had **visited**[1] the Soviet Union. I answered that I had spent about three months there **on my way**[2] to China. For several weeks I translated letters from English to Russian and then **went on.**[3] Ten years later (In ten years) I went to China on **vacation.**[4] Going through the Soviet Union, I stopped off to see an old comrade.   5

"I'll hang your coat in the wardrobe, and then **let's**[5] **play**[6] cards," said Stepán Dmítrievič, having sat me down in a chair. "It seems to me that I'm constantly hanging caps up and seating people. I see that you brought your violin with you. You would probably like to **play**[6] violin. But I don't want to listen to your music. Please stand the violin **on the floor.**"[7]   10

The old judge Glafíra Petróvna entered the room. She had made me acquainted with Stepán when I was here the last time. I asked her if she was **acquainted**[8] with the lawyer Nadéžda Petróvna Nikoláeva. "I myself don't know her," she answered, "but I know a person **acquainted**[8] with her. Aren't you that person, Stepán Dmítrievič? And isn't it true that Nádja is a well-known   15 scholar?"

"It is true," he answered coldly. "And I'm not only acquainted with Nádja; I'm even marrying her next week."

"**Really?**[9] I thought she was already married. So she's marrying you. I would have wanted her to marry a worker or a soldier. But now she has no   20 future. And I think you're marrying her because of money."

NOTES

1. "Visit, be in a place once" may be **побыва́ют** (NB) perfective only, an intransitive verb; compare the transitive verb **посети́ть** – **посеща́ют** in Lesson I.

2. **Пу́ть** is a *masculine* noun with a unique declension (see vocabulary). "On the way" is **по пути́**.

3. **Да́льше** 'further' may also mean "Go on" or "Next" in recitation.

4. A "vacation" in the academic world is **кани́кулы** (**на**). Otherwise, **о́тпуск** (**в**) is normally used.

5. An imperfective verb may form a first plural imperative by adding **бу́дем** to the infinitive. A preceding **дава́й(те)** softens the imperative (cf R3 note 11).

6. "Play" an instrument is **игра́ют на** *prp*; "play" a sport is **игра́ют в** *acc*.

7. **на́ пол**. The student must learn the instances of prepositional stress as he goes along. The phenomenon is prominent in set expressions (cf. R8.C) but is giving way to stem stress in many cases.

8. **Знако́м(ый)** is like the adjectives described in R9.E.

9. The "really" which expresses the speaker's doubt of or surprise at a statement which has been made is often translated by **ра́зве** or, if the response is more emphatic, by **неуже́ли**. The words may stand alone, as the above sentence to be translated calls for, or they may be used in a clause, which they would normally introduce:

Ра́зве о́н тако́й у́мный? (!)	Is he really so intelligent? (!)
Неуже́ли вы́ меня́ не узна́ете? (!)	Do you really not recognize me? (!)

III
LESSONS I TO X

LESSON
I

АМЕРИКА́НСКИЙ СТУДЕ́НТ РАССКА́ЗЫВАЕТ О СЕБЕ́

Америка́нскому студе́нту Ви́ктору Мо́ссу повезло́. Он всю жизнь хоте́л посети́ть Сове́тский Сою́з, но ему́ ника́к не удава́лось пое́хать. Он был сли́шком за́нят, да и де́нег бы́ло ма́ло. Но неда́вно его́ оте́ц почему́-то про́дал свою́ автомаши́ну за ты́сячу до́лларов и дал э́ти де́ньги Ви́ктору на пое́здку в **СССР**.[4]

Ви́ктор ра́довался э́той пое́здке, представля́л себе́ Москву́ и сове́тских люде́й. Наконе́ц мы ви́дим его́ на Кра́сной пло́щади. Предста́вьте себе́ его́ сча́стье. Про́сто невероя́тно. Он и сам с трудо́м э́то понима́ет.

Как то́лько он прие́хал, его́ пригласи́л к себе́ обе́дать оди́н сове́тский студе́нт, Влади́мир Васи́льевич Марты́нов. Бу́дем называ́ть его́ Воло́дей. Ви́ктора мы бу́дем называ́ть по-ру́сски, Ви́тей. Воло́дя представля́ет Ви́тю свои́м колле́гам и начина́ет задава́ть вопро́сы своему́ америка́нскому го́стю:

Воло́дя.   Меня́ о́чень интересу́ет америка́нский о́браз жи́зни. Я хоте́л бы зада́ть вам не́сколько вопро́сов. Расскажи́те нам о себе́, пожа́луйста. Наприме́р, отку́да вы ро́дом, когда́ вы роди́лись и где вы вы́росли?

Ви́тя.   Я роди́лся в (**ме́сто**[6]) (число́) и вы́рос в (**ме́сто**[6]).

Воло́дя.   В како́й сре́дней шко́ле вы учи́лись?

Ви́тя.   Сре́днее образова́ние я получи́л в сре́дней шко́ле в моём родно́м го́роде ———. Учи́лся я в ней с о́сени ——— го́да и че́рез четы́ре го́да, то́-есть ле́том ——— го́да, око́нчил её.

Воло́дя.   Что вы де́лали **по́сле того́ как**[1] око́нчили сре́днюю шко́лу? Продолжа́ли ли учи́ться в вы́сшей шко́ле?

5

10

15

20

149

Ви́тя.   Продолжа́л. Я поступи́л в _____-ский университе́т (колле́дж) в
25   _____ году́ и тепе́рь учу́сь в нём уже́ _____ год. Но поско́льку заня́тия
ко́нчились на ле́тний пери́од, мне удало́сь сде́лать э́ту пое́здку.

Воло́дя.   Кто ваш оте́ц, где он живёт и что он де́лает?

Ви́тя.   Мой оте́ц — врач. Тепе́рь он живёт в _____ и там рабо́тает.

Воло́дя.   Кем вы хоти́те быть по́сле того́ как око́нчите университе́т?

30   *Ви́тя.*   Я ещё не зна́ю, но мой оте́ц хоте́л бы, что́бы я стал то́же врачо́м.

Воло́дя.   Больша́я ли у вас семья́?

Ви́тя.   Больша́я. Кро́ме отца́ и ма́тери у меня́ два бра́та и одна́ сестра́.
Ста́рший брат поступи́л на госуда́рственную слу́жбу в Вашингто́не.
Мла́дший брат слу́жит в вое́нно-морско́м фло́те, но ско́ро вернётся в
35   **шта́тскую**[5] жи́знь. Сестра́ преподаёт в нача́льной шко́ле и ду́мает
вы́йти за́муж за одного́ молодо́го челове́ка.

Воло́дя.   А где вы бу́дете служи́ть: в а́рмии и́ли во фло́те?

Ви́тя.   Я не о́чень хочу́ быть на вое́нной слу́жбе. Но уж е́сли пойду́, то в
вое́нно-возду́шный флот.

40   *Воло́дя.*   Вы ча́сто посеща́ете ва́ших роди́телей и́ли други́х свои́х родны́х
(ро́дственников)?

Ви́тя.   Да. Я е́зжу к ним дово́льно ча́сто и всегда́ ра́дуюсь возмо́жности
ви́деть их.

Воло́дя.   Быва́ли ли вы когда́-нибудь за грани́цей? (Е́здили ли вы когда́-
45   нибудь за грани́цу?)

Ви́тя.   Два го́да наза́д я е́здил во Фра́нцию и в Герма́нию. Я провёл три
ме́сяца в Евро́пе.

Воло́дя.   **На каки́х языка́х**[8] вы говори́те?

Ви́тя.   Кро́ме англи́йского я говорю́ свобо́дно по-испа́нски, хорошо́ по-
50   неме́цки и сно́сно по-ру́сски.

Воло́дя.   Нет, вы отли́чно говори́те по-ру́сски. Без труда́ отвеча́ете на
ка́ждый вопро́с. Но скажи́те, отку́да вы зна́ете испа́нский язы́к? Быва́-
ва́ли ли вы в Ю́жной Аме́рике и́ли на Ку́бе.

Ви́тя.   На Ку́бу е́здить сейча́с тру́дно, но в Ю́жной Аме́рике я о́чень хоте́л
55   бы побыва́ть.

Воло́дя.   Жи́ли ли вы когда́-нибудь на **за́паде**[3] Аме́рики (**США**[4])?

Ви́тя.   Да, но о́чень ма́ло. Не́сколько лет (тому́) наза́д я жил пять неде́ль
в Лос-Анжело́се и в Сан-Франци́ско. На ю́ге США я жил два го́да, во
Флори́де. На се́вере я никогда́ не жил, а на восто́ке то́лько учи́лся.

60   *Воло́дя.*   Вы меня́ извини́те, но ра́зве Ке́мбридж не на се́вере? Я ду́мал, что
он нахо́дится в шта́те Массачу́сетс, в Но́вой А́нглии.

Ви́тя.   Соверше́нно пра́вильно. Вы отли́чно зна́ете геогра́фию. Ке́мбридж
нахо́дится на се́веро-восто́ке США.

Воло́дя.   А в како́й ча́сти Массачу́сетса нахо́дится Ке́мбридж?

Ви́тя.   Он в восто́чной ча́сти, как ра́з о́коло Босто́на, недалеко́ от мо́ря.   65

Воло́дя.   Ну́, что́ мы́ с ва́ми де́лаем, Ви́тя. Прие́хали в го́сти, а попа́ли на допро́с. Зна́ете на́шу ру́сскую **посло́вицу**:[7] В гостя́х хорошо́, а до́ма лу́чше. Она́ ту́т о́чень к ме́сту.

Ви́тя.   Не́т, что́ вы́! Я с удово́льствием отвеча́ю на ва́ши вопро́сы.

Воло́дя.   Ну́, здо́рово. Тогда́ дава́йте пойдём вы́пьем ча́шку ко́фе. Сюда́ к   70
нам идёт ещё оди́н колле́га; подождём, **пока́**[2] он **не** придёт. **Пока́**[2] мы́ ждём, мо́жем продолжа́ть на́ш разгово́р.

1. Notice the difference between the prepositions **до**, **перед**, **по́сле** used with nouns or pronouns (**до войны́**, **перед ва́ми**) and the related adverbs **до того́ как**, **перед те́м как**, **по́сле того́ как** used with verbs:

По́сле университе́та о́н поступи́л в а́рмию. (Око́нчивши университе́т, о́н . . .)	After the university he entered the army.
По́сле того́ как о́н око́нчил ку́рс, о́н поступи́л в а́рмию. (Око́нчивши ку́рс, о́н . . .)	After he finished the course, he entered the army.
До войны́ (Перед войно́й) о́н служи́л в Евро́пе.	Before the war he served in Europe.
До того́ (Перед те́м) как о́н поступи́л на рабо́ту, о́н бы́л студе́нтом.	Before he went to work, he was a student. (*Cf.* R9 note 1 *on the difference between* до *and* перед.)
До того́ (Пе́ред те́м) как война́ нача́ла́сь, мы́ жи́ли в Евро́пе.	Before the war began, we lived in Europe.
По́сле того́ как о́н прие́хал, я́ позвони́л его́ сестре́.	After he arrived, I called his sister.

To express "before X-ing," **перед те́м как** or **пре́жде че́м** plus infinitive may be used; the logical performer of both the subordinate and the main action must be the same, however:

Перед те́м как⎱ уйти́, о́н мне́ да́л⎰ это. Пре́жде че́м	Before leaving⎱ he gave me this. Before he left,

По́сле, used by itself, has essentially the same meaning as **пото́м** (cf. R7.A5): "afterwards, later (on)":

Э́то вы́ мо́жете сде́лать по́сле.	You can do that later.

2. The conjunction **пока́** introduces action which is simultaneous with the action in the main clause. If the action it introduces is continuous, it usually corresponds to English "while" or "during the time that":

Пока́ мы́ рабо́тали, о́н про́сто та́м сиде́л.	While we were working, he was just sitting there.
Поговори́м, пока́ вы́ не рабо́таете.	Let's talk while you're not working.
Ка́ждое у́тро, пока́ я́ бы́л бо́лен, Ири́на приходи́ла ко мне́ пи́ть ко́фе.	Every morning during the time that I was sick, Irina came to drink coffee with me.
Пока́ мы́ шли́ на ста́нцию, пошёл до́ждь.	While we were going to the station, it started to rain.
На́м на́до ко́нчить свою́ рабо́ту, пока́ о́н зде́сь.	We must finish our work while he is here.

(Note that **пока́** in these usages is close to **когда́**, but it emphasizes duration rather than a stage of the action: "during," rather than "at" a time.)

When **пока́** introduces a *negated* noncontinuous action, the English translation is usually "until." For example:

Мы́ бу́дем зде́сь, пока́ мы́ не[1] око́нчим ку́рс.	We will be here until we finish the course.
Они́ жда́ли, пока́ две́рь не откры́лась.	They waited until the door was opened.
Я́ не уйду́, пока́ о́н не ска́жет пра́вду.[2]	I won't leave until he tells the truth.

Note that "not until" may also be translated by a positive verb plus **то́лько (по́сле)**:

Я́ уйду́ то́лько по́сле того́ как мне́ отве́тят.	I won't leave until they answer me. (I'll leave only after they answer me.)

Remember that the conjunction **пока́** is used only with verbs; "until" with time expressions is usually translated by **до**; "not until" (negated verb plus "until") often by **то́лько** (cf. the example with a verb, above).

Она́ бу́дет зде́сь до суббо́ты.	She'll be here until Saturday.
Мы́ рабо́тали до шести́ (часо́в).	We worked until six (o'clock).
Я́ уйду́ то́лько в ше́сть часо́в.	I won't leave until six o'clock.

Пока́ used as an *adverb* has the same meaning of simultaneity. It is treated in V.5.

3. "In/to" with a compass point is expressed by **на**; e.g. **на ю́ге** 'in the south,' **на ю́г** 'to the south'; **к ю́гу** means "toward the south, southward."

---

[1] Note that **пока́** plus the future *without* **не** is colloquial for the same meaning.

[2] A direct object after **пока́ не** is in the accusative, not the genitive.

Note the compounds **се́веро-за́пад, ю́го-за́пад, се́веро-восто́к, ю́го-восто́к**, and observe their secondary stress (see paragraph 4, below).

4. The question of *secondary stress* in Russian is too complex to deal with in detail here, but a few general things may be noted about compound words (words with more than one root) and abbreviations. Most compound words have a single stress, usually on the final root, as in:

самолёт [səmal'ót]	airplane
земледе́лие [z'iml'id'э́l'ijə]	agriculture
Ленингра́д [l'in'ingrát]	Leningrad
восемьсо́т [vəs'imsót]	eight hundred

Certain compounds, however, notably new formations in which the component elements are still felt as somewhat independent, are likely to have secondary stress (reference works which mark secondary stress, and not all do, usually use a "grave" accent: ò). As such compounds become more familiar and begin to be felt as units, there is an increasing tendency to reduce them to a single stress. Usage may vary among different words and speakers. Compare, for example:

о̀бщепоня́тный understood by all	*but*	общепри́нятый recognized by all
новорождённый newborn	*but*	но̀вооткры́тый newly opened

Hyphened words, like the examples in paragraph 3 above, almost always have secondary stress: **сѐверо-восто́к, воѐнно-морско́й**, etc.

Abbreviations used as independent words are treated as compounds with secondary stress, but some of the commoner ones become subject to the process described above; others retain the secondary stress. For example:

го̀рсове́т (*from* городско́й сове́т) [gòrsav'ét] 'city council'
полѝтрабо́та 'political work' (political education of the people)
but политру́к 'political instructor' (in a military unit)

Very common abbreviations, such as **СССР** and **США**, may manifest extreme phonetic reduction, as well as weakening or loss of secondary stress:

СССР   formerly [èsèsèsér], now approximately [èšér] (š̄ designates long [s])
США   formerly [èssàá], now approximately [sšá] or even [šá]

5. Note that **штат** is specifically a "state" of the United States or similar country, a territorial unit. **Госуда́рство** is "state" in the sense of a particular political structure. **Прави́тельство** is the "government," the specific organ which manages the state. The adjectives from **госуда́рство** and **прави́тельство** are **госуда́рственный** and **прави́тельственный**, but note: "Government service" is usually **госуда́рственная слу́жба** ("state" service).

Шта́тский is not the adjective for **штат**, but means "civil" or "civilian," the opposite of **вое́нный**; e.g. **шта́тское пла́тье** 'civilian clothes.'

6. Non-Russian place-names are regularly treated as Russian masculine nouns if they end in a consonant or as feminines if they end in **-a**. If they end in any other vowel, they are indeclinable, and as a rule masculine in gender, although names in **-o** may be neuter.

Here are the names of the states as used in contemporary Soviet sources. Occasional variations in spellings are possible. Sometimes one finds translated forms like **Но́вая Ме́ксика** or **Но́вый Джерси** and, conversely, nontranslated forms like **Са́ут**. Spellings and stress do not always exactly reflect English spelling and/or pronunciation; the most obvious noncorrespondences are in boldface. Note that "h" is rendered by both **x** and **г**.

Treated as ordinary masculines or feminines:

Арканза́с, Вайо́минг, Вашингто́н, Вермо́нт, Виско́нсин, Де́лавэр, Илли-но́йс, Ка́нзас, Конне́ктикут, Массачу́сетс, Мичига́н, Мэн, Мэ́риленд, Нью-Ге́мпшир, Нью-Йо́рк, Орего́н, Род-А́йленд, Теха́с

А́йова, Алаба́ма, Аля́ска, Аризо́на, Вирджи́ния, За́падная Вирджи́ния, Се́верная Дако́та, Южная Дако́та, Джо́рджия, Индиа́на, Калифо́рния, Се́верная Кароли́на, Южная Кароли́на, Луизиа́на, Миннесо́та, Мон-та́на, Небра́ска, Нева́да, Оклахо́ма, Пенсильва́ния, Флори́да, Ю́та

Note also: Кана́да, Ме́ксика

Indeclinable neuters:

Айдахо, Колора́до, Нью-Ме́ксико, Ога́йо

Indeclinable masculines:

Гава́йи, Кенту́кки, Миссиси́пи, Миссу́ри, Нью-Джерси

Cities follow the same rules:

Нью-Йо́рк, Чика́го, Лос-А́нжелос, Филаде́льфия, Детро́йт, Кли́вленд, Сент-Лу́ис, Пи́тсбург, Майа́ми, Босто́н

NOTE: In some foreign words *ja, jo*, etc. may be rendered by **йа, йо**, . . . , instead of by the normal **я, ё**, . . . ; e.g. **Майа́ми, Нью-Йо́рк**.

7. Russians make far more liberal use of traditional proverbs and sayings than Americans do. The proverb (**посло́вица**) theoretically is a succinct statement with a definite, often didactic point (**Повторе́ние — мать уче́ния** 'Repetition is the mother of learning'), while the saying (**погово́рка**) is merely a neat way of expressing an idea (**У него́ не всё до́ма** 'He is not all there'). In practice the two are not always distinct.

From time to time we will encounter examples of **посло́вицы** and **пого-**

во́рки. It will be noted that certain linguistic features occur more frequently in them than in normal literary Russian. The second singular verbal form, with or without the pronoun ты,[1] conveys "general person," very like the English general "you"; e.g. **От посло́вицы не уйдёшь** 'You (one) can't get away from proverbs.' Often conjunctions are omitted, the most usual instance being the omission of "*if* . . ., *then* . . ."; e.g. **Ре́же ви́дишь — бо́льше лю́бишь**. The conjunction да (always unstressed, [də] (schwa)) is used where и or а might be expected; it suggests that the addition is an afterthought (cf. line 3 of the lesson text). None of these elements is restricted to proverbs; all are typical of spoken Russian as well (the second singular in the "general person" usage is particularly common). The **то́, что́** constructions described in Lesson III are also very frequent in proverbs and sayings.

8. Note that **по-ру́сски, по-францу́зски**, etc. are fixed expressions and cannot be broken up or otherwise elaborated. To do something "in X language" may always be translated **на Х-ом языке́**, and this construction must be used when **по-Х-ски** is not appropriate. Examples:

He speaks Russian.		Он говори́т по-ру́сски.
	or	Он говори́т на ру́сском языке́.
Her report was written in German.		Её докла́д бы́л напи́сан по-не́мецки.
	or	Её докла́д бы́л напи́сан на неме́цком языке́.
Her report was written in good German.	*only*	Её докла́д бы́л напи́сан на хоро́шем неме́цком языке́.
How many languages does he speak?	*only*	На ско́льких языка́х о́н гово́рит?

TRANSLATION INTO ENGLISH

1. Его́ реше́ние поступи́ть на госуда́рственную слу́жбу о́чень обра́довало все́х его́ ро́дственников. **2.** Мы́ о́чень ра́дуемся прие́зду на́ших госте́й. Наде́емся то́лько, что обе́д уда́стся. **3.** Мо́й оте́ц роди́лся и вы́рос на ю́ге, в восто́чном Теха́се. Он та́м жи́л всё вре́мя, пока́ не поступи́л в университе́т в Чика́го. **4.** На́м с америка́нцами сейча́с везёт. Наприме́р, вчера́ попа́л к на́м оди́н студе́нт из Нью-Йо́рка, кото́рый с удово́льствием расска́жет на́м о сре́днем образова́нии в своём родно́м шта́те. **5.** Скажи́те ему́, чтобы о́н зашёл ко мне́, до того́ как пойдёт в кино́. **6.** Пре́жде чём

5

---

[1] This construction carries no connotation of familiarity and is used when addressing both familiar and strange persons.

поехать в Ленингра́д, на́м пришло́сь спроси́ть, ка́к лу́чше попа́сть туда́.
7. Каки́м о́бразом о́н попа́л в а́рмию? Я ду́мал, что ему́ о́чень нра́вится
шта́тская жи́знь. Да не преподаёт ли о́н где́-нибудь? Ра́зве учителя́ должны́
служи́ть? 8. Мо́й лу́чший дру́г ро́дом с за́пада. Но́ о́н тепе́рь живёт в
се́верной ча́сти За́падной Вирджи́нии. 9. Мо́й племя́нник тепе́рь в военно-
возду́шном фло́те. Но́ о́н ма́ло лета́ет и никогда́ не попада́ет за грани́цу.
Он слу́жит в юго-восто́чной ча́сти США. Я то́лько с трудо́м представля́ю
себе́ его́ жи́знь. 10. Подожди́те, пока́ я не верну́сь, пока́ вы́ ждёте, вы́
мо́жете чита́ть э́тот журна́л. 11. Таки́х люде́й не найдёшь в на́шем прави́-
тельстве. Ре́дко встре́тишь бо́лее у́много челове́ка. 12. Ти́ше е́дешь —
да́льше бу́дешь. 13. На́ш профе́ссор говори́т на мно́гих языка́х. Он про-
во́дит ка́ждое ле́то за грани́цей. Бу́дущим ле́том о́н ду́мает посети́ть По́ль-
шу. Он уже́ побыва́л в СССР. 14. У ни́х та́м ведётся допро́с на по́льском
языке́. Зайди́те, вы́ без труда́ всё поймёте. 15. Бы́ло вре́мя, когда́ госуда́р-
ства не́ было. 16. Никто́ не зна́ет, где́ прохо́дит госуда́рственная грани́ца
ме́жду э́тими стра́нами. 17. На́ши дела́ иду́т отли́чно. Прави́тельство
посла́ло на́с на се́вер, и мы́ полу́чим до́м как ра́з на мо́ре. Жена́ ужа́сно
лю́бит морску́ю во́ду, да роди́тели её живу́т недалеко́. К ю́гу от на́с на-
хо́дится нача́льная шко́ла; туда́ бу́дет ходи́ть на́ш ма́льчик. Говоря́т, что
та́м отли́чно преподаю́т все́ языки́. Таки́м о́бразом, Ва́ня смо́жет продол-
жа́ть учи́ться англи́йскому языку́. 18. Вы́ говори́те, что Степа́н Ильи́ч
несно́сный челове́к. Объясни́те мне́ приме́ром. 19. Мо́й сы́н сейча́с
ока́нчивает университе́т. По-мо́ему, о́н уже́ слу́жит прекра́сным приме́ром
образо́ванного сове́тского челове́ка. 20. Я верну́лся домо́й, но́ её о́браз
до́лго не выходи́л из мое́й головы́. 21. Он то́лько сре́дний учени́к. 22.
Ли́дия Петро́вна не ра́з приглаша́ла меня́ к себе́ и всегда́ представля́ла
меня́ са́мым интере́сным лю́дям. 23. Я ре́дко продаю́ свои́ со́бственные
ве́щи, но́ прода́м ва́м мои́ часы́. 24. Бу́дучи солда́том, о́н ма́ло живёт на
ро́дине, но́ о́н всё вре́мя слу́жит ей.

TRANSLATION INTO RUSSIAN

1. I have finally succeeded in visiting the Soviet Union. A colleague of my
father invited me there, and after finishing studies at the university, I sold my car
for five hundred dollars. 2. You can imagine that I sold it without trouble, inasmuch as it was almost new. 3. What happiness! Every day people introduce
me to new students, who ask me the most improbable questions about the
American way of life. 4. Just after I arrived a very interesting Soviet mechanic
invited me to his place. He wanted to ask me a few questions about my native
state. 5. For some reason this trip has made me very happy. At first I wasn't
very happy about it, but now I must say that I have been very lucky. 6. How

did I get to Germany? Well, just before I was supposed to enter the university I had a talk with my older brother, who was serving in the air force at that time. "You ought to think about military service," he said. "You will probably be sent abroad and in this way will be able to visit many countries. In the army, for instance, the average soldier travels over his whole native land and often gets abroad as well." **7.** What languages do you speak besides your own (native)? **8.** In high school she was an average student (pupil), and she got into the university only with great difficulty. **9.** How would an educated person have acted? That's what you must ask yourself. **10.** Please continue to tell us about your government service. **11.** I'll with great pleasure tell you about myself; for instance, I'm from the eastern part of North Dakota, where my parents still live. I went to an elementary school in the western part of South Dakota. The teaching was very good there (they taught well there). I received my high school education in central Iowa. Before entering the university I went to Europe and this trip gave me the opportunity to visit many universities where Russian is taught. **12.** I want my children to grow up in the West. **13.** Our city is growing very rapidly. Before the war it grew very slowly. **14.** My nephew entered the navy, but he wound up in Alaska, where he spent three years. **15.** Don't disturb him while he's working. Wait until he finishes his work. **16.** You (use second singular) don't see such a teacher every day. **17.** I'll stay until you sell me your car. **18.** What is your profession? **19.** I teach geography in an elementary school in the northern part of Virginia. In addition, I am preparing a report for the government in Washington. In Washington there is little living space; thus I must live in Virginia. **20.** Now I am serving abroad. But in five years I hope to return to my native land.

СЛОВА́РЬ

а́вто-маши́н-а automobile, car
(не)-**вер-о-я́т-**/н-ый (im)probable
во-ѐн-н-о-воз-ду́ш-н-ый фло́т air force
во-ѐн-н-о-мор-ск-о́й фло́т navy
во-ѐн-н-ый **ВОЙ**[1]-н military, war *adj*
восто́к (на) east I.3; восто́ч-н-ый eastern
вра́ч *E* physician, doctor CL3.4
вы́с-ш-ий higher; —ее образова́ние higher education; —ая шко́ла college-level school

геогра́фи-я geography
го́сть *M E pl obl* guest; иду́т – ходи́ть в —и go to visit; бы́ть в —я́х be visiting
го́сть/я *F (gen pl* го́стий) guest
госуда́р-ств-енн-ый state *adj* I.5
госуда́р-ств-о state *n* I.5
гран-и́ц-а boundary, border; за —ей *гдѐ*, за —у *куда́*, из-за —ы *отку́да* abroad
да (да и) and, but, for that matter, furthermore I.7, CL5.4

---

[1] The numbers 1, 2, etc. following roots in the vocabularies refer to the similarly numbered roots in the Root List, where the numbers serve to distinguish roots with identical spelling but different origin. See also the last footnote on page 324 of the Root List.

до́ллар dollar
до-**про́с** (на) interrogation
за *кого́/что́* for (IV.4b)
заня́тия *pl* studies, school session
за́-пад (на) west; за́-пад-н-ый western I.3
здо́рово *colloq* fine, great; greatly
здоро́в-ый (*comp* здорове́е) healthy
как ра́з just right, precisely:
  Э́то как ра́з то́. That's just (precisely)
  the right thing.
карье́р-а career
колле́г-а colleague
колле́дж college (English or American)
кро́ме *кого́/чег ó* except (for), besides
кро́ме того́ furthermore, in addition
ме́ст-о: к ме́сту appropriate, in place
мо́р-е *E pl* (*gen pl* море́й) sea, large lake
мор-ск-о́й maritime, sea *adj*
нача́ль-н-ый **Ч/Н** beginning, elementary
наприме́р for example, for instance
о́браз ОБ-РАЗ[1] form, image, shape, manner; гла́вным —ом mainly, chiefly;
  каки́м —ом in what way, how; таки́м
  —ом in that/this way, thus; Х-ым —ом
  in X way/manner
от-ли́ч-/н-ый excellent
пери́од period
пло́щадь *E pl obl* city square; space
по-**гово́р**-/к-а saying I.7
по-**е́зд**-/к-а trip, journey
пока́ I.2
по-**сло́в**-иц-а proverb I.7
почему́-то for some reason
прав-и́-тель-ств-енн-ый government *adj* I.5
прав-и́-тель-ств-о government *n* I.5
при-**ме́р** example; приведу́т – приводить
  — give/cite an example

профе́сси-я profession
ро́д: ро́дом by birth/origin:
  Отку́да вы́ ро́дом? Where were you
  born?
  Óн ро́дом из Кана́ды. He is from/was
  born in Canada; a native of Canada.
ро́д-ин-а (на) native land, motherland
род-и́-тел-и *pl* parents
род-н-о́й native
род-н-ы́е *pl* relatives *sub adj*
ро́д-ств-енн-ик relative
свобо́д-а freedom
свобо́д-/н-ый free
се́вер (на) north I.3; се́вер-н-ый northern
  I.3
сейча́с now; very soon, right away
семь-/я́ **СЕМ-ЕН** *S pl* (*gen pl* семе́й) family
слу́ж-б-а (на) service
(не)-с-**но́с**-/н-ый (in)tolerable; *positive also
  means* fair, middling
со-**верш**-ён-/н-ый perfect, absolute
(не)-со-**верш**-ён-н-ый **ви́д** (im)perfective
  aspect
сре́д-н-ий middle, central; average; —ее
  образова́ние high school education;
  —яя шко́ла high school
сча́сть-е happiness, luck
тру́д *E* work, labor, trouble, difficulty; с
  —о́м with difficulty; без —а́ without
  difficulty
у-**дово́ль**-ств-и-е pleasure; с —ем with
  pleasure
уж really
флóт *E pl* fleet
шта́т state I.5
шта́т-ск-ий civilian I.5
юг (на) south I.3; **юж**-н-ый southern I.3

ГЛАГО́ЛЫ

(по)-**вёз**-ёт *кому́/чему́ imps* be lucky,
  have luck:
  Ему́ о́чень повезло́. He was very
  lucky.

при-**глас**-и́-ть – приглаша́ют *куда́* invite
  n приглаше́ние
за́-**да**-ть – задава́ть **ДАЙ** give, assign, set:
  — вопро́с *кому́/чему́* ask a question;

— то́н set the tone/fashion

n зада́ние assignment; *cf.* зада́ча task, problem, assignment; дома́шнее зада́ние homework

пре-по-да-ва́-ть *что́ кому́* teach

про̀-да-ть – продава́ть sell

n прода́жа sale

у-да́-ть-ся (*past* уда́лся, -а́сь, -о́сь, -и́сь) – удава́ться be a success (of person or thing); —ся *кому́ inf* (*imps*) succeed in X-ing

n уда́ча

про-до́лж-и-ть – продолжа́ют continue *tr*; —ся be continued, continue *intr*

n продолже́ние

о-ко́нч-и-ть – ока́нчивают finish (particularly some set program, *e.g.* око́нчить шко́лу)

n оконча́ние ending (*also gr*)

образ-ова́-ть *both P and I, or I* образ-о́в-ывай-ут form; образо́ванный *PPP* formed; well-educated

n образова́ние formation; education

по-па̀д-ут – попада́ют *куда́* strike, hit (mark); get (to), arrive, "wind up," "land (in)"

по-сет-и́-ть – посеща́ют visit (*ch 5*)

n посеще́ние ‖ (об)-ра́д-ова-ть make happy *tr*; —ся *кому́/чему́* be happy about; *I may mean* look forward to *something in future*

раст-у́т (ро́с, росла́) **РОСТ** grow, grow up; increase

вы̀-раст-ут (вы́рос, вы́росла) – выраста́ют grow up

род-и́-ть-ся – рожда́ются *P and I* be born

n рожде́ние   (*ch 5*)

служ-и́-ть *кому́/чему́* serve

n слу́жба

пред-ста́в-и-ть – представля́ют represent, present, introduce (a person); — себе́ imagine

n представле́ние

по-ступ-и́-ть – поступа́ют act, take a step *fig*; — *куда́* enter, enroll

n поступле́ние enrollment, entering; посту́п/о/к act

LESSON
II

Conversation about education

АМЕРИКА́НСКИЙ СТУДЕ́НТ РАССКА́ЗЫВАЕТ
ОБ УНИВЕРСИТЕ́ТЕ

Воло́дя. Что́ вы изуча́ете[7] в университе́те?

Ви́тя. В э́том семе́стре я слу́шаю ле́кции по[5] эконо́мике,[4] хи́мии[4] и ру́сской исто́рии[4] восемна́дцатого и девятна́дцатого веко́в.

Воло́дя. Како́й ваш гла́вный предме́т?

5 *Ви́тя.* Мой гла́вный предме́т — фи́зика. Когда́ я око́нчу э́тот курс (Когда́ я получу́ сте́пень бакала́вра), я собира́юсь поступи́ть в аспиранту́ру и рабо́тать в о́бласти а́томной фи́зики.

Воло́дя. Что́ вам э́то даст?

Ви́тя. Наде́юсь, что э́то мне́ даст возмо́жность получи́ть до́кторскую сте́-

10 пень. Но э́то ещё в далёком бу́дущем. На́до бу́дет писа́ть мно́го рабо́т, выступа́ть со мно́гими докла́дами, слу́шать мно́го ле́кций. Зате́м на́до бу́дет сдава́ть экза́мены.

Воло́дя. Каки́е вы бу́дете держа́ть экза́мены?

Ви́тя. Экза́мены быва́ют и пи́сьменные и у́стные. Са́мые тру́дные — э́то

15 у́стные. Сиди́шь, по кра́йней ме́ре, три часа́ перед все́ми профессора́ми, обсужда́ешь с ни́ми все изу́ченные предме́ты. Это всё изве́стные учё-ные, зна́ют вся́кие[3] подро́бности во все́х областя́х. Да и любо́й[3] специали́ст мо́жет прийти́ на твой экза́мен и задава́ть вопро́сы. На-стоя́щий у́жас. Едва́ ли вы́держишь.

20 *Воло́дя.* Ну, а что́ е́сли прова́лят?

160

Ви́тя. Прова́лишься, зна́чит, опя́ть ну́жно бу́дет сдава́ть. Сдаёшь, пока́ не сда́шь.

Воло́дя. А что́ по́сле? Диссерта́ция?

Ви́тя. Диссерта́ция. Почти́ **невозмо́жно**[1] себе́ предста́вить, кака́я э́то рабо́та. И вы́брать **те́му, на кото́рую**[6] лу́чше бу́дет писа́ть, ужа́сно тру́дно. Вы́бор те́мы игра́ет огро́мную ро́ль в успе́хе или неуспе́хе диссерта́ции. Говоря́т, что диссерта́цию **мо́жно**[1] сравни́ть с жено́й; **бу́дто**[2] же́нишься на не́й. Це́лый ве́к с не́й живёшь.   25

Воло́дя. Я неда́вно прочита́л одну́ передову́ю статью́ в «Пра́вде», в кото́рой шла ре́чь о ску́чном содержа́нии мно́гих диссерта́ций. И оди́н изве́стный учёный неда́вно вы́ступил с ре́чью, где́ о́н то́же си́льно критикова́л сове́тские диссерта́ции настоя́щего вре́мени.   30

Ви́тя. Соверше́нно пра́вильно. Любо́й челове́к ва́м ска́жет, что диссерта́ции да́же передовы́х учёных ча́сто соде́ржат вся́кий вздо́р.

1. Both **возмо́жно (невозмо́жно)** and **мо́жно (нельзя́)** refer to physical or mental possibility (impossibility), but only **мо́жно (нельзя́)** can express the idea of permission (prohibition). For example:

Мо́жно (Возмо́жно) бы́ло поня́ть его́ слова́.	It was possible to understand his words.
Нельзя́ (Невозмо́жно) купи́ть здесь ру́сских газе́т.	It is impossible to buy Russian newspapers here.

but only

Кури́ть здесь мо́жно.	Smoking is permitted here.
Кури́ть здесь нельзя́.	Smoking is not permitted here.

Возмо́жно, but not **мо́жно**, is combined with **что** in the meaning "it is possible that . . .":

Возмо́жно, что о́н придёт.	It's possible that he will come.

or it may be used parenthetically in the meaning "might/may, perhaps"; here it is synonymous with **мо́жет быть**:

О́н, возмо́жно, зна́ет её а́дрес.	He might (may) know her address.
О́н, мо́жет быть, зна́ет её а́дрес.	Perhaps he knows her address.

Возмо́жно is also used in the meaning "as X as possible," akin to **как мо́жно** plus comparative (cf. R5.A4);

Принеси́те кни́гу возмо́жно скоре́е.	Bring the book as soon as possible.

Unlike **мо́жно, возмо́жно** *is not used with a dative.*

Нельзя, in addition to impossibility and prohibition, frequently has a more strictly modal sense: "must not":

Вам нельзя говорить так.	You must not talk like that.

2. **Будто**, **как будто**, and **будто бы**, as conjunctions or particles, express approximately "as if, just like, allegedly":

Он идёт быстро и уверенно, как будто уже ходил здесь.	He is walking quickly and confidently, as if he had already walked here.
Говорят, будто он уехал.	They're talking as if he had left. (*Or simply* They say he's left.)
Он дал мне два будто бы очень важных письма.	He gave me two allegedly very important letters.

3. **Всякий** and **любой** are essentially interchangeable in the general meaning "any/every" in the *singular*. For example:

Вы их найдёте в любом (во всяком) магазине.	You'll find them in any (every) store.

"Anybody/everybody" is **всякий** by itself or **любой человек**:

Всякий (Любой человек) вам это скажет.	Anybody/everybody will tell you that.

In the plural, however, there is some divergence. **Всякие** usually means "all kinds of," but **любые** retains its sense of "any . . . you like" (cf. the roots: **ВС** "all" vs. **ЛЮБ** "like"). Examples:

Всякие ходят к этому врачу.	All kinds of people go to that doctor.
Я выбрал всякие книги.	I selected all kinds of books.

but

Выберите любые три книги.	Select any three books you like.

Note the important construction **без всяк-** NOUN 'without any NOUN (at all)':

без всякого интереса   without any interest (at all)
без всяких вопросов   without any questions (at all)

(Remember that "without" plus a verb ("X-ing" or "having X-ed") is often translated by a negated gerund (cf. R9.D)):

Она вышла, не ответив.	She went out without answering (having answered).
Я приехал, не зная русского языка.	I arrived without knowing Russian.

4. Below we list some branches of science with the corresponding scientists and adjectives pertaining to the science. Observe that many of the relationships are quite regular (as are some of the stress patterns within a single group):

Russian:	-ло́гия	-′лог	-логи́ческий
English	-logy	-logist	-logical

Russian:	-гра́фия	-′граф	-графи́ческий
English:	-graphy	-grapher	-graphical

Russian:	-ика	-ик	-и́ческий
English:	-ics/-ic	-ician/-icist/-ist	-ical

The student should not, however, expect perfect correspondences. Examples:

нау́ка	учёный	нау́чный
антрополо́гия	антропо́лог	антропологи́ческий
археоло́гия	архео́лог	археологи́ческий
астроно́мия	астроно́м	астрономи́ческий
биоло́гия	био́лог	биологи́ческий
геогра́фия	гео́граф	географи́ческий
геоло́гия	гео́лог	геологи́ческий
исто́рия	исто́рик	истори́ческий
картогра́фия	карто́граф	картографи́ческий
психоло́гия	психо́лог	психологи́ческий
социоло́гия	социо́лог	социологи́ческий
теоло́гия	тео́лог	теологи́ческий
фотогра́фия	фото́граф	фотографи́ческий
филосо́фия	филосо́ф	филосо́фский
хи́мия	хи́мик	хими́ческий
акаде́мия	акаде́мик	академи́ческий
тео́рия	теоре́тик	теорети́ческий
бота́ника	бота́ник	ботани́ческий
диале́ктика	диале́ктик	диалекти́ческий
кри́тика	кри́тик	крити́ческий
лингви́стика	лингви́ст	лингвисти́ческий
ло́гика	ло́гик	логи́ческий
матема́тика	матема́тик	математи́ческий
педаго́гика	педаго́г	педагоги́ческий
фи́зика	фи́зик	физи́ческий
эконо́мика	экономи́ст	экономи́ческий

Эконо́мика is "economics (science)" or "economy (economic structure or system)," and should be kept carefully distinct from **эконо́мия**, which almost always means "economy (of time, money, etc.)."

5. **По** plus the dative has a number of important usages in addition to those connected with location or motion (R4 note 6) or time (R7.A7):

a. "About" often in a somewhat formal or official sense ("on the subject of"), notably with certain words, such as **вопро́с** or **предме́т**:

Ма́слов говори́т по э́тому вопро́су.	Maslov is speaking about this question.
Что́ о́н сказа́л по э́тому предме́ту?	What did he say on that subject?

Or in the somewhat more extended sense "in connection with" (cf. paragraph 6 below):

Они́ е́дут в Москву́ по одному́ ва́жному де́лу.	They're going to Moscow about (in connection with) an important matter.
Мы́ здесь по вопро́су о рабо́чих права́х.	We're here in connection with (about) the question of workers' rights.

b. Closely related to the usage just discussed is **по** *dat* in the sense "with respect/relation/regard to X, as far as X is concerned":

Он меха́ник по профе́ссии.	He's a mechanic by profession.
Он крестья́нин по происхожде́нию.	He's a peasant by origin.
дешёвый по цене́	cheap in price
не злой по душе́	not bad at heart
пе́рвая кома́нда по футбо́лу	first (best) team in soccer
ма́льчик по и́мени Ива́н	boy by the name of Ivan

And note the related usage pertaining to personal relationships:

бра́т по отцу́	stepbrother (same father)
ро́дственники по ма́тери	relative on my mother's side
това́рищ по рабо́те	*fellow* worker
това́рищ по университе́ту	*fellow* university student
това́рищ по ко́мнате	room*mate*
това́рищ по шко́ле	school*mate*

c. "According to, in correspondence with, on the basis of":

Мы́ рабо́таем по пла́ну.	We work according to a plan.
Мы́ поступа́ем по пра́вилам.	We act according to the rules.
по жела́нию, по вы́бору	by desire, by choice

Я узна́л ва́с по го́лосу.	I recognized you by your voice.
по на́шему мне́нию, по-на́шему	in our opinion
рабо́та по си́лам	work commensurate with (our) strength

d. "Because of, due to":

Она́ сде́лала э́то по оши́бке.	She did that by mistake.
Он не пришёл на заня́тия по боле́з-ни.	He didn't come to class because of illness.
Он поступи́л та́к по мо́лодости.	He acted that way because of his youth.
поэ́тому, по э́той причи́не	therefore, for that reason

6. In addition to **по** *dat*, Russian has a number of other expressions generally corresponding to "about, on the subject of, in connection with, with respect/relation[1]/regard to," and others. These expressions are not always interchangeable, and each may have a more specific reference in certain contexts, but the student may begin by being able to recognize them in the above senses:

насчёт *gen* (very common, particularly in conversation):

Спроси́ насчёт обе́да.	Ask about dinner.
Что́ о́н сказа́л насчёт э́того?	What did he say in regard to that?
Ка́к насчёт экза́мена?	What about the exam?

по по́воду *gen* (slightly more formal):

Он ска́жет не́сколько сло́в по по́-воду но́вой матема́тики.	He will say a few words about the new mathematics.

в связи́ с *inst* (*lit* 'in connection with, owing to, due to'):

Он здесь в связи́ с одни́м ва́ж-ным де́лом.	He's here in connection with an important matter.
В связи́ с прие́здом но́вого ко-манди́ра, всё солда́ты мно́го рабо́тают.	Owing to the arrival of a new commander, all the soldiers are working very hard.

"About" a fairly definite "subject" is often **на те́му о** *prp* 'on the subject of' (NB: do not say **о предме́те**):

Он говори́т на те́му о второ́й миро-во́й войне́.	He is speaking on the subject of the Second World War.

If the subject is not specified, **на ... те́му** or **по ... предме́ту** may be used:

---

[1] See IV.6 for some "about" words based on **отнёсу́т – относи́ть** 'relate.'

Он бу́дет до́лго говори́ть на э́ту те́му (по э́тому предме́ту).	He will speak for a long time on that subject.

7. The student has probably already encountered a number of verbs meaning "teach," "study," "learn." Here are the most usual correspondences:

TEACH

(на)учи́ть 'teach' someone (*acc*) something (*dat or inf*):

Он у́чит на́с матема́тике.	He teaches us mathematics.
Я ва́с научу́ е́здить верхо́м.	I will teach you to ride horseback.

преподава́ть *impf only* 'teach' someone (*dat*) something (*acc*) (cf. Lesson I Text):

Она́ преподаёт хи́мию в сре́дней шко́ле.	She teaches chemistry at the high school.

STUDY and LEARN[1]

учи́ть *and* вы́учить – вы́учивают 'study/learn' (commit to memory) *acc*:

Я учу́ ро́ль.	I'm learning (studying) the role.
Мы́ у́чим уро́к.	We're learning (studying) the lesson.
Она́ вы́учила слова́ (наизу́сть).	She learned the words (by heart).

(на)учи́ться 'study/learn' *dat or inf*:

Я учу́сь ру́сскому языку́.	I'm studying Russian.
Я научи́лся ру́сскому языку́.	I learned Russian.
Я учу́сь пла́вать.	I'm learning to swim.
Я научи́лся пла́вать.	I've learned to swim.

изучи́ть – изуча́ют *acc* 'study, make a (thorough) study of, get to know the details of something through study':

Я реши́л изучи́ть ру́сский язы́к.	I've decided to study Russian (become competent in it, study it systematically).
Он изучи́л вое́нную исто́рию.	He has made a study of military history.
Мы́ изуча́ем э́тот вопро́с.	We are studying this question.

занима́ются *impf only*[2] *inst* 'study, work at something'; (without complement) 'study, work' (carry on some mental activity):

---

[1] Verbs meaning "study" are often imperfectives corresponding to perfectives meaning "learn." Cf. R2.A4

[2] This meaning is simply a part of the broader sense of займу́тся (*past tense E*) – занима́ются 'occupy oneself with, be engaged in, go in for, do.'

Он занима́ется в университе́те.	He studies at the university.
Он занима́ется англи́йским язы-ко́м в университе́те.	He studies English at the university.
Я иду́ домо́й занима́ться.	I'm going home to do some work (studying).

TRANSLATION INTO ENGLISH

1. Расскажи́те мне́ насчёт ва́шей програ́ммы в университе́те. **2.** Мо́й гла́вный предме́т поли́тика, но́ я́ та́кже занима́юсь экономи́ческой геогра́фией. **3.** В э́том семе́стре я́ слу́шаю ле́кции профе́ссора Семёнова по филосо́фии. **4.** Я сейча́с гото́влю докла́д по по́воду изуче́ния сове́тского пра́ва настоя́щего вре́мени. **5.** Мо́й това́рищ по ко́мнате рабо́тает над диссерта́цией по сове́тскому пра́ву. Он изуча́ет изве́стные статьи́ сове́тской конститу́ции. **6.** Оди́н из мои́х това́рищей по шко́ле уже́ сде́лался изве́стным учёным. Он рабо́тает в о́бласти физи́ческой хи́мии и написа́л мно́го ва́жных стате́й. Он неда́вно вы́ступил с ре́чью в одно́й из изве́стных лаборато́рий здесь в го́роде, но я́ не по́мню, на каку́ю те́му о́н говори́л. **7.** Я слу́шаю ку́рс ру́сского языка́. Мы́ де́лаем перево́ды с ру́сского языка́ на англи́йский и с англи́йского на ру́сский. **8.** Ва́ше зада́ние на за́втра — проче́сть э́ту передову́ю (статью́) из «Пра́вды». **9.** Не́сколько ра́з в семе́стр мы́ должны́ выступа́ть с докла́дами. **10.** Вы́учите все́ но́вые слова́, чтобы мы́ могли́ обсуди́ть э́тот вопро́с на ру́сском языке́. **11.** Вы́ говори́те, как бу́дто вы́ ча́сто обсужда́ли содержа́ние мое́й диссерта́ции. **12.** Жи́ть в на́шем го́роде для тако́го челове́ка невозмо́жно. Он изве́стный учёный и не хо́чет, чтобы его́ де́ти учи́лись в на́ших шко́лах. На на́ших собра́ниях в Москве́ о́н не ра́з выступа́л про́тив на́ших сре́дних шко́л, и сего́дня ве́чером о́н вы́ступит с ре́чью на те́му о сре́днем образова́нии в на́шей респу́блике. Я ему́ говори́л, что хотя́ и мо́жно критикова́ть на́шу систе́му, но нельзя́ сра́внивать её с моско́вской систе́мой. **13.** Вы́ до изве́стной сте́пени пра́вы. Но́ пока́ на́ши передовы́е учёные в э́той о́бласти не изуча́т э́тот вопро́с бо́лее подро́бно, я́ не могу́ вполне́ согласи́ться с ва́ми. **14.** Эта да́ма поёт настоя́щие по́льские наро́дные пе́сни. Она́ выступа́ет в Центра́льном теа́тре и бу́дет та́м, по кра́йней ме́ре, две́ неде́ли. **15.** Этот аспира́нт сда́ст сво́й у́стный экза́мен без вся́кого труда́. Он до́лго гото́вился к нему́: четы́ре го́да занима́лся и уже́ хорошо́ разбира́ется во все́х подро́бностях. **16.** Мы́ все́ зна́ем о его́ большо́м успе́хе. Спроси́те любо́го учёного в э́той о́бласти, о́н ва́м расска́жет о Бе́льском. Это настоя́щий у́м. Но́ о́н не лю́бит кри́тики. **17.** Середи́н — э́то челове́к без вся́кого образова́ния. Но́ о́н всё-таки гото́в говори́ть на любу́ю те́му. Говоря́т, что о́н когда́-то давно́ бы́л в университе́те, сдава́л экза́мены, но провали́лся на ни́х. С э́того вре́мени о́н де́ржит себя́, бу́дто о́н изве́стный хи́мик. И о́н на са́мом де́ле разбира́ется неплохо́

35 в э́том предме́те, или, по кра́йней ме́ре, лю́ди та́к говоря́т. **18.** Его́ но́вую
рабо́ту мо́жно сравни́ть со вздо́ром, напи́санным по э́тому предме́ту
две́сти ле́т тому́ наза́д. **19.** Ужа́сно! Она́ уе́хала то́лько в четы́ре часа́,
зна́чит, прие́дет сюда́ то́лько в се́мь. **20.** Он три́ го́да занима́лся геоло́гией,
зна́чит, до́лжен разбира́ться в э́том вопро́се. **21.** Я научу́ ва́с води́ть авто-
40 моби́ль. **22.** Я ви́дел со́н, как бу́дто я́ шёл по ле́су. **23.** Педаго́гика е́сть
са́мая сло́жная и разнообра́зная нау́ка. **24.** Это о́чень сло́жный вопро́с;
без во́дки не разберёшься. **25.** На́ши лю́ди хотя́т рабо́тать по возмо́ж-
ности в специа́льных областя́х.

TRANSLATION INTO RUSSIAN

1. These students are discussing the reports without reading them (having
read them). Can one really pass an examination in that way? In my opinion, it's
impossible. **2.** You ought to take a course in psychology. Choose any course;
you'll learn a great deal. **3.** My colleague is giving a report tomorrow evening.
5 He will speak on the subject of the teaching of botany in American high schools.
4. You are an intolerable person without any education at all, as if you'd never
been to high school. **5.** Let's now discuss Soviet college-level schools. What
about the courses? Is it true that one must take courses without any choice at
all? Or is one permitted freely to choose any course? **6.** It is impossible to dis-
10 cuss the contents of that article without comparing them with the rubbish he
wrote when he was a graduate student. **7.** You are taking a real examination.
You will either fail it or pass it. The success or failure of your reports will also
play a role. **8.** Much is now being said about Soviet dissertations of the present
time. Last night they were discussed for a long time at our meeting. I terribly
15 wanted to criticize them, and, finally, couldn't hold out any longer. **9.** Wait
until he delivers the speech. **10.** He may not understand that he is not working
in the right area (R5, note 11). But he is, at least, making a thorough study of
Russian. Later he will take written and oral state exams. He thinks that this will
give him the possibility of getting the doctor's degree. **11.** I know that editorial
20 well, as if I wrote it myself. **12.** It seems to me that you are holding that newspaper as if you don't want to read it. I know that all the journalists are coming
out against your plan, but are you really so afraid of criticism? **13.** How many
articles have you read on this subject (*two ways*)? **14.** Júrij Vasíl'evič is working in the field of biology. I never studied biology. **15.** If you study the content
25 of this article, I think you will understand why I chose this subject for my dissertation. **16.** Anthropologists occupy themselves with all kinds of sociological
questions. **17.** A bacteriologist works in (the field of) bacteriology in this new
bacteriological institute. For this reason we will call him a real scientist. **18.**
One should select a wife not for love, but for economic reasons. **19.** The govern-
30 ment is constantly shouting about economy. **20.** Anybody will tell you that in

order to get a bachelor's degree, one must take certain exams. It's horrible at these exams. At the oral exam you just sit, as at an interrogation. And an oral exam *is* an interrogation. You can't smoke. They ask you all kinds of questions. Any specialist can visit the exam. My roommate told me about it last year. He failed two years ago, but last year studied a great deal, and at the end of last semester passed his exams with an "excellent." He has now made great progress in his field. He isn't a scholar yet, but it is already possible to call him a specialist in archaeology. **21.** You'll recognize this well-known critic by his tall black hat. **22.** Study this role until you learn it. **23.** Let me say a few words with regard to our program. **24.** Bring the report as soon as possible. **25.** I want only good teachers to teach in our college-level schools. But our directors are always thinking about economy. **26.** I don't like her folk songs, but she has the right to perform in any theater. **27.** Mathematics is a very complex science, and I don't understand it (use **разбира́ются в** *prp*). **28.** It's a very complicated matter. But we've got to get to the bottom of it. **29.** I have the right to smoke in my own house. **30.** I rarely have dreams, but last night I had a dream in which (**бу́дто**) I was living in the fifteenth century. It was horribly interesting. I could tell you all the details.

35

40

45

СЛОВА́РЬ

аспира́нт, аспира́нт/ка graduate student
аспирант-у́р-а graduate course
бу́дто, как бу́дто, бу́дто бы II.2
ве́к *E pl* -á century; age, lifetime
вз-до́р rubbish, nonsense
(не)-воз-мо́ж-/н-ый II.1
(не)-воз-мо́ж-н-ость (im)possibility, opportunity
вполне́ quite, fully, entirely
вс-я́к-ий II.3
дире́ктор *E pl* -á director
диссерта́ци-я dissertation
до-кла́д report
ду́х spirit; не в — out of spirits
зна́чит *paren without* что thus, so, this means that
из-ве́ст-/н-ый ВЕД-т well-known, (a) certain; до —ой сте́пени to a certain degree/extent
кра́й-н-*ий* extreme, last; по —ей ме́ре at least; кра́йне extremely
кри́тик-а criticism
ку́рс (academic: по чему́) course; rate of

exchange; слу́шают — take a course; бы́ть в —е дел(а) be in the know
лаборато́ри-я laboratory
люб-о́й II.3
наизу́сть by heart
наро́дная пе́сня: *see* пе́сня
на-у́к-а science
на-сто-я́щ-ий real, actual; present; в —ее вре́мя at the present time; в —ем вре́мени in the present tense
насчёт *кого*/*чего* II.6
не-у-спе́х failure
о́бласть об-ВЛАД *E pl obl* region; area, field (of knowledge, etc.)
о-гро́м-/н-ый enormous, huge
отли́чно: сдать экза́мен на — pass an exam with an "excellent"
перёд-ов-о́й foremost, leading; —áя статья́ editorial
пе́-с/н-я ПЕЙ (*gen pl* пе́сен) song; наро́дная — folk song
пи́сь-м-енн-ый written, writing *adj*
по́-вод: по по́воду *чего* II.6

по-дро́б-н-ость detail
по-дро́б-/н-ый detailed, in detail
пра́в-о *E pl* right; *sg* law (science); име́ют
— *inf* have the right
пред-ме́т object; subject; по э́тому —y on
this/that subject
при-чи́н-а cause, reason; по X-ой —e for X
reason
програ́мм-а program
ре́чь РЁК *E pl obl* speech; a speech; вы́-
ступить – выступа́ют с ре́чью make a
speech; — идёт о *ко́м/чём* X is being
discussed
ро́ль *E pl obl* role; (с)игра́ют (*P* сыгра́ют)
— play role *also fig*
свя́зь: в связи́ с *ке́м/чём* II.6
семе́стр semester
си́л-а strength, force; *pl* forces
си́ль-/н-ый strong, powerful
систе́м-а system
сло́ж-/н-ый complicated, complex; *gr* compound
с/о́/н sleep, dream; ви́деть со́н/сны́ dream,
have a dream/dreams
специал-и́ст specialist

специа́ль-/н-ый special
стать-/я́ article
сте́пень *E pl obl* degree; до изве́стной/
не́которой —и to a certain degree;
— бакала́вра bachelor's degree; маги́-
стерская — master's degree; до́ктор-
ская — doctor's degree
те́м-а subject, theme; на —y о *ко́м/чём* II.6;
на X-ую —y II.6
у́жас horror, terror
ужа́с-/н-ый horrible, terrible, *fig* of very bad
quality; ужа́сно terribly, awfully
(much, badly)
у-спе́х (< успе́ют – успева́ют) success;
успе́хи *pl* progress; (с)де́лают успе́хи
make progress
у́ст-н-ый oral
уч-ён-ый learnèd; scholar, scientist *sub adj*
фи́зик physicist; фи́зик-а physics; физи́ч-
еск-ий physical
хи́мик chemist; хи́ми-я chemistry; хими́ч-
еск-ий chemical
эконо́м-ика economics, economy II.4
эконо́ми-я economy (thrift) II.4

ГЛАГОЛЫ

вы́-б/р-ать (вы́берут) – выбира́ют choose,
select; — *кого́ чём* elect X (as) Y
n вы́бор; *pl* election
раз/о/-бр-а-ть-ся (разберу́тся) – разбира́-
ются в *чём* investigate, gain an understanding of, figure out; *I only* know, be
versed in
n разбо́р
про-ва́л-и-ть – прова́ливают (на экза́ме-
не) fail, flunk *colloq tr*; —ся (на экза́-
мене) fail, flunk *intr*
n прова́л
с-да́-ть – сдава́ть экза́мен *P* pass examination; *I* take an exam
n сда́ча
держ-а́-ть hold, keep; — экза́мен take
examination
вы́-держ-а-ть – выде́рживают sustain,
hold out; — экза́мен *P* pass exam

со-держ-а́-ть contain
n содержа́ние content(s)
за-ним-а́й-ут-ся *чём or without complement*
II.7
критик-ова́-ть *P and I* criticize
кур-и́-ть smoke
с-равн-и́-ть – сра́внивают compare
n сравне́ние
вы́-ступ-и-ть – выступа́ют step/come out/
forward, perform publicly; — с ре́чью
make a speech; — с докла́дом deliver
a report; — с пе́сней perform a song
n выступле́ние performance, speech
об-су́д-и-ть – обсужда́ют discuss, talk over
n обсужде́ние *(Ch5)*
уч-и́-ть(ся), вы́-уч-и-ть – выу́чивают, из-
уч-и́-ть – изуча́ют II.7
n уче́ние, изуче́ние

РАЗГОВОР МЕЖДУ ЛЕНИНЫМ И СТАЛИНЫМ

Советский драматург Всеволод Витальевич Вишневский родился в Петербурге в 1900 году в семье инженера. Он учился в военизированной мужской гимназии. В 1914 году, когда началась война с Германией, он поступил в морской флот и затем служил в армии. Он активно принимал участие в Октябрьской революции. ⁵

Свою литературную работу он начал **во время**⁶ гражданской войны (1920). **За последние тридцать лет**⁶ своей жизни (он умер в 1951) он написал много пьес, одна из которых, написанная в 1949 году, даёт нам возможность познакомиться с великими вождями Советской революции, В. И. Лениным и И. В. Сталиным. Пьеса, из которой мы взяли следующий разговор, называется «Незабываемый 1919-й». ₁₀

Май 1919 года. Кремль. В. И. Ленин сидит в своём кабинете за бумагами. Входит секретарша.

Секретарша.   Вы вызывали товарища Сталина. Он пришёл.
Ленин.   Просите, просите, я жду. ₁₅

Секретарша выходит. Через короткое время в кабинет входит И. В. Сталин.

Ленин.   Здравствуйте, товарищ Сталин. Очень, очень хотел вас видеть. С фронта опять плохие новости. Я хотел вам сказать о том, что меня

20 беспоко́ит — и уже́ не пе́рвый де́нь. Мы́ **ведь**[3] с ва́ми открове́нны до
конца́ — не та́к ли?

Ста́лин. Коне́чно та́к, Влади́мир Ильи́ч. Я говорю́ то́, что ду́маю, хотя́
иногда́ э́то мо́жет не́которым **и**[1] не нра́виться.

Ле́нин. Во́т **и**[1] я хоте́л бы сказа́ть то́, о чём давно́ уже́ ду́маю, и что́, на-
25 верняка́, не понра́вится на́шему Революцио́нному Вое́нному Сове́ту.
Я начина́ю ду́мать, что на́ш Реввоенсове́т не рабо́тает как сле́дует.

Ста́лин. Соверше́нно согла́сен с ва́ми. Несмотря́ на опа́сное положе́ние,
они́ всё стара́ются на́с успока́ивать, уверя́ют на́с, что всё в поря́дке.
Это явля́ется своего́ ро́да обма́ном.

30 *Ле́нин.* Ио́сиф Виссарио́нович, я вы́звал ва́с, чтобы от и́мени Центра́ль-
ного Комите́та проси́ть отпра́виться на Петрогра́дский фро́нт. Я хочу́,
чтобы вы́ при́няли все́ необходи́мые ме́ры в связи́ с опа́сным та́м
положе́нием. Бе́лая а́рмия на́с атаку́ет.

Ста́лин. Сове́тская Росси́я не мо́жет отда́ть Петрогра́д да́же на са́мое
35 коро́ткое вре́мя. Этот го́род име́ет огро́мное значе́ние для на́с. Ведь
э́то[2] Петрогра́д пе́рвый восста́л про́тив буржуази́и.

Ле́нин. То́лько по́мните, — проти́вник опа́сный, души́ть уме́ет.

Ста́лин. **Это**[2] мы́ и́х заду́шим. Не беспоко́йтесь, мы́ на фро́нте всё при-
ведём в поря́док.

40 *Ле́нин.* И наконе́ц ко́нчится э́та ужа́сная гражда́нская война́ и откро́ется
ми́рное строи́тельство. Жела́ю ва́м всего́ до́брого. До свида́ния.

> [Adapted from A. Dubovikov and E. Severin, *Russkaja Sovetskaja
> literatura*, Moscow, 1954, pp. 702–706 and 732]

Equational (то́, что́) constructions

The "equational" principle underlying what we may call **то́, что́** (NB
stressed **что́**) constructions in complex sentences is fundamental in Russian and
is not new to you. You have already seen it in **(то́т)** . . . , **кото́рый** constructions
and, quite possibly, in comparisons of the type **та́к же** . . . **ка́к (и)** and **тако́й
же . . . , како́й (и)**:

Я ви́жу (ту́) кни́гу, кото́рую вы́ чи-та́ете.	I see the book (that/which) you are reading.
Мо́й бра́т та́к же высо́к, ка́к и вы́.	My brother is as tall as you.
Ива́н пи́шет та́к же хорошо́, ка́к Пётр.	Ivan writes as well as Pjotr.
Это така́я же зада́ча, кака́я была́ у на́с вчера́.	This is the same sort of problem as we had yesterday.

Notice the structural similarity between these and the following sentences:

Он рабо́тает та́к, ка́к я́ рабо́таю.	He works like I do.
Он де́лает то́, что́ я́ де́лаю.	He does what I do.
Он лю́бит того́, кого́ я́ люблю́.	He loves the (same) person I do.
Он живёт та́м, где́ я́ живу́.	He lives where I do.
Он ку́рит тогда́, когда́ я́ курю́.	He smokes when I do.

All of these sentences and the many others below have the same basic formula: *demonstrative* **то́** word plus *comma* plus an *interrogative* (relative) **что́** word. **То́** words begin in **т-**; **что́** words usually in **к-** or **ч-**.

An important difference between the Russian and the English is that *Russian* often *retains*[1] the demonstrative where *English* often *omits* it or paraphrases it in various ways. Compare:

Он де́лает то́, что́ я́ де́лаю.	He does what I do.
⊙	He does the things I do.

The English structural equivalent "that which" is not usual here.

Он живёт та́м, где́ я́ живу́.	He lives where I live.
	He lives in the place I live.

The structural equivalent "there where" is impossible.

We recall also that Russian **кото́рый** may not be omitted although the English equivalent may often be:

Он зна́ет (одну́) де́вушку, кото́рую я́ зна́ю.	He knows a girl whom I know.
	He knows a girl I know.

То́, что́ constructions may begin a sentence, or the **то́** and **что́** elements may be separated (as they frequently are in proverbs), but the relationships are the same:

То́, что́ о́н де́лает, мне́ не нра́вится.	What he's doing doesn't please me.
Та́м, где́ бы́л на́ш до́м, стро́ят шко́лу.	They're building a school where our house was.
Та́м хорошо́, где́ на́с не́т.	Wherever we aren't is a nice place.
Чему́ бы́ло нача́ло, тому́ и бу́дет коне́ц.	Whatever has a beginning has an end.

When the elements of **то́, что́** constructions are declinable, their case is determined by their function in the clause in which they occur (we recall this principle from **то́т . . . , кото́рый** constructions):

---

[1] But note in the examples below that Russian may omit an accusative **то́** or genitive **того́** functioning as a direct object. There are, in fact, cases where inclusion of **то́** produces a clumsy or stylistically different sentence from the sentence without **то́**.

Он понима́ет (то),		что́ я де́лаю.
Он не понима́ет (того́),		о чём мы ду́маем.
Он бои́тся того́,	**WHAT**	над чем мы рабо́таем.
Он говори́т о то́м,		чему́ я ра́д.
Он ра́д тому́,		чего́ я не понима́ю.
Он интересу́ется те́м,		чём я занима́юсь.

Translate these combinations orally into English.

The same rules apply to **всё, что́**, or, when more concrete, **всё то́, что́** 'everything/all (that/which)'; **всё** simply replaces **то́** in all instances:

Он ви́дит всё, что́ я де́лаю.	He sees everything (all) that I do.
Я бою́сь всего́ того́, над чём о́н рабо́тает.	I'm afraid of everything he's working on.

"The one who" may be rendered by the appropriate forms of **то́т, кото́рый** (usually a specific person is in mind or has just been mentioned) or **то́т, кто́** (usually in general statements):

Это сде́лал то́т, кото́рый зде́сь бы́л.	The one who was here did that.
Не ошиба́ется то́т, кто́ ничего́ не де́лает.	One who does nothing never makes mistakes.

Sometimes **то́т** can be omitted:

Сча́стлив (то́т), кто́ э́то ви́дел свои́ми глаза́ми.	Happy is he who saw it with his own eyes.

"The ones (The people) who" and "everyone who" are **те́, кто́** and **все́, кто́**. Note that **кто́** may take either a singular (always masculine) or a plural verb:

Те́, Все́,	кто́ хоте́л(и), ушли́ ра́но.	Those Everyone	who wanted to left early.
Те́, Все́,	у кого́ бы́ли де́ньги, запла́тили.	Those Everyone	who had money paid.
Те́м, Все́м,	кто́ провали́лся(лись) на экза́мене, придётся яви́ться к профе́ссору.	Those Everyone	who failed will have to report to the professor.

"Everyone who" in the sense of "each one who" may be **ка́ждый, кто́**:

За обе́дом о́н разгова́ривал с ка́ждым, кто́ подходи́л к столу́.	At dinner he talked with everyone who came up to the table.

SUBORDINATE POINTS

1. И is ordinarily translatable as "and" or, when repeated in the appropriate context, as "both" (R8 note 3). When not translatable as "and," however, **и** may mean:

"also" ("too," "as well"):

Мы́ уве́рены, что о́н **и** ва́с пригласи́т на ве́чер.	We are sure that he will invite you also to the party.
Он **и** в э́том ошиба́ется.	He's mistaken in that as well.

"even":

Таки́е плохи́е но́вости могли́ беспоко́ить **и** Ле́нина.	Such bad news could disturb even Lenin.
Она́ **и** спаси́бо не сказа́ла.	She didn't even say thank you.
И в Москве́ э́то ре́дко встреча́ется.	You rarely encounter that even in Moscow.

"in fact" ("as a matter of fact," "just," "precisely"): *confirmation* of expressed or implicit expectation (close to the idea in **и́менно** or **как ра́з**). This **и** is frequently used before a verb after words like **во́т**, **та́к**, **э́то**, and others:

Та́к э́то **и** бы́ло.	That's the way it was as a matter of fact.
Этого я́ **и** ожида́л.	I was expecting that in fact.
Он здесь **и** живёт.	It's here that he lives (in fact).
Это **и** е́сть моё мне́ние.	That *is* (in fact) my opinion.
Во́т мы́ **и** прие́хали.	Here we are. (Well, we've arrived.)
Вот я́ ва́м **и** говорю́.	That's just what I'm telling you.

2. A similar meaning is conveyed by the following usage of **э́то**:

Это Ива́н пи́шет на доске́.	That's Ivan writing on the board.
Это, должно́ быть, игра́ет Ойстрах.	That must be Ojstrax (Oistrakh) playing.
Это Ива́н не рабо́тает ка́к сле́дует.	Ivan's the one who's not working as he should.
Это его́ я́ встре́тил вчера́.	It was he (whom) I met yesterday.
Что́ э́то вы́ та́м де́лаете?	What is it you're doing there?
Где́ э́то вы́ служи́ли в а́рмии?	Where was it that you served in the army?

NOTE: Do not use **кото́рый** in such expressions.

3. The *stressless* particle **ведь** (pronounced [v'it']) most often corresponds to "after all" in English, but the expressions "you know, you see, surely, why, of course" may also be appropriate translations:

Коне́чно вы́ э́то слы́шали, ведь я́ са́м ва́м сказа́л.	Of course you heard that—after all (why) I told you myself.
Я не могу́ прийти́, я́ ведь за́нят по вечера́м.	I can't come—I'm busy evenings, you know (you see, after all).
Ведь о́н на́м помо́жет.	Surely he'll help us (won't he?).

4. Notice also:

Он жи́л то́ в Омске, то́ в То́мске.	He lived now in Omsk, now in Tomsk.
Она́ то́ крича́ла, то́ пла́кала.	Now she shouted, now she wept.
Он приходи́л то́ по утра́м, то́ по вечера́м.	He came now mornings, now evenings.

5. Notice that English "unless" is approximately equivalent to "if . . . not," which in Russian is rendered by **е́сли . . . не**:

Я приду́, е́сли до́ждь не пойдёт.	I'll come unless it rains.
	I'll come if it doesn't rain.

6. Action concurrent with time is handled in various ways in Russian:

a. **За** or **в** plus the accusative of a time expression means "during the course of." Used with a *perfective* verb, these prepositions indicate an action *completed* during a *specific period* (**за** is particularly common here):

За э́ту неде́лю я́ написа́л статью́.	During that week I wrote an article.
Она́ за пя́ть ме́сяцев мно́гому научи́лась.	She learned a lot in five months.
За (В) после́днее вре́мя рабо́чие всё акти́внее принима́ют уча́стие в э́том де́ле.	Recently the workers have been taking part more and more actively in this affair.

(Note that when "recently" refers to a point in time, it is usually translated by **неда́вно**: **Он прие́хал неда́вно** 'He arrived recently.')

b. **В тече́ние** (and, less commonly **в продолже́ние** and **на протяже́нии**) used with an *imperfective* verb describes action going on *over a period of time*:

В тече́ние э́той неде́ли я́ писа́л статью́.	During that week I was writing an article.
В продолже́ние у́жина о́н мно́го говори́л.	He talked a great deal during supper.
На протяже́нии 19-ого ве́ка Росси́я остава́лась в состоя́нии засто́я. (Karpovich)	Over the nineteenth century Russia remained in a condition of stagnancy.

c. **В течéние** also has the meaning "at some/any stage" of time, "in the course" of something. **Во врéмя** (also plus genitive) has the same meaning, but it is most often used with historical events, natural phenomena, and other activities with which the coinciding action has only an incidental connection. **Во врéмя** is not normally used with periods of time: **в течéние** (not **во врéмя**) **недéли**:

Он э́то сказа́л в течéние своегó докла́да.	He said that in the course of his report. (*Verb related to the report.*)
Он роди́лся во врéмя войны́.	He was born during the war. (*Verb unrelated in this and next two examples*)
Они́ пришли́ во врéмя грозы́.	They arrived during a thunderstorm.
Во врéмя лéкции нельзя́ кури́ть.	Smoking is forbidden during the lecture.

NOTE: Do not confuse **во врéмя** *gen* with **вóвремя** "on time": **Мы́ пришли́ вóвремя** 'We came on time.'

TRANSLATION INTO ENGLISH

1. Случи́лось тó, чегó всé боя́лись. **2.** Ктó вéсел, тóт смеётся. **3.** Я не тóт, за когó вы́ меня́ принима́ете. **4.** Он тóлько что верну́лся отту́да, куда́ собира́ется éхать мóй бра́т. **5.** Он получи́л тóт же отвéт от всéх, когó óн об э́том спра́шивал. **6.** Это как ра́з тó, что я́ хотéл купи́ть для Белóвой. **7.** Почему́ та́к случи́лось, ведь я́ при́нял всé необходи́мые мéры в связи́ с э́тим дéлом? **8.** Чтó вы́ собира́етесь дéлать в связи́ с тéм, что случи́лось? **9.** Вóт я́ ва́м и говори́л. Дóктора легкó найти́ тóлько тогда́, когда́ óн не ну́жен. **10.** Он служи́л тó в Москвé, тó в Ленингра́де. **11.** Моя́ жена́ совершéнно не согла́сна со мнóй в э́том. Она́ меня́ всё увера́ет, что её бра́т рабóтает как слéдует, нó ведь меня́ увéрить в э́том мóжет тóлько óн са́м. **12.** Несмотря́ на всé мéры, при́нятые на́ми, мы́ с фрóнта опя́ть получа́ем тóлько плохи́е нóвости. **13.** Лéнин всегда́ отправля́л Ста́лина туда́, гдé нарóд восстава́л прóтив буржуази́и. **14.** Мы́ всегда́ беспокóимся, когда́ на́ши воéнные дела́ иду́т плóхо. **15.** Успокóйтесь, пожа́луйста. Това́рищ Иóсиф Виссариóнович Ста́лин, вели́кий вóждь нарóда, увера́ет, что в э́той мировóй войнé бу́дут принима́ть уча́стие тóлько тé, ктó не служи́л(и) в пéрвой. **16.** Это Лéнин сказа́л, что у ва́с нéт никакóго поря́дка. Нó э́то Ста́лин увéрил меня́, что положéние опа́сное. **17.** Лéнин сегóдня не принима́ет. **18.** Откровéнно говоря́, я́ ду́маю, что в Революциóнном Воéнном Совéте далекó не всё в поря́дке. **19.** На́ша гражда́нская война́ имéет для всегó ми́ра огрóмное значéние. Она́ даёт на́м возмóжность задуши́ть всéх проти́вников Совéтского Сою́за и потóм откры́ть ми́рное строи́тельство. **20.** Проти́вник ско́ро бу́дет атакова́ть по всему́ фро́нту. Он наверня́ка займёт и наш го́род. **21.** Ты́ отда́й то́, что взя́л у меня́! (Отве́т) Я у тебя́ ничего́ не бра́л. **22.** Во вре́мя заня́тий о́чень тру́дно найти́ ко́мнату о́коло университе́та. **23.** В тече́ние не́скольких секу́нд о́н стоя́л та́м и не говори́л ни сло́ва. **24.** Га́ля ничего́ не сказа́ла об э́том в тече́ние на́шего разгово́ра. Она́ наверняка́ мне ска́жет за́втра во вре́мя ле́кции. **25.** Через два́ часа́ вы́ бу́дете сдава́ть экза́мен. То́лько не беспоко́йтесь. Ведь за э́то вре́мя вы́ без труда́ вы́учите все́ слова́. Я уве́рен, что вы́ отли́чно напи́шете экза́мен, е́сли вы́ не забу́дете слова́. Это в поря́дке веще́й. **26.** Мы́ зна́ем, что у ва́с е́сть изве́стный поря́док, но ведь и у на́с е́сть своего́ ро́да поря́док. **27.** Что́ вы́ ду́маете де́лать в связи́ с э́тим де́лом? **28.** Если вы́ не согласи́тесь привести́ свои́ дела́ в поря́док, я ва́с вы́зову на объясне́ния. **29.** В ва́шем положе́нии я́ бы поступи́л по-друго́му. **30.** Мо́й оте́ц всегда́ стара́лся бы́ть хоро́шим солда́том. **31.** Я постара́юсь объясни́ть ва́м всё. **32.** Пра́вильно, но́ всё же настоя́щее положе́ние меня́ ужа́сно ду́шит. **33.** Этот челове́к име́ет свя́зи; придётся пригласи́ть его́ на ве́чер. Тогда́ о́н наверняка́ согласи́тся на на́ш ма́ленький обма́н. **34.** Эта пье́са име́ет мирову́ю изве́стность. **35.** В э́том магази́не име́ются вся́кого ро́да кни́ги. **36.** В настоя́щее вре́мя о́чень опа́сно писа́ть на таку́ю те́му. Не на́до выступа́ть про́тив того́, что́ име́ет свя́зь с интере́сами наро́да. **37.** Игорь меня́ не ра́з обма́нывал, но́ я́ ничего́ не име́ю про́тив него́.

Посло́вицы и погово́рки

1. Кто́ лю́бит труди́ться, тому́ без де́ла не сиди́тся. **2.** Чего́ себе́ не хо́чешь, того́ дру́гу не жела́й. **3.** Чего́ не лю́бишь, того́ и не ку́пишь. До́ма е́шь то́, что хо́чешь, а в гостя́х, что даю́т. **4.** У кого́ рабо́та, у того́ и хле́б. Кто́ не рабо́тает, то́т не е́ст. **5.** Чего́ мно́го, то́ и дёшево, а чего́ ма́ло, то́ и до́рого. **6.** Кто́ говори́т, что́ хо́чет, услы́шит, чего́ и не хо́чет. **7.** У дурака́ что́ на уме́, то и на языке́. **8.** То́т труда́ не бои́тся, кто́ уме́ет труди́ться. **9.** На́до взя́ть от жи́зни всё, что она́ мо́жет да́ть.

DRILL

From the sentences **Он зна́ет э́то** and **Я зна́ю э́то** we build an equational sentence **Он зна́ет то́, что́ я́ зна́ю.** Make similar sentences from the following:

1. Я принёс э́то. Ты́ проси́л э́то. **2.** Он смеётся над э́тим. Я занима́юсь э́тим. **3.** Мы́ говори́ли о ни́х. Мы́ и́х неда́вно ви́дели. **4.** Она́ бои́тся э́того. Вы́ у́читесь э́тому. **5.** Она́ ра́да всему́ э́тому. Вы́ говори́ли об э́том. **6.** Это случи́лось. Это не должно́ повтори́ться. **7.** Мы́ пое́дем туда́. Та́м жду́т на́с друзья́. **8.** Я не ве́рю всему́. Вы́ говори́те э́то.

TRANSLATION INTO RUSSIAN

1. Did you notice what she gave him? **2.** They are worrying about what might happen, unless Véra Pávlovna comes on time. **3.** Give my secretary everything she has chosen. She wants everything we need in connection with our new work. **4.** He works now for the Revolutionary Military Council, now for Lenin himself. **5.** He who works at the university as he should (properly) will not have to serve in the army. **6.** Please translate what this man is trying to say. **7.** He's trying all the time, but one can't say that he is making progress. **8.** Bring each one what he needs. **9.** In five years he has read 250 books. **10.** In the course of the lesson we began to understand what the teacher was trying to say. **11.** The leader of the Soviet people loves all people who were born during the October Revolution. **12.** I took him for a professor, but he turned out to be the dramatist who wrote a play about the civil war. How is it you haven't heard of him? Why, his book has enormous significance. He was the one who kept assuring Lenin that the situation at the front was dangerous. It's such people who participate actively in the peaceful construction of socialism. **13.** Please send Comrade Stalin to the front and tell him to take all the necessary measures. The news from the front doesn't calm me at all; military affairs are going badly today and will go badly tomorrow as well, unless the Kremlin immediately summons Iósif Vissariónovič there. **14.** We are all agreed that even Lenin should be invited to this party. It isn't far from here to the Kremlin, you know. Well, (then) I'll invite him (и before verb). **15.** Frankly speaking, it seems to me that our position is a dangerous one. I am certain that the people will soon revolt against their leaders, if we don't succeed in quieting them down. In connection with this Vladímir Il'íč is setting out for the front today. Two weeks ago Lenin's words would have provoked great joy, but now the people are afraid of some sort of deceit. They aren't sure that Lenin always acts properly. He keeps trying to convince them that everything is all right, in spite of all kinds of bad news. According to this news, the situation is so bad that we will have to give up Petrográd. The people are challenging Lenin to (на *acc*) frankness, are asking that he make a speech, but I don't think he'll agree to this. He likes to talk at parties, at which everybody agrees (use verb) with him, where he asks questions and all the other people only answer them. A conversation with him is (use являются), in its way, an interrogation. **16.** I should not have agreed with what you said. **17.** You have deceived me. And in spite of what you say, I never deceive anybody. **18.** I have nothing against this agreement with the enemy. But I will never agree to his participation in the formation of our new government. **19.** This revolt is indispensable for our revolution.

СЛОВА́РЬ

акти́в-/н-ый active

буржуази́-я bourgeoisie

ведь III.3

ве́чер (на) *E pl* -á evening; (evening) party (*also* вечери́нка)

во́ждь *ME* leader

гимна́зи-я high school (in prerevolutionary Russia and in certain other countries)

гражд-а́н-ск-ий **ГРАД**[1] civil; —ая война́ civil war

драмату́рг playwright, dramatist

дур-а́к *E* (ду́р-а *F*) fool, idiot

и́мя: от и́мени in the name of, on behalf of

кабине́т study

Кре́мль *M E* Kremlin

ме́р-а measure; по кра́йней —е at least

ми́р *E pl* peace; world

ми́р-/н-ый peaceful

мир-ов-о́й world(wide)

наве́рно probably

наверняка́ surely, for sure

на-ро́д people, the people, the nation; ру́с-ский — the Russian people

наро́д-н-ый popular, people's, national

не-об-хо́д-и́м-ый indispensable, necessary; необходи́мо *inf*/чтобы it is necessary (in order) to

несмотря́ на что́ in spite of, despite

но́в-ость *E pl obl* piece of news; novelty; но́вости news

об-ма́н deceit, deception, fraud

о-гро́м-/н-ый enormous, huge, immense

октя́бр[2]-ск-ий October *adj*

о-па́с-/н-ый dangerous

от-кров-е́н-/н-ый **КРОЙ**[1] frank, sincere, open

по-ря́д-/о/к order; в —ке in order, all right; приведу́т – приводить в — put/set in order; в —ке веще́й natural, in the nature of things

про́тив кого́/чего́ against; opposite

проти́в-ник opponent, enemy

пьес-а (stage) play

революци́-о́н-н-ый revolutionary

револю́ци-я revolution

ро́д: своего́ —a X in its/a way, a special kind of X; *cf. also* вся́кого —a X all kinds of X; тако́го —a X such X

с-вя́зь connection, communication, liaison; love affair; II.6

как сле́дует as one should/ought to, properly

со-ве́т advice; council, Soviet

со-гла́с-/н-ый *used mostly in short-form predicate*; — с ке́м/че́м agree with; — на что́ agree to; согла́сно кому́/чему́ according to

стро-и́-тель-ств-о building, construction

ум *E* mind, wit, intellect; на —é on (one's) mind; с/о/йдут – сходить с —á go out of one's mind; приду́т – приходить кому́ на — come into one's head, occur to one

фро́нт (на) *E pl* front

у-ча́ст-ие participation; interest, sympathy; share; при́мут – принима́ют — в чём take part, participate in

ГЛАГО́ЛЫ

атак-ова́-ть *P and I* attack

n ата́ка

у-ве́р-и-ть — уверя́ют в чём assure, convince of; я уве́рен I'm sure/certain

n увере́ние

со-глас-и́-ть-ся – соглаша́ются с ке́м/че́м

agree with; — на что́ consent to

n соглаше́ние agreement; согла́сие consent

от-да́-ть – отдава́ть give back; give up, surrender

n отда́ча

(за)-**душ**-и-ть strangle, suffocate; *fig* crush, oppress

вы́-з/в-а-ть(вы́зовут) – вызыва́ют call out, summon, challenge, provoke, cause

n вы́зов call; challenge

знач-и-ть mean

n значе́ние meaning, significance, import; име́ют значе́ние have significance

при͡-м-ут – принима́ют ЙМ receive, accept, take, assume; — ме́ры take measures; — уча́стие в *чём* participate/take part in

n приня́тие reception, taking; приём reception (guests, etc.), receiving

по-**лож**-и-ть – кладу́т

n положе́ние position, situation

об-**ма͡н**-ну-ть – обма́нывают deceive, cheat

n обма́н fraud, deception

бес-**поко́й**-и-ть upset, disturb; —ся о *ко́м/ чём* be/become upset/disturbed about

у-с-**поко́й**-и-ть – успока́ивают calm, quiet down *tr*; —ся calm/quiet oneself down

n успокое́ние

от-**пра́в**-и-ть – отправля́ют send off; —ся set/start off

n отправле́ние

вос-**ста́н**-ут – восстава́ть revolt, rise up (in a rebellion)

n восста́ние

тёк-у́т flow

n тече́ние flow, current, course; в тече́ние *чего́* III.6

про-**тя͡г**-ну-ть – протя́гивают stretch, extend

n протяже́ние; на протяже́нии *чего́* III.6

LESSON IV

Fact-oriented constructions:
A. то, что (*unstressed*)
B. то, *interrogative*

БОРЬБА́ ЗА МИ́Р И ДРУ́ЖБУ

Важне́йшим истори́ческим собы́тием яви́лся 22-ой съезд Коммунисти́ческой Па́ртии Сове́тского Сою́за, кото́рый указа́л пу́ть вперёд, в све́тлое бу́дущее **всему́ челове́честву**.⁴ᵃ Большо́е значе́ние э́того съе́зда заключа́ется в то́м, что впервы́е в исто́рии ста́ло возмо́жным поста́вить на пове́стку дня́ практи́ческую програ́мму построе́ния коммуни́зма. Эта програ́мма представля́ет собо́й филосо́фское, экономи́ческое и полити́ческое обоснова́ние строи́тельства коммуни́зма. В не́й определены́ конкре́тные зада́чи Сове́тского наро́да в о́бласти промы́шленности, се́льского хозя́йства, национа́льных **отноше́ний**,⁶ нау́ки, культу́ры.

Програ́мма э́та исхо́дит из того́, что социали́зм тепе́рь ока́зывает реша́ющее влия́ние на хо́д мировы́х собы́тий. Но она́ **не мо́жет не**¹ принима́ть во внима́ние та́кже и то́, что, пока́ существу́ет империали́зм, сохраня́ется и опа́сность войны́. Собы́тия после́дних ле́т пока́зывают, что монополисти́ческая буржуази́я (капитали́зм) продолжа́ет проводи́ть поли́тику агре́ссии и вое́нных авантю́р. Это в пе́рвую о́чередь **отно́сится**⁶ к то́й её ча́сти, кото́рая свя́зана с вое́нным произво́дством. Де́ло в то́м, что руководи́тели капиталисти́ческих корпора́ций, производя́щих вооруже́ние, ока́зывают са́мое серьёзное противоде́йствие сове́тским мероприя́тиям, напра́вленным на сохране́ние ми́ра, на всео́бщее и по́лное разоруже́ние, **вообще́ говоря́**,⁷ на поли́тику ми́рного сосуществова́ния с За́падом.

Всё э́то привело́ к тому́, что Сове́тский Сою́з, как са́мое мо́щное в экономи́ческом и вое́нном отноше́нии госуда́рство ла́геря социали́зма, до́лжен держа́ть свои́ вооружённые си́лы на высо́ком у́ровне. Внима́тель-

182

ные лю́ди во всех стра́нах ми́ра **не мо́гут не**[1] **ви́деть, как**[2]   Сове́тский
Сою́з, вме́сте со всем социалисти́ческим ла́герем, бо́рется **за**[4b] ми́р и   25
дру́жбу. Мы́ твёрдо уве́рены в то́м, что на́ше де́ло пра́вое; мы́ убеждены́,
что побе́да оста́нется за на́ми. Ну́, присту́пим к де́лу. Вперёд к побе́де
коммуни́зма!

[Adapted from M. Baturin and S. Tarov, *Vnešnjaja politika
Sovetskogo Sojuza na sovremennom ètape*, Moscow, 1962]

A. То́, что (unstressed)

Я понима́ю (то́), **что́** вы́ чита́ете.	I understand *what* you are reading.
Я понима́ю (то́), **что** вы́ чита́ете.	I understand *that* you are reading.
То́, **что́** вы́ чита́ете, интересу́ет меня́.	What you are reading interests me.
То́, **что** вы́ чита́ете, интересу́ет меня́.	The fact that you are reading interests me.

The sentences in these pairs are superficially rather similar but are fundamentally diverse in structure, meaning, and pronunciation. The first of each pair
is an equational **то́, что́** sentence of the type treated in Lesson III. In the second
sentences the (stressless) **что** is a mere connective "that," and the **то́** is not a
demonstrative; it is a purely grammatical or "dummy" word with no real
meaning of its own. When translated at all, it is usually rendered by "the fact
that," "a situation in which," or similar expressions.

Many sentences with which you have been working for a long time are in
fact **то́, что** sentences with the **то́** omitted. An accusative **то́** or genitive **того́**
functioning as a direct object is almost always omitted unless there is particular
emphasis on "the fact that," and (unlike **то́, что́** types) the **то́** word may be
omitted in the oblique cases as well:

Я по́мню (то́), что о́н сде́лал э́то.	I remember (the fact) that he did it.
Я не зна́л (того́), что о́н зде́сь.	I didn't know (the fact) that he was here.
Я бою́сь (того́), что о́н э́то ска́жет.	I fear (the situation) that he'll say it.
Я ра́д (тому́), что вы́ зде́сь.	I'm glad (of the fact) that you are here.
Я уве́рен (в то́м), что о́н зде́сь.	I'm sure (of the fact) that he is here.

With more complex statements, particularly in written language, the **то́** word is
often included. After prepositions, of course, it is mandatory:

О то́м, что они́ пожени́лись, я уз-на́л случа́йно.	I found out by chance about their having gotten married.

Мы́ недово́льны те́м, что о́н заплати́л за э́то.	We're displeased with the fact that he paid for it.
Не ну́жно забыва́ть и того́, что За́падная Герма́ния сильна́.	Nor should one forget (the fact) that West Germany is strong.
Спаси́бо за то́, что вы́ сде́лали э́то.	Thanks for having done it.
Несмотря́ на то́, что о́н живёт здесь уже́ давно́, о́н почти́ ничего́ не зна́ет о на́шей стране́.	In spite of the fact that he's lived here a long time, he knows almost nothing about our country.
Ясно то́лько то́, что никто́ не хо́чет войны́.	The only thing that is clear is that no one wants war.

То́, что, like **то́, что́**, may be split up:

Не то́ ва́жно, что оди́н челове́к у́мер, а ва́жны причи́ны его́ сме́рти.	What is important is not that this one person died, but the reasons for his death.

Note the important expression **де́ло в то́м, что** (and other **де́ло в** *prp*):

Де́ло в то́м, что мы́ за ми́р.	The fact is that we are for peace.
В чём ту́т де́ло?	What's going on (What's involved) here?
Не в то́м де́ло.	That isn't what's involved.
Всё де́ло в вы́боре.	The whole thing is in the choice.

Note also the useful expression **те́м, что** 'in that':

Ва́ш пла́н хоро́ш те́м, что о́н всё принима́ет во внима́ние.	Your plan is good in that it takes everything into account.
Она́ помога́ет на́м те́м, что не рабо́тает для проти́вника.	She helps us in that she doesn't work for the enemy.

B. То́, interrogative

Observe the following examples:

Это зави́сит от того́, чья́ жена́ лу́чше зна́ет ру́сский язы́к.	That depends on whose wife knows Russian best.
Мы́ э́то сде́лаем согла́сно тому́, ка́к вы́ посове́туете.	We will do that in accordance with how you (will) advise.
О то́м, когда́ о́н прие́хал, не́ было ни сло́ва.	No one said anything about when he came.
О то́м, прие́хал ли о́н, не́ было ни сло́ва.	No one said anything about whether he came.
Всё зави́сит от того́, хоро́ший ли о́н студе́нт.	Everything depends on whether he is a good student.

Я поражён тем, как хорошо он пишет.	I'm struck with how well he writes.
Я возмущён тем, где вы живёте.	I'm indignant about where you live.

NOTE:

Мы спорили о том, кто пришёл.	We argued about which one came. *Or:* We argued about the one who came.

The written Russian is the same, but in the first (fact-oriented) statement the **кто** receives a stronger stress than the **кто** in the second (**то, что**) statement. The same difference emerges in the graphic homonyms:

Я интересуюсь тем, что вы читаете. (то, *interrogative type*)	I'm interested in what it is you're reading (in the *fact* of what it is).
Я интересуюсь тем, что вы читаете. (то, что *type*)	I'm interested in what you're reading (in the actual material).

If the **то** in a **то**, *interrogative* sentence is syntactically a direct object, it is omitted, and the homonymity described above is avoided, even though the English translation of the **то**, *interrogative* and **то, что** sentences might be the same:

Я помню, что он сказал.	(то, *interr*)	⎫
Я помню то, что он сказал.	(то, что)	⎬ I remember what he said. ⎭

Я не понимаю, за что мы боремся.	(то, *interr*)	⎫ I don't understand what we
Я не понимаю того, за что мы боремся.	(то, что)	⎬ are fighting for. ⎭

SUBORDINATE POINTS

1. The student should always note the position of the particle **не** in a sentence. If the **не** does not directly precede the verb, the meaning is significantly changed; what is denied is not the action but whatever the **не** precedes. Note the following examples:

Я не веду урока.	I'm not conducting the lesson.
Не я веду урок.	I'm not the one conducting the lesson (but someone is conducting it).
Я не урок веду.	It's not a lesson I'm conducting.
Я не еду в Лондон.	I'm not going to London.
Не я еду в Лондон.	I'm not the one going to London.
Я не в Лондон еду.	It isn't London I'm going to.

Я сего́дня не получи́л письма́.	I didn't get a letter today.
Я не сего́дня получи́л письмо́.	It wasn't today I got a (the) letter.
Он ни ра́зу не говори́л э́того.	He never said that once.
Он не ра́з говори́л э́то.	He said that more than once.

Compare also:

| Я о́чень не люблю́ её. | Это совсе́м не я́сно. |
| Я не о́чень люблю́ её. | Это не совсе́м я́сно. |

and

| Он взя́л не ту́ доро́гу.[1] | He took the wrong road. |

Compare the following carefully:

Вы́ не мо́жете согласи́ться с э́тим.	You can't agree with that.
Вы́ мо́жете не согласи́ться с э́тим.	You may not agree with that.[2]
Вы́ не мо́жете не согласи́ться с э́тим.	You can't not agree with that. (You can't help agreeing with that.)

Translate:

Это не мо́жет игра́ть та́м ро́ли.
Это мо́жет не игра́ть та́м ро́ли.
Это не мо́жет не игра́ть та́м ро́ли.

2. To *perceive* somebody doing something is: *verb of perception* plus comma plus **ка́к**. Do not translate **ка́к** by "how" in such sentences:

Я ви́дел, ка́к о́н ушёл.	I saw him leave.
Я ви́дел, ка́к они́ уходи́ли.	I saw them leaving.
Я слы́шал, ка́к о́н задава́л вопро́сы.	I heard him asking questions.
Я заме́тил, ка́к о́н положи́л что́-то в карма́н.	I noticed him put something into his pocket.

Compare **Я ви́дел, что о́н ушёл** 'I saw that he had left.' **Что** instead of **ка́к** indicates not perception of the action, but awareness after the fact.

3a. The numeral **о́ба** (*masc/neu*) – **о́бе** (*fem*) means "both/the two." In the nominative/accusative it acts like **два́ – две́**; i.e. takes a noun in the genitive

---

[1] Note that **не то́т**, like **ничто́, никто́**, etc., is "split" by a preposition:

| Он рабо́тает не в то́й о́бласти. | He's working in the wrong field. |

[2] The sense is "You possibly don't agree with that" or "You don't have to agree with that."

singular and an adjective in the genitive plural if the noun is masculine or neuter, in the nominative plural if the noun is feminine:

óба нóвых столá   óбе нóвые кнѝги
óба нóвых перá

In the oblique cases it behaves like a plural adjective: **обóих – обéих, обóими – обéими, обóим – обéим**, agreeing with the case of the plural noun or pronoun:

Я вѝжу ѝх обóих.	I see them both.
Я довóлен обéими студéнтками.	I am satisfied with both students (*fem*).

A verb used with **óба – óбе** is always in the plural: **Оба онѝ пришлѝ**.

Note that **óба – óбе** used with a negated verb may be translated as "neither":

Онѝ óба не пришлѝ.	Neither of them came.

b. When the noun or pronoun is not mentioned, "both" ("neither") may be expressed by **и тóт и другóй** (**ни тóт ни другóй**) in the appropriate case and gender. Where the thing talked about is not specific or has no specifiable gender, or if specific objects of different genders are involved, the impersonal **и тó и другóе** (**ни тó ни другóе**) is used:

Какóй из э́тих двýх городóв вы бóльше лю́бите? Я люблю́ и тóт и другóй.	Which of the two cities do you like best? I like both.
Вы лю́бите игрáть в кáрты ѝли в шáхматы? Я люблю́ и тó и другóе.	Do you like to play cards or chess? I like both.
Я ни о тóм ни о другóм не говорю́.	I'm not talking about either one (of those things, ideas, etc.).

4. The meanings conveyed by the English preposition "for" are represented in a variety of ways in Russian:

a. **Для** has denotations including purpose, application, and use, as well as "for the sake of" and, in addition, the "for" which suggests disproportionateness ("big for his age"):

учéбник для нерýсских шкóл	a textbook for non-Russian schools
библиотéка для детéй	a library for children
Эта статья́ необходѝма для моéй рабóты.	This article is indispensable for my work.
Очень жáрко для Москвы́.	It's very hot for Moscow.

In certain contexts **для** plus the genitive in the meaning "for" may be replaced by the *dative* case without a preposition (the so-called "ethical dative"). The first sentence of the text above:

в све́тлое бу́дущее всему́ челове́че-   into a bright future *for* all mankind
ству

illustrates this type of dative, but more common examples in everyday speech are such sentences as:

Во́т ва́м письмо́.   Here's a letter *for* you.
Я ва́м э́то сде́лаю.   I'll do that *for* you.

Для plus the genitive is also possible, of course, in all these examples.

b. **За** plus the accusative[1] often expresses "for" in the sense of requital, compensation, replacement, or favor:

Я заплати́л ему́ за статью́.   I paid him for the article.

Спаси́бо за папиро́сы. Не́ за что.   Thanks for the cigarettes. Don't mention it.

Мы́ бо́ремся за свобо́дную, демо-карти́ческую Слобо́вию.   We are fighting for a free, democratic Slobovia.

Я сча́стлив за Ва́ню.   I'm happy for Vanja.

Compare:

Сде́лайте э́то { для меня́. / за меня́. }   Do this { for me (for my benefit/sake). / for me (in my place). }

c. **На** plus the accusative often has the meaning "for" in the sense of assignment, allocation, or distribution; it is quite close to and sometimes interchangeable with **для** in such meanings:

зада́ние на за́втра (на четве́рг)   assignment for tomorrow (for Thursday)

биле́т на Москву́   a ticket for Moscow
по кни́ге на ка́ждого   a book for each person
гара́ж на 500 автомоби́лей   garage for 500 cars
Эти де́ньги иду́т на раке́ты.   This money goes for rockets.
На что́ ва́м э́то ну́жно?   What do you need that for?

The **на** in sentences like **Он прие́хал сюда́ на 10 дней** belongs here also. Note also the adverbs **навсегда́** 'forever' and **надо́лго** 'for a long time':

---

[1] Do not confuse with за *inst* used with verbs of "fetching" ("to go/send for"); **сходить за молоко́м, посла́ть за до́ктором. За** *inst* may also mean "at" (some activity) **за обе́дом,** or, sometimes, "due to" **за ста́ростью ле́т.**

Он уе́хал навсегда́.	He's left for good.
Вы́ надо́лго к на́м?	Are you coming for a long time?

5. Уро́к is the most general word for "lesson" in all senses. It sometimes means "homework," though this is more likely to be **дома́шняя рабо́та** or **дома́шнее зада́ние** (assignment—*n* from **за́дать – задава́ть**). **Заня́тие** (*n* from **за́ймут(ся) – занима́ют(ся)**) means "occupation, pursuit" in the singular; in the plural it means "business that is going on" or, in an academic context, "studies, lessons, classes":

Э́то бу́дет хоро́ший уро́к для него́.	That will be a good lesson for him.
Все́ бы́ли на уро́ке/на заня́тиях.	Everyone was at the lesson/at class(es).
Каки́е у ва́с заня́тия в университе́те?	What sort of studies do you have at the university?
часы́ заня́тий	hours of operation: office hours, school hours, etc.

6. The verbs and verbals built with **от-НЁС – от-НОС-и** 'relate' form a particularly useful group: **отнесу́т – относи́ть** (*n* **отнесе́ние**) 'relate, put down to, ascribe'; **отнесу́тся – относи́ться** (*n* **отноше́ние**) к *dat* 'relate oneself to, treat, have X attitude to'; **относи́тель/ный** 'relative.'

То́, что ска́зано о фи́зике, мо́жно отнести́ и к други́м областя́м есте́ственных нау́к.	What has been said about physics pertains to other branches of the natural sciences as well.
Наско́лько мы́ зна́ем, э́то зда́ние отно́сится к четы́рнадцатому ве́ку.	As far as we know, this building dates back to the fourteenth century.
Он хорошо́ отно́сится к на́м.	He treats us well (has a good attitude toward us).
Ка́к вы́ отно́ситесь к моему́ пла́ну.	What is your attitude toward my plan?
Э́то к де́лу не отно́сится.	That's beside the point.
Его́ отве́т не име́ет ни мале́йшего отноше́ния к вопро́су.	His answer hasn't the slightest relation to the question.
Отноше́ния ме́жду двумя́ госуда́рствами тепе́рь немно́го лу́чше.	The relations between the two states are now a little better.
В э́том отноше́нии я́ с ва́ми соверше́нно согла́сен.	In this respect I'm completely in agreement with you.
У него́ отноше́ние к рабо́те о́чень серьёзное.	His attitude toward his work is a very serious one.

Он с на́ми в о́чень плохи́х отно-ше́ниях.	He's on very bad terms with us.
Что́ вы́ ска́жете относи́тельно э́того пла́на (по отноше́нию к э́тому пла́ну)?	What do you have to say with respect to this plan?
Мо́ре бы́ло относи́тельно споко́й-но.	The sea was relatively calm.
Оди́н изве́стный учёный выступа́ет про́тив тео́рии относи́тельности.	A well-known scholar is coming out against the theory of relativity.

7. В о́бщем means "generally, on the whole." **Вообще́** may have the same meaning,[1] but often is more categorical and means "in general" in the sense of "always, altogether," sometimes with the idea of "in the first place." It is used when the speaker has said (or there has been implied) something partial about something and decides to extend it to the whole. In a negative or interrogative context, **вообще́** is once again categorical, meaning "(not) at all," while **в о́бщем** again simply means "generally":[2]

В о́бщем вы́шло о́чень глу́по.	On the whole it turned out very stupidly.
Вообще́ вы́шло о́чень глу́по.	It turned out very stupidly altogether.
Я в о́бщем не курю́.	I don't generally smoke.
Я вообще́ не курю́.	I don't smoke at all.

Here are some more sentences containing **вообще́**:

Вы́пьем не за одни́х то́лько на́ших жён, но́ и за все́х же́нщин во-обще́.	Let's drink not only to our wives, but to all women in general.
Я сего́дня не в ду́хе, я пло́хо спа́л, голова́ боли́т, я́ вообще́ себя́ пло́хо чу́вствую.	I'm out of sorts today: I didn't sleep well, my head aches, I feel bad altogether.
Ему́ вообще́ на́до бы́ло э́то зна́ть.	He should have known that in the first place.
Ве́ра вообще́ така́я.	Vera is always like that.
Ива́н вообще́ не придёт.	Ivan won't come at all.
Придёт ли Ива́н вообще́?	Will Ivan come at all?

---

[1] Notably, in **вообще́ говоря́** 'generally speaking.'

[2] For students familiar with German, **вообще́** corresponds very closely to *überhaupt*, **в о́бщем** to *im allgemeinen*.

TRANSLATION INTO ENGLISH

1. На э́том съе́зде не ра́з ука́зывали на то́, что социалисти́ческий ла́герь до́лжен сохраня́ть свои́ вооружённые си́лы на высо́ком у́ровне. **2.** То́, что пове́стка дня́ была́ при́нята все́ми прису́тствующими на съе́зде (не́ было отсу́тствующих), не мо́жет не понра́виться всему́ сове́тскому наро́ду. **3.** Смерть э́того челове́ка явля́ется ва́жным истори́ческим собы́тием (представля́ет собо́й ва́жное истори́ческое собы́тие). Она́ важна́ тем, что даёт нам возмо́жность вы́брать но́вого вождя́. **4.** Наконе́ц ста́ли определя́ть на́ши зада́чи по отноше́нию к построе́нию коммуни́зма. **5.** На́ша систе́ма хорошо́ рабо́тает во всех областя́х. **6.** Вопро́с не в том, существу́ет ли ещё империали́зм (в том, что он ещё существу́ет, не тру́дно убеди́ться), а в том, како́е влия́ние мы́ са́ми ока́зываем на хо́д мировы́х собы́тий. **7.** В пе́рвую о́чередь сле́дует приня́ть во внима́ние то́, что монополисти́ческая буржуази́я продолжа́ет проводи́ть поли́тику агре́ссии и вое́нных авантю́р. **8.** О́чередь тепе́рь за на́ми. Несмотря́ на то́, что нам бу́дет ока́зано серьёзное противоде́йствие, мы́ бу́дем идти́ вперёд к коммуни́зму, твёрдо убеждённые в коне́чном успе́хе на́шего де́ла. **9.** Мы́ твёрдо стои́м за ми́р и за всео́бщее и по́лное разоруже́ние. На́ша поли́тика напра́влена и на то́ и на друго́е. (Отве́т) Неуже́ли? А почему́ ва́ши де́йствия (посту́пки) ничего́ не име́ют о́бщего с ва́шими убежде́ниями. Вы́ де́йствуете, как бу́дто вы́ ни за то́ ни за друго́е. **10.** Я́ хочу́ указа́ть на то́, что для высо́кого у́ровня вое́нного произво́дства и вооруже́ния нам ну́жно соде́йствие всех капиталисти́ческих корпора́ций. И я́ уве́рен в том, что они́ нам ока́жут э́то соде́йствие. **11.** Экономи́ческое и полити́ческое обоснова́ние строи́тельства коммуни́зма тре́бует бо́лее то́чного определе́ния. **12.** Внима́ние! (Прошу́ внима́ния). Ста́ньте в о́чередь, получи́те биле́ты; бу́дут места́ для всех ва́с, они́ ука́заны на ва́ших биле́тах. Сохраня́йте биле́ты до конца́ представле́ния. **13.** Приступа́я к э́той на́шей зада́че, мы́ должны́ бу́дем исходи́ть из бо́лее конкре́тного положе́ния. **14.** Уже́ начина́ются предвари́тельные перегово́ры по вопро́су всео́бщего и по́лного разоруже́ния. Мы́ исхо́дим из того́, что Сове́тский Сою́з явля́ется са́мым мо́щным в экономи́ческом и вое́нном отноше́нии госуда́рством ла́геря социали́зма. **15.** Стара́ясь да́ть нам теорети́ческое обоснова́ние свои́х де́йствий, он привёл не́сколько интере́сных приме́ров. **16.** Мы́ здесь прово́дим поли́тику ми́ра и дру́жбы. Все́ на́ши мероприя́тия на э́то и напра́влены; всё, что мы́ де́лаем, свя́зано с сохране́нием ми́ра. **17.** Мы́ всегда́ де́йствуем согла́сно тому́, что говоря́т на́ши руководи́тели. Зато́ мы́ име́ем пра́во тре́бовать де́йствия и от ни́х. **18.** Само́ произво́дство вооруже́ния представля́ет собо́й опа́сность. Поэ́тому мы́ должны́ всегда́ ока́зывать вся́кое противоде́йствие но́вому вооруже́нию. **19.** В на́ших национа́льных отноше́ниях культýра игрáет большýю рóль. **20.** Мы́ дóлго обсуждáем вопрóс о тóм, какóе у нáс отношéние к национáльной проблéме. Конéчно, мы́ пострóили для ни́х большýю промы́шленность, и они́ принимáют учáстие во всéх съéздах, во всём, чтó свя́зано с наýкой и культýрой. Но́ в други́х отношéниях тó, что мы́ дéлаем для национáльностей оставля́ет желáть лýчшего. **21.** Вéсь ми́р не мóжет не ви́деть, как капиталисти́ческий лáгерь выступáет за ми́р и дрýжбу мéжду нарóдами. **22.** Если ты́ реши́шь всé задáчи сегóдня вéчером, ты́ мóжешь не рабóтать зáвтра. **23.** В какóм из лáгерей вы́ хотéли бы бы́ть? Я́ не хотéл бы бы́ть ни в тóм ни в другóм. **24.** Вы́ меня́ не тáк понимáете. Мы́ бóремся не за однó тóлько нáше дéло, нó и за всé междунарóдные делá. **25.** Нáм обóим я́сно, что онá люби́ла не егó, а вáс. Нó люби́ла онá вáс не за тó, что вы́ хорóший человéк, а за тó, чтó вы́ могли́ ей дáть. **26.** Чтó меня́ в Амéрике бóльше всегó порази́ло, э́то тó, что ничегó не порази́ло. **27.** Нáш руководи́тель бы́л возмущён тéм, что мы́ тáк пóздно приступи́ли к дéлу. **28.** Успéх нáшей прогрáммы зави́сит от тогó, каки́е мéры мы́ при́мем в связи́ с нéй. **29.** Вы́ мóжете не принимáть во внимáние тó, что он скáжет насчёт нарóдного хозя́йства Совéтского Сою́за. Ведь óн вообщé не разбирáется в эконóмике. **30.** В óбщем всё кóнчилось хорошó. **31.** Её успéх меня́ нискóлько не поражáет. Онá всегдá хорошó знáет свóй предмéт, всегдá сдаёт экзáмены на отли́чно — онá вообщé óчень ýмная дéвушка. **32.** Проезжáя ми́мо аэродрóма, Лихачёв напрáвил внимáние на стоя́щие тáм огрóмные самолёты: «Это впервы́е в истóрии самолёты на двéсти человéк», сказáл óн. **33.** Нáм нýжно тóчно определи́ть своё отношéние к Твардóвскому. **34.** Мы́ встрéтились в определённый чáс. **35.** Культýра в нерýсских зéмлях должнá бы́ть национáльная по фóрме, социалисти́ческая по содержáнию. Этого трéбовал Влади́мир Ильи́ч Лéнин, нó пóмните, что Лéнин вообщé говори́л óбщими местáми. Рáзве мóжно говори́ть о существовáнии культýры при нáшем жи́зненном ýровне?

DRILL

Combine the following sets of phrases into fact-oriented **тó, что** or **тó,** *interrogative* sentences:

1. Я́ хорошó понимáю э́то.	Он дéлает успéхи.
2. Онá интересýется э́тим.	Мы́ зáвтра съéздим в гóрод.
3. Мы́ говори́м об э́том.	Кáк вы́ рабóтаете?
4. Мы́ говори́м об э́том.	Вы́ ужáсно мнóго рабóтаете.
5. Мы́ рáды э́тому.	Ивáну хорошó.
6. Всё зави́сит от э́того.	Мóй дрýг дурáк.
7. Всё зави́сит от э́того.	Мóй дрýг дурáк?

8. Всё зави́сит от э́того.   Где́ о́н бу́дет жи́ть?
9. Я поражён э́тим.   Каки́е ве́щи о́н вы́брал?
10. Я возмущён э́тим.   Кого́ вы́ вы́брали президе́нтом?

Changed word order (**то́** element comes first):

11. Э́то совсе́м я́сно.   Они́ уже́ до́лго слу́жат.
12. Э́то я хорошо́ понима́ю.   Вы́ отли́чный челове́к.
13. В э́том я глубоко́ уве́рен.   Вы́ де́лаете оши́бку.
14. Несмотря́ на э́то — ты́ лу́чше   Он хорошо́ игра́ет.
    его́.
15. В связи́ с э́тим — я зайду́ то́ль-   Вы́ зде́сь до́лго бу́дете.
    ко на бу́дущей неде́ле.

TRANSLATION INTO RUSSIAN

1. The fact is that the success of this program depends on the influence which it will exert on the course of world events. **2.** For the first time in history people are beginning to define their tasks concretely, are beginning to understand and take into account the enormous significance of universal and complete disarmament. **3.** We are firmly convinced that in spite of the fact that people at first had a bad attitude toward it, the agenda will still be accepted by all those present at the congress. **4.** It is well known that the danger of war exists. But although our cause is in fact the right one, we ought to remember that the preservation of peace is more important than victory. **5.** The cause of peaceful coexistence is not served by those who produce armaments. Generally speaking our attitude toward the socialist camp will depend on what level their armed forces are at. **6.** We saw him help the girl. We saw him helping the girl. **7.** We can't help noticing him go to the store every day. **8.** The important thing (What is important) is that all are present; nobody is absent. **9.** We must discuss the question of whether we can continue this bloody struggle or not. **10.** Many of our former colleagues are now offering us opposition. It's hard for us to function without any cooperation at all. **11.** This congress is an important historical event almost in all respects. **12.** The premier pointed out that our agriculture is not operating as it should. This in turn (in its turn) causes difficulties in many areas of our industry. And this can't help influencing our national relations. **13.** Are you going to be at the preliminary congress or at the preparatory *meeting* ? I won't be at either one. **14.** You may not understand what we are fighting for. Our struggle for peace and friendship is very important in that it points out the path into a bright future for all mankind. At last it has become possible to determine the directions of our science and culture; that is, if our science and culture exist in the first place. **15.** I will direct you to the leaders of the foremost

capitalist corporations. These people exert a great influence on economic and military affairs. You can't fail to take into account the fact that in both these respects the monopolists are conducting a policy of aggression. **16.** I landed at
30 the wrong meeting and was told that I wasn't the one they were waiting for. "Go away," they said, "we are just getting down to business." "I'm going," I answered, "but in what direction?" **17.** I would like to say a few words in connection with your having arrived late. **18.** He has a very serious attitude toward everything which is connected with science and culture. **19.** What we will
35 be discussing at this congress is already known to all members of the Communist Party. **20.** Yes, that is, in its way, an economic and political basis for the construction of communism. **21.** Now it's our turn to criticize the low level of military production. **22.** We are now discussing the question of how long mankind will exist. **23.** I am struck by the fact that the most powerful nation in the
40 world finds itself in such a situation. **24.** This is what your policy has led to. All the people are working in the wrong factories; they are working for (replacing) each other the whole time. A terrible situation! It is preventing us from preserving good relations among ourselves. **25.** The whole matter depends not on you but on how much your friends have done. **26.** You will receive a defi-
45 nite assignment in a short time. **27.** The party never demanded his death. **28.** Our living standard, in general, is not very high, but (to make up for it) the level of our agriculture is growing with every day. And our industry is also going forward. And we are making progress in a cultural respect as well. Think of the works of our leading writers. **29.** Our country is disarming; we now have the
50 right to demand a higher standard of living. And we advise you to take into account our demands; otherwise you will provoke indignation.

СЛОВАРЬ

авантю́р-а adventure (*us pej*)
борь-б-а́ fight, struggle; *cf.* боро́ться
в-ним-а́-тель-/н-ый attentive, thoughtful
вообще́ IV.7
впервы́е for the first time
вперёд *куда́* ahead, forward
вс-ё-о́бщ-ий universal, general
де́й-ств-и-е action, function; act in play; *cf.* де́йствовать
де́л-о *E pl* matter, affair, business, cause; де́ло в чём IV.A
дру́ж-б-а friendship
империал-и́зм imperialism; —и́ст imperialist; —и́ст-и́ческ-ий imperialist(ic)
капитал-и́зм capitalism; —и́ст capitalist;

—и́ст-и́ческ-ий capitalist(ic)
коммун-и́зм communism; —и́ст communist; —и́ст-и́ческ-ий communist(ic)
конкре́т-/н-ый concrete
кров-а́в-ый **КРОВ**[2] bloody
культу́р-а culture
культу́р-/н-ый cultural; cultured
ла́герь *M E pl* -я́ camp; *nom pl* ла́гери (in sense of political grouping)
ме́р-о-при-я́-т-и-е measure
монополист-и́ческ-ий monopolist(ic)
мо́щ-/н-ый powerful
национа́ль-н-ость nationality (both status and group)
национа́ль-/н-ый national, nationality *adj*

о́бщ-ий general, common; не име́ют ниче́го —его с *ке́м/че́м* have nothing in common with; в —ем IV. 7; —ее ме́сто platitude

о-пре-**дел**-ён-/н-ый (*adj/PPP* < определи́ть – определя́ют) definite, specific, certain, fixed

о́-**черед**ь *E pl obl* turn, line; ста́нут – станови́ться в — get into line; стоя́ть в —и stand in line; в свою́ — in its (one's) turn; в пе́рвую — first of all; — за ва́ми *or* ва́ша — it's your turn

па́рти-я (political) party

пере-**говор**-ы (на) *pl only* talks, negotiations

по-**бе́д**-а victory; *cf.* победи́ть – побежда́ют; — за на́ми the victory is ours; — оста́нется за нами the victory will be ours

по-**вест**-/к-а дня́ (на) **ВЕД**-т agenda; (по)ста́вить на —у дня́ place on the agenda

под-**готов**-и-тель-н-ый preparatory

поли́тик-а politics; policy

пра́ктик-а practice

практи́ч-еск-ий practical

пред-вар-и-тель-н-ый preliminary

програ́мм-а program

про-из-**во́д**-ств-о production, manufacture; *cf.* произведу́т – производить

про-**мы́шл**-ен-н-ость industry

про-**мы́шл**-ен-н-ый industrial

против-о-дей-ств-и-е opposition, counter-action; *cf.* противоде́йствовать

раке́т-а rocket

рук-о-**вод**-и́-тель *M* leader

свет-/л-ый light, bright; светло́ it is light

се́ль-ск-ое **хозя́й**-ств-о agriculture, *lit* rural economy

серьёз-/н-ый serious

с-**мер**ть *M/P E pl obl* death

со-**дей**-ств-и-е assistance, cooperation; *cf.* соде́йствовать

социал-и́зм socialism; —и́ст socialist; —ист-и́ческ-ий socialist(ic)

съ-**езд** (на) congress, convention

твёрд-ый hard, firm

у́-**ров**-/е/нь **РОВ**[1] *M* level; жи́зненный — standard of living

хо́д motion; — собы́тий course of events

хозя́й-ств-о economy

человеч-е-ств-о mankind

чле́н member

ю́мор humor

ГЛАГО́ЛЫ

у-**бед**-и́-ть – убежда́ют в *чём* convince of; —ся в *чём* become convinced of, convince oneself of

    n убежде́ние

бор-о-ть-ся fight, struggle

    n борьба́

про-**вёд**-у́т – проводить conduct, carry on

    n проведе́ние

про-из-**вёд**-у́т – производить produce; carry out, execute

    n произведе́ние production, work (of art, of a writer, etc.); произво́дство production (economic manufacture)

за-**ви́с**-е-ть от *кого́/чего́* depend *on*

с-**вяз**-а-ть – свя́зывают connect, tie

    together

    n свя́зь III Vocab

дей-ств-ова-ть act, operate, function

    n де́йствие

против-о-**дей**-ств-ова-ть *кому́/чему́* oppose, counteract

    n противоде́йствие

со-**дей**-ств-ова-ть *кому́/чему́ P and I* assist further, promote

    n соде́йствие

в-**ним**-а́-н-и-е (< *an older* внима́ют) attention; при́мут – принима́ют во — take into account/consideration

за-н-**я**-т-и-е (< за́-йм-ут(ся) – занима́ют(ся)) IV.5

о-каз-а-ть – ока́зывают render, show; — противоде́йствие *кому́/чему́* oppose; — соде́йствие *кому́/чему́* assist, render assistance to; — влия́ние на *кого́/чтó* influence, exert influence on
n оказа́ние

у-каз-а-ть – ука́зывают *кого́/чтó or кому́* на *кого́/чтó* indicate, point out
n указа́ние indication; *pl* instructions

за-ключ-а́й-ут-ся в *чём* consist in

в-лий-а́-н-и-е (< (по)-в-лий-а́й-ут на *кого́/чтó*) influence; оказа́ть – ока́зывают — на *кого́/чтó* influence

воз-мут-и́-ть – возмуща́ют make indignant; —ся *кéм/чéм* be/become indignant about
n возмущéние   (Ch 5)

от-нёс-у́т – относить,   от-нёс-у́т-ся – относиться IV. 6

во-оруж-и́-ть – вооружа́ют arm *tr*; вооружённые си́лы armed forces; —ся arm *intr*
n вооружéние arming; *pl* arms

раз-оруж-и́-ть – разоружа́ют disarm *tr*; —ся disarm *intr*
n разоружéние

об-основ-а́-ть   (обосну́ют) – обоснóвывают ground, base, substantiate
n обоснова́ние

на-пра́в-и-ть – направля́ют direct
n направлéние

о-пре-дел-и́-ть – определя́ют пре-ДЕЛ[1] determine, define, specify, fix
n определéние

по-раз-и́-ть – поража́ют РАЗ[1] *fig* strike; amaze; —ся be struck/amazed
n поражéние *NB* defeat

(по)-совéт-ова-ть ВЕТ *кому́* advise
n совéт

(по)-спóр-и-ть argue
n спóр

пред-ставл-я́й-ут собóй be

при-ступ-и́-ть – приступа́ют к *чему́* begin, get at, get down to (work, task, etc.)

от-су́т-ств-ова-ть be absent
n отсу́тствие

при-су́т-ств-ова-ть be present
n прису́тствие

сущ-е-ств-ова́-ть exist
n существова́ние

со-сущ-е-ств-ова́-ть coexist
n сосуществова́ние

(по)-трéб-ова-ть *когó/чегó or когó/чтó* demand, require
n трéбование

ис-ход-и-ть из *чегó* depart from, take as a point of departure

со-хран-и́-ть – сохраня́ют retain, keep, preserve
n сохранéние

АМЕРИКА́НЕЦ В ИРКУ́ТСКЕ

Лю́ди из-за грани́цы е́здят в Сове́тский Сою́з обы́чно в ка́честве тури́стов. Почти́ все́ тури́сты **остана́вливаются**[1] в гости́ницах, руководи́мых госуда́рственным аге́нтством «Интури́ст». Ме́сто в э́тих помеще́ниях должно́ бы́ть зака́зано (заброни́ровано) **задо́лго до**[3] прие́зда го́стя, **что**[10] позволя́ет Интури́сту зара́нее назна́чить ему́ ко́мнату. Гости́ницы быва́ют 5 ра́зного ка́чества, но́ коли́чество и́х, осо́бенно в небольши́х города́х, стро́го ограни́чено. Тури́ст, попа́вший в да́нный го́род, ещё не име́ет ни мале́йшего поня́тия о то́м, где́ его́ помести́ли. Одна́ко, вме́сто того́, чтобы ограни́читься одни́ми таки́ми обобще́ниями, я́ лу́чше расскажу́ ва́м **про**[8] оди́н слу́чай, име́вший ме́сто в го́роде Ирку́тске, находя́щемся в восто́чной 10 Сиби́ри.

Оди́н америка́нский коммерса́нт, Ка́рл Джо́нсон, пое́хал в Евро́пу по дела́м, в командиро́вку. Привы́кши бы́ть в Евро́пе, о́н не обраща́л осо́бого внима́ния на её достопримеча́тельности и всё вре́мя рабо́тал. Таки́м о́бразом, ему́ удало́сь зако́нчить свои́ дела́ за де́сять дне́й до назна́ченного 15 отбы́тия в Аме́рику. Зна́чит, вре́мя е́сть и не́чего де́лать. Ка́рл Джо́нсон реши́л пое́хать в Сове́тский Сою́з, к одному́ ста́рому знако́мому, Петру́ Ю́рьевичу Кондрашо́ву, живу́щему в восто́чной Сиби́ри, в го́роде Ирку́тске.

Джо́нсон при́был в Ирку́тск, и его́ **отвезли́**[6] пря́мо в бюро́ обслу́жива- 20 ния Интури́ста. Та́м жда́л его́ са́м Кондрашо́в, **что**[10] Джо́нсона о́чень

197

обра́довало, поско́льку о́н всё вре́мя боя́лся, что до́лго бу́дет разы́скивать своего́ знако́мого. Кондрашо́в кре́пко пожа́л ему́ ру́ку, сказа́в: — Добро́ пожа́ловать в Ирку́тск, — и зате́м помо́г ему́ при оформле́нии докуме́нтов,

25 что́ в Сове́тском Сою́зе вообще́, **не говоря́ уже́ о**[2] тако́м небольшо́м го́роде ка́к Ирку́тск, занима́ет нема́ло вре́мени. Бу́дучи коммерса́нтом, Джо́нсон уже́ давно́ привы́к ко вся́кого ро́да волоки́те и хорошо́ уме́л обраща́ться с чино́вниками. Те́м не ме́нее, к тому́, что сейча́с сказа́л ему́ оди́н тако́й чино́вник, сотру́дник Интури́ста, Джо́нсон ниско́лько не́ был гото́в:

30 *Сотру́дник Интури́ста.* К сожале́нию, ва́ше прибы́тие совпада́ет с междунаро́дной вы́ставкой в на́шем го́роде. В гости́ницах сейча́с не́где останови́ться.

Джо́нсон. **Что́ вы!**[10] Ме́сто для меня́ уже́ давно́ зака́зано (заброни́ровано).

Сотру́дник Интури́ста. Ва́м не́ о чем беспоко́иться. Через не́сколько дне́й

35 но́мер для ва́с освободи́тся. А **пока́**[5] вы́ бу́дете жи́ть у своего́ знако́мого Кондрашо́ва.

Джо́нсон. Я ничего́ не име́ю про́тив э́того. Наоборо́т, я́ о́чень ра́д. Но́, Пе́тя, ра́зве у ва́с ме́ста хва́тит для меня́? Да и к тому́ же вы́ писа́тель, рабо́таете до́ма. Я не хочу́, чтобы ва́ша рабо́та прекрати́лась из-за

40 меня́.

Кондрашо́в. Ах, переста́ньте беспоко́иться. И ме́ста для ва́с хва́тит, и рабо́та из-за ва́с не прекрати́тся. Не бо́йтесь, мы́ о́чень ра́ды име́ть ва́с у себя́ в ка́честве го́стя.

Джо́нсон. Кака́я у ва́с кварти́ра?

45 *Кондрашо́в.* Её нетру́дно описа́ть. Она́ небольша́я, но све́тлая — в ка́ждой ко́мнате **по два́ окна́**[7] — и с хоро́шей обстано́вкой (ме́белью). **Гости́ная**,[9] две́ спа́льни, ку́хня, ва́нная, убо́рная и пере́дняя. Отде́льной столо́вой не́т; мы́ обе́даем в гости́ной. Кварти́ра на девя́том этаже́. Прекра́сный ви́д на го́род.

50 *Джо́нсон.* Ясно, что кварти́ра удо́бная. Ли́фт, — наде́юсь, е́сть?

Кондрашо́в. Бо́же мо́й! Како́е у ва́с представле́ние о на́шем о́бразе жи́зни. Мы́ кре́пкий наро́д, но ра́зве мо́жно поднима́ться и спуска́ться по ле́стнице, когда́ живёшь на девя́том этаже́? Ли́фт, коне́чно, е́сть, о́н де́йствует самообслу́живанием. Ну́, хва́тит. Переста́нем спо́рить. Вы́,

55 наве́рно, уста́ли и хоти́те отдохну́ть. За́втра пое́дем на о́зеро Байка́л.

Джо́нсон. Прекра́сно, но я́ всё-таки бою́сь что́-нибудь пропусти́ть. Не пойдём ли мы́ сейча́с осма́тривать го́род. Я, в о́бщем, о́чень ре́дко устаю́.

Кондрашо́в. Го́род мы́ успе́ем осмотре́ть послеза́втра. Не́чего спеши́ть.

60 Пое́дем домо́й, отдохнём.

Они́ спусти́лись на пе́рвый эта́ж, вы́шли на у́лицу и останови́ли такси́.

не- plus the infinitive

The stressed particle **не-**, prefixed to interrogative pronominal and adverbial stems and used with an infinitive, imparts the sense "there is no . . . to (VERB)." The result is an impersonal construction whose logical subject is expressed by the dative or, occasionally, **у** plus *gen*; in general statements this dative is usually omitted:

На́м не́кого бы́ло спроси́ть.	There was no one for us to ask.
Не́кого бы́ло спроси́ть.	There was no one to ask.

Do not confuse this construction with the familiar **ни** . . . **не** type:

Мы́ никого́ не спроси́ли.	We didn't ask anyone.

Other examples:

Не́чего де́лать. Не́чем занима́ться.	There's nothing to do.
Ребёнку не́ с кем игра́ть.	There's no one for the child to play with.
На́м не́куда идти́.	There's nowhere for us to go.
Не́ у кого бу́дет останови́ться.	There'll be no one to stay with.
Не́чего и не́кого боя́ться.	There's nothing and no one to fear.
Ему́ не́откуда бы́ло э́то зна́ть.	There was nowhere he could have known that from.
Мне́ тепе́рь не́когда идти́ в о́перу.	I have no time to go to the opera now.
Не́когда ходи́ть в о́перу.	There's no time to go to the opera.

Не́кому requires special comment. In a sentence such as:

На́м не́кому бы́ло э́то посла́ть.	There was no one for us to send it to.

it is parallel to the above examples. More often, however, **не́кому** takes over the role of logical subject and means "there is no one who":

Не́кому бы́ло э́то посла́ть.	There was no one to send it.
Не́кому э́то сде́лать.	There's no one to do it.

Не́чего, in addition to its above usage, may also mean "there is no reason to, it is of no use to." **Не́зачем** has approximately the same meaning:

Не́чего разгова́ривать.	There's no use talking.
Не́чего бы́ло та́к мно́го рабо́тать.	There was no reason to work so much.
Не́зачем писа́ть об э́том.	There's no point writing about that.

We have already seen that **не-** added to interrogative stems may have the positive indefinite sense "some, certain." Some special cases of this will be treated in Lesson VIII.

Positive expressions corresponding to не plus the infinitive

The corresponding positive "there is . . . to (VERB)" is handled by **есть** plus the appropriate interrogative. The logical subject is expressed by the dative or **у** plus genitive:

У неё есть с кéм говори́ть.	There is someone for her to talk to.
У ни́х есть что́ рассказа́ть.	They have something to relate.
На́м бу́дет куда́ идти́.	We will have somewhere to go.

And, parallel to

Не́кому бы́ло реши́ть э́тот вопро́с.	There was no one to decide that question.

is

Есть кому́ реши́ть э́тот вопро́с.	There is someone to decide that question.

We may note, parenthetically, that in conversational language interrogatives may occur with indefinite meaning without **-нибудь**:

Éсли что́ случи́тся, позвони́.	If something happens, phone.
Éсли вы́ найдёте кого́ в пере́дней, спроси́те его́ ка́к попа́сть в спа́льню.	If you find someone in the front hall, ask him how to get to the bedroom.
Я хочу́ узна́ть, не ви́дел ли его́ кто́ из ва́с.	I want to find out if one of you didn't see him.
Бога́тый бе́дного ра́зве когда́ поймёт?	Do you really think a rich man will ever understand a poor one?
Тепе́рь кто́ кого́.	Now everybody's on his own. (Who can get who(m).)

SUBORDINATE POINTS

1. The idea of "stop" in English is usually expressed in Russian by one of four verbs:

Остановить – остана́вливают means "bring to a halt, stop something's or someone's motion"; **остановиться – остана́вливаются** is the intransitive equivalent "cease, halt of one's own accord" and also has the sense "stop/stay" in a place. **Прекрати́ть – прекраща́ют** is to stop or *discontinue* something which is in progress but *not in motion*. Both **остановить – остана́вливают** and **прекра-**

ти́ть – прекраща́ют take direct objects and are *not used with verbs*. **Переста́нут – переста́вать** means to "cease doing something," and the action is expressed by an *imperfective infinitive*. **Переста́нут – переставать** is intransitive and is *never* used with nouns alone. Examples of these three verbs:

Солда́ты останови́ли и́х на у́лице.	The soldiers stopped them on the street.
Мы́ останови́лись перед гости́ницей.	We stopped in front of the hotel.
Я́ всегда́ остана́вливаюсь у бра́та.	I always stop (stay) at my brother's.
Мы́ прекрати́ли на́ш разгово́р.	We stopped our conversation.
Я́ хочу́ прекрати́ть на́шу подпи́ску.	I want to discontinue our subscription.
Прекрати́ли произво́дство а́томного ору́жия.	They ceased production of atomic weapons.
Он до́лжен переста́ть кури́ть.	He must stop smoking.
Она́ говори́ла, не перестава́я.	She talked incessantly (without stopping).
До́ждь переста́л идти́.	It stopped raining.

(По)меша́ют plus dative (of the person hindered) plus infinitive means "stop" in the sense of "prevent from doing":

Это помеша́ет ему́ прийти́.	This will stop him from coming.
Это не меша́ет на́м де́йствовать.	This does not stop us from functioning.

2. Note the expression **не говори́ть уже́ о** *prp* 'to say nothing of, not to mention,' whose most frequent usage is the gerundial **не говоря́ уже́ о**:

Я́ не люблю́ а́втора самого́, не говоря́ уже́ о его́ ужа́сных кни́гах. *Or:* . . . , я́ уже́ не говорю́ о его́ ужа́сных кни́гах.	I don't like the author himself, to say nothing of his awful books.

3. За plus the accusative of a time expression plus **до** means "earlier (by), before." This construction is parallel to **через** plus accusative of a time expression plus **по́сле** 'later (by), after,' although in conversation **через** is sometimes omitted, while **за** almost never is:

Оте́ц прие́хал **за** неде́лю до э́того.	My father arrived a week before that.
Оте́ц прие́хал **(через)** неде́лю **по́сле** э́того.	My father arrived a week after that.
Я́ написа́л ему́ **за** ше́сть ме́сяцев **до** того́ как о́н уе́хал.	I wrote him six months before he left.

Он привы́к к на́шей жи́зни уже́ за-до́лго до того́ как прие́хал сюда́.	He had gotten used to our life a long time before he moved here.

4. The noun **пора́** 'time' is used principally in set expressions which serve as temporal adverbs or conjunctions:

До каки́х пор ну́жно жда́ть?	Until when must one wait?
С каки́х пор он здесь?	How long has he been here?
С э́тих пор мы бу́дем говори́ть об э́том то́лько на о́бщих собра́ниях.	From now on we will speak about this only at general meetings.
Я до сих пор интересу́юсь му́зыкой.	I'm interested in music to this day.
С тех пор как он прие́хал, он рабо́тает с Па́вловым.	Ever since he arrived he's been working with Pavlov.

And note: **до тех пор, пока́ . . . не** 'until (such time as)':

Мы оста́немся здесь до тех пор, пока́ Серге́й не зако́нчит де́ло.	We'll stay here until Sergej completes the case.

5. The adverb **пока́**, like the conjunction (I.2), expresses the idea of simultaneity; it has the meaning, "for the time being, for now, so far, as yet." **Пока́ что** has about the same sense: "for now, in the meanwhile":

Я пока́ подожду́.	I'll wait for the time being.
Они́ пока́ ещё здесь.	As yet they're still here.
По́чты пока́ ещё нет.	There's no mail as yet.
Он пока́ что напи́шет э́ти пи́сьма.	In the meanwhile he'll write those letters.
Мы пока́ что здоро́вы.	For the time being we're well.
Пока́. (*colloq*)	So long (for now).

6. **От** prefixed to **несу́т**, **везу́т**, or **веду́т** may give the compound the meaning of "take to a place, deliver":

Отвези́те его́ на ста́нцию.	Take him to the station.
Я отнёс письмо́ на по́чту.	I brought the letter to the post office.

7. The preposition **по** with the dative may have a distributive meaning:

Де́ти получа́ют по (одному́) карандашу́.	The children are getting a pencil each.
По ско́льку? По одному́ каранда́шу.	How many each? One pencil each.

With numerals other than **оди́н**, the accusative is used:

Берите по́ два́/две́.   Take two each.

Они́ получа́ют по две́сти рубле́й.   They get 200 rubles each.

8. The preposition **про** takes the accusative and has the same meaning as **о** plus prepositional, which it frequently replaces in conversation. It is used in both written and spoken Russian in the expression **про себя́** 'to oneself':

Он мно́го расска́зывал $\begin{cases}\text{про ва́с.} \\ \text{о ва́с.}\end{cases}$ He has told us a lot about you.

Про меня́ забы́ли.   They forgot about me.

Кто́ зна́ет, что́ они́ про себя́   Who knows what they are thinking
ду́мают.   to themselves.

«Это не та́к», сказа́ла она́ про себя́.   "That's not so," she said to herself.

But note:

Он мно́го расска́зывал $\begin{cases}\text{про себя́.} \\ \text{о себе́.}\end{cases}$ He talked a lot about himself.

9. Many Russian words for rooms are adjectives in **-ая** used as nouns. The gender derives from the word **ко́мната**, which is, however, only rarely used with them:

столо́вая   dining room, restaurant, (often students' or workers') cafeteria

гости́ная   sitting room, living room

приёмная   reception room

операцио́нная   operating room

Note that **ва́нная** is the room with the bathtub (**ва́нна**) in it; in Russia, as generally in Europe, the toilet is usually in a separate room, the **убо́рная**, a word which serves for public rest rooms as well.

10. Stressed **что́** has two more uses not mentioned in Lessons III and IV:

a. It may replace a whole clause, in which case it may be rendered in English by "a fact that/which," "something which," or simply "which":

Он опозда́л, что́ бы́ло стра́нно.   He was late, (a fact) which was strange.

Он пришёл ра́но, чему́ мы́ бы́ли   He came early, which pleased us.
ра́ды.

Его́ назна́чили на́шим секретарём,   They appointed him our secretary,
что́ на́м о́чень помогло́.   (something) which helped us a great deal.

b. It may mean "why" or express some other sort of question:

Что́ вы́ не рабо́таете?	Why aren't you working?
Что́ она́ всё та́к бе́гает?	Why does she keep running around like that?
Что́ э́то вы́ всё ещё лежи́те?	Why is it that you're still in bed?
Что́ ва́ша голова́?	How's your head?
Что́ диссерта́ция?	How's the dissertation coming?

And note:

Что́ вы́? (!)	Why are you doing that, reacting like that, why did you say that, what do you mean? (*Surprise or indignation*)
Что́ вы!	You don't say so!

TRANSLATION INTO ENGLISH

1. На́м пока́ не́ за что боро́ться. **2.** Мы́ живём в отде́льной ко́мнате, а ме́ста всё равно́ не хвата́ет. **3.** Таки́е слу́чаи, отде́льно взя́тые, не позво́лят на́м сравни́ть э́ти две́ систе́мы. **4.** На́до привы́кнуть к тому́, что не всё на́ши гости́ницы вы́сшего ка́чества. **5.** Мы́ прие́хали на грани́цу за де́нь до назна́ченной встре́чи. **6.** Пока́ ещё неизве́стно, бу́дут ли свобо́дные места́ в э́том теа́тре. Всё зави́сит от коли́чества тури́стов в Москве́ в да́нное вре́мя. **7.** Мы́ подняли́сь на второ́й эта́ж в конто́ру администра́ции. Та́м сиде́л оди́н сотру́дник и обслу́живал люде́й, стоя́щих в о́череди, и говори́л и́м: — Зака́зывайте по одному́ биле́ту, пожа́луйста, чтобы всём хвати́ло. Не на́до та́к. Ведь у на́с изве́стный поря́док. — Над сотру́дником висе́л кра́сный плака́т, на кото́ром бы́ло напи́сано: — Насто́йчиво бори́тесь за культу́рное обслу́живание наро́да. **8.** В на́шей кварти́ре оказа́лось по три́ сту́ла в ко́мнате; на́до бы́ло проси́ть по пя́ть или по ше́сть на вся́кий слу́чай. Ну́, де́лать не́чего, во вся́ком слу́чае сту́льев на́м хва́тит. В кра́йнем слу́чае бу́дем сиде́ть на полу́. **9.** С те́х по́р как меня́ назна́чили на э́ту рабо́ту, меня́ ни ра́зу не посыла́ли в командиро́вку. **10.** До си́х по́р не́ было ни одного́ тако́го слу́чая. **11.** В связи́ с но́выми собы́тиями мы́ реши́ли стро́го ограни́чить коли́чество чле́нов в на́шей па́ртии. **12.** Обрати́те внима́ние на обслу́живание в э́той гости́нице. Определи́те ка́к мо́жно точне́е, ско́лько вре́мени тре́буется для оформле́ния докуме́нтов, зака́за биле́тов, и т.д. **13.** Не́ с кем зде́сь обсужда́ть э́ту те́му. **14.** Получи́лось, что мне́ с не́й не́ о чем бы́ло спо́рить. Снача́ла, я ду́мал, что у неё не хвата́ет ума́, а пото́м ста́ло я́сно, что она́ хорошо́ уме́ет обраща́ться с людьми́ и про́сто не хо́чет со мно́й вступа́ть в спо́р. **15.** Не на́до сра́внивать Ирку́тск с каки́м-либо больши́м го́родом ка́к, наприме́р Москва́. Но в Ирку́тске есть, всё-таки, свои достопримечательности. Я недавно был там; разыскал одного родственника. **16.** — В новой квартире и обстановка должна быть новая, — сказала жена. **17.** Когда международная обстановка станет лучше? **18.** Какое совпадение! На выставке, где я работаю, к нам недавно назначили одного человека, который оказался моим старым товарищем по школе. **19.** Врач посоветовал ему перестать курить. **20.** Военные действия пока прекратились, но следовало бы прекратить войну вообще. Ведь от будущей войны некуда будет бежать. **21.** У вас есть чем писать? **22.** Нам будет где остановиться. **23.** Они ничего не имеют против освобождения народа, что каждому ясно. Наоборот, они готовы оказывать нам всякое содействие. Гораздо важнее знать, как относится империалистический лагерь к этому делу. По-моему, империалисты уверяют, что народ пока что не готов к освобождению, не говоря уже о том, что уровень их технического и экономического развития, вероятно, не позволит этого. **24.** Крепко жму вашу руку (пишется в конце письма). **25.** Чиновник сказал только что прибывшему из Польши гостю: — Добро пожаловать! **26.** Нам нужно вести серьёзную борьбу с бюрократизмом и волокитой. **27.** Я знал заранее, что это вам не удастся. Нечего вам было так стараться. **28.** Я иду вместо брата. ‖Зачем он пришёл? Ему незачем было приходить. **29.** Что вы так поздно пришли? **30.** Что ваша жена? **31.** А что же вы мало едите? — Видите, ем, всё будет съедено. **32.** Без секретаря я не знаю, где что лежит, куда что послать. **33.** — Как вас зовут? — спросил её солдат. — Шурой, иногда Сашей называют, кто как. **34.** Она была красивая и, что ещё важнее, умная женщина. **35.** Что это ты всё смеёшься? **36.** Ваша работа поднимает вас в глазах всего мира. **37.** Ребёнка спустили на пол и опять подняли. **38.** Мы вас поместим в гостинице «Националь». Там удобно и светло. **39.** Ему нужно обратиться к врачу. **40.** Я имею ясное представление о положении дел. Из-за того, что сами боятся критики, эти люди теперь спешат критиковать ведение нашего хозяйства. **41.** Выборы у нас имеют место в ноябре. К сожалению, мы в то время будем отдыхать на юге. **42.** Опишите нам жизнь вашей матери. **43.** Мы спешим отдохнуть в парке культуры и отдыха. **44.** Он хорошо со всеми обращается, причём и к вам относится неплохо. **45.** Его идеи были ограниченны, но определённы. **46.** Мы сейчас пойдём осматривать достопримечательности Москвы. Я не знаю, пропустят ли нас в Кремль. Остановим милиционера, спросим его. **47.** Некому рассказать о себе, да и рассказывать нечего. — Неправда, рассказывайте, можете пропускать подробности. Никто не мешает вам говорить, но старайтесь ограничиться важными пунктами. **48.** Не будем останавливаться на описании всех озёр вообще, я для этого слишком устал. Байкал — это самое глубокое озеро в мире — вот и всё. **49.** Принимается подписка на литературные журналы

на 1965 г. Для оформле́ния зака́за на подпи́ску тре́буется во́семь неде́ль.
50. По на́шим да́нным ру́сские ре́дко ку́рят иностра́нные папиро́сы. **51.**
Ну́, э́того ещё не хвата́ло! Ока́зывается, что Оля не име́ет ни мале́йшего
представле́ния о то́м, когда́ самолёты прибыва́ют в Смоле́нск. К тому́ же
она́ поня́тия не име́ет о гости́ницах в э́том го́роде. **52.** Расскажи́те, кто́ из
дете́й что́ де́лает. **53.** До́ждь ско́ро ко́нчился, что́ все́х о́чень обра́довало.
54. Он звёзд с не́ба не хвата́ет (зна́чит: о́н не ге́ний).

TRANSLATION INTO RUSSIAN

1. Unfortunately, during the international exhibition there will be no-
where to put you up. In spite of the fact that you ordered a hotel room ten
weeks before the opening of the exhibition, there wasn't enough room for you.
2. We stopped at the Hotel Moscow. There is an enormous number of tourists
there, but the rooms are of low quality. **3.** Our director indicated that one must
not limit oneself to examples from the present time. Instead of that one must
generalize the most important out of what science has given during the period
from Marx to Lenin. **4.** Elections are going on now. If Vinográdov isn't elected,
there will be nobody for me to turn to. **5.** It was very interesting, and you will have
something to tell about when you get home. However, you shouldn't have missed
the lecture. **6.** As yet we are paying no attention to the registration of the docu-
ments of a given tourist. But if worst comes to worst, we will have to treat the
tourists a little more strictly. **7.** I've already gotten used to Irkútsk, but you
probably want to inspect the city. But let's limit ourselves to the   *main*
sights. **8.** I had no one to look up in L'vov. So they brought me straight to the
Intourist service bureau. **9.** You will have to order the room in advance.
10. Don't pay any attention to that. He has nothing against a specific program;
on the contrary, I think he will demand it. Not long ago he came out against the
cessation of negotiations. **11.** From now on we're going to live separately. You
have no idea at all about how to get along with people. Tomorrow I will address
myself to my lawyer. **12.** Waitress (Де́вушка), the service here is awful.
13. Will you have enough money for that? **14.** Describe your work at that
hotel. I work there as (in the capacity of) an elevator operator. Sometimes the
elevator doesn't work; in general (altogether) it functions rather badly. Then
people have to go up and down by the stairs. It's very inconvenient for everybody except me. I go out into the Park of Culture and Rest. But I don't rest
there. I'm a robust person and seldom get tired. **15.** You know comparatively
little about our way of life. Of course we have bedrooms, living rooms, kitchens,
etc. **16.** She and I had nothing to talk about; the situation was a very awkward
one. She raised her eyes to me (на *acc*) and said, "I'm awfully tired." **17.** Our
relatives all live in this apartment building, but on different floors. **18.** We're

finishing up our affairs now. **19.** I won't permit you to go until you take measures which will stop him from making that speech. **20.** I know nothing about Moscow, to say nothing about L'vov. **21.** For the time being it is very comfortable here. **22.** My teacher is an especially strict person. **23.** Let's go down 35
to the dining room. Hurry! (Quickly). What do you mean! There's no reason to hurry. **24.** After your inspection of the city you must put your affairs in order. **25.** Businessmen rule your country. That's why there's such red tape there. Your leaders are always on business trips. They do not occupy themselves with individual problems but limit themselves to generalizations about the world 40
situation. Thus, the quality of their work is not especially high. Nevertheless, inasmuch as you're here, I'll try to give you an idea of how our government operates. **26.** Our data show clearly that people in general haven't the slightest idea about international relations or foreign affairs. **27.** "Anna, give every man a glass of beer." "My Lord," Anna said to herself, "that's all I needed." 45

СЛОВА́РЬ

аге́нт-ств-о agency

администра́ци-я administration, management

бóг *E pl obl* god

бóже мóй my God! CL3.7

бюрó *N indecl* office, bureau

ва́нн-а bathtub

ва́нн-ая bathroom V.9

ви́д view, appearance, form; *gr* aspect VIII. 8

вме́сто *когó/чегó* instead of

волок-и́т-а red tape; ladies' man

вы́-став-/к-а (на) (< вы́ставить – выставля́ют) exhibition, exhibit, display

гост-и́н-ая living room V.9

гост-и́н-иц-а hotel

да́-н-н-ый (*PPP* < дать – дава́ть) (а) given, specific, present; да́нные data *sub adj*

Добрó пожа́ловать *куда́* Welcome (to)

докуме́нт document

досто-при-меч-á-тель-н-ость thing/place worthy of interest; *pl* sights (of city, etc.)

задóлго до *чего* V.3

зара́нее beforehand, in advance

иде́-я idea

ин-о-стра́н-н-ый foreign

Интури́ст (*short for* иностра́нный тури́ст) bureau for foreign travel

к томý же in addition, moreover

ка́ч-е-ств-о quality; в —е *когó/чегó* as, in the capacity of

коли́ч-е-ств-о quantity

команд-ир-óв-/к-а(в) (< командирова́ть) mission, business trip

коммерс-áнт businessman, merchant

кре́п-/к-ий strong, firm, robust

культу́р-/н-ый cultural; cultured, polite, refined

ку́х/н-я (в *or* на) (*gen pl* ку́хонь) kitchen

ле́стниц-а ЛЕЗ[1] stairs, stairway; ladder

-либо = -нибудь

ли́фт elevator, lift

лифтёр elevator/lift operator

мал-е́йш-ий (the) least/slightest; ни —его not the least, not the slightest

ме́бель furniture

между-нарóд-н-ый international

ме́сто: *see* име́ют ме́сто

наоборóт об-**ВОРОТ** on the contrary

на-стóй-чив-ый persistent

ниско́лько **КОЛИК** not at all

нóмер *E pl* -á number; size; issue (number) of magazine, etc.; hotel room

об-**ста́н**-о́в-/к-а *sg only* situation, conditions, circumstances; furniture

одна́ко however

о́зёр-о *pl* (*nom* озёра) lake

о-со́б-енн-ый (e)special, particular

от-де́ль-н-ый **ДЕЛ**[2] separate, individual

о́т-дых (на) (< отдохну́ть – отдыха́ют) rest, relaxation, vacation (rest)

пере́д-н-яя front hall, anteroom V.9

плака́т placard, poster

под-**пи́с**-/к-а (< подписа́ться – подпи́сываются на *кого́/что́* subscribe to) subscription

причём VIII. 2

про *кого́/что́* V.8

ра́з-н-ый different, various

слу́ч-ай case, occasion, incident, opportunity; во вся́ком слу́чае in any case, anyway; на вся́кий слу́чай just in case; в кра́йнем слу́чае if the worst comes to worst

со-**тру́д**-ник co-worker, collaborator, employee

сп-а́-ль/н-я (*gen pl* спа́лен) bedroom

стол-о́в-ая dining room, restaurant, (students' or workers') cafeteria   V. 9

стро́г-ий strict, stern, severe

тём не ме́нее nevertheless

у-**бо́р**-н-ая lavatory, room with a toilet V.9

у-**до́б**-/н-ый comfortable, convenient

у́м *E* mind, wit, intellect

чин-о́в-ник official, bureaucrat

эта́ж *E* floor, story

ГЛАГО́ЛЫ

(за)-**брон**-и́р-ова-ть order, reserve, confirm (official language)

о́т-**бы**-ть – отбыва́ют depart from, leave (*esp* on planes, trains, etc.)

n отбы́тие

при́-**бы**-ть – прибыва́ют arrive (*esp* on planes, trains, etc.)

n прибы́тие

от-**вёз**-у́т – отводи́ть V.6

рук-о-**вод**-и́-ть *кем/чем* rule, govern VII.6

n руково́дство

поз-**во́л**-и-ть – позволя́ют (по-и́з) *кому́/чему́ что́/inf* allow, permit

n позволе́ние

об-**рат**-и́-ть – обраща́ют об-**ВРАТ** turn; — внима́ние на *кого́/что́* pay attention to; —ся к *кому́/чему́* за *чем* turn to X for Y, address oneself to X for Y

обраща́ются с *кем/чем* get along with, treat (people and things)

n обраще́ние

при-**вы́к**-(ну)-ть – привыка́ют к *кому́/чему́* get used to, become accustomed to

n привы́ч/ка habit

о-**грани́ч**-и-ть – ограни́чивают **ГРАН**-иц limit, restrict; —ся *кем/чем* limit/restrict oneself to, be limited/restricted to

n ограниче́ние

от-**дох**-ну́-ть – отдыха́ют rest, take a rest/vacation

n о́тдых

со-**жал**-е́-н-и-е (< сожале́ют *кому́* о *ко́м/чём* or *что*) pity, regret; к —ю unfortunately

по-**жа́л**-ова-ть: *see* Добро́ пожа́ловать

(по)-**жм**-ут – пожима́ют press, squeeze; — *кому́* ру́ку shake someone's hand

n пожа́тие

на-**зна́ч**-и-ть – назнача́ют assign, appoint, fix

n назначе́ние

раз-**ыск**-а-ть – разы́скивают **ИСК** look for, look up; *P* find

n ро́зыск

им-е́й-ут **ме́ст**-о take place, go on

по-н-**я́**-т-и-е (< по́-**йм**-у́т – понима́ют) concept, notion; не име́ют (никако́го)

—я о *чём* have no idea (at all) of

под-ни́м-ут – поднима́ют raise, lift; —ся *past tense E* go up, rise

n подня́тие, подъём

за-ка́з-а-ть – зака́зывают order (as food, a room, etc.)

n зака́з

за-ко́нч-и-ть – зака́нчивают **КОН-Ц** finish (up)

пре-крат-и́-ть – прекраща́ют V.1

n прекраще́ние

по-мест-и́-ть – помеща́ют *гдé* place, locate, house

n помеще́ние (action of) housing; lodgings, premises

об-общ-и́-ть – обобща́ют generalize, summarize

n обобще́ние

со-в-пад-у́т – совпада́ют с *чём* coincide with

n совпаде́ние

о-пис-а-ть – опи́сывают describe

n описа́ние

про-пуст-и-ть – пропуска́ют let through; omit, skip, miss

n про́пуск admission; pass; omission

с-пуст-и-ть – спуска́ют lower; —ся descend, go down

n спуск

о-свобод-и́-ть – освобожда́ют liberate, set free

n освобожде́ние

об-служ-и-ть – обслу́живают wait on, serve *tr*

n обслу́живание service

о-смотр-е-ть – осма́тривают inspect, examine, look at

n осмо́тр

у-спе́й-ут – успева́ют *inf* have time to; succeed in; — на *чтó or* к *чему́* be in time for, make (something on time)

n успе́х success

(по)-спеш-и́-ть *куда/inf* hurry

пред-ста́вл-ен-и-е (< пред-ста́в-и-ть – представля́ют) (re)presentation; idea, concept; не име́ют (никако́го) —я о *ком/чём* have no idea (at all) of

пере-ста́н-ут – перестава́ть V.1

о-стан-ов-и-ть V.1; —ся V.1

n остано́в/ка stop (*both action and place*; *e.g.* bus stop)

у-ста́н-ут – устава́ть be tired, get tired; я уста́л *inf* I'm tired/I've become tired of

n устава́ние getting tired

о-фо́рм-и-ть – оформля́ют make official, formalize, register

n оформле́ние

хват-и-ть – хвата́ет CL3-5 Vocab. R8. C

LESSON
VI

The infinitive

ВОПРО́С О БЕССМЕ́РТИИ ДУШИ́

Вожди́ коммуни́зма не ра́з ука́зывали на то́, что коммуни́зм и рели́гия — несовмести́мые поня́тия. «Рели́гия е́сть о́пиум для наро́да», писа́л Ма́ркс. Ле́нин разделя́л э́то мне́ние и **счита́л**,[2] что па́ртия не мо́жет бы́ть нейтра́льна в отноше́нии рели́гии и должна́ вести́ пропага́нду про́тив все́х религио́зных «предрассу́дков». Ста́лин име́л таки́е же взгля́ды, и его́ насле́дники та́кже не допуска́ют возмо́жности отказа́ться хоть части́чно от маркси́стского уче́ния о рели́гии. **Пра́вда**,[3] во вре́мя войны́ напа́дки на це́рковь со стороны́ прави́тельства вре́менно прекрати́лись, но э́то примире́ние не пережило́ конца́ войны́. Сего́дня молоды́м лю́дям в СССР почти́ не́т **де́ла до**[4] рели́гии; большинство́ из ни́х про́сто атеи́сты.

Но да́же к атеи́зму е́сть ра́зные подхо́ды. Бы́ть атеи́стом во́все не зна́чит ни во что́ не ве́рить. Мно́гие ду́мают, что ве́ра в коммуни́зм до изве́стной сте́пени замени́ла ве́ру в Бо́га. Но е́сть и други́е то́чки зре́ния. Быва́ют лю́ди, кото́рые не вполне́ отрица́ют бессме́ртие души́, впро́чем они́ воспринима́ют э́то бессме́ртие ина́че, чем обыкнове́нные христиа́не. Ка́к нам э́то поня́ть? Рассмо́трим оди́н отры́вок из по́вести В. Ф. Тендряко́ва «Чрезвыча́йное». Дире́ктор одно́й сре́дней шко́лы, Анато́лий Матве́евич, разгова́ривает с одно́й из свои́х учени́ц, ве́рующей в Бо́га. Они́ иду́т по мо́крой, дереве́нской у́лице. Она́ говори́т ему́:

Учени́ца. Анато́лий Матве́евич, скажи́те, вы́ ду́мали о то́м, что вы́ когда́-нибудь умрёте, а э́то всё . . . — Всё, всё оста́нется. И э́ти лу́жи бу́дут лежа́ть, и кто́-то обходи́ть и́х бу́дет . . . Кто́-то, а не мы́. Умрём, и всё!

Анато́лий Матве́евич.   Хо́чешь ве́рить в бессме́ртие души́? Бои́шься ис-
че́знуть совсе́м? Та́к я́ скажу́ тебе́: да́, существу́ют бессме́ртные чело-
ве́ческие ду́ши или почти́ бессме́ртные . . . Удивлена́, что э́то говорю́   25
я́, не ве́рящий ни в бо́га, ни в чёрта, ни в переселе́ние безгре́шных ду́ш
в ра́йские ку́щи. А во́т ско́лько ра́з ты́ слы́шала стихотворе́ние «На
хо́лмах Гру́зии лежи́т ночна́я мгла́»? По́мнишь: «Мне́ гру́стно и легко́,
печа́ль моя́ светла́ . . .» Ко́сти Пу́шкина давно́ истле́ли, а э́то живёт.
Душа́ живёт, вну́тренний ми́р! Умрём мы́, бу́дет жи́ть и по́сле на́с.   30
Придёшь домо́й, возьмёшь кусо́к хле́ба — заду́майся. Растёртое в
муку́ зерно́, вода́, дро́жжи, со́ль — то́лько ли э́то должно́ насы́тить
тебя́? Не́т, мука́, дро́жжи, со́ль, а ещё и ду́ши, да́, ду́ши многочи́слен-
ных, безве́стных, о́чень далёких пре́дков . . . Опя́ть удивля́ешься. На-
ве́рно, счита́ешь меня́ и́ли сумасше́дшим старико́м, и́ли ве́рующим на   35
сво́й ла́д . . . Кусо́к хле́ба! Что́ мо́жет бы́ть про́ще? Но да́же в нём
зало́жены наблюде́ния, соображе́ния, дога́дки не со́тен, а мно́гих
ты́сяч люде́й, духо́вные проявле́ния огро́мной а́рмии, жи́вшей в ра́з-
ные века́, в ра́зных стра́нах. Кто́ пе́рвый догада́лся насади́ть на о́сь
колесо́? Никто́ не зна́ет. Духо́вный вкла́д! Он живёт и сейча́с в любо́й   40
автомаши́не, в любо́м самолёте. Бессме́ртна душа́ э́того неизве́стного
челове́ка! . . . Тебе́ отме́рено ше́сть, се́мь и́ли во́семь десятиле́тий,
суме́й[5] их испо́льзовать, подари́ что́-то но́вое, пу́сть ма́ленькое, но́
своё, подари́ его́ те́м, кто́ ста́нет жи́ть по́сле тебя́. Бессме́ртие то́лько в
э́том, **друго́го**[1] не существу́ет . . .   45

[Third and fourth paragraphs adapted from V. F. Tendrjakov,
Črezvyčájnoe, Moscow, 1962, pp. 32–33]

THE INFINITIVE

The infinitive is already well known to us as a "neutral" or "dictionary"
form lacking tense and person and expressing only aspect and voice. We are
familiar with its role as a complement to such verbs as **хоте́ть, люби́ть, обе-
ща́ют**, with its denotation of future or incipient action with forms of **бу́дут** and
ста́нут; we have encountered it as a complement to **чтобы** in purpose clauses
(and in Lesson IX we will see it with **чтобы** in other contexts) and to predicates
like **пора́** or **на́до** in impersonal constructions. Let us consider certain other
usages:

A. As subject

An infinitive or infinitive phrase may serve as the subject of a sentence; the
English equivalent is often the present participle:

Учи́ться — всегда́ интере́сно.	Studying (To study) is always interesting.
Кури́ть — вре́дно для здоро́вья.	Smoking is injurious to health.
Жи́ть во Владивосто́ке нелегко́.	Living in Vladivostok is not easy.
О́чень опа́сно стоя́ть на краю́ платфо́рмы.	It's very dangerous to stand at the edge of the platform.

B. With е́сли

Е́сли plus the infinitive is used when the hypothetical subject of the subordinate clause is unspecific or of no importance to the main clause:

Е́сли взя́ть э́тот пери́од как приме́р, уви́дим, что . . .	If one takes this period as an example, one sees that . . .
Е́сли спроси́ть его́, о́н отве́тит, что ничего́ не зна́ет.	If you ask (one asks) him, he will answer that he knows nothing.

C. With dative complement

An infinitive used with a dative complement, or used independently, implying a dative, expresses a range of meanings connected with possibility and/or desirability and may be said to have a modal function. Such an infinitive may correspond to English "can/could/is to/should/ought/shall," etc. or to an imperative, according to the context:

1. Interrogatives:

Ка́к пройти́ на Кра́сную пло́щадь?	How does one get to Red Square? *Or:* How is one to, can one, shall one, should one, ought one to, could one, etc.
Как (мне́, ему́, etc.) . . .?	(*Or substitute specific pronouns*)
Где́ (мне́) иска́ть э́ту кни́гу?	Where can one (am I to, etc.) look for this book?
Ско́лько на́м жда́ть?	How long must we (are we to) wait?
Где́ посмотре́ть фи́льм «Судьба́ челове́ка»?	Where can we see the film *Fate of a Man*?
Когда́ мне́ ва́м позвони́ть?	When shall (should) I call you?
Что́ бы́ло сказа́ть?	What was to be said?
К кому́ ему́ бу́дет тогда́ обрати́ться?	Whom will he have to turn to then?
Ва́м помо́чь?	Can I help you?
Сказа́ть?	Should I tell?

Máма, намáзать тебé хлéб мáс- лом?	Mama, can I fix you a bread and butter?
Кáк нáм бы́ть?	How are we to manage?
Зачéм молчáть?	Why be quiet?
Почемý допускáть такýю возмóж- ность?	Why allow such a possibility?

2. Statements:

Офицéром такóму солдáту не бы- вáть.	Such a soldier should (would, could, ought . . . to) never be (become) an officer.
Егó идéя — емý и бы́ть учи́телем.	It's his idea; let him be the teacher.
Не éй емý э́то сказáть, а емý éй.	It's not she who ought to tell him, but he who should tell her.
Вáм лýчше искáть рабóту . . .	You'd better look for work.
Об э́том лýчше никомý не го- вори́ть.	You'd better not tell anyone about that.
Тебé говори́ть, а нáм слýшать.	It's for you to talk and for us to listen.

The modal quality of the infinitive may be enhanced by the addition of the
particle **бы**, which introduces a conditional element:

Стáть бы офицéром.	If I could only become an officer.
Вáм бы обращáться с ни́м осто- рóжнее.	You ought to treat him more care- fully.
Тóлько бы жи́ть.	If only I (we, etc.) could live.
Если тáк нýжно, давáй перегово- ри́м. А лýчше бы спáть. (Толстóй)	If it's so necessary, let's talk. But it would be better to go to sleep.

Compare:

| Кáк мнé э́то сдéлать? | How can I do that? |
| Кáк бы мнé э́то сдéлать? | How could I do that? |

3. Commands: Here the infinitive (with the dative only implied) may convey an unspecified notion of duty or necessity, the exact significance being made
clearer by the context. On public signs or directions it serves as a reminder or
mild command:

По травé не ходи́ть.	Don't walk on the grass.
Не кури́ть. Не кантовáть.	No smoking. This side up (Don't tip).
Не высóвываться.	Don't lean out (the train window).

Less stereotyped or more personal commands or instructions on signs are usually expressed in the imperative:

Береги́сь по́езда.	Watch out for trains (a train).
Уважа́йте дру́г дру́га.	Show respect for one another.

Pronounced with the intonation of a command, the infinitive takes on a more definitely imperative sense. Military commands directed at a group may be infinitives:

Молча́ть!	Be silent! Keep quiet!
Взя́ть его́.	Grab him!
Все́м бы́ть на места́х. Через ча́с собра́ться зде́сь.	Everyone to be in their places. Meet here in an hour!
В строю́ не разгова́ривать.	Don't talk in ranks!

SUBORDINATE POINTS

1. The student, who is already familiar with **есть** and **нет** constructions, may now begin to notice a similar pattern with various verbs and other predicate constructions. The positive has a normal subject-verb format, while the corresponding negative consists of an impersonal (third singular form) verb with a *genitive* complement. Such constructions are particularly common when the negated item is a pronoun. **Ничего́** is used for **ничто́** with particular frequency:

Что́ из э́того вы́шло?	What came of that?
Из э́того **ничего́** не вы́шло.	Nothing came of that.
С ни́м **что́-то** случи́лось.	Something happened to him.
С ни́м **ничего́** не случи́тся.	Nothing will happen to him.
Что́ у ва́с боли́т?	What hurts?
Ничего́ не боли́т.	Nothing hurts.
Оста́лись то́лько мы́ с сестро́й.	Only my sister and I were left.
Кро́ме ни́х **никого́** не оста́лось.	Outside of them nobody was left.
Таки́е явле́ния существу́ют.	Such phenomena exist.
Таки́х явле́ний не существу́ет.	Such phenomena do not exist.
С друго́й стороны́ ко́мнаты на́м бы́л ви́ден неме́цкий **солда́т**.	From the other side of the room we could see a German soldier.
Отсю́да не ви́дно **го́рода**.	The city isn't visible from here.
Ста́л слы́шен шу́м реки́.	The noise of the river became audible.
В э́той ко́мнате **ничего́** не слы́шно.	One can't hear anything in this room.

Мне́ нужна́ но́вая **кварти́ра**.　　　I need a new apartment.

Мне́ **ничего́ (никого́)** не ну́жно.　　I don't need anything (anybody).

2. The important verb **счита́ют** (imperfective) has a number of meanings: "count, regard, consider"; it is perfectivized in various ways depending on the meaning:

(со)счита́ют 'count (numbers)':

Э́тот ма́льчик уме́ет счита́ть до ста́.

The boy knows how to count to 100.

с/о/чту́т (счесть) – счита́ют что *or кого́/что́ ке́м/че́м (or* за *кого́/что́)* 'consider, regard that *or* X as Y':

Я счита́ю, что вы́ име́ете на э́то пра́во.

I consider that you have a right to that.

Я счита́ю его́ у́мным челове́ком./ Я счита́ю его́ за у́много челове́ка.

I consider him (as) an intelligent person.

Я э́то счита́ю мои́м до́лгом.

I regard that as my duty.

Он счёл ну́жным всё рассказа́ть. (*The direct object is the infinitive phrase* всё рассказа́ть.)

He considered it necessary to tell everything.

Счита́ется 'be considered' is a passive (cf. X.H):

Он счита́ется хоро́шим специали́стом.

He is considered a good specialist.

Счита́ется, что на́м лу́чше прекрати́ть на́ши де́йствия.

It is considered that we had better cease our operations.

Счита́ются should be distinguished from счита́ют себя́ *inst* or за *acc* 'consider oneself'; compare (cf. also X.B):

Он счита́ется вели́ким писа́телем.

He is considered a great writer.

Он счита́ет себя́ вели́ким писа́телем.

He considers himself a great writer.

(по)счита́ются с *inst* 'reckon with':

С таки́ми соображе́ниями я́ не счита́лся.

I didn't reckon with such considerations.

Finally, note:

Э́то не счита́ется.

That doesn't count.

не счита́я X *gen*

not counting X

3. Note that **пра́вда**, as a parenthetical word set off by commas, has a concessive meaning: "to be sure, true, while it is true," etc.:

Он, пра́вда, написа́л письмо́, но́ ещё не отпра́вил его́.	He's written the letter, to be sure, but he hasn't sent it off yet.
Пра́вда, о́н умён, но́ . . .	True, he's bright, but . . .

4. Notice the expression *dat pers* **де́ло до** *gen*:

Како́е на́м де́ло до э́того?	What business is that of ours?
На́м не́т де́ла до э́того.	That's no business of ours.

5. The perfective verb **суме́ют** is not a partner of **уме́ют**; it does not mean "know how" but rather "prove able to, succeed in":

Он не суме́ет э́того сде́лать.	He won't be able to do that.
Она́ суме́ла его́ убеди́ть.	She succeeded in convincing him.

TRANSLATION INTO ENGLISH

1. Како́го вы́ мне́ния об э́том? Мы́ обраща́емся к ва́м ка́к к челове́ку без вся́ких предрассу́дков. (Отве́т) Ну́, что́ ва́м сказа́ть? Я не счита́ю себя́ нейтра́льным в э́том отноше́нии: К тому́ же е́сли я́ ва́м отве́чу, то́ мои́ взгля́ды бу́дут изве́стны все́м. Я до́лжен счита́ться с те́м, ка́к на меня́ бу́дут
5   смотре́ть мои́ насле́дники. 2. Я не отрица́ю то́чки зре́ния ве́рующих в бессме́ртие души́; напро́тив я́ вполне́ допуска́ю таку́ю возмо́жность. А сказа́ть о свои́х со́бственных взгля́дах нелегко́. Не лу́чше ли мне́ молча́ть? 3. Что́ де́лать? В гости́нице не оказа́лось ме́ста. 4. Вре́мя идёт, и ника́ких реши́тельных ме́р не принима́ется. 5. Это то́лько части́чное при-
10 мире́ние. Мы́ не ду́маем прекрати́ть на́шу борьбу́ навсегда́. 6. Вы́ до изве́стной сте́пени пра́вы. Но́ не бу́дет ли всё зави́сеть от того́, како́й бу́дет у ни́х подхо́д? Ведь мы́ не зна́ем, ка́к они́ воспри́мут на́шу иде́ю. Суме́ют ли они́ вообще́ её поня́ть, не говоря́ уже́ об обсужде́нии? 7. Спаси́бо, я́ себя́ прекра́сно чу́вствую. Умере́ть? Напро́тив, я́ бу́ду жи́ть до бесконе́ч-
15 ности. 8. Не́кому его́ замени́ть. Мы́ счита́ем его́ еди́нственным на́шим руководи́телем. 9. По́езд исче́з с по́ля зре́ния. 10. Её засте́нчивость посте́пенно исчеза́ла. 11. Я удивля́юсь ка́честву ва́шей по́вести. Я до сих по́р счита́л ва́с за отли́чного писа́теля. 12. Стари́к глубоко́ заду́мался: «Что́ меня́ беспоко́ит? Я живу́ ти́хо, берегу́ своё здоро́вье, всегда́ де́йствую со-
20 гла́сно о́бщим пра́вилам и зако́нам. Все́ лю́ди меня́ уважа́ют. Чего́ ещё не хвата́ет? А во́т чего́. Я не занима́юсь вопро́сом о мое́й душе́. А ка́к нача́ть? Не́ во что ве́рить. Ну́ и вздо́р! С ума́ схожу́! Не бу́ду боро́ться с э́тим вопро́сом. Откажу́сь — и всё.» 13. В на́шем го́роде всё бо́льше и бо́льше

хо́дят в це́рковь. Через не́сколько лет неве́рующих не оста́нется совсе́м. Пра́вда, вы спро́сите, отку́да э́тим лю́дям бу́дет взять таку́ю ве́ру? А я отве́чу, что тут соверше́нно обы́чное явле́нче, что в нём нет ничего́ чрезвыча́йного. **14.** Таки́х явле́ний про́сто не быва́ет. **15.** На́до знать жизнь во всех её проявле́ниях. **16.** Этот челове́к проявля́ет са́мые лу́чшие ка́чества. **17.** Появле́ние его́ сестры́ в Москве́ нас всех удиви́ло. **18.** Из-за горы́ появи́лся большо́й самолёт. **19.** Мы до́лго и подро́бно обсужда́ли э́тот вопро́с. Он за́нял пе́рвое ме́сто на на́шей пове́стке дня. Мы ка́ждый день рассма́тривали все его́ сто́роны, мы испо́льзовали зна́ния вся́кого ро́да учёных, име́вших с э́тим де́ло, мы вызыва́ли сюда́ всевозмо́жных специали́стов. Мы ча́сто заду́мывались и над ва́шими наблюде́ниями; сло́вом, мы сде́лали всё возмо́жное в связи́ с э́тим вопро́сом. **20.** Мы неда́вно пересели́лись на но́вую кварти́ру. **21.** Како́е мне де́ло до ва́шей духо́вной жи́зни? (Отве́т) Вы соверше́нно пра́вы, вам нет де́ла до моего́ вну́треннего ми́ра. **22.** В его́ рабо́те не оказа́лось стихотворе́ний на духо́вные те́мы. Впро́чем, мы не зна́ем, отказа́лся ли Бра́ун от свои́х пре́жних убежде́ний. **23.** Он, наве́рно, ма́ло зна́ет о вне́шней поли́тике Фра́нции. Ина́че бы он сказа́л своё мне́ние. С друго́й стороны́, на́до счита́ться с тем, что он живёт там уже́ пять лет. **24.** Нам без ва́шей по́мощи не обойти́сь. **25.** Умо́м Росси́ю не поня́ть. **26.** Но́вость обошла́ весь го́род. **27.** На э́тот раз мы про́сто обойдём вопро́с о забасто́вке рабо́чих. **28.** Нам пришло́сь отказа́ть рабо́чим в большинстве́ их тре́бований. Поэ́тому они́ и забастова́ли. **29.** Мне не́ было слы́шно его́ се́рдца. **30.** Мы замолча́ли и стари́к заговори́л о свои́х греха́х. **31.** По́сле исчезнове́ния его́ жены́ печа́ль его́ не зна́ла грани́ц. **32.** Они́ жи́ли в ра́зные века́, но име́ли одина́ковые взгля́ды. **33.** Когда́ я ду́маю о том, ско́лько она́ пережива́ет, у меня́ гру́стно на душе́. **34.** Он е́дет с сумасше́дшей ско́ростью. **35.** Бери́ э́тот кусо́к хле́ба, нама́зывай. Сейча́с переда́м соль. **36.** Я влюби́лся в неё с пе́рвого взгля́да. **37.** На пе́рвый взгля́д показа́лось, что он хоро́ший челове́к. А тепе́рь я уже́ не могу́ быть того́ мне́ния. **38.** Колесо́ — э́то исхо́дный пу́нкт вся́кого тра́нспорта. **39.** В тече́ние э́того десятиле́тия мно́гие учёные подари́ли что́-то но́вое нау́ке. **40.** На́ша страна́ неда́вно пережила́ револю́цию. **41.** Пожа́луйста, не разгова́ривайте. Мы сейча́с му́чимся над о́чень тру́дной пробле́мой. Этой рабо́той мы наде́емся внести́ хотя́ бы ма́ленький вклад в о́бщее де́ло. **42.** Меня́ му́чит вот како́й вопро́с. Допу́стим, оди́н изве́стный фи́зик уже́ внёс значи́тельный вклад в нау́ку. Но он то́лько что написа́л о́чень глу́пую кни́гу. До́лжен ли я отрица́ть его́, переста́ть уважа́ть его́? **43.** Что тако́е зако́н? Эри́ксен счита́л, что зако́н представля́ет собо́й выраже́ние во́ли большинства́ люде́й да́нного о́бщества. Как вы отно́ситесь к э́той то́чке зре́ния? **44.** Весёлые де́вушки дари́ли солда́там цветы́. **45.** Многоуважа́емый тов.(гр.) Жда́нов . . . Дорого́й Ва́ня . . .

TRANSLATION INTO RUSSIAN

1. I don't consider it necessary to have such views. I consider them prejudices. **2.** What's your opinion about the Marxist teaching about the church? **3.** I regard your approach as a denial of our existence itself. **4.** It will be difficult to replace him. He has never refused to work and has never refused us any help. **5.** How can I share your opinion? You ought to understand that other points of view are possible as well, and that they aren't all incompatible. **6.** What business is that of theirs? **7.** Ordinary Christians, perhaps most Christians, believe in the immortality of the soul. **8.** This time let's examine the matter from a new viewpoint. **9.** From the whole conversation only fragments were audible. **10.** Our workers constantly think of the contribution they are making to society and to humanity. That's why they never strike. **11.** Fate measures off for you seven or eight decades. Be able to use them, but one must rest also. One shouldn't torment oneself over hard work all the time. **12.** I immediately guessed that she was an American. She said her husband had disappeared but that she had not been very surprised by his disappearance. **13.** That didn't happen. **14.** There's nothing extraordinary in that; why does it strike you so? **15.** Everybody apprehends life in his own way (по-своему). **16.** I often fall into thought about Puškin's poems. **17.** Nothing has come of these negotiations. The workers are tired of arguing, they are indignant about our demands, and I am afraid that they will suddenly go on strike. **18.** Your observations have turned out to be correct. It is obvious that the majority of the workers very much respect their leaders, and I am sure that, if we refuse the workers their demands, there will be a strike. **19.** I know that it is considered that he has great influence, but I don't think that he will prove able to reconcile our two sides. Furthermore, he knows only one side of the question. **20.** If it turns out that there isn't enough bread, the people will revolt. **21.** Your spiritual life is no business of mine, but I respect you for the high quality of your work. **22.** Why should I watch out for your children? **23.** Talent is a relatively rare phenomenon. **24.** Not long ago a new young man appeared, whom my daughter liked very much. She told me, "His former sins don't interest me. I can't get along without him." **25.** How does he manifest this feeling of love? **26.** Next month we will move our parents to the city. Have you gone out of your mind? Then it will be too hot. **27.** We used all available data, and are now pondering over your observations. But so far we know only the external side of the matter. **28.** From where we were standing the woman was not visible, but her voice was audible. **29.** Working in your store isn't very interesting. Well, we don't need you. You serve (wait on) people poorly, you don't know how to treat them, and when there's nobody to wait on, you don't do a damn thing. **30.** One should not circumvent laws and regulations. **31.** We are only conjecturing about what our ancestors experienced. Such conjectures can lead to the allowing of serious errors. **32.** Take any person, even the stupidest, and he will agree with that. **33.** You ought to share my grief at least partially. **34.** These attacks on the party come from all sides. **35.** We must conduct a neutral policy in this regard. **36.** Our director has very definite views. He says that the only manifestation of immortality of the soul consists in what a man has done during his life. **37.** There are ten people here, not counting Gláša Zórina. **38.** Igor' considers music a manifestation of the soul. **39.** Be silent! Don't talk thus about Stalin! After all, he was a native of Georgia. The people there believed in him. **40.** It is extremely difficult to say whether our descendants will believe what we say now. After all, we all ought to know that one can't believe everything our ancestors said. **41.** Our only gift to our descendants is hope.

СЛОВА́ ТО́ЛЬКО К Э́ТОМУ УРО́КУ

без-ве́ст-/н-ый unknown, obscure
без-гре́ш-/н-ый sinless, without sin
дро́жж-и (long, soft ž') E pl obl yeast
ку́щ-а hut, abode obs poet
лу́ж-а puddle
мгл-а́ haze; shadows poet
мук-а́ **МУК**[2] flour

о́пиум opium
о́сь E pl obl axle
ра́й paradise
ра́й-ск-ий heavenly
хо́лм E hill; stem stress in Pushkin's poem
    is for prosodic reasons

ГЛАГО́ЛЫ

ис-тле́й-ут – истлева́ют rot, decay
на-**сад**-и-ть – наса́живают set/place on
    n наса́д/ка
на-**сы́т**-и-ть – насыща́ют satiate,
    saturate

n насыще́ние
раз-/о/**тр́**-ут – растира́ют grind, rub
    over
    n расти́рка

О́БЩИЙ СЛОВА́РЬ

атеи́зм, atheism; атеи́ст, atheist; атеис-
    ти́ческий atheist(ic)
бес-**смерт**-и-е immortality
бес-**смерт**-/н-ый immortal
больш-ин-ств-о́ **БОЛ**[2] (pl большинства́)
    кого́/чего́ majority, most
вз-**гляд** (<взгляну́ть – взгля́дывают)
    glance, look; view, opinion
вид-/н-ый visible; eminent (lg f only)
    VI.1; ви́дно, что . . . it's obvious
    that . . .

в-**клад** (<вложи́ть – вкла́дывают put in)
    contribution; investment; внесу́т –
    вноси́ть — в что́ make contribution
    to (nonfinancial)
внеш-/н-ий external, outside; —яя поли́-
    тика foreign policy
внутр-енн-ий internal, inside
вол-я will
вполне́ completely
впро́чем however, though
времен-/н-ый temporary

всё: ... , и всё ... and that's all there is to it: Он ге́ний, и всё. He's a genius and that's all there is to it.

гре́х *E* sin

Гру́з-и-я Georgia (Soviet republic); гру-зи́н(ка), грузи́нский Georgian

гру́ст-/н-ый sad

де́ло: де́ло до *кого́/чего́* VI.4

дерев-е́н-ск-ий rural, village, country *adj*

десяти-ле́т-и-е decade

дире́ктор *E pl* -а́ director

до-га́д-/к-а guess, conjecture; *cf.* дога-да́ются – дога́дываются

дух-о́в-н-ый spiritual; ecclesiastical

душ-а́ *S pl acc sg* soul; person (*as in* на ду́шу per capita)

еди́н-ств-ен/н-ый the only

за-баст-о́в-/к-а (workers') strike; *cf.* за-бастова́ть

за-ко́н law (a law or law in general); law as studied = пра́во

за-сте́н-чив-ый bashful

зёрн-о́ *S pl* grain

иде́-я idea

ина́че otherwise *adv and conj*

кол-ёс-о́ (*pl* колёса) wheel

ко́сть *E pl* bone

кус-/о́к piece, bit, lump

ла́д: на свой ла́д in one's own (often peculiar) fashion

люб-/о́вь (*gen* любви́, *inst* любо́вью) love

маркс-и́зм Marxism; маркс-и́ст Marxist

мног-о-чи́сл-ен/н-ый numerous

мо́к-р-ый wet

на-де́жд-а hope

на-па́д-/к-и *pl only* (*gen* напа́док) attacks (often verbal: criticism); *cf.* нападу́т – напада́ют attack

напро́тив on the contrary; opposite, on the other side, across the street, etc.

на-сле́д-ник successor, heir

нейтра́ль-/н-ый neutral

не-со-в-ме́ст-и́-м-ый incompatible

один-а́к-ов-ый the same, identical

о-сторо́ж-/н-ый careful

от-ры́в-/о/к fragment; passage, extract (of a text)

печа́ль grief, sorrow

по́-весть ВЕД-т *E pl obl* tale, story, novelette

под-хо́д approach; *cf.* под/о/йду́т – под-ходи́ть

пото́м-/о/к descendant

пра́в-ил-о rule, regulation

пре́д-/о/к ancestor, forefather

пред-рас-су́д-/о/к prejudice

пре́ж-н-ий previous

пропага́нд-а propaganda

пу́сть even if, even though

раб-о́ч-ий РАБ–ОТ worker *sub adj*; workers', labor *adj*

рели́ги-я religion

религио́з-/н-ый religious

се́рд-/ц-е *E pl* (*gen pl* серде́ц) heart

слы́ш-/н-ый audible VI.1

со́б-ств-ен/н-ый own, proper; со́бственно говоря́ strictly speaking

со́ль *E pl obl* salt

со́т-/н-я (*gen pl* со́тен) (a) hundred

стих-о-твор-е́н-и-е (normal-length) poem; a longer, narrative poem = поэ́ма

сторон-а́ *S nom pl acc sg* side, direction; со —ы́ *кого́/чего́* from, on the part of; с мое́й —ы́ for my part; с одно́й —ы́ ..., с друго́й —ы́ ... on the one hand ..., on the other hand ...

судь-/б-а́ *S pl* (*gen pl* су́деб) fate

с-ум-а́-с-ше́д-ш-ий mad, out of one's mind; с/о/йду́т – сходи́ть с ума́ go out of one's mind

сух-о́й dry

то́ч-/к-а point; period; — зре́ния point of view; с —и зре́ния *кого́/чего́* from the point of view of

уч-ен-и́к *M*, уч-ен-и́ц-а *F* pupil (through high school)

фа́кт fact

хотя́ бы if only, if even; at least

христиан-и́н (*pl* христиа́не) Christian

христиа́н-ств-о Christianity
церк-о́в-н-ый church *adj*
це́рк/о/вь (*gen*/*dat*/*prp* це́ркви, *inst* це́р-
  ковью) *E pl obl* (це́ркви, -ве́й, -ва́м,
  etc.) church

челове́ч-еск-ий human
челове́ч-е-ств-о mankind, humanity
чрез-**выч**-а́й-/н-ый extraordinary, out of
  the ordinary
чу́в-ств-о feeling

ГЛАГО́ЛЫ

баст-ова́-ть strike
  n басту́ющий striker
за-баст-ова́-ть *P only* go on strike
  n забасто́в/ка strike
берёг-у́т (*us P* сберегу́т) save, guard,
  watch; —ся *кого́*/*чего́* beware, watch
  out for:
  Береги́сь соба́ки. Beware of the dog.
на-блюд-а́й-ут observe; — за *ке́м*/*че́м*
  supervise, watch over
  n наблюде́ние < *an older* наблюду́т
у-**важ**-а́й-ут respect, esteem; *adj* уважа́е-
  мый respected, esteemed; (мно́го)ува-
  жа́емый X Dear X (*respectful; more intimate is* Дорого́й)
  n уваже́ние < *an older* ува́жить
(по)-**ве́р**-и-ть *кому́*/*чему́* believe; — в
  кого́/*что* believe in
  n ве́ра faith, belief
ве́р-ова-ть в *кого́*/*что* believe in
  n (не)ве́рующий (non)believer
до-**гад**-а́й-ут-ся – дога́дываются о *ко́м*/
  чём or что guess, conjecture
  n дога́д/ка
за-**говор**-и́-ть *P only* start to speak
пе́ре-да́-ть – передава́ть give/hand/pass
  over, transmit
  n переда́ча
(по)-**дар**-и-ть *кому́* present, give (a gift)

  n пода́р/о/к gift, present
раз-**дел**-и́-ть – разделя́ют divide, distrib-
  ute, share
  n разделе́ние
у-**див**-и́-ть – удивля́ют surprise; —ся
  кому́/*чему́* be surprised at; *cf.* я
  удивлён *ке́м*/*че́м and* я удивля́юсь
  кому́/*чему́* I'm surprised at
  n удивле́ние
за-**ду́м**-ай-ут-ся – заду́мываются become
  lost in thought *P*; ponder *I*
пе́ре-жив-ут – пережива́ют experience, live
  through, survive
  n пережива́ние experience, emotional experience
зр-е́н-и-е (< зре́ть) vision, sight; то́чка
  —я: *see* то́чка
вы́-йд-ут – выходить come/turn out
об-/о/-**йд**-у́т – обходить go all over;
  go around; avoid; —ся без *кого́*/*чего́*
  get along without
  n обхо́д
вос-при-**м**-ут – воспринима́ют **ЙМ** perceive, understand; interpret
  n восприня́тие
†от-**каз**-а́-ть – отка́зывают *кому́* в *чём*
  refuse/deny, reject; —ся *inf* refuse; —
  от чего́ refuse, renounce
  n отка́з

---

† Do not confuse отказа́ть(ся) – отка́зывают(ся) with отрица́ют:

Он отказа́л ей в по́мощи.   He denied her help.
Он отказа́лся от по́мощи.   He refused help.
Он отказа́лся вы́полнить про́сьбу. He refused to carry out the request.
Я отрица́ю, что . . .   I deny that . . .
Он отрица́ет таки́е взгля́ды.   He rejects such views.

за-лож-и-ть – закла́дывают put, lay (as a foundation)

в-люб-и-ть-ся – влюбля́ются в *кого́*/*что́* fall in love with

на-ма́з-а-ть – нама́зывают smear, spread

за-мен-и-ть – заменя́ют replace
  n заме́на

от-ме́р-и-ть – отмеря́ют/отме́ривают measure off

при-мир-и́-ть – примиря́ют reconcile; —ся с *ке́м*/*че́м* reconcile oneself to, become reconciled to
  n примире́ние

мн-е́н-и-е (< *an older* мни́ть) opinion; бы́ть Х-*ого* —я о *ко́м*/*че́м* be of X opinion about; по *моему́*/*ва́шему* —ю, etc. in my/your, etc. opinion

молч-а́-ть be silent
  n молча́ние

за-молч-а́-ть *P only* fall silent

му́ч-и-ть torment, harass; —ся над *ке́м*/*че́м* torment/worry oneself over
  n муче́ние, му́ка

в-нёс-у́т – вноси́ть: — вкла́д во *что́* make contribution to (nonfinancial)

со-о́браз-и-ть – сообража́ют consider, weigh, reason
  n соображе́ние

ис-по́льз-ова-ть *P and I* use VIII.9
  n испо́льзование

до-пуст-и-ть – допуска́ют allow, permit; допу́стим, . . . let us assume/suppose . . .
  n допуще́ние assumption

†от-риц-а́й-ут РЁК deny, disclaim, reject
  n отрица́ние

пере-сел-и́-ть – переселя́ют move to a new location *tr*; —ся move to a new location *intr*, (transmigrate
  n переселе́ние

рас-смотр-е-ть – рассма́тривают examine, consider
  n рассмотре́ние

с-ум-е́й-ут VI.5

ис-че́з-(ну)-ть – исчеза́ют disappear
  n исчезнове́ние

с/о/-чт-ут – счита́ют VI.2

явл-е́н-и-е (< яви́ться – явля́ются be) phenomenon

по-явл-е́н-и-е (< появи́ться – появля́ют-ся appear) appearance

про-я́в-и-ть – проявля́ют manifest, display, show, reveal; —ся manifest/show itself, reveal itself
  n проявле́ние

---

† See footnote, p. 221.

СЛАВЯ́НСКИЕ ЯЗЫКИ́

Ско́лько мы́ ни изуча́ем ру́сский язы́к, мы́ всё-таки удивля́емся тому́, что э́тот восточнославя́нский язы́к, по своему́ происхожде́нию и положе́нию среди́ языко́в ми́ра, те́сно свя́зан с це́лым ря́дом западноевропе́йских языко́в, в то́м числе́ и с на́шим англи́йским, по происхожде́нию, герма́нским, языко́м. Славя́нские языки́, та́к же ка́к и герма́нские, принадлежа́т к 5 большо́й языково́й семье́, кото́рую при́нято называ́ть индоевропе́йской. Э́та семья́ **состои́т**[3a] из девяти́ и́ли десяти́ языковы́х гру́пп (среди́ ни́х мо́жно назва́ть герма́нские, рома́нские, ке́льтские, славя́нские, балти́йские, индоира́нские, гре́ческий, армя́нский и алба́нский языки́). Но́ при всём э́том многообра́зии индоевропе́йские языки́ **составля́ют**[3b] то́лько одну́ из 10 о́чень мно́гих языковы́х семе́й в ми́ре. Таки́м о́бразом, на́до счита́ть, что, ка́к бы на́м э́то ни каза́лось стра́нным, ру́сский язы́к нахо́дится в дово́льно те́сной свя́зи с англи́йским.

Совреме́нные славя́нские языки́ разделя́ются обы́чно на три́ гру́ппы:

ЮЖНОСЛАВЯ́НСКИЕ: слове́нский, сербохорва́тский, македо́нский, 15 болга́рский
ЗА́ПАДНОСЛАВЯ́НСКИЕ: че́шский, слова́цкий, по́льский, ве́рхне- и ни́жнелужи́цкий
ВОСТО́ЧНОСЛАВЯ́НСКИЕ: ру́сский, белору́сский, украи́нский

Все́ э́ти языки́ восхо́дят к одному́ языку́-осно́ве, кото́рый получи́л в 20 нау́ке назва́ние праславя́нского языка́. Изуче́ние э́того языка́ име́ет ва́жное значе́ние, та́к как позволя́ет установи́ть древне́йшую структу́ру славя́нской ре́чи и определи́ть тенде́нции разви́тия отде́льных славя́нских языко́в.

Праславя́нский язы́к устана́вливается и путём сравни́тельной лингви́стики и при по́мощи пе́рвого славя́нского литерату́рного языка́, та́к 25

223

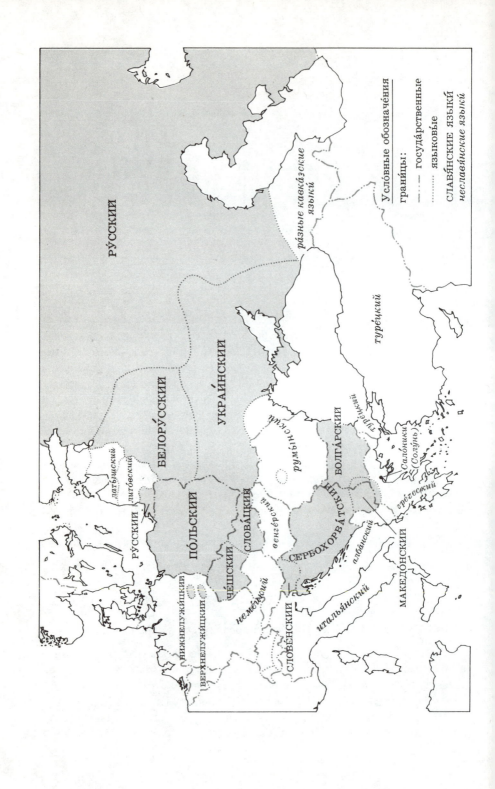

РУ́ССКИЙ

ра́зные кавка́зские языки́

туре́цкий

БЕЛОРУ́ССКИЙ

УКРАИ́НСКИЙ

латы́шский

лито́вский

РУ́ССКИЙ

ПО́ЛЬСКИЙ

СЛОВА́ЦКИЙ

ЧЕ́ШСКИЙ

НИ́ЖНЕЛУ́ЖИЦКИЙ

ВЕ́РХНЕЛУ́ЖИЦКИЙ

СЛОВЕ́НСКИЙ

неме́цкий

венге́рский

румы́нский

БОЛГА́РСКИЙ

СЕРБОХОРВА́ТСКИЙ

МАКЕДО́НСКИЙ

алба́нский

туре́цкий

гре́ческий

Сало́ники
(Солу́нь)

италья́нский

Усло́вные обозначе́ния

грани́цы:

— — — госуда́рственные

· · · · · · языковы́е

СЛАВЯ́НСКИЕ ЯЗЫКИ́

несл‌авя́нские языки́

называемого старославянского (или церковнославянского) языка. Этот язык был создан в девятом веке апостолами Константином-Кириллом и Мефодием для распространения и утверждения христианства в Великой Моравии и перешёл оттуда к словенам, чехам, хорватам, болгарам и, через **последних**,[5] к русским. Кирилл и Мефодий родились в Солуни, и их язык имел некоторые типично южнославянские черты (многие из которых выступают в русском языке в хорошо известных нам церковнославянизмах), но, в общем, мы можем считать его письменным выражением праславянского языка позднего варианта.

Старое деление Европы на два больших культурных общества, — с одной стороны, западное, латинское, и, с другой стороны — восточное, греческое, — выражается в употреблении двух совершенно различных азбук: западные славяне и словенцы пишут латиницей, восточные **же**[1] славяне, болгары и македонцы — кириллицей. Единственным славянским языком, **располагающим**[6] обеими азбуками, является сербохорватский: сербы пользуются кириллицей — хорваты латиницей. В остальном же их языки мало отличаются друг от друга.

[Partly adapted from the introduction to Rajko Nahtigal, *Slavjanskie jazyki*, Moscow, 1963, translated from the Slovenian by N. M. Ëlkina]

Expressions with ни

The particle **ни** expresses negation when it is used with some other negational element as in the following, mostly familiar types:

У нас нет ни школы ни церкви.	We have neither a school nor a church.
Ни один студент не провалился на экзамене.	Not one student failed the exam.
Нельзя опаздывать ни на минуту.	One can't be a minute late.
Ни слова больше! (Не говорите *is understood*.)	Not another word!

As part of negative pronouns like **никто, ничто, никакой, ничей**:

Мы никого не знаем.	We don't know anybody.
Мы ни с кем ни о чём не советовались.	We didn't consult with anyone about anything.
Для него не оказалось места ни в чьём автомобиле.	There turned out to be no room for him in anybody's car.
Он не занимается никаким языком.	He's not studying any language at all.

When, however, **ни** follows an interrogative word and is used *without* another negative element, it imparts a generalizing meaning frequently corresponding to English "-ever" ("whenever, whoever, whatever," etc.). The imperative singular may be used in such sentences to express the general subject "one, you":

Кто́ ни придёт, скажи́те, что меня́ нет до́ма.	Whoever comes, say I'm not home.
Что́ он ни говори́т, всё ерунда́.	Whatever he says, it's all nonsense.
Куда́ ни смотри́, везде́ де́ти.	Wherever you look, there are children.
Как ни сло́жен э́тот вопро́с, мы́ должны́ на него́ отве́тить.	However complicated the question may be, we must answer it.
Ско́лько ни труди́сь, никогда́ всего́ не ко́нчишь.	No matter how much you work, you never finish everything.
Ка́к ни по́здно, но́ я́ до́лжен зако́нчить перево́д статьи́.	Late as it is, I have to complete the translation of the article.
Ка́к я́ ни стара́лся, я́ не суме́л спра́виться с э́тим перево́дом.	Try as I would, I couldn't cope with this translation.
Каки́е ни е́сть у ва́с кни́ги, мы́ их всё ку́пим для на́шей библиоте́ки.	Whatever books you have, we'll buy them all for our library.

In the above examples the verbal action is presented as real; for example, in the first the implication is that at least one person will definitely come. In the type of sentence below, the presence of **бы** denotes that the action is viewed by the speaker as hypothetical and the meaning is even more generalized. The use of **бы**, of course, requires the past tense form, whether past meaning is indicated or not:

Кто́ бы ни пришёл, скажи́те, что меня́ нет до́ма. (*Compare with first sentence in preceding examples.*)	No matter who comes (or might come—I'm not definitely expecting anyone), say I'm not home.
Ско́лько бы э́то кре́сло ни сто́ило, я́ его́ куплю́.	Whatever that armchair costs, I'll buy it.
Где́ бы то́ ни́ было, а я́ вас всё равно́ найду́.	No matter where you are, I'll find you (anyway).
С ке́м бы ни знако́мился Семён, о́н со все́ми спо́рил.	No matter whose acquaintance Semën made, he argued with everyone.
Ка́к бы то́ ни́ было, мы́ о́сенью вернёмся домо́й.	Be that as it may, we will return home in the fall.

С каки́м бы учи́телем о́н ни занима́лся, о́н всё равно́ ничему́ не нау́чится.	Whatever teacher he works with, he still won't learn anything.

The **ни** usually precedes the verb directly, but on occasion may precede another element, if this element is emphasized:

Ка́к ни кре́пко о́н спа́л, услы́шав свою́ фами́лию, о́н то́тчас же откры́л глаза́.	As deeply as he may have been sleeping, he opened his eyes immediately on hearing his name.

Note the idiom **во что́ бы то́ ни ста́ло** 'no matter what (happens), without fail,' and observe that the **что́** and **бы** are two separate elements; they are not the stressless conjunction **чтобы**.

Во что́ бы то́ ни ста́ло, позвони́те Ива́ну Никола́евичу на заво́д.	No matter what, call Ivan Nikolaevič at the factory.

And notice that **како́й ни е́сть** 'no matter what kind' may in colloquial speech be strengthened by adding **на**:

Како́й ни **на** е́сть, а всё же о́н челове́к.	No matter what kind, he's still a human being.

The perfective present

The Russian perfective present has thus far represented for us simply a single action in the future. It has also, however, certain uses in which it portrays a *present frequentative* meaning with the force of a *general statement*, often with strong *modal* tones. Sometimes the English equivalent has (or "will have"— this very sentence is a case in point) a "will" in it but, as with the Russian, the statement is not future but general in nature, with a degree of modality (speaker's opinion and/or involvement).[1] The frequentative or general sense of this usage emerges in the fact that words like **всегда́** and **ча́сто** may readily be used with these perfectives:

Вре́мени ника́к не найду́.	I just can't find the time.
О́н ва́м э́то всегда́ сде́лает.	He can (He'll) do it for you any time.
Вы́ от него́ ча́сто услы́шите таки́е ве́щи.	You hear such things from him quite often.
С э́тим я спра́влюсь без вся́кого труда́.	I can cope with that with no trouble at all.
Таки́х люде́й встре́тите (встре́тишь) в любо́м о́бществе.	You find (You can find, You'll find) such people in any society.

---

[1] With respect to possibility, desirability, etc. Cf. R3.B.

These present perfective general statements are frequently combined with the **ни** described above, which, as we have seen, is modal in character. The perfective can occur in the **ни** clause, independent clause, or both.

Куда́ он ни пойдёт, всю́ду встре́тит (встреча́ет) знако́мых.	Wherever he goes, he meets acquaintances.
Что́ он ни ска́жет, интере́сно.	Whatever he says is interesting.
Ско́лько ни принесу́ Ва́не книг, он всё (про)чита́ет.	No matter how many books I bring Vanja, he reads everything.
Что́ он ни де́лает, де́лает хорошо́.	Whatever he does, he does well.

The English present in all these sentences could be replaced by the future with no real change in meaning; e.g. "Whatever he'll do, he'll do well."

Finally, the present perfective may have a general meaning in a certain type of conditional construction; the perfective present usually appears in both clauses of the complex sentence:

Е́сли он заме́тит оши́бку, он неме́дленно обрати́т внима́ние на неё.	If he notices an error, he immediately calls attention to it.
Е́сли он сде́лает оши́бку, он сейча́с же попра́вит её.	If he makes an error, he corrects it right away.

Sometimes in colloquial speech **е́сли** plus personal pronoun is omitted. This elliptical usage is also characteristic of certain proverbs. Examples:

Заме́тит э́то — сейча́с же ска́жет ва́м.	If he notices that, he tells you right away.
Сло́во — не воробе́й, вы́летит — не пойма́ешь. (*Perfective verb*)	A word isn't a sparrow—once it's flown out, you can't catch it.

Omission of **е́сли** is also quite common in ordinary, non-contrary-to-fact conditionals with a clear future reference; e.g. **Не придёт — скажу́** 'If he doesn't come, I'll tell.' Such elliptical usages should be recognized, but are best avoided by the student at this time (cf. IX.B2).

SUBORDINATE POINTS

1. The particle **же**, which serves the general purpose of emphasizing the preceding word, may attach an adversative meaning:

Он бога́т, я же бе́ден.	He's rich; I, however, am poor.
Все ему́ ве́рят, я же не ве́рю.	Everybody believes him, but I, for one, do not.
Ру́сский язы́к я зна́ю пло́хо, неме́цкий же хорошо́.	I know Russian badly but German well.

2. The verb **сто́ить** (*impf only*) takes a direct object when it means "cost," but tends to take a genitive complement when it means "be worth" or "cost" in a less concrete sense. For example:

Э́то ва́м бу́дет сто́ить сто́ рубле́й.	That will cost you a hundred rubles.
Э́то сто́ило ему́ большо́го труда́.	That cost him much effort.
Чего́ э́то сто́ит?	What is that worth?
Что́ (Ско́лько) э́то сто́ит?	What does that cost?
Не сто́ит благода́рности.	Don't mention it (It isn't worth thanks).

And note:

Э́то сто́ит проче́сть.	That's worth reading.

Сто́ить (*impf only*) *imps* (*dat*) plus infinitive corresponds approximately to "all one has to do is, one has only to . . . , (and something will happen, be true, etc.)." **То́лько** is often added for emphasis:

На́м сто́ит то́лько подня́ться на э́ту го́рку, и до́м бу́дет ви́ден.	All we have to do is climb this hill, and the house will be visible.
На́м сто́ит попа́сть в ру́ки проти́вника, и всё бу́дет поте́ряно.	We have only to fall into the hands of the enemy, and all will be lost.
Сто́ило то́лько обрати́ть его́ внима́ние на э́то.	All that had to be done was call his attention to it.

3. Do not confuse the verbs **состоя́ть** (*impf only*) and **соста́вить – составля́ют**.

a. **Состоя́ть** is intransitive (cf. **стоя́ть**) and means "be, consist":

Он состои́т чле́ном э́того нау́чного о́бщества.	He is a member of this scientific society.
Он состои́т на слу́жбе.	He is in the service.
В чём состои́т значе́ние э́того собы́тия?	What does the significance of this event consist in?
Ра́зница состои́т в то́м, что . . .	The difference consists in the fact that . . .
Вода́ состои́т из водоро́да и кислоро́да.	Water consists of hydrogen and oxygen.
Их гру́ппа состоя́ла из десяти́ челове́к.	Their group consisted of ten persons.

The verbal noun **состоя́ние** means "state, condition." Note particularly the expression **бы́ть в состоя́нии** *inf* 'be able to, be in a position to':

Больно́й находи́лся в плохо́м состоя́нии.	The sick man was in bad condition.

Он подробно описа́л состоя́ние пого́ды.	He described in detail the state of the weather.
Он в состоя́нии купи́ть э́то.	He can afford it.
Вы ско́ро бу́дете в состоя́нии ходи́ть в шко́лу.	You will soon be able to attend school.
Он не в состоя́нии ока́зывать нам противоде́йствие.	He is not in a position to oppose us.

b. **Соста́вить – составля́ют** is transitive (cf. **ста́вить**) and means "compose, put together, compile" and also "constitute, comprise, represent (be)." The verbal nouns are **составле́ние** 'putting together' and **соста́в** 'composition, make up':

Соста́вили по́езд.	They made up the train.
Я составля́ю себе́ мне́ние о нём.	I am forming an opinion about him.
Они́ рабо́тают над составле́нием но́вого словаря́.	They are working on the compilation of a new dictionary.
Меня́ интересу́ет соста́в морско́й воды́ о́коло Босто́на.	I am interested in the composition of the sea water around Boston.
На́ши офице́ры в по́лном соста́ве.	Our officers are at full strength.
Всё э́ти ча́сти составля́ют це́лое предложе́ние.	All these parts comprise a whole sentence.
Сде́лать э́то не составля́ет большо́го труда́.	Doing that isn't (doesn't constitute) a great deal of trouble.

4. In addition to its primary sense "it's all the same (to me, us, etc.)," **всё равно́** often has the meaning "anyway, even so":

Не сто́ит та́к му́читься над э́той пробле́мой. Вы её не реши́те, да и учи́тель всё равно́ не придёт.	It isn't worth it to torment yourself over that problem. You won't solve it, and the teacher won't come anyway.

5. После́дний may have the meaning "latter" and may, like the English word, refer to either an animate or inanimate, singular or plural, noun. "Former . . . latter" is **пе́рвый . . . после́дний**.

6. Russian has a number of verbs with meanings connected with the ideas of *possession* or *control* which take an *instrumental* complement:

На́шей страно́й **руководя́т** те́, кто са́ми вы́шли из рабо́чих и крестья́н.	Our country is ruled by people who have themselves come from the workers and the peasants.
Проти́вник не **располага́ет** артилле́рией.	The enemy has no artillery at his disposal.

Сестра́ уме́ет **управля́ть** тра́ктором.	My sister knows how to drive a tractor.
Э́то сло́во **управля́ет** да́тельным падежо́м.	This word governs the dative case.
Кто́ **управля́ет** страно́й?	Who runs the country?
Э́тот челове́к **облада́ет** большо́й си́лой во́ли. (облада́ют (об-**ВЛАД**) 'possess')	That man has great will power.
Он **владе́ет** ру́сским языко́м. (владе́ют 'possess, be master of')	He has a command of Russian.

Such verbs are almost always imperfective only, since they designate generally *states* of possession or control.

It may be noted that the English counterparts of these verbs are almost always transitive, and that passive participles (present), which ideally may be formed only from transitive verbs, are formed from most of these verbs; e.g. **руководи́мый**, **управля́емый**, **облада́емый**, etc. (cf. R9.C2).

TRANSLATION INTO ENGLISH

1. Что́ ни говори́те, а у се́рбов и хорва́тов одина́ковый язы́к. Отлича́ются и́х языки́ то́лько а́збукой. 2. Те́рмином «праязы́к» мы́ обознача́ем язы́к, о́бщий для гру́ппы ро́дственных языко́в: существова́ние тако́го языка́ предполага́ется на основа́нии сравни́тельных материа́лов э́тих языко́в. 3. Како́го бы происхожде́ния ни́ был мо́й оте́ц, о́н америка́нец. 5 4. Что́ бы э́тот офице́р ни говори́л, не ве́рьте ему́. Ему́ ведь не́откуда зна́ть соста́в на́шей администра́ции. 5. Большинство́ лингви́стов предполага́ют существова́ние о́бщего балтославя́нского языка́ по́сле распа́да индоевропе́йского еди́нства. 6. На что́ бы он ни взгляну́л, о чём бы ни поду́мал, всё представля́лось ему́ све́тлым, ра́достным и счастли́вым. 7. Тако́й челове́к 10 всегда́ ку́пит са́мое лу́чшее пальто́. 8. Ка́к бы то́ ни́ было, всё студе́нты сда́ли экза́мен успе́шно. 9. На́ш до́м про́дан; тепе́рь о́н принадлежи́т како́му-то чино́внику. 10. Моя́ пе́рвая любо́вь принадлежи́т к числу́ действи́тельно не совсе́м обыкнове́нных. 11. На́ша гла́вная гру́ппа состои́т из мно́гих ма́леньких гру́пп. 12. Она́ принадлежи́т к вы́сшему 15 о́бществу. 13. Ру́сский, белору́сский и украи́нский языки́ составля́ют восто́чную гру́ппу славя́нских языко́в. 14. Мы́ все наблюда́ем постепе́нный распа́д систе́мы империали́зма. 15. Мы́ живём о́чень те́сно, ме́ста не хвата́ет. Но́ мо́й дя́дя всё равно́ пересели́тся к на́м. Моя́ ма́ть бу́дет ра́да ему́, но я́ не разделя́ю её ра́дости. 16. В о́бщем совреме́нный челове́к не 20 зло́й челове́к, но о́н не всегда́ де́йствует по убежде́нию. Он счита́ет, что ве́ра — э́то усло́вное де́ло. 17. Я тепе́рь вообще́ не пишу́ или пишу́ о́чень

ма́ло, та́к что обеща́ние да́ть могу́ то́лько усло́вно: напишу́ расска́з, е́сли не помеша́ет боле́знь. **18.** Все́ славя́нские языки́, в то́м числе́ и ру́сский, восхо́дят к праславя́нскому языку́. **19.** Этот па́мятник восхо́дит к пятна́д-цатому ве́ку. **20.** Францу́зский, италья́нский, испа́нский, португа́льский и румы́нский языки́ восхо́дят к одному́ языку́-осно́ве. Лати́нский язы́к клас-си́ческого вре́мени представля́ет собо́й пи́сьменный вариа́нт прарома́н-ского языка́. Прарома́нский язы́к, в свою́ о́чередь, восхо́дит к праитали́й-скому языку́, кото́рый мо́жно установи́ть то́лько путём сравни́тельной лингви́стики и при по́мощи не́скольких о́чень ста́рых па́мятников. Лати́н-ский язы́к распространя́лся по все́й сре́дней и ю́жной Евро́пе. Со вре́менем о́н замени́л ме́стные языки́ и бы́л при́нят ка́к о́бщий язы́к. Пото́м лати́нский язы́к в ка́ждой стране́ ста́л развива́ться по-сво́ему. **21.** Мы́ устана́вливаем связь с э́тим генера́лом, но́ до сих по́р не установи́ли. **22.** Нау́ка устано-ви́ла, что в то́ вре́мя э́тот язы́к употребля́лся везде́. **23.** Годнёва взгля-ну́ла на него́ — и бо́же! — ско́лько любви́ вы́разил э́тот коро́ткий взгля́д. **24.** «Ми́лая Ма́ша, к чему́ употребля́ть таки́е выраже́ния?» **25.** Древнеру́с-ский язы́к отлича́ется от совреме́нного ру́сского языка́ во мно́гих отно-ше́ниях. Он име́л бо́льшее коли́чество южнославя́нских че́рт, чём совре-ме́нный язы́к. **26.** Этот челове́к не со́здан для э́того, во́т и всё. **27.** Для э́того посту́пка име́ется ря́д причи́н. **28.** Созда́ние мо́щного моско́вского госуда́рства привело́ к исчезнове́нию ме́стных диале́ктов и к разви́тию одного́ ру́сского литерату́рного языка́, в осно́ву кото́рого лёг (в осно́ве кото́рого лежи́т) средневеликору́сский диале́кт. **29.** Это мне́ние получа́ет большо́е распростране́ние. **30.** Эта систе́ма была́ устано́влена уже́ давно́ в на́шей стране́. Но ско́лько я ни рабо́таю при ней, ка́к хорошо́ я ни зна́ю её, я́ ника́к не привы́кну к ней. **31.** Скажи́те, пожа́луйста. Ка́к мне́ дойти́ до Кра́сной пло́щади? (Ответ) Я ва́м не скажу́. **32.** Я утвержда́л, что ни-когда́ не́ жил та́м. **33.** Я на́чал диску́ссию с утвержде́ния, что фа́кты, устано́вленные на́шим комите́том, до си́х по́р сохраня́ют своё значе́ние. **34.** Я положу́ ва́ши уче́ния в осно́ву мое́й рабо́ты. **35.** Он про́тив ва́с, я́ же на ва́шей стороне́. Позво́льте мне́ рабо́тать с ва́ми, э́то ва́ша еди́нственная возмо́жность. **36.** Мы́ оказа́ли по́мощь ме́стному комите́ту. **37.** Он мо́й еди́нственный сы́н, но́ о нём лу́чше молча́ть. Он принадлежи́т к Па́ртии. Я уве́рен, что о́н отли́чно спра́вится с любы́м зада́нием. Об остально́м не бу́дем говори́ть. **38.** Мы́ предполага́ем разви́ть агита́цию среди́ ру́сских рабо́чих. Сто́ит поду́мать об э́том, чтобы поня́ть ва́жность э́того. **39.** Предполо́жим, вы́ реши́те э́ту зада́чу. А ка́к ва́м спра́виться с остальны́ми? **40.** Назови́те языки́ в Югосла́вии. Да́йте мне́ э́ти папиро́сы, каки́е они́ ни е́сть. **41.** Я о́чень высо́кого мне́ния о не́й. В её перево́де почти́ не оказа́-лось граммати́ческих оши́бок. Те́, что бы́ли, я поправил за пя́ть мину́т. **42.** Не поправля́йте его́. Не на́до теря́ть на э́то вре́мя. На ва́ши попра́вки о́н всё равно́ не бу́дет обраща́ть внима́ния. **43.** Я не в состоя́нии отказа́ть челове́ку на основа́нии одни́х то́лько предположе́ний. **44.** У на́с при́нято 65 обознача́ть ре́ки голубы́ми ли́ниями. **45.** Я сейча́с располага́ю вре́менем. Могу́ ва́м рассказа́ть о то́м, ка́к получи́лось ру́сское сло́во «го́род» от праславя́нского *гордъ (сравни́те неме́цкое сло́во 'Garten,' англи́йское 'garden'). Де́ло в то́м, что в восточнославя́нских языка́х *гордъ разви́лось в «го́род» путём так называ́емого «полногла́сия». Вопро́с о полногла́сии 70 сто́ит ва́шего внима́ния. **46.** Ду́ня мне́ написа́ла це́лый ря́д пи́сем, но́ в то́ вре́мя я́ не́ был в состоя́нии отве́тить на ни́х. **47.** Вы́ ви́дите то́лько ра́зни-цу на́ших взгля́дов. Ра́зве не мо́жет бы́ть еди́нства? **48.** Таки́х веще́й не происходи́ло, когда́ я́ бы́л у вла́сти. **49.** Мы́ ду́маем по́льзоваться но́вым ти́пом карандаша́. **50.** Что́ та́м происхо́дит? 75

TRANSLATION INTO RUSSIAN

1. The diversity of political ideas in the world amazes me. But there exists a certain unity as well. **2.** Are you of German origin? Yes, but I have lived in many countries, including the Soviet Union. **3.** Whatever party he belongs to, I con-sider him a stupid man. **4.** Our party consists of five groups. **5.** Which lan-guages comprise the South Slavic group? **6.** Lenin defined law as an expression 5 of the will of the people. **7.** These scholars long ago reconstructed a proto-language on the basis of materials from related modern languages and with the aid of written monuments. **8.** We were rendered great aid in our study of these phenomena. **9.** German and English are closely related languages which have (use **располага́ют**) almost identical alphabets. **10.** Different peoples use differ- 10 ent alphabets. **11.** The West Slavs belong to Western cultural society. **12.** That's a very widespread phenomenon. **13.** We must create a strong army; the development of industry we will leave to our successors. **14.** Macedonian is spoken in southern Yugoslavia, southwestern Bulgaria, and certain parts of northern Greece. It has only one alphabet; Serbo-Croatian, on the other hand, 15 has two (instrumental is **двумя́**). **15.** Old Church Slavonic long exerted a great influence on Russian; hence the large number of typically South Slavic traits in Modern Russian. **16.** The most important West Slavic languages are Polish, Czech, and Slovak; the latter, however, shares a number of features with Slo-venian, a South Slavic language. **17.** Drop in on him, no matter what happens. 20 **18.** Let's assume you are right; we have no monuments from ancient times at our disposal. We will then have to limit ourselves to a study of the modern lan-guage. **19.** They ought to build him a monument; it was he who created mod-ern Russian literature. **20.** The study of the literary language already occupies all our time; we will never cope with all the variants. **21.** He likes to use learned 25 terms and expressions; altogether he considers himself an intelligent man. **22.**

We are now observing the gradual development of the socialist state. The majority of people agree that the disintegration of capitalism gave the socialists the opportunity to come to power, but about everything else there exists no
30 unity of views. **23.** You have asserted that Belorussian differs little from Russian. That's true, but in what? It is asserted that in Belorussian there is manifested a strong influence from (**со стороны́**) Polish. **24.** If you want to convince yourself of how crowded it is at our place, all you have to do is drop in on us in our apartment. **25.** French, Italian, and Rumanian all go back to one proto-
35 language. **26.** It's our custom to treat guests very well. **27.** In every society there exists conventional truth and conventional deceit. **28.** There's nothing constant in this world; everything is relative, arbitrary. **29.** Local industry is developing slowly. Our local economy is still based on agriculture (translate: At the base of our local economy lies agriculture.) **30.** Your assumptions have led
40 to nothing; let's start from the beginning. Let's assume that an established order already exists. **31.** He agreed to make the speech but refused us in everything else. He said the rest wasn't worth his time anyway. **32.** Please correct the errors in this translation. **33.** We have designated the unknown by X (**йкс**).
34. The general was standing at the map and designating the direction of our
45 attack. "It is clear that the enemy is in no position to cope with our army," he said. "Victory will be ours." **35.** On the one hand one must consider that Cyril and Methodius were typical apostles of that time. On the other hand one can't deny that they created a language which spread over (**на** *acc*) half of Eastern Europe. **36.** I would say that this man is characterized by all the traits of the
50 new Soviet man, and I know that type well. He's not stupid, but he expresses himself in conversation unclearly; I would not permit him to lead our group.
37. We have on our agenda a number of questions. **38.** What's going on here? I think someone lost his money. **39.** She is not noted for anything. When she led our group, we all quickly lost respect for (**к**) her.

СЛОВА́ ТО́ЛЬКО К Э́ТОМУ УРО́КУ

Алба́н-и-я Albania; албáн-ск-ий Albania n

апо́стол apostle

Армéн-и-я Armenia; армя́н-ск-ий Armenian

балт-и́й-ск-ий Baltic

балт-о-**слав-я́**н-ск-ий Balto-Slavic

Бел-о-ру́сс-и-я Belorussia; бел-о-ру́с-ск-ий, бел-о-ру́с, бел-о-ру́с-/к-а Belorussian (*not* White Russian)

Болга́р-и-я Bulgaria; болга́р-ск-ий, болга́р-ин (*pl* болга́ры, болга́р), болга́р-/к-а Bulgarian

Вéнгр-и-я Hungary; венгéр-ск-ий Hungarian

верх-н-ё-лужи́ц-к-ий Upper Lusatian

герма́н-ск-ий Germanic, German

Грéц-и-я Greece; грéч-еск-ий Greek

Евро́п-а Europe; европ-éй-ск-ий European

индоевроп-éй-ск-ий Indo-European

индоира́н-ск-ий Indo-Iranian

итал-и́й-ск-ий Italic (*pert. to tribes and languages of ancient Italy*)

Кавка́з (на) Caucasus; кавка́з-ск-ий Caucasian

ке́льт-ск-ий Celtic

Кири́лл Cyril

Ла́тв-и-я Latvia; латв-и́й-ск-ий *or* латы́ш-ск-ий Latvian

лати́н-ск-ий Latin

Литв-а́ Lithuania; лито́в-ск-ий Lithuanian

Македо́н-и-я Macedonia; македо́н-ск-ий, македо́н-/е/ц, македо́н-/к-а Macedonian

Мефо́дий Methodius

Мора́в-и-я Moravia (central Czechoslovakia)

ниж-н-ё-лужи́ц-к-ий Lower Lusatian

По́ль-ш-а ПОЛ² Poland; по́ль-ск-ий Polish; пол-я́к, по́ль-/к-а Pole

рома́н-ск-ий Romance

Румы́н-и-я Rumania; румы́н-ск-ий Rumanian

Сало́ники Salonika (Greece)

Се́рб-и-я Serbia; се́рб-ск-ий, се́рб, се́рб-/к-а Serbian, Serb

серб-о-хорва́т-ск-ий Serbo-Croatian

Слова́к-и-я Slovakia; слова́ц-к-ий, слова́к, слова́ч-/к-а Slovak(ian)

Слове́н-и-я Slovenia; слове́н-ск-ий, слове́н/е/ц, слове́н-/к-а Slovene, Slovenian

Солу́нь *older name for* Salonika (Greece)

сред-н-ё-**велик**-о-**ру́с**-ск-ий Central Great Russian (dialect)

Ту́рц-и-я Turkey; туре́ц-к-ий Turkish

Украи́н-а (у кра́я) Ukraine; украи́н-ск-ий, украи́н-/е/ц, украи́н-/к-а Ukrainian

Хорва́т-и-я Croatia; хорва́т-ск-ий Croatian; хорва́т, хорва́т-/к-а Croat

Че́х-и-я Bohemia; че́ш-ск-ий, че́х, че́ш-/к-а Czech

Чех-о-слова́к-и-я Czechoslovakia; чех-о-слова́ц-к-ий Czechoslovak(ian)

О́БЩИЙ СЛОВА́РЬ

агита́ци-я agitation

а́збук-а alphabet

вариа́нт variant

везде́ everywhere

вла́сть ВЛАД-т *E pl obl* power, authority, rule; ruling power/authority; быть у —и be in power; приду́т – приходить к —и come to power

всю́ду (*or* повсю́ду) everywhere

гру́пп-а group

дей-ств-и́-тель-/н-ый real, actual; valid

диале́кт dialect

дре́в-н-ий old, ancient

еди́н-ств-о unity

за-во́д (на) plant, factory

зл-о́й, з/о́/л evil, malicious

кири́лл-иц-а Cyrillic alphabet

класси́ч-еск-ий classical

комите́т committee

лати́н-иц-а Latin alphabet

лингви́ст linguist; лингви́ст-ик-а linguistics; лингвист-и́ч-еск-ий linguistic

литерату́р-a literature

литерату́р-н-ый literary

материа́л, материа́лы material(s)

ме́ст-н-ый local

мног-о-**обра́з**-и-е diversity

общ-е́-ств-енн-ый social, society *adj*

о́бщ-е-ств-о society

осно́в-а basis; stem; на —е *чего́* on the basis of; *что́* лежи́т в —е *чего́* X is the basis of Y; *что́* лёг в —у *чего́* X is/was the basis of Y; положи́ть – кла́дут *что́* в —у *чего́* make X the basis of Y

о-**сталь**-н-о́й **СТАН** remaining, other, rest

пальто́ *N indecl* (over)coat

па́мят-ник М/Н¹ monument

папирóс-а cigarette (Russian style, with a cardboard holder)

пере-вóд translation; *cf.* переведýт – переводить

пó-мощь МОГ помогут – помогáют help

по-прáв-/к-а correction; repair; *cf.* попрáвить – поправля́ют

по-слéд-н-ий VII.5

по-степéн-/н-ый gradual

пра-язы́к protolanguage

при́нято (< при́мут – принимáют) ЙМ it is the custom to, it is accepted/customary

путём *чегó* by means of

рáз-н-иц-а difference

рáз-н-ый different; various

рас-пáд disintegration, decay; *cf.* распадýтся – распадáются disintegrate

рóд-ств-енн-ый related

ря́д *E pl* row, line; series; в —ý in row, rank; в —е in series; ря́д (цéлый ря́д) + *gen pl* a number of (a large number of, whole bunch of)

слав-ян-и́н (*pl* славя́не) Slav

слав-я́н-ск-ий Slavic, Slavonic

со-времéн-/н-ый modern, contemporary

с-рав-н-и́-тель-н-ый comparative

со-стáв VII.3

среди́ *когó/чегó* among, amidst

стар-о-слав-я́н-ск-ий Old Church Slavic/Slavonic

структýр-а structure

тéрмин term

тéс-/н-ый close, narrow, crowded

ти́п type

тип-и́ч-/н-ый typical

тóтчас (*often with* же) immediately

у-слóв-/н-ый conditional; conventional, prearranged; arbitrary

церков-н-о-слав-ян-и́зм Church Slavonicism; церков-н-о-слав-я́н-ск-ий Church Slavonic

черт-á line; trait, feature

чис/л-ó *S pl* number; date; в тóм —é (и) including

язык-ов-óй linguistic, language *adj*

ГЛАГÓЛЫ

раз/о/-вий-ут – развивáют develop *tr*; —ся develop *intr*

  n разви́тие

вз-гля́д-ну-ть – взгля́дывают на *когó/чтó* look/glance at

  n взгля́д view, opinion

дел-éн-и-е (< дел-и́-ть(-ся)) division

разделя́ются на *чтó* be divided into

  n раздéл, разделéние

сóз-да-ть – создавáть create (*falsely assimilated to* дать – давáть *from* со-зд-а-ть ЗД build)

  n создáние

обо-знáч-и-ть – обозначáют designate, mark

  n обозначéние

про-из-/о/йд-ýт – происходи́ть happen, go on; — *откýда* come from

  n происхождéние origin, extraction (of a person)

при-над-лёж-á-ть *комý/чемý or* (*with groups often*) к *комý/чемý* belong

рас-по-лаг-áй-ут *кéм/чéм* have at one's disposal; have

  n расположéние disposition, arrangement

от-лич-и́-ть – отличáют distinguish; —ся *I only* от *когó/чегó* чéм/в чём differ from X with respect to Y; —ся *I only* чéм be noted/notable for, be characterized by

  n отли́чие

пред-по-лóж-и-ть – предполагáют assume, suppose; предполóжим (*like* допýстим) let us assume/suppose

  n предположéние

основ-а́-н-и-е (< основа́ть (осну́ю) – осно́-
вывают) base; на —и *чего́* on the
basis of

по́льз-ова-ть-ся *ке́м/че́м* use VIII.9
n по́льзование

с-пра́в-и-ть-ся – справля́ются с *ке́м/че́м*
cope with

вы́-раз-и-ть – выража́ют **РАЗ**[1] express;
—ся express oneself
n выраже́ние

со-ста́в-и-ть – составля́ют VII.3b
n соста́в, составле́ние

у-стан-ов-и-ть – устана́вливают establish; reconstruct (a language); —ся
establish oneself

n установле́ние

со-стой-а́-ть VII.3a
n состоя́ние

рас-про-**стран**-и́-ть – распространя́ют
spread *tr*; —ся spread *intr*
n распростране́ние

у-**твержд**-а́й-ут assert, affirm
n утвержде́ние (< *an older* утверди́ть)

(по)-**тер**-я́й-ут lose
n поте́ря

у-по-**треб**-и́-ть – употребля́ют use VIII.9
n употребле́ние

вос-**ход**-и-ть к *кому́/чему́* go back to, derive from

РÓЛЬ ВОДЫ́ В ПРИРÓДЕ

В младéнческом вóзрасте земли́, когда́ температу́ра на её повéрхности достига́ла нéскольких ты́сяч гра́дусов, из водорóда и кислорóда начала́ образóвываться вода́. Дальнéйшая истóрия всéй твёрдой земнóй коры́ теснéйшим óбразом свя́зана с водóй. *Возника́вшие в жи́дкой распла́вленной массе минера́лы* ча́стью включа́ли её в свой хими́ческий соста́в, ча́стью,
5   застыва́я под больши́м давлéнием, удéрживали водянóй па́р (наряду́ с други́ми га́зами) в ви́де раствóра. Если кусóк, напримéр, грани́та нагрéть вы́ше 1000° (ты́сячи гра́дусов), óн выделя́ет га́зы, объём котóрых **во мнóго ра́з**[5] превыша́ет егó сóбственный, **причём**[2] бóльшая ча́сть вы́деленного объёма прихóдится на водянóй па́р.
10   **При**[1] дальнéйшем охлаждéнии земнóй коры́ *оста́вшаяся несвя́занной вода́* перешла́ в жи́дкое состоя́ние и покры́ла óколо 3/4 (трёх четвертéй) земли́. *Образова́вшиеся тёплые моря́* послужи́ли средóй для зарождéния жи́зни: и́менно в ни́х, по-ви́димому, возни́кли и в течéние дóлгих геологи́ческих эпóх развива́лись пéрвые комóчки живóй матéрии. Впослéдствии
15   жи́знь части́чно перешла́ на су́шу, одна́ко вода́ оста́лась *основны́м необходи́мым для её поддержа́ния веществóм.*

Óбщее коли́чество воды́ на землé оцéнивается в $2 \cdot 10^{18}$ (два́ **на**[5] дéсять в восемна́дцатой стéпени) тóнн. Óколо трёх пя́тых э́того коли́чества сосредотóчено в моря́х и океа́нах. На протяжéнии извéстных на́м геологи́-
20   ческих перио́дов коли́чество свобóдной воды́ сохраня́лось приблизи́тельно постоя́нным. Хотя́ и в настоя́щее врéмя протека́ют нéкоторые процéссы, при котóрых она́ вступа́ет в прóчные соединéния, одна́ко имéют мéсто и *уравновéшивающие э́ту потéрю обра́тные процéссы.* В глубóких слоя́х земнóй коры́, в результа́те *протека́ющих при высóких температу́рах и дав-
25   лéниях хими́ческих реа́кций*, образу́ются та́к называ́емые «ювени́льные»

238

во́ды, кото́рые зате́м выно́сятся на пове́рхность **в ви́де**[8] горя́чих и холо́д-
ных ключе́й. И те́ и други́е мо́гут образова́ться та́кже за счёт обы́чных под-
по́чвенных во́д и ча́сто соде́ржат растворённые со́ли и га́зы. Тогда́ они́
называ́ются минера́льными исто́чниками и части́чно **испо́льзуются**[9] для
лече́бных и промы́шленных це́лей.   30

Больша́я теплоёмкость воды́ (приблизи́тельно в 3300 ра́з превыша́ю-
щая теплоёмкость во́здуха) определя́ет ро́ль океа́нов в климати́ческом
отноше́нии. Мо́щные тёплые и холо́дные тече́ния обусло́вливают кли́мат
омыва́емых и́ми часте́й су́ши. Наприме́р, благодаря́ влия́нию тёплого
океа́нского тече́ния Гольфстри́ма, Му́рманск явля́ется незамерза́ющей   35
га́ванью, **в то́ вре́мя ка́к**[1] *располо́женный значи́тельно южне́е Ленингра́д-
ский по́рт* зимо́й замерза́ет. Мя́гкость кли́мата все́й за́падной Евро́пы обу-
сло́влена и́менно влия́нием нагре́той воды́ Гольфстри́ма, кото́рая смягча́ет
ре́зкость температу́рных колеба́ний. В противополо́жность **тако́му**[7] «мор-
ско́му» кли́мату, «континента́льный» кли́мат *удалённых от океа́на стра́н*   40
характеризу́ется ре́зкой сме́ной температу́ры по времена́м го́да. Всле́д-
ствие то́й же причи́ны — большо́й теплоёмкости воды́ — ра́зница тем-
перату́р дня́ и но́чи, о́чень ре́зкая для стра́н с континента́льным кли́матом,
стано́вится почти́ незаме́тной на острова́х океа́на.

[Adapted from B. V. Nekrasov, *Kurs obščej ximii*,   45
Moscow. 1945, vol. I, pp. 148–149]

Scientific Russian

Scientific Russian differs little, except in its vocabulary, from nonscientific
scholarly prose or, for that matter, from the somewhat more jargonized, didactic
prose of which the text in Lesson IV is a typical example. Certain types of constructions are particularly frequent: instrumental predicates, impersonal constructions (third singular verb with genitive or dative complement), gerunds and
participles, most notably participial constructions in which the participle and
everything that goes with it precedes the noun it modifies (R9.C3); these constructions are italicized in the text on the preceding page. All these features,
however, are quite common in nonscientific scholarly prose as well.

One usage which is very typical in technical writing and is beginning to
enter colloquial speech is **за счёт** *gen* in the meaning "owing to, due to," rather
than in the usual sense "at the expense of"; for example:

Его́ ко́мнату увели́чили за счёт ку́хни.	His room was enlarged at the expense of the kitchen.
И те́ и други́е мо́гут образова́ться за счёт подпо́чвенных во́д.	Both can form due to subterranean water. (*From the text*)

SUBORDINATE POINTS

1. A number of words or expressions which have nothing in their primary meaning or makeup to indicate negativity or opposition may, in fact, acquire an adversative or concessive meaning in the proper context. The versatile preposition **при** (R9 note 4) usually has the general meaning "close to, in the presence of" and, on a more abstract level, "in view of, given, when one considers that . . ."; however, under circumstances it may assume a meaning like "in spite of, in the face of, for all . . . ." Compare:

При таки́х тала́нтах о́н мо́г дости́гнуть бо́льшего.	In view of such talents he could have accomplished more.
При всём своём образова́нии, о́н не о́чень у́мный челове́к.	In spite of (For all) his education, he isn't a very intelligent person.

В то́ вре́мя как, тогда́ как, and **ме́жду те́м как** are all concessive conjunctions with meanings close to "whereas, while." The adverb **ме́жду те́м** may mean "meanwhile" or have the adversative sense "nevertheless." The parenthetical **пра́вда,** discussed in VI.3, has the concessive sense "to be sure."

2. The conjunction **причём** conveys the primary idea of **при,** but its usage and translation frequently give rise to problems. Occasionally it has the meaning "furthermore, in addition," but it is usually weaker; the action it introduces may clarify or elaborate the main action, rather than add directly to it. The English verb describing the subordinate action frequently emerges as a present participle:

К на́м назна́чили де́сять челове́к, причём ка́ждый име́л свою́ специа́льность.	Ten men were assigned to us, each having his own specialty.
Он рабо́тал в о́бласти лингви́стики, причём обраща́л осо́бое внима́ние на герма́нские языки́.	He worked in the area of linguistics, paying special attention to the Germanic languages.
Он зна́ет ру́сский язы́к о́чень хорошо́, причём и диале́кты зна́ет непло́хо.	He knows the Russian language well and knows the dialects fairly well too.

(Study the use and translation of **причём** in the first paragraph of the text at the beginning of the lesson.)

The conjunction **прито́м** means "moreover," often with the idea "in the bargain, at that." Examples:

Она́ вдова́ и прито́м бе́дная.	She's a widow and a poor one at that.
Он умён и прито́м о́чень до́бр.	He's intelligent and very nice in the bargain.

3. In Lesson V we discussed a negative usage of the stressed particle **не-**, but it should be remembered that **не-** much more frequently conveys a positive, "indefinite" meaning, "some, (a) certain," as in **несколько** and **некоторый** (R6.A2). Here are some other, less frequent uses of indefinite **не-**:

    a. The pronoun **нечто** (only nominative/accusative) occurs primarily with adjectives:

Случилось нечто замечательное.	Something remarkable happened.
Он нам показал нечто очень странное.	He showed us something very strange.

    b. The pronoun **некто** occurs rarely in the meaning "someone" (where it is identical with the far more common **кто-то**); e.g. **Некто вам звонил** 'Someone called you.' It may also be combined with **по имени** and a proper name in the meaning "a certain X, one X." The bookish **некий** is also used in this way:

Некто по имени (Некий) Иванов был здесь.	A certain Ivanov was here. (One Ivanov was here.)

    c. The adverb **некогда** may mean "once, at one time, in the old days." It is used fairly frequently:

Он некогда работал там.	He once worked there.
Она некогда жила в Москве.	She lived in Moscow in the old days.

4. The element **кое-**,[1] prefixed to a pronoun or an adverb, imparts the sense of "one or two, but not all," "a few places, but not everywhere," or, depending on the emphasis, "not all, but (still) one or two," "not everywhere, but (still) a few places," and so on:

Он кое-где побывал за это лето.	He's been a few places this summer.
Он кое-кого знает.	He knows one or two people.
Я кое-что сделал.	I've done something (in my life— something, though not much, *or* not much, but something).
Дайте кое-какие примеры.	Give an example or two.
Он был здесь кое с какими товарищами.	He was there with a couple of comrades.

(**Кое-какой**, like **никакой**, **никто**, etc., may be divided by a preposition, but some Russians keep the pronoun intact: **с кое-какими**.)
    Кое-как usually has the sense "any old way, carelessly":

Работа была сделана кое-как.	The work was done carelessly.
Она одевается кое-как.	She dresses any old way.

---

[1] Or, colloquially, **кой-**.

5. Notice the use of **на** *acc* in the sense "to the degree of, to the amount of, by." A comparative is often expressed or implied:

Он похудéл на пять килогрáммов.	He lost (got thinner by) five kilograms.
Мы опоздáли на дéсять минýт.	We were ten minutes late.
Онá на пять лéт стáрше мýжа.	She is five years older than her husband.
Он нá год молóже меня.	He's a year younger than I.
Мáльчик умнóжил шéсть на дéвять.	The boy multiplied six by nine.
Мы стáли намнóго сильнéе.	We have become much stronger.
Мы должны намнóго улýчшить кáчество нáшей продýкции.	We must greatly improve the quality of our production.

Where the *number of times more* is specified, however, **в** *acc* plus the word **рáз** is used:

Онá в стó рáз милéе Тáни.	She's a hundred times nicer than Tanja.
Нóвый пáрк в дéсять рáз длиннéе стáрого.	The new park is ten times as long as the old one.

For five times and under, the expressions **вдвóе, втрóе, вчéтверо,** and **впятеро** are quite frequent, though **в двá рáза, в три рáза,** etc. are also used:

Онá вдвóе стáрше своегó брáта.	She is twice as old as her brother.
В этом магазине всё вéщи втрóе дорóже чéм в других.	In this store everything is three times as expensive as in others.

Finally, note **во мнóго рáз** 'by many times (more)' and **в нéсколько рáз** 'by several times (more)':

Вы богáче нáс во мнóго (в нéсколько) рáз.	You´are many (several) times richer than we.

6. The series **во-пéрвых, во-вторых, в-трéтьих, в-четвёртых,** etc. means "in the first (second, third, fourth, etc.) place":

Я не пойдý с вáми потомý что, во-пéрвых я устáл, во-вторых мнé нéкогда, и в-трéтьих у меня нéт дéнег.	I won't go with you because in the first place I'm tired, in the second I have no time, and in the third I have no money.

7. Note that **такóй** 'such' may be extended to mean "the thing itself" rather than "such a thing". Hence it may be translated by "this" or "that":

В тако́м слу́чае я́ приду́.	In that case I'll come.
Я тако́го не хочу́. Возьму́ тако́й.	I don't want that one. I'll take that one.

It is used in the same manner in the expressions:

Кто́ тако́й? Кто́ таки́е?	Who is it? Who are they?
Кто́ вы́ тако́й? Что́ э́то тако́е?	Who are you? What is that?
Что́ тако́е?	What's the matter? (What happened?)

8. The word **вид** 'view, form, aspect, sort, kind' has certain special uses:

в ви́де *gen* X, в X-ом ви́де	in the form of X, in X form
ввиду́ *gen* X, ввиду́ того́, что	in view of X, in view of the fact that
име́ют в виду́	have (bear) in mind
Име́йте в виду́, что . . .	Keep in mind that, remember that . . .
де́лают ви́д, что	pretend that

9. We have already met several Russian verbs which convey the English verb "use," with varying shades of meaning. Selection of the proper verb is often difficult, and sometimes variants are possible. The most general verb is **употреби́ть – употребля́ют**, a transitive verb, *n* **употребле́ние**. **По́льзоваться** *inst*, *n* **по́льзование**, is also quite general, while **воспо́льзоваться** *inst* may serve as a perfective of the former but more often conveys the idea of "avail oneself of, take advantage of." The transitive verb **испо́льзовать** (both perfective and imperfective), *n* **испо́льзование**, often emphasizes the secondariness of the thing used: "use something for some other purpose." Finally, the transitive verb **примени́ть – применя́ют**, *n* **примене́ние**, often refers to the use of something new and is frequently translated by "apply."

Я ре́дко употребля́ю э́то сло́во.	I rarely use this word.
Я употреби́л на э́то два́ часа́.	I used two hours for that.
для вну́треннего употребле́ния	for internal use
Он никогда́ не по́льзуется ли́фтом.	He never uses the elevator.
По́льзуйтесь услу́гами «Бюро́ до́брых де́л».	Use the services of the Bureau of Good Works.
о по́льзовании словарём	about the use of the dictionary
Ма́льчик воспо́льзовался те́м, что ма́ть была́ занята́, и вы́бежал.	The boy took advantage of the fact that his mother was busy and ran out.
Мы́ воспо́льзовались слу́чаем сказа́ть ему́ э́то.	We used (availed ourselves of) the opportunity to tell him that.

В своёй диссертáции óн испóльзовал всé новéйшие дáнные.

He used all the latest data in his dissertation.

В э́том дéле нáм придётся использовать специалиста.

For this matter we'll have to use a specialist.

Потóм мы́ бýдем обсуждáть вопрóс об испóльзовании áтомной энéргии в ми́рных цéлях.

Later we will discuss the question of the use of atomic energy for peaceful purposes.

Мы́ примени́ли нóвый мéтод, и óн дáл хорóшие результáты.

We applied the new method, and it gave good results.

В строи́тельстве применя́ют тепéрь нóвый ви́д пластмáссы.

A new type of plastic is now being used in construction.

Нóвая маши́на ещё не нашлá своегó применéния.

The new machine has yet to find an application.

Пóльзоваться, in addition, has the meaning "have, enjoy" (cf. Lesson VII.6).

Онá пóльзуется больши́м успéхом у мужчи́н.

She enjoys great success with men.

Нáш дирéктор пóльзуется больши́м авторитéтом.

Our director has great authority.

Он пóльзуется мировóй извéстностью.

He has worldwide fame.

TRANSLATION INTO ENGLISH

1. Мы́ наконéц дости́гли нáшей цéли. Тепéрь мы́ пóльзуемся горя́чей поддéржкой нáших бы́вших проти́вников. **2.** Мы́ с женóй почти́ одногó вóзраста. Онá молóже меня́ на двá мéсяца. **3.** Мы́ намнóго превы́сили нáшу нóрму. Нý, сóбственно говоря́, э́то не совсéм тáк. Я вáм скажý нéсколько слóв насчёт нáших нóрм. Во-пéрвых, у нáс нéт постоя́нных нóрм, во-вторы́х, почти́ нельзя́ оцéнивать нáши достижéния по нóрмам, и, в трéтьих, применéние нóрм к любóй рабóте — весьмá услóвное дéло. **4.** Вы́ставка достижéний нарóдного хозя́йства СССР располóжена далекó от цéнтра Москвы́. Тудá и обрáтно за оди́н чáс доéхать нельзя́. Мы́ мóжем опоздáть на полчасá. **5.** От нáс трéбуют перевыполнéния нóрмы на 15 процéнтов. **6.** Коли́чество кислорóда в вóздухе значи́тельно бóльше на повéрхности земли́, чéм на высотé нéскольких киломéтров. **7.** Нéкоторые водорóдные соединéния явля́ются опáсными для жи́зни. **8.** Пролетáрии всéх стрáн, соединя́йтесь! **9.** У меня́ возни́кло чýвство, что на меня́ окáзывают какóе-то давлéние. **10.** Я взя́л с собóй кóе-каки́е кни́ги. **11.** Я хочý рассказáть тебé кóе о чём. **12.** Вслéдствие образовáния комитéта по капитáльному строи́тельству, нóвые городá стáли возникáть по всéй странé.

13. Вода обыкновенно бывает в жидком состоянии. Если она перейдёт в твёрдое состояние, то получится лёд, а если в газовое состояние, то получится водяной пар. 14. Некогда здесь было озеро. Но оно, видно, исчезло. Странное дело. 15. Нечто странное случилось. 16. Надо воспользоваться этим случаем, чтобы удержать его от такого поступка. 17. Мы сейчас имеем дело с вопросом о зарождении жизни. Наши учёные уже кое-что знают в этой области, но их успехи пока только частичные. 18. Узкая дорога была покрыта снегом. 19. Его литературное творчество невелико по объёму, но оно ставит его в ряд наших лучших писателей. 20. Многие из моих коллег не в состоянии правильно оценить творчество современных писателей. 21. При реакции это соединение выделило кислород. 22. Реакция представляет собой всякое противодействие развитию нового, передового. 23. Мы нашли горячую поддержку во всех слоях общества. 24. Он, по-видимому, не в состоянии нас больше поддерживать. 25. Возникновение жизни обусловлено существованием некоторых органических веществ. 26. При всей разнице между Александром Первым и Николаем Первым, в политике их, а особенно в результатах их политики, было много общего. 27. Очень хорошо будет провести эти реформы хотя бы в этом виде. 28. При коммунизме вся власть будет сосредоточена в руках трудящихся. 29. Подобные процессы протекают постоянно. 30. Болезнь протекает нормально. ‖ Между тем как Ленин думал о мировой революции, Сталин имел в виду революцию и развитие социализма в одной стране. 31. Мы использовали имеющиеся исторические источники. 32. Есть холодные и горячие ключи, вода которых содержит несколько высший процент растворённых солей, причём почва около них тоже содержит небольшое количество соли. 33. Вот вам ключ от моей квартиры. 34. Это слово уже вышло из употребления. 35. Он выполняет свою работу пока хорошо, хотя сначала все думали, что он располагает только поверхностными знаниями. 36. Радость, пусть даже самая маленькая, не бывает без причин: всегда она обусловлена победой или успехом. 37. Мы атаковали и на суше и на море. 38. Эти поля хорошо омыты дождём. 39. Командиры уже расположили свои части, причём всё в полном составе. 40. Он расположил её к себе... и всё ещё пользуется её расположением. 41. Благодаря расположению нашего дома на берегу, мы имеем прекрасный вид на океан. 42. Река опять замёрзла. Несколько южнее, ближе к океану, климат значительно мягче. 43. Я имею в виду именно этот случай. 44. Ввиду этого вам придётся смягчить ваши условия: а то противник будет колебаться, и, возможно, их вовсе не примет. 45. Тут борьба противоположностей. 46. Мы не колеблемся, потому что наша позиция прочная. 47. В противоположность его симпатичной наружности, его голос был резкий, неприятный. 48. Его поступок подобен поступку героя.

49. Он удали́лся от те́мы. **50.** Его́ удали́ли из ко́мнаты. **51.** На́м не удало́сь обнару́жить причи́ны таки́х ре́зких колеба́ний температу́ры. **52.** На́ша соба́ка всегда́ обнару́живает свою́ ра́дость при ви́де отца́. **53.** У него́ е́сть да́р сло́ва и прито́м прия́тная нару́жность. Я уве́рен, что о́н понра́вится все́м на вечери́нке. **54.** Мо́й сы́н де́лает ви́д, что живёт на со́бственный счёт, когда́, на са́мом де́ле, живёт на мои́ де́ньги. **55.** — Мы́ сейча́с стро́им большу́ю жи́знь, — продолжа́л Серге́ич, — ка́ждый челове́к, е́сли о́н хо́чет, мо́жет примени́ть у на́с свои́ си́лы. **56.** Мы́ идём в обра́тном направле́нии. **57.** Деле́ние — де́йствие обра́тное умноже́нию. **58.** Вероя́тно, я отказа́л ей таки́м то́ном, кото́рый не допуска́л дальне́йших разгово́ров. **59.** Озёра уже́ покры́ты льдо́м, зна́чит, то́чка замерза́ния дости́гнута. Зима́, по-ви́димому, бу́дет ра́нняя. **60.** Дальне́йшее разви́тие наро́дного тво́рчества уже́ не бу́дет зави́сеть от усло́вий жи́зни, тогда́ как в про́шлом, при ни́зком жи́зненном у́ровне, просты́е лю́ди не могли́ зна́ть ра́дости тво́рчества. **61.** Он всегда́ бы́л про́тив включе́ния и́менно э́того вопро́са в на́шу програ́мму. **62.** Лю́ди жи́ли та́м уже́ задо́лго до возникнове́ния Москвы́. **63.** Он располага́ет то́лько немно́гими и прито́м пове́рхностными зна́ниями. **64.** Эти постоя́нные измене́ния языка́ в о́бласти ле́ксики, веду́щие к тому́, что слова́рный соста́в языка́ стано́вится всё бога́че и разносторо́ннее, происхо́дят преиму́щественно за счёт разли́чных проце́ссов словообразова́ния на ба́зе существу́ющих в языке́ сло́в.

TRANSLATION INTO RUSSIAN

1. When the temperature at the earth's surface reaches 1000 degrees, certain gases form whose chemical composition includes minerals. **2.** These substances form owing to the cooling of hydrogen and oxygen. **3.** Such questions rarely come up. **4.** We are no longer in a position to maintain our attack. **5.** These gases are under great pressure, but their volumes nevertheless exceed by six times the volumes of the substances that contain them. At very high temperatures the reverse processes take place. It's obvious that we know a thing or two about chemistry. **6.** We must use the reports of these scientists in our work on our dissertations. **7.** A certain Mr. Morózov was here. **8.** For all the mildness of the climate on this island, the temperature here varies rather strongly, whereas farther south, where there are only warm ocean currents, there are no such variations. **9.** Both hot and cold springs are used for medicinal purposes. **10.** That's only a partial improvement. I want our production to exceed the present level by 30 percent. **11.** Thanks to the large contribution you made to our work, next year we will be able to operate without the support of the government. **12.** When you talk about "substance," what do you have in mind? **13.** I saw something unusual. **14.** She has traveled to a few places in her time. **15.** Don't forget how much you're late by when you use (**пóльзоваться**) that transportation. **16.** In the first place you're four times as rich as your brother; in the second place you know how to dispose people toward you, whereas your brother does not enjoy any success in society. In view of all this I think that only with great difficulty will you be able to take advantage of his help. **17.** I never use such expressions. **18.** Recently they began to exert on me significantly greater pressure. **19.** A continental climate, unlike a maritime climate, is characterized by sharp variations of temperature. **20.** The mildness of our maritime climate is caused (conditioned) by the influence of warm currents, whose water is heated by the Gulf Stream. **21.** He's a likable person and reveals a great talent. But in view of what happened we can accept him only under the condition that he will restrain himself from such acts in the future. **22.** The enemy has only a few separate units at his disposal. He must attack now. — Yes, precisely, if he hesitates, all will be lost. **23.** What is his disease characterized by (two possible verbs)? **24.** Much time has passed by since then. **25.** He subsequently took part in many decisions; however, he seldom pondered over what the results would be. **26.** In contrast to your description of the results of our plan, we have actually achieved a level in our production at least five times higher than yours. But all our leading people assert that we must improve its quality. **27.** How are we to evaluate the achievements of Russian science? **28.** We can't help valuing very highly Puškin's creative work. But we must include in our discussion other writers as well. **29.** We are now in a position to concentrate all our forces on one front. In that way we will increase the enemy's losses by 50 percent. **30.** Port A differs from Port B in that it does not freeze in the winter. **31.** Yes, I have precisely those islands in mind. The air there is remarkably clean and cold in comparison with ours; there's a noticeable difference. One must reckon with the influence of the ice and the masses of cold air from the north. **32.** I want to unite my fate with yours. **33.** Whatever you say, the enemy will not agree to such conditions. **34.** He's pretending that everything is in order. **35.** To be sure, we believe in freedom, but at this period of our development authority is authority. Subsequently, after we have established a sound peace, it will be possible to speak of a softening in the conducting of our policies. **36.** Our good relations are based on a friendship which has long existed between our peoples (use **лёжáть в оснóве**). **37.** People lived there long before the emergence of Moscow. **38.** These minerals are covered only by a superficial (surface) layer of soil. **39.** We are making a trip to the reverse side of the moon. **40.** Our leaders are demanding not only fulfillment of the norms but overfulfillment as well. As a consequence of this the workers may go on strike.

СЛОВА́ ТО́ЛЬКО К Э́ТОМУ УРО́КУ

бо́ж-ий God's, of God

вод-о-ро́д hydrogen

вод-о-ро́д-н-ый hydrogen *adj*

вод-ян-о́й water *adj*

га́вань harbor, haven

Гольфстри́м the Gulf Stream

грани́т granite

капита́ль-н-ое стро-и́-тель-ств-о capital construction

кисл-о-ро́д oxygen

ком-о́ч-/е/к (*dim of* ком-/о́/к) lump, clod

кор-а́ crust; rind, bark

континента́ль-н-ый continental

леч-е́б-н-ый medical, medicinal

матéри-я matter; material (fabric)

млад-е́нч-еск-ий infantile; (of time) earliest

океа́н-ск-ий ocean *adj*

па́р *E pl obl* steam, vapor

психи́ч-еск-ий mental, psychical

рас-тво́р solution; *cf.* раствори́ть – растворя́ют

су́ш-а (на) land (*vs.* sea)

тёпл-о-ём-к-ость thermal capacity

то́нн-а ton

ювени́ль-н-ый juvenile

хими́ч-еск-ий chemical

ГЛАГО́ЛЫ

при-д-у́т-ся – приходи́ться ЙД turn out (as), emerge (as)

о-мо́й-ут – омыва́ют wash against/around

рас-пла́в-и-ть – расплавля́ют melt (down) *tr*; —ся melt (down) *intr*
    n расплавле́ние

об-усло́в-и-ть – обусло́вливают stipulate, make a condition; cause, provoke,

create the conditions for; *cf.* усло́вие

за-сты́н-ут *or* за-сты́д-ну-ть – застыва́ют congeal (in cooling)
    n застыва́ние

рас-твор-и́-ть – растворя́ют dissolve *tr*; —ся dissolve *intr*
    n раство́р, растворе́ние

О́БЩИЙ СЛОВА́РЬ

авторите́т authority

благ-о-дар-я́ *кому́/чему́* thanks to, due to; *ger* < (по)благодари́ть *tr* thank

весьма́ B/C highly, greatly, very

вещ-е-ств-о́ substance

во́з-дух air

во́з-раст age (of someone or something); в —е пяти́ ле́т at the age of five

впосле́дствии subsequently, afterwards (*do not confuse with* всле́дствие *чего́* as a consequence of)

вре́мя: в то́ — как VIII.1

всле́дствие *чего́* as a consequence of, owing to, due to

вы́с-от-а́ (*pl* высо́ты) height; elevation

га́з gas

гор-я́ч-ий hot; ardent; —ая вода́ hot water (*but* hot weather/climate жа́ркая пого́да/жа́ркий кли́мат)

гра́дус degree (temperature; angles, etc.; *Soviets use centigrade*)

даль-н-е́йш-ий further, subsequent; в —ем subsequently

да́р gift, donation; да́р *чего́* gift of; да́р ре́чи gift of speech

жи́д-/к-ий liquid *adj*

жи́д-к-ость liquid

за-ме́т-/н-ый noticeable, marked

за-меч-а́-тель-/н-ый remarkable, splendid

зем-н-о́й terrestrial, earth *adj*

и́мен-но namely; just, precisely: Именно. Yes, that's just it.

ис-то́ч-ник **ТОК**[2] spring; source
килогра́мм kilogram
киломе́тр kilometer
кли́мат climate
клю́ч *E* key; spring
л/ё/д (на льду́) ice
ма́ло того́ CL5.2
ма́сс-а mass
ме́жду те́м, ме́жду те́м как VIII.1
ме́тод method
ми́л-ый nice, sweet; (spoken address) dear
минера́л mineral
мя́г/к-ий soft, mild, gentle
нару́ж-н-ость (< нару́жный exterior) exterior, (outside) appearance
наряду́ с *ке́м/че́м* together with, side by side with; equal with
но́рм-а norm, standard; вы́полнить – выполня́ют —y fulfill norm; перевы́полнить – перевыполня́ют —y overfulfill norm
об-ра́т-н-ый об-**ВРАТ** reverse, return, opposite
объ-ём volume, size, extent
одна́ко however
о́стров *E pl* -а́ island
пери́од period
по-**ве́рх**-н-ость surface
по-**ве́рх**-н-ост-/н-ый superficial, surface *adj*
по – **ви́**димому apparently, to all appearances
под-**де́рж**-/к-а support; *cf.* поддержа́ть – подде́рживают
по-**до́б**-/н-ый similar, like; ничего́ —ого nothing of the sort; и тому́ —ое and so forth
по́рт (в порту́) *E pl obl* port, harbor
по-**сто́**-я-н-/н-ый constant
по́чв-а soil

при-**близ**-и́-тель-/н-ый approximate
прогре́сс progress
пролета́рий, пролета́р/к-а, пролета́р-ский proletarian
против-о-по-ло́ж-н-ость opposite; в — кому́/чему́ unlike, in contrast to
проце́нт percent
проце́сс process
про́ч-/н-ый solid, stable, durable
реа́кци-я reaction
ре́з-/к-ий sharp
ре́з-к-ость sharpness; sharp words
результа́т result; в —е *кого́/чего́* as a result of
симпати́ч-/н-ый likable, attractive
сло́й (в сло́е *or* в слою́) *E pl* layer
с-**ме́н**-а shift, replacement; *cf.* смени́ть – сменя́ют change, replace
соба́к-а dog
сред-а́ *S pl* environment, milieu, medium; — *S nom pl acc sg* Wednesday
с-**чёт** (ac)count, bill, score; *cf.* с/о/чту́т – счита́ют VI. 2; за — *кого́/чего́* VIII; на X — on X account; насчёт *кого́/чего́* II.6
тала́нт talent
тво́р-че-ств-о creation, creative work (*often* works *of creator*)
температу́р-а temperature
тёп-/л-ый warm
тогда́ как VIII.1
у-**сло́в**-и-е condition, term; *pl only* conditions, circumstances; рабо́чие —я working conditions; ни при каки́х —ях under no conditions; при —и, что on the condition that
це́ль goal, purpose, aim
эпо́ха epoch, era

ГЛАГО́ЛЫ

у-**вели́ч**-и-ть – увели́чивают increase, enlarge; —ся increase *intr*
n увеличе́ние

пре-**вы́с**-и-ть – превыша́ют exceed
n превыше́ние

на-**гре́й**-ут – нагрева́ют heat (up), warm (up)

n нагрева́ние

давл-е́н-и-е (< давить) pressure; ока-за́ть – ока́зывают — на *кого́/что́* exert pressure on

у-**дал**-и́-ть – удаля́ют remove, move off *tr*; —ся move off, withdraw *intr*

n удале́ние

вы́-**дел**-и-ть – выделя́ют single out, apportion; secrete, give off

n выделе́ние

под-**держ**-а-ть – подде́рживают support, maintain

n подде́рж/ка support; поддержа́ние maintenance; подде́рживание supporting, maintaining

у-**держ**-ать — уде́рживают retain, hold, restrain; —(ся) от *кого́/чего́* restrain (oneself) from; —ся hold fast *intr*

n удержа́ние, у́держ *us in expression* без у́держу unrestrainedly

со-**един**-и́-ть – соединя́ют unite, combine, join, connect *tr*; —ся *intr*

n соедине́ние compound (chemistry)

в-**ключ**-и́-ть – включа́ют *кого́/что́ в что́* include; switch on

n включе́ние

(по)-**колеб**-а́-ть *S pres and impv* (*PPP* поколе́блен) shake; —ся oscillate; fluctuate, vary; hesitate

n колеба́ние

по-**кро́й**-ут – покрыва́ют cover

n покры́тие covering (of expenses); roofing; покро́в cover; shroud, pall *fig*

у-**лу́чш**-и-ть – улучша́ют improve

n улучше́ние

за-**мёрз**-(ну)-ть – замерза́ют freeze *intr*; то́чка замерза́ния freezing point

у-**мно́ж**-и-ть – умножа́ют increase, multiply

n умноже́ние

с-**мягч**-и́-ть – смягча́ют soften, ease, mollify

n смягче́ние

об-**нару́ж**-и-ть – обнару́живают reveal, display, discover

n обнаруже́ние

воз-**ни́к**-(ну)-ть – возника́ют arise, come up, emerge, originate

n возникнове́ние

о-**позд**-а́-ют – опа́здывают be late

n опозда́ние

вы́-**полн**-и-ть – выполня́ют fulfill

n выполне́ние

пере-вы́-**полн**-и-ть – перевыполня́ют overfulfill

n перевыполне́ние

рас-по-**лож**-и́-ть – располага́ют dispose, arrange, place, locate; dispose (incline); — *кого́ к кому́/чему́* dispose, incline to/toward

n расположе́ние

за-**рожд**-ён-и-е **РОД** (< зароди́ть(ся) – зарожда́ют(ся)) origin, conception

у-**равн**-о-**ве́с**-и-ть – уравнове́шивают balance, counterbalance, equalize

n уравнове́шивание

со-**сред**-о-**то́ч**-и-ть – сосредото́чивают concentrate

n сосредото́чение

до-**сти́г**-(ну)-ть (*or* дости́чь) – достига́ют *чего́* achieve, accomplish, reach

n достиже́ние

теч-е́н-и-е (< тёку́т) current

про-**тёк**-у́т – протека́ют flow (through), leak; pass, elapse (of time); go on (of a process), proceed, progréss

n протека́ние

характер-из-ова́-ть *P and I* characterize; —ся *чéм* be characterized by

о-**хлад**-и́-ть – охлажда́ют cool (off); dampen (feelings)

n охлажде́ние

о-**цен**-и-ть – оце́нивают (*PPP* оценён) evaluate, estimate

n оце́н/ка

Modal expressions

ДОСТОЕВСКИЙ

Фёдор Миха́йлович Достое́вский роди́лся в Москве́ 30 октября́ 1821 г. По слова́м жены́ писа́теля, Анны Григо́рьевны, о́н «охо́тно вспомина́л о своём счастли́вом, безмяте́жном де́тстве и с горя́чим чу́вством говори́л о ма́тери.» Одна́ко, из ра́зных исто́чников мы́ доста́точно зна́ем, чтобы сомнева́ться в правоте́ э́того заявле́ния; едва́ ли де́тство Достое́вского бы́ло 5 таки́м безмяте́жным. Сама́ ма́ть называ́ла Фе́дю «настоя́щий ого́нь», и с отцо́м бы́ло нема́ло столкнове́ний. Оте́ц вообще́ бы́л челове́к тяжёлого нра́ва, вспы́льчивый, подозри́тельный и угрю́мый. Он бы́л ужа́сно ску́п и беспреры́вно жа́ловался на бе́дность, хотя́ на са́мом де́ле у него́ бы́ло доста́точно де́нег, чтобы купи́ть име́ние, состоя́щее из дву́х дереве́нь. Он 10 заставля́л сы́на в го́ды его́ студе́нчества постоя́нно проси́ть де́нег да́же на ча́й, оде́жду, и т.д. (бе́дность — одна́ из важне́йших те́м в произведе́ниях Достое́вского). Со свои́ми крестья́нами оте́ц Достое́вского обраща́лся насто́лько жесто́ко, что они́, наконе́ц, уби́ли его́ (задуши́ли поду́шкой). В перепи́ске писа́теля мы́ не найдём ни одного́ упомина́ния о траги́ческой 15 сме́рти отца́, и его́ совреме́нники сообща́ют, что «об отце́ Достое́вский реши́тельно не люби́л говори́ть и проси́л о нём не спра́шивать». Но тру́дно пове́рить, чтобы уби́йство отца́ не произвело́ о́чень си́льного впечатле́ния на восемнадцатиле́тнего сы́на. Воображе́ние Достое́вского бы́ло потрясено́ не то́лько драмати́ческой обстано́вкой сме́рти старика́, но и чу́вством 20

251

своей вины́ перед ни́м. Он не люби́л его́, жа́ловался на его́ ску́пость, незадо́лго до его́ сме́рти написа́л ему́ раздражённое письмо́. И тепе́рь чу́вствовал свою́ отве́тственность за его́ смерть. Это нра́вственное потрясе́ние подгото́вило зарожде́ние паду́чей. Пробле́ма отцо́в и дете́й, преступле́ния и наказа́ния, вины́ и отве́тственности встре́тила Достое́вского на поро́ге созна́тельной жи́зни. Это была́ его́ физиологи́ческая и душе́вная ра́на. И то́лько в са́мом конце́ жи́зни, в «Бра́тьях Карама́зовых», он освободи́лся от неё, преврати́в её в созда́ние **иску́сства**.[4]

Достое́вский про́жил глубоко́ траги́ческую жи́знь. Его́ одино́чество бы́ло безграни́чно. Пробле́мы гениа́льного а́втора «Преступле́ния и наказа́ния» бы́ли недосту́пны совреме́нникам; они́ ви́дели в нём то́лько пропове́дника гума́нности, певца́ «бе́дных люде́й», «унижённых и оскорблённых». Лю́дям 19-го ве́ка мир Достое́вского представля́лся фантасти́ческим. Турге́нев, Гончаро́в и Лев Толсто́й **эпи́чески**[2] изобража́ли незы́блемый строй ру́сского «ко́смоса». — Достое́вский крича́л, что э́тот «ко́смос» непро́чен, среди́ всео́бщего благополу́чия он оди́н говори́л о кри́зисе культу́ры и о надвига́ющихся на мир неслы́ханных катастро́фах. Достое́вский был про́зван «больны́м, жесто́ким тала́нтом» и ско́ро забы́т. Духо́вная связь ме́жду писа́телем и поколе́ниями 80-х и 90-х годо́в порвала́сь. В нача́ле 20-го ве́ка символи́сты откры́ли Достое́вского. Автор «Бе́сов» стал их духо́вным учи́телем; они́ бы́ли охва́чены его́ проро́ческой трево́гой, в их кни́гах и статья́х впервы́е раскры́лась филосо́фская диале́ктика Достое́вского, впервы́е была́ оценена́ произведённая им духо́вная револю́ция. Тво́рчество писа́теля приобрело́ тре́тье измере́ние: метафизи́ческую глубину́. Заслу́га символи́стов состои́т в преодоле́нии чи́сто психологи́ческого подхо́да к созда́телю «рома́нов-траге́дий». 20-й век уви́дел в Достое́вском не то́лько тала́нтливого психопато́лога, но и вели́кого религио́зного мысли́теля.

Поколе́ние символи́стов откры́ло Достое́вского — фило́софа; поколе́ние совреме́нных иссле́дователей открыва́ет Достое́вского — худо́жника. Миф об эстети́ческой бесфо́рменности и стилисти́ческой небре́жности а́втора «Карама́зовых» разру́шен оконча́тельно. Изуче́ние поэ́тики писа́теля, его́ компози́ции, те́хники и сти́ля вво́дит нас в эстети́ческий мир вели́кого романи́ста.

> [Adapted from K. Močul'skij, *Dostoevskij: žizn' i tvorčestvo*,
> Paris, YMCA Press, 1947, pp. 7–12]

A. Constructions with чтобы

1. The modal conjunction **чтобы (чтоб)** introduces clauses with a variety of meanings connected with desirability or possibility; notably purpose, but

also wish, necessity, command, and the like, and sometimes combinations of these elements. Several of these patterns are already familiar to you:

Он рабо́тает (для того́), что́бы жи́ть.	He works in order to live.
Он говори́т гро́мко, что́бы всё его́ слы́шали.	He is speaking loudly, so that everyone will hear him.
Он хо́чет, что́бы вы́ рабо́тали.	He wants you to work.
Он про́сит, что́бы бы́ли при́няты всё необходи́мые ме́ры.	He is asking that all the necessary measures be taken.

We recall that **что́бы** expressing purpose may be omitted after a verb of motion. If the purpose is negative, however, **что́бы** is obligatory:

Он ушёл рабо́тать.	He went away to work.
Он ушёл, что́бы не меша́ть на́м.	He went away so as not to bother us.

2. The modal nature of **что́бы** emerges very clearly when it is contrasted with **что** in similar or identical contexts; the hypothetical is opposed to the factual. Compare:

Ва́жно, что всё обсуди́ли вопро́с.	It is important that everyone discussed the question. (*And they did.*)
Ва́жно, что́бы всё обсуди́ли вопро́с.	It is important that everyone (should) discuss the question. (*Hypothetical.*)
Он объясни́л та́к, что мы́ всё его́ по́няли.	He explained in such a way a way that we all understood him. (*We did understand.*)
Он объясни́л та́к, что́бы мы́ всё его́ по́няли.	He explained in such a way that we all might understand him. (*Not certain that we all did, in fact, understand.*)

3. Notice also the following sentences with **что́бы**:

Ну́жно (Необходи́мо), что́бы всё отказа́лись.	It is necessary (indispensable) that everyone refuse (*or* should refuse).
Он наста́ивает (на то́м), что́бы мы́ оста́лись.	He insists that we stay.
Тре́буется, что́бы писа́тель изобража́л, а не то́лько расска́зывал, что придёт ему́ в го́лову.	A writer must depict and not just relate whatever comes into his head.
На́ш команди́р приказа́л, что́бы мы́ никуда́ не ходи́ли.	Our commander has ordered us not to go anywhere.

Смотри́те, что́бы ва́ши де́ти бо́льше к на́м не приходи́ли.	See to it that your children don't come to see us any more.
Всé рефо́рмы напра́влены к тому́, что́бы улу́чшить рабо́чие усло́вия.	All the reforms are directed toward improving working conditions.
Мы́ стреми́мся к тому́, что́бы вы́ бы́ли хоро́шими солда́тами.	We are striving (to the end) that you may be good soldiers.

4. **Что́бы** clauses are regularly used after **доста́точный(-о)** 'enough, sufficient(ly),' **недоста́точный(-о)** 'not enough, insufficient(ly),' **не тако́й** 'not of such quality, not such that,' **не насто́лько** 'not to such an extent, not so, not so much,' **сли́шком** 'too, too much,' and certain similar expressions. In some sentences it may be more or less appropriate to insert **для того́** before **что́бы**, but this usage rests on rather complex syntactic and stylistic considerations and is almost always optional in any case:

Тепе́рь доста́точно тепло́, что́бы ходи́ть без пальто́.	It's warm enough now to go without an overcoat.
Доста́точно бы́ло взгляну́ть на него́, что́бы уви́деть, что э́тот челове́к бы́л на фро́нте.	It was enough to look at him to see that this man had been on the front.
Вы́ недоста́точно зна́ете литерату́ру для того́, что́бы оцени́ть произведе́ния Турге́нева.	You don't know enough about literature to evaluate the works of Turgenev.
У э́тих аспира́нтов не хвата́ло зна́ний для того́, что́бы спра́виться с э́тим экза́меном.	These graduate students *did* not have enough knowledge to cope with this examination.
Пого́да сего́дня не така́я, что́бы де́ти могли́ игра́ть на дворе́.	The weather today isn't such that the children can play outside.
Cf. Пого́да сего́дня така́я, что де́ти мо́гут игра́ть на дворе́.	The weather today is such that the children can play outside.
Сейча́с не насто́лько тепло́, что́бы мо́жно бы́ло ходи́ть без пальто́.	It's not warm enough now so that one can go without an overcoat.
Cf. Сейча́с насто́лько тепло́, что уже́ мо́жно ходи́ть без пальто́.	It's warm enough now so that one can go without an overcoat.
Мы́ сли́шком уста́ли, для того́, что́бы идти́ да́льше.	We're too tired to go on.
Он мно́го рабо́тает, но́ у него́ сли́шком мно́го недоста́тков для того́, что́бы его́ вы́брали президе́нтом.	He works a great deal, but he has too many shortcomings to be elected president.

5. Note also the following expressions:

без того́ чтобы (*often with* не)[1]	without X-ing
вме́сто того́ чтобы	instead of X-ing
кро́ме того́ чтобы	besides X-ing
состои́т в том, чтобы	consists in X-ing

Examples:

Он не мо́жет жи́ть без того́ чтобы не ходи́ть в теа́тр (без того́ что-бы не встреча́ться с друзья́ми).	He can't live without going to the theater (without meeting with his friends).
Вме́сто того́ чтобы взя́ть такси́, он прошёл ве́сь пу́ть пешко́м.	Instead of taking a taxi, he walked the whole way.
Кро́ме того́ чтобы написа́ть ему́ письмо́ об э́том, мы́ должны́ бы́ли и поговори́ть с ни́м.	Besides writing him a letter about it, we had to have a talk with him too.
На́ша зада́ча состои́т в то́м, чтобы созда́ть лу́чшие рабо́чие усло́вия в на́шем о́бществе.	Our task consists in creating better working conditions in our society.

6. **Чтобы** may also be used with verbs of saying, thinking, or perception used negatively or in some other manner questioned or denied. Most often the reference is to past or present meaning. Usage is inconsistent, and sometimes either **что** or **чтобы** may be used. Note also the compared examples in paragraph A4 on the preceding page.

Тру́дно пове́рить, чтобы она́ могла́ сде́лать таку́ю ве́щь.	It's hard to believe that she could do (*or* have done) such a thing.
Я никогда́ не представля́л себе́, чтобы о́н та́к поступи́л.	I never imagined that he would act (*or* would have acted) thus.
Я никогда́ не ви́дел, чтобы челове́к попа́л в тру́дности из-за э́того.	I never saw a person get into trouble over that.
Он никогда́ не ду́мал, чтобы э́тот солда́т когда́-нибудь ста́л ге-нера́лом.	He never thought that one day that soldier would be a general.
Я не ве́рю, что о́н придёт. *Or:* Я не ве́рю, чтобы о́н пришёл.	I don't believe he'll come.

Verbs of fearing may take **чтобы** when the dependent clause is affirmative in meaning, and the so-called pleonastic **не** may be added (compare the same phenomenon in French: *Je crains qu'il ne vienne* 'I am afraid that he will come'

---

[1] This usage is akin to a double negative (which Russian, unlike English, employs freely) and is similar to the pleonastic **не** described in paragraph 6 below.

Я бою́сь, что́бы он не пришёл.).[1] **Что́бы** may also be used with **сомнева́ются** 'to doubt':

Я бою́сь, что она́ ска́жет пра́вду. *Or:* Я бою́сь, ка́к бы она́ не сказа́ла пра́вду.	I'm afraid she will tell the truth.
Cf. Я бою́сь, что она́ не ска́жет пра́вды.	I'm afraid she won't tell the truth.
Я боя́лся, что она́ придёт. *Or:* Я боя́лся, ка́к бы она́ не пришла́.	I was afraid she would come.
Cf. Я боя́лся, что она́ не придёт.	I was afraid she wouldn't come.
Я сомнева́юсь, понра́вится ли ва́м мо́й бра́т. *Or:* Я сомнева́юсь, что́бы ва́м понра́вился мо́й бра́т.	I doubt whether you will like my brother.

7. Finally, **что́бы** in certain cases may have the effect of an imperative or a mild warning:

Чтоб(ы) ва́с не́ было.	Go away.
Чтоб(ы) все́ кни́ги бы́ли о́тданы в библиоте́ку.	Make sure all the books are returned to the library.

B. Conditionals: бы and the imperative

In conditional sentences, the dependent clause is called the *protasis* and the main clause is called the *apodosis*; or we may call them simply *if clause* and *consequence clause*, respectively.

1. The normal type of conditional is already familiar to the student. The protasis may either precede or follow the apodosis. When it precedes, the particle **то́** may be used at the beginning of the apodosis (this element is omitted in translation into English, or is rendered by "then"):

Я бы зна́л об э́том, е́сли бы о́н сде́лал э́то.	I would have known about it if he had done it.
Е́сли бы о́н сде́лал э́то, (то́) я́ бы зна́л об э́том.	If he had done it, (then) I would have known about it.

2. Occasionally, **е́сли** may be omitted, and the verb and subject in both the protasis and the apodosis inverted; the protasis always precedes:

Не опозда́ли бы вы́ к по́езду, не познако́мился бы я́ с ва́ми.	If you hadn't been late for the train, I wouldn't have become acquainted with you.

---

[1] **Что́бы** after verbs of fearing is usually replaced by **ка́к бы.**

Пришёл бы о́н, ви́дел бы его́.	If he had come, I would have seen him.
Придёт о́н — скажу́ ему́.	If he comes, I'll tell him.

3. As in English, the protasis is sometimes merely implied:

О́н да́л бы ва́м де́сять рубле́й.	He would give you ten rubles. (*Some if clause is implied.*)

4. Sometimes only the protasis is expressed, with **е́сли** omitted, and the subject and verb inverted; the apodosis is implied. The result is equivalent to English "If only . . . , (then, . . . (implied))":

Да́л бы о́н ва́м де́сять рубле́й.	If only he would give you ten rubles. (*You could buy a new shirt, etc.*)
Бы́л бы о́н зде́сь.	If only he were here.

5. Occasionally the second singular imperative is used to render contrary-to-fact conditions. Such constructions are particularly likely in conversation or informal prose:

Зна́й я́ како́й-нибудь иностра́нный язы́к, рабо́тал бы перево́дчиком.	If I knew some foreign language, I would work as a translator.
Окажи́сь у меня́ сейча́с де́ньги, я́ бы обяза́тельно купи́л маши́ну.	If I were to get some money now, I would definitely buy a car.

The expressions **бу́дь то́** 'though it were' and **не бу́дь** *gen* 'but for' belong here:

Бу́дь то́ са́м президе́нт, я́ не поступи́л бы ина́че.	Though it were the president himself, I would not have acted differently.
Не бу́дь ва́с, она́ исче́зла бы.	But for you, she would have disappeared.

6. "But for" may also be rendered by **е́сли бы не** plus the nominative:

Если бы не кри́зис (Не бу́дь кри́зиса), мы́ сейча́с отдыха́ли бы в Крыму́.	But for (If it weren't for) the crisis, we would now be resting in the Crimea.

7. **Ра́з** is another conditional conjunction, with a somewhat colloquial flavor. It means "once (given the fact that), now that, since":

Расска́зывайте до конца́, ра́з на́чали.	Finish your story to the end, now that you've started.
Ра́з (э́то) та́к, есть что́ обсужда́ть.	If that's so, there is something to be discussed.

C. Other modal uses of the imperative form

In paragraph B5 we described a use of the imperative to convey conditional meaning. Here are two additional, quite specialized uses of the imperative form which are highly modal, but have nothing directly to do with command:

1. An action (often unpleasant) arbitrarily imposed; often this action is compared to a pleasant action engaged in by someone else:

Он всё время играет в карты с друзьями, а я работай на кухне.	He plays cards all the time with his friends, and I have to work in the kitchen.
Муж оставайся дома, а жена — в театр.	The husband has to stay home, while his wife goes to the theater.

2. An unexpected or sudden action which interrupts or hampers in some way another action; frequently **возьми да** is placed before the imperative:

Всё весело гуляли и пели, а он — возьми да вернись домой.	Everybody was strolling along gaily and singing, and he, all of a sudden (darn him), goes home.
Всё отдыхают, а он — возьми да побеги.	Everybody's resting and he, all of a sudden (darn him), starts to run.

Verbs of type 1 are usually imperfectives; verbs of type 2 are likely to be perfectives. In all these special uses of the imperative form, it should be noted that only the basic form is used (i.e. -те is never added) and this form serves for both numbers and for all persons.

SUBORDINATE POINTS

1. The adjective **(не)достаточ/ный** means "(in)sufficient":

(не)достаточные средства	(in)sufficient means
достаточная сумма, причина	a sufficient sum, reason
недостаточная помощь	insufficient help

The indeclinable **(не)достаточно** '(not) enough, (in)sufficient' takes a genitive complement (cf. **хватить – хватают**, CL3–5 Vocab):

достаточно молока	enough milk
недостаточно денег	not enough money
Достаточно пяти минут.	Five minutes is enough.

The indeclinable **довольно** also takes a genitive complement and has approximately the same meaning as **достаточно**, but is more likely to be used when the primary emphasis is on the sufficiency itself rather than on sufficiency for some specified purpose. Hence it is not used in sentences of the type in paragraph A4, but is frequent in more independent contexts, where the thing which is sufficient is not specified or is abstract (though **доста́точно** may also be used in most of these contexts):

Мы́ получи́ли дово́льно (доста́точно) хле́ба.	We received enough bread.
Мы́ получи́ли дово́льно (доста́точно).	We received enough.
Я чу́вствую в себе́ дово́льно (доста́точно) си́лы на э́то.	I feel enough strength in me for that.
Ей бы́ло дово́льно, что о́н на свобо́де.	It was enough for her that he was free.
Дово́льно.	That's enough. Stop it.
Дово́льно с него́. (Хва́тит с него́.)	That's enough for (from) him.
Дово́льно спо́рить.	That's enough arguing. Stop arguing.

The student is probably already acquainted with **дово́льно** as an adverb meaning "rather" and with the adjective **(не)дово́льный** (short forms required in predicate usage) *plus inst* 'satisfied (with)':

Он дово́льно ску́чный челове́к.	He's a rather boring person.
Она́ игра́ет дово́льно хорошо́.	She plays pretty well.
Я дово́лен ва́шей рабо́той.	I am satisfied with your work.
Президе́нт, недово́льный у́ровнем произво́дства, сде́лает заявле́ние об э́том за́втра.	The president, dissatisfied with the level of production, will make a statement about it tomorrow.

2. The preposition **по** connected by a hyphen to the dative form of an adjective X has the meaning "in an X manner":

Мы́ на́чали жи́ть по-но́вому.	We started to live in a new manner.
Заявле́ние прави́тельства бы́ло встре́чено по-ра́зному.	The announcement of the government had a mixed reception.

Most adjectives built with the suffix **-ск** (which makes adjectives denoting primarily persons and places) do not form adverbs at all. Those which do exist are in **-ски**, often with a prefixed **по-**:

дру́жеский: *adv* дру́жески *or* по-дру́жески	in a friendly manner
ле́нинский: *adv* по-ле́нински	according to Lenin's manner

If the adjective can mean a language, the adverb may mean "in X language," but it may also mean "in the manner of X people":

по-ру́сски in Russian (the language), in the Russian manner

Finally, many of the very substantial "international" adjectives in -**и́ческий** have adverbs in -**ски** (without the **по-**):

герметически	hermetic ally
геройчески	heroic ally

3. The idea of joining a group or entering the ranks of something is sometimes expressed by a *motion verb* plus **в** plus an *accusative plural*, which does *not* assume the genitive form for animates and, hence, is equivalent to the nominative plural. Examples:

Она́ вы́шла в лю́ди.	She took her place in society. (She came out.)
Он поступи́л (пошёл) в солда́ты.	He went into the army.

4. The Russian word for "art" in the broad sense is **иску́сство**. The adjective **иску́сственный**, however, means "artificial"; "artistic" or "art" (adjective) is **худо́жественный** (from **худо́жество**, a word now archaic, except for certain special uses). **Худо́жник** means "artist" in both the broad sense of the word and in the narrower sense (painter), while **арти́ст** almost always refers to a stage or screen performer: "actor, singer, dancer," etc., but may have the broader sense of "artist" in colloquial speech. The more specific word for "actor, actress" is **актёр/актри́са**. "Painting" in general is **жи́вопись**. **Худо́жественный** is more commonly used than "artistic" in English; it refers to things for art, decoration, or entertainment as opposed to things practical or didactic; e.g. **худо́жественная литерату́ра** 'belles lettres,' **худо́жественный фи́льм** 'feature film.'

TRANSLATION INTO ENGLISH

1. Он заявля́ет, что в э́том не мо́жет быть никаки́х сомне́ний. **2.** Вме́сто того́ чтобы до́лго и подро́бно объясня́ть вам сове́тскую вне́шнюю поли́тику, я вам сове́тую проче́сть са́мое после́днее заявле́ние сове́тского прави́тельства. **3.** Солда́т по́дал заявле́ние о том, чтобы его́ произвели́ в
5 офице́ры. **4.** Не забы́ли ли вы её? Напро́тив, я её ещё ча́ще вспомина́ю. **5.** Из ра́зных исто́чников сообща́ют, что команди́р ско́ро посети́т наш ла́герь. **6.** Я не ду́маю, чтобы тако́й челове́к возмути́лся, когда́ речь идёт о его́ со́бственных недоста́тках. Наоборо́т, таки́е лю́ди охо́тно говоря́т о свои́х сла́бых сторона́х и, кро́ме того́, стремя́тся к тому́, чтобы никто́ не
10 знал о их побе́дах. **7.** Как вам описа́ть моё де́тство? Открове́нно говоря́, я то́лько с трудо́м вспомина́ю его́. **8.** Ни одно́й зимы́ не проходи́ло без того́ чтобы к нам не приходи́ли го́сти. **9.** Неуже́ли она́ в нём сомнева́ется? (Отве́т) Едва́ ли. **10.** Иногда́ я сомнева́юсь, в состоя́нии ли ты продолжа́ть на́шу борьбу́. **11.** Мне нере́дко приходи́лось ста́лкиваться с тако́го ро́да
15 людьми́. **12.** Он едва́ не упа́л в ого́нь. Не будь ма́тери (Е́сли бы не мать),

óн упáл бы. **13a.** Пройдú вы́ огóнь и вóду, вы́ всё равнó не достúгнете вáшей цéли. **13b.** Он пúшет, не знáя своегó дéла, а я́ читáй его вздóр. **13c.** Всé берегýт э́ти вéщи, а óн — возьмú да потеря́й её. **14.** Вáжно, что-бы вы́ по-настоя́щему вéрили в правотý нáшего дéла. Я увéрен, что в дальнéйшем бýдет немáло столкновéний с врагóм. **15.** Это слúшком тяжёлое наказáние для тогó, чтобы óн пóсле негó стáл лýчше. Напрóтив, онó егó унúзит, оскорбúт. И всю́ жúзнь емý бýдет на чтó жáловаться. Он и тáк с сáмого дéтства жáлуется на свою́ судьбý, бýдто бы всё врéмя жúл в сáмых тяжёлых услóвиях. Лýчше бы бы́ло наказáть егó по-другóму и не тáк стрóго. Однáко нельзя́ отрицáть, что э́тот человéк явля́ется врагóм нарóда. **16.** Кáк нáм вестú себя́? По-прéжнему ли? Кáк нáм доказáть свою́ правотý, рáз всé нáши бы́вшие друзья́ и коллéги стоя́т на противопóлóжной тóчке зрéния? **17.** Вúдите, нáс пропускáют в гóрод. По-вúдимому, солдáты не нашлú ничегó подозрúтельного в нáшем поведéнии. **18.** Беспреры́вный дóждь наконéц застáвил нáс брóсить нáш проéкт. **19.** Онú отказáлись со-общúть подрóбности своегó решéния. По послéдним сообщéниям печáти у протúвника положéние плохóе. **20.** Нáши дéти óчень небрéжно обращáются со своéй одéждой. Онú всё врéмя рвýт её. Я дóлжен смотрéть (за тéм), чтобы онú бéрежно обращáлись с нéй. **21.** Скóро стáло я́сно, что крестья́не получúли слúшком мáло землú для тогó, чтобы онú моглú прóчно стáть нá ноги. **22.** Вмéсто тогó чтобы продолжáть и постепéнно расширя́ть рефóрмы, правúтельство Алексáндра Трéтьего стремúлось э́ти рефóрмы остановúть. **23.** В своúх произведéниях óн опúсывает своúх герóев тáк, что онú кáк бы существýют в нáшем воображéнии. **24.** Нáша задáча состоúт в тóм, чтобы создáть по возмóжности сúльную áрмию. Этого достáточно. Остальнóе остáвим правúтельству. **25.** Прикажú мнé сейчáс Аракчéев идтú на вáс, — ни на секýнду не задýмаюсь и пойдý. **26.** Нельзя́ повéрить, чтобы жестóкое убúйство нáшего велúкого вождя́ никогó не потряслó. По-мóему э́то действúтельно потрясáющее собы́тие. **27.** Я виновáт перед вáми. Я не имéл нрáвственного прáва отказáть вáм в такóм пустякé. **28.** Нрáвственное — э́то всё, чтó отнóсится к нóрмам поведéния человéка в óбществе. **29.** Я отрицáю свою́ винý и настáиваю на своём прáве об-ратúться к адвокáту. **30.** По настоя́нию своéй жены́ Пётр дóлжен бы́л рассказáть тóтчас же и дáже с большúми подрóбностями всю́ истóрию прóшлой нóчи. **31.** Врáч совéтовал не раздражáть больнóе мéсто. **32.** Он раздражáется из-за пустякóв. **33.** Я не могý сдéлать э́то, хоть убéй. **34.** Вы́ слúшком сознáтельно меня́ мýчили, чтоб я́ вáм мóг простúть э́то. **35.** Извинúте, господá, что я́ застáвила вáс ждáть. **36.** Бýдем откровéнны, óн убúл человéка и дóлжен нестú пóлную отвéтственность за своё престу-плéние. **37.** Я вáм никогдá не прощý э́того постýпка. **38.** У негó сознá-тельное отношéние к трудý. **39.** Тýт наблюдáется закóн превращéния и сохранéния энéргии. **40.** Литвúнов тóтчас её узнáл, хотя́ онá успéла измени́ться с тех пор, как он ви́дел её в после́дний ра́з: из де́вушки она́ преврати́лась в же́нщину. **41.** Я не бою́сь одино́чества. Ка́к-нибудь проживу́ э́ти де́сять лет без тебя́. **42.** Хо́д собы́тий измени́лся к лу́чшему. **43.** Подхо́д к реке́ вполне́ досту́пен, и тече́ние её ти́хое и споко́йное. **44.** Произведе́ние иску́сства должно́ бы́ть досту́пно челове́ческому понима́нию. **45.** В на́шем поколе́нии появи́лся це́лый ря́д гениа́льных писа́телей и кри́тиков, кото́рые высоко́ по́дняли на́шу литерату́ру, сде́лали её мирово́й. **46.** Он не та́к глу́п, как его́ изобража́ют. **47.** В своём рома́не а́втор суме́л изобрази́ть действи́тельность тако́й, кака́я она́ е́сть. **48.** Он всё вре́мя кричи́т, что среди́ всео́бщего благополу́чия далеко́ не всё в поря́дке, что мы́ стои́м перед кри́зисом культу́ры. **49.** Я кри́кнул от ра́дости. **50.** Ты — дру́г мо́й, но мо́жет случи́ться, что на́ша дру́жба порвётся. **51.** Буржуа́зный стро́й во всём ми́ре переживёт революцио́нный кри́зис. **52.** Мне нра́вится направле́ние его́ мы́слей и чу́вств. **53.** Я не согласи́лся с его́ оце́нкой, и э́то не́сколько раздражи́ло его́. **54.** В на́шей стране́ о́чень жесто́кие нра́вы. **55.** Твоё больно́е воображе́ние мо́жет увести́ тебя́ бо́г зна́ет куда́. **56.** Всё э́то я́сно пока́зывает, что худо́жник не мо́жет жи́ть отде́льно от о́бщества и что иску́сство те́сно свя́зано с духо́вным содержа́нием худо́жника. **57.** Никако́е иску́сство не мо́жет та́к заста́вить забы́ть всё, как му́зыка. **58.** Он удивля́ет свои́х сосе́дей иску́сством жи́ть хорошо́ и откры́то при незначи́тельных сре́дствах. **59.** Он всегда́ жи́л не по сре́дствам. **60.** При коммуни́зме всё сре́дства произво́дства принадлежа́т рабо́чим, и́ли, по кра́йней ме́ре, та́к утвержда́ют коммуни́сты. **61.** Его́ недоста́точные сре́дства заставля́ют его́ жи́ть в бе́дности. **62.** Через не́сколько дней э́та забасто́вка охвати́ла всю страну́. **63.** Он вы́шел из кварти́ры и, охва́ченный у́жасом, побежа́л по у́лице. **64.** Трево́га молодёжи за бу́дущее произво́дит на меня́ большо́е впечатле́ние. **65.** Через ча́с начала́сь возду́шная трево́га. **66.** Рабо́чие на э́том заво́де о́чень пло́хо зараба́тывают. **67.** Мы́ живём в госуда́рстве рабо́чих и крестья́н. **68.** Ка́к сове́тскому челове́ку оцени́ть свои́х родны́х худо́жников? Ведь о́н не в состоя́нии сра́внивать и́х тво́рчество с произведе́ниями иску́сства на За́паде; они́ ему́ ма́ло досту́пны. **69.** Ва́ш подхо́д к психологи́ческим вопро́сам приобрета́ет всё бо́льшее значе́ние. **70.** Приобрети́ ты плоху́ю репута́цию, и я тебя́ оста́влю навсегда́.‖Он допусти́л э́ту оши́бку то́лько по небре́жности. **71.** — Бо́же мо́й, — ду́мал он, вспомина́я, ка́к врачи́ то́лько что иссле́довали его́. — Они́ поня́тия не име́ют о психиа́трии. **72.** На сме́ну ста́ршему поколе́нию фи́зиков иду́т молоды́е иссле́дователи. **73.** Гончаро́в явля́ется пре́жде всего́ худо́жником, уме́ющим вы́разить полноту́ явле́ний жи́зни. **74.** Во всём создава́емом о́н проявля́ет большо́й вку́с и худо́жественное мастерство́. **75.** Карти́ны располо́жены с больши́м зна́нием и вку́сом. **76.** Мы́ встре́тили певца́ у вхо́да для арти́стов. **77.** Он никогда́ не изменя́ет свои́х мне́ний, всё ещё де́ржится одни́х и те́х же взгля́дов. **78.** Худо́жник сиде́л перед то́лько что напи́санным и́м портре́том и ду́мал, не́т ли зде́сь како́й-нибудь та́йной свя́зи с его́ со́бственной судьбо́й. **79.** Ники́та Ильи́ч принадлежи́т к како́му-то та́йному о́бществу.‖ Он рабо́тает перево́дчиком, зараба́тывает 103 рубля́ в ме́сяц. **80.** Любо́вь была́ не настоя́щая, иску́сственная, но ведь мне́ каза́лось тогда́, что она́ настоя́щая. **81.** На́м ча́сто приходи́лось относи́ться к пробле́мам чи́сто теорети́чески. **82.** Ме́жду его́ слова́ми и поведе́нием заме́тно глубо́кое противоре́чие. **83.** Я не понима́ю смы́сла э́того си́мвола. **84.** Он винова́т в то́м, что не во́время сообщи́л после́дние но́вости своему́ генера́лу. Но́ вообще́ у него́ больши́е заслу́ги перед страно́й. **85.** В свое́й ре́чи о́н не ра́з упомина́л о достиже́ниях сове́тской нау́ки и те́хники. Он говори́л, что мы́ стои́м на поро́ге но́вой жи́зни, что всё тру́дности мо́жно преодоле́ть. **86.** Ю́жная ча́сть го́рода была́ разру́шена авиа́цией. **87.** Сде́латься жено́й — о́ нет, прости́те! Челове́к до́лжен стреми́ться к вы́сшей це́ли.

100

105

110

СЛОВА́ ТО́ЛЬКО К Э́ТОМУ УРО́КУ

без-грани́ч-/н-ый **ГРАН**-иц boundless, infinite

без-мят-е́ж-/н-ый serene, tranquil

бес-фо́рм-енн-ость formlessness, shapelessness

вс-пы́ль-чив-ый hot-tempered

гума́н-н-ость humanity, humaneness

диале́ктик-а dialectic(s)

драмати́ч-еск-ий dramatic

импе́ри-я empire

компози́ц-я composition

метафизи́ч-еск-ий metaphysical

ми́ф myth

не-зы́бл-ем-ый stable, immovable

пад-у́ч-ая (боле́знь) epilepsy

пев-/е́/ц singer

под-у́ш-/к-а pillow

поро́г threshold

портре́т portrait

поэ́тика poetics

прое́кт project

про-по-ве́д-ник preacher, advocate

про-ро́ч-еск-ий (< проро́к prophet) prophetic

психиа́три-я psychiatry

психи́ч-еск-ий psychic(al), mental

психопато́лог psychopathologist

романи́ст novelist

тала́нт-лив-ый talented

траги́ч-еск-ий tragic

угрю́м-ый sullen, gloomy

фантасти́ч-еск-ий fantastic

физиологи́ч-еск-ий physiological

эне́рги-я energy

эпи́ч-еск-ий epic

эсте́тик-а aesthetics

эстети́ч-еск-ий aesthetic

ГЛАГО́ЛЫ

на-дви́г-ну-ть-ся – надвига́ются be imminent, impend

про-зв-а-ть (прозову́т) – прозыва́ют name, call; nickname

п прозва́ние, про́звище

им-е́-н-и-е (< име́ют) estate, landed property

ÓБЩИЙ СЛОВÁРЬ

áвтор author

артúст IX.4

бéд-н-ость poverty

бéреж-н-ый careful, cautious (*note the corresponding negative* небрéж/ный *has ChS root*)

бéс devil, demon; «Бéсы» "The Devils" *or* "The Possessed," a novel by Dostoevskij

бес-пре-рьíв-/н-ый uninterrupted, unbroken

благ-о-полýч-и-е well-being

вин-á *S pl* guilt

вин-овáт-ый в *чём* guilty of (*used most commonly in short-form predicate:* я виновáт it's my fault); — перед *кém/чém* guilty before

в-кýс taste

врáг *E* enemy

в-хóд entrance; *cf.* в/о/йдýт – входить

гениáль-/н-ый genius *adj*, brilliant

гéний genius

герóй hero

глуб-ин-á (*pl* глубúны) depth

дéт-ств-о childhood

до-вóль-/н-ый, довóльно IX.1

до-стáт-оч-/н-ый, достáточно IX.1, IX.A4

до-стýп-/н-ый *комý/чемý* accessible (to), within reach (of)

душ-éв-н-ый emotional, mental; cordial

едвá (ли) hardly; — не almost

жест-óк-ий cruel, severe

за-слýг-а merit, desert; service; *cf.* заслужить – заслýживают; — перед *кém/чém* service to; по —ам according to deserts/services

ис-кýс-ств-ен/н-ый IX.4

ис-кýс-ств-о IX.4

ис-слéд-ова-тель investigator, researcher

картúн-а picture, painting; film *colloq*

катастрóф-а catastrophe

командúр commander

кóсмос cosmos

кресть-я́н-ин (*pl* крестья́не) peasant (*confusion with root in* Христóс Christ)

крúзис crisis

-либо = -нибудь

лúни-я line

лúч-н-ый personal

мáстер-ств-ó mastery, craftsmanship

молод-ёжь youth (young people)

мысл-и́-тель thinker

мы́сль thought, idea

настóлько so, so much

не-брéж-/н-ый careless, slipshod; *cf. pleo* бéрежный

не-до-стá-т-/о/к **СТАН** insufficiency, defect, drawback

не-об-хо́д-и́м-ый indispensable

нрáв disposition, temper; *pl* morals, customs

нрáв-ств-ен/н-ый moral

ог/ó/нь fire (general); light; a fire (conflagration) = пожáр

один-óч-е-ств-о loneliness

о-конч-á-тель-/н-ый final, definitive

оснóв-н-óй basic; в — óм basically

от-вéт-ств-ен/н-ый за *когó/чтó* responsible

о-хóт-н-о willingly

офицéр officer

пере-вóд-чик translator

пере-пúс-/к-а correspondence; *n* < перепúсываются (с *кém*) correspond (with)

под/о/зр-и́-тель-/н-ый suspicious (provoking or manifesting suspicion)

по-колéн-и-е generation (young, old, present, etc.)

полн-от-á fullness, completeness

прав-от-á rightness, correctness

президéнт president

прóтив-о-рéч-и-е contradiction

психологи́ч-еск-ий psychological

пуст-я́к *E* trifle (*often pl*):

Это пустякú. That's nothing.

ра́з IX.B7
ра́на wound
репута́ци-я reputation
реш-и́-тель-/н-ый decisive; decidedly, abso-
    lutely *adv*:
    Он реши́тельно ничего́ не де́лает. He
    does absolutely nothing.
ру́бль *M E* ru̇ble
секу́нд-а second (time)
си́мвол symbol; символ-и́ст symbolist
скуп-о́й stingy
с-мы́сл sense, meaning
со-**време́н**-ник contemporary
со-зд-а́-тель creator
со-**зна́**-тель-/н-ый **ЗНАЙ** conscious; con-
    scientious
сре́д-ств-о means, way; сре́дства *pl* means
    (material; money)
стар-и́к *E* old man
сти́ль *M* style

стро́й system, order; *cf.* (по)стро́ить
студе́нч-е-ств-о student days; students
    colloq
та́й-н-ый secret
те́хник-а technique(s); technology, engin-
    eering; machinery
траге́ди-я tragedy
трево́г-а alarm
тяж-ёл-ый (*E sh f*) heavy, difficult, hard
у-**би́й**-ств-о murder; *cf.* убий-ут – убива́ют
униж-ён-/н-ый humble, oppressed; *cf.* уни́-
    зить – унижа́ют
филосо́ф philosopher; филосо́фи-я philos-
    ophy; филосо́ф-ск-ий philosophical
фи́льм film
худо́ж-е-ств-ен/н-ый IX.4
худо́ж-ник IX.4
шир-от-а́ (*pl* широ́ты) width; latitude
    (geography)

ГЛАГО́ЛЫ

у-би́й-ут – убива́ют kill, murder
    n уби́йство
в-**вё**д-у́т – вводить lead in, introduce
    n введе́ние
(по)-**вё**д-у́т себя́ behave, conduct oneself
    n поведе́ние
про-из-**вё**д-у́т – производить в *acc pl* pro-
    mote (in rank) IX.3; *other meanings* IV
    Vocab
    n произведе́ние
пре-**врат**-и́-ть – превраща́ют в *кого́/что́*
    transform, turn into *tr*; —ся turn into
    intr
    n превраще́ние
под-**гото́в**-и-ть – подготовля́ют –
    приготавливают prepare
    n подгото́в/ка, подготовле́ние
по̄-да-ть – подава́ть hand, serve, give
    n пода́ча
держ-а́-ть-ся *кого́/чего́* hold to, adhere to
пре-о-дол-е́й-ут – преодолева́ют **ДОЛ**[2]

overcome
    n преодоле́ние, преодолева́ние
раз-**драж**-и́-ть – раздража́ют annoy, irri-
    tate
    n раздраже́ние
(по)-**жа́л**-ова-ть-ся на *кого́/что́* complain
    against
    n жа́лоба
до-**каз**-а-ть – дока́зывают prove; *I* point
    out
    n доказа́тельство
на-**каз**-а-ть – нака́зывают punish
    n наказа́ние
при-**каз**-а-ть – прика́зывают *кому́/чему́*
    order (command)
    n прика́з
кри́к-ну-ть – крича́ть shout, cry
    n кри́к
рас-**кро́й**-ут – раскрыва́ют uncover, dis-
    close, open
    n раскры́тие

из-**мен**-и-ть – изменя́ют change *tr*; —ся change *intr*
 n измене́ние
из-**мен**-и-ть – изменя́ют *кому́/чему́* betray, be unfaithful to
 n изме́на
из-**ме́р**-и-ть – измеря́ют measure
 n измере́ние measuring; dimension
со-**мн**-е-ва́й-ут-ся в *чём* doubt IX.A6
 n сомне́ние
у-**ни́з**-и-ть – унижа́ют humble, humiliate, debase (*note adj* унижённый humbled; *cf. PPP* уни́женный)
 n униже́ние
во-**образ**-и́-ть – вообража́ют imagine
 n воображе́ние
из-**образ**-и́-ть – изобража́ют depict
 n изображе́ние
со-**общ**-и́-ть – сообща́ют communicate, impart, report
 n сообще́ние
у-**па́д**-ут – **па́**дают fall
 n упа́д/о/к decline; collapse; паде́ние falling, downfall
в-**печат**-л-е́н-и-е impression; *cf.* впечатля́ют *I only colloq* impress; произведу́т – производить — на *кого́/ что́* make impression on; оста́вить – оставля́ют — leave an impression
у-**по-мя-ну**-ть – упомина́ют *кого́/что́* or о *ко́м/чём* mention
 n упомина́ние
вс-**по́-мн**-и-ть – вспомина́ют *кого́/что́* or о *ко́м/чём* recall
 n вспомина́ние recalling *or, commoner,* recollection, memoir, *often pl* memoirs, reminiscences
прост-и́-ть – проща́ют *кого́* or *кому́ что́*
 n проще́ние
при-**обрёт**-у́т – приобрета́ют acquire, get
 n приобрете́ние
за-**рабо́т**-ай-ут – зараба́тывают earn
 n за́работ/о/к

(по)-**рв**-а-ть tear, break *tr*; —ся tear, break *intr*
раз-**ру́ш**-и-ть – разруша́ют destroy, ruin
 n разруше́ние
о-**свобо́д**-и-ть – освобожда́ют от *кого́/ чего́* become free of, free/rid oneself of
 n освобожде́ние
о-**скорб**-и́-ть – оскорбля́ют insult, outrage
 n оскорбле́ние
ис-**сле́д**-ова-ть *P and I* investigate, examine, research
 n иссле́дование
за-**ста́в**-и-ть – заставля́ют *кого́ inf* force to
на-**сто́й**-а́-ть – наста́ивают на *чём* insist on IX.A3
 n настоя́ние, наста́ивание
у-**стран**-и́-ть – устраня́ют remove, eliminate
 n устране́ние
стрем-и́-ть-ся к *чему́* or *inf* strive/aim/aspire to/toward
 n стремле́ние
пре-**ступ**-и́-ть – преступа́ют transgress, violate (law, etc.)
 n преступле́ние crime
с-**толк**-ну́-ть-ся – ста́лкиваются с *ке́м/ чём* collide/clash with; come into contact with
 n столкнове́ние
по-**тряс**-у́т – потряса́ют shake; shock
 n тря́с/ка shaking, bumping; потрясе́ние shock; *cf.* землетрясе́ние earthquake
о-**хват**-и́-ть – охва́тывают grip; envelop; include
 n охва́т
за-**яв**-и́-ть – заявля́ют announce, declare, state
 n заявле́ние; подать – подава́ть заявле́ние на *что́* submit an application for
по-**яв**-и́-ть-ся – появля́ются appear
 n появле́ние

LESSON
X

ХАРАКТЕРИ́СТИКА ЦАРЯ́ ИВА́НА ГРО́ЗНОГО

Ца́рь Ива́н роди́лся в 1530 г. От приро́ды о́н получи́л у́м бо́йкий и ги́б-кий, вду́мчивый и немно́го насме́шливый, настоя́щий великору́сский, моско́вский у́м. Но́ обстоя́тельства, среди́ кото́рых протекло́ де́тство Ива́на, ра́но испо́ртили э́тот у́м, да́ли ему́ неесте́ственное, боле́зненное разви́тие. Ива́н ра́но осироте́л, на четвёртом году́ лиши́лся отца́, а на восьмо́м потеря́л и ма́ть. Он с де́тства ви́дел себя́ среди́ чужи́х люде́й. В душе́ его́ ра́но и глубоко́ вре́залось и всю жи́знь сохраня́лось чу́вство сиро́тства, бро́шенности, одино́чества. Отсю́да его́ ро́бость, ста́вшая основно́й черто́й его́ хара́ктера. Ка́к все́ лю́ди, вы́росшие среди́ чужи́х, Ива́н ра́но усво́ил себе́ привы́чку ходи́ть, огля́дываясь и прислу́шиваясь. Это разви́ло в нём подозри́тельность, кото́рая с лета́ми преврати́лась в глубо́кое недове́рие к лю́дям. В де́тстве ему́ ча́сто **приходи́лось**[7] испы́тывать равноду́шие или пренебреже́ние со стороны́ окружа́ющих. В торже́ственные, церемониа́ль-ные слу́чаи, при вы́ходе или приёме посло́в, его́ окружа́ли ца́рственной пы́шностью, станови́лись вокру́г него́ с раболе́пным смире́нием, а в бу́дни те́ же лю́ди не церемо́нились с ни́м, поро́й балова́ли, поро́й дразни́ли. Игра́ют они́, **быва́ло**,[2] с бра́том Юрием в спа́льне поко́йного отца́, а пе́р-венствующий боя́рин кня́зь И. В. Шу́йский разва́лится перед ни́ми на ла́вке, обопрётся ло́ктем **о посте́ль**[4] поко́йного госуда́ря, и́х отца́, и но́гу на неё поло́жит, не обраща́я на дете́й никако́го внима́ния, ни оте́ческого, ни да́же власти́тельного. Го́речь, с како́ю Ива́н вспомина́л об э́том 25 ле́т спустя́,

5

10

15

20

267

даёт почу́вствовать, ка́к ча́сто и си́льно его́ серди́ли в де́тстве. Его́ ласка́ли, ка́к госуда́ря, и оскорбля́ли, ка́к ребёнка. Но́ в обстано́вке, в како́й шло́ его́ де́тство, о́н не всегда́ мо́г то́тчас и пря́мо обнару́жить чу́вство доса́ды или
25 зло́сти, и э́та необходи́мость сде́рживаться пита́ло в нём раздражи́тельность и молчали́вое озлобле́ние про́тив люде́й.

Безобра́зные сце́ны боя́рского своево́лия и наси́лий, среди́ кото́рых ро́с Ива́н, бы́ли пе́рвыми полити́ческими его́ впечатле́ниями. Они́ преврати́ли его́ ро́бость в не́рвную пугли́вость, из кото́рой с лета́ми развила́сь накло́н
30 ность преувели́чивать опа́сность, образова́лось то́, что называ́ется стра́хом с вели́кими глаза́ми. Ве́чно трево́жный и подозри́тельный, Ива́н ра́но привы́к ду́мать, что окружён то́лько врага́ми; мы́сль, что во́т-во́т из-за угла́ на него́ бро́сится не́друг, ста́ла привы́чным, ежемину́тным его́ ожида́нием. Всего́ сильне́е рабо́тал в нём инсти́нкт самосохране́ния. Всё уси́лия его́
35 бо́йкого ума́ бы́ли обращены́ на разрабо́тку э́того гру́бого чу́вства.

Чита́я пи́сьма царя́ к кня́зю Ку́рбскому (Ива́н вообще́ бы́л одни́м из лу́чших моско́вских ора́торов и писа́телей 16-го ве́ка), поража́ешься бы́строй сме́ной в а́вторе са́мых разнообра́зных чу́вств, поры́вы великоду́шия и раска́яния, про́блески глубо́кой задуше́вности череду́ются с гру́бой
40 шу́ткой, жёстким озлобле́нием, холо́дным презре́нием к лю́дям. Тако́й нра́вственной неро́вностью, чередова́нием высо́ких подъёмов ду́ха с са́мыми посты́дными паде́ниями объясня́ется и госуда́рственная де́ятельность Ива́на. Ца́рь соверши́л или заду́мывал мно́го хоро́шего, у́много, да́же вели́кого, и ря́дом с э́тим наде́лал ещё бо́льше посту́пков, кото́рые
45 сде́лали его́ предме́том у́жаса и отвраще́ния для совреме́нников и после́дующих поколе́ний. Разгро́м Но́вгорода по одному́ подозре́нию в изме́не, моско́вские ка́зни, уби́йство сы́на и митрополи́та Фили́ппа, безобра́зия с опри́чниками в Москве́ и Алекса́ндровской слободе́ — чита́я обо всём э́том, поду́маешь, что э́то бы́л зве́рь от приро́ды. Он не́ был таки́м, но по
50 приро́де или воспита́нию о́н бы́л лишён усто́йчивого нра́вственного равнове́сия, и на́до сказа́ть, что при мале́йшем жите́йском затрудне́нии о́н охо́тнее склоня́лся в дурну́ю сто́рону.

[Adapted from V. Ključevskij, *Kurs russkoj istorii*,
Lekcija XXX (Part II pp. 199–202, Moscow, 1937)]

VOICE AND VERBS IN ся[1]

The verbal category of voice involves various relationships between the action and its subject and its object, if there is an object. In Russian voice be-

---

[1] Parts of this section are reprinted from my article by the same title in *The Slavic and East European Journal*, XI, 2, 1967.

comes, for practical purposes, a matter of the transitivity or intransitivity of the action. Russian verbs are transitive: e.g. **ви́деть, люби́ть, мо́ют**; or intransitive: e.g. **рабо́тают, ходи́ть, мо́ются**; and a few may be transitive in one usage and intransitive in another: e.g. **говори́ть** is transitive when it means "say" (paired with **сказа́ть**) but intransitive when it means "talk" (imperfective only). There is no special grammatical marker for transitivity in Russian verbs, and many intransitive verbs carry nothing to identify them as such. A great many other intransitive verbs, however, including a number of important semantic categories, are marked by the particle **ся**.

Verbs built with the particle **ся** are frequently called "reflexive" verbs (Russian **возвра́тные глаго́лы**), yet it is plain that this is far too broad a use of the term. "Reflexive" implies some sort of reflection of the action back on the subject, and the majority of verbs in **ся** do not fulfill this condition. In fact, it cannot be said that verbs in **ся** share any general property other than intransitivity; they never take a direct object. It is possible to isolate certain categories of verbs in **ся**: "true" reflexives, reciprocals, passives, and certain others we will discuss below, but a very large number display no special feature other than their intransitivity; we may call these simply *general* **ся** verbs. Let us discuss these *general* **ся** verbs first and then turn to some of the more important subcategories.

A. General ся verbs

A certain number of *general* **ся** verbs have no corresponding non-**ся** verbs in the language:

боя́ться (*gen*)	fear, be afraid
смея́ться (над *inst*)	laugh (at)
оста́нутся – остава́ться	remain

A substantially greater number of general **ся** verbs have corresponding non-**ся** verbs which are almost always transitive. The precise semantic relationships existing between the transitives and corresponding **ся** verbs vary a great deal depending on the verbs involved:

возврати́ть – возвраща́ют return (*tran*)	*vs.*	возврати́ться – возвраща́ются return (*intr*)
остановить – остана́вливают stop (*tran*)	*vs.*	остановиться – остана́вливаются stop (*intr*)
продо́лжить – продолжа́ют continue (*tran*)	*vs.*	продо́лжиться – продолжа́ются continue (*intr*)
изменить – изменя́ют change (*tran*)	*vs.*	измениться – изменя́ются change (*intr*)

In translation to and from English it should be remembered that English syntax often allows the same verb to express both transitive and intransitive action, but Russian rules do not permit this. Hence, when a Russian transitive verb is converted to an intransitive it *always* carries the **ся** marker, whereas English frequently expresses the shift by the same verb without any object. The student should not allow this superficial identity to cause him to omit the **ся** when it is needed:

Он возврати́л кни́ги.	He returned the books.
Он возврати́лся.	He returned.
Он измени́л свои́ взгля́ды.	He has changed his views.
Его́ взгля́ды измени́лись.	His views have changed.
Она́ слу́шает ма́ть.	She listens to her mother.
Она́ слу́шается ма́тери.	She obeys her mother.
Солда́ты занима́ют го́род.	The soldiers are occupying the city.
Солда́ты занима́ются ру́сским язы-ко́м.	The soldiers are studying Russian.

As in the last two pairs of example sentences above, often a non-**ся** verb and the corresponding **ся** verb are lexically distinct, or at least seem so from their English translations. Translation in itself, of course, is not a solid basis for establishing semantic distinction or similarity. Transitivity and intransitivity in Russian and English by no means always correspond, as the above examples demonstrate. The arbitrariness of translation is evident in such an example as **Я бою́сь Ни́ны** 'I fear Nina.'

Let us now turn to some of the more specific types of verbs in **ся**.

B. Reflexive ся verbs

These "true" reflexives are those in which the subject is also the object of the action. The most obvious type concerns direct, physical action upon oneself (see also CL4.1):

(вы́)мо́ются	wash oneself (*or*, *simply*, wash)
оде́нутся – одева́ются	dress oneself (*or*, *simply*, dress)
причеса́ться – причёсываются	comb oneself (*or*, *simply*, comb)

Some grammarians consider such "physical" verbs to be the only "true" reflexives. However, it seems reasonable to regard as reflexive also such verbs as:

защити́ться – защища́ются	defend oneself
берегу́тся	guard oneself

сдержа́ться – сде́рживаются	hold oneself back, control oneself
отличи́ться – отлича́ются	distinguish oneself

Some verbs may be reflexive in some meanings and nonreflexive in others, allowing no clear-cut analysis: **освободи́ться – освобожда́ются** 'get free' may signify "free oneself" (reflexive) or "become free" (general **ся** verb).

The criterion of reflexiveness is whether the **ся** may logically be replaced by **себя́**. Indeed, reflexive meaning is normally expressed by the reflexive pronoun **себя́**,[1] used as the object of a transitive verb:

Он лю́бит себя́. *Not* *Он лю́бится.	He loves himself.
Он ви́дит себя́. *Not* *Он ви́дится.	He sees himself.

Frequently verb-**ся** and verb-**себя́** coexist, but the meanings are almost always distinct:

Он счита́ет себя́ хоро́шим солда́том.	He considers himself a good soldier.
Он счита́ется хоро́шим солда́том. (*Passive; see below.*)	He is considered a good soldier. (Cf. VI.2.)
Он постоя́нно руга́ет себя́.	He's constantly scolding himself.
Он руга́ется ка́к изво́зчик. (*General characteristic; see below.*)	He swears like a trooper (coachman).
Мы́ ви́дели себя́ в зе́ркале.	We saw ourselves in the mirror.
Мы́ не ви́делись це́лое ле́то. (*Reciprocal; see below.*)	We haven't seen each other all summer.

Note, however, that a reflexive verb-**ся** may coexist with a semantically equivalent verb-**себя́** which may replace it if the reflexive meaning is to be emphasized, e.g. both **защити́ться – защища́ются** and **защити́ть – защища́ют себя́** mean "defend oneself," but the sentence "I am defending *myself*, and not you" would be **Я защища́ю себя́, а не ва́с** (**защища́юсь** is impossible in this instance).

C. Reciprocal ся verbs

Reciprocals are sometimes understood to be limited to those verbs whose subjects are also the direct objects of their reciprocal actions (i.e. **ся** means only **дру́г дру́га**). The very nature of the category, however, calls for the inclusion of verbs whose subjects are also objects of the preposition **с** (i.e. **ся** means **дру́г с дру́гом** as well as **дру́г дру́га**). For example:

---

[1] **(По)чу́вствовать себя́** 'feel' is exceptional; it does not have a reflexive meaning.

Мы́ встре́тились на у́лице.	We met on the street.
Мы́ ви́делись ка́ждый де́нь.	We saw each other every day.
Гали́на и Зо́я помири́лись.	Galina and Zoja reconciled.

Or:

Я встре́тился с Ива́ном на у́лице.	I met Ivan on the street. (And he met me.)
Я ви́делся с ни́м ка́ждый де́нь.	I saw him every day. (And he saw me.)
Гали́на помири́лась с Зо́ей.	Galina reconciled with Zoja. (And Zoja reconciled with Galina.)

Note also such reciprocal types as:

Жи́тели дере́вни объедини́лись в колхо́з.	The inhabitants of the village combined (with each other) into a collective farm.
Ка́ждый де́нь мы́ де́лимся зна́ниями и о́пытом.	Every day we share (with each other) our knowledge and experience.
Мы́ обменя́лись взгля́дами.	We exchanged glances (with each other).

D. General characteristic

A **ся** verb may express a general characteristic of the subject; often, a non-**ся** verb exists, expressing the corresponding action. The action may or may not be transitive. The characteristic may be either something the subject does or a property of the subject:

Соба́ка куса́ет ребёнка.	The dog bites the child.
Соба́ка куса́ется.	The dog bites (is a biter).
Де́вочка рвёт своё пла́тье.	The little girl is tearing her dress.
Э́ти пла́тья не рву́тся.	These dresses don't tear.
Э́ти стака́ны легко́ бью́тся.	These glasses break easily.
Э́та крапи́ва жжётся.	This nettle burns.

Sometimes a **ся** verb of this type acquires a special meaning, as in:

Он ча́сто руга́ет свою́ жену́.	He frequently scolds his wife.
Он ча́сто руга́ется.	He often swears.

E. Intensification of action; modality of ся

Somewhat related to the preceding type are **ся** verbs expressing intensification or concentration of the actor on some specific aspect or, often, on the result of his action. Compared with the corresponding non-**ся** verbs with a neutral meaning, these **ся** verbs often reflect the personal involvement of the speaker in the effect his action will have. This concern with result suggests that **ся** has a modal role, in effect, the expression of purpose.

Some examples of this verb type (with the corresponding non-**ся** verbs) are these:

пла́кать	cry, weep
пла́каться	cry to attract attention or sympathy; complain
грози́ть	threaten
грози́ться	threaten (*More personal; the subject is interested in the effect of the threat, which itself may be empty.*)
стуча́ть	knock
стуча́ться	knock (*More specific:* knock at a door, knock with the purpose of being heard)
звони́ть	ring (*General*)
звони́ться	ring at door
реши́ть – реша́ют	decide
реши́ться – реша́ются	decide, make up one's mind (*More personal involvement; often* dare to, bring oneself to)

F. Impersonal ся verbs

Action somehow independent of the will of the actor may be expressed by **ся** added to the impersonal (third singular) forms of an intransitive (or, less often, a transitive verb, but the usage is never connected with the transitive meaning). Exact translation into English is sometimes difficult, although "can (can't)" or "do (not) feel like" is often close:

Хорошо́ спи́тся под у́тро в дере́вне.	One feels like sleeping in the morning in the country.
Мне́ не спи́тся.	I can't get to sleep./I don't feel like sleeping./I am not sleepy.
Ка́к ва́м живётся?	How's life treating you?
Мне́ здесь про́сто не пи́шется.	I just can't/don't feel like writing here.
Та́м хорошо́ рабо́тается.	One can work well there./One feels like working there.

The idea of "feel like" or "not feel like" is more definitely expressed by **хо́чется/не хо́чется** plus the infinitive. Note the difference from the stronger **хоте́ть** 'want': **Мне́ (не) хо́чется рабо́тать** 'I (don't) feel like working' vs. **Я́ (не) хочу́ рабо́тать** 'I (don't) want/intend to work.'

G. The use of ся with certain prefixes

Ся used in conjunction with various verbal prefixes may intensify the meaning of the prefix or lend a special meaning to the action. The underlying stem is usually intransitive. In those cases where the prefix suggests completion or attainment, usage may be largely restricted to the perfective. Some prefixes (**с** and, less often, **пере, раз, до**) may lend themselves to reciprocal meaning; cf. section C on page 271:

вы...ся   successful conclusion:
Я хорошо́ вы́спался.

I had a good sleep (slept myself out).

до...ся   attainment of goal:
Я звони́л ва́м, но́ не дозвони́лся.

I tried to call you but didn't get through.

до...ся   attainment of goal/reciprocal:
Мы́ договори́лись о дне́ встре́чи.

We arranged (reached an agreement with each other about) the day of the meeting.

за...ся   overdoing or extreme:
Э́тот студе́нт заучи́лся.

This student has become foggy from studying.

из...ся   exhaustion:
Он исписа́лся.

He's written himself out.

на...ся   satiation or excess:
Молоды́е лю́ди натанцева́лись.

The young people danced their fill.

о...ся   do badly:
Она́ зна́ла доро́гу и ни ра́зу не оступи́лась.

She knew the road and didn't once stumble.

пере...ся   exchange (reciprocal):
Мы́ с не́й давно́ перепи́сываемся.

She and I have been corresponding for a long time.

раз...ся   diffusion (reciprocal):
Солда́ты разошли́сь.
Мы́ расхо́димся в свои́х мне́ниях.

The soldiers dispersed.
We differ in our opinions.

с...ся   together (reciprocal):
Они́ сошли́сь.
Они́ сошли́сь в свои́х вку́сах.

They have come together (physical).
They have come together in their tastes.

H. The passive in Russian

The student is by now doubtless familiar with passive constructions, but he may not be aware of certain notions relevant to their proper analysis and of certain restrictions in their use. For example, it is true that any passive verb in **ся** may be converted into an active phrase consisting of the corresponding transitive verb and a direct object which is the subject of the passive verb; for example:

Кни́га пи́шется Ива́ном.   implies   Ива́н пи́шет кни́гу.

But it is not true that any active transitive phrase with a direct object may be transformed into a passive verb in **ся**. Indeed, we shall see below that if the transitive verb is perfective, it almost never may be transformed into a passive by adding **ся**; i.e. the perfective and a purely passive **ся** are incompatible. In addition, animate subjects may only rarely be the subjects of passive verbs, and may never be if the verb describes a physical action. The student, faced with a verb in **ся** following an animate subject, should look for a nonpassive meaning, even if the verb in **ся** is commonly used as a passive with *inanimate subjects*:

Эти кни́ги возвраща́ются в би- блиоте́ку студе́нтами.	These books are being returned to the library by the students.

This is a true passive; it implies the active phrase:

Студе́нты возвраща́ют э́ти кни́ги в библиоте́ку.	The students are returning these books to the library.

But the sentence **Студе́нты возвраща́ются в библиоте́ку** is *not* a passive; it does not mean "The students are being returned to the library" (that would have to be **Студе́нтов возвраща́ют в библиоте́ку**). No one is returning them. Nor is it a reflexive; they are not "returning themselves." The sentence means simply: "The students are returning (going back) to the library"; the verb is a typical *general* **ся** verb.

Or compare **Автомоби́ли мо́ются** 'The cars are being washed,' a passive, with **Лю́ди мо́ются**, which can mean only "The people are washing themselves," a reflexive.

Passives in **ся** are not **ся** verbs of the types described in sections A to G above. Rather, they are **ся** forms of active, non-**ся**, transitive verbs. In the sentences

Кни́ги возвраща́ются мной.	The books are being returned by me.
Кни́ги возвращены́ мной.	The books have been returned by me.

both verbs rest on the active **возврати́ть – возвраща́ют** and have nothing to do with the intransitive **возврати́ться – возвраща́ются**. Similarly, the sentences

| Я удивлён э́тим. | I am surprised *by* that. |
| Я удивля́юсь э́тому. | I am surprised at that. |

differ fundamentally in their structure. The first is a passive based on the active transitive **удиви́ть**, while the second is a nonpassive general **ся** verb taking a dative complement.

A very few verbs describing nonphysical actions may have animate subjects:

| Он все́ми счита́ется хоро́шим рабо́чим. | He is considered by all a good worker. |
| Таки́е писа́тели ре́дко иссле́дуются. | Such writers are rarely investigated. |

Present tense passives, or past and future passives in which the speaker does not wish to specify or emphasize completion of the action, are expressed simply by the present, past, and future imperfective verbs in **ся**:

Этот до́м стро́ится на́шими рабо́чими.	This house is being built by our workers.
Эти вопро́сы сейча́с обсужда́ются.	These questions are now being discussed.
Этот до́м до́лго стро́ился.	This house was being built a long time (i.e. a long time being built).
Эти вопро́сы до́лго обсужда́лись.	These questions were discussed for a long time.
Этот до́м бу́дет до́лго стро́иться.	This house will be a long time being built.
Эти вопро́сы бу́дут до́лго обсужда́ться.	These questions will be discussed for a long time.

Completed passive actions, however, are usually rendered by the past passive participle, with the appropriate form of **бы́ть** (which is zero when the tense corresponds to the English present perfect). In the past and future these forms will be much commoner than the **ся** forms, above. In the following sentences, for example, **ся** forms would be bad usage or impossible:

Этот до́м бы́л постро́ен на́шими рабо́чими. (*Not* постро́ился . . .)	This house was (had been) built by our workers.
Эти вопро́сы бы́ли обсуждены́ вчера́. (*Not* обсуди́лись . . .)	These questions were (had been) discussed yesterday (and their discussion was completed).
Этот до́м постро́ен на́шими рабо́чими. (*Not* постро́ился . . .)	This house has been built by our workers.

Эти вопро́сы уже́ обсуждены́. (*Not* обсуди́лись . . .)	These questions have already been discussed.
Этот до́м бу́дет постро́ен. (*Not* постро́ится . . .)	This house will be built.
Эти вопро́сы бу́дут обсуждены́. (*Not* обсу́дятся . . .)	These questions will be discussed.

Since the **ся** form is limited to imperfective passives, there is no reason to mistake for passives perfective **ся** verbs bearing a superficial resemblance to them. **Кни́га найдётся** means "The book will turn up (be located in general)," whereas "The book will be found (by somebody)" can only be **Кни́га бу́дет найдена́**. Similarly, **Ива́н уби́лся** in colloquial usage means "Ivan smashed himself to death (as in a fall)" or "Ivan bruised himself," but the sentence "Ivan was killed (by somebody)" can only be **Ива́н бы́л уби́т**.

It should be remembered that the past passive participle may lose some of its passive-verbal force and become more or less adjectival. For example, from the foregoing we realize that **Две́рь откры́лась** 'The door opened' is not a passive (even though someone may, in fact, have opened the door). But **Две́рь была́ откры́та** does not convey a passive in the sense **Кни́га была́ найдена́** does; it does not mean "The door was open*ed*" but rather "The door was open"; i.e. **откры́та** is an adjective, not a participle. Under such conditions, Russians usually resort to an active construction; the best way to render "The door was opened (by somebody)" is by the (third plural form) impersonal **Две́рь откры́ли**. Frequent usage has probably contributed to the adjectivization of participles like **уве́рен, убеждён, окружён**, and others. **Я уве́рен** no longer means "I have been assured" but simply "I am sure"; while to express "I have been assured . . .," one must resort to **Меня́ уве́рили** . . . (cf. above). The same considerations apply to the other two and to similar cases.[1]

Indeed, with all passives the student should keep in mind the possibility and, frequently, the desirability of their replacement by a corresponding active construction. Note that passives without a specified instrumental agent are readily convertible into (third plural form) impersonals:

> До́м стро́ится > До́м стро́ят
> До́м стро́ился > До́м стро́или
> До́м бу́дет стро́иться > До́м бу́дут стро́ить
> До́м бу́дет постро́ен > До́м постро́ят
> До́м бы́л постро́ен/До́м постро́ен > До́м постро́или

---

[1] Note that in the case of 'convince' **убеди́ть – убежда́ют** a similar situation exists in English; "I was convinced . . ." may be ambiguous, and the English speaker might prefer to render the passive meaning by an active construction (e.g. "People (had) convinced me . . ."), just as Russians would say **Меня́ убеди́ли** . . . .

Students frequently attempt to translate such English constructions as "I was told" or "I was given" by Russian passives (usually with past passive participles; e.g. **Я был сказан, Я был дан,** etc.). Such mistakes can be avoided if the student remembers that the subject of the passive must have been the direct object in the active, and in the above sentences "I" was dative, not accusative: **Мне сказали, Мне дали.** Hence, the only passives possible are **Мне было сказано, Мне было дано.**

Finally, we may note a special impersonal construction expressing a passive with a physical meaning only. The agent is always inanimate and is frequently some unspecified natural force or physical object which, if expressed, is in the instrumental. The action is rendered by an impersonal transitive verb:

Во время перестрелки убило майора и комиссара.	During the exchange of fire the mayor and commissar were killed.
В одну минуту дорогу занесло снегом.	In one minute the road was covered with snow.
Варьке хочется спать. Голову тянет вниз, шея болит.	Var'ka is sleepy. She can hardly hold her head up, her neck hurts.
Его тянет в город.	He has an urge to go to the city.
Город залило водой.	The city was inundated by water.

SUBORDINATE POINTS

1. The preposition **в** plus the accusative may have the meaning "as, in the capacity of, for, as a form of":

Он сказал это в шутку (в насмешку).	He said that as a joke (gibe).
Она не в шутку больна.	She is seriously ill.
Возьмём в пример ...	Let's take as/for an example ...
В ответ на ваш вопрос ...	As an answer to your question ...
Что он привёл в доказательство?	What did he offer as proof?

2. The verb **бывают** should be regarded as a nondetermined verb, relating to **быть** as, for example, **ходить** to **идут.** As such it often has a frequentative sense, but does not exclude the meaning "always." Hence:

Он часто бывает у нас.	He's at our place frequently.
У нас бывает колбаса.	We have sausage from time to time.

but

Вечером он всегда бывает дома.	He's always home evenings.
У нас колбаса всегда бывает.	We always have sausage.

The negative of **быва́ют** is at least as categorical as the negative of **бы́ть**:

Я никогда́ не быва́л в Крыму́.	I have never been in the Crimea.
Таки́х кни́г у на́с не быва́ет.	We don't carry such books.

Note that the following usages also correspond to **ходи́ть**:

Собра́ния быва́ют три́ ра́за в ме́сяц.	Meetings are held three times a month.
Пи́во зде́сь быва́ет хоро́шее.	The beer is good here.

Быва́ет (быва́ло), что is equivalent to **Случа́ется (Случа́лось), что** 'It (sometimes) happens/used to happen that . . .' **Быва́ло** is also used as a parenthetic expression with past imperfectives or *present perfectives* (see page 227).

Он,быва́ло,е́здил (съе́здит)в го́род.	He (frequently) used to go into the city.

3. The unstressed particle **бы́ло** means "nearly, on the point of, was about to, would have (but for), wanted to." It is used with past tense verbs. It frequently occurs in the construction **чу́ть бы́ло не** 'nearly':

Он бы́ло сказа́л на́м об э́том, но́ разду́мал.	He was about to tell us but changed his mind.
Я вошёл бы́ло в ко́мнату, но́ мо́й оте́ц удержа́л меня́.	I wanted to enter the room, but my father restrained me.
Он чу́ть бы́ло не забы́л.	He very nearly forgot.
Он чу́ть бы́ло не уе́хал.	He was just about to leave.

4. The preposition **о (об)** plus the *accusative* has the meaning "against/on (the surface of something)":

Он оперся́ рука́ми о сто́л.	He leaned against the table with his hands.
Он уда́рился ного́й о ка́мень.	He struck his foot on a rock.

And note:

бо́к о́ бок, плечо́ о́ плечо	side by side, shoulder to shoulder
живут стена́ о́б стену	live in close quarters

5. The pronoun **каков** (end-stressed) replaces **какой** in certain purely predicate usages; it refers to the quality or general nature of persons or things and may be used in interrogative, relative, or exclamatory contexts:

Я слы́шал, что вы́ познако́мились с но́вым студе́нтом. Каков он?	I've heard you've gotten to know the new student. What kind of person is he?

На́до узна́ть, какова́ о́бщая ли́ния па́ртии.	One must find out what the general party line is.
Како́в результа́т?	What is the result?
Неуже́ли о́н действи́тельно та́к ду́мает? Каковы́ взгля́ды!	Does he really think that way? What views he has!
Никто́ не ска́жет, каковы́ бу́дут на́ши оши́бки через де́сять ле́т.	No one can say what the nature of our mistakes will be in ten years.

Note also **каково́** for **ка́к**:

Каково́ ва́м сего́дня?	How are you today?
Он и са́м до́лжен зна́ть, каково́ крестья́не живу́т.	He himself ought to know how the peasants are living.

The pronoun **тако́в** (end-stressed) bears essentially the same relationship to **тако́й** as **како́в** to **како́й**, except that **таково́** is not used adverbially:

Како́в офице́р, тако́в и его́ солда́т.	A soldier is (just) the way his officer is.
Она́ такова́, ка́к ты́ о не́й расска́зывал.	She's (just) as you described her to me.
Таковы́ бы́ли вы́воды центра́льного комите́та.	Such were the conclusions of the central committee.

Occasionally, a bookish long form (but still predicate only) **таково́й** is found, most commonly in the set expression **как таково́й** 'as such':

любо́вь как такова́я	love as such
Я говорю́ о рома́не как таково́м.	I'm speaking about the novel as such.

6. Notice the useful expression **тако́й-то** 'such and such a':

в тако́й-то ча́с	at such and such a time
Допу́стим, тако́й-то челове́к живёт на тако́й-то у́лице.	Let's assume that such and such a person lives on such and such a street.

7. Придётся – приходи́ться *plus dat* may, particularly when used in the imperfective, be weaker than "must" and mean simply "have occasion to":

Мне́ не ра́з приходи́лось его́ ви́деть в то́ вре́мя.	I more than once had occasion to see him in those days.
Мне́ ча́сто прихо́дится име́ть с ни́м де́ло.	I often have occasion to deal with him.

8. In addition to **стреми́ться** 'strive' (Lesson IX) there are three Russian verbs which, used with the infinitive, may render the English "try to":

(по)пробовать is neutral, implies no result, means simply "try"; the idea is often "try out," similar to the transitive verb: **(по)пробовать** *acc* 'try (out)'; e.g. food or a dress.

(по)пытаются suggests the existence of an obstacle and the possibility or probability of failure.

(по)стараются suggests application of effort, a concentrated endeavor.

In many instances, however, two or all three of these verbs may be more or less interchangeable. Here are some examples of their usage:

a. Этого ещё никто в здешних местах   No one around these parts has tried
   не пробовал (пытался) делать.   to do that yet.

Пробовал is neutral; **пытался** suggests difficulty in attaining the result (which is probably the reason no one has "tried" to do it yet). **Старался** is impossible because there is no interest in the effort itself, simply in whether the effort has been made.

b. Он пытался (старался) сохранить   He tried to retain his balance, but his
   равновесие, но ноги разъехались в   legs shot out in different direc-
   разные стороны, и мальчик опять   tions, and the boy again fell on the
   упал на лёд.   ice.

Пытался implies difficulty or improbability of success; **старался** a great effort. **Пробовал** would suggest that he was more or less impartially testing his balance; the fall would be more expected and less serious.

c. Я пытался (старался) объяснить   I tried to explain to him my view of
   ему свой взгляд на его поступок,   his action, but he didn't under-
   но он не понял меня.   stand me.

Approximately the same considerations apply as in the above sentence.

d. Надо попробовать (попытаться)   We must try to give the patient a
   дать больному новое лекарство,   new medicine; perhaps the pains
   может быть, боли уменьшатся.   will decrease.

Попробовать is the most likely choice here, since the context is neutral ("try out giving him") and there is no suggestion of difficulty in getting the patient to take the medicine. If there were, **попытаться** would be appropriate. **Постараться** is unlikely for the reason given in example a.

e. Мальчик старается (пытается, про-   The boy is trying, through a chink
   бует) в щель между досками за-   between the boards in the fence, to
   бора рассмотреть, что же делают   perceive what the children in the
   дети во дворе.   yard are doing.

All possibilities exist; choice would depend on the circumstances attending the "trying."

f. Examples of transitive **(по)про́бовать** *acc*:

Попро́буйте на́ше пи́во.	Try our beer.
Певцы́ про́буют свои голоса́.	The singers are trying out their voices.
Попро́буй (то́лько)! (Это *or some infinitive understood*)	Just try it! (*A threat or negative warning*)

TRANSLATION INTO ENGLISH

1. Ца́рь Ива́н роди́лся четы́реста со́рок ле́т тому́ наза́д. **2.** Ко́жа всего́ скоре́е по́ртится в жа́рком кли́мате. По́сле не́которого вре́мени она́ рвётся та́к же легко́, ка́к бума́га. **3.** Не чита́й при тако́м све́те! По́ртишь зре́ние. **4.** Солда́т бы́л не о́чень бо́ек от приро́ды. **5.** Ру́сский наро́д — э́то бо́йкий наро́д. **6.** Когда́ о́н говори́т, то́ у него́, как вообще́ у насме́шливых люде́й, улыба́ются одни́ то́лько глаза́. **7.** Я зна́ю, что ва́м тру́дно говори́ть об э́том, но́, пожа́луйста, попыта́йтесь объясни́ть на́м всё обстоя́тельства де́ла. **8.** Я ра́но осироте́л, лиши́лся свои́х роди́телей в во́зрасте пяти́ ле́т. **9.** Пожа́луйста, сравни́те сле́дующие три́ фра́зы: Он *лиши́лся* жи́зни (то́ есть, о́н у́мер, поги́б); Он *лиши́л себя́* жи́зни (то́ есть, соверши́л самоуби́йство); Он *лиши́л* царя́ жи́зни (то́ есть, уби́л царя́). **10.** В э́том столкнове́нии автомоби́лей поги́бло пя́ть челове́к. **11.** Журнали́сты испо́льзовали чужи́е непра́вильные исто́чники, и за э́то и́х лиши́ли пра́ва печа́таться в газе́тах. **12.** Ти́хо откры́лась две́рь, ро́бко вошла́ жена́ писа́теля. **13.** Ца́рь не до́лжен испы́тывать ро́бость. **14.** За оди́н ме́сяц и́м бы́ли усво́ены все́ четы́ре арифмети́ческих пра́вила. **15.** Ско́лько оте́ц ни би́лся со мно́ю, я́ не мо́г усво́ить а́збуки с пе́рвого взгля́да. **16.** Он огляну́лся, чтобы посмотре́ть, ка́к далеко́ от него́ идёт Лари́са. **17.** Этим посту́пком Анна Григо́рьевна лиша́ется моего́ дове́рия к ней. **18.** Этот челове́к по́льзуется везде́ по́лным дове́рием. **19.** На́до всегда́ прислу́шиваться к го́лосу наро́да. **20.** Эта же́нщина испыта́ла почти́ всё в жи́зни. **21.** Кто́ испыта́л наслажде́ния тво́рчества, для того́ всё други́е наслажде́ния не существу́ют. **22.** На́ше прави́тельство тре́бует неме́дленного прекраще́ния термоя́дерных испыта́ний. **23.** Ки́ти не за́мужем и больна́, больна́ от любви́ к челове́ку, кото́рый пренебрёг е́ю. **24.** Он ужа́сно пренебрега́ет рабо́той. **25.** Он не пренебрега́ет никаки́ми сре́дствами в связи́ с э́той зада́чей. **26.** Пренебреже́ние к лише́ниям жи́зни счита́ется положи́тельным ка́чеством челове́ка. **27.** Каковы́ результа́ты? Отрица́тельны? **28.** Ну, такова́ на́ша оце́нка. В ней, ка́к ви́дишь, ма́ло положи́тельного. **29.** Тепе́рь, с Го́голя, всё до того́ охва́чено отрица́тельным направле́нием, что положи́тельный ти́п лица́ почти́ невозмо́жен в литерату́ре. **30.** Его́ хара́ктер лишён отрица́тельных че́рт. **31.** Не́которые ду́мают, что наде́жды бо́льше не́т. Го́род окружён. Но́ мы́ ещё де́ржимся и бу́дем держа́ться. **32.** Ведь пре́жде всего́ ему́ ну́жно бы́ло окружи́ть себя́ надёжными людьми́. **33.** На э́тот ра́з сотру́дники посо́льства бы́ли приглашены́, хотя́ на таки́е торже́ственные приёмы обыкнове́нно приглаша́ются то́лько послы́. **34.** На́м ча́сто приходи́лось встреча́ться у вы́хода из музе́я. **35.** Он заста́вил себя́ подро́бно изучи́ть приёмы все́х изве́стных совреме́нных писа́телей. **36.** Приём, кото́рым о́н нака́зывал дете́й, бы́л оди́н: молча́ние, то́ есть, о́н перестава́л говори́ть с ка́ждым винова́тым ребёнком. **37.** Его́ пы́шные францу́зские фра́зы ужа́сно рассерди́ли все́х прису́тствующих. **38.** Одни́м то́лько появле́нием свои́м коро́ль Ка́рл привёл в смире́ние ливо́нских ры́царей. **39.** Солда́ты ста́ли огля́дываться вокру́г. **40.** Мы́ се́ли вокру́г стола́. **41.** Мы́ соверши́ли пое́здку вокру́г све́та. **42.** Входи́те, пожа́луйста, раздева́йтесь. Прошу́ не церемо́ниться. **43.** Этого бе́дного ребёнка то́ балова́ли, то́ дразни́ли. **44.** По суббо́там и воскресе́ньям вы́ бу́дете мои́ми гостя́ми. А в бу́дни бу́дем рабо́тать по-настоя́щему. **45.** — Осторо́жнее, кня́зь! Обопри́тесь на мою́ ру́ку, — крича́ла Ма́рья Алекса́ндровна. **46.** Де́вушка останови́лась о́коло ли́пы, оперла́сь о неё руко́й, и запла́кала. **47.** Я вполне́ опира́юсь на ва́ши фа́кты и на вы́воды, сде́ланные из ва́ших наблюде́ний. **48.** Он сади́лся в кре́сло, протя́гивал но́ги на сту́л, и, разва́ливаясь, таки́м о́бразом, начина́л чита́ть. **49.** Он занима́л тако́е ва́жное перве́нствующее положе́ние, что каку́ю бы глу́пость о́н ни сказа́л, её принима́ли за у́мные мы́сли. **50.** Снача́ла, благодаря́ свое́й спосо́бности усва́ивать чужи́е мы́сли и то́чно передава́ть и́х, о́н в пери́од уче́ния, в среде́ уча́щих и уча́щихся всегда́ име́л пе́рвенство. **51.** Все́ рабо́чие, спосо́бные к труду́, должны́ яви́ться на заво́д как мо́жно скоре́е. **52.** Он о́чень спосо́бен к му́зыке, да и вообще́ о́н спосо́бный челове́к. **53.** Он на всё спосо́бен, на вся́кое наси́лие, о́н соверши́т любо́е преступле́ние. **54.** Я откры́то выступа́ю про́тив вся́кого примене́ния наси́лия над челове́ком. **55.** Он здо́рово се́рдится на меня́ за то́, что я́ вёл себя́ та́к ду́рно вчера́ ве́чером. **56.** Этот учёный успе́л приобрести́ мно́го сторо́нников, но́ не все́ они́ оста́лись и́ми до конца́. **57.** Они́ уе́хали спустя́ три́ дня́. **58.** Мы́, быва́ло, сиде́ли на рассве́те и мо́лча кури́ли. ‖ А ра́з уже́ ты́ бро́сил кури́ть, то́ и мы́ должны́ бы́ли бро́сить э́то прия́тное заня́тие. **59.** Всё, что́ о́н де́лает, броса́ется в глаза́. **60.** Не на́до преувели́чивать значе́ние э́того письма́. **61.** Ли́почка обнару́живает накло́нность к са́мому гру́бому поведе́нию. **62.** Все́ ва́ши уси́лия напра́сны. Это ва́м не уда́стся. **63.** Люби́ меня́, какова́ я́ е́сть, со все́ми мои́ми сла́бостями. **64.** Мы́ сейча́с разраба́тываем пла́н для прое́кта. **65.** Он бьётся ка́к ры́ба об лёд (то́ есть, нахо́дится в тяжёлых материа́льных усло́виях). **66.** Серёжа руга́ет все́х, кого́ встреча́ет, а времена́ми то́лько молчи́т, обнару́живая холо́дное презре́ние к окружа́ющим. **67.** Быва́ло, мы́ всё собира́лись у друзе́й и пе́ли.[1] **68.** Он вста́л из-за стола́ в поры́ве зло́бы, охва́ченный жела́нием крича́ть, руга́ться, би́ть кулака́ми о сто́л и сте́ны. **69.** Мо́й дя́дя ча́сто проявля́ет великоду́шие и доброту́, зато́ нере́дко на́м пока́зывает и свою́ дурну́ю сто́рону. **70.** Он вдру́г почу́вствовал раска́яние за гру́бости, ска́занные и́м во вре́мя разгово́ра с тётей. **71.** На́м бы́ло прика́зано ко́нчить рабо́ту, но́ на́м и без того́ не рабо́талось. **72.** На́м не ве́рится, что э́то та́к случи́лось. **73.** На́ш учи́тель череду́ет шу́тки с серьёзными разгово́рами. **74.** Среди́ ру́сских согла́сных наблюда́ется мно́го чередова́ний, в осно́ве кото́рых лежи́т смягче́ние не́которых шу́мных и и́х перехо́д в щипя́щие. Наприме́р к, г, х череду́ются с ч, ж, ш. **75.** И та́к хорошо́ она́ пе́ла, про́сто и задуше́вно, что ка́ждому ду́малось о свое́й люби́мой. **76.** Выступа́ла с пе́снями не́мка с отли́чным го́лосом; я́ не мо́г наслу́шаться э́тих пе́сен. **77.** Ко́жа на его́ лице́ из жёсткой постепе́нно превраща́лась в мя́гкую. **78.** Моро́зило. Стоя́л жёсткий моро́з. **79.** Дава́йте заброни́руем места́ не в мя́гком, а в жёстком ваго́не. Та́м ме́нее удо́бно, но зато́ деше́вле, и встреча́ются лю́ди бо́лее интере́сные. **80.** Мы́ повсю́ду чу́вствовали озлобле́ние наро́да про́тив па́ртии. Лю́ди руга́ют свои́х руководи́телей, а са́ми рабо́тают пло́хо. **81.** Я во́все не разбира́юсь в причи́нах неожи́данного подъёма произво́дства автомоби́лей. **82.** Она́ удиви́лась э́той его́ быстроте́ и лёгкости при подъёме на го́рку. **83.** Неда́внее паде́ние це́н, быть мо́жет, ока́жет положи́тельное влия́ние на хозя́йство. **84.** Счита́ют, что о́н сде́лал э́то в шу́тку. По-мо́ему, о́н сде́лал э́то в зна́к свое́й дру́жбы. **85.** От него́ тре́буют, чтобы о́н то́тчас же прекрати́л свою́ революцио́нную де́ятельность. **86.** При всём отвраще́нии к э́тому челове́ку Ку́нину вдру́г ста́ло жа́ль его́. **87.** Мы́ стреми́мся к по́лному разгро́му не́мцев. **88.** Он о́чень ча́сто ука́зывал мне́ на преувеличе́ния, допуска́емые мно́ю в расска́зах. **89.** Опри́чник — э́то дворяни́н, состоя́вший в ряда́х опри́чнины. Опри́чнина — э́то была́ систе́ма чрезвыча́йных мероприя́тий, совершённых Ива́ном Гро́зным для разгро́ма боя́рско-кня́жеской оппози́ции и укрепле́ния ру́сского централизо́ванного госуда́рства. **90.** Он не челове́к, а зве́рь. **91.** Я убеждён, что це́ль на́шего воспита́ния состои́т не то́лько в то́м, что́бы воспита́ть челове́ка, спосо́бного с наибо́льшим эффе́ктом принима́ть уча́стие в строи́тельстве госуда́рства. **92.** На́до воспи́тывать в де́тях уваже́ние к ста́ршим. **93.** Хоро́шее воспита́ние сейча́с же даёт о себе́ зна́ть. **94.** При вся́ких затрудне́ниях о́н пыта́ется сохрани́ть вну́треннее равнове́сие. **95.** В про́шлом о́н стара́лся держа́ться о́бщей ли́нии, а в после́днее вре́мя всё бо́льше склоня́ется к на́шему мне́нию. **96.** На́м сле́дует склони́ть его́ на на́шу сто́рону. **97.** Несмотря́ на все́ на́ши уси́лия, на все́

---

[1] От *соберёмся* у друзе́й и *начнём* пе́ть

стара́ния измени́ть его́ дурно́й хара́ктер, о́н остаётся таки́м, каки́м всегда́ был. **98.** Из э́того ничего́ не получи́лось, но́ на́до сказа́ть, что э́то на́ша пе́рвая попы́тка. **99.** Мы́ пыта́емся служи́ть Ро́дине, ка́к уме́ем. **100.** Вы́ гро́зны на слова́х, попро́буйте на де́ле. **101.** Пре́жде че́м се́сть на сту́л, он попро́бовал его́. **102.** У на́с еда́ хоро́шая, попро́буйте её. **103.** Меня́ тя́нет на ро́дину. Ка́к хо́чется верну́ться! **104.** «Ка́к я ра́д тебя́ ви́деть» — сказа́л Фёдор, целу́ясь с бра́том и кре́пко пожима́я ему́ ру́ки. **105.** Де́вушки тако́го во́зраста, ка́к пра́вило, не целу́ются. **106.** Мы́ жда́ли его́ и, наконе́ц, дожда́лись. **107.** Вы́ меня́ дождётесь, не пра́вда? Я ско́ро верну́сь. **108.** Евге́ний хоте́л что́-то сказа́ть, но сдержа́лся. **109.** Я всё вре́мя стара́юсь освободи́ться от свои́х предрассу́дков. Но я́ всё ещё пита́ю чу́вство любви́ к ста́рым времена́м. **110.** Я всегда́ ра́д дождю́, о́н пита́ет на́шу по́чву — здесь су́хо. **111.** Ва́ше се́рдце пита́ется зло́стью и доса́дой. **112.** По приро́де о́н молчали́в, но зато́ ка́к умён. **113.** В э́том я́ ви́жу молчали́вое соглаше́ние с на́шим реше́нием. **114.** Его́ жена́ побледне́ла от зло́сти. **115.** Бы́ли Октя́брьские пра́здники, са́мые торже́ственные на сове́тской земле́. Но я́ не о́чень люблю́ быва́ть на таки́х торже́ственных пра́здниках, и почти́ ни на оди́н не ходи́л. **116.** Равноду́шие к обще́ственному де́лу бы́ло всео́бщее; на вы́боры е́здили о́чень немно́гие. **117.** Та́ня уе́хала с неопределённым чу́вством доса́ды. **118.** Не́ на кого бы́ло опере́ться, не́ от кого бы́ло жда́ть по́мощи, сове́та, сло́ва уча́стия. Все́ бы́ли ко мне́ равноду́шны. **119.** Если ва́с не затрудни́т, то́, пожа́луйста, пришли́те его́ а́дрес. **120.** Этот вопро́с, каза́лось, затрудни́л го́стя. **121.** Ско́ро найдётся вы́ход из э́того затрудне́ния. **122.** Всё ожида́ли вы́ход его́ кни́ги в све́т. **123.** Та́м идёт како́е-то безобра́зие. Иди́те туда́ разобра́ться. **124.** Он гру́б в обраще́нии со вся́ким наро́дом. **125.** Уже́ в его́ ра́нних произведе́ниях встреча́ются про́блески вели́кого тала́нта. **126.** Все́ ли́пы поги́бнут от моро́за. **127.** Же́ня чу́ть бы́ло не упа́ла. **128.** Ка́к на́м не заду́мываться? Сейча́с прави́тельство грози́тся лиши́ть на́с пра́ва печа́таться в журна́лах. Зна́чит, мы́ лиши́мся того́ ва́жного обме́на о́пытом и мне́ниями, кото́рым мы́ до си́х по́р по́льзуемся. **129.** В све́те после́дних да́нных мо́жно сказа́ть, что кулаки́ исчеза́ют. Им грозя́т по́лным лише́нием земли́, и, есте́ственно, что они́ ухо́дят в города́. Кула́к, по ле́нинскому определе́нию, явля́ется крестья́нином, живу́щим чужи́м трудо́м, ста́вшим бога́тым не свои́ми уси́лиями. **130.** Я ужа́сно сержу́сь на бра́та, когда́ о́н не сде́рживается от э́того гру́бого сме́ха. **131.** Это са́мый посты́дный посту́пок. Вы́ не сдержа́ли обеща́ния, измени́ли жене́. Вы́ безобра́зный челове́к. **132.** У него́ о́чень ги́бкий у́м, но в э́том де́ле о́н не име́ет о́пыта. **133.** Ве́сь де́нь несли́ поко́йного царя́. **134.** Ну́ каково́ бы́ло? Проигра́ли? Не́т, вы́играл сто́ ты́сяч. **135.** Свои́м тво́рчеством о́н вы́играл во мне́нии о́бщества. **136.** Сравни́те сле́дующие фра́зы: (1) Ца́рь заду́мал мно́го хоро́-

шего./Ца́рь глубоко́ заду́мался. (2) Кни́ги собира́ются все́ми студе́нтами./ Студе́нты собира́ются в за́л.   /Студе́нты собира́ются в за́ле. (3) Она́ причёсывается ка́ждый де́нь./У кого́ она́ причёсывается? (4) Э́то стихотворе́ние не перево́дится./Мне́ не перево́дится. (5) Он вы́рос в дере́вне./Он жени́лся и вы́растил до́чь.

СЛОВА́ ТО́ЛЬКО К Э́ТОМУ УРО́КУ

бро́ш-енн-ость abandon

бо-я́р-ин (*pl* боя́ре, боя́р) boyar (member of old Russian nobility)

бо-я́р-ск-ий boyar *adj*

бо-я́р-ств-о boyars *collec*

в-ду́м-чив-ый thoughtful

велик-о-ру́с-ск-ий Great Russian *as distinct from Belorussian or Ukrainian* (*Little Russian*)

власт-ели́н-ск-ий ВЛАД-т *adj* < властели́н lord, sovereign

го́р-к-а hill

жи-т-е́й-ск-ий ЖИВ everyday (from everyday life) *adj*

за-бо́р Б/Р fence

зе́р-к-ал-о Е *pl* mirror

из-во́з-чик coachman, cabman

инсти́нкт instinct

кома́нд-а command; crew, team

ливо́н-ск-ий Livonian

ли́п-а linden tree (*Eng* lime)

ло́к/о/ть М Е *pl obl* elbow

материа́ль-/н-ый material *adj*

митрополи́т metropolitan *eccles*

не́-друг enemy, foe

о-при́ч-ник oprichnik

о-при́ч-н-ин-а oprichnina

ора́тор orator

пе́рв-ен-ств-о championship

про́-блеск flash (of talent, etc.; *often in plural*)

пуг-ли́в-ый easily frightened

пы́ш-н-ый splendid, magnificent; luxuriant

раб-о-ле́п-/н-ый servile

сво-ё-во́л-и-е willfulness, self-will

сирота́ (*pl* сиро́ты) *M and F* orphan

сиро́т-ств-о state of being an orphan; loneliness

слобод-а́ *S nom pl* (сло́боды) settlement (often a special part of a city where residents had special privileges)

термо-я́дер-н-ый ЯД/Р thermonuclear

футбо́ль-н-ый soccer *adj*

ца́р-ств-ен-/н-ый kingly, regal; tsar(ist) *adj* = ца́р-ск-ий

церемониа́ль-н-ый ceremonial

щип-я́щ-ий hushing *ling* (ж, ш, ч, щ)

ГЛАГО́ЛЫ

раз-**вал**-и-ть-ся – разва́ливаться fall/ tumble down; sprawl

о-**гляд**-е́-ть-ся – огля́дываются look around (in different directions)

о-**гляд**-ну-ть-ся – огля́дываются look around (behind)

n огля́д/ка; с огля́дкой with care, with caution

на-**говор**-и́-ть *что́ or чего́ P only* say a lot of (often bad or silly) things

драз-н-и-ть tease

(по)-**ду́й**-ут blow *intr*

кус-а́й-ут bite *tr*; —ся bite X.D

ласк-а́й-ут caress, fondle, treat (often too) nicely

n ла́ска

за-**лий**-ут – залива́ют flood, inundate X.H

моро́з-и-ть *I only* freeze *tr*; be freezing *intr*

n моро́з

за-**моро́з**-и-ть – замора́живают freeze *tr*;

cf. за-мёрз-(ну)-ть – замерзáют freeze *intr*

за-нёс-ёт – заносить carry, waft X.H
n занóс snowdrift

пéрвенств-овá-ть (*cf.* пéрвенство) have priority; первенствýющие *sub adj* the most important

ис-пис-а-ть-ся – исписываются write oneself out X.G

(вы)-раст-и-ть – вырáщивают grow, rear, cultivate *tr*; *cf.* (вы)-раст-ут – вырастáют

в-рéз-а-ть-ся – врезáются в *когó/чтó* cut into

свет-áй-ёт *imps* dawn

(о)-сирот-éй-ут become an orphan; *cf.* сирот-á

о-сирот-й-ть *P only* make an orphan

на-слад-й-ть-ся – наслаждáются *кéм/чéм* enjoy, take pleasure in

n наслаждéние

при-слýш-ай-ут-ся – прислýшиваются к *комý/чемý* listen, lend an ear to, perk up one's ears

на-смотр-е-ть-ся *когó/чегó P only* look to one's fill X.G

вы-сп-а-ть-ся (*like* спать) – высыпáются get a good sleep X.G

о-ступ-и-ть-ся – оступáются stumble X.G

на-танц-ёвá-ть-ся *P only* dance one's fill X.G

за-уч-и-ть-ся – заучиваются overstudy, get foggy from studying X.G

централ-из-овá-ть *P and I* centralize

церемóн-и-ть-ся stand on ceremony:
Не церемóнься. Make yourself at home.

при-чёс-а-ть (причéшут) – причёсывают comb; —ся comb oneself X.B
n причёска combing; coiffure

ÓБЩИЙ СЛОВÁРЬ

без-обрáз-и-е ugliness, deformity; an ugly, disorderly scene in public, often a loud argument with bystanders involved

без-обрáз-/н-ый hideous; ugly; disgraceful, outrageous

бóй-/к-ий brisk, sharp, pert, animated; busy

бол-éзн-ен/н-ый sickly, ailing; morbid; causing pain

бýд-/н-и БУД¹ *M pl only* (*gen* бýдней) working days, nonholidays

бывáло БУД² X.2

было БУД² X.3

велик-о-дýш-и-е generosity

велик-о-дýш-/н-ый generous

вокрýг *prep* (*когó/чегó*) *and adv* around

врáг *E* enemy

вы-вод conclusion; withdrawal; *cf.* выведут – выводить lead out, draw conclusion

вы-ход going out, way out, exit; *cf.* выйдут – выходить

гиб-/к-ий flexible, pliant

гóр-ечь bitterness; bitter taste

госудáрь sovereign, tsar

грóз-/н-ый threatening, terrible

грýб-ый crude, coarse

двóр *E* court, yard, courtyard; на —é outside

двор-ян-ин (*pl* дворя́не) noble(man), man of the nobility

двор-я́н-ск-ий nobility *adj*; noble act or person = благ-о-рóд-/н-ый

двор-я́н-ств-о nobility, nobles

дéрев-о (*pl* дерéвья, дерéвьев) tree

дéт-ств-о childhood

дé-я-тель-н-ость activity, work, activities

(не)до-вéр-и-е к *комý/чемý* (lack of) faith, trust, confidence in; *cf.* доверя́ют к *комý/чемý*

до-каз-á-тель-ств-о proof; *cf.* до-каз-а-ть – докáзывают

до-сáд-а vexation, annoyance; a pity:
Какáя —! How annoying!

дур-/н-óй bad, evil; (*sh f us with* собóй) ugly:
Он дýрен собóй. He is ugly.

ед-а́ food

ест-е́-ств-енн-ый natural

жёст-/к-ий tough, hard, rough; —ий вагóн "hard" class coach

за-душ-е́в-н-ость sincerity

зверь *M E pl obl* (wild) beast, brute

здéш-н-ий here *adj*

зл-óб-а spite; anger

зл-ость malice; ill-naturedness, fury

из-мéн-а betrayal, treachery, infidelity; *cf.* изменить – изменя́ют *комý/чемý* betray

кáзнь execution, death penalty

как-óв X.5

кáм/е/нь *M E pl obl* stone, rock

кня́ж-е-ств-о principality

кня́зь (*pl* князья́) prince

кóж-а skin; hide; leather

корóль *M E* king

кулáк *E* fist; kulak (wealthy peasant)

лáв-/к-а bench; store, shop

люб-и́м-ый favorite, loved one

молч-а-ли́в-ый silent, taciturn

морóз frost; freezing weather

на-клóн-н-ость к *комý/чемý* inclination, leaning

на-прáс-/н-ый vain, futile; напрáсно in vain; useless

на-си́л-ие violence

на-смéш-лив-ый *derisive*

не-вóль-н-ый involuntary

не-об-хóд-и́м-ость necessity, indispensability

нéрв-/н-ый nervous

нрáв-ств-енн-ый moral

об-стó-я́-тель-ств-о circumstances

один-óч-е-ств-о loneliness

ó-пыт experience; experiment, trial

оснóв-н-óй basic; в —óм basically

отéч-е-ск-ий ОТ/Ц paternal

от-риц-á-тель-/н-ый negative

о-хóт-н-о willingly

под/о/-зр-и́-тель-/н-ый suspicious (provoking or manifesting suspicion)

подъ-ём rise, raising, lifting; *cf.* подни́мут(ся) – поднимáют(ся)

покóй-н-ый deceased; calm

пóлностью completely, entirely

по-лóж-и-тель-н-ый positive (as opposed to negative)

порóй at times, now and then

по-слéд-у-ющ-ий succeeding, subsequent

по-с/ó/л ambassador

по-сóль-ств-о embassy

по-стыд-/н-ый shameful

прáзд-ник holiday; festive occasion

при-ём reception, receiving; device; *cf.* при́мут – принимáют

равн-о-вéс-и-е balance, equilibrium

равн-о-дýш-и-е к *комý/чемý* indifference to

равн-о-дýш-/н-ый к *комý/чемý* indifferent to

раз-грóм destruction; total rout

раз-драж-и́-тель-н-ость irritability, shortness of temper

разн-о-обрáз-и-е diversity

разн-о-обрáз-/н-ый diverse

раз-рабóт-/к-а elaboration, working out; *cf.* разрабóтают – разрабáтывают

рас-свéт (на) dawn, daybreak

рóб-/к-ий timid

рóб-ость timidity (*note that the* к *is omitted in the abstract noun*)

ры́царь *M* knight

ря́дом с *кéм/чéм* next to; together with, in addition to

сам-о-у-би́й-ств-о suicide; соверш́́ить – совершáют — commit suicide

свéт world; light; на —е in the world; на тóм —е in the other world; в —е in society; при —е *чегó* by the light of; в —е *чегó* in the light of

с-клáд warehouse; case, mold

снóва again, new

спосóб-н-ость capability, ability

спосóб-/н-ый capable; — к *чемý* ability, talent in; — на *чтó* capable of: Он спосóбен ко всемý. He can do anything/is capable *in* everything. Он спосóбен на всё. One can expect anything (often bad) from him.

спустя́: 3 дня́ — three days afterwards

сторо́н-н-ик supporter, adherent, partisan
сце́н-а stage; scene
так-о́в X.5
так-ов-о́й X.5
так-о́й-то X.6
торж-é-ств-енн-ый grand, solemn; festive
трево́ж-/н-ый disturbed; disturbing
у-би́й-ств-о murder

у-си́л-и-е effort
у-сто́й-чив-ый steady, firm, *stable*
хара́ктер character
характери́стик-а characterization
ца́рь *M E* tsar
шу́м-/н-ый noisy, loud
шу́т-/к-а joke
эффе́кт effect

ГЛАГО́ЛЫ

(из)-бал-ова́-ть spoil, pamper
 n баловство́
бы-ва́й-ут БУД² X.2
бий-ут break *tr*; —ся break *intr* X.D.
пре-не-брёг-у́т – пренебрега́ют *кéм/чéм*
 neglect, ignore, shun, *disdain*
 n пренебреже́ние
(по)-вёд-у́т себя́ behave, conduct oneself
 n поведе́ние
пре-у-вели́ч-и-ть – преувели́чивают exaggerate
 n преувеличе́ние
со-верш-и́-ть – соверша́ют do, make, accomplish, complete, commit
 n соверше́ние
от-вращ-е́н-и-е к *кому́/чему́* aversion/repugnance to; *cf.* отврати́ть – отвраща́ют avert
пре-врат-и́-ть – превраща́ют в *кого́/что́* turn into *tr*; —ся в *кого́/что́* turn into *intr*
по-ги́б-(ну)-ть – погиба́ют perish, be killed (in accident, catastrophe, war, etc., as opposed to illness or age)
гор-е́-ть burn *intr*
 n горе́ние
гроз-и́-ть *кому́ чéм* threaten X with Y; — *inf* threaten to; —ся X.E
 n угро́за
пере-да́-ть – передава́ть give, hand over, transmit, reproduce
 n переда́ча
с-де́рж-а-ть – сде́рживают hold in, keep back, repress; *P only* keep (word,

promise); —ся control oneself, hold oneself in
за-ду́м-ай-ут – заду́мывают conceive, plan; —ся become lost in thought *P*, ponder *I*
объ-един-и́-ть unite, join *tr*; —ся unite *intr* X.C
 n объедине́ние
жг-у́т (жéчь, жёг, жгла́, etc., жёгши) burn *tr*
до-жд-а-ть-ся — дожида́ются *кого́/чего́* wait for X until X comes/happens X.G
звон-и́-ть-ся ring at the door X.E
до-звон-и́-ть-ся *P only* call and get an answer, get through by phone *X. G*
под/о/-зр-é-н-и-е (< *an older P* подозре́ть, *modern* подозрева́ют *I only* suspect) suspicion
пре-зр-é-н-и-е (< *an older P* презре́ть, *modern* презира́ют *I only* despise, hold in contempt) contempt, scorn
вы́-игр-ай-ут – выи́грывают win
про-игр-а́й-ут – прои́грывают lose (game, war, etc.)
на-йд-у́т – находить (*PPP* на́йден, найдена́, на́йдено) find; —ся turn up; *I only* be located
раз/о/-йд-у́т-ся – расходиться go apart, disperse, diverge X.G
с/о/-йд-у́т-ся – сходиться с *кéм/чéм* come together X.G
до-каз-а́-ть – дока́зывают prove; *I only* point out
 n доказа́тельство

рас-ка́й-а-ть-ся – раска́иваются о *ко́м/
чём* repent, regret
n раска́яние

с-клон-и́-ть – склоня́ют к *кому́/чему́* incline, bend; —ся к *кому́/чему́ intr*
incline, bend, tend toward
n склоне́ние *has certain special meanings,
including* declension *gr*

у-креп-и́-ть – укрепля́ют strengthen *tr*;
—ся strengthen *intr*
n укрепле́ние

о-круж-и́-ть – окружа́ют surround, encircle; я́ окружён *ке́м/чём* I'm surrounded by; окружа́ющие *sub adj*
associates, people who are around
n окруже́ние

лиш-и́-ть – лиша́ют *кого́/что́ кого́/чего́*
deprive X of Y; лиши́ть – лиша́ют
себя́ *кого́/чего́* deprive self of; —ся be/
become deprived of, lose
n лише́ние

пре-у-ме́ньш-и-ть – преуменьша́ют underestimate, understate, belittle
n преуменьше́ние

об-мен-я́й-ут-ся – обме́ниваются *ке́м/
чём* с *ке́м/чём* exchange X with Y
n обме́н

(по)-мир-и́-ть reconcile *tr*; —ся с *ке́м/чём*
reconcile oneself to, become reconciled
with X.C

с-мир-е́н-и-е (< смири́ть(ся) – смиря́ют-
(ся) subdue, humble (submit, resign
oneself)) humility, meekness

пад-е́н-и-е falling, downfall; *cf.* упаду́т
(паду́т) – па́дают

(на)-печа́т-ай-ут print, type; write for a
printed publication; —ся write for a
printed publication, get/be in print
n печа́тание

в-печат-л-е́н-и-е impression IX *Vocab*

пере-пи́с-ывай-ут-ся с *ке́м* correspond X.G
n перепи́ска

пит-а́й-ут feed, nourish; nourish (some
feeling); —ся *чём* feed on, live on;
пита́ются хорошо́ eat well

n пита́ние

вос-пит-а́й-ут – воспи́тывают bring up,
rear, educate; —ся be brought up, be
reared
n воспита́ние

пла́к-а-ть weep, cry; —ся X.E
n плач

за-пла́к-а-ть *P only* begin to cry/weep,
break out in tears

(ис)-по́рт-и-ть spoil, damage; —ся become
spoiled/damaged
n по́рча

обо-пр-у́т-ся (опере́ться, оперся́, оперла́сь) – опира́ются на *кого́/что́* lean
on, rest on (*also fig,* be guided by) `
(по)-про́б-ова-ть *кого́/что́* or *inf* try (out)
X.8
n про́ба

ис-пыт-а́й-ут – испы́тывают test, try out;
experience
n испыта́ние

(по)-пыт-а́й-ут-ся *inf* try X.8
n попы́т/ка

(по)-рв-а́-ть tear *tr*; —ся tear *intr* п порыв
рв-а-ть-ся tear *intr* X.D

при-обрёт-у́т – приобрета́ют get, obtain
n приобрете́ние

реш-и́-ть-ся – реша́ются decide X.E

руг-а́й-ут *I only* scold, abuse, criticize; —ся
swear, curse X.D; scold/abuse/criticize
each other X.C
n ру́гань

о-свобод-и́-ть – освобожда́ют free, liberate; —ся X.B
n освобожде́ние

у-сво́й-и-ть – усва́ивают (себе́) adopt, assimilate, master
n усвое́ние

(рас)-серд-и-ть *кого́* на *кого́/что́* make X
angry at Y; —ся на *кого́/что́* get/be
angry at

(по)-слу́ш-ай-ут-ся *кого́* obey
n послуша́ние

за-ста́в-и-ть – заставля́ют *кого́ inf* force X
to Y

(по)-**стар**-áй-ут-ся *inf* try X.8

  n старáние

пре-**ступ**-и-ть – преступáют *что* transgress, violate (law)

  n преступлéние

стуч-á-ть knock, rap; —ся X.E

  n стýк

за-**труд**-н-и́-ть – затрудня́ют hamper

  n затруднéние

(по)-**тя**ѓ-ну-ть draw, drag; *imps* be pulled toward, long for X.H:

  Егó тя́нет в теáтр. He longs for the theater.

про-**тя**ѓ-ну-ть – протя́гивают stretch, extend; —ся stretch/extend *intr*

  n протяжéние; *cf.* на протяжéнии *чего́* during the extent of III.6

удáр-и-ть – ударя́ют *кого́ | что́* по *чему́*

hit, strike; —ся *чéм* о (*что́*) hit/strike one's X on Y

  n удáр

о-**хват**-и-ть – охвáтывают grip; envelop; include

  n охвáт

(по)-**цел**-овá-ть kiss; —ся kiss one another X.C

цел-овá-ть-ся X.D

  n поцелýй

черед-овá-ть alternate tr; —ся с *кéм/чéм* alternate with *intr*

  n чередовáние

за-**щит**-и́-ть – защищáют defend; —ся defend oneself; *cf.* защити́ть – защищáют себя́ X.B

  n защи́та

IV

CONVERSATION LESSONS 1 TO 5

CONVERSATION LESSON
1

В РЕСТОРА́НЕ. РАЗГОВО́Р МЕ́ЖДУ
МИХАЙЛОМ И АЛЕКСЕ́ЕМ

М. Куда́ ты́ идёшь сейча́с?

А. Я иду́ в рестора́н обе́дать: сейча́с уже́ два́ часа́, и я́ о́чень го́лоден. А ты́ уже́ обе́дал?

М. Не́т, я́ то́же ещё не обе́дал. Я обыкнове́нно обе́даю и у́жинаю до́ма, но́ сего́дня моя́ жена́ с детьми́ ещё с утра́ уе́хала к свое́й ма́тери и я́ до́лжен бу́ду обе́дать в како́м-нибудь рестора́не. 5

А. Та́к пойдём и пообе́даем вме́сте. Зде́сь за угло́м е́сть небольшо́й, недо-рого́й, но́ хоро́ший рестора́н. Еда́ та́м отли́чная, официа́нты подаю́т бы́стро и, поэ́тому, не ну́жно до́лго жда́ть.

М. С удово́льствием. Я ра́д, что мы́ проведём э́то вре́мя вме́сте: во-пе́р-вых я́ давно́ тебя́ не ви́дел, а во-вторы́х я́ не люблю́ быва́ть в рестора́-нах оди́н. 10

А. Ну́, во́т мы́ и пришли́. Ся́дем за то́т сто́лик в углу́. Зде́сь подаёт о́чень хоро́шенькая, ми́лая и любе́зная официа́нтка, и я́ всегда́ сажу́сь за э́тот сто́лик, когда́ о́н свобо́ден. (Обраща́ясь к официа́нтке) — Что́ у ва́с сего́дня на обе́д? 15

О. Во́т, пожа́луйста, меню́. Сего́дня кро́ме ра́зных заку́сок вы́ мо́жете полу-чи́ть уху́, грибно́й су́п, прекра́сный бо́рщ и́ли ки́слые щи́. На второ́е у на́с жа́реная ры́ба, свины́е котле́ты, бифште́кс, ро́стбиф, гуля́ш и шни́цель. Е́сли жела́ете — мо́жете заказа́ть инде́йку и́ли цыпля́т. На сла́дкое — компо́т, кисе́ль и́ли моро́женое. 20

М. Ну́, что́ же мы́, Алёша, зака́жем?

A. Да́йте на́м, пожа́луйста, графи́нчик во́дки, селёдку, све́жую икру́ и не́-
сколько горя́чих мясны́х пирожко́в. Пото́м бо́рщ, моему́ дру́гу ро́ст-
25 биф, а мне́ шни́цель. На сла́дкое — компо́т и сли́вочное моро́женое . . .
не́т, принеси́те лу́чше шокола́дное. И, коне́чно, чёрный ко́фе с ликёром.

М. Ну́, одна́ко, я́ ви́жу, что у тебя́ о́чень хоро́ший аппети́т. Я никогда́ не
е́м та́к мно́го.

А. Зде́сь о́чень хоро́ший по́вар, и о́н та́к вку́сно гото́вит, что да́же е́сли ты́
30 и не о́чень го́лоден, то́ мо́жешь ску́шать мно́го. Ты́ зна́ешь францу́з-
скую посло́вицу: «Аппети́т прихо́дит во вре́мя еды́».

О. Во́т, пожа́луйста, во́дка и заку́ски. Когда́ вы́ око́нчите заку́сывать, я́
принесу́ ва́м всё остально́е.

А. (*Налива́я во́дку*) — За твоё здоро́вье! Прия́тного аппети́та! (*чо́каются,*
35 *едя́т*) Ну́, ку́шай, ку́шай на здоро́вье. Как нра́вятся тебе́ э́ти пирожки́?

М. Они́ о́чень вку́сные, осо́бенно к во́дке.

А. Не сказа́л ли я́ тебе́, что зде́сь о́чень разнообра́зный и вку́сный сто́л, и
не ну́жно до́лго жда́ть?

М. Да́, действи́тельно, э́то та́к.

40 А. А во́т и счёт. Ви́дишь, о́н о́чень небольшо́й и це́ны не дороги́е.

М. На́до ли что́-нибудь да́ть официа́нтке на ча́й?

А. Не́т, её чаевы́е уже́ запи́саны в э́тот счёт. Ви́дишь, зде́сь стои́т: " 10% за
услу́ги».

М. Я жале́ю, что никогда́ ра́ньше не быва́л в э́том рестора́не, но́ тепе́рь
45 бу́ду всегда́ ходи́ть сюда́, когда́ не смогу́ обе́дать до́ма.

А. Я обыкнове́нно обе́даю в столо́вых, потому́ что та́м деше́вле, но́ зато́
еда́ в ни́х значи́тельно ху́же.

1. Beside the general verb (съ)éсть 'eat (eat up),' there is a synonym
(с)ку́шают. This verb is considered "polite" than éсть and is used particularly
in the second person:

Что́ вы́ бу́дете ку́шать?	What are you going to eat?
Вы́ не ку́шаете сла́дкого?	Don't you eat dessert?
Ску́шайте ещё кусо́к.	Have another piece.
Я не е́м мя́са.	I don't eat meat.
Мы́ е́ли, пи́ли, говори́ли.	We ate, drank, and talked.
Ребёнок съе́л всю икру́.	The child ate up all the caviar.

Individual Russians, however, vary considerably in their feelings about when
éсть and ку́шают should be used.

2. Just before beginning a meal, one may say прия́тного аппети́та (жела́ют
gen understood), a formula which has no equivalent in English, but corresponds
to French *Bon appetit* or German *Guten Appetit* or *Mahlzeit*.

3. "First," "second," "dessert," "meat" course are **пéрвое, втор́ое, слáдкое, жарќое (блю́до); блю́до** means "course" or "dish" ('my favorite dish' **моё люб́имое блю́до). Чт́о б́удет на пéрвое?** 'What's for the first course?'

4. To "drink to" somebody or something is **(вы́)пьют за** *acc*. "Let's drink to health, friendship" is **Вы́пьем за здор́овье, др́ужбу. Ќушайте, пéйте на здор́овье** means "Eat, drink to your heart's content"; **На здор́овье** by itself may be used as a reply to expressed thanks and may mean approximately "You're welcome." The most frequent expression for drinking a general toast ("Cheers" or "Prosit") is **Б́удь(те) здор́ов(ы).**

5. The conjunction **зат́о** means "however, on the other hand," frequently with the idea "to make up (compensate) for it," more often implied than expressed:

Он м́ало в́идит, зат́о мн́ого сл́ышит.	He sees little but hears a great deal.
Он тепéрь мéньше зараб́атывает, н́о зат́о мéньше уст́аёт.	He now earns less; however (on the other hand), he gets less tired.

СЛОВ́АРЬ

аппет́ит appetite; при́ятного аппет́ита CLɪ.2

бифштéкс (beef)steak

блю́д-о CLɪ.3

б́орщ *E* borscht, beet soup

в-ќус taste

в-ќус-/н-ый tasty

в́од-/к-а vodka

втор-́ое CLɪ.3

гол́од-/н-ый, ѓолоден, голодн́а, ѓолодны hungry

гор-́яч-ий hot

граф́ин-чик small decanter

гр́иб *E* mushroom

гриб-н-́ой mushroom *adj*

гул́яш goulash

дéй-ств-и́-тель-/н-ый real, actual; valid

др́уж-б-а friendship

ед-́а food; meal (eating)

ж́ар-ен-ый fried, roasted, grilled

жар-к-́ое *sub adj* meat course CLɪ.3

за-ќус-/к-а snack; *pl* hors d'œuvres, refreshments

зат́о CLɪ.5

здор́овь-е health; за — CLɪ.4; на — CLɪ.4

знач-́и-тель-/н-ый significant

икр-́а caviar

индéй/к-а turkey

кис-éль *M E* kissel (jellylike dish)

ќис-/л-ый sour; (chemistry) acid *adj*

комп́от stewed fruit

котлéт-а cutlet

кр́оме *коѓо/ чеѓо* except (for), besides

кус-/́о/к piece, bit, lump

ликёр liqueur

люб-́ез-/н-ый amiable, polite, nice

меню́ *N indecl* menu

мор́ож-ен-ое *sub adj* ice cream

мяс-н-́ой meat *adj*

м́яс-о meat

о-стáль-н-́ой **СТАН** remaining, left

от-л́ич-/н-ый excellent

офици́ант waiter

офици́ант-/к-а waitress

пéрв-ое CLɪ.3

пирож-/́о/к little meat pie, patty

п́о-вар *E pl* -́а cook

под *когó*/*чтó* with, to (accompanying)
по-**слóв**-иц-а proverb
рáд, **рáда**, **рáды** *sh f only* glad; — *inf* glad
    to; — *что* glad that; — *комý*/*чемý*
    glad about
рáз-н-ый **РАЗ**[2] different, various
разн-о-**обрáз**-/н-ый diverse, diversified
ры́б-а fish
свéж-ий fresh
свин-óй pig *adj*
свинь-/**я́** *S pl* (*exc gen* свин/é/й) pig
селёд-/к-а herring
слáд-/к-ий (*comp* слáще) sweet; слáдкое
    sub adj dessert
с-**лив**-/к-и **ЛЬЙ** *pl only* cream
с-**лив**-оч-н-ый cream *adj*; слúвочное мо-
    рóженое vanilla ice cream
стóл *E* table (*also* cuisine)
стóл-ик little table
стол-óв-ая dining room; restaurant (often
a cafeteria or dining hall in a university, factory, etc.)
с-**чёт** **Ч/Т** (< с/о/чт-ýт – считáют) bill,
    account, calculation
ýг/о/л (в/на углý) *E* corner; за углóм
    around the corner
у-**дóль**-ств-и-е pleasure; с —ем with
    pleasure
у-**слýг**-а service
ух-**á** fish soup
хорóш-ень-к-ий pretty
цен-á *S pl acc sg* price
цыпл-ён-/о/к (*nom pl* цыплáта, *gen pl* цы-
    плáт) chicken
ча-ев-ы́е *sub adj* gratuities
чáй: дать – давáть на чáй tip, give a tip
шнúцель *M* schnitzel
шоколáд chocolate
шоколáд-н-ый chocolate *adj*
щ-й *pl only* cabbage soup

ГЛАГÓЛЫ

про-**вёд**-ýт – проводить врéмя spend time
об-**рат**-и́-ть-ся – обращáются к *комý*/*чемý*
    об-**ВРАТ** turn to, address
(при)-**готóв**-и-ть prepare; cook
пó-**да**-ть – подавáть give, hand, serve
(по)-**жал**-éй-ут regret, be sorry
(по)-**жел**-áй-ут *когó*/*чегó or чтобы or inf*
    wish, desire
им-éй-ут have, possess
за-**каз**-а-ть – закáзывают order (food,
room, etc.)
(с)-**кýш**-ай-ут CL1.1
за-**кус**-и-ть – закýсывают have a snack;
    eat introductory part of meal
на-**лий**-ут – наливáют *комý что*/*чегó*
    pour, fill someone's glass with (liquid)
за-**пис**-а-ть – запúсывают write down
чóк-ну-ть-ся – чóкаются с *кéм* clink glasses
    (toast, etc.)

CONVERSATION LESSON
2

ЖЕ́НСКАЯ БОЛТОВНЯ́. РАЗГОВО́Р МЕ́ЖДУ МАРИ́ЕЙ ИВА́НОВНОЙ И НАДЕ́ЖДОЙ НИКОЛА́ЕВНОЙ

М.И. Зна́ете ли вы́, ми́лая Наде́жда Никола́евна, инжене́ра Смирно́ва Никола́я Ильича́?

Н.Н. Кто́ о́н тако́й? Я не зна́ю никако́го инжене́ра Смирно́ва.

М.И. Э́то то́т челове́к, кото́рого мы́ вчера́ встре́тили в кино́. Он высо́кого ро́ста, у него́ широ́кие пле́чи, кру́глое лицо́, высо́кий ло́б, о́чень большо́й и некраси́вый но́с, то́лстые гу́бы, седы́е во́лосы и больши́е у́ши. 5

Н.Н. А, тепе́рь я́ зна́ю. Он вчера́ бы́л, ка́жется, со свое́й жено́й, по́лной же́нщиной невысо́кого ро́ста в очка́х.

М.И. Да́, да́! Его́ жена́ уже́ ста́рая же́нщина, но она́ хо́чет каза́ться моло́же 10 свои́х ле́т. Она́ всегда́ но́сит о́чень крича́щие пла́тья и шля́пы. На не́й всегда́ таки́е коро́ткие пла́тья, едва́ до коле́н.

Н.Н. А скажи́те, ка́к вы́ нахо́дите Людми́лу Никола́евну?

М.И. О, она́ о́чень ми́лая, споко́йная и серьёзная же́нщина. Она́ о́чень умна́ и симпати́чна. У неё таки́е не́жные щёки, таки́е краси́вые голу- 15 бы́е глаза́ и тако́е ми́лое выраже́ние лица́, что с не́й всегда́ быва́ет прия́тно встреча́ться.

Н.Н. Я с ва́ми вполне́ согла́сна, но не зна́ю, согла́сен ли с на́ми му́ж Людми́лы Никола́евны. Говоря́т, что до́ма она́ совсе́м не така́я, что она́ про́сто чёрт в ю́бке (дья́вол в ю́бке). 20

М.И. Да́, я то́же ко́е-что слы́шала об э́том. Я слы́шала, что её му́ж о́чень не́жный и ми́лый, но́ что она́ с ни́м ча́сто ссо́рится. Не зна́ю то́лько почему́. Кста́ти, говоря́т, что она́ о́чень похо́жа на свою́ ма́ть.

Н.Н. На э́ту худу́ю длиннон́осую стару́ху в чёрных очка́х и с огро́мными ко́льцами на па́льцах?

М.И. Да́, на неё. Эта стару́ха о́чень несимпати́чная же́нщина. Она́ всегда́ лю́бит критикова́ть все́х и никогда́ ни о ко́м не говори́т ничего́ хоро́шего.

Н.Н. Ах, э́то та́к пло́хо. Я не люблю́ таки́х же́нщин. Я никогда́ никого́ не критику́ю.

М.И. И я то́же. А зна́ете вы́ её сы́на, э́того бледноли́цего ю́ношу в очка́х с бородо́й и дли́нным но́сом. По-мо́ему, о́н о́чень у́мный молодо́й челове́к.

Н.Н. Да́, мо́жет бы́ть, но е́сли о́н похо́ж на свою́ ма́ть, то вря́д ли э́то та́к. Ведь она́ о́чень глупа́.

М.И. А заме́тили ли вы́ ка́к о́н бы́л оде́т вчера́? На нём бы́л тако́й я́ркий га́лстук и таки́е крича́щие носки́, что я про́сто была́ в у́жасе.

Н.Н. О да́, э́то бы́ло ужа́сно.

Numerous adjectives are formed by adding adjectival endings to certain roots denoting parts of the body and prefixing an adjectival root or the preposition **без-** plus **-о-**. The meanings of the adjectives below will be clear, if the component parts are known.

желтоли́цый, красноли́цый, круглоли́цый; черноволо́сый, безволо́сый; низколо́бый; синегла́зый, голубогла́зый, быстрогла́зый, одногла́зый, безгла́зый; краснощёкий, полнощёкий; широкопле́чий; седоборо́дый; редкозу́бый; безру́кий; толстоно́гий

СЛОВА́РЬ

бле́дн-о-ли́ц-ый pale-faced
бо́лт-ов-н-я́ chatter, gossip
борода́ *S nom pl acc sg* beard
ведь after all III.3
вря́д ли hardly, scarcely, I doubt . . .
вы-раж-е́н-и-е expression; *cf.* вы́разить –
    выража́ют
га́лстук necktie
глу́п-ый stupid, foolish
губа́ *S nom pl* lip
дли́нн-о-но́с-ый long-nosed

дья́вол devil
едва́ (ли) hardly, scarcely
инжене́р engineer
ко́е-что́ something, a little VIII.4
коль-/ц-о́ *S pl (gen* коле́ц) ring
крич-а́-щ-ий *part <* крич-а́-ть shout
кру́г-л-ый round
к-ста́т-и СТАН by the way; to the point
ло́б/б (на лбу́) forehead
ми́л-ый nice, sweet, dear
не́ж-н-ый tender, loving; delicate

нóс (на носу́) *E pl* nose
нос-/ó/к sock
оч-к-й (*gen pl* очкóв) (eye)glasses; в —áх
  with glasses on
пáл/е/ц (*gen* пáльца) finger
плáть-е (*gen pl* плáтьев) dress
плеч-ó *S* (*nom pl*/ плéчи) shoulder
пóлн-ый full; stout, plump
по-хóж-ий на *когó/чтó* like R9.E
прáв-ый right
раз-**говóр** conversation *cf.* разговáривают
рóст growth, increase; height; —ом in
  height; (не)высóкого —а (not) tall;
  ни́зкого —а short
сед-óй gray(-haired)

серьёз-/н-ый serious
симпати́ч-/н-ый sympathetic
со-**глáс**-/н-ый с *кéм/чéм* in agreement with
с-**покóй**-/н-ый quiet, calm
стар-ýх-а old woman
тём-/**н**-ый dark
тóлст-ый thick, fat
ýх-о *E pl obl* (*pl* ýши, ушéй, ушáм) ear
худ-óй (*comp* худéе) thin
чёрт *E pl obl* (*pl* чéрти) devil CL3.6
шля́п-а hat
щёк-á *S nom pl acc sg* cheek
ю́б-к-а skirt
ю́н-ош-а *M* (*gen pl* ю́ношей) youth
я́р-/к-ий bright

ГЛАГÓЛЫ

критик-овá-ть criticize
за-**мéт**-и-ть – замечáют notice, remark
  n замéт/ка note; замечáние remark

(по)-с-**сóр**-и-ть-ся quarrel
  n ссóра

CONVERSATION LESSONS 3 TO 5

Conversation Lessons 3 to 5 comprise a playlet entitled «Я хочу́ уви́деть Кра́сную пло́щадь,» consisting of two acts and a conclusion. Act 1 (Акт пе́рвый) is the text for CL3, Act 2 (Акт второ́й) the text for CL4, and the Conclusion (Заключе́ние) the text for CL5. The vocabulary for these lessons follows CL5.

я́ хочу́ уви́деть кра́сную пло́щадь

Пье́са в дву́х а́ктах с заключе́нием (Автор предпочита́ет оста́ться неизве́стным)

Де́йствующие ли́ца: америка́нский тури́ст Бра́ун: Б
советский ги́д (Интури́ста) Соколо́в: С
медсестра́: МС

CONVERSATION LESSON
3

Я́ ХОЧУ́ УВИ́ДЕТЬ КРА́СНУЮ ПЛО́ЩАДЬ

Акт пе́рвый

Америка́нский тури́ст Бра́ун всю́ жи́знь слы́шал о Кра́сной пло́щади, всю́ жи́знь чита́л о то́м, ка́к по Кра́сной пло́щади прохо́дят больши́е та́нки и марширу́ют солда́ты. Он стра́стно хо́чет посети́ть изве́стные достопримеча́тельности, хра́м Васи́лия Блаже́нного, зда́ние Истори́ческого музе́я, Госуда́рственный универса́льный магази́н (ГУМ), мавзоле́й Ле́нина. В Кремле́ он наме́рен основа́тельно осмотре́ть ба́шни, дре́вние собо́ры, зда́ние прави́тельства, зда́ние Прези́диума Верхо́вного Сове́та СССР. Но́, бо́льше всего́, о́н хо́чет уви́деть огро́мные кра́сные плака́ты, кото́рые вися́т на стена́х Кремля́. 5

Но в де́нь назна́ченного посеще́ния Кра́сной пло́щади Бра́ун лежи́т на спине́ в посте́ли. Не хо́чется встава́ть. Он **чу́вствует себя́**[1] ужа́сно. У него́ боли́т всё те́ло с головы́ до но́г. Он смо́трит на часы́. Бо́же мо́й, уже́ де́вять часо́в! Кто́-то стучи́т в две́рь. Должно́ быть, Соколо́в, его́ ги́д из Интури́ста. 10

С. Здра́вствуйте, ми́стер Бра́ун. Ещё не вста́ли? Хорошо́ вы́ вы́спались? 15

Б. Да́, спаси́бо. Но я́ проспа́л, извини́те меня́!

С. Ничего́. Когда́ бу́дете гото́вы, пое́дем на Кра́сную пло́щадь. Пого́да сего́дня прекра́сная. Ка́к ва́ше здоро́вье?

Б. Я бою́сь, что я́ чём-то **заболе́л.**[2] Я вчера́ ве́чером просиде́л це́лый ча́с в холо́дной ва́нне и простуди́лся. У меня́ на́сморк и ка́шель. 20

С. Така́я боле́знь ско́ро пройдёт. Полежи́те, прими́те лека́рство. Вы́ через де́нь попра́витесь.

303

Б.   Ту́т[3] де́ло не в на́сморке. Я вообще́ ча́сто простужа́юсь. Но́ тепе́рь у
      меня́ боля́т го́рло, гру́дь, голова́, у́ши, сло́вом, всё те́ло.

25 С.   Зна́чит, ва́м ну́жно серьёзно лечи́ться. Я позову́ **врача́**.[4] Где́ телефо́н?
      (*Поднима́ет телефо́нную тру́бку и набира́ет но́мер. Отвеча́ет меди-
      ци́нская сестра́ из городско́й больни́цы* **и́мени В. И. Ле́нина**.)[5]

    МС.   Говори́т городска́я больни́ца и́мени Ле́нина.

    С.   Я звоню́ из гости́ницы Украи́ны. Здесь заболе́л оди́н америка́нский
30   тури́ст.

    МС.   Давно́ ли о́н боле́ет?

    С.   Не́т, вчера́ ве́чером бы́л ещё здоро́в.

    МС.   Че́м о́н бо́лен? Кака́я у него́ температу́ра?

    С.   Ка́к мне зна́ть кака́я у него́ температу́ра? Ведь у меня́ не́т термо́метра.

35 МС.   Вы́ должны́ бы бы́ли име́ть при себе́ термо́метр. А скажи́те, како́й у
      него́ пу́льс. Са́ми пощу́пайте.

    С.   **Чёрт возьми́!**[6] Я не вра́ч! Я не уме́ю счита́ть пу́льса!

    МС.   Ах, **бо́же мо́й**.[7] А ка́к се́рдце?

    С.   Се́рдце **бьётся**.

40 МС.   Коне́чно, бьётся. У на́с все́х се́рдце бьётся. Я ту́т ничего́ не понима́ю.
      Привези́те его́ сюда́ в больни́цу. Здесь его́ и бу́дем лечи́ть, пока́ не
      вы́лечим.

    С.   Хорошо́, привезём. И я́ ту́т ни черта́ не понима́ю.

По доро́ге в больни́цу Бра́ун и Соколо́в разгова́ривают о боле́знях и о
45 *достопримеча́тельностях Москвы́.*

    1. **(По)чу́вствовать себя́** is quite unique in its use of transitive verb plus
себя́ to convey a nontransitive meaning. (Cf. X.B.)
    2. "I'm sick" may be:

Я бо́лен	'I'm sick'	short form of боль/но́й 'sick'
Я боле́ю	'I'm ailing'	боле́ют (*impf only*) 'be sick, ail'
Я заболе́л	'I have become ill'	заболе́ют/заболева́ют 'become ill'

"With X" is expressed by the instrumental of X (*NB* by itself, not **c** *inst*).
    Do not confuse **боле́ют** and **заболе́ют** – **заболева́ют** *inst* with **боле́ть** and
заболе́ть – **заболева́ют** with **y** *gen* of person (*3 pers only*) 'hurt,' which have to
do with *pain* rather than illness. Examples of both groups:

Мо́я жена́ заболе́ла гри́ппом.	My wife has fallen ill with the grippe.
В про́шлом году́ я́ ча́сто заболева́л.	Last year I used to get sick a lot.
Её му́ж боле́ет (бо́лен) уже́ не́-сколько ле́т.	Her husband has been ill for several years.

У меня́ боли́т голова́.	My head aches (hurts).
У меня́ у́ши заболе́ли.	My ears began to ache.
У меня́ живо́т всё вре́мя боле́л.	My stomach hurt the whole time.

"Sick person, patient" is **больно́й** (*sub adj*). Compare:

Мо́й оте́ц бо́лен.	My father is sick.
Мо́й оте́ц больно́й.	My father is a sick man.

3. Both **ту́т** and **та́м**, in addition to their primary meanings, may express more abstract concepts. **Ту́т** may mean "in *this* case, under *these* circumstances," and, sometimes, "then" (**зде́сь**, less often, also may have these meanings). **Та́м** may mean "in *that* case, under *those* circumstances":

Что́ мы́ должны́ ту́т сде́лать?	What should we do in this case?
Мы́ ве́село разгова́ривали. А ту́т и оте́ц с ма́терью пришли́.	We were conversing gaily. And then father and mother came.
Что́ он та́м сде́лает?	What will he do under those conditions?

4. The correct word for "doctor" when the meaning is "physician" is **вра́ч**. **До́ктор**, strictly speaking, refers to the academic degree or, more commonly, to the holder of that degree; however, it may mean "physician" colloquially. With specialties or official titles only **вра́ч** may be used: **де́тский вра́ч** 'children's doctor," **глазно́й вра́ч** 'eye doctor.' "Dentist" is **зубно́й вра́ч**. As in English, however, the Latin or Greek term may be preferred: **педиа́тр, окули́ст, данти́ст**—'pediatrician,' 'oculist,' 'dentist.'

5. The "(А. Р.) Chekhov Municipal Hospital" would be **городска́я больни́ца и́мени (А. П.) Че́хова**. How would one designate the V. I. Lenin Municipal Library (in Moscow)?

6. **Чёрт**, *gen* **чёрта**, *pl* **че́рти, черте́й** 'devil, deuce' is used in some mild oaths; for example:

Чёрт с ни́м!	The hell with him!
Иди́ к чёрту!	Go to hell!
Чёрт возьми́!	Damn!
Како́го чёрта он та́м де́лает?	What the devil is he doing there?

Note the special end-stressed form in "don't X a damn thing."

Я ни черта́ не понима́ю/не ви́жу.	I don't understand/see a damn thing.

7. The form **Бо́же** in **Бо́же мо́й** 'My God!' (**бо́г** 'god') is a vestige of the old *vocative*, which comprised a set of forms used in direct address.

CONVERSATION LESSON
4

Об у́треннем туале́те

Я́ ХОЧУ́ УВИ́ДЕТЬ КРА́СНУЮ ПЛО́ЩАДЬ

Акт второ́й

Америка́нский тури́ст Бра́ун *попра́вился*[1] *и верну́лся* в гости́ницу. При-
е́хавши, о́н сра́зу *разде́лся* и наде́л се́рый хала́т и ночны́е ту́фли. Хотя́ о́н и
бы́л здоро́в, но чу́вствовал себя́ ещё сла́бым. Со́н – по ста́рой америка́н-
ской посло́вице — лу́чше вся́кого лека́рства. Бра́ун бро́сился на крова́ть и
5 *засну́л* глубо́ким сно́м. Он кре́пко спа́л и никаки́х сно́в не ви́дел.

На друго́е у́тро о́н *проснулся* в полови́не седьмо́го. Или, точне́е, его́
разбуди́л Ги́мн Сове́тского Сою́за, кото́рый ка́ждое у́тро гро́мко *раздаётся*
по ра́дио и бу́дит ка́ждого, кто́ не вы́ключил своего́ радиоаппара́та. Бра́ун
бы́стро встаёт и идёт в ва́нную. Ещё боя́сь холо́дной воды́, о́н **ду́мает**[2] то́ль-
10 ко *побри́ться* и *умы́ться*. Но́, сла́ва Бо́гу, **на э́тот ра́з**[3] из кра́на *льётся*
горя́чая вода́. С ра́достным кри́ком о́н впры́гивает в ва́нну. До́лго, до́лго
о́н сиди́т и *мо́ется*, да́же поёт ру́сские пе́сни. Кака́я ро́скошь!

> Не слышны́ в саду́ да́же шо́рохи
> Всё здесь за́мерло до утра́.
> 15 Если б зна́ли вы́, ка́к мне́ доро́ги
> Подмоско́вные вечера́!

Стуча́т в две́рь. Должно́ быть, Соколо́в.

С. (*Про себя́*) Како́го чёрта о́н та́м де́лает? Ра́зве э́то му́зыка? Невозмо́жно.

Б. Войди́те, пожа́луйста. Я в ва́нной, ещё *мо́юсь*. Сейча́с выхожу́. Бо́же
20 мо́й, ка́к вре́мя лети́т! Ка́к э́то вы́ всегда́ во́время прихо́дите?

С. Я берегу́ своё вре́мя и чужо́е. (*Б выхо́дит из ва́нной, на нём то́лько ни́жнее*

306

бельё, рубáшка и корúчневые тýфли.) Здрáвствуйте, óчень рáд вáс вúдеть ужé здорóвым.

Б. Извинúте, что я́ не одéт. Сейчáс *одéнусь.* (*Надевáет брю́ки и пиджáк. Снимáет тýфли и надевáет ботúнки.*)   25

С. Кáк э́тот костю́м вáм к лицý. Я́ óчень люблю́ э́тот тёмно-зелёный цвéт. Совéтую вáм вы́брать вóт э́тот гáлсутк.

Б. Спасúбо, óн отлúчно подхóдит к э́тому костю́му.

С. Дéло в тóм, что у меня́ хорóший вкýс насчёт одéжды. Дáже женá говорúт, что хорóший. Я́ выбирáю для неё всé плáтья, а иногдá и ю́бки и   30 блýзки.

Б. Кáк интерéсно. Моя́ женá óчень не **лю́бит когдá**[4] я́ говорю́ об её одéжде. *Обижáется.* Нý, ничегó. Я́ дóлжен ещё вы́чистить зýбы и *причесáться;* тогдá и бýду готóв.

С. Дá, тогдá и поéдем на Крáсную плóщадь.   35

По дорóге на Крáсную плóщадь Брáун и Соколóв разговáривают об одéжде и о рýсских и совéтских пéснях.

Подмосковные Вечерá[1]

Рéчка *двúжется* и не *двúжется*	А рассвéт ужé всё замéтнее
Вся́ из лýнного серебрá.	Тáк, пожáлуйста, бýдь добрá,
Пéсня *слы́шится* и не *слы́шится*	Не забýдь и ты́ э́ти лéтние
В э́ти тúхие вечерá.	Подмоскóвные вечерá . . .

40

1. For a full discussion of **ся** verbs see Lesson X. Act II has several "true" reflexive **ся** verbs (in which the subject is the object of the action); e.g. **раздéнутся – раздевáются, (по)брéются**, and others, and a number of *general* intransitive **ся** verbs; e.g. **попрáвиться – поправля́ются, вéрнуться – возвращáются**. There is also an instance of two verbs with opposite but parallel meanings, where one of these verbs is a **ся** verb and the other is not:

просы́нуться – просыпáются   wake up
засы́нуть – засыпáют   go to sleep

Such an instance illustrates the general nature of **ся**; the only meaning common to all **ся** verbs is *intransitivity*. (NOTE: All **ся** verbs in the text are italicized.)

2. **Дýмают** (*impf only*) plus infinitive may mean "intend to, plan to":

Чтó вы́ дýмаете дéлать?	What do you intend to do?
Я́ дýмаю поступúть в университéт.	I am planning to enter the university.
Я́ не дýмаю говорúть с нúм.	I don't intend to speak with him.

[1] Two more verses; the first verse is given above.

3. "This time (right now)" is often **на э́тот ра́з**. Otherwise, **ра́з** takes **в**; e.g. **в бу́дущий ра́з, в друго́й ра́з, в пе́рвый ра́з**, or **в э́тот ра́з** '(at) *that* time":

В э́тот ра́з мы́ поступи́ли ина́че.	That time we acted differently.

4. To "like it when (that) somebody (does something)" is **люби́ть** plus **когда́** or **что́бы** with the past tense (the latter primarily with a negative construction):

Я люблю́ когда́ игра́ют на роя́ле.	I like to hear the piano played.
Я не люблю́, когда́ хо́дят (что́бы ходи́ли) ко мне́ с про́сьбами.	I don't like it when people come to me with requests.

CONVERSATION LESSON
5

Я́ ХОЧУ́ УВИ́ДЕТЬ КРА́СНУЮ ПЛО́ЩАДЬ
Заключе́ние

Прие́хавши на Кра́сную пло́щадь, Бра́ун нема́ло удивлён, что она́, в о́бщем, оказа́лась дово́льно пусто́й. **Не то́, что**[1] не́т люде́й — лю́ди е́сть, наприме́р, перед ле́нинским мавзоле́ем стои́т дли́нная о́чередь, — но́ шу́ма не́т, пра́здничная атмосфе́ра во́все отсу́тствует. Бра́ун **не то́, что**[1] ожида́л та́нков — о́н прекра́сно зна́ет, что они́ прохо́дят по пло́щади то́лько пе́рвого ма́я и седьмо́го ноября́ — но́ всё-таки ему́ ка́жется, что чего́-то не хвата́ет. Вдру́г ему́ прихо́дит в го́лову (на у́м), чего́ и́менно не хвата́ет. На стена́х, окружа́ющих пло́щадь, не́т ни одного́ кра́сного плака́та. Но́ **ма́ло того́**,[2] на Кра́сной пло́щади вообще́ не́т ничего́ кра́сного. Куда́ ни взгля́нешь — всё се́рое, кори́чневое. Еди́нственное, что́ мо́жно бы бы́ло **счита́ть**[3] чуть-чу́ть кра́сным — э́то сте́ны дре́внего Кремля́ — **и то́**[4] они́ о́чень тёмного ржа́вого **цве́та**.[5] Бра́ун не́сколько разочаро́ван, но́ о́н дово́льно любопы́тный челове́к и **всё равно́**[6] хо́чет узна́ть, отку́да Кра́сная пло́щадь получи́ла своё назва́ние. Он обраща́ется к Соколо́ву с про́сьбой объясни́ть происхожде́ние э́того назва́ния.

Соколо́в объясни́л ему́, что кра́сные плака́ты вися́т то́лько по больши́м торже́ственным пра́здникам. А **что́ каса́ется**[7] происхожде́ния назва́ния, то́ Кра́сная пло́щадь во́все не означа́ет пло́щадь кра́сного цве́та. В древнеру́сском, **да и**[4] в бо́льшей ча́сти совреме́нных славя́нских языко́в, «кра́сный» означа́ет «краси́вый», а в совреме́нном ру́сском языке́ э́то первонача́льное значе́ние измени́лось (хотя́ оно́ сохраня́ется в ря́де сло́в церко́внославя́нско-

5

10

15

20

309

го происхождéния; напр. *прекрáсный, красноречие*). Чéм э́то объясня́ется? Мóжет быть, рýсские лю́ди счита́ли кра́сный цвéт са́мым краси́вым.

Отвéт ги́да удовлетвори́л любопы́тство Брáуна, нó óн не мóг скры́ть своегó разочарова́ния по пóводу отсýтствии кра́сного цвéта на Кра́сной плóщади.

Москва́

Утро кра́сит нéжным свéтом
Стéны дрéвнего Кремля́,
Просыпа́ется с рассвéтом
Вся́ Совéтская земля́.
Холодóк бежи́т за вóрот,
Шýм на ýлицах **сильнéй.**[8]
С дóбрым ýтром,[9] ми́лый гóрод,
Сéрдце рóдины моéй!

Кипу́чая, могу́чая,[10]
Никéм не **победи́мая,**[11]
Страна́ моя́, Москва́ моя́, —
Ты́ са́мая **люби́мая!**[12]

1. The idea of "It isn't that . . . (but something else)" is often rendered by Russian **не тó, что** or **не тó, чтобы**:

Не тó, что нéт людéй — лю́ди éсть, . . .	It isn't that there are no people; there are people . . . (*From the text*)
Брáун не тó, что ожида́л та́нков — . . . , нó . . .	It wasn't that Brown expected tanks . . . but . . . (*From the text*)
Не тó, чтобы я́ нé был твои́м дру́гом, нó я́ прóсто не могý идти́ с ва́ми.	It isn't that I'm not your friend; I just can't go with you.
Не тó, что тяжёлого, а вообщé никакóго физи́ческого труда́ на такóм произвóдстве нéт.	It isn't that there's no heavy labor, there's no physical labor at all in such production.

2. **Ма́ло тогó** is sometimes translated as "moreover," but in addition it belittles the importance of whatever precedes it and often has a meaning close to "but that's nothing, the most (more) important thing is . . .":

. . . , нéт ни одногó кра́сного плака́та. Нó, ма́ло тогó, на Кра́сной плóщади вообщé нéт ничегó кра́сного.	. . . there isn't one red placard. But this is nothing (isn't the half of it); there isn't anything red on Red Square at all. (*From the text*)

Я да́м ва́м по́лную свобо́ду. Ма́ло того́, я скажу́, чтобы ва́м бо́льше не меша́ли.	I will give you full freedom. Moreover (and more important), I'll tell people not to disturb you any more.

3. For a discussion of **с/о/чту́т – счита́ют** see VI.2.

4. The conjunctions **и то́**, **да и то́**, and **да и** all mean approximately "for that matter, even X (even here, even in this case, even considering this)":

Еди́нственно, что́ мо́жно бы бы́ло счита́ть чуть-чу́ть кра́сным — э́то сте́ны дре́внего Кремля́ — и то́ они́ о́чень тёмного, ржа́вого цве́та.	The only thing which could be considered even the slightest bit red is the walls of the ancient Kremlin, and even those are of a dark, rusty color. (*From the text*)
В древнеру́сском, да и в бо́льшей ча́сти совреме́нных славя́нских языко́в . . .	In Old Russian, and for that matter in most modern Slavic languages . . . (*From the text*)

5. **Цве́т, цве́та**, *pl* **цвета́** is "color." "What color is X?" is **Како́го цве́та** X? "Of a red color" is **кра́сного цве́та**, etc. **Цве́т** may mean "flower" in the sense of "bloom" (**в по́лном цвету́** 'in full flower/bloom'), but "flower" in the normal sense is **цвет/о́/к**, *pl NB* **цветы́**. Hence the plural oblique cases of "flower" and "color" are ambiguous: **цвето́в – цвета́м – цвета́ми – цвета́х**.

6. See VII.4.

7. **Косну́ться – каса́ются** *plus gen* means "touch, touch on" in both physical and abstract senses, **каса́ются**   particularly in the latter:

На́ши разгово́ры не каса́лись бу́дущего.	Our conversations didn't touch on the future.
Мне́ до́рого всё, что́ тебя́ каса́ется.	Everything which touches (concerns, has to do with) you is dear to me.

Note the expression: **Что́ каса́ется** *gen* X 'As far as X is concerned':

Что́ каса́ется меня́, (то) я согла́сен на вся́кие ме́ры, кото́рые о́н ду́мает та́м приня́ть.	As far as I am concerned, I am agreed to any measures he's planning to take in that case.

8. The simple comparative is occasionally used as an adverb with an emphatic meaning; the form is likely to be in **-ей** rather than **-ее**. The context is frequently imperative, but does not have to be:

Пиши́те ча́ще и подро́бнее о свое́й жи́зни.	Write frequently and in detail about your life. (*Emphasis—in a letter*)
Иди́ скоре́й!	Come quickly!

9. Certain greetings, welcomes, and congratulations are expressed by **c** plus the instrumental, with which we understand (or may include) the verb **поздра́вить – поздравля́ют** 'wish, congratulate':

С Рождество́м.	Merry Christmas.
С Но́вым го́дом.	Happy New Year.
Позво́льте поздра́вить ва́с с при-е́здом.	Let me welcome you here.
Они́ поздра́вили его́ с рожде́нием но́вого сы́на.	They congratulated him on the birth of a new son.
Поздравля́ю.	Congratulations.

10. **Кипу́чий** and **могу́чий** belong to a group of adjectives in **-у(ю)чий** (connected with verbs whose third plural is **-у(ю)т** and, occasionally, with verbs with third plural in **-а(я)т**); or **-а(я)чий** (connected with verbs whose third plural is **-а(я)т**). These adjectives have meanings which are similar to the corresponding participles but have become stabilized in some specific usage. Here are some examples:

могу́щий (могут)	being able to (*participle*)
могу́чий	powerful, mighty
кипя́щий (кипе́ть)	boiling (*participle*)
кипу́чий	seething, ebullient (*Note that the adjective is in* -учий *despite* -ят.)
летя́щий (лете́ть)	flying (*participle*)
летуу́чий (лету́чая ры́ба/мы́шь)	flying (fish, mouse; i.e. bat); volatile (*chemistry*) (-учий *despite* -ят)
стоя́щий (стоя́ть)	standing (*participle*)
стоя́чий (стоя́чая вода́)	standing (stagnant water)
сидя́щий (сиде́ть)	sitting (*participle*)
сидя́чий (сидя́чая жи́знь)	sitting (sedentary life)
горя́щий (горе́ть)	burning (*participle*) (*intr*)
горя́чий	hot
горю́чий (горю́чее *sub adj*)	combustible (fuel) (-ючий *despite* -ят)

Participles, of course, may also acquire certain specific meanings, in addition to their participial function; examples are:

теку́щий (тёку́т)	flowing (*participle*); *but also* current (year, affairs, events, etc.).
теку́чий	fluid (*physiol.*), fluctuating, unstable

11. There is no positive adjective corresponding to **непобеди́мый** 'invincible.' The division into **не** and **победи́мый** is due to **нике́м**.

12. **Люби́мый**, the present passive participle of **люби́ть**, may be used as an adjective in the meaning "favorite," or as a substantivized adjective meaning "loved, beloved, dear one," in addition to its participial use.

СЛОВА́РЬ

а́втор author
а́кт act (*approximately the same meanings as in English*)
атмосфе́р-а atmosphere
ба́ш/н-я (*gen pl* ба́шен) tower
бель-ё linen; washing; ни́жнее — underwear
блу́з-/к-а blouse
бо́г god; Бо́же мо́й! My God, Heavens! CL3.7
бол-е́-знь disease, illness
боль-/н-о́й, бо́лен, больна́, больно́, больны́ sick, ill CL3.2; бо́льно painful(ly)
боти́н/о/к (*gen pl* боти́нок) shoe (with laces; the type usually worn by men)
брю́к-и *pl only* (*gen pl* брю́к) trousers
ва́нн-а bathtub V.9
ва́нн-ая bathroom (room with bathtub) V.9
верх-о́в-н-ый supreme; Верхо́вный Сове́т Supreme Soviet
в-ку́с КУС¹ taste; в-ку́с-/н-ый tasty
во́все quite; — не at all
вообще́ IV.7
во́рот collar
вра́ч *E* physician CL3.4
га́лстук necktie
ги́д guide (person)
ги́мн hymn; anthem
гла́з *E pl* (*gen pl* гла́з) eye
глаз-н-о́й eye *adj*
голов-а́ *S nom pl acc sg* head; приду́т – приходи́ть *кому́* в —у come into one's head
го́рл-о throat
го́род-ск-о́й municipal, city *adj*
гор-я́ч-ий hot; ardent
гри́пп (в гриппу́) grippe

гру́дь (в груди́) *E pl obl* breast, chest
да: да и, да и то́ CL5.4
де́йствующие ли́ца cast of characters
де́ло в чём IV.A
дл-и́н-/н-ый long (measure); lengthy
досто-при-меч-а́-тель-н-ость thing/place worthy of interest; *pl* sights (of a city, etc.)
дре́в-н-ий old, ancient
еди́н-ств-ен/н-ый (the) only
жив-о́т stomach
за-ме́т-/н-ый noticeable
здоро́в-ый (*comp* здорове́е) healthy
здоро́вь-е health
зем/л-я́ *S pl* (*exc gen* земе́ль) *acc sg* earth, land, ground
зу́б *E pl obl* tooth
зуб-н-о́й dental, tooth *adj*
и́мя: и́мени CL3.5
и́менно namely, precisely, just: Именно. That is just it. Precisely.
Интури́ст *short for* Иностра́нный тури́ст state bureau for foreign travel
и то́ CL5.4
ка́ш/е/ль *M* cough
кип-у́ч-ий seething CL5.10
кор-и́ч-н-ев-ый brown
костю́м suit
кра́н faucet
крас-н-о-ре́ч-и-е eloquence
креп-/к-ий strong, firm, robust
кри́к shout, cry
крова́ть bed(stead), bed without bedclothes (*but may also refer to a bed with clothes, which is* посте́ль)
лек-а́р-ств-о (a) medicine, remedy
лиц-о́ *S pl* face; personage; *see also* дей-

ствующие ли́ца
Это ва́м к —у́. That becomes you.

лун-а́ *S pl* moon

лу́н-н-ый lunar, moon *adj*

люб-и́м-ый CL5.12

люб-о-пы́т-/н-ый curious (both senses)

люб-о-пы́т-ств-о curiosity

мавзоле́й mausoleum

ма́ло того́ CL5.2

медици́н-ск-ая сёстр-а́ (медсестра́) nurse

мог-у́ч-ий powerful CL5.10

му́зык-а music

на-ме́р-ен-н-ый intentional; я наме́рен *inf*
    I intend to . . .

на́-сморк head cold; a more general cold =
    про-сту́д-а

не́ж-/н-ый tender, delicate (of substance,
    taste, health, etc.); loving

не-по-бед-и́м-ый invincible CL5.11

не то́, что CL5.1

ни́ж-н-ий lower; *see* бельё

но́мер *E pl* -а́ number; size; hotel room

ноч-н-о́й nocturnal, night *adj*

о́бщ-ий: в о́бщем IV. 7

о-де́жд-а clothes, clothing

основ-а́-тель-/н-ый thorough, substantial;
    well-grounded

от-ли́ч-/н-ый excellent; сдать – сдава́ть
    экза́мен на отли́чно pass examination
    with an "excellent"

от-су́т-ств-и-е absence

о́-чередь *E pl obl* line; turn

пара́д-н-ый parade *adj*

перв-о-нача́ль-н-ый Ч/Н primary; original,
    initial

пе́-сн-я ПЕЙ (*gen pl* пе́сен) song

пиджа́к jacket, (suit) coat

плака́т placard, poster

пла́ть-е (*gen pl* пла́тьев) dress

пло́щ-адь *E pl obl* (city) square

под-моско́в-н-ый (situated) near Moscow

по-сте́ль bedclothes, bed with clothes; *cf.*
    крова́ть

пра́зд-ник holiday, festive occasion, cele-
    bration

пра́зд-нич-н-ый holiday *adj*, festive

прези́диум presidium

при-су́т-ств-и-е presence

про́сь-б-а request, favor; *cf.* (по)проси́ть

пу́льс pulse

пье́с-а (stage) play

пуст-о́й empty

равно́: всё равно́ VII.4

ра́дио *N indecl* radio

радиоаппара́т radio (set)

ра́д-ост-/н-ый glad, joyous

раз РАЗ[1]: на э́тот ра́з CL4.3

рас-све́т dawn, daybreak; на рассве́те at
    (the) dawn *also fig*

рж-а́в-ый rusty, rust-colored

Рожд-е-ств-о́ Christmas

ро́скошь luxury

руба́ш-/к-а shirt

се́рд-/ц-е *E pl* (*gen pl* серде́ц) heart

серебр-о́ silver

серьёз-/н-ый serious

си́ль-/н-ый strong

сла́б-ый weak

сла́в-а *кому́/чему́* glory to

слы́ш-/н-ый audible

со-бо́р cathedral; council, synod

со-ве́т council; Soviet; advice

со-време́н-/н-ый modern, contemporary

спин-а́ *S pl acc sg* back

с/о́/н *С/П* sleep; dream

сра́зу immediately

стра́ст-/н-ый СТРАД-т passionate

стра́сть СТРАД-т *E pl obl* passion

та́нк tank (military)

те́л-о *E pl* body

тём-/н-ый dark; темно́ it is dark

температу́р-а temperature

термо́метр thermometer

ти́х-ий quiet, still; slow

торж-е́-ств-ен/н-ый grand, festive, auspi-
    cious, solemn

тру́б-/к-а tube, pipe; телефо́нная — tele-
    phone receiver

тури́ст tourist

ту́ф/л-я (*gen pl* ту́фель) low shoe without
    laces; slipper, loafer

у́м *E* mind, wit, intellect; приду́т – приходить *кому́* на — come into one's head

универса́ль-/н-ый universal

хала́т bathrobe, dressing gown

хо́лод/о́/к chill, chilly air

хра́м temple

цве́т *E pl* -á color CL5.5

цвет/о́/к (*nom pl* цветы́) flower CL5.5

чёрт *E pl obl* (*nom pl* че́рти, *gen pl* черте́й) devil CL3.6

чуж-о́й somebody else's; alien

чуть–чу́ть the slightest bit

шо́рох rustle

шу́м noise, sound

ю́б-/к-а skirt

ГЛАГО́ЛЫ

би́й-ут-ся beat *intr* X.A

берёг-у́т keep, save, watch, guard

бол-é-ть: за-бол-é-ть – заболева́ют CL3.2

бол-éй-ут: за-бол-éй-ут – заболева́ют CL3.2

   n заболева́ние

на-б/р-а-ть (наберу́т) – набира́ют но́мер dial number

(по)-бре́й-ут (бри́ть) shave *tr*; —ся shave oneself CL4.1

   n бритьё

брóс-и-ть – броса́ют throw; —ся throw oneself

(раз)-бу́д-й-ть wake (up) *tr*

оби́д-е-ть – обижа́ют об-ВИД offend, insult; —ся be/get offended

   n оби́да

из-ви́н-й-ть – извиня́ют *кого́* за *что́ or кому́ что́* excuse; —ся excuse oneself

   n извине́ние

вис-é-ть hang *intr*

об-рат-й́-ть-ся – обраща́ются об-ВРАТ к *кому́/чему́* turn/apply to; address

   n обраще́ние

вз-гля́д-ну-ть – взгля́дывают на *кого́/что́* look at, glance at

   n взгля́д look; view, opinion

раз-гова́р-ивай-ут converse

раз-да-ть-ся – раздава́ться resound, be heard

дви́г-ну-ть-ся – дви́гаются move *intr*

   n движе́ние

на-де́н-ут – надева́ют put on (clothes, etc.)

о-де́н-ут – одева́ют dress *tr*; —ся get dressed, dress oneself CL4.1

раз-де́н-ут – раздева́ют undress *tr*; —ся get undressed, undress oneself CL4.1

у-ди́в-й-ть – удивля́ют surprise; —ся *чему́* be surprised at

   n удивле́ние

у-до́в/л-е-твор-й-ть – удовлетворя́ют satisfy

   n удовлетворе́ние

ду́м-ай-ут CL4.2

о-жид-а́й-ут *кого́/чего́ or кого́/что́* expect

   n ожида́ние

на-зв-а-ть(назову́т) – называ́ют call, name

   n назва́ние name, appellation, title (of a book)

по-здра́в-и-ть – поздравля́ют *кого́* с *чем* congratulate CL5.9

   n поздравле́ние

на-знáч-и-ть – назнача́ют assign, appoint, fix

   n назначе́ние

о-знач-а́й-ут mean, signify

под-/о/йд-у́т – подходить к *кому́/чему́* come up to, approach; — *кому́/к чему́* suit, fit, be suitable for

   n подхо́д

про-из-/о/йд-у́т – происходить take place, happen; — *отку́да* come from

   n происхожде́ние origin, birth, extraction

по́д-ним-ут – поднима́ют raise, lift; —ся go up, ascend, rise

   n подня́тие, подъём

с-ним-ут – снима́ют take down; take away; take off (clothes); photograph

n сня́тие, сни́м/о/к photograph
кас-а́й-ут-ся: *see* кос-ну́-ть-ся
вы́-клю́ч-и-ть – выключа́ют turn off, switch off
   n выключе́ние
за-клю́ч-и́-ть – заключа́ют conclude; enclose, imprison
   n заключе́ние; приду́т – приходи́ть к заключе́нию come to a conclusion
кос-ну́-ть-ся – каса́ются CL5.7
(по)-кра́с-и-ть paint, dye; *I only* adorn
   n кра́шение
с-кро́й-ут – скрыва́ют conceal, hide *tr*; —ся hide/conceal oneself
о-круж-и́-ть – окружа́ют surround, encircle
   n окруже́ние
леч-и́-ть treat, attempt to cure; —ся be treated
   n лече́ние (medical)
вы́-леч-и-ть – выле́чивают *кого́* от *чего́* cure; —ся от be cured of; recover from
лий-ут pour *tr and colloq intr*; —ся flow, pour *intr*
люб-и́-м-ый CL5.12
марш-ир-ова́-ть march
   n марширова́ние
из-мен-и́-ть – изменя́ют change *tr*; —ся change *intr*
   n измене́ние
(вы́)-мой-ут – вымыва́ют wash, bathe *tr*; —ся wash/bathe oneself CL4.1
   n мытьё
у-мой-ут – умыва́ют wash face and hands *tr*; —ся wash one's own face and hands CL4.1
за́-мр-ут – замира́ют stop, die down (of noise, activity, etc.)
   n замира́ние
(с)-пой-ут (петь) sing
   n пе́ние
по-пра́в-и-ть – поправля́ют correct, repair; —ся recover, get well; correct oneself
в-пры́г-ну-ть – впры́гивают *куда́* jump
род-и́-ть-ся – рожда́ются be born

n рожде́ние; де́нь рожде́ния birthday
про-сид-е́-ть – проси́живают sit (for a certain period)
о-смотр-е́-ть – осма́тривают examine, inspect, look at (sights of a city)
   n осмо́тр inspection, survey
вы́-сп-а-ть-ся – высыпа́ются get a good rest, sleep oneself out
про-сп-а-ть-ся – просыпа́ются oversleep, sleep through
за-сп-ну́-ть – заспыпа́ют go to sleep CL4.1
про-сп-ну́-ть-ся – просыпа́ются wake up *intr* CL4.1
про-студ-и-ть-ся – простужа́ются catch a cold
хват-и́-ть – хвата́ет *imps кого́/чего́ кому́* suffice:
   Ему́ хвати́ло вре́мени. He had enough time.
   Хва́тит. That's (will be) enough.
   Этого ещё не хвата́ло. That's all we needed. That's the last straw.
происхожде́ние: *see* про-из-/о/йд-у́т – происходи́ть
раз-о-ча́р-ова́-ть – разочаро́вывают disappoint; —ся в *ком/чём* be disappointed in
   n разочарова́ние
при-чёс-а-ть(приче́шут) – причёсывают comb, brush; —ся comb/brush oneself CL4.1
   n причёс/ка brushing; coiffure
(вы́)-чи́ст-и-ть зу́бы brush teeth
чи́ст-и-ть clean
   n чи́ст/ка cleaning; purge
пред-по-чт-у́т (предпоче́сть, -чёл, -чла́, -чли́) – предпочита́ют *кого́/что́ кому́/чему́* prefer X to Y
с/о/-чт-у́т (счесть: счёл, сочла́, сочли́) – счита́ют *кого́/что́ ке́м/че́м* consider X as (to be) Y VI. 2
(по)-чу́в-ств-ова-ть feel (mentally) *tr*; —себя́ feel *adv or adj in inst* CL3.1
(по)-щу́п-ай-ут touch, feel *tr*

APPENDIX

GENITIVE:

Я получи́л пи́сьма от	ста́	сорока́	одного́	но́вого	студе́нта
			одно́й	но́вой	студе́нтки
			дву́х		
	двухсо́т	пяти́десяти	трёх	но́вых	студе́нтов
			четырёх		
	пятисо́т	девяно́ста	пяти́		студе́нток
			восьми́		
			оди́ннадцати		

PREPOSITIONAL:

Де́ло идёт о (об)	ста́	сорока́	одно́м	но́вом	студе́нте
			одно́й	но́вой	студе́нтке
			дву́х		
	двухста́х	пяти́десяти	трёх	но́вых	студе́нтах
			четырёх		
	пятиста́х	девяно́ста	пяти́		студе́нтках
			восьми́		
			оди́ннадцати		

DATIVE:

Показа́ли э́то	ста́	сорока́	одному́	но́вому	студе́нту
			одно́й	но́вой	студе́нтке
			дву́м		
	двумста́м	пяти́десяти	трём	но́вым	студе́нтам
			четырём		
	пятиста́м	девяно́ста	пяти́		студе́нткам
			восьми́		
			оди́ннадцати		

INSTRUMENTAL:

Я говорю́ с (со)	ста́	сорока́	одни́м	но́вым	студе́нтом
			одно́й	но́вой	студе́нткой
			двумя́		
	двумяста́ми	пятью́десятью	тремя́	но́выми	студе́нтами
			четырьмя́		
	пятьюста́ми	девяно́ста	пятью́		студе́нтками
			восьмью́[1]		
			оди́ннадцатью		

[1] Ог восемью́.

A. THE OBLIQUE CASES OF THE CARDINAL NUMERALS

The table opposite summarizes the oblique cases of the cardinal numerals.
Note that the only numbers to assume a genitive form in the animate accusative are 2, 3, and 4, when they stand alone; e.g. **Я ви́дел дву́х студе́нтов.** When they are the last digits of a longer number, the accusative rather than the genitive is used; e.g. **Я ви́дел сто́ три́дцать два студе́нта.**

In using longer numbers, Russians make an effort to avoid the oblique cases; e.g. instead of **Он говори́л с двумяста́ми шестью́десятью тремя́ профессо́рами,** they might be inclined to say something like **Бы́ло две́сти шестьдеся́т три профе́ссора. Я говори́л со все́ми и́ми.** However, there are instances where the oblique forms cannot reasonably be avoided, and they are definitely used in formal speech (e.g. on the radio) or when numerals are spelled out in writing, and under such conditions the rules are carefully observed.

B. THE COLLECTIVE NUMERALS

The collective numerals are decreasing in importance in Russian, but certain usages remain.

Forms. The nominative/inanimate accusative forms of the collectives are:

дво́е, тро́е, че́тверо, пя́теро, ше́стеро, се́меро, во́сьмеро, де́вятеро, де́сятеро

They take the *genitive plural*. Collectives above 10 built with **ер** are occasionally found in colloquial speech, but we may disregard them.

The oblique cases of the collectives are the following:

двоих	троих	четверых	пятерых	Others like пятеро: шестерых,
двоим	троим	четверым	пятерым	семерым, восьмерыми
двоими	троими	четверыми	пятерыми	

Usage. 1. The collectives up to four *must* be used with nouns which have no singular form. From five on, the collective or cardinal may be used:

одни часы	one watch	двое часов	two watches
одни ножницы	one pair of scissors	четверо ножниц	four pairs of scissors
одни ворота	one gate	шестеро/шесть ворот	six gates
одни сутки	one day (24 hours)	пятеро/пять суток	five days

For the oblique cases, however, the cardinals are more usual with inanimate and feminine animate nouns, the collectives with masculine animate nouns: **с** *двумя* **ножницами, менее** *пяти* **суток, на** *шести* **воротах, с** *тремя* **студентками; с** *троими* **студентами.**

2. Collectives *may* be used for the plural of paired objects:

двое сапог (*zero gen pl* of сапог *M E*)   two pairs of boots
трое перчаток (перчат/ка)   three pairs of gloves

However, it is simpler and more usual to use **пара** 'pair' plus the genitive plural: **две пары сапог, три пары перчаток.**

3. The collectives *may* be used with nouns denoting *male* persons, including the plural nouns **люди** and **дети**, but cardinals are also possible:

двое людей		два человека
двое детей	*or*	два ребёнка
двое братьев		два брата

Usage varies with specific words and contexts, but the collectives seem to be receding. This is particularly true with the oblique cases:

четырёх детей	*more usual than*	четверых детей
с тремя товарищами	*more usual than*	с троими товарищами, etc.

Note that the collective may be used without the noun:

Двое пришли.   Two came.

4. The collectives may be used with personal pronouns. Note particularly the following types:

Нас было трое.   There were three of us.
Четверо их приехали на ночь.   Four of them came for the night.

The oblique forms are quite common here:

Мы́ встре́тили и́х **трои́х**.	We met the three of them.
Cf. Мы́ встре́тили **трёх** това́рищей.	
Мы́ говори́ли с ни́ми **трои́ми**.	We spoke with the three of them.
Cf. Мы́ говори́ли с **тремя́** това́рищами.	

Collectives six through ten are much less common than are two through five.

TRANSLATION INTO ENGLISH

1. Письмо́ лежа́ло под тремя́ больши́ми кни́гами. **2.** Это све́тлая ко́мната с четырьмя́ больши́ми о́кнами. **3.** В дву́х тёмных угла́х стоя́ли шкафы́. **4.** В пе́рвых десяти́ уро́ках о́коло трехсо́т но́вых сло́в. **5.** Я до́лжен позвони́ть семи́ това́рищам до полови́ны седьмо́го. **6.** Наконе́ц о́н уе́хал с пятью́ ру́сскими студе́нтами. **7.** Он, вероя́тно, пошёл показа́ть го́род э́тим пятна́дцати ру́сским студе́нтам. **8.** Вы́ познако́мились с девятью́ студе́нтами, кото́рые то́лько что верну́лись из восьми́ ра́зных стра́н? **9.** В ско́льких журна́лах об э́том писа́ли? В двадцати́ дву́х и́ли в двадцати́ одно́м. **10.** Он купи́л тро́е дороги́х часо́в. **11.** Шли́ тро́е: дво́е мужчи́н и же́нщина. **12.** То́лько мы́ дво́е оста́лись зде́сь./На́с оста́лось то́лько дво́е. **13.** Мы́ с не́й увели́ *двои́х* молоды́х студе́нтов и *трёх* краси́вых де́вушек. **14.** Тро́е молоды́х студе́нтов говори́ли с *тремя́* краси́выми де́вушками. **15.** Три́ краси́вых де́вушки смея́лись над двумя́ молоды́ми студе́нтами. **16.** Ка́к до́лго вы́ бу́дете говори́ть об э́тих трои́х студе́нтах? **17.** Мы́ е́дем на аэродро́м встре́тить сто́ два́дцать одного́ ру́сского студе́нта, кото́рые прилетя́т на две́ неде́ли. **18.** Мы́ везём с собо́й сто́ три́дцать одну́ краси́вую де́вушку, чтобы всем бы́ло ве́село. **19.** Мы́ нашли́ та́м два́дцать две́ студе́нтки./Мы́ нашли́ та́м то́лько дву́х студе́нток. **20.** Нельзя́ бы́ло не смея́ться над ва́шими четырьмя́ ма́ленькими сыновья́ми. **21.** Моя́ тётя, ма́ть трои́х дете́й, оста́лась у на́с на э́тот ра́з всего́ четы́ре дня́. **22.** Оба согласи́лись спроси́ть трои́х проезжа́вших ми́мо и́х до́ма старико́в. **23.** Вы́ давно́ живёте в Москве́? Нет, неда́вно, всего́ о́коло дву́х ме́сяцев. **24.** Та́м я́ познако́мился с двумяста́ми семью́десятью тремя́ учителя́ми и профессора́ми из ста́ девяно́ста одного́ университе́та. **25.** На́ша гру́ппа состои́т из сорока́ пяти́ челове́к. **26.** Стара́ясь не смея́ться, дво́е дете́й бе́гали о́коло на́с. **27.** Их до́м нахо́дится между двумя́ широ́кими у́лицами, веду́щими пря́мо в це́нтр го́рода. **28.** Этот учи́тель сейча́с даёт уро́ки трём де́вушкам. **29.** Он мно́го расска́зывает о свои́х четырёх бра́тьях. **30.** На́ша ста́рая кварти́ра тепе́рь за́нята семью́ неда́вно прие́хавшими япо́нскими студе́нтами. **31.** На́с бы́ло че́тверо в ко́мнате. **32.** Мы́ ви́дели и́х трои́х в кино́.

TRANSLATION INTO RUSSIAN

Write in Russian (write out all numerals using oblique cases wherever possible; translate "more than" by **бо́лее** *gen*):

1. I can't imagine where the judge met those three actresses. **2.** Somebody give the two writers some beer. I think they will drink in all about (use **о́коло**) twenty-four glasses. **3.** Here are more than 45 interesting letters, written by 58 of my 79 students to 82 acquaintances. **4.** I showed to 622 of my 891 students more than 452 reports written by 144 students. **5.** Ask Véra Pávlovna, perhaps she'll agree to go with the three of us. **6.** This book contains only five of Petróv's eighteen plays, but on the other hand it contains more than sixty letters. **7.** Five (*m*) left in the two automobiles, and the rest left on twelve buses. **8.** I have only three pairs of glasses (two ways). **9.** He lives with his parents, three sisters, and four brothers. **10.** There were six of us in the restaurant, but later, in Nikíta's apartment, there were only three of us. **11.** Grandmother always goes to church with her two sons and four daughters. **12.** The teacher was satisfied with the first five exercises. **13.** I've lived in eight apartments in the course of only four months. **14.** She promised the eleven children that she would return in eleven days with eight pretty pictures. **15.** In the twenty-six letters there was not one word about the three students he's been living with for four months. **16.** I was sorry for the two weeping girls. **17.** There were more than eighty words in the last three lessons. **18.** He saw 222 American teachers (*f*). **19.** My brother has three children. **20.** This student has only two watches, but he walks around with seven watches. **21.** We were there two days (use **су́тки**). **22.** There is only one gate there; we have four.

ROOT LIST

This Root List is a working list for practical use; it is neither exhaustive, nor does it pretend to solve all the problems raised by analysis of individual roots. The considerations and criteria discussed in the Introduction on roots in general apply. A final root paired consonant is regarded as neither hard nor soft. All roots are designated as nominal, adjectival, or verbal (N, A, or V); the decision is usually clear, though in certain cases opinions may vary as to the status assigned a root. In a few cases, a root has split into two parts of speech; often an older nominal root has become verbalized; for example, **БЕД, РЯД, ГОЛОС** (nominal) but **ГЛАС** (the ChS variant: verbal).

The list contains about 650 common roots, not including variants. Most of the important adjectival and verbal roots are included; nominal roots are given in most cases only if they build words not directly related to their concrete meaning; for example, **РУК** and **ГОЛОВ – ГЛАВ** are given because they build words like **вы́ручить** 'rescue,' **поручить** 'entrust a task' as well as **рука́** 'hand'; **гла́вный** 'main,' **заголо́в/о/к** 'headline' as well as **голова́** 'head,' but not **НОГ** or **ГЛАЗ**, because their derivatives are directly connected with 'foot/leg' and 'eye.' On the other hand such roots may be given if they are very important or if they coincide with other roots; for example, **ВОД** 'water' homonymous with **ВОД** from **ВЁД – ВОД** 'lead.'

The most "basic" possible variant of the root is given in all cases; variants showing truncation and consonant mutation are not given except in unusual or unpredictable cases.* Most of the unpredictable or isolated variants (particularly those resulting from vowel alternations (cf. pages 18–19) are listed and referenced

---

* I.e. only **ЗНАЙ** and **ВОЗ** are given, not **ЗНА** and **ВОЖ**. Root variants reduced by truncation or isolated processes to a single consonant; e.g. **ЙД > Д** in **при-д-ут** 'they will come'; **ГБ > Г** in **г-ну-ть** 'bend,' are not included in the list.

to one of the variants; for example, **СЛЫХ** to **СЛУХ**). Syllabic variants* of non-syllabic roots are referenced to the nonsyllabic root, Church Slavonic roots are referenced to the pleophonic variant (where one exists), and variants in **O** to variants in **Ě**; for example, **МЁР** and **МОР** to **М/Р**, **ГЛАВ** to **ГОЛОВ**, and **ВОЗ** to **ВĚЗ**. If a root ever occurs with ё in a word, it is listed with **Ě**, even if one or more other words have the root in the stressed **é** (cf. page 10).

БАВ v add; amuse
БАЛ v indulge, spoil
Б/Д v be alert; cf. БУД
БЕГ v run
БЕД N trouble, disaster; v defeat,
   -vince, vic-
БЕЛ A white
БЕР *See* Б/Р
БЕРЁГ¹ v guard, save†
БЕРЕГ² N bank, shore
БЕРЕМ-ЕН (БЕРЕМ-Я) N burden
БЕС N devil, fury
БИВ *See* БЬ/Й
БИЙ *See* БЬ/Й
БЛАГ A good
БЛЕД/Н A pale
БЛЁСК – БЛЕСТ v shine, brilliance
БЛИЗ A near
БЛИСТ *See* БЛЁСК – БЛЕСТ
БЛУД N error, wandering
БЛЮД v observe
БОГ N god; wealth
БОГ-АТ A rich
БОД *See* Б/Д
БОЙ¹ v fear
БОЙ² *See* БЬ/Й
БОК N side
БОЛ¹ N sickness, pain
БОЛ² A large
БОЛТ v shake, stir, chatter
БОР¹ v fight, struggle
БОР² *See* Б/Р

БОРОН v fight, defend; cf. БРАН
Б/Р v take
БРАН v scold; cf. БОРОН
БРЁГ *See* БЕРЁГ¹
БРЁД v wander
БРЕЙ v shave
БРЕМ-ЕН *See* БЕРЕМ-ЕН
БРИЙ *See* БРЕЙ
БРОД *See* БРЁД
БРОН N armor; reservation,
   guarantee
БРОС v throw
БУД¹ v wake
БУД² *See* БЫВ
БЫВ v be
БЫЛ *See* БЫВ
БЫТ *See* БЫВ
БЬ/Й v beat, fight

ВАГ N weight, esteem; daring
ВАЛ v throw; pile up, wave, bank
ВАР v cook
ВЕД v know; tell
ВЁД v lead, *-duce*
ВЁЗ v convey
ВЕЙ v blow
ВЕК N century, eternity
ВЕЛ v command; cf. ВОЛ
ВЕЛ-ИК A great
ВЕР v believe
ВЕРГ v *-ject*, throw
ВЕРЕД N harm

---

* Syllabic variants in *i* of the type found in derived imperfectives and verbal nouns from nonsyllabic verb stems are not ordinarily listed; e.g. **МИР** 'die,' **СЫЛ** 'send.'

† Roots numbered 1, 2, etc. are regarded by most etymologists as distinct from one another in origin.

ВЕРЕТ *See* ВОРОТ
ВЁРТ *See* ВОРОТ
ВЕРХ N top
ВЕС V hang (tran)
ВЕСЁЛ A gay
ВЕТ V say, speak
ВЕТХ A decrepit
ВЕЩ N thing, substance
ВИВ *See* ВЬ/Й
ВИД V see, *vid-*
ВИЙ *See* ВЬ/Й
ВИН N guilt
ВИС V hang (intr)
ВИТ V live
ВЛАГ N moisture
ВЛАД *See* ВОЛОД
ВЛАСТ (< ВЛАД-Т) N power
ВЛАК *See* ВОЛОК
ВЛЁК *See* ВОЛОК
ВН N outside, away; cf. ВОН
ВН-УТР N inside
ВОД¹ *See* ВЁД
ВОД² N water
ВОЗ *See* ВЁЗ
ВОЙ¹ N war, fighting
ВОЙ² V howl
ВОЛ N will, freedom
ВОЛК *See* ВОЛОК
ВОЛН N wave, agitation
ВОЛОД V possess, control
ВОЛОК V drag, *-tract*
ВОН N smell
ВОР *See* ТВОР²; о-твор became
    от-вор in отворить 'open'
ВОРОГ N magic; cf. ВРАГ
ВОРОТ V turn
В/Р V lie, talk nonsense
ВРАГ N enemy; cf. ВОРОГ
ВРАТ *See* ВОРОТ
ВРЕД *See* ВЕРЕД
ВРЕМ-ЕН (ВРЕМ-Я) N time
В/С A all, entire
ВСТРЕТ (В-С(Т)-РЕТ) V meet
ВС-ЯК A every, any; cf. В/С
ВТОР A second

ВЫЙ *See* ВОЙ²
ВЫК V become accustomed/habitu-
    ated
ВЫС A high
ВЬ/Й V wind, *-velop*
ВЯД V fade, wither
ВЯЗ V bind, tie

ГАД¹ V guess
ГАД² N vileness
ГАР *See* ГОР¹
ГАС V extinguish
Г/Б V bend; cf. Г/Н²
ГИБ V perish, bend; cf. Г/Б
ГЛАВ *See* ГОЛОВ
ГЛАД¹ A smooth
ГЛАД² *See* ГОЛОД
ГЛАС V call, sound; cf. ГОЛОС
ГЛОТ V swallow
ГЛОХ *See* ГЛУХ
ГЛУБ A deep
ГЛУП A stupid
ГЛУХ A deaf
ГЛЯД V look, glance
Г/Н¹ V chase; distill
Г/Н² V bend; cf. Г/Б and ГИБ
ГНЁТ V oppress
ГНИЙ V rot
ГНОЙ *See* ГНИЙ
ГОВОР V speak, talk
ГОД N goodness, advantage
ГОЛ A naked
ГОЛОВ N head
ГОЛОД N hunger
ГОЛОС N voice
ГОН *See* Г/Н¹
ГОР¹ V burn (intr); N sorrow,
    bitterness
ГОР² N mountain
ГОРБ N hump
ГОРД A proud
ГОРОД V enclose, partition
ГОСПОД N master, lord, God
ГОСТ N guest
ГОСУД *See* ГОСПОД

ГОТОВ A ready; V prepare
ГРАБ V grab, rob; cf. ГРЁБ
ГРАД¹ V reward (originally with a castle)
ГРАД¹ *See* ГОРОД
ГРАД² N hail
ГРАН N border
ГРЁБ V dig, row
ГР-ЕЙ V heat; cf. ГОР¹
ГРЕМ V ring out, thunder
ГРЕХ и sin
ГРОБ *See* ГРЁБ
ГРОМ *See* ГРЕМ
ГРУБ A crude
ГРУЗ V load
ГРУСТ N sadness (< ГРУЗ-ТЬ)
ГРЫЗ V gnaw
ГРЯЗ N dirt
ГУБ V (Г/Б) bend; destroy
ГУД V hum
ГУЛ V stroll
ГУСТ A thick

ДАВ¹ V squeeze, press
ДАВ² (usually ДАВ-Н) A long ago
ДАД *See* ДАЙ
ДАЙ V give
ДАЛ A far
ДАН *See* ДАЙ
ДАР¹ *See* ДАЙ
ДАР² V ДАР in УДАР 'hit' is related to Д/Р
ДАТ *See* ДАЙ
ДВЕР N door
ДВИГ V move, -mot-
ДВОР N court (yard); cf. ДВЕР
ДЕВ N maiden, girl
ДЕД¹ N grandfather
   ДЕД² (ДЕЖ/ДЕЖД) V put, lay*
   ДЕЙ V put, lay; do, act, operate*
   ДЕЛ¹ V do, make*
   ДЕН V put, lay*
ДЕЛ² V divide

---

* Related roots.

ДЕР *See* Д/Р
ДЁРГ V pull; cf. ДЕРЖ
ДЕРЖ V hold; cf. ДЁРГ
ДЕРЕВ N wood, country
ДЕРЗ A bold
ДЕШЁВ A cheap
ДИВ N wonder
ДИК A wild
ДЛ A long
Д/Н¹ N day
Д/Н² N bottom
ДОБ N suitability, convenience
ДОБ-Р A good, kind; cf. ДОБ
ДО-В/Л (ДО-В/О/Л) N satisfaction; cf. ВОЛ
ДОЙ V milk
ДОЛ¹ N valley, down
ДОЛ² N divide, share; cf. ДЕЛ²
ДОЛ-Г A long; cf. ДЛ
ДОЛГ N obligation
ДОР *See* Д/Р
ДОРОГ¹ A dear, expensive
ДОРОГ² N road
ДОСТО- (< ДО plus СТОЙ²) N worth, sufficiency
ДОХ *See* ДЫХ
Д/Р V tear, fight
ДРАГ *See* ДОРОГ¹
ДРАЖ V annoy; cf. ДРАЗ
ДРАЗ V tease; cf. ДРАЖ
ДРЕВ N antiquity; cf. ДЕРЕВ
ДРОБ N small pieces, fraction
ДРОВ N wood; cf. ДЕРЕВ
ДРОГ V tremble, shake
ДРУГ N friend; A other
ДУЙ V blow
ДУМ V think
ДУР A foolish, bad, homely
ДУХ N atmosphere, breath, spirit
ДЫХ V breathe; cf. ДУХ

ЕД¹ V eat
ЕД² *See* ЕЗД
ЕДИН *See* ОД(И)Н
ЕЗД V ride

ЁМ   *See* Й/М
ЕХ   *See* ЕД²
ЕСТ   v be, *natur-*

ЖА(М)   *See* Ж/М
ЖА(Й)   *See* Ж/Н
ЖАД   N greed, thirst
ЖАЛ¹   N pity, regret
ЖАЛ²   N sting
ЖАР   v burn; cf. ГОР¹
ЖАС (cf. ГАС)   *See* У-ЖАС
Ж/Г   v burn (tran)
Ж/Д   v wait
ЖЁГ   *See* Ж/Г
ЖЕЛ   v wish
ЖЁЛТ   A yellow
ЖЁН   N woman, *fem-*
ЖЁРТВ   N sacrifice
ЖЁСТ   A hard, cruel
ЖИВ   v live
ЖИД   A liquid
ЖИР   N fat
Ж/М   v press
Ж/Н   v reap
ЖОГ   *See* Ж/Г
ЖОР   *See* Ж/Р
Ж/Р   v gorge, eat

ЗАБОТ   N care, concern
ЗАД   N back
З/В   v call, *-voke, voc-*
ЗВЕН   v ring
ЗВЕР   N beast
ЗВОН   *See* ЗВЕН
ЗВУК   N sound; cf. ЗВЕН
З/Д   v build, *edif-*
ЗДОРОВ   A healthy
ЗДРАВ   *See* ЗДОРОВ
ЗЁВ   v yawn
ЗЕЛЁН   A green
ЗЕМ (ЗЕМ-Л)   N earth, land
ЗЕР   *See* З/Р
ЗИМ   N winter
ЗИН   *See* ЗЁВ
З/Л   A evil, bad; angry

ЗЛАТ   *See* ЗОЛОТ
ЗЛ-ОБ   *See* З/Л
ЗНАЙ   v know
ЗНАК   N sign; cf. ЗНАЙ
ЗНАМ-ЕН (ЗНАМ-Я)   N banner; cf.
   ЗНАЙ
ЗОВ   *See* З/В
ЗОД   *See* З/Д
ЗОЛОТ   A gold
ЗОР   *See* З/Р
З/Р   v see
ЗРЕЙ   v ripe
ЗЫБ   v vacillate, shake

ИГ/Р   v play
ИД   *See* ЙД
ИМ   *See* Й/М
ИМ-ЕН (ИМ-Я)   N name
ИН   A other
ИСК   v seek
ИСТ   A genuine

ЙД   v go
Й/М   v take, have

КАЗ¹   v show, render
КАЗ²   v deform
КАК   A how, *qual-*
КАЛ   v temper, heat
КАМЕН   N stone
КАП – КАП-Л   N drop, drip
КАС   *See* КОС¹
КАТ   v roll
КИВ   v nod
КИД   v throw
КИП   v boil
КИС   v become sour
КЛАД   v place
КЛАН   *See* КЛОН
КЛЁВ   v peck
КЛЕВЕТ   v slander; cf. КЛЁВ
КЛЕЙ   v paste
КЛИК   v shout, hail
КЛИН   *See* КЛЯН
КЛОН   v bow, *-cline*

КЛЮЙ   *See* КЛЁВ
КЛЮЧ   N key; V -*clude*, close
КЛЯН   V vow, curse
КОВ   V forge
КОЙ   *See* ПО-КОЙ; cf. ЧИЙ
КОЛ¹   N circle
КОЛ²   V prick
КОЛОТ   V strike, break, thrash
КОЛЕБ   V shake, waver, vacillate
КОЛИК – КОЛЬК   A how many/
    much, *quant-*
КОН   N beginning, end, order; cf.
    Ч/Н
КОН-/Ц   N end
КОП   V dig, heap
КОР¹   V reproach; subject
КОР²   N rind
КОРМ   V feed
КОРОТ   A short
КОС¹   V cut; touch
КОС²   A slanted, awry
КРАД   V steal
КРАЙ   N edge, extreme
КРАС   N beauty, color
КРАТ¹   *See* КОРОТ
КРАТ²   N time (number of times)
КРЕП   A strong
КРЕС   V raise/rise up, resurrect
КРЁСТ   N cross
КРИВ   A crooked
КРИК   V shout
КРОВ¹   *See* КРОЙ¹
КРОВ²   N blood
КРОЙ¹   V cover
КРОЙ²   V cut (cloth)
КРОТ   A tame
КРУГ   N circle, round
КРУП-/Н   A coarse, large, major
КРУТ   A steep; V turn, twist
КРЫЙ   *See* КРОЙ¹
КУЙ   *See* КОВ
КУК   V be bored, burdened
КУП¹   V buy
КУП²   V bathe
КУР¹   V smoke

КУР²   N poultry
КУС¹   V bite, piece
КУС²   V test
КУТ   V wind, wrap

ЛАГ   *See* ЛЁГ¹
ЛАД   N harmony, good
ЛАЗ   *See* ЛЕЗ¹
Л/Г   V prevaricate
ЛЕВ   A left
ЛЁГ¹   V lie, lay, place, -*pose*, -*pone*
ЛЁГ²   N; ЛЁГ-К   A light, easy
ЛЕЗ¹   V climb
ЛЕЗ²   *See* ПО-ЛЬ/З
ЛЕК   V heal
ЛЕН   A lazy
ЛЕП   V stick, paste; beautiful; cf. ЛЬ/П
ЛЕСТ   *See* ЛЬ/СТ
ЛЕТ   N year, summer
ЛЁТ   V fly
ЛИВ   *See* ЛЬ/Й
ЛИЙ   *See* ЛЬ/Й
ЛИК   N face, person, identity
ЛИП   *See* ЛЬ/П
ЛИХ¹   N extra, superfluity
ЛИХ²   A bad; wild, daring
ЛОВ   V catch
ЛОГ   *See* ЛЁГ¹
ЛОЖ   *See* Л/Г
ЛОМ   V break
ЛОП   V burst
ЛУК   N onion; bend, bow; ray;
    V bind, separate
ЛУЧ   V give, permit (получить,
    случиться)
ЛЬ/З   *See* ПО-ЛЬ/З (ЛЁГ-/К)
ЛЬ/Й   V flow, *flu-*
ЛЬ/П   V stick, adhere
ЛЬ/СТ   V flatter, charm
ЛЮБ   V love, like
ЛЮД   N people
ЛЯГ   *See* ЛЁГ¹

МАЗ   V smear
МАЛ   A little

МАН v entice, lure
МАТ (МАТЕР) N mother
МАХ v wave; miss
М/Г N moment, instant; wink
МЕД N copper
МЁД N honey
МЕЖ – МЕЖД N between, *inter-*
МЕЛ v grind; fine, minor; shallow
МЕН[1] v change
МЕН[2] A less
МЕР v measure
МЁР *See* М/Р
МЕРЗ A vile
МЁРЗ *See* МОРОЗ
МЁРК *See* МОРОК
МЁРТВ A dead; cf. М/Р
МЁРЦ – МЁРК *See* МОРОК
МЕС *See* МЕХ
МЕСТ[1] N place
МЕСТ[2] *See* М/СТ
МЕТ v notice, mark, aim
МЁТ v sweep, throw
МЕХ v mix, hinder; cf. МЕС
МИГ *See* М/Г
МИЛ A dear, nice
МИН v pass, go by
МИР N peace; world
М/К v close, join; rush
МЛАД *See* МОЛОД
М/Н[1] v think
М/Н[2] v crumple
МНОГ A many, *multi-*
МОГ v can, able to
МОЙ v wash
МОК *See* М/К
МОК – МОК-Р A wet
МОЛ[1] v pray, implore
МОЛ[2] *See* МЕЛ
МОЛВ v say
МОЛК v be silent
МОЛОД A young
МОР *See* М/Р
МОРОЗ N frost, severe cold
МОРОК N darkness
МОЧ (< МОГ-Т) N power

МОЩ *See* МОЧ
М/Р v die
МРАК *See* МОРОК
М/СТ v avenge
МУДР A wisdom
МУЖ N man, male
МУК[1] v torture
МУК[2] N grain
МУТ v confusion, dullness
МЫВ *See* МОЙ
МЫЙ *See* МОЙ
МЫСЛ – МЫШЛ v think
МЯГ/К A soft
МЯ(Н) *See* М/Н[1], М/Н[2]

НАГ A bare
НА-РУЖ N exterior, outside
НЕГ N luxury, tenderness
НЕМ A mute
НЁС v carry
Н/З v penetrate, cut
НИЗ A low
НИК v appear, emerge, go; bend
НОВ A new
НОЙ v ache; whimper
НОРОВ N moral(e), custom
НОС[1] *See* НЁС
НОС[2] N nose
НРАВ *See* НОРОВ
НУД N need, boredom, coercion
НУЖ *See* НУД
НЫЙ *See* НОЙ

ОБ-РАЗ (РАЗ[1]) N form
ОБ-РЁТ v find, get; cf. ВСТРЕТ
ОБЩ A general
ОДИН – ОД/Н A one
ОК N eye
ОПТ *See* ОБЩ
О-РУД N tool, instrument; cf. РУД[2]
О-РУЖ N weapon, arm(s)(ament); cf.
    РУЖ[1]
О-СНОВ v base
ОСТ/Р A sharp
ОТ/Ц N father, *patr-*

ПАД v fall, -*cide*
ПАЛ v burn
ПАС v tend, watch; save
ПАХ¹ v smell; blow, sweep
ПАХ² v plow
ПЕЙ v sing
ПЁК v bake; take care of
ПЁР   *See* П/Р
ПЕРВ A first
ПЕРЁД N front, forward part, *fore-*
ПЕРЁК N direction across, against
ПЁСТР A multicolored
ПЕХ A on foot
ПЕЧ-АЛ (ПЁК) N sadness
ПЕЧ-АТ (ПЁК) N press, print, seal
ПИВ   *See* ПЬ/Й
ПИЙ   *See* ПЬ/Й
ПИС v write, -*scribe*
ПИСК v squeal
ПИТ v nourish, feed
ПЛАВ v swim; melt, fuse; cf. ПЛЫВ
ПЛАК v weep
ПЛАМ-ЕН (ПЛАМ-Я) N flame
ПЛАТ N cloth; v pay (cloth is an
   ancient means of payment)
ПЛЁВ v spit
ПЛЕН N *capt-* (captive, captivate)
ПЛЁСК v clap, splash
ПЛЁТ v weave
ПЛОВ   *See* ПЛЫВ
ПЛОД N fruit
ПЛОСК A flat
ПЛОТ N flesh
ПЛОТ-/Н A dense, close
ПЛОХ A bad
ПЛЫВ v swim
ПЛЮЙ   *See* ПЛЁВ
П/Н v string up; kick
ПОЗД A late
ПОЙ¹   *See* ПЬ/Й
ПОЙ²   *See* ПЕЙ
ПО-КОЙ N rest, peace; cf. ЧИЙ
ПОЛ¹ N half; sex
ПОЛ² N field
ПОЛ³ N floor

ПО-ЛЕЗ   *See* ПО-ЛЬ/З
ПОЛЗ v crawl
ПОЛ/Н A full
ПОЛ/О/Н¹   *See* ПОЛ/Н
ПОЛОН²   *See* ПЛЕН
ПОЛОС N strip(e)
ПОЛОСК A rinse
ПО-ЛЬ/З N use (ЛЁГ in ЛЁГ-/К)
ПО-М/Н v remember
ПО-МЯН   *See* ПО-М/Н
ПОР¹ v rip, slash, beat; time
ПОР²   *See* П/Р
ПОРОЖН A idle, empty
ПОРТ¹ v spoil
ПОРТ¹ N trousers, clothes
ПО-ШЛ (по-йдýт) A banal, vulgar
П/Р v shut; support; press
ПРАВ A right, *rect-*
ПРАЖН   *See* ПРАЗДН
ПРАЗДН   *See* ПОРОЖН
ПРЕД   *See* ПЕРЁД
ПРЕЙ v rot
ПРЁК v reproach; cf. ПЕРЁК
ПРЕТ v forbid; cf. ПРОТ-ИВ
ПРОБ N attempt
ПРОК A other, away; benefit,
   solidity
ПРОС v ask, *quest-*
ПРОСТ A simple
ПРОТ-ИВ N against
ПРУГ N spring, resilience; cf.
   ПРЫГ, ПРЯГ
ПРЫГ v jump, spring; cf. ПРУГ,
   ПРЯГ
ПРЯГ v harness, tension; cf. ПРУГ,
   ПРЫГ
ПРЯД v spin (yarn)
ПРЯМ A straight
ПРЯТ A hide
ПУГ v frighten
ПУСК   *See* ПУСТ
ПУСТ v let, loose; A empty
ПУТ¹ v tangle, confuse
ПУТ² N route, travel
ПУХ v swell

ПЫЛ N flame, fire; dust
ПЫТ v try, test
ПЫХ v flare, flame; cf. ПУХ
ПЬ/Й v drink
ПЯ(Н) *See* П/Н

РАБ N slave; cf. РОБ
РАБ-ОТ N work; cf. РАБ
РАВ *See* РОВ[1]
РАВ/Н *See* РОВ-/Н
РАД A glad
РАЗ[1] v strike
РАЗ[2] *See* РОЗ
РАЗ-/Н – РОЗ-Н *See* РАЗ[2]
РАН[1] A early
РАН[2] N wound
РАСТ *See* РОСТ
Р/В v tear
Р/Д A red; cf. РУД[1]
Р/Ж N rust; cf. Р/Д
РЕД A rare
РЕЗ v cut
РЕЙ v swarm
РЕК N river
РЁК v speak, say
РЁТ v find, obtain; cf. ВСТРЕТ
РЕШ v decide, solve
РИЦ *See* РЁК
РОБ A timid; cf. РАБ
РОВ[1] A equal, even, exact
РОВ[2] *See* РОЙ[1]
РОВ-/Н *See* РОВ[1]
РОД N birth, *gen-*
РОЗ N difference, variety
РОЙ[1] v dig
РОЙ[2] *See* РЕЙ
РОК *See* РЕК
РОН v lose, drop
РОП/Т (РОПОТ) v murmur
РОС[1] N dew
РОС[2] *See* РОСТ
РОСТ v grow
РУБ v chop
РУГ v scold
РУД[1] A red, rusty

РУД[2] *See* О-РУД; cf. РЯД
РУЖ[1] N gun; cf. О-РУЖ weapon,
    arm(s); related to РУГ
РУЖ[2] *See* НА-РУЖ
РУК N hand
РУС N Russia
РУХ v crash, destruction
РЫВ *See* Р/В
РЫЖ A red, rusty; cf. Р/Д, РУД[1]
РЫЙ *See* РОЙ[1]
РЫХ *See* РУХ
РЯД N row, order; v set in line/order

САД v set, make sit; cf. СЕД[1]
САМ A self, *auto-*
СВЕЖ A fresh
СВЕТ N light, world
СВИСТ v whistle
СВОБОД N freedom
СВОЙ A own, *prop(e)r-*
СВЯТ A holy
СЕБ N person, own, self
СЕВ *See* СЕЙ
СЕВЕР N north
СЕД[1] v sit down, set(tle) (intr)
СЕД[2] A gray (haired)
СЕЙ v sow
СЕК (СЁК) v chop, whip
СЕЛ v settle; cf. СЕД[1]
СЕМ-ЕН (СЕМ-Я) N seed; cf. СЕЙ
СЕР A gray
СЕРД N warmth, anger; cf. СЕРЕД
СЕРД-/Ц N heart; cf. СЕРД and
    СЕРЕД
СЕРЕД N middle, center; cf.
    СЕРД-/Ц
СЕТ[1] N net
СЕТ[2] v guest
СИД v sit; cf. СЕД[1]
СИЯЙ v shine, radiance
СИЛ N strength, force
СКАК – СКОК v jump, gallop
СКОЛЬЗ v slip, slide
СКОР A quick, soon

СКОРБ N sadness
СКРЁБ V scrape
СКРИП V squeak
С-КУК N boredom; cf. КУК
СКУП A stingy
С/Л V send
СЛАБ A weak
СЛАВ N glory; cf. СЛОВ and СЛЫВ
СЛАД A sweet; cf. СОЛОД
СЛЕД N track, trace
СЛЕП A blind
СЛОВ N word; cf. СЛАВ and СЛЫВ
С-ЛОГ N complex, compound, complicated
С-ЛОЙ N layer; cf. ЛЬ/Й
СЛОН V lean
СЛУГ V serve
СЛУХ V listen, hear
СЛЫВ V pass for; cf. СЛАВ and СЛОВ
СЛЫХ   See СЛУХ
СМЕЙ¹ V dare
СМЕЙ² V laugh
СМЕЛ A bold; cf. СМЕЙ¹
С-МЕР-Т N death; cf. М/Р
СМЕХ   See СМЕЙ²
СМОТР V look at
С/Н   See С/П
СНОВ   See О-СНОВ
СОБ   See СЕБ
СОВ V thrust
СОЛ¹ N salt
СОЛ²   See С/Л
СОЛОД N malt; cf. СЛАД
СОР N trash; quarrel
СОС V suck
СОХ   See СУХ
С/П V sleep; cf. С/Н
СПЕЙ V be on time, succeed, ripe
СПЕХ   See СПЕЙ
С-ПОР N argument (П/Р)
С-ПО-СОБ N capability
СРЕД   See СЕРЕД
СТАВ V stand (tran), -pose; cf. СТАН and СТОЙ¹

СТАН V take a standing position; become; cf. СТАВ and СТОЙ¹
СТАН-ОВ V stand (tran); cf. СТАН
СТАР A old
СТЁГ V stitch, button; whip
СТЕЛ   See СТ/Л
СТЕН N wall
СТЕПЕН N degree; cf. СТУП
СТЕРЁГ V watch, guard
СТИГ V achieve, reach
СТ/Л V spread, cover
СТОЙ¹ V stand (intr), -sist; cf. СТАН and СТАВ
СТОЙ² V cost
СТОЛ   See СТ/Л
СТОН V groan
СТОРОГ   See СТЕРЁГ
СТОРОН N side, strange, foreign
СТ/Р V stretch
СТРАГ   See СТОРОГ
СТРАД V suffer
СТРАН   See СТОРОН
СТРАХ N fear
СТРЕК V excite, incite
СТРЕЛ N arrow, shot
СТРЕМ V go headlong, strive
СТРИГ V shear
СТРОГ A strict, stern; cf. СТЕРЁГ
СТРОЙ V build, -struct, order
СТРУЙ N stream
СТУД A cold
СТУК V knock
СТУП V step
СТЫД N shame; cf. СТУД
СТЫН V cool off; cf. СТУД (СТЫД-Н)
СУД N judgment
СУЙ   See СОВ
СУТ V be, exist, essen-
СУХ A dry
С-ЧАСТ N happiness, fortune
С-ЧЁТ   See С-Ч/Т
С-Ч/Т V consider, calculate
СЫП V pour, strew
СЫР A raw, bitter

СЫТ A satiated
СЯГ v seize, obtain; swear
СЯД *See* СЕД¹
СЯЗ *See* СЯГ

ТАЙ¹ v hide
ТАЙ² v melt
ТАСК v drag, pull
ТВАР *See* ТВОР¹
ТВЁРД A hard, firm
ТВОР¹ v create
ТВОР² v close
ТЁК v flow, run
ТЁМ-/Н A dark; cf. Т/М
ТЁП-/Л A hot
ТЕР v lose
ТЁР *See* Т/Р
ТЕРП v bear, endure
ТЕС-/Н A close, dense
ТЕХ v console, amuse; cf. ТИХ
ТИСК v press, clamp
ТИХ A quiet, calm; cf. ТЕХ
Т/К v poke; weave
ТЛ N decay
Т/М N darkness; cf. ТЬ/М
ТОК¹ N point; cf. Т/К
ТОК² *See* ТЁК
ТОЛК¹ N sense, interpretation
ТОЛК² *See* ТОЛОК
ТОЛОК v pound, shove
ТОЛСТ A thick, fat
ТОМ N weariness; cf. ТЁМ-Н
ТОН A thin
ТОП¹ v sink, drown
ТОП² N heat; cf. ТЁП-/Л
ТОП/Т (ТОПОТ) v stamp
ТОРГ¹ N trade; solemnity, triumph
ТОРГ² v tear, thrust
ТОРК v protrude
ТОСК N yearning, melancholy
ТОЩ A emaciated, worn
Т/Р v rub
ТРАТ v waste, lose
ТРЕБ v demand, require
ТРЕВОГ N alarm

ТРЕЗВ A sober
ТРЕСК v crack(le)
ТРОГ v touch
ТРУД N work, -labor-
ТРЯС v shake
ТУГ A taut; N sadness; cf. ТЯГ
ТУП A blunt, dull
ТУХ¹ v extinguish
ТУХ² v become rotten
ТЬ/М N darkness; cf. Т/М
ТЯГ v pull, drag; cf. ТУГ, ТЯЗ
ТЯЗ *See* ТЯГ

УВ *See* УЙ
У-ДАР v hit; cf. ДАР²
У-ЖАС N horror, terror; cf. ГАС
УЗ A narrow
УЗД N bridle
УЙ v shoe (verb)
УК v teach, learn
УЛ N street
УМ N mind, intellect
УСТ N mouth
УТР¹ N interior; cf. ВН-УТР
УТР² N morning
УХ N ear

ФОРМ N form

ХВАЛ v praise
ХВАТ v grasp, grip; be sufficient
ХИТ v grab, ravish; crafty
ХЛАД *See* ХОЛОД
ХЛОП v slam, bang
ХМУР A dark, cloudy; frown
ХОД v go on foot; cf. Ш/Д and
    ШЕД
ХОЗЯЙ N host, ownership
ХОЛОД N cold
ХОРОН v keep, save, preserve
ХОРОШ A good; good looking
ХОТ v want (includes о-хот-а both
    "wish" and "hunt")
ХРАБР A brave
ХРАН *See* ХОРОН

ХРОМ A lame
ХУД A thin; bad
ХУДОЖ N art

ЦАР N tsar, ruler
ЦВЁТ v bloom
ЦЕЛ¹ A whole; healthy, great
ЦЕЛ² N aim, purpose
ЦЕН N price; v evaluate, appreciate
ЦЕП N chain, hook

ЧА(Н)   *See* Ч/Н
ЧАЙ v expect, hope
ЧАР N magic, spell
ЧАСТ¹ v part
ЧАСТ² A often
ЧЕЗ v disappear
ЧЕРЕД N line, row, turn
ЧЁРК v sketch, draw; cf. ЧЕРТ
ЧЁРН A black
ЧЕРП v draw up, scoop
ЧЕРТ N line; cf. ЧЁРК
ЧЁС v scratch, comb
ЧЕСТ (< Ч/Т-Т) N honor
ЧЁТ   *See* Ч/Т
ЧИЙ v rest; cf. КОЙ
ЧИН N rank, order; v cause, fix
ЧИСЛ N number; cf. Ч/Т
ЧИСТ A clean
ЧЛЕН N member
Ч/Н v begin; cf. КОН
ЧРЕД   *See* ЧЕРЕД
Ч/Т v regard, consider
ЧУВ   *See* ЧУЙ
ЧУД¹ N marvel
ЧУД (ЧУЖ)² A not one's own,
    alien

ЧУЙ v feel, *sens-*
ЧУТ   *See* ЧУЙ

ШАГ N step
ШАТ v shake, wobble
Ш/В   *See* ШЬ/Й
Ш/Д (Ш/Д-Л)   *See* ХОД
ШЕД   *See* Ш/Д
ШЁПОТ   *See* ШЁП/Т
ШЁП/Т v whisper
ШЕСТ   *See* Ш/Д (ШД/-Т (ШЕД-Т))
ШИБ v hit
ШИВ   *See* ШЬ/Й
ШИЙ   *See* ШЬ/Й
ШИР A wide, broad
ШОВ   *See* ШЬ/Й
ШУМ N noise
ШУТ N joke
ШЬ/Й v sew

ЩАД v spare
ЩЕД-Р A generous; cf. ЩАД
ЩИП v pinch, pluck
ЩИТ v defend
ЩУП v feel, probe
ЩУТ   *See* ЧУТ

ЮГ N south
ЮН A young
ЮТ v shelter

Я(М)   *See* Й/М
ЯВ v manifest, show
ЯД N poison
ЯД/Р N nucleus
ЯС/Н A clear
ЯТ   *See* Й/М

GENERAL VOCABULARY

RUSSIAN-ENGLISH VOCABULARY

а то́ otherwise, or else
авантю́ра adventure (*us pejorative*) IV
авиа́ция aviation; air force I
авто́бус bus
автомаши́на automobile R4 note 5; truck I
автомоби́ль (на) automobile R4 note 5
а́втор author CL3
авторите́т authority VIII
аге́нтство agency V
агита́ция agitation (political) VII
агре́ссия aggression IV
адвока́т lawyer
администра́ция administration, management
а́дрес *E pl* -а́ address
а́збука alphabet VII
А́зия Asia
-айший R5.A2
акаде́мия academy
а́кт act
актёр actor IX.4; актри́са actress IX.4
акти́вный active III
Аме́рика America; америка́н/е/ц, америка́н/ка American *n*; америка́нский American *adj*
(про)анализи́ровать analyze
англи́йский English *adj*; англича́нин (*pl* англича́не, англича́н) Englishman;

англича́н/ка Englishwoman; А́нглия England
апо́стол apostle
аппети́т appetite CL1.2; прия́тного —а bon appetit, Guten Appetit
арестова́ть *both P and I* arrest; *I also* аресто́вывают
а́рмия army
арти́ст actor; artist IX.4
аспира́нт, —/ка graduate student II
аспиранту́ра graduate course II
атакова́ть *I and P* attack III
атеи́зм, atheism; атеи́ст atheist VI
атмосфе́ра atmosphere CL.3
А́фрика Africa
ах! oh!
аэропо́рт airport

ба́буш/ка grandmother
бакала́вр: *see* сте́пень
Баку́ *indecl* Baku
ба́нк bank (for money)
баскетбо́л basketball
бастова́ть strike; басту́ющий striker *sub adj* VI
ба́ш/ня (*gen pl* ба́шен) tower CL.3
бе́гают *nondet* run
бе́глый fluent; cursory; *gr* mobile, inserted: — гла́сный mobile vowel

бе́д/ный poor (not rich; object of pity: Ах ты́ бе́дная!)

бежа́ть, бегу́, бежи́шь, бегу́т *det* run; flee

безли́чный impersonal *gr*

безопа́сность security

без того́, чтобы IX.A5

бейсбо́л baseball

белору́с Belorussian *n*; Белору́ссия Belorussia; белору́сский Belorussian *adj* VII

бе́лый white

бельё linen, washing; ни́жнее — underwear CL4

бензи́н gasoline

бе́рег (на берегу́) *E pl* -á bank, shore

берёгу́т save, keep, guard, watch VI; —ся *кого́/чего́* watch out for, beware: Береги́сь соба́ки! Beware of the dog!

беспоко́ить disturb, upset III; —ся о *ко́м/чём* be disturbed, upset (about)

бессме́ртие immortality VI; бессме́рт/ный immortal

ближа́йший nearest R5.A, p. 86 n.1

биле́т ticket V

би́ться *see* бий-утся

бифште́кс (beef)steak CL1

благодаря́ *кому́/чему́* thanks to, due to VIII

бле́д/ный pale; бледноли́цый pale-faced CL2

бли́же *comp of* бли́зкий

бли́з/кий к *кому́/чему́ or* от *кого́/чего́* near, close

блу́з/ка blouse CL4

блю́до dish, course CL1.3

бо́г *E pl obl* god VI

бога́тый rich; *comp* бога́че

бо́же мо́й my God! Lord! CL3.7

болга́рин (*pl* болга́ры, болга́р), болга́р/ка Bulgarian *n*; Болга́рия Bulgaria; болга́рский Bulgarian *adj* VII

бо́лее R5.A1; — того́ R5 note 5

боле́знь sickness, disease, illness CL3.2

боле́ть у *кого́* CL3.2

боле́ют CL3.2

болтовня́ chatter, gossip CL1

боль/но́й (*sh f* бо́лен, больна́, больны́, *no N*) sick, a sick person; painful, tender, sore *also fig*; бо́льно *кому́* painful, it hurts CL3; больно́й вопро́с sore subject; больно́е ме́сто sore spot

большеви́к *E* Bolshevik; большеви́стский Bolshevik *adj*

бо́льший larger R5.A1; *cf* большо́й large бо́льше *comp* R6 note 3; бо́льше не R3 note 18; бо́льшей ча́стью for the most part

большинство́ (*pl* большинства́) majority VI

борода́ *S nom pl acc sg* beard CL1

боро́ться с *ке́м/чём* struggle (with) IV; — за *кого́/что́* struggle for; — про́тив *кого́/чего́* struggle against

бо́рщ *E* borscht, beet soup CL2

борьба́ fight, struggle IV

боти́нок (*us pl* боти́нки, *gen pl* боти́нок) shoes (with laces, the type usually worn by men) CL4

боя́ться *кого́/чего́* fear, be afraid of; — не *pleonastic* не IX.A6

(по)бре́ют (бри́ть) shave *tr*; —ся shave oneself CL4.1

(за)брони́ровать order, reserve, give (official) priority

бро́сить – броса́ют throw CL4; —ся throw oneself

брю́ки *pl only* (*gen* брю́к) trousers CL4

бу́дем + *I inf* R10 note 5

(раз)буди́ть wake up, awaken *tr* CL3

бу́дто (бы) II.2

бу́дучи (*pres ger* < бы́ть) being (since) R5.D1, R9.A, p. 131

бу́дущий future *adj*; next R7.A6; бу́дущее вре́мя future tense *gr*; бу́дущее *sub adj* (the) future

бу́дь: бу́дь то IX.B5; не бу́дь IX.B5

бу́ква (*gen pl* бу́кв) letter (of the alphabet)

бума́га paper

буржуази́я bourgeoisie III

буты́л/ка bottle

бы R3.B, IX.B; *with inf* VI.C2

быва́ет X.2

быва́ло X.2

быва́ют X.2, R5.D2

бы́вший (*PAP of* бы́ть) former, ex-

бы́ло X.3

бы́ть *inst pred* R5.D1

бий-утся beat *intr* CL4.1

бюро́ *N indecl* office; bureau V

во *что́ per unit time* R7.A2; *times* VIII.5; as a, in the capacity of X.1; *time* III.6; *acc pl form of animates* IX.3
«в» *words vs.* «на» *words* R4.B
ва́ж/ный important; нева́жный unimportant; mediocre, bad
ва́нна bathtub CL.3, V.9
ва́нная bathroom (room with tub) V.9
вариа́нт variant VII
введу́т – вводи́ть introduce
    n введе́ние introduction
вво́дное сло́во parenthetic word *gr*
вдруг suddenly
ведь III.3
везде́ everywhere VII
(по)везёт, (по)везло́ *кому́/чему́* be lucky, have luck I
век *E pl* -á century; в 19-ом —e in the nineteenth century; на своём —ý in one's age, eternity, *also colloq*
вели́кий great (*sh f S* вели́к, вели́ка); large (*sh f only E* вели́к, велика́)
велича́йший the greatest
веля́рный velar *ling* (к, г, х)
Ве́нгрия Hungary; венге́рский Hungarian
(по)ве́рить *кому́/чему́* believe VI; — в *кого́/что́* believe in
    n ве́ра belief, faith
верну́ть(ся): *see* возврати́ть(ся)
ве́р/ный true, loyal; верне́е rather, more precisely R3 note 14
ве́ровать в *кого́/что́* believe VI
ве́рующий believer
вероя́тный probable II
верхо́вный supreme CL3
верхо́м: е́здить верхо́м ride horseback
верши́на (на) top, summit; acme
весёлый, ве́сел, ве́село, ве́селы, весела́ gay, merry
вес/на́ *S pl* spring; весно́й in the spring
весьма́ greatly, highly VIII
ве́т/е/р wind
ве́чер *E pl* -á (на) evening; party III
вече́рний evening *adj* R7.D
ве́чность eternity VI
ве́ч/ный eternal
ве́шают: *see* пове́сить – пове́шают

вещество́ substance VIII
вещь *E pl obl* thing
взаи́мный mutual; *gr* reciprocal
взволнова́ть: *see* (вз)волнова́ть
взгляну́ть – взгля́дывают на *кого́/что́* look at, glance at VII
    n взгляд look, glance; view, opinion VI; на мой — in my opinion; на пе́рвый — at first glance; с пе́рвого —a from the first glance, at first sight
вздор rubbish, nonsense II
взро́слый adult, grown-up *adj and sub adj*
взять: *see* возьму́т
вид view, form, appearance, aspect VIII.8; (не)соверше́нный — (im)perfective aspect
ви́деть R8 note 4
ви́д/ный visible VI; ви́дный eminent, notable; ви́дно obvious, it is obvious
ви́л/ка fork
вини́тельный (паде́ж) *gr* accusative (case)
вино́ *S pl* wine
висе́ть hang *intr* CL3
вклад contribution, investment, deposit VI; внесу́т – вноси́ть вклад в что́ make a contribution to
включи́ть – включа́ют turn on; в *кого́/что́* include
вкус taste CL4
вку́с/ный tasty CL1
владе́ют *кем/чем* possess, be master of; — X-ым языко́м speak, have command of X language VII.6
Владивосто́к Vladivostok
власть ВЛАД *E pl obl* power, (the) power VII; быть у —и be in power R4.B; приду́т – приходи́ть к —и come to power R4.B
влия́ние на *кого́/что́* influence IV; оказа́ть – ока́зывают — на *кого́/что́* exert influence
влюби́ться – влюбля́ются в *кого́/что́* fall in love with VI
вме́сто *кого́/чего́* in place of III; — того́ что́бы + *inf* IX.A5
вне *кого́/чего́ adv or prep* outside (of)
внесу́т – вноси́ть вклад: *see* вклад
вне́шний outside, external; foreign VI
вниз *куда́* down(stairs), to the bottom

внизу́ *гдé* down(stairs), at the bottom

внима́ние < *an older* внима́ют attention IV; обрати́ть – обраща́ют — на *когó/чтó* pay attention to; при́мут – принима́ют во — take into account; Внима́ние! Attention!

внима́тель/ный attentive, thoughtful

внук grandson

внуч/ка granddaughter

вну́тренний inside, internal; domestic VI

внутри́ *когó/чегó adv or prep* inside (of)

во вре́мя: *see* вре́мя

во́время on time, in time III.6c

во́все quite; во́все не not at all CL5

во-вторы́х in the second place VIII.6

вода́ *S nom pl acc sg* water

води́ть (маши́ну, автомоби́ль) drive (a car) R5 note 7

вод/ка vodka

водоро́д hydrogen VIII; водоро́дный hydrogen *adj* VIII

вое́нно-возду́шный (флóт) air (force) I

вое́нно-морско́й (флóт) naval (navy) I

вое́нный military, war *adj* I

вождь *M E* leader III; — наро́да leader of the people

возврати́ть – возраща́ют *or* вёр̯ну́ть *P only*; return *tr* X; —ся return *intr* CL4.1, X.A

возвра́тный *gr* reflexive; — глагóл reflexive verb; —ое местоиме́ние reflexive pronoun

во́здух air VIII

вози́ть drive (convey) R5 note 7

во́зле *adv or prep когó/чегó* by, near, beside

возмо́жность possibility, opportunity, chance; по возмо́жности II.1

возмо́ж/ный possible II; возмо́жно possible, might, may II.1; возмо́жно + *comp* = как мо́жно + *comp* II.1

возмути́ть – возмуща́ют make indignant IV; —ся *ке́м/чéм* be indignant at; я возмущён *кéм/чéм* I am indignant at

возни́к(ну)ть – возника́ют arise, come up, emerge, originate *n* возникнове́ние VI

возрази́ть – возража́ют про́тив *когó/чегó* object to

возьми́ (да) IX.C2

возьму́т (взять) – беру́т (брать) take

война́ *S pl* war; гражда́нская — civil war III

вокру́г *когó/чегó adv or prep* around

Во́лга Volga

волна́ *S pl or E pl obl* wave

(вз)волнова́ть excite, agitate; —ся о *кóм/чём* be (get) excited, agitated

волоки́та red tape; ladies' man V

во́лос *E pl obl (gen pl* волóс) hair CL1

во́ля will VI

вообще́ IV.7

вооружи́ть – вооружа́ют arm IV; воору-жённые си́лы armed forces *n* вооруже́ние armament, arming

во-пе́рвых in the first place VIII.6

вопро́с; used with по II.5

вопроси́тельный *gr* interrogative; — знак question mark

во́рот collar CL5

воро́та *pl only* gates; *see* Appendix B.1

восклица́тельный знак exclamation point

во ско́лько (часóв) at what time R6.A3

воспо́льзоваться: *see* (вос)пóльзоваться VIII.9

воспри́мут – воспринима́ют perceive, apprehend, interpret, understand *n* восприя́тие (*по* н; *cf.* заня́тие)

восста́нут – восстава́ть revolt, rise up, rebel *n* восста́ние revolt

восто́к (на) east; восто́чный eastern I; восточнославя́нский East Slavic VII

восходи́ть к go back to, derive from VII

вот R5 note 1

впервы́е for the first time IV

вперёд *кудá* ahead, forward

впереди́ *гдé* ahead, in front

вполне́ completely VI

впосле́дствии subsequently, later on VIII

впро́чем however, though

впры́гнуть – впры́гивают jump in(to) CL.4

врач *E* physician, doctor CL3.4

вре́менный temporary VI

вре́мя time; *gr* tense; в настоя́щее — now, at the present time; в своё — R6 note 8; в то — ка́к whereas VIII.1; во — чегó III.6c

вря́д ли hardly, scarcely; I doubt it/that . . . CL1

всё, кто́ III

всего́ in all, a total of, only, all R6 note 9; их — пя́ть there are five of them in all

всео́бщий universal, general IV

всё: всё + *verb* X keep (kept) X-ing R4 note 7; я всё чита́л I kept reading; всё ещё still R4 note 7; всё же all the same, still; . . . , и всё . . . and that's all there is to it: Он ге́ний, и всё. He's a genius and that's all there is to it.

всё X-е(е) и X-е(е) X-er and X-er; R5.A3

всё вре́мя R4 note 7

всё равно́ VII.4

всё (то), что III

всле́дствие *чего́* as a consequence of VIII

вста́нут – встава́ть из-за R9 note 7

вступи́тельный introductory

всю́ду everywhere VII

вся́кий every, any; *pl* all kinds of II.3; вся́кого ро́да of all kinds

второ́е CL1.3

в-тре́тьих in the third place VIII.6

вход (*n* < войду́т – входить) entrance

в-четвёртых in the fourth place VIII.6

вы́брать (вы́берут) – выбира́ют choose, select, elect II; — *кого́ чём* elect X as Y *n* вы́бор choice II; —ы (на) elections

вы́делить – выделя́ют pick out; secrete VIII

вы́держать – выде́рживают hold out, sustain, endure; —экза́мен *P only* pass an exam; держа́ть экза́мен take an exam I

вы́звать (вы́зовут) – вызыва́ют call, call out, summon; challenge, provoke; cause *n* вы́зов call, challenge

вы́йдут – выходить за́муж за *кого́* marry (of a woman) R5 note 9

вы́йдет – выхо́дит, что *or adv* turn out, come out: Всё вы́шло хорошо́. It all turned out fine. *n* вы́ход

вы́ключить – выключа́ют turn off, switch off CL4

вы́лечить – выле́чивают cure CL3

вы́моют(ся): *see* (вы́)мо́ют(ся)

вы́мыть(ся): *see* (вы́)мо́ют(ся)

вы́полнить – выполня́ют fulfill, carry out VIII; — но́рму fulfill norm *n* выполне́ние

вы́пий-ут – выпива́ют drink up; (вы́)пи́й-ут за *кого́/что́* drink to CL1.4; *see* R2.A5

вы́разить – выража́ют express VII *n* выраже́ние expression

вы́растут (вы́рос, вы́росла) – выраста́ют **РОСТ** grow up I

высо́кий (*sh f* высо́к, высока́, высо́ко, высо́ки) high, tall

высота́ (*pl* высо́ты) height, elevation

высоча́йший highest

вы́спаться (*like* спать) – высыпа́ются get a good rest, sleep oneself out CL3

вы́став/ка exhibition, fair V (*n* < вы́ставить – выставля́ют)

вы́ступить – выступа́ют *no mut in I* step (come) out (forward), perform publicly II; — с докла́дом give a report; — с пе́сней sing a song; — с ре́чью make a speech *n* выступле́ние

вы́сший higher, highest R5.A1; —ая шко́ла college-level school

вы́учить II.7

вы́ход exit, way out; *also fig* (*n* < вы́йдут – выходить)

выходно́й д/е́/нь day off

вы́чистить: *see* (вы́)чистить

вы́чистить – вычища́ют clean CL4

вы́ше *comp of* высо́кий

газ gas VIII

газе́та newspaper

га́лстук (neck)tie

где́ *place where* R4.B

генера́л general (military)

геогра́фия geography I

Герма́ния Germany VII; герма́нский German(ic)

герои́ня heroine

геро́й hero; protagonist

ге́ний genius; гениа́ль/ный of genius (*not* genial)

гид guide (for tourists) V

гимн hymn, anthem VIII; Гимн Советского Союза Soviet national anthem

главный main, chief

глагол *gr* verb; взаимный — reciprocal verb; возвратный — reflexive verb; — движения verb of motion; — на -ся *sja*-verb; (не)переходный — (in)transitive verb

глагольный verb(al); *cf.* отглагольный

глаз (в глазу) *E pl* -á (*gen pl* глаз) eye CL1; карие —á brown eyes; смотреть *кому* в —á look someone in the eyes

глазной врач eye doctor

гласный (звук) *gr* vowel (sound); гласная (буква) *gr* vowel (letter)

глубже *comp of* глубокий

глубокий (*sh f* глубок, глубока, глубоко, глубоки) deep

глубочайший deepest

глупый stupid, foolish CL1, VI

глухой deaf; *gr* voiceless

гнездо *S pl* nest

говорить: — на X-ом языке speak X language II; — с *кем* talk with *or* to R3.F; говорить – сказать, чтобы R3.F; уже не — о: не говоря уже о much less, not to mention V.2

год: в X-ых годах R8.A

голова *S nom pl acc sg* head; придут – приходить *кому* в —у come into somebody's head

голод/ный (*sh f* голоден, голодна, голодны) hungry CL2

голос *E pl* -á voice

голубой *no sh f* (light) blue CL1

гольф golf

гора *S nom pl acc sg* mountain; в —у uphill; под —y downhill

гораздо (*with comp* X) much X-er R5.A8; — лучше much better

горе grief, woe VII

гореть burn *intr*

горло throat CL3

город *E pl* -á city; за город(ом) to (in) the country/suburbs

городской municipal, city *adj* CL3

горячий *sh f E* hot; ardent CL4, C 5.10; горячая вода *but* жаркая погода

господин *pl* господа, госпожа R5.B

гостиная living room *sub adj* V

гостиница hotel V.9

гость *M E pl obl* guest I; идут – ходить в —и go visiting; быть – бывают в —ях be visiting

государство state I.5

государственный government(al), state *adj* I.5

(при)готовить *or* приготовить – приготовляют (к) prepare; cook; —ся (к) prepare oneself (for)

готовый (*sh f* готов, готова) к *чему or* на *что* ready, prepared R9.E

градус degree (*Soviets use centigrade*) VIII

гражданин (*pl* граждане, *gen pl* граждан), граждан/ка citizen R5.B

гражданский civil III; —ая война civil war

грамматика grammar; a grammar book

грамматический grammatical

граница boundary, border, frontier I; за —ей be in a foreign land; за —у go to a foreign land; из-за —ы come from a foreign land

графинчик small decanter CL1

грех *E* sin VI

Греция Greece; грек, гречанка Greek *n*; греческий Greek *adj* VII

гриб *E* mushroom CL1; грибной mushroom *adj*

грипп (в гриппу) grippe CL3

гром/кий loud

громче *comp of* громкий

грудь (в *or* на груди) *E pl obl* breast, chest CL3

группа group VII

груст/ный sad VI

грязь (в грязи) mud, dirt; *also fig*

грязный muddy, dirty; *also fig*

губа *S nom pl* lip CL1

губной **lip** *adj*; *gr* labial

гуляш goulash CL1

гуляют take a walk, stroll; have good time

ГУМ Государственный Универсальный Магазин State Department Store

да for that matter; and; but; let; да и (то) I.7,CL5.4

давáй(те) R3 note 11; давáй(те) бýдем + *I inf* R10 note 5

давить press, crush

   n давлéние pressure

дáвний of long ago; давнó long ago

дáлее: и тáк дáлее (и т.д.) and so forth, et cetera, etc.

далёкий (*sh f* далёк *E*) (от *когó/чегó*) far (from); далекó не by far/a long way not

дальнéйший further, subsequent VIII; в —ем subsequently

дáльше (*comp of* далёкий) further; Go on! Proceed! R10 note 3

дáма lady; queen (in cards)

дáнный given, present III; — вопрóс the question under consideration; this; дáнные *pl only* facts

дáр *E pl* gift, donation VIII; — *чегó* gift of (по)дарúть *чтó комý* give (a gift)

дáтельный (падéж) *gr* dative (case)

дать – давáть let, allow; — *комý* + *inf* R7 note 9

дáча (на) dacha, (summer) cottage

двúнуть – двúгают *or* двúгать move *tr* CL5; move part of body *intr*; — рукóй, ногóй move arm, leg; —ся move *intr*

   n движéние motion

двоетóчие *gr* colon

двор *E* court, yard; на —é outside; при —é at court

дéвоч/ка little girl

дéвуш/ка girl (unmarried, but physically mature); waitress R9 note 10

дéдуш/ка grandfather

деепричáстие *gr* gerund

дéйствие action, function; act (of a play) IV

действúтельный real, actual; valid CL1, VII; действúтельно really, in actual fact, indeed, actually

действúтельный залóг *gr* active voice

дéйствовать act, function, operate *intr*

(по)дéйствовать на *когó/чтó* act on, influence

дéйствующие лúца cast of characters, dramatis personae CL3

(с)дéлаются *кéм/чéм* become R5.D7

делúть divide, share VII; —ся на *чтó* be divided into

дéло *E pl* affair, matter, business, cause IV; В чём дéло?. IV.A; делá business, affairs; Дéло в тóм, что IV.A; имéют дéло с have to do with; Какóе мнé дéло до VI.4; Мнé нéт дéла до VI.4; на сáмом дéле in actual fact; по делáм on business; *cf.* по (однóму) дéлу on a certain (single) matter

демократúческий democratic; Демократúческая пáртия Democratic Party

д/é/нь: выходнóй дéнь day off; на днях the other day (a day or so ago) *or* one of these days (in a day or so); трéтьего дня day before yesterday

дерéв/ня *E pl obl* (*gen pl* деревéнь) country; village; в —е in the country; в —ю to the country

дéрево (*pl* дерéвья, *gen pl* дерéвьев) tree

держáть hold, keep; —ся *чегó* hold to, adhere to; — экзáмен take exam; *cf.* вúдержать экзáмен pass exam

десятилéтие decade VI

дéти, детéй, дéтям, детьмú, дéтях *pl of* ребёнок

дефúс *gr* hyphen

дешéвле *comp of* дешёвый

дешёвый cheap, inexpensive

дéнь/ги, дéнег, деньгáм, деньгáми, деньгáх money; живýт на —и live on money; игрáют на —и play for money

дé ятельность activity

диалéкт dialect VII

дивáн couch, sofa, divan

(про)диктовáть dictate

диктóв/ка dictation

дирéктор *E pl* -á director VI

дискýссия discussion

диссертáция dissertation (Ph.D.), thesis II

длúн/ный long (physical or, less often, time) CL5; дóлгий long (time); длúнный *or* дóлгий доклáд

длиннонóсый long-nosed CL2

для *genitive vs. ethical dative* R5 note 12; IV.4a

для тогó чтобы in order to R7.C, IX.A1

днём in the afternoon; in the daytime

Днепр *E* Dnepr

до *vs.* перед R9 note 1

до up to, as far as; от . . . до (place) R4.B, (time) R8.A

до того как I.1

до: за X до Y X time before Y V.3

добива́ются, доби́ться: *see* доби́й-утся

добро́ good (*opposed to* зло́ evil)

Добро́ пожа́ловать в *что* Welcome (to)

до́брый, до́бр, добра́, добро́, добры́ good-hearted, kind; good (quality) *only in certain phrases*: до́брый де́нь, до́брый ве́чер; бу́дьте добры́ please (be so kind as to)

доби́й-утся – добива́ются *кого́/чего́* gain, achieve; — своего́ gain one's ends; — успе́ха achieve success

дово́льно R5 note 13, IX.1

дово́льный IX.1; — *ке́м/че́м* (*without* с) satisfied with R9.E

догада́ются – дога́дываются о *ко́м/чём* conjecture, guess (*P* successfully)

n дога́д/ка guess, conjecture VI

договори́ться – догова́риваются о *ко́м/ чём* come to an agreement; *P only* make arrangements: Договори́лись? Okay? Have we arranged it? Is it a date? etc.

доказа́ть – дока́зывают prove R2.A4

докла́д report II; вы́ступить – выступа́ют с —ом give a report; (с)де́лают — give a report

до́ктор *E pl* -а́ CL3.4

до́кторский: *see* сте́пень

докуме́нт document, paper

до́л/гий, до́лог long (of time)

долж/е/н R6.C

должно́ быть probably, must (in sense of probability) R6.C

доли́на valley

до́ллар dollar

до́льше *comp of* до́лгий

до́м (жило́й до́м) *E pl* –а́ house; apartment building

дома́шний *adj* house, home, domestic

До́н (на Дону́) Don (river)

дополне́ние addition, supplement; *gr* object, complement; ко́свенное — indirect object; прямо́е — direct object

допро́с (на) interrogation I (< допроси́ть – допра́шивают)

допусти́ть – допуска́ют allow, permit VI; допу́стим let us suppose, assume; — оши́бку allow an error

доро́га road; желе́зная — railroad

дорого́й, до́рог expensive, dear; dear (familiar address in letters)

доро́же *comp of* дорого́й

дос/ка́ *S nom pl acc sg* (*gen pl* досо́к) board, blackboard

доста́вить – доставля́ют deliver, provide, supply VII; — удово́льствие *кому́* give pleasure

доста́нут – достава́ть get, obtain

доста́точно IX.1; — . . ., чтобы IX.A4

доста́точный IX.1; — . . ., чтобы IX.A4

дости́г(ну)ть (*or* дости́чь) – достига́ют *чего* (*see* p. 135) achieve, accomplish *n* достиже́ние achievement

достопримеча́тельность thing worthy of note; *us pl* sights V

драмату́рг playwright

древнеру́сский Old Russian CL5, VII

дре́вний old, ancient CL5, VII

дру́г дру́га each other X.C

друго́й: и то́т . . . и друго́й IV.3b, R7 note 1; на друго́й , ѣнь R7.A6

дру́жба friendship

ду́мают intend to CL4.2; (believe) R6 note 17

дура́к *E* fool, idiot III

ду́х spirit; breath II; не в —е out of spirits

духо́вный spiritual; spiritual (ecclesiastical, religious) VI

душа́ *S pl acc sg* soul VI; soul (person); на ду́шу (населе́ния) per capita

(за)души́ть strangle, suffocate III

дуэ́ль duel VII

дья́вол devil CL2

дя́дя *M* (*gen pl* дя́дей) uncle

Евро́па Europe; европе́/е/ц (*gen* европе́йца), европе́й/ка European *n*; европе́йский European *adj*

еда́ (*n* < есть/едя́т) food; meal (eating) CL1

едва́ hardly, scarcely, only, just CL1: едва́ ли: Едва́ ли о́н здесь. He can hardly be here. I doubt if he is here. едва́ ли не: Он едва́ ли не са́мый лу́чший студе́нт. He is almost (probably) the best student.

едва́ не: Он едва́ не упа́л. He almost fell.

еди́нственный (the) only, sole VI

еди́нственное число́ *gr* singular number

еди́нство unity VI

еди́ный unified, united; only, alone CL4

еже- *prefix* every *time unit*, -ly; ежедне́вный every day, daily; ежеме́сячный monthly; еженеде́льный weekly

е́здить drive R5 note 7

-ей *vs.* -ee in comparatives CL5.8

-ейший R5.A2

е́сли *conditional, but not* whether R3.C
     IX.B1; omission of, VII, p. 228, IX.B2

е́сли + *inf* VI.B

е́сли бы не but for IX.B6

е́сли . . . не unless, if . . . don't III.5

есте́ственный natural

есть: *see* съе́сть – съеда́ют eat up CL1.1; *see also* R2.A5

есть *or* и е́сть is, are R5.D4

есть кому́ *or* у кого́ (*positive*) *corresponding to* не V

есть R4.C; како́й ни на — VII, p. 227

есть ли *confusion with* е́сли R3.C

ещё *vs.* уже́ R3 note 18; — *vs.* бо́льше R6.3

(по)жале́ют кого́/что́ be sorry for; — о ко́м/чём *or* что be sorry that, regret

жаль кому́ кого́ X *dat* is sorry for Y *acc* R5; жаль it's a pity

жара́ heat (weather)

жа́реный fried, roasted, grilled

жа́р/кий, жа́рок hot (of weather, sun, etc.); *but* hot water = горя́чая вода́

жарко́е meat course CL1.3

жа́рче *comp of* жа́ркий

жгут (жечь, жёг, жгла́) burn *tr*

(под/о/)жда́ть кого́/что́ *or* кого́/чего́ (*pres ger* ожида́я) wait (for)

же *emphasizes preceding element, adversative* VII.1

(по)жела́ют *us* кого́/чего́ desire, wish CL1; *see also* R9 note 9
     n жела́ние wish, desire; пожела́ние wish (get well, birthday)

желе́зный iron; —ая доро́га railroad

жёлтый yellow

желу́д/о/к stomach CL.3

жё.ла *S pl* wife

жена́т(ый) на ко́м married (of a man to a woman) R5 note 9

жени́ться на ко́м *both P and I* marry (of a man) R5 note 9; жени́ть *P and I* marry off

жени́тьба marriage

жени́х *E* fiancé; bridegroom

же́нский female, woman's, feminine; — ро́д *gr* feminine gender

же́чь: *see* жгут

живо́й alive; live, lively

живопи́с/е/ц (*gen* живопи́сца) painter IX

живопи́сь painting (in general) IX.4

жи́д/кий liquid *adj* VIII

жи́дкость liquid *n* VIII

жи́же *comp of* жи́дкий

жилпло́щадь living space

(по)жмут – пожима́ют press, squeeze, shake hand(s); (Кре́пко) жму Ва́шу (Твою) ру́ку *a closing in a letter*

журна́л periodical; magazine, journal

журнали́ст, журнали́ст/ка journalist; журнали́стика journalism

за кого́/что́ during III.6; for IV.4b; (time) before V.3

за ке́м/чём go for, go after, pick up R4 note 4; due to IV.4b; at (some activity) IV.4b

за- *prefix to motion verb*: drop in R4 note 4

забастова́ть: *see* бастова́ть VI

забасто́в/ка (workers') strike VI

заболе́ть – заболева́ют CL3.2
     n заболева́ние

(по)забо́титься о ко́м/чём worry about; take care of, concern oneself with
     n забо́та

забастова́ть go on strike VI

заброни́ровать: *see* (за)брони́ровать

зави́сеть *or* depend on (a condition; *not* rely on) IV

заво́д (на) factory, plant VII

за́втрак breakfast; lunch

(по)за́втракать have breakfast; lunch

заговори́ть *P only* start to speak VI

задать – задавáть give (assignment), set a task for; — вопрóс *комý* ask a question R3.F

n задáние assignment; task; *cf.* задáча task, problem

зáдний back *adj*

задóлго до long before V.3

задýмаются – задýмываются нáд *чем* become lost in thought *P*; ponder *I* VI

задушить: *see* (за)душить

заинтересовáть *P only* arouse (someone's) interest; —ся *кéм/чéм* become interested in

зáймут – занимáют occupy, take up, interest; займýтся (*past tense E*) – занимáются *кéм/чéм* occupy oneself with

n занятие occupation, pursuit; заня́тия studies, lessons IV.5

заказать – закáзывают order (dinner, a room, etc.) V

n закáз order

заклáдывают: *see* заложить

заключить – заключáют conclude (finish, draw a conclusion) IV; —ся в *чём I only* consist in IV

n заключéние conclusion; придýт – приходить к —ю come to a conclusion

закóн a law, law in general (law as a course or science = прáво) VI

закусить – закýсывают eat snack, eat introductory part of meal CL1

закýс/ка snack, hors d'œuvres; закýски refreshments

зáл hall, auditorium

залóг guarantee; *gr* voice; действи́тельный — active voice; страдáтельный — passive voice

заложить – заклáдывают: *see* оснóва VI

заменить – заменя́ют replace VI

n замéна replacement

замёрз(ну)ть – замерзáют freeze *intr* VIII

замéтить – замечáют notice; remark CL1

n замéт/ка note; замечáние remark (make notes)

замéт/ный noticeable CL5

замечáтель/ный remarkable, splendid VIII

замолчáть fall silent; *cf.* молчáть VI

зáмрут – замирáют stop, come to a standstill (of noise, activity), die down CL5

зáмуж: вы́йдут – выходить зáмуж за *когó* marry (of a woman) R5 note 9

зáмужем: бы́ть зáмужем за *кéм* be married (of a woman) R5 note 9

занимáются *кéм/чéм and without complement* II.7

заня́тия studies, classes; hours of operation; school session IV

занятóй, зáнят busy; *cf.* зáнятый (*PPP of* зáймут) occupied, busy, R9.B, p. 132

занять: *see* зáймут

зáпад west X; западнославя́нский West Slavic; зáпадный western X

записать – запи́сывают write down CL2

запи́с/ка note (a note left for somebody)

заплáкать *P only* begin to weep; *cf.* плáкать

запрети́ть – запрещáют *комý чтó* forbid

запятáя *sub adj, gr* comma

зарáнее beforehand, in advance V

зарождéние (*n < зароди́ть*) conception, origin

засмея́ться *P only* begin to laugh; *cf.* смея́ться

засну́ть – засыпáют fall asleep CL4.1

засте́нчивость bashfulness VI

затéм then, next R7.A5

затó on the other hand, however CL1.5

захотéть *or* захотéться *комý P only, imps* get the desire; *cf.* хотéть(ся)

зачéм why, what for R10.B

защити́ть — защищáют defend; —ся defend oneself X.B

(по)звáть (зовýт) R5.D7

звёздá *S pl* star

(по)звони́ть *комý* (по телефóну) *кудá* ring; call (on the telephone) R8 note 6;

n звон/ó/к ring, bell; telephone call

звóнкий ringing, clear; *gr* voiced

звýк sound; глáсный — *gr* vowel; соглáсный — *gr* consonant; *cf.* R10.A

здáние building (structure); *n < previous* здáть build; *cf.* создáть

здорóвый, здорóв, здорóва healthy R9.E; здоровéе *comp*; здóрово *colloq* marvellous(ly); great!

здорóвье health CL1; за — CL1.4; на — CL1.4

здра́вствовать be well, prosper, thrive
CL4; здра́вствуй(те) (greeting) hello;
да здра́вствует long live (*lit* Let
flourish, prosper)
зелёный (*sh f* зе́лен, зелена́, зе́лено, зе́ле-
ны) green; *cf.* зеленее CL4
зем/ля́ *S pl* (*exc gen* земе́ль) *acc sg* earth,
land, ground CL5; Земля́ the Earth
земно́й, terrestrial, earth *adj* VIII
зёрно́ grain VI; зёрна *S pl* grains, cereals
зима́ *S pl acc sg* winter; зимо́й in the winter
зло́ evil, bad (*opposed to* добро́ good)
з/ло́й, зол evil, malicious; angry; зол
на *кого́/что́ sh f only* be angry at
зна́к sign, symbol, mark III; в — as a sign
of X; вопроси́тельный — question
mark; восклица́тельный — exclamation point
(по)знако́мить *кого́* с *кем* make acquainted
with; —ся с *кем* get acquainted with
знако́мый, знако́м, знако́ма *кому́* familiar
to R10 note 8, R9.E; — с *кем* acquainted with; *sub adj* acquaintance
знамени́тый famous, eminent
зна́мя, зна́мени (*sg like* вре́мя; *pl* знамёна,
знамён, знамёнам) banner, standard
CL4
зна́ние (*n* < зна́ют) *freq pl* knowledge:
У него́ больши́е —я. He has great
knowledge.
значе́ние (*n* < зна́чить) meaning, significance, importance III; име́ют —е have
significance
зна́чит *paren* thus, then, this means that II:
Он жи́л в Росси́и, зна́чит, уже́ ви́дел
на́шу ро́дину. He's lived in Russia, so
he's already seen our motherland.
значи́тель/ный significant, important CL.2
зна́чить *3 pers only* mean
  n значе́ние meaning; significance
(по)зову́т: *see* (по)зва́ть
зо́лото gold
зре́ние (*n* < зре́ть *obs* see) (eye)sight,
vision VI; то́чка —я point of view; с
то́чки —я from the point of view of
зу́б *E pl obl* tooth CL3
зубно́й tooth *adj* CL3; — вра́ч dentist CL3
и III.1; *emphatic* R5.D4

и . . . и . . . both . . . and . . . R8 note 3
и то CL5.4
игра́ *S pl* game
(с)игра́ют (*P* сыгра́ют) play R10 note 6;
— в *что́* play a sport; — на *чём* play
an instrument; — ро́ль play a role
иде́я idea VI
идио́м *or* идио́ма idiom
иду́т (*inf.* идти́) come R4 note 15; run,
function (of trains, etc.) R7 note 12
из (*отку́да of* в *words*) R4.B
изве́ст/ный (well-)known, familiar; (a) certain II; до —ой сте́пени to [a]certain
degree
извини́ть – извиня́ют *кого́* за *что́ or кому́*
что́ excuse somebody for something
CL3; —ся excuse oneself
измени́ть – изменя́ют change *tr* CL5;
—ся в *кого́/что́* change into/to *intr*; *gr*
(of sounds) X.A
из-за (*отку́да of* за) R4.B; due to, because
of; from behind; *see* грани́цы (из-за)
из-за того́, что because R10.B
из-под (*отку́да of* под) from under R4.B
изучи́ть – изуча́ют II.7
изъяви́тельное наклоне́ние indicative
mood
икра́ caviar CL1
и́кс X (unknown, etc.)
или . . . или . . . either . . . or . . . R8 note 3
имени́тельный (паде́ж) nominative (case)
и́менно namely; precisely, exactly, just
CL5, III:
Во́т и́менно. Yes, that's just it.
име́ют have, possess R9 note 12; — де́ло с
have to do with, have business with;
— ме́сто *3 pers only* take place, go on
V; — в виду́ keep/have in mind
име́ются be found, be available; име́ющие-
ся available
импера́тор emperor
императри́ца empress
империали́зм imperialism; империали́ст
imperialist; империалисти́ческий im-
perialist(ic)
и́мени *gen of* и́мя CL3.5
и́мя, и́мени (like вре́мя) name (first name of
person); R5.B *gr* noun, substantive; —
прилага́тельное adjective; — со́б-

ственное proper name/noun; — существительное noun; — числительное numeral

йна́че otherwise, in another way VI

индей/ка turkey (hen) CL2

инжене́р engineer CL1

иногда́ sometimes

иной other; йна́че *adv* otherwise, in another way; ин(о)- other-

иностра́нный foreign CL3, V

институ́т institute

интере́с/ный interesting; (of a person) attractive

интересова́ть interest *tr*; интересова́ться *кем/чем* be interested in

Интури́ст *short for* Иностра́нный тури́ст Intourist (Soviet bureau for foreign travel) V

инфинити́в *gr* infinitive

иска́ть *кого́/что́ or кого́/чего́* look for, search

исключи́ть – исключа́ют except, exclude, rule out, expel VII
    n исключе́ние
    за исключе́нием *кого́/чего́* with the exception of

иску́сствен/ный artificial IX.4

иску́сство art IX.4; skill

испа́н/е/ц, испа́н/ка Spaniard; Испа́ния Spain; испа́нский Spanish

испо́льзовать *I and P* use VIII.9

исто́рия history; story

исто́чник spring; source VIII

исходи́ть из *чего́* take as a point of departure, depart from, be based on IV; исхо́дный пу́нкт point of departure

исче́з(ну)ть – исчеза́ют disappear
    n исчезнове́ние VI

Ита́лия Italy; италья́н/е/ц, италья́н/ка Italian *n*; италья́нский Italian *adj*

и т.д., и та́к да́лее and so forth

и т.п., и тому́ подо́бное and so forth

итти́ *variant of* идти́

йо́т j, jot, *or* jod *gr*

к (*куда́ of* «у» *words*) R4.B

кабине́т study

Кавка́з (на) Caucasus

ка́ждый every, each; *imposes accusative without preposition regardless of time unit* R7.A1

ка́ждый, кто́ III

ка́жется – каза́лось *paren* apparently:
    Он, ка́жется, её бра́т. He is, apparently, her brother.

(по)каза́ться *кем/чем or* что seem R5.D7

ка́к *or кем/чем* as R8 note 13; *as conjunction with verbs of perceiving*, that *instead of* how IV.2

ка́к бы IX.A6

ка́к мо́жно *comp of* X   as X as possible R5.A4

как ра́з just, exactly R6 note 2, I, III:
    Это как ра́з то́. That's just it (the thing).

ка́к: та́к как since

како́в, какова́, каково́, каковы́ X.5

календа́рь *M E* calendar

ка́ль/ка (*gen pl* ка́лек) calque *ling*; loan translation

кани́кулы (на) *pl only* (*gen* кани́кул) vacation (in academic world) R10 note 4

капитали́зм capitalism; капитали́ст capitalist; капиталисти́ческий capitalistic IV

капита́льное строи́тельство capital construction VIII

капита́н captain

ка́рий brown, hazel R7.D; —е глаза́ brown/hazel eyes

ка́рта map, chart; playing card

карти́на picture; *also fig*; painting

карье́ра career I

каса́ются: *see* косну́ться CL5.7

ка́сса box office, cashier's office

ката́ются на *чём* roll, ride

катего́рия category

ка́федра (на) college or university department

ка́чественный qualitative

ка́чество quality V; в ка́честве *кого́/чего́* in the capacity of, as

ка́ша porridge

ка́ш/е/ль *M* cough CL3

кварти́ра (в *or* на) apartment

килогра́мм kilogram

кило́метр kilometer

кино́ *N indecl* cinema, movies *colloq*, movie house, theater

кинотеа́тр movie theater

кипу́чий seething CL5.10

Кири́лл Cyril VII; кири́ллица Cyrillic alphabet VII

кисе́ль *M* kissel (jellylike dish) CL1

кислоро́д oxygen VIII; кислоро́дный oxygen *adj* VIII

кис/лый, ки́сел sour; acid (chemistry) CL1

кита́/е/ц, китая́н/ка Chinese *n*; Кита́й China; кита́йский Chinese *adj*

клад́ут: *see* положи́ть – клад́ут

кла́сс class, classroom; заня́тия classes

класси́ческий classical VII

кла́сть: *see* положи́ть – клад́ут

кли́мат climate VIII

клуб club

клю́ч *E* key; spring (water) VIII

ко́е- VIII.4

ко́е-ка́к carelessly VIII.4

(по)колеба́ть *S all pres and impv* (*PPP* поколе́блен) shake VIII; —ся oscillate, hesitate; vary, fluctuate; *n* колеба́ние

колбаса́ (*pl* колба́сы) sausage

коле́но (*pl* коле́ни, коле́ней) knee CL2

колесо́ *S pl* wheel VI

коли́чественный quantitative; —ое числи́тельное cardinal numeral

коли́чество quantity, amount V; большо́е — large number

колле́га *M* colleague

коллекти́в collective *n*; коллекти́вный collective *adj*

колхо́з (коллекти́вное хозя́йство) collective farm, kolkhoz; колхо́зник, колхо́зница collective farmer

кольцо́ *S pl* (*gen pl* коле́ц) ring CL2

команди́р commander

командиро́в/ка business trip, official mission V; бы́ть в —е be on a business trip; е́хать в —у go on a business trip

комите́т committee VII

коммерса́нт businessman, merchant V

коммуни́зм communism; коммуни́ст communist; коммунисти́ческий communist(ic) IV

ко́мната room V.9; R10.A

компози́тор composer

компо́т stewed fruit CL2

конве́рт envelope

коне́чно of course; *also concessive meaning*

конкре́т/ный concrete IV

конститу́ция constitution

констру́кция construction; *also gr*

контине́нт continent; континента́льный continental VIII

конто́ра office

конце́рт (на) concert

концла́герь (*nom pl* концлагеря́) (концентрацио́нный ла́герь) concentration camp

копе́й/ка kopeck (100 to a ruble)

ко́р/е/нь *M E pl obl* root

коридо́р corridor, hall

кори́чневый brown CL4; ка́рие глаза́ brown eyes

коро́ва cow

коро́т/кий, ко́роток, коротка́, ко́ротко́, ко́ротки́ short

коро́че *comp of* коро́ткий

корпора́ция corporation

ко́свенный indirect; oblique (cases: genitive, instrumental, prepositional, dative); —ое дополне́ние indirect object; —ая ре́чь indirect speech

косну́ться – каса́ются CL5.7

кость (в кости́) *E pl obl* bone VI

костю́м suit; costume CL4

кото́рый R4.D, III; *substitutions for participles* R9.A; *avoided in* э́то *constructions* III.2

котле́та cutlet CL1

ко́фе *M indecl* coffee

кошёл/ё/к, кошёлька purse

ко́ш/ка cat II

кра́й (в/на краю́) (*E pl* края́) edge, border; land, region, territory II

кра́йний extreme; last II; *no sh f, but note adv* кра́йне extremely; по кра́йней ме́ре at least

кра́йность extremity

кра́н faucet; crane (machine) CL4

крапи́ва nettle

краси́вый beautiful, pretty

(по)кра́сить paint; *I only* adorn CL5

красноре́чие eloquence CL5

кра́с/ный red CL5

кра́т/кий short, concise (*more abstract than* коро́ткий)

Кре́мль *M E* Kremlin III, CL3

кре́п/кий strong, robust, firm III

кре́пче *comp of* кре́пкий

кре́с/ло armchair

кри́к shout CL4

кри́кнуть – крича́ть shout

кри́тика criticism II

критикова́ть criticize CL2

крича́ть: *see* кри́кнуть

крича́щий (*pres act part* < крича́ть) loud, flashy

крова́вый bloody IV

крова́ть bed(stead) CL3 Vocab

кро́вь (в крови́) *E pl obl* blood

кро́ме *кого́/чего́* except; besides I

кро́ме того́ (чтобы) furthermore IX.A5

кру́глый, кру́гл round; complete CL2

кру́п/ный large, big; important, major (*freq opposite of* ме́лкий)

Кры́м (в Крыму́) Crimea

кста́ти by the way; to the point, appropriate(ly) CL1

кто́ тако́й X? who is X? R5 note 3

куда́ *place to* R4.B; *with comp* R5.A8

культу́ра culture IV

культу́р/ный cultural; cultured; polite

куп/е́/ц merchant

купить – покупа́ют buy

курить smoke II

ку́рс course (academic по *чему́*) II.5; rate of exchange II; бы́ть в —е (де́л(а)) be in the know; слу́шают — take a course

кус/о́/к piece, bit, lump VII, CL1

куха́р/ка cook *F*

ку́х/ня (в *or* на) (*gen pl* ку́хонь) kitchen

ку́шают (ску́шают) eat CL1.1

лаборато́рия laboratory

ла́герь *E pl* -я́ camp (military, boy scout, etc.); *nom pl* ла́гери camp (sociopolitical) IV

ла́мпа lamp

лати́ница Latin (Roman) alphabet VII

лати́нский Latin VII

ле́вый left; *see also* нале́во, сле́ва

лёг/кий, лёгок, легка́, легко́, легки́ easy; light (of weight)

ле́гче *comp of* лёгкий

легча́йший easiest

л/ё/д, льда́ (на льду́) ice VIII

лёжа́ть R8.B

лейтена́нт lieutenant

лека́рство medicine (remedy) CL3

ле́ксика lexicon

лекси́ческий lexical

ле́кция lecture

лени́вый lazy

ле́с (в лесу́) *E pl* -а́ forest

ле́стница stairs, stairway; ladder V

лета́ют fly *nondet*

лете́ть fly *det*

ле́то   summer; ле́том in the summer

лётчик, лётчица flier

лечить treat, attempt to cure CL3; —ся undergo cure, receive treatment

ле́чь: *see* ля́гут(ле́чь) – ложи́ться

ли R3.C

ликёр liqueur CL1

лингви́ст linguist; лингви́стика linguistics; лингвисти́ческий linguistic VII

ли́ния line

литерату́ра literature VII

литерату́р/ный literary

ли́ть(ся): *see* лий-ут(ся)

ли́фт elevator V

лифтёр elevator operator

лицо́ *S pl* face; person, *also gr*; де́йствую-щие —а cast of characters; к —у́ becoming, appropriate:

Э́то ва́м к —у́. That's becoming to you.

Э́то не к —у́. That isn't becoming.

ли́чный personal, *also gr*; —ое местоиме́-ние personal pronoun

лишь only

л/о́/б (на лбу́) forehead CL2

ло́д/ка boat

ло́ж/ка spoon

ложи́ться R8.B

ло́шадь *E pl obl* horse

луна́ *S pl* moon CL5

лу́нный lunar, moon *adj* CL5

лу́чше все́х *vs.* лу́чше всего́ R5.A7

лу́чший best R5.A

лы́жа ski

льд-: *see* лёд

лий-ут pour *tr and colloq intr* VIII; —ся
flow, pour *intr*

любéз-ный amiable, nice CL1; бýдьте
любéзны please (be so kind as)

любúмый favorite CL5.12

любить R4 note 13; — когдá *or* чтобы like
it when (that) CL4.4

люб/ó/вь, любви́, любóвью love VI

любóй any II.3

любопы́т/ный curious (*both* worthy of *and*
manifesting curiosity) CL5

любопы́тство curiosity CL5

ля́гут (лечь *past* лёг, легла́, легло́, легли́) –
ложи́ться R8.B

мавзолéй mausoleum CL3

магази́н store; универса́льный — department store

маги́стерский: *see* стéпень

майóр major *n*

Македóния Macedonia VII; македóнский
Macedonian VII

малéйший least, slightest III, V; без —его
without the least, slightest; ни —его
not the least, slightest

ма́ло R6.A2, R4 note 14

ма́ло тогó CL5.2

ма́лый small; ма́л, мала́, мало́, малы́ too
small

маркси́зм Marxism; маркси́ст Marxist *n*;
маркси́стский Marxist *adj*

маршировáть march CL3

ма́с/ло E *pl* (*exc gen pl* ма́сел) butter, oil

ма́сса mass VIII; ма́ссы *pl* (the) masses

математика mathematics

материа́л(ы) material(s) VII

матрóс sailor

маши́на machine; *colloq* car

маши́н/ка (пи́шущая) typewriter

мéбель furniture V

медици́на medicine (field)

медици́нская сестра́ (медсестра́ *or* сестра́)
nurse

междомéтие *gr* interjection

мéжду тéм VIII.1; мéжду тéм как VIII.1

междунарóдный international V

мéл (в/на мелу́) chalk

мéл/кий small, fine; shallow; petty

мéльче *comp of* мéлкий

мельча́йший smallest, minutest

мéнее R5.A1

мéньший R5.A

меню́ N *indecl* CL1

мéра measure III; по кра́йней —е at least;
при́мут – принима́ют —ы take measures

мероприя́тие measure IV

мёртвый dead

мéстный local; *gr* locative VII

мéсто E *pl* -á place

местоимéние *gr* pronoun; возвра́тное —
reflexive pronoun; ли́чное — personal
pronoun; относи́тельное — relative
pronoun; отрица́тельное — negative
pronoun; притяжа́тельное — possessive pronoun; указа́тельное — demonstrative pronoun

мета́лл metal; металли́ческий *adj*

мéтод method

метрó N *indecl* subway, metro

Мефóдий Methodius VII

меха́ник mechanic

мечта́ dream (while awake and *fig*), daydream, fantasy (dream (asleep) = сóн;
pl is normally мечта́ния)

мечта́ют dream (while awake and *fig*), daydream; *but* dream (asleep) = ви́деть
сóн

(по)меша́ют disturb, bother; — + *inf*
stop V.1

n помéха

мили́ция police

милиционéр policeman

ми́лый nice, sweet; (direct address) dear
CL1, VIII

ми́ля mile

ми́мо когó/чегó past

минера́л mineral; минера́льный *adj*

ми́нус minus (A minus = A с ми́нусом)

мину́та minute

ми́р E *pl* peace III; world III

ми́рный peaceful

мировóй world *adj*, worldwide

мла▨▨▨ческий infantile; (of time) earliest

мла́дший younger, youngest, junior R5.A1

мнéние opinion VI; бы́ть X-ого —я о be
of X opinion about; Какóго вы́ —я о

What's your opinion about; по моему
—ю = по-мо́ему
мно́гие *vs.* мно́го R6.A2
мно́го R4 note 14; *vs.* мно́гие R6.A2
мно́го *vs.* о́чень R4 note 3
многокра́т/ный repeated, multiplex; —
ви́д frequentative aspect *gr*
многообра́зие diversity, variety VII
многообра́з/ный diverse, varied
многочи́слен/ный numerous VI
мно́жественное число́ plural (number)
могу́чий powerful CL5.10
мода́льный modal
мо́жет быть *NB stress* perhaps CL5
мо́жно R5.C, II.1; ка́к мо́жно + *comp of*
X as X as possible R5.A4
молодёжь youth
моло́же *comp of* молодо́й
молоко́ milk; моло́чный *adj*
мо́лча silently R9.B, p. 133
молча́ть be silent; *cf.* замолча́ть VI
монополи́ст monopolist; монополисти́-
ческий monopolistic
мо́ре *E pl* -я́ (*gen pl* море́й) sea I
моро́женое (*sub adj* < моро́зить) ice
cream; сли́вочное — vanilla ice cream;
шокола́дное — chocolate ice cream
моро́з cold, frost, freezing weather:
Сего́дня си́льный —. It's freezing
weather today.
морско́й maritime, sea *adj* I
морфе́ма morpheme
морфологи́ческий *gr* morphological
морфоло́гия *gr* morphology
морфофоне́ма morphophoneme
Москва́ *song* CL5
моско́вский Muscovite, Moscow *adj*
мо́ст (на мосту́) *E pl* bridge
мо́щ/ный powerful IV
(вы́)мо́ют wash *tr*; —ся wash oneself CL4,
X.B
му́ж (*pl* мужья́, муже́й) husband
мужско́й masculine, men's, male; — ро́д *gr*
masculine gender
мужчи́на *M* man (as distinct from woman)
музе́й museum
му́зыка music CL4
музыка́нт, музыка́нтша musician
мундшту́к *E* cigarette holder VII

му́чить torment VI; —ся torment oneself
n му́ка
мы́сль thought, idea
мы́ть(ся): *see* мо́ют(ся)
мя́г/кий soft, mild, gentle VIII; — согла́с-
ный soft consonant
мя́гкость mildness
мя́гче *comp of* мя́гкий
мя́со meat CL1; мясно́й meat *adj*
мя́ч *E* ball

на *acc or prp* R4.B; for (a period of time
with change of location) R7.A3; for
IV.4; by, to the extent of VIII.5; in:
Э́то сло́во конча́ется на гла́сный.
This word ends in a vowel.
«на» words *vs.* «в» words R4.B, R4 note 5;
(compass points) I.3
на Х-ом языке́ in X language I.8
набира́ют: *see* набра́ть
наблюда́ют ка́к watch, observe how something is done VI; — за ке́м/че́м observe, follow; watch over, supervise
n наблюде́ние (< *an older* наблюду́т)
remark, observation
наб/ра́ть(наберу́т) – набира́ют (но́мер)
dial (number) CL3
наве́ки forever CL4
наве́рно *paren* probably; III surely *arch*
наверняка́ surely, certainly III
наве́рх (*куда́*) up, upward, upstairs
наверху́ (*где́*) above, upstairs
нагре́ют – нагрева́ют heat, warm up VIII
наде́жда hope VI
надёж/ный reliable, dependable CL4
наде́нут – надева́ют put on (clothes) CL4
наде́яться, что hope that; — на кого́/что́
rely/depend on
на́до: не на́до R6.C
наза́д (*куда́*) back R5; Иди́ наза́д Go back;
X тому́ наза́д X ago (тому́ *may be
omitted*)
назва́ть (назову́т) – называ́ют name, call
R5.D7, CL5
n назва́ние name, title (of a book or
thing, but not of a person) R5.B
назна́чить – назнача́ют appoint, assign,
fix V
назову́т: *see* назва́ть

называемый *pres pass part* < называют; так — so-called

называются *кём/чём I only* be called, give a name R5.D7

наиболее + *adj* X the most X; — интересная книга the most interesting book

наименее + *adj* X the least X; — интересная книга the least interesting book

найдут – находить find; —ся *see* p. 277

накануне R7.A6

наклонение *gr* mood; mode; изъявительное — indicative mood; повелительное — imperative mood; сослагательное — subjunctive mood; условное — conditional mood

наконец finally, at last VII

наконечное ударение end stress

налево (*куда, где*) to/at the left

наливают: *see* налий-ут

налить: *see* налий-ут

налий-ут – наливают *кому что/чего* pour, fill (up) someone's glass with (liquid) CL1

намазать – намазывают smear, spread on VI

намеренный intentional, deliberate CL3
  n намерение intention; я намерен, намерена + *inf* I intend to

намного + *comp* much, by far VIII.5

наоборот (напротив) on the contrary; the wrong way around III; как раз — quite the contrary

напад/ки *pl only* (*gen* нападок) (< нападут – нападают) attacks (*us* verbal); criticism

напечатают: *see* (на)печатают

направить – направляют direct IV
  n направление direction (also political)

направо (*куда, где*) to/at the right

напрас/ный vain, futile; напрасно in vain; useless, it's no use, there is no use in it

например for example

напротив (наоборот) on the contrary; *adv* across the street; — кого/чего opposite, on the other side of

наречие *gr* adverb

народ people, the people, nation, folk III; много —у many people R8.C; русский

— the Russian people

народ/ный people's, popular, national; —ая песня folk song

наружность exterior, personal appearance, looks

наряду с *кём/чём* together with, side by side with; on a level with VIII

насколько to the extent that, as far as

наследник successor, heir VI

населить – населяют settle, populate
  n население population

насморк head cold (a more general cold = простуда) CL3

настолько so, so much; не —; —, чтобы IX.A4

настоять – настаивают на *ком/чём* insist on

настоящий real, actual; present II; в —ее время now, at the present time; —ее время *gr* present tense; по- —ему properly; really, truly

насчёт II.6

наука science; Академия наук Academy of Sciences

научить(ся) II.7 R2.B4

находиться *I only* be located/found R5.D5

национальн/ый national, nationality *adj*
  n национальность IV

начало beginning

начальный beginning, elementary I; —ая школа elementary school

не- V; "*indefinite*" *meaning* VIII.3; *see* несколько, некоторый R6.A2

не *vs.* нет R4.C, p. 77

не *position in sentence* IV.1, R8 note 7

не *pleonastic* (*after verbs of fearing*) IX.A6

не + *verb* + *gen compl* VI.1

не: не раз more than once IV.1; не тот not the right, wrong R5 note 11, IV.1; не то, что (бы) it isn't that CL5.1

небо (*pl* небеса) sky; *pl* skies, heavens; небоскрёб skyscraper

небольшой small, not large

неверующий nonbeliever, atheist VI

невеста fiancée; bride

невозмож/ный impossible II; невозможно impossible

недавний recent; недавно recently, not long ago

недово́ль/ный IX.1
недоста́точ/ный IX.A4, IX.1; недоста́точно IX.A4; IX.1
не́ж/ный tender, loving; delicate (of taste, health, etc.), gentle CL2, CL5
не́зачем V
не́ за что don't mention it IV.4b
незнако́м(ый) *кому́* unfamiliar (to); — с *ке́м/че́м* unacquainted with
неизве́стный unknown
нейтра́ль/ный neutral VI
не́кий someone VIII.3b
не́когда have no time V; once, at one time VIII.3c
не́кому V
не́который some, a certain; *pl* some, certain, VIII.3; —ые из R6.A2
не́кто someone VIII.3b
некульту́р/ный uncultured
нельзя́ II.1, R5.C
не́м/е/ц, не́м/ка German *n*
немно́гие some, a few; few R6.A2; то́лько немно́гие only a few R4 note 14
немно́го some, a bit, a little R4 note 14
немно́го *vs.* немно́гие из R6.A2
немно́жко *colloq* a little bit
нену́ж/ный unnecessary; useless
необходи́мый necessary; indispensable; *stronger than* на́до *or* ну́жно; необходи́мо *inf/*чтобы it is necessary (in order) to III
неопределён/ный indefinite, undetermined, unspecific; — вид nondetermined aspect *gr*
непа́рный согла́сный unpaired consonants
непобеди́мый invincible CL5.11
непра́виль/ный incorrect; *gr* irregular
непра́вый, непра́в, неправа́, непра́вы wrong; incorrect; unjust IV
непреме́нно definitely, certainly
несклоня́емый *gr* indeclinable
не́скольки- *vs.* не́которые из R4 note 14, R6.A2
не́сколько R4 note 14, R6.A2
неслоговой *gr* nonsyllabic
несмотря́ на *кого́/что́* in spite of, despite III
несоверше́н/ный imperfect, not perfect; — вид *gr* imperfective aspect

несовмести́мый incompatible VI
несча́ст/ный unhappy
не́т R4.C; —ещё R3 note 18
не́т *vs.* не R4.C, p. 77
неударя́емый unstressed
неудо́б/ный uncomfortable; inconvenient, awkward V; —ое положе́ние awkward situation
неуже́ли really? is it possible? R10 note 9
неуспе́х failure II, VII; неуспе́ш/ный unsuccessful
нефть oil (petroleum)
не́чего V
не́что something VIII.3a
ни VII; *after interrogatives* VII; *used with pronouns* R3 note 5; *double negative* R3 note 5
ни . . . ни neither . . . nor R8 note 3
ни оди́н R4 note 9, R8 note 9
ни ра́зу not once
ни сло́ва not a word
ни то́т, ни друго́й IV.3b
-нибудь *omission of* V; -нибудь *vs.* -то R3 note 2
нижа́йший lowest R5.A, p. 87 n.1
ни́же *comp of* ни́зкий
ни́жний lower; —ее бельё underwear
ни́з/кий low
ни́зший lower, lowest R5.A
«-ний» *adjectives in soft* n' R7.D
никако́й *separation by preposition* R3 note 5, R8 note 9
никто́ *separation by preposition* R3 note 5
ниско́лько not at all, not in the least V
но́вость *E pl obl, sg* piece of news; *pl* news III; —и дня́ news of the day
нога́ *S pl acc sg* leg, foot
но́ж *E* knife
но́жницы *pl only* (*gen* но́жниц) scissors; *see* Appendix B
но́мер *E pl* -á number; size; issue (number); hotel room/suite
но́рма norm, standard VIII; вы́полнить – выполня́ют —у fulfill norm; перевы́полнить – перевыполня́ют —у overfulfill norm
но́с (на носу́) *E pl* nose CL2
носи́ть wear (clothes)
носки́: *see* носо́к

нос/о́/к (*pl* носки́) sock(s) CL2
ночно́й night *adj*, nocturnal CL4; —ы́е
    ту́фли night slippers
но́чь (в ночи́) *E pl obl* night; на — for the
    night; споко́йной —и good-night
(по)нра́виться *кому́* like R4 note 13
ну́жно R6.C; — чтобы IX.A3
нулево́й zero *adj*; —о́е оконча́ние zero-
    ending
ну́ль *M E* zero
ну́ Well . . . , now . . .

о *кого́/что́* X.4
о́ба/о́бе both IV.3a
обе́д: за обе́дом at dinner
(по)обе́дают eat dinner, dine CL1
(по)обеща́ют *or* обеща́ют *кому́ что́ I and P*
    promise
оби́деть – обижа́ют offend, insult CL4;
    —ся be/get offended/insulted CL4
облада́ют *кем/чем* possess VII.6
о́бласть *E pl obl* area, region; field (area of
    knowledge) II; в о́бласти *чего́* in the
    field of
обма́н deception, deceit, fraud III
обма́|нуть – обма́нывают deceive, trick
    III
обнару́жить – обнару́живают reveal, dis-
    play VIII; —ся reveal/display itself
обобщи́ть – обобща́ют generalize V
обозна́чить – обознача́ют designate, mark
    VII
об/о/йду́т – обходить go over; go
    around; avoid VI; —ся без get along/
    do without
обоснова́ть – обосно́вывают base,
    ground, substantiate
    n обоснова́ние basis
обра́довать(ся): *see* (об)ра́довать(ся)
о́браз shape, form, manner, image; X —ом
    in X way/manner; гла́вным —ом
    mainly, chiefly; каки́м —ом how, in
    what way; таки́м —ом thus, in this/
    that way; — жи́зни way of life
о́браз *E pl* -а́ icon
образова́ть *P and I or* образо́вывают form
    tr; *PPP* образо́ванный (well-)edu-
    cated; —ся form *intr*
    n образова́ние formation, education

VIII; вы́сшее образова́ние higher edu-
    cation
обрати́ть – обраща́ют turn V; —внима́-
    ние на *кого́/что́* pay attention to;
    —ся к *кому́* за *чем/с чем* turn to,
    address oneself to for/with:
    Я обрати́лся к врачу́ за по́мощью. I
    turned to the doctor for help.
    Он обрати́лся к учи́телю с про́сьбой.
    He addressed the teacher with a re-
    quest.
обраща́ются с *кем/чем I only* get along
    with/treat (people); treat, handle
    (objects)
обра́тный opposite, reverse, back *adj* VIII;
    —ая сторона́ луны́ reverse side of the
    moon; туда́ и обра́тно there and back;
    round trip
обслужи́ть – обслу́живают serve, wait on V
    n обслу́живание service; *pl* facilities
обстано́вка furniture; situation, condi-
    tions, circumstances V
обсуди́ть – обсужда́ют (*PPP* обсужде́н)
    discuss, talk over II
обусло́вить – обусло́вливают make a con-
    dition, stipulate; cause VIII
обще́ственный social, of society
о́бщество society VII
о́бщий general, common, overall, total
    VIII; в —ем, вообще́ IV.7; име́ют
    мно́го —его have much in common;
    —ее де́ло common cause
объём volume VIII
объясни́ть – объясня́ют explain
    n объясне́ние
обыкнове́н/ный usual, ordinary, common-
    place
обы́ч/ный usual, ordinary, customary
обяза́тель/ный obligatory; обяза́тельно
    obligatory; definitely, certainly:
    Я обяза́тельно приду́. I'll definitely
    come.
о́вощи *pl only, E pl obl* vegetables
ограни́чить – ограни́чивают limit, restrict
    V; —ся *чем* limit oneself/be limited to
ограни́чен/ный limited
огро́м/ный enormous, immense, huge III
одева́ют(ся): *see* оде́нут(ся)
оде́жда clothes, clothing CL4

одéнут – одевáют dress *tr*; —ся get
  dressed, dress oneself CL4, X.B
одéть(ся): *see* одéнут(ся)
одúн one, alone, only, (a) certain, a R5
  note 8; the same R5 note 10; *see also*
  ни одúн
одинáковый the same, identical VI
однáжды once (upon a time), one day
однáко however VIII
однослóж/ный *gr* monosyllabic
одолéют – одолевáют overcome VI
ожидáют *когó*/*чегó* expect
означáют mean, signify CL5
оказáть – окáзывают render, exert, show
  IV; — влияние на *когó*/*чтó* exert influence on; — пóмощь *комý*/*чемý*
  render aid to; — противодéйствие
  комý/*чемý* oppose; — содéйствие
  комý/*чемý* cooperate; —ся *кéм*/*чéм or*
  что turn out R5.D7:
    Он оказáлся хорóшим человéком.
    He turned out to be a good man.
    оказáлось, что it turned out that
океáн ocean; океáнский ocean *adj*
окнó: (по)смотрéть в окнó look out the
  window R8 note 5
óколо *когó*/*чегó* near; around, about; approximately R7 note 7
окончáние termination, ending; *gr* ending
окóнчить – окáнчивают finish (particularly a set program, a school course, etc.) I
окружúть – окружáют surround, encircle
  CL5; окружáющие surrounding
  people CL5; я окружён XH, p. 277
октя́брьский October *adj*
омóют – омывáют wash against
омывáют: *see* омóют
омы́ть: *see* омóют
опáздывают: *see* опоздáют
óпера (на) opera
описáть – опúсывают describe V
  n описáние description
оплóт stronghold, bulwark CL4
опоздáют – опáздывают be late; — на
  чтó or к *чемý* be late for; на *чтó* time:
    Он опоздáл на дéсять минýт. He was
    ten minutes late.
    n опоздáние
определён/ный (*PPP* < определúть –

определя́ют) definite, fixed, determined; — вид *gr* determined aspect
определéние determination; definition; *gr*
  attribute
определúть – определя́ют define, determine, fix, specify IV
опя́ть again
организáция organization
организовáть *P and I or* организóвывают
  organize
орфогрáфия orthography
освободúть – освобождáют liberate, free
  VI; —ся от free/rid oneself of X
óсень fall, autumn; óсенью in the fall/
  autumn
осмотрéть – осмáтривают look at, inspect
  V, CL3; —ся look around, get one's
  bearings
  n осмóтр
оснóва basis VI; заложúть – заклáдывают
  —у lay foundation; лежáть в —е *чегó*
  (ля́гут (лéчь) – ложúться в —у *чегó*) be
  (become) the basis of; положúть – кла-
  дýт X в —у *чегó* take X as a basis of;
  на —е *чегó* on the basis of; —на глáсный, соглáсный, сонóрный, шýмный
  gr consonant, vowel, resonant, obstruent
  stem; пóлная — *gr* full stem
основáние (*n* < основáть found) basis,
  reason, grounds, foundation; на тóм
  —и, что on the grounds that
основáтель/ный thorough CL3
осóба person *us F*
осóбенный special, particular V
осóбый special, particular
остáваться: *see* остáнутся
остáвить – оставля́ют leave *tr* R4 note 16.
  R7 note 3
остальнóй remaining, other CL1, VII
остановúть – останáвливают stop V.1;
  —ся stop *intr* V.1, X.A
  n останóв/ка stop, halt; stop (place where
  things—bus, etc.—stop)
остáнутся – остáваться stay, remain;
  accusative of time or на *когó*/*чтó* (for)
  R7.A3, R7 note 3, R5.D7
остáться: *see* остáнутся
осторóж/ный careful, cautious
óстрый, óстр sharp; остёр *E* sharp, quick-

witted
о́стров (на) *E pl* island
от (*отку́да* «у» *words*) R4.B
от . . . до . . . *place* R4.B; *time* R8.A
отбы́ть – отбыва́ют (из) depart
   n отбы́тие
отвёду́т – отводить V.6
отвёзу́т – отвозить V.6
отве́тить – отвеча́ют *кому́* на вопро́с
   answer someone's question
   n отве́т; в отве́т in/as an answer X.1
отглаго́льный (formed) from a verb, deverbative; —ое существи́тельное *gr*
   deverbative noun
отда́ть – отдава́ть give up; give back III
   n отда́ча
отдели́ть – отделя́ют separate, divide
   n отделе́ние separation, division, department, section
отде́льный separate, individual V
отдохну́ть – отдыха́ют rest, take a rest; be
   on vacation V.I
о́тдых (на) rest V; *see* отдохну́ть – от-
   дыха́ют
отдыха́ют: *see* отдохну́ть
оте́чество fatherland CL4
отказа́ть – отка́зывают *кому́ в чём* refuse/
   deny; reject; —ся от *чего́* refuse, renounce
   n отка́з VI
открове́нность frankness III
открове́н/ный frank, open III
откро́ют – открыва́ют discover
   n откры́тие
открыва́ют: *see* откро́ют
откры́тый *adj* vs. *part* R9.B, p. 132, p. 277
откры́ть: *see* откро́ют
отку́да *place whence* R4.B
отличи́ть – отлича́ют distinguish VII;
   —ся distinguish oneself X; отлича́ют-
   ся *чём* be notable for; —ся от *чего́*
   or в *чём* differ from in, be distinguished
   from by
   n отли́чие
отли́ч/ный excellent CL1, I; сдать экза́мен
   на отли́чно pass an examination with
   an "excellent"
отме́рить – отме́ривают *or* отмеря́ют
   measure off VI

отме́т/ка (< отме́тить – отмеча́ют) note,
   grade (in school)
отнесу́т – относить IV.6, V.6; —ся IV.6
относи́тельно *кого́/чего́* IV.6
относи́тель/ный relative, *also gr*
отноше́ние IV.6
отпра́вить – отправля́ют send (off) III;
   —ся set out for III
о́тпуск vacation R10 note 4
отрица́тель/ный negative, *also gr*
отрица́ют *I only* deny, reject VI
   n отрица́ние denial; *gr* negation
отры́в/о/к fragment; passage VI
отста́нут – отстава́ть от lag behind, fall
   behind; run slow (of clock)
отступи́ть – отступа́ют step away from
отсу́тствие absence IV
отсу́тствовать be absent
отсю́да from here, hence
оттого́, что because R10.B
отту́да from there, from that, from that it
   is clear that
отчего́ why R10.B
о́тчество patronymic
отъе́зд departure V
отыска́ть – оты́скивают find, look for
   R2.A4
офице́р officer
официа́нт waiter CL1
официа́нт/ка waitress CL1
офо́рмить – оформля́ют make official, formalize, write up officially, register V
   n оформле́ние
охлади́ть – охлажда́ют cool (off), *also fig*
   VIII
оцени́ть – оце́нивают (*PPP* оценён) estimate, value, evaluate VIII
   n оце́н/ка evaluation, estimate
о́чень vs. мно́го R4 note 3
о́чередь *E pl obl* line; turn IV; в пе́рвую —
   primarily; в свою́ — in its turn; ста́-
   нут – станови́ться в — take place in
   line; стоя́ть в —и stand in line
очки́ *pl only* (*gen* очко́в) (eye)glasses; в
   очка́х wearing glasses
ошиби́ться (ошибу́сь, ошибу́тся, ошибся,
   ошиблась) – ошиба́ются make a mistake
   n оши́б/ка mistake

па́дают: *see* упаду́т
паде́ж *E* case *gr*
палатализа́ция palatalization
палатализова́ть palatalize; палатализо́-
ванный palatalized
палата́льный *gr* palatal
па́л/е/ц (*gen* па́льца) finger; toe CL2
пальто́ (over)coat VII
пальц-: *see* па́лец
па́мятник monument; literary monument/
document VII
папиро́са cigarette (*Russian style with
holder* = мундшту́к) VII
па́ра pair
пара́д parade
паради́гма *gr* paradigm
пара́дный parade *adj* CL5
па́рк park VIII; — культу́ры и о́тдыха
park of culture and rest
па́рный согла́сный paired consonant
парти́й/ный party *adj* IV
парти́йность party membership; party
spirit/principles (*us* Communist Party)
па́ртия party (political) IV; съе́зд —и party
congress
пассажи́р passenger
пе́рвое CL1.3
пе́рвый first; former VII.5
первонача́льный primary, original, initial
CL5
переведу́т – переводи́ть transfer, move
across; — с *чего́ на что́* translate from
X to Y R4.B
n перево́д translation; transfer VII
перево́дчик, перево́дчица translator
перевооружи́ть – перевооружа́ют rearm
n перевооруже́ние rearmament
перевы́полнить – перевыполня́ют overfulfill VIII; — но́рму overfulfill norm
n перевыполне́ние
перегласо́в/ка *gr* vowel shift
перегово́ры (на) *pl only* negotiations, talks
перед *vs.* до R9 note 1
перед те́м как I.1
пере́дний front *adj*
пере́дняя *sub adj* anteroom, front hall V.9
передово́й foremost, front, leading II; *sub
adj* front line (military); —ая статья́
editorial

переживу́т – пережива́ют experience, live
through; survive VII
n пережива́ние experience
перейду́т – переходи́ть в/на что́ change to;
«т» перехо́дит в «ч» "t" changes to
"č"
n перехо́д
переоде́нут – переодева́ют change someone's clothes CL4; —ся change (one's
own) clothes
переоде́ть(ся): *see* переоде́нут(ся)
пересели́ть – переселя́ют move to a new
location *tr* VI; —ся move to a new
location *intr*, migrate
n переселе́ние move, migration
переста́нут – перестава́ть + *inf* stop V.1
переста́ть: *see* переста́нут
перехо́д (< перейду́т – переходи́ть)
change, mutation
пери́од period I
перо́ *S pl* (*nom pl* пе́рья, *gen pl* пе́рьев)
feather; pen
пе́с/ня (*gen pl* пе́сен) song; вы́ступить –
выступа́ют с —ей sing a song (performance); наро́дная —я folk song
(с)пе́ть: *see* (с)пою́т
печа́ль grief, sorrow VI
печа́ль/ный sad, sorrowful
(на)печа́тают print; type on a typewriter;
—ся be published, appear in print (of
a writer)
печа́ть the press
пи́во beer
пиджа́к *E* jacket, (suit) coat CL4
пирож/о́/к little pie, patty CL1
писа́тель, писа́тельница writer
пи́сьменность written language; literature
пи́сьменный written (not oral); writing II;
— стол (writing) desk; — экза́мен
written exam
пить: *see* пьют
пи́шущая: — маши́н/ка typewriter
пи́ща food
пла́вают *nondet* swim
плака́т placard, poster CL3
пла́кать weep, cry; *cf.* запла́кать
план plan
плат/о́/к kerchief, shawl; носово́й —
handkerchief

пла́тье (*gen pl* пла́тьев) clothes; (woman's) dress CL2

племя́нник nephew

племя́нница niece

плечо́ *S* (*nom pl* пле́чи) shoulder CL2

пло́щадь (на) *E pl obl* (city) square; space I;. жила́я — (жилпло́щадь) living space

плыву́т *det* swim

плюс plus; A с —ом A plus

по чему́ II.5; *motion about, all over a surface* R4 note 6; *each—distributive* V.7; по + *dat pl* (*time expressions*) R7.A7; с . . . по R8.A; по-Хому, по-Хски in an X manner IX.2

по- (*prefix*) *perfectivizing plus inceptive meaning* R2.A3, R4.A2; *for a while* R3 note 7, R8.B

по- (*prefix*) + *comp* a little X-er R5.A5

по-Хски *vs.* на X-ом языке́ I.8

-победи́мый CL5.11

победи́ть – побежда́ют defeat;
  n побе́да victory (*but* defeat = пораже́ние); — бу́дет за на́ми we shall have the victory

побре́ют(ся): *see* (по)бре́ют(ся)

побри́ть(ся): *see* (по)бре́ют(ся)

побыва́ют (*где verb*) *P only, intr* visit, be in a place R10 note 1

по́вар *E pl* -а́ cook (male) CL1

по-ва́шему in your opinion

повезёт – повезло́: *see* (по)везёт

повели́тельное наклоне́ние *gr* imperative mood

пове́рить: *see* (по)ве́рить

повер̧ну́ть – повора́чивают turn *intr*: Он поверну́л нале́во. He turned left.

пове́рхност/ный superficial VIII

пове́рхность surface; area VIII

пове́сить – ве́шают hang *tr*

пове́стка дня́ (на) agenda IV

по́весть *E pl obl* tale, novelette VI

повиди́мому apparently, to all appearances VIII

по́вод: по по́воду II.6

повора́чивают: *see* повер̧ну́ть

повсю́ду (*куда*) everywhere

повтори́ть – повторя́ют repeat
  n повторе́ние

поговор/ка saying, maxim I.7

под *что* with/to (accompanying); под *кого*/*что*/*кем*/*чём* under R4.B; под *чём* near, in the environs of R8 note 15

подари́ть: *see* (по)дари́ть
  n пода́р/о/к gift VIII

по́дать – подава́ть give, hand, serve (food and in sports) CL1; — заявле́ние submit application
  n пода́ча service (sports)

подви́жно́е ударе́ние movable/shifting stress

подготови́тельный preparatory IV

поддержа́ть – подде́рживают support, maintain VIII
  n поддержа́ние maintenance; подде́ржка support

по́дле *кого*/*чего* next to, beside

подлежа́щее *sub adj, gr* subject

подмоско́вный near Moscow *adj* CL5; Подмоско́вные Вечера́ *song* CL5

по̆дни́мут – поднима́ют raise, lift CL3; —ся (подня́лся, -а́сь, -о́сь, -и́сь) go up, ascend, rise
  n подня́тие, подъём

подо́б/ный similar, like; this VIII; и тому́ —ое (и т.п.) and so forth, etc.

подожда́ть: *see* (под/о/)жда́ть

под/о/йду́т – подходи́ть к approach, come up to; — *кому*/*чему* suit, fit, be suitable for VIII
  n подхо́д

подро́бность detail II

подро́б/ный detailed II

подру́га friend (female)

подтверди́ть – подтвержда́ют confirm, substantiate
  n подтвержде́ние

подхо́д approach VI

подъём (*n* < по̆дни́мут – поднима́ют) rise, ascent

по́езд *E pl* -а́ (на) train

пое́зд/ка trip, journey I

пожале́ют: *see* (по)жале́ют

пожа́ловать: Добро́ пожа́ловать *куда* Welcome to V

пожа́луй perhaps VI

пожа́р fire (conflagration)

пожела́ют: *see* (по)жела́ют

пожениться R5 note 9

пожмут: *see* (по)жмут

позабо́титься: *see* (по)забо́титься

поза́втракать: *see* (по)за́втракать

позади́ (*где́*) behind, in back

позва́ть: *see* (по)зва́ть

позво́лить – позволя́ют *кому́ что́* permit, allow V

   n позволе́ние

позвони́ть: *see* (по)звони́ть

поздне́е *comp of* по́здний

по́здний late; по́здно *adv* late, too late

поздра́вить – поздравля́ют с *чём* wish, congratulate on CL5.9

   n поздравле́ние

по́зже *comp of* по́здний

пози́ция position

познако́мить(ся): *see* (по)знако́мить(ся)

позову́т: *see* (по)зва́ть

поймут – понима́ют understand

   n поня́тие concept, idea; понима́ние understanding

(с)пой-ут (пе́ть) sing

пока́ while I.2; for the time being V.5; — не until I.2; — что for now V.5

показа́ть – пока́зывают *кому́ что́* show; — на *кого́/что́* point to/at; —ся: *see* (по)каза́ться

   n пока́з show, demonstration

поко́й rest, peace III

поколеба́ть(ся): *see* (по)колеба́ть(ся)

покра́сить: *see* (по)кра́сить

покро́ют – покрыва́ют cover VIII

покупа́ют: *see* купи́ть – покупа́ют

пол half R7 note 6

пол (на полу́) *E pl* floor R10 note 7

пол- *prefix* R7 note 6

по́ле *E pl* -я (*gen pl* поле́й) field

полёжа́ть R8.B

поли́тика politics; policy, policies IV

пол/ка shelf

полногла́сие *gr* polnoglasie, pleophony; полногла́сный polnoglasie *adj*

по́л/ный, по́лон *чего́* full (of); complete; (of a person) stout, plump CL2

полови́на half; в —е второ́го at 1:30; —a пе́рвого 12:30 R6.A3, R7 note 6; X с —ой X and a half

положе́ние (< положи́ть – кладу́т) position; situation III

положи́тель/ный positive; —ая сте́пень *gr* positive degree

положи́ть – кладу́т R?.F

   n положе́ние position, situation

пол/о/н: *see* по́лный

полтора́ *M and N,* полторы́ *F; obl* полу́тора one and a half

полу-: *see* пол-

получи́ться – получа́ются obtain *intr*, be obtained, occur; —, что turn out/ happen that

полчаса́ (*obl* получа́са) half an hour R7 note 6

(вос)по́льзоваться use VII, VIII.9

по́льзоваться *кем/чём* enjoy VIII.9; — авторите́том enjoy authority; — успе́хом enjoy success

   n по́льзование

поль/ка (*gen pl* по́лек) Pole *F*; по́льский Polish *adj* VII; По́льша Poland; поля́к Pole *M*

помести́ть – помеща́ют (*где́*) place, locate; house, put up

   n помеще́ние V

помеша́ют: *see* (по)меша́ют

помеще́ние (*n* < помести́ть – помеща́ют) building, premises, insides of building V

по́мнить remember

помогу́т (помогу́, помо́жешь) – помога́ют *кому́/чему́* help

   n по́мощь help, aid

по-мо́ему in my opinion

помо́чь: *see* помогу́т – помога́ют

по́мощь (*n* < помогу́т – помога́ют) help, aid

понима́ние (*n* < поймут – понима́ют) understanding

понра́виться: *see* (по)нра́виться

поня́тие (*n* < поймут – понима́ют) concept, idea

пообе́дают: *see* (по)обе́дают

пообеща́ют: *see* (по)обеща́ют

попаду́т – попада́ют (*куда́*) *S past* strike/ hit mark; arrive, get (to), "wind up," "land" I

попра́вить – поправля́ют correct; repair

CL4.1; —ся get well, recover; correct self

n попра́в/ка, поправле́ние

попро́бовать: *see* (по)про́бовать

попроси́ть: *see* (по)проси́ть

популя́р/ный popular

попыта́ются: *see* (по)пыта́ются

пора́ *S nom pl acc sg* time V.4; — *кому́ inf* it is time to R9 note 8

порази́ть – поража́ют strike, *fig* amaze IV; я́ поражён *ке́м/че́м* I am struck by; —ся be struck/amazed

n пораже́ние hitting; defeat

по́рт (в порту́) *E pl obl* port VIII

портре́т portrait

портфе́ль *M* briefcase

поря́дковое числи́тельное *gr* ordinal numeral

поря́д/о/к order, system; sequence III; в —е all right, in order; —а *чего́* (mathematics) of the order of; — сло́в *gr* word order

посади́ть – сажа́ют seat R8.B; — в тюрьму́ put into prison

по-сво́ему in its/his/her/their own way

посети́ть – посеща́ют visit I

n посеще́ние

посиде́ть R8.B

поско́льку so far as, as far as; since, inasmuch as R9 note 3

посла́ть (пошлю́т) – посыла́ют send

n посы́л/ка sending; package

по́сле *кого́/чего́ prep* after; по́сле *adv* afterwards

по́сле того́ как I.1

после́дний last, latter R7.A6, VII.5

после́довательность consistency; sequence; — времён *gr* tense sequence

после́доватсль/ный consistent

после́довать: *see* (по)сле́довать

после́дствие consequence VIII

после́дующий ensuing, subsequent

послеза́втра day after tomorrow

посло́вица proverb I.7

послу́шают(ся): *see* (по)слу́шают(ся)

посмотре́ть: *see* (по)смотре́ть

посове́товать: *see* (по)сове́товать

пос/о́/л ambassador

посо́льство embassy

поспеши́ть: *see* (по)спеши́ть

поспо́рить: *see* (по)спо́рить

поссо́риться: *see* (по)ссо́риться

постара́ются: *see* (по)стара́ются

посте́ль bed CL3

постепе́н/ный gradual VII

поста́вить: *see* (по)ста́вить R8.B

постоя́н/ный constant; —ое ударе́ние *gr* fixed stress

постоя́ть R8.B

постро́ить: *see* (по)стро́ить

поступи́ть – поступа́ют (*куда́*) enter, enroll; act, take a step

n поступле́ние entering, enrollment; посту́п/о/к act, step taken

посу́да dishes; мо́ют посу́ду wash dishes

посчита́ются: *see* (по)счита́ются

посыла́ют: *see* посла́ть

по-тво́ему in your opinion

поте́ря (*n* < (по)теря́ют) loss VIII

потеря́ют: *see* (по)теря́ют

потол/о́/к ceiling

пото́м then, afterward R7.A5

потому́ что R10.B

пото́м/о/к descendant VI

потре́бовать: *see* (по)тре́бовать

потрясе́ние shock (*n* < (по)трясу́т)

поу́жинают: *see* (по)у́жинают

похо́жий на *кого́/что́* like, similar; (бы́ть) —*freq sh f* resemble R9.E:

Она́ похо́жа на сестру́. She resembles her sister.

по́чва soil VIII

почему́ R10.B

почему́-то for some reason

по́чта (на) post office; mail; по —е by mail

почу́вствовать: *see* (по)чу́вствовать

пошл-: *see* посла́ть

пощу́пают: *see* (по)щу́пают

поэ́т poet

поэ́тому therefore

(с)пою́т(пе́ть) *see* (с)пой-ут (пе́ть)

появи́ться – появля́ются appear

n появле́ние appearance

пра- proto-; праязы́к protolanguage

пра́вда truth; *paren with concessive sense:* (it is) true VI.3:

Пра́вда. It is true.

Не пра́вда ли? Isn't it so?

пра́вило regulation, rule VI; как — as a rule

пра́вильный correct, true; *gr* regular

прави́тельственный government *adj*

прави́тельство government I.5

пра́вить *ке́м/че́м* rule, govern VII

пра́во *E pl* law (science or study); right; *cf.* зако́н; име́ют — have the right

правописа́ние spelling, orthography

пра́вый right (*vs.* wrong); (hand) R9.E, IV, CL2; он прав he's right R9.E

пра́здник holiday, festival, festive occasion CL5

пра́здничный holiday *adj*, festive

пра́ктика practice IV; на —e in practice

практи́ческий practical

пре- *prefixed to adjective intensifies meaning*: most

превосхо́д/ный excellent, first-rate; —ая сте́пень *gr* superlative degree

превы́сить – превыша́ют exceed VIII

предвари́тельный preliminary IV

предло́г excuse; *gr* preposition

предложи́ть – предлага́ют offer, suggest
n предложе́ние offer, suggestion, proposal; *gr* sentence, clause; *see also* предло́г

предло́жный (паде́ж) prepositional (case)

предме́т object; subject II.5

пре́д/о/к ancestor, forefather VI

предпочту́т (предпоче́сть) – предпочи-та́ют *кого́/что́ кому́/чему́ or inf* prefer X to Y, prefer to CL3

предположи́ть – предполага́ют assume, suppose VII; предполага́ют *inf* intend/propose to; предполо́жим (допу́стим) let us suppose, let us assume
n предположе́ние

предпри́мут – предпринима́ют undertake
n предприя́тие undertaking, enterprise

предрассу́д/о/к prejudice VI

председа́тель chairman

представи́тель, представи́тельница representative

предста́вить – представля́ют represent, present, introduce (a person) I; — себе́ imagine, represent to oneself; предста́вь(те) себе́ imagine!; представля́ют собо́й *кого́/что́* be (something)

R5.D6, IV
n представле́ние presentation, representation; performance (play, etc.); idea (conception); он не име́ет ни мале́йшего представле́ния о he hasn't the least idea of

пре́жде *adv* before, earlier R9 note 1

пре́жде че́м I.1

пре́жний previous VI

президе́нт president

прези́диум presidium CL3

прекра́с/ный beautiful, magnificent; прекра́сно wonderful! great!

прекрати́ть – прекраща́ют stop V.1

премье́р premier

препина́ние: зна́ки —я punctuation marks

преподава́ть (*like* дава́ть) teach I, II.7, R5 note 4

пре́фикс *gr* prefix

при R9 note 4, VIII.1

при всём то́м: *see* при

приблизи́тель/ный approximate

прибы́ть – прибыва́ют arrive (on train, plane, etc.) V
n прибы́тие arrival

приведу́т – приводить bring; — в поря́док put in order; — приме́р give example

приве́т greeting(s); hello! *colloq*; переда́й(те) приве́т give regards

приве́тствовать welcome, greet; *also fig*

привы́к(ну)ть – привыка́ют к *кому́/чему́* get used to, get accustomed to
n привы́ч/ка habit

пригласи́ть – приглаша́ют (*куда́*) invite I

приго́товить(ся) – приготовля́ют(ся): *see* гото́вить(ся)

придётся – приходиться *кому́/чему́ imps* must, have to R7 note 2; turn out (as), emerge as VIII; have the occasion to X.7

прие́зд arrival

признаю́т – признава́ть recognize, admit; —ся в *чём* confess to X

прийти́сь *see* придётся

прилага́тельное (и́мя) adjective

примени́ть – применя́ют apply VIII.9
n примене́ние application

приме́р example I; наприме́р for example

примири́ть – примиря́ют reconcile VI;
—ся become reconciled with

при́мут – принима́ют receive, accept,
take III; — во внима́ние take into account; — ме́ры take measures; —
уча́стие в *чём* participate in; при́нято
inf it is the custom (to), it is accepted by
everyone (to) VII

принадлежа́ть *кому́/чему́* (к *кому́/чему́*)
belong to (a group or organization)
VII; — к числу́ belong to the number
(of those who . . . etc.)

принесу́т – приноси́ть bring

при́нято: *see* при́мут – принима́ют

приро́да nature VII; от —ы, по —е
by nature, naturally; явле́ние —ы
natural phenomenon

приста́в/ка *gr* prefix

приступи́ть – приступа́ют к begin, get at/
to something IV

прису́тствие presence IV

прису́тствовать be present IV

прито́м VIII.2

притяжа́тельный *gr* possessive

приходи́ться: *see* придётся

причём VIII.2

прича́стие X-ого зало́га Y-ого вре́мени
participle of X voice (and) of Y tense;
— действи́тельного зало́га active
participle; — страда́тельного зало́га
passive participle; — настоя́щего/про-
ше́дшего вре́мени present/past participle

причёсать – причёсывают comb *tr* CL4;
—ся comb oneself CL4, X.B

причи́на reason, cause II

прия́тно: Очень прия́тно (познако́миться
с ва́ми). I'm glad to meet you.

прия́т/ный pleasant

про *кого́/что́* about *colloq* V.8; — себя́ V. 8

про- *prefix* (for/through) (a specific period)
R8.B

проанализи́ровать: *see* (про)анализи́ро-
вать

пробле́ма problem

(по)про́бовать try (out) X.8

провали́ть – прова́ливают fail *tr, colloq*
II; —ся (на экза́мене) collapse; (fail)
n прова́л

проведу́т – проводи́ть carry on/out, conduct, lead IV, CL1; — вре́мя spend
time R8 note 11; — неде́лю spend a
week

програ́мма program IV

прогре́сс progress VIII

про́дать – продава́ть sell
n прода́жа

продиктова́ть: *see* (про)диктова́ть

продо́лжить – продолжа́ют continue *tr* I;
—ся continue *intr*
n продолже́ние continuation; в продол-
же́ние III.6

продукти́в/ный productive, *also gr*

проживу́т – прожива́ют live through,
spend (time)

произведу́т – производи́ть produce, create
IV
n произведе́ние production, work; *cf.*
произво́дство; произведе́ние иску́с-
ства work of art; произведе́ния Пу́ш-
кина works of Pushkin; произво́дство
production, manufacture, produce (*in
concrete sense*; *i.e.* turn out *autos
per year* = вы́пустить – выпуска́ют)
IV

произнесу́т – произноси́ть pronounce; —
то́ст pronounce a toast
n произнесе́ние utterance (as of a toast);
произноше́ние pronunciation

произо/йду́т – происходи́ть *3 pers only*
take place, happen, VII; come from
n происхожде́ние origin; он ру́сского
происхожде́ния he's of Russian ori-
gin/extraction

пройду́т – проходи́ть go/pass through; —
уро́к go through lesson

пролёжа́ть R8.B

пролета́рий proletarian:
Пролета́рии всех стра́н, соединя́й-
тесь! Workers of the world, unite!

промы́шленность industry IV

пропага́нда propaganda VI

пропусти́ть – пропуска́ют miss, omit V

просиде́ть – проси́живают sit for/through
a period of time CL3, R8.B

(по)проси́ть *vs.* спроси́ть – спра́шивают
R3.F

просклоня́ют: *see* (про)склоня́ют

просл́нуться – просыпа́ются wake up *intr* CL4.1

проспа́ть (*like* спа́ть) – просыпа́ют oversleep CL3

проспряга́ют: *see* (про)спряга́ют

прости́ть – проща́ют forgive

про́сто simply, merely R6 note 2

просто́й simple

простоя́ть R8.B

простуди́ться – просту́живаются catch cold CL3

просыпа́ют(ся): *see* проспа́ть *and* проснуться

про́сьба request, favor CL5 (*n* < (по)проси́ть)

протёку́т – протека́ют flow, leak; pass (elapse), proceed VIII

про́тив *кого́/чего́* against; име́ют — R9 note 12

проти́вник enemy, opponent III

проти́в/ный opposite; offensive, repulsive; в —ом слу́чае otherwise

противоде́йствие opposition IV; оказа́ть – ока́зывают — *кому́/чему́* oppose

противоде́йствовать *кому́/чему́* oppose

противополо́жность opposition, contrast VIII; в — *кому́/чему́* unlike X, in contrast to X

противополо́ж/ный opposite; opposed; —ые интере́сы opposed/opposite interests

протяже́ние (*n* < протя́гнуть – протя́гивают): на протяже́нии III.6 stretch, extend

профе́ссия profession I

профе́ссор *E pl* -á professor; *see* R3 note 6

прохла́дный cool

проце́сс process VIII

проце́нт percent VIII

прочёл, проче́сть, прочл-: *see* прочту́т

прочита́ют = прочту́т *P of* чита́ют

про́ч/ный solid, firm, durable VIII

прочту́т – прочита́ют – (прочи́тывают): проче́сть, прочёл, прочла́; *see* R2.A5

проше́дшее вре́мя *gr* past tense

про́шлое *sub adj* the past

про́шлый past; last R7.6

про́ще *comp of* просто́й

прояви́ть – проявля́ют manifest, display,

show VI; —ся manifest/display itself
n проявле́ние manifestation

прямо́й straight, direct; пря́мо directly; openly; *also gr.* паде́ж, ре́чь, дополне́ние

психи́ческий mental, psychical

пти́ца bird

пу́блика public (in a theater, etc.); audience

пульс pulse CL3

пункт point

пуска́й = пусть

пусти́ть – пуска́ют let

пусто́й empty

пусть let (*introduces 3 pers impv*); even if, if only (хотя́ бы, хоть) VI; -нибудь *after* — *and* пуска́й R3 note 2

путь way, path, road R10 note 2; like 3 decl noun (две́рь) except has end stress and inst sg путём); по —й on the way; путём *чего́* by means of VII

(по)пыта́ются X.8
n попы́т/ка

пье́са (stage) play; musical piece CL3

пий-ут drink; *cf.* вы́пий-ут – выпива́ют; *see also* R2.A5

рабо́та (на) work

рабо́тают над *чём* work on something R6 note 19

рабо́чий *adj* workers', labor; *sub adj* worker, working man, laborer VI

ра́венство equality

равно́: всё равно́ *кому́/чему́* it's all the same to; it doesn't matter; anyway, nevertheless VII.4

ра́в/ный equal

равноХ-ый: равнозна́ч/ный meaning the same; равнопра́в/ный with equal rights

равноду́ш/ный indifferent

ра́д, ра́да, ра́ды *sh f only* glad CL1, R9 note 11; — *inf* glad to; — что glad that; — *кому́/чему́* glad of: Мы́ ра́ды го́стю. We're glad of our guest, glad that he came.

ра́ди *кого́/чего́* prep (*sometimes follows gen*) for the sake of; — бо́га for God's sake; шу́тки — for the sake of a joke

ра́дио *N indecl* radio CL4; по — on the radio; радиоаппара́т radio (set)

(об)ра́довать make glad/happy I; —ся
кому́/чему́ be glad/happy about/of I

ра́дость joy, gladness

ра́дост/ный glad, joyous CL4

ра́з E pl (gen pl ра́з) time(s), occasion
R7.A8; в пе́рвый — for the first time;
на э́тот — this time (right now) CL4.3;
не — more than once; ни —y not once

ра́з once, since IX.B7

разбира́ются в ко́м/чём know, be versed
in; see also раз/о/бра́ться

разбуди́ть: see (раз)буди́ть

ра́зве really? (Do you mean it?) R10 note 9

развёд/ка intelligence (branch of government or military) II

развива́ют, разви́тие, разви́ть: see раз/о/
вий-ут – развива́ют

разгова́ривают converse, talk CL3

разгово́р conversation CL2

разда́ться (разда́лся other past E) – раз-
дава́ться resound, be heard

раздели́тельный роди́тельный partitive
genitive

раздели́ть – разделя́ют share VI; — на
что́ divide (something) into X; —ся на
X be divided into X

разде́нут – раздева́ют undress tr; —ся get
undressed, undress intr, take coat off
CL4.1

разде́ть(ся): see разде́нут(ся)

разли́ч/ный different, differing; diverse VII

ра́зница difference VII; кака́я — (ме́жду)
what's the difference (between)

разнообра́з/ный varied, diverse CL1

ра́зный different, various VI, CL1

раз/о/вий-ут – развива́ют develop tr VII;
—ся develop intr
n разви́тие development

раз/о/бра́ться – разбира́ются в ко́м/чём
investigate, gain understanding of, figure out, get to the bottom of II

разоде́нут P only dress up tr CL4; —ся P
only dress up intr

разоде́ть(ся): see разоде́нут(ся)

разоружи́ть – разоружа́ют disarm IV
n разоруже́ние disarmament

разочарова́ть – разочаро́вывают disappoint CL5; —ся в be disappointed
in/about

n разочарова́ние

разреши́ть – разреша́ют кому́ что́ permit

разыска́ть – разы́скивают look up V

райо́н region, area

раке́та rocket IV

ра́нний early; ра́но adv

ра́ньше comp of ра́нний; before, previously
R9 note 1

распа́д disintegration, decay VII (< распа-
ду́тся – распада́ются)

располага́ют ке́м/чём have at one's disposal, have VII.6; see also располо-
жи́ть

расположи́ть – располага́ют dispose,
place, arrange VIII; — к dispose to, incline to tr
n расположе́ние

распространи́ть – распространя́ют spread
tr VII; —ся spread intr

рассве́т dawn, also fig CL5; на —е at dawn,
also fig at the dawn

рассказа́ть – расска́зывают tell, narrate,
relate R3.F, R7 note 10
n расска́з

рассмотре́ть – рассма́тривают examine/
consider (a question, etc.) VI
n рассмотре́ние

раствори́ть – растворя́ют dissolve VIII

расту́т (расти́: ро́с, росла́, росли́) grow
n рост

реа́кция reaction VIII

ребён/о/к (pl де́ти) child

революцио́н/ный revolutionary III

револю́ция revolution III

ре́д/кий rare, seldom

ре́же comp of ре́дкий

ре́з/кий sharp, harsh VIII

ре́зкость sharpness; pl sharp words

результа́т result VIII; в —е чего́ as a result
of

ре́зче comp of ре́зкий

река́ S nom pl acc sg river

религио́з/ный religious VI

рели́гия religion VI

ремо́нт repair(s); в —е being repaired

респу́блика republic CL4

республика́нский republican; Республи-
ка́нская Па́ртия Republican Party

рестора́н restaurant CL1

ре́чь *E pl obl* speech; a speech II; вы́сту-
пить – выступа́ют с ре́чью make a
speech; о чём —? what's being discussed?; — идёт о *ко́м/чём* X is being
discussed; *gr* speech

реши́ть – реша́ют decide; solve
n реше́ние

реши́тель/ный decisive, decided, resolute

ржа́вый rusty, rust-colored CL5

Рим Rome; ри́мский Roman

ро́в/ный even; ро́вно в 5 часо́в at exactly
5 o'clock

род (в роду́) *E pl* birth, family (in broad
sense); *gr* gender; вся́кого —а X all
kinds of X; мужско́й/же́нский —
masculine/feminine gender; type, sort;
своего́ —а X an X in its way, in a way
(in some special way); тако́го —а X
X of that type, such an X
Откуда́ вы —ом? Where were you
born?

ро́дина (на) native land, motherland CL5

роди́тели *us pl* parents I

роди́тельный (падеж) genitive (case); —ый
раздели́тельный partitive genitive

роди́ть *both P and I or I* рожда́ют give
birth CL5; роди́ться – рожда́ются be
born
n рожде́ние

родно́й native I

родны́е *pl sub adj* relatives I

ро́дственник relative I

ро́дствен/ный related VII

рожа́ют: *see* роди́ть

рожда́ют(ся): *see* роди́ть(ся)

рожде́ние (*n* < роди́ть(ся)) birth

Рождество́ Christmas; рожде́ственские
кани́кулы Christmas vacation CL5

ро́ль *E pl obl* role II; игра́ют — play a
role

рома́н novel

рос, росла́, росли́: *see* расту́т

ро́скошь luxury CL4

Росси́я Russia

рост (*n* < расту́т) growth, increase; height
CL2; (не)высо́кого —а (not) tall;
ни́зкого —а short
Он —ом с вас. He is about your
height. (с кого́/что́ approximately)

ро́стбиф roast beef CL1

р/о́т, рта́ (во рту́) mouth

роя́ль piano

р/т-: *see* ро́т

руба́ш/ка shirt CL4

рубль *E* ruble

ружь/ё *S pl* (*nom pl* ру́жья, *gen pl* ру́ж/е/й)
gun

рука́ *S nom pl acc sg* hand, arm; за́ руку by
the hand; под руку by the arm

руководи́тель leader IV

руководи́ть *кем/чем I only* rule, govern,
lead V, VII.6

ру́копись manuscript

Румы́ния Rumania, Romania; румы́нский
Rumanian, Romanian

ру́сский: на ру́сском языке́ *vs.* по-ру́сски
I.8

Русь (на Руси́) (*obl* Руси́, *but* Ру́сью) *old
word for* Росси́я CL4

ры́ба fish CL1

ряд (в ряду́) *E pl* ряды́ (*after numbers 2/3/4*
ряда́) rank, row; series; — X (*gen pl*)
a number of X; це́лый — a number; a
whole bunch, a lot

с since (*in time expressions*) R6 note 1

с ... по ... R8.A

с (*откуда of «на» words*) R4.B

сад (в саду́) *E pl* garden

сади́ться: *see* ся́дут (се́сть) – сади́ться

сажа́ют: *see* посади́ть – сажа́ют R8.B

сам *vs.* са́мый R4 note 11, R5 note 2

самова́р samovar

самолёт (на) airplane

са́мый *no sh f* (*do not confuse with* сам X-
self); the very R4 note 11; са́мый X
(*adj*) the most X, the X-est R4 note 11,
R5.A2; тот же (са́мый) the (very)
same

сапо́г *E* (*gen pl* сапо́г) boot; *see* Appendix
B2

са́хар *E pl* -а́ sugar

сва́дьба (на) (*gen pl* сва́деб) wedding

све́жий fresh CL1

сверх- super-, over-; —уро́чная рабо́та
overtime work; —челове́к superman

све́рху (*откуда*) from above/the top

свет light; world X

све́т/лый, све́тел, све́тло; *adv* светло́ (в
 ко́мнате светло́) light, bright IV
свида́ние meeting, rendezvous; до —я
 good-bye
свино́й *pig adj* CL1
свинь/я́ *S pl* (*gen pl* свине́й) pig
свобо́да freedom I
свобо́д/ный free (*also* unoccupied) I; го-
 вори́ть свобо́дно (на X языке́) speak
 X language fluently R9.E
сво́й R3 note 8
связа́ть – свя́зывают connect, tie, link IV
 n связь (*prp* свя́зи) connection, communication, liaison, link, love affair III; в
 связи́ с in connection with, with regard
 to; due to II.6, III
сдать – сдава́ть surrender; hand in II,
 R2.A4; —ся surrender *intr*; — экза́-
 мен *I* take; *P* pass exam R2.A4
 n сда́ча surrender; handing in
сде́лаются: *see* (с)де́лаются
себе́: *see* себя́
себя́ *vs.* -ся X.B
себя́ *reflexive pronoun* R7.B3
себя́: *see* про себя́
се́вер (на) north I; северо-восто́к (-чный)
 northeast(ern); северо-за́пад (-ный)
 northwest(ern); се́верный northern I
седо́й gray(-haired) CL1
сей, сего́, сих, сию́ *arch pronoun for* э́тот
сейча́с now; very soon, right away:
 — ва́м скажу́. I'll tell you right away.
 Что́ вы — де́лаете? What are you
 doing now?
сейча́с же immediately, right away
секрета́рша secretary (female); секрета́рь
 M E secretary (male or female)
секу́нда second
селё́д/ка herring *colloq* CL1
село́ *S pl* (peasant) village
се́льский of the village, rural
се́льское хозя́йство agriculture, *lit* rural
 economy IV
семе́стр semester II
семь/я́ *S pl* (*gen pl* семе́й) family I
серб, се́рб/ка Serb
Се́рбия Serbia; се́рбский Serbian
сербохорва́тский Serbo-Croatian VII
се́рд/це *E pl* (*gen pl* серде́ц) heart CL3

серебро́ silver CL5
се́рый gray
серьё́з/ный serious CL2, IV
сестра́: *see* медици́нская сестра́
сесть: *see* ся́дут(се́сть) – сади́ться
сза́ди (*гдé, откýда*) (from) behind
Сиби́рь Siberia
сига́ра cigar
сигаре́та cigarette without holder VII
сиде́ть R8.B; си́дя *vs.* сидя́ R9.B, p. 133
си́ла strength II; —ы forces; вооружё́нные
 —ы armed forces
си́ль/ный strong, powerful II
симпати́ч/ный likable, attractive VIII, CL2
симфо́ния symphony
си́ний (dark) blue
си́нтаксис *gr* syntax
синтакси́ческий *gr* syntactic
систе́ма system II
сих: *see* сей; до сих по́р V.4
сказа́ть – говори́ть, чтобы R3.F
-ски *and* по-X-ски IX.2; по-X-ски *vs.* н а
 X-ом языке́ I.8
склоне́ние *gr* declension
(про)склоня́ют *gr* decline
ско́б/ки *pl only* (*gen pl* ско́бок) parentheses,
 brackets; в ско́бках in parentheses/
 brackets
скольк- R6.A2
ско́лько вре́мени how much time, how
 long; what time is it? R6.A2
скоре́е (скоре́й) (*comp of* ско́рый) rather,
 sooner R5.A9
ско́рость velocity
ско́рый soon; fast, quick; до —ого свида́-
 ния see you soon; —ая по́мощь first
 aid; —ый по́езд express train
скри́п/ка violin
скро́ют – скрыва́ют conceal, hide *tr* CL5;
 —ся conceal self, hide *intr* X
скрыва́ют(ся): *see* скро́ют(ся)
ску́ч/ный boring
скуша́ют: *see* ку́шают
сла́бый weak CL4
сла́ва glory CL4; — бо́гу glory to God,
 thank God
славяни́н (*nom pl* славя́не, *gen pl* славя́н)
 Slav VII
славя́нский Slavic, Slavonic VII

слад/кий sweet CL1

слáдкое CL1

слáть (шлют) send

слáще *comp of* слáдкий

слéва (*гдé, откýда*) on/from the left

слéд (в следý) *E pl gen sg* trace VI

(по)слéдовать *комý/чемý or* за *кéм/чéм* follow

слéдует – слéдовало *комý/чемý plus inf* should, ought; кáк слéдует properly, as one should; не слéдует – слéдовало should not, ought not R6.C

слéдствие consequence VIII

слéдующий next, following на слéдующий дéнь R7.A6; *see also* R9.B, p. 132

слúв/ки *pl only* (*gen pl* слúвок) cream CL1

слúвочный cream *adj*; —ое морóженое vanilla ice cream

слúшком IX

Словáкия Slovakia VII; словáцкий; словáк, словáч/ка Slovak VII

Словéния Slovenia VII; словéнский; словéн/е/ц, словéн/ка Slovene (-ian) VII

словообразовáние *gr* word-formation

словáрь *M E* dictionary

слóг *E pl obl, gr* syllable

слоговóй *gr* syllabic

слóж/ный complicated; *gr* compound

слóй (в слою) *E pl* layer VIII

служúть *комý/чемý* serve I

n слýжба (на) service I

слýчай case; occasion, instance; incident; opportunity V; в крáйнем —е if worst comes to worst (in an extreme case); в протúвном —е otherwise; в такóм (этом) —е in that case; во всяком —е in any case; anyway; на всякий — just in case

случúться – случáются *3 pers only* happen: Случúлось, что ... It happened that ...
Чтó случúлось? What happened?

(по)слýшаются *когó/чегó* obey

слыш/ный audible VI

смéна change, shift VIII (*n* < сменúть – сменяют)

смéрть *E pl obl* death

смéх laughter

смеш/нóй funny, ridiculous, humorous

смеяться над *кéм/чéм* laugh (at); *see also* X.A; *cf.* засмеяться

(по)смотрéть look (at) R4 note 10, R8 notes 4 *and* 5

смотрéть за *кéм/чéм* look after; смотрéть чтобы *past/impv* see to it that

смотря depending on, according to; — кáк/ когдá depending on how/when; — по томý, кáк это бýдет сдéлано depending on how it will be done

смягчúть – смягчáют soften, ease, mollify VIII

n смягчéние softening; *gr* palatalization, softening

сн-: *see* сóн

сначáла at first

снéг (в/на снегý) *E pl* -á snow; — идёт it's snowing

снúзу (*откýда*) from below/the bottom

снúм/о/к (*n* < снúмут – снимáют) photograph

снúмут – снимáют take off; photograph CL4

n снятие

снóс/ный tolerable, bearable I

собáка dog VI

собирáтельное числúтельное *gr* collective numeral

собирáют(ся): *see* собрáть(ся)

собóй: R7.B3

собóр cathedral CL3

собрáть (соберýт) – собирáют gather, collect *tr*; —ся gather, collect *intr*; get ready to, intend to, be about to

n собирáние collecting; собрáние (на) collection; — meeting

сóбственный own; R3 note 8; сóбственно говоря strictly speaking; —ое úмя proper name; свóй —ый one's own

событие event IV

совершён/ный perfect, absolute; — вúд perfective aspect; *vs.* совершённый R9.B

совéт advice; council, Soviet IV

(по)совéтовать *комý/чемý* advise IV

совéтский Soviet; Совéтский Союз Soviet Union

совпадýт – совпадáют (с) coincide (with) V

n совпадéние coincidence

совреме́нник contemporary

совреме́н/ный modern, contemporary VII

совсе́м: совсе́м не not at all; не совсе́м not entirely

согласи́ться – соглаша́ются с *кем/чем* agree with; — на *что* or *inf* agree/consent to III

 n соглаше́ние agreement; согла́сие consent

согла́с/ный in agreement; — с *кем/чем* in agreement with; — на *что* in agreement to:

 Я согла́сен с э́тим. I agree with that.

 Я согла́сен на э́то. I agree to that.

согла́сно *кому/чему* according to

согла́сный (звук) *gr* consonant

согласова́ть – согласо́вывают с *кем/чем* coordinate, make agree with, *also gr*; —ся agree with (correspond to, be coordinated with), *gr* agree with

 n согласова́ние agreement (correspondence), grammatical agreement

соде́йствие assistance, cooperation IV; оказа́ть – ока́зывают — *кому/чему* render assistance, show cooperation

соде́йствовать *кому/чему* assist

содержа́ть (*pres part* содержа́щий) contain II

 n содержа́ние content(s)

соедини́ть – соединя́ют unite, combine, join VIII; Соединённые Шта́ты United States

сожале́ние regret, pity V; к —ю unfortunately

созда́ть – создава́ть (*conjugated like* дать/ дава́ть, *but origin is* со-ЗД- build; *cf.* зда́ние) create

 n созда́ние creation

с/о/йду́т – сходить go down, come off, get off; — с ума́ go out of one's mind

солда́т (*gen pl* солда́т) soldier

со́лнце sun; лежа́ть на — lie in the sun

соль *E pl obl* salt VI

сомнева́ются в *ком/чем pleonastic* не IX. A6

с/о/н sleep; dream CL3; ви́деть — have dream

соно́рный согла́сный *gr* resonant consonant

сообрази́ть – сообража́ют consider, weigh, reason, figure out; при́мут – принима́ют в соображе́ние = при́мут – принима́ют во внима́ние take into account, consideration

 n соображе́ние consideration

сосе́д (*pl* сосе́ди) neighbor; сосе́д/ка neighbor (female)

сослага́тельное наклоне́ние *gr* subjunctive mood

сосредото́чить – сосредото́чивают concentrate VIII

соста́вить – составля́ют: *cf.* состоя́ть(ся) VII.3b

 n составле́ние; соста́в composition, makeup; staff VIII; входить в — *кого/чего* belong to, make up (the composition of)

составно́й compound, *also gr*; composite

состоя́ть VII.3a; состои́т в то́м, чтобы IX.5

 n состоя́ние state, condition; бы́ть в —и be in a position to

состоя́ться *P only* VII.3a;

сосуществова́ть coexist IV

 n сосуществова́ние coexistence

(со)счита́ют count VI.2

со́т/ня (*gen pl* со́тен) hundred VI; со́тни *кого/чего* hundreds of

сотру́дник employee, collaborator, co-worker V

сотру́дничество collaboration

сохрани́ть – сохраня́ют retain, keep, preserve IV

 n сохране́ние

социали́зм socialism; социали́ст socialist; социалисти́ческий socialist(ic) IV

с/о/чту́т (счесть) – счита́ют VI.2

 n счёт

сою́з union; *gr* conjunction; Сою́з Сове́тских Социалисти́ческих Респу́блик Union of Soviet Socialist Republics

спа́ль/ня (*gen pl* спа́лен) bedroom V

спаси́бо: спаси́бо за *что* thanks for IV

спать (сплю, спишь, спят, *impv* спи) sleep

спекта́кль *M* (на) spectacle; spectator event‖спеть: *see* (с)пою́т

специали́ст по *кому/чему* specialist (in) II

(по)спеши́ть hurry; run fast (clock) V

спина́ *S pl acc sg* back (part of body) CL3

спи́ч/ка match (to light a fire)

споко́й/ный calm, quiet, peaceful III; споко́йной но́чи good-night

(по)спо́рить argue IV

спо́рт *sg only* sport, sports; занима́ются —ом (play) sports

спою́т: *see* (с)пою́т

спра́ва (*где́, отку́да*) on/from the right

справедли́вый fair, just

спра́виться – справля́ются с *кем/чем* cope with VII

спроси́ть – спра́шивают *vs.* (по)проси́ть R3.F

(про)спряга́ют *gr* conjugate

спряже́ние *gr* conjugation

спусти́ть – спуска́ют lower; —ся descend, go down

   n спуск descent

сравни́тельный comparative VII; —ая сте́пень *gr* comparative degree; сравни́тельно comparatively

сравни́ть – сра́внивают compare II

   n сравне́ние comparison; по сравне́нию с compared with

сра́зу immediately, at once CL4

среда́ *S pl* environment, milieu, medium; *S nom pl acc sg* Wednesday VIII

среди́ *кого́/чего́* among, amidst VII

сре́дний middle, central; average I; в —ем on the average; сре́дне *colloq* so-so; fair; — род *gr* neuter gender; —яя Азия Central Asia; —яя шко́ла high school

сре́дство means; *pl* material means

(по)ссо́риться quarrel CL2

   n ссо́ра

СССР USSR: *see* сою́з; *pronunciation* I.4

(по)ста́вить R8.B

стака́н glass

станови́ться: *see* ста́нут – станови́ться

ста́нут – станови́ться *кем/чем* become R8.B, R5.D7; *inf, P only* begin to; во что́ бы то́ ни ста́ло no matter what (happens) VII

ста́нция (на) station

(по)стара́ются try X.8

старе́е *comp of* ста́рый R5.A1

стари́к *E* old man

старославя́нский (язы́к) Old Church Slavic (Slavonic) VII

стару́ха old woman CL2

ста́рше *comp of* ста́рый *refers only to age of persons or seniority in rank*; *cf.* старе́е R5.A1

ста́рший older, senior

ста́ть: *see* ста́нут

статья́ (*gen pl* стате́й) article (in newspaper, law code, constitution) II; передова́я — editorial

стена́ *S nom pl acc sg* wall

сте́пень *E pl obl* degree II; до изве́стной (не́которой) —и to a certain extent/degree; до́кторская — doctor's degree; маги́стерская — master's degree; положи́тельная — *gr* positive degree; превосхо́дная — superlative degree; сравни́тельная — comparative degree; — бакала́вра bachelor's degree

стихотворе́ние (normal-length) poem (longer, narrative poem = поэ́ма) CL4

сто́ить *кому́/чему́ что́* cost; *чего́* be worth VII.2; — (то́лько) VII.2

стол *E* table; cuisine CL1; (*verbs of motion and rest used with*) R9 note 7 пи́сьменный — (writing) desk

столи́ца capital city

столо́вая dining room; restaurant (workers', university, etc.) CL1

сто́лько so much; сто́лько . . . ско́лько as much as

сторона́ *S nom pl acc sg* side VI; в —у *кого́/чего́* in the direction of; на —é *кого́/чего́* on the side of; на Х-ой —é on X side; с мое́й —ы́ on/for my part; со —ы́ *кого́/чего́* from/on X's part

стоя́ть R8.B; сто́я *vs.* стоя́ R9.B, p. 133

страда́тельный зало́г *gr* passive voice

(по)страда́ют suffer

страна́ *S pl* country

страни́ца page

стра́н/ный strange

стра́ст/ный passionate CL3

стра́сть *E pl obl* passion

страх fear

стра́ш/ный fearful, terrible, *also fig*; мне стра́шно, I'm afraid/scared

стреми́ться к *чему́ or inf* strive, try IX
стро́гий strict, severe, stern V
стро́же *comp of* стро́гий
строи́тельство building, construction III
(по)стро́ить build
   n строй system, order
стро́ч/ка line (of a page); *also* строка́
структу́ра structure VII
судь/ба́ *S pl (gen pl* су́деб) fate VI
судь/я́ *M S pl (gen pl* суде́й) judge
сумасше́дший mad; out of one's mind VI;
   cf. сойду́т – сходи́ть с ума́
суме́ют *P only* prove able to, succeed in
   VI.5
су́м/ка purse
су́п *E pl* soup CL1
су́т/ки *pl only (gen* су́ток) one day; *see*
   Appendix
су́ть essence IV; по —и де́ла in actual fact;
   — де́ла essence of the matter
сухо́й dry VI
су́хость dryness VI
су́ша (на) dry land (opposed to sea)
существи́тельное (и́мя) noun
существова́ть exist IV
   n существова́ние existence
су́ффикс *gr* suffix; словообразова́тельный
   — formant
сходи́ть round trip R4.A2
счастли́вый (*sh f* сча́стлив) happy; lucky;
   счастли́во so long, best of luck; —ого
   пути́ bon voyage
сча́стье happiness; (good) fortune, luck I;
   к —ю fortunately
сче́сть(ся): *see* сочту́т(ся)
счёт (*n* < сочту́т – счита́ют) *E pl obl or E
   pl* -а́ calculation; bill; (ac)count CL1;
   за — кого́/чего́ at the expense of; due
   to VIII; насчёт II.6
(со)счита́ют VI.2
счита́ют(ся): *see* сочту́т(ся)
(по)счита́ются с VI.2
США Соединённые Шта́ты Аме́рики
   USA
съезд congress, convention IV; — па́ртии
   party congress
съесть (*like* есть) – съеда́ют eat up CL4;
   cf. есть
сыгра́ют: *see* (с)игра́ют

сы́р *E pl* cheese
-ся *pronunciation* R1.A4d; глаго́л на -ся
   sja verb (*in detail*) X; R7.B; CL4.1
-ся *vs.* -сь R7.B1
ся́дут (се́сть) R8.B, CL4

та́к: и та́к as it is, anyway; не та́к wrong,
   not right; та́к как since R9 note 3; та́к
   называ́емый so-called; та́к себе́ so-so,
   middling; та́к что so that (result, not
   purpose); *cf.* та́к, чтобы so that (purpose) IX.A2
та́кже also
тако́в X.5
таково́й X.5; ка́к таково́й X.5
тако́й such; this VIII.7; кто́ —? VIII.7, R5
   note 3; не — ... чтобы IX.A4; —
   (же), како́й III; что́ тако́е? R5 note 3
тако́й-то such and such a X.6
такси́ *N indecl* taxi
тала́нт talent VIII
тала́нтливый talented
та́м there, then; in that case CL3.3; та́м
   (*где́*) III
та́н/е/ц dance
та́нк tank (military) CL3
танцева́ть dance
таре́л/ка dish, plate
твёрдый hard, firm IV; —ый согла́сный *gr*
   hard consonant
твори́тельный (паде́ж) *gr* instrumental
   (case)
тво́рчество creation, creative work (of an
   artist, writer, etc.) VIII
т.е., то́ есть that is
теа́тр theater
телегра́мма telegram
телеграфи́ровать *P and I* telegraph
телефо́н telephone; (по)звони́ть по —у
   call on the telephone
телефо́нный telephone *adj*
те́ло *E pl* body CL3
те́м: *see* чём . . . те́м
те́м + *comp*(X) для so much the X for
   R5.A6
те́м бо́лее, что the more so as R5.A6
те́м не ме́нее nevertheless V
те́ма theme, subject, topic; на —у о on the
   subject of II.6

тём/ный, тёмен *others* E dark CL2, CL4:
Темно́. It is dark.

температу́ра temperature V

те́ннис tennis

тёп/лый, тёпел *others* E warm VIII

те́рмин term VII

термо́метр thermometer CL3

(по)теря́ют lose (general); *but* lose a game
= проигра́ют – прои́грывают VII
n поте́ря

те́с/ный close, narrow VII; те́сно closely;
cramped, crowded

тетра́д/ка, тетра́дь notebook

тётя (*gen pl* тётей) aunt

те́хника technique(s); technology

те́хникум technical (engineering) school

тече́ние (*n* < тёку́т) flow; current VIII; в
— in the course of III.6

тип type VII

типи́ч/ный typical VII

тире́ [t'iré] *gr* dash

ти́хий quiet, still; slow CL5

ти́ше *comp of* ти́хий

то́ *in set expressions* R3.D

то́: да и то́ *or* и то́ for that matter CL5.4;
не то́, что (чтобы) CL5.1; -то *emphatic particle*: э́того-то я́ и хоте́л that's
just what I wanted; то́ (*particle*)
е́сли . . ., (то́) if . . ., then; то́ есть that
is; то́ . . ., то́ now . . . now III.4; то́,
что́ III, IV.A, IV.B; то́, что IV.A,
IV.B⁻

-то *vs.* -нибудь R3 note 2

това́рищ comrade, fellow; — (address)
Comrade, Mr. R5.B; — по *чему́*
-mate, fellow in II.5b; — по ко́мнате
roommate II; — по рабо́те fellow
worker II; — по шко́ле schoolmate
II

тогда́ then, in that case R7.A5; тогда́ как
while, whereas VIII.1; тогда́, когда́
III

то́лстый fat, thick

то́лще *comp of* то́лстый

то́лько not until, only; R9 note 5; only,
just R6 note 2

то́лько *vs.* то́лько что R6 note 2

то́лько что just R6 note 2:
Я́ — — бы́л та́м. I was just there.

тому́: тому́ наза́д ago; к тому́ же furthermore

то́н tone; зада́ть – задава́ть — give/set the
tone

то́н/кий thin

то́ньше *comp of* то́нкий

торго́вля trade

торго́вый commercial, trade *adj*

торже́ствен/ный grand, festive, auspicious,
solemn CL5

то́ст toast; произнесу́т – произноси́ть —
pronounce a toast

то́т: *see* э́тот/то́т, *also* R3.D

то́т же (са́мый) the (very) same

то́т, кото́рый III

то́т, кто́ III

(не) то́т: *see* не то́т

(ни) то́т, ни друго́й: *see* ни то́т, ни друго́й

то́тчас (*often with* же) immediately VII

то́ч/ка point, period VI; — зре́ния point of
view; — зре́ния *кого́/чего́* from the
point of view of; — с запято́й *gr* semicolon

то́ч/ный exact, accurate; точне́е rather,
more exactly R3 note 14

трава́ S *pl* grass

тра́ктор tractor

трамва́й tram, trolley, streetcar

транскри́пция transcription

транслитера́ция transliteration

тра́нспорт transport, transportation VI

(по)тре́бовать *кого́/чего́* demand, require;
—(ся) чтобы + *past* demand/require
that IX.A3
n тре́бование demand, requirement

тре́т/и/й third; *declension type* R6 note 6

тре́тьего дня́ the day before yesterday

тро́й/ка troika

тролле́йбус trolleybus (trackless)

тротуа́р sidewalk

тру́б/ка tube, pipe; telephone receiver CL3

тру́д E work, labor; trouble I; без —á
without difficulty; с —о́м with difficulty

труди́ться work, toil VII; трудя́щийся
worker, toiler (*used in more abstract
contexts*; *pl* toilers, laboring masses)

тру́д/ность difficulty

туале́т toilet

тури́ст tourist CL3

ту́т here; *meaning* in this situation CL3.3

туф/ля (*us pl* ту́фли, *gen pl* ту́фель) loafer, slipper (low shoe without laces) CL4

тюрь/ма́ *S pl* (*gen pl* тю́рем) prison; посади́ть – сажа́ют в —у́ put in prison

тяжёлый *sh f E* heavy, difficult, painful

у *кого́* at someone's place R4.B

-у (-ю) *locative* R3 note 15

-у (-ю) *partitive genitive* R8.C

убеди́ть – убежда́ют *кого́* в *чём* convince X of Y IV; я́ убеждён I'm convinced X.H, p. 277; —ся в *ко́м/чём* convince oneself, make certain

n убежде́ние persuasion; conviction

убо́рная *sub adj* room with toilet V.9

уважа́ют respect, esteem VII; уважа́емый *pres part* respected, esteemed; многоуважа́емый X Dear X (formal address in letters)

n уваже́ние (ува́жить *is not used*) respect, esteem

увели́чить – увели́чивают increase, enlarge VIII

n увеличе́ние

уве́рить – уверя́ют *кого́* в *чём* assure/convince X of Y; я уве́рен I'm certain/sure X.H, p. 277; —ся в *чём* be convinced of

n уве́рение

уви́деть see, catch sight of; *cf.* R2.A2

уговори́ть – угова́ривают persuade R2.A4

уго́дно -ever, any- at all:

Что́ ва́м —? What can I do for you/ What do you want?

Возьми́те ско́лько —/каки́е —. Take as many as you like/whichever ones you like.

у́г/о/л *others E* CL1; в/на углу́ corner, angle; за угло́м around the corner

у́г/о/ль *M* coal

удали́ть – удаля́ют remove *tr* VIII; —ся remove oneself, go away from

n удале́ние

ударе́ние *gr* stress, accent; — на пе́рвом/ после́днем сло́ге stress on the first/last syllable; — па́дает на пе́рвый/после́дний слог stress falls on the first/ last syllable

ударя́емый *gr* stressed

уда́ться (уда́лся, -а́сь, -о́сь, -и́сь) – удава́ться be a success; I; на́м удало́сь *inf* we succeeded in; обе́д уда́лся the dinner was a success; — *кому́ imps inf* succeed in X-ing

удержа́ть – уде́рживают hold fast; retain; restrain VIII; —ся от *чего́* restrain oneself from

удиви́ть – удивля́ют surprise, amaze; я́ удивлён *ке́м/че́м* I'm surprised by X.H, p. 276; —ся *кому́/чему́* be surprised at X.H, p. 276

n удивле́ние

удо́б/ный comfortable, convenient V; удо́бно (*кому́*) comfortable, convenient, (person) at ease

удовлетвори́ть – удовлетворя́ют *кого́/ что́ and кому́/чему́* satisfy

n удовлетворе́ние

удово́льствие pleasure, satisfaction I, CL1; доста́вить – доставля́ют — give/ bring pleasure; с —ем with pleasure

у́ж really, certainly I

у́жас horror, terror II

ужа́с/ный terrible, horrible; very bad (of quality) II; ужа́сно terribly, awfully; very bad

уже́ *vs.* ещё R3 note 18

уже́ не no longer R3 note 18

у́же *comp of* у́зкий

у́жин supper; за —ом at supper

(по)у́жинают have supper

у́з/кий narrow

узна́ют – узнава́ть find out, recognize

указа́тельный *gr* demonstrative

указа́ть – ука́зывают *кому́ кого́/что́ or* на *кого́/что́* indicate, point to, point out IV

n указа́ние: *pl* instructions, directions

Украи́на (на) Ukraine; украи́нский; украи́н/е/ц, украи́н/ка Ukrainian VII

улу́чшить – улучша́ют improve VIII

n улучше́ние

улыбну́ться – улыба́ются smile

n улы́б/ка smile

ум *E* mind, wit, intellect CL5; приду́т – приходи́ть *кому́* на у́м come into one's r..ind/head

уменьши́тельный *gr* diminutive

умере́ть: *see* умру́т

уме́ют know how to, be able to (in general) R3 note 17

  n уме́ние

умира́ют: *see* умру́т

умно́жить – умножа́ют increase VIII; — на *что́* multiply by

  n умноже́ние

у́м/ный, умён, умна́, у́мно́, у́мны́ intelligent, smart, bright

умо́ют – умыва́ют wash face and hands *tr*; —ся wash one's own face and hands CL4

у́мрут – умира́ют, у́мер, уме́рший die

у́мственный mental, intellectual

умыва́ют(ся), умы́ть(ся): *see* умо́ют(ся)

универма́г (универса́льный магази́н) department store

универса́ль/ный universal

университе́т university

упаду́т – па́дают fall

употреби́ть – употребля́ют use VII, VIII.9

  n употребле́ние

управля́ют *ке́м/че́м*; *see* p. 135 govern *also gr*, rule VII.6; маши́ной drive R5 note 7; управля́ет X-ым падежо́м takes X case

  n управле́ние

упражне́ние exercise

Ура́л (на) Urals

у́ров/е/нь *M* level IV; жи́зненный — living standard

уро́к lesson IV.5; на —е at the lesson IV

усеку́т – усека́ют *gr* truncate

  n усече́ние *gr* truncation

уси́лить – уси́ливать strengthen, intensify VII

  n усиле́ние

усло́вие condition, term; *pl* conditions (*both* terms *and* circumstances) VII

усло́в/ный conditional, conventional, prearranged, arbitrary VII; —ое накло-не́ние *gr* conditional mode

услу́га service; *pl* services CL1

услы́шать hear R2.A2

усну́ть *P only* fall asleep

успе́ют – успева́ют have time to, be on time; succeed in V

  n успе́х success II; (с)де́лают —, make progress

успе́ш/ный successful

успоко́ить – успока́ивают calm/quiet down *tr* III; —ся calm/quiet (oneself) down *intr*

  n успокое́ние

уста́лость tiredness

уста́лый *no sh f* tired; *cf.* уста́нут

установи́ть – устана́вливают establish, determine; reconstruct (a language) VII

  n установле́ние

уста́нут – устава́ть be/get tired V; я́ ре́дко устаю́ I rarely am/get tired; я́ уста́л I'm tired, I have become tired

уста́ть: *see* уста́нут

у́стный oral II; —ый экза́мен oral exam

устро́ить – устра́ивают arrange, organize; —ся get arranged/organized/settled

  n устро́йство

утвержда́ют assert, affirm

  n утвержде́ние

у́тро morning; *shift in stress in certain set expressions* R7 note 5

у́тренний morning *adj*

уха́ fish soup CL1

у́хо *E pl obl* (*nom pl* у́ши, *gen pl* уше́й) ear CL4

уча́стие participation; interest, sympathy III; при́мут – принима́ют — в *чём* participate in, take part in

учёба studies, training

уче́бник textbook

уче́бный educational, school *adj*; — го́д school/academic year

уче́ние (*n* < учи́ть(ся)) study

учени́к, учени́ца pupil/student in elementary or high school (precollege) VI

учёный learned *adj*; scholar *n*; scientist *n* II; — по *чему́* scholar/scientist in

учи́ть II.7, R5 note 4, R2.A4; —ся II.7

ую́т/ный comfortable, cozy

фа́брика (на) factory

фа́кт fact VI

факульте́т (на) faculty, department

фами́лия last name

фи́зик physicist; фи́зика physics; физи́чес-кий physics *adj*

физи́ческий physical

фи́льм film

фи́рма (business) firm
фле́ксия *gr* inflection
фло́т fleet I; военно-возду́шный — air
    force; военно-морско́й — navy
фоне́ма *gr* phoneme
фоне́тика *gr* phonetics
фоноло́гия *gr* phonology
фо́рма form, *also gr*
фотоаппара́т camera
фотогра́фия photograph
фра́за phrase; sentence
Фра́нция France; францу́жен/ка French-
    woman; францу́з Frenchman; фран-
    цу́зский French *adj*
фро́нт (на) front (military *and fig*) III
фру́кт (*us pl* фру́кты) fruit(s)
футбо́л soccer

хала́т bathrobe, dressing gown CL4
хара́ктер character, nature
характеризова́ть *P and I* characterize VIII;
    —ся *кем/чем* be characterized by
хвати́ть – хвата́ет *imps кому́ кого́/чего́* be
    enough/sufficient; R8.C, CL3–5 Vocab:
    У ни́х хвата́ет де́нег. They have
    enough money.
    Хва́тит. That's enough, that will be
    enough.
хи́мик chemist R.3 note 13
хими́ческий chemical
хи́мия chemistry
хле́б bread; loaf of bread R 6 note 11
хо́д motion, speed, march, course IV; —
    собы́тий course of events
ходи́ть make a round trip R4.A2; — в
    шко́лу/университе́т attend a school/
    university R4 note 12
хозя́ин (*pl* хозя́ева, *gen pl* хозя́ев) pro-
    prietor, landlord, host, master
хозя́й/ка hostess, mistress
хозя́йство economy (large or small scale)
    IV; дома́шнее — household; се́льское
    — agriculture
хокке́й hockey
хо́лод cold, the cold
холодне́е *comp of* холо́д/ный
холо́д/ный, хо́лоден, холодна́, хо́лодно,
    хо́лодны cold
холодо́к chill, chilly air CL5

Хорва́тия Croatia; хорва́тский; хорва́т,
    хорва́т/ка Croatian
хоро́шенький pretty, nice CL1
хоро́ший: хоро́ш, хороша́, хорошо́, хо-
    роши́ good; good-looking (*particularly
    with* собо́ю/собо́й); она́ хороша́ со-
    бо́ю she is good-looking
хоте́л *inf* was about to (wanted to) R5 note
    14, R8 note 14
хоте́л бы R3 note 12

хоте́ться *кому́* feel like X.F
хоть although *colloq*; at least; even if (only)
    VI
хотя́ although; at least; even if (only) VI:
    Он придёт, хотя́ бы на де́сять мину́т.
    He'll come, if only for ten minutes.
хра́м temple CL3
христиани́н (*pl* христиа́не, *gen pl* хри-
    стиа́н) Christian VI; христиа́нский
    Christian *adj*; христиа́нство
    Christianity
худо́жествен/ный artistic IX.4
худо́жество art *arch* IX.4; *see* иску́сство
худо́жник, худо́жница artist (*in general
    sense and in sense of* painter) IX.4
худо́й (*comp* худе́е) thin
худо́й (*comp* ху́же) bad
ху́дший worse R5.A1
ху́же (*comp of* худо́й *and* плохо́й) bad

цари́ца tsarina/czarina
ца́рь *M E* tsar/czar
цве́т *E pl* -á color CL5.5
цвет/о́к (*pl* цветы́) flower CL5.5
це́лый whole, a whole, entire, all II
це́ль goal, purpose VIII
цена́ *S pl acc sg* price, cost CL1
це́нтр center
центра́льный central
церковнославяни́зм *gr* Church Slavonic-
    ism
церковнославя́нский Church Slavonic VII
церко́вный ecclesiastical, church *adj*
це́рк/о/вь (*inst* це́рковью), *E pl obl* (це́ркви,
    церкве́й *but* церква́м, церква́ми,
    церква́х church VI
цыплён/о/к (*pl* цыпля́та, *gen pl* цыпля́т)
    chicken

чаевы́е *sub adj* gratuities CL1

ча́й *E pl* tea; дать – дава́ть на — tip

части́ца particle, *also gr*

части́ч/ный partial VI

ча́стный private

ча́стый frequent

ча́сть *E pl obl* part; unit (military); бо́ль-
шей ча́стью for the most part, mostly;
— ре́чи *gr* part of speech; ча́стью partly

ча́ш/ка cup

ча́ще *comp of* ча́стый

ч/é/й declension R6 note 6; *usage* R4 note 21

челове́к (*gen pl* челове́к R8 note 2); моло-
до́й челове́к R9 note 10

челове́чество mankind, humanity (people)
IV

чём . . . тём R5.A6

чемода́н suitcase

чему́: к чему́ R10.B

чередова́ть alternate *tr*; —ся alternate *intr*,
also gr

n чередова́ние alternation, *also gr*

через *что́* in (after a period of time has
elapsed) R7.A4; by the way of, via R4
note 20; every, every other R7.A4

чёр/ный black

чёрт (*nom pl* че́рти) *E pl obl* CL3.6; ни
черта́:
я ни черта́ не ви́жу/зна́ю. I don't see/
know a damn thing.

черта́ feature, trait; line IX

че́ст/ный honest

че́тверть *E pl obl* fourth, quarter

че́х Czech

Че́хия Bohemia

Чехослова́кия Czechoslovakia VII; чехо-
слова́цкий Czechoslovak(ian)

че́ш/ка Czech (female)

че́шский Czech VII

-чий *vs.* -щий CL5.10

чино́вник official, bureaucrat V

числи́тельное (и́мя) numeral; коли́че-
ственное — cardinal numeral; поря́д-
ковое — ordinal numeral;
собира́тельное — collective numeral

число́ *S pl* (*gen pl* чи́сел) number; date VII;
в то́м —é (и) including

(вы́)чистить зу́бы brush/clean one's teeth
CL4

чи́стый clean

(про)чита́ют = прочту́т; *see also* R2.A5

чи́ще *comp of* чи́стый

член member IV; — па́ртии party member

чрезвыча́й/ный extraordinary VI

что *vs.* чтобы IX.A2

что́ what/why/Why V.10; which (a fact
which) V.10; то́, что III, IV; что тако́е
R5 note 3
Что вы! What's the matter with you!
Come on!

что *unstressed conjunction* that R3 note 10;
то́, что IV.A

чтоб(ы) *in detail* IX.A; purpose R7.C, R3.B;
with negated verbs IX.A6; *mild imperative* IX.A7; для того́, чтобы so that,
in order that X

чу́вство feeling VI

(по)чу́вствовать feel *tr* CL3; (по)чу́вство-
вать себя́ *adv or adj* (*inst*) feel *intr* X.B,
p. 271 *fr.*; он чу́вствует себя́ хорошо́/
сла́бым he feels good/weak; —ся be
felt

чу́д/ный wonderful

чу́до *E pl* (*nom pl* чудеса́)

чужо́й somebody else's; strange CL4

чу́ть hardly, barely; чу́ть не almost, nearly;
чуть-чу́ть the slightest bit CL5

ша́п/ка cap

ша́хматы *pl only* (*gen pl* ша́хмат) chess;
игра́ют в — play chess

шипя́щий (согла́сный) hushing (consonant)
(ш, ж, щ, ч)

ши́ре *comp of* широ́кий

широ́кий, широ́к, широка́, широ́ко́ wide,
broad

шка́ф (в/на шкафу́) *E pl* wardrobe, cupboard

шко́ла: вы́сшая/нача́льная/сре́дняя
шко́ла college-level/elementary/high
school

шл'-: *see* слать

шля́па hat CL2

шни́цель *M* schnitzel CL1

шокола́д chocolate CL1

шокола́дный chocolate *adj*; —ое моро́же-
ное chocolate ice cream

шо́рох rustle CL5
шта́т state (territorial unit) I.5.; Соединённые Шта́ты United States
шта́тский civilian, civil I.5
шум noise, sound CL5
шу́м/ный noisy, loud; — (согла́сный) *gr*
  obstruent (consonant)

щека́ *S nom pl acc sg* cheek CL2
щи *pl only* cabbage soup CL1
-щий *vs.* -чий CL5.10
(по)щу́пают feel, touch *tr* CL3; — пульс
  feel pulse

экза́мен (на) по *чему́* examination in; вы́-
  держать – сдать экза́мен pass exam;
  держать – сдава́ть экза́мен take exam
эконо́мика economics; economy (economic
  structure) II.4
эконо́мика *vs.* эконо́мия II.4
эконо́мия economy (thrift); *but note* по-
  лити́ческая — political economy II.4
эконо́мия *vs.* эконо́мика II.4
электри́ческий electric
электри́чество electricity
элеме́нт element
эпо́ха epoch
эта́ж (на) *E* story, floor
эта́п stage (of development, etc.)
этимоло́гия etymology
этимологи́ческий etymological
э́то *translation of* it R3.E
э́то: Кого́ э́то вы зна́ете? *and other*

examples III.2
э́то *vs.* то́ R3.D
э́тот: э́тот/то́т R3.D

юб/ка skirt CL2
юг (на) south I; юго-восто́к (- чный) south-
  east(ern); юго-за́пад (-ный) south-
  west(ern)
югосла́в, югосла́в/ка Yugoslav *n*; Юго-
  сла́вия Yugoslavia VII; югосла́вский
  Yugoslav *adj*
южнославя́нский South Slavic VII
ю́жный southern I
ю́мор humor
ю́ноша *M* (*gen pl* ю́ношей) youth CL2
юри́ст lawyer; law student

яви́ться – явля́ются be (*statements and frequently* (*esp I*) *in definitions*); он
  явля́ется руководи́телем he is the
  leader; — *куда́* appear, present oneself, show up for, report for
n явле́ние phenomenon R5.D3
языкове́дение linguistics
языково́й linguistic, language *adj* VII
языкозна́ние linguistics
Я́лта Yalta
япо́н/е/ц Japanese *m*; Япо́ния Japan;
  япо́н/ка Japanese *F*; япо́нский Japanese *adj*
я́р/кий bright
я́с/ный, я́сны clear *also fig*, bright

ENGLISH-RUSSIAN VOCABULARY

a оди́н R5 note 8

able: be able to бы́ть в состоя́нии; prove able to суме́ют *P only*

about о ко́м/чём; про кого́/что́; *also* II.6, II.5a, IV.6; (approximation) о́коло R7 note 7; was — to R5 note 14, X.3

above вы́ше

abroad (*где́*) за грани́цей (*куда́*) за грани́цу, (*отку́да*) из-за грани́цы

absence отсу́тствие

absent: be — отсу́тствовать

academic year уче́бный го́д

academy акаде́мия

accent(ed): *see* STRESS(ED)

accept при́мут – принима́ют; —ed при́нято

accompanying (to food/music) под *что́*

accomplish дости́г(ну)ть – достига́ют

accomplishment достиже́ние

according to согла́сно *кому́/чему́*; (depending on) смотря́ по *кому́/чему́*; по *чему́*

account счёт; take into — при́мут – принима́ют во внима́ние/в соображе́ние

accurate то́чный

accusative case вини́тельный паде́ж

accustom: become —ed to привы́к(ну)ть – привыка́ют к *кому́/чему́*

achieve дости́г(ну)ть – достига́ют *чего́*; добью́тся – добива́ются *чего́*

achievement достиже́ние

acid *adj* ки́слый

acme верши́на

acquaint (по)знако́мить

acquaintance знако́мый

acquainted знако́м(ый); become — with (по)знако́миться с *кем/чём*

across the street напро́тив

act де́йствовать, поступи́ть – поступа́ют; (behave) (по)веду́т себя́; — on (по)де́йствовать на *кого́/что́*; *n* а́кт, посту́пок; (of a play) де́йствие, а́кт

action де́йствие, посту́пок

active акти́вный; *gr* действи́тельный

activity де́ятельность

actor актёр, арти́ст

actress актри́са, арти́стка

actual действи́тельный; —ly действи́тельно в/на са́мом де́ле

addition: in — кро́ме того́, к тому́ же

address а́дрес; — oneself to обрати́ться – обраща́ются к *кому́/чему́*

adjective и́мя прилага́тельное

administration администра́ция

admit признаю́т – признава́ть

379

adorn красить, украсить – украшают
adult взрослый *adj and sub adj*
advance: in — заранее
advantage: take — of (вос)пользоваться *кем/чем*
adventure *pej* авантюра
adverb наречие
advice совет
advise (по)советовать
affair дело (*pl* дела); love — связь
affirm утверждают
afraid: be — бояться, страшно *кому/чему*
Africa Африка
after после, после того как
after all ведь III.3, в конце концов, уж
afternoon: in the — днём
afterwards потом
again ещё раз, опять, снова
against против; have nothing – ничего не имеют против
age век
agency агентство
agenda повестка дня
aggression агрессия
agitate (вз)волновать
agitation агитация (political)
ago (тому) назад; long ago давно; not long ago недавно
agree согласиться – соглашаются, быть соглас/е/н; — to согласиться – соглашаются, быть соглас/е/н на *что*; — with согласиться – соглашаются, быть соглас/е/н с *кем/чем*; — on (arrangements) договориться – договариваются о *чём*
agreement соглашение; come to — договориться *P only*; in — with согласный с *кем/чем*
agriculture сельское хозяйство, земледелие
ahead (*куда*) вперёд, (*где*) впереди
aid помощь; first — скорая помощь; render — оказать – оказывают помощь *кому/чему*
ail болеют
air воздух; *adj* воздушный; — force военно-воздушный флот, авиация
airplane самолёт
airport аэродром

alive живой
all: not at — вовсе не, совсем не; that's — there is to it и всё; in — всего
alliance союз
allow позволить – позволяют, разрешить – разрешают; (errors, etc.) допустить – допускают
almost почти, чуть не
alone один, единый
along по *чему*; get — with обращаются с *кем/чем*; get — without об/о/йдутся – обходиться без *кого/чего*
alphabet азбука, алфавит
all right хорошо, в порядке
also тоже; и III.1
alternate чередовать; alternation чередование
although хотя (и), несмотря на то, что
amaze: *see* SURPRISE, STRIKE; I'm —d я поражён *кем/чем*
ambassador посол
America Америка; —n американский; американец, американка
amiable любезный
amid(st), among(st) среди
amount количество
analyze (про)анализировать
ancestor предок
ancient древний
and и, а; да *stressless* CL5.4; Tanja — I мы с Таней R4 note 1
angle угол
angry з/лой; be — at быть з/о/л на *кого/что*
answer ответ; in — to в ответ на *кого/что*
anteroom передняя
anthem гимн
any -нибудь, любой, угодно; not — никакой; without — X без вся́к- X
anybody (anyone), anything R3 note 5
anyone: *various translations* p. 62
anyway всё равно VII.4; во всяком случае, и так
apartment квартира; — building/house дом
apostle апостол
apparently повидимому
appear появиться – появляются, явиться – являются, показаться –

показываются; — in public выступить – выступают
appearance появле́ние; (exterior) нару́жность
appearances: to all — по-ви́димому
appetite аппети́т CL1.2
application примене́ние; заявле́ние
apply примени́ть – применя́ют; по́дать заявле́ние на *что́*
appoint назна́чить – назнача́ют
apprehend воспри́мут – воспринима́ют
approach под/о/йду́т – подходи́ть (к *кому́/чему́*); подхо́д (к *кому́/чему́*)
appropriate кста́ти, к ме́сту, уме́стный
approximate приблизи́тельный; —ly о́коло *чего́*, *inversion of noun and numeral* R7 note 7
arbitrary усло́вный
ardent горя́чий, стра́стный
area (region, field) о́бласть; (space) пло́щадь (жилпло́щадь)
argue (по)спо́рить
arise (come up) возни́к(ну)ть – возника́ют; (stand up) вста́нут – встава́ть
arm рука́; вооружи́ть(ся) – вооружа́ют(ся)
armament вооруже́ние
armchair кре́сло
armed forces вооружённые си́лы
army а́рмия
around о́коло *adv or prep*; (approximation) R7 note 7; вокру́г *кого́/чего́*; go — об/о/йду́т – обходи́ть
arrange устро́ить – устра́ивают; (physical) расположи́ть – располага́ют; make arrangement договори́ться – догова́риваются о *ко́м/чём*
arrest арестова́ть *both P and I or* аресто́вывают
arrival прие́зд, прибы́тие
arrive при́быть – прибыва́ют
art иску́сство, худо́жество *arch* IX.4
article статья́
artificial иску́сственный IX.4
artist худо́жник, худо́жница; арти́ст IX.4
artistic худо́жественный IX.4
as ка́к, *ке́м/че́м*, в ка́честве *кого́/чего́*; че́м; *see also* SINCE; — X — possible ка́к

мо́жно *comp of adj* X; — if (как) бу́дто II.2; — it is и та́к; — such как таково́й
ascend поднима́ются (*past tense E*) – поднима́ются; ascent подъём
Asia А́зия; Central — Сре́дняя А́зия
ask R3.F; (information) спроси́ть – спра́шивают; (request) (по)проси́ть; — question зада́ть – задава́ть вопро́с
asleep: I'm — я сплю́; fall — засну́ть – засыпа́ют, усну́ть *P only*
aspect ви́д; *see also* PERFECTIVE, IMPERFECTIVE, DETERMINED, NONDETERMINED
assert утвержда́ют
assign назна́чить – назнача́ют, зада́ть – задава́ть
assignment назначе́ние, зада́ние; homework — дома́шнее зада́ние
assistance соде́йствие, по́мощь; render — оказа́ть – ока́зывают соде́йствие, по́мощь, соде́йствовать
assume (take on) при́мут – принима́ют; (suppose) предположи́ть – предполага́ют; let's — предположи́м, допу́стим
assumption предположе́ние
assure уве́рить – уверя́ют
at в *чём* R4.B; на *чём* R4.B; — person's place у *кого́*; — activity за *чём* IV.4b
at last наконе́ц
at least по кра́йней ме́ре; (if only) хоть, хотя́
at once сейча́с (же), сра́зу
atheism атеи́зм; atheist атеи́ст, неве́рующий; atheistic атеисти́ческий
atmosphere атмосфе́ра
attack ата́ка; —s (verbal) напа́дки; *v* нападу́т –напада́ют
attend (school, etc.) ходи́ть (*куда́*)
attention внима́ние; Attention! Внима́ние!; pay — to обрати́ть – обраща́ют внима́ние на *кого́/что́*
attentive внима́тельный
attitude отноше́ние IV.6
What is your — toward ...? Как вы отно́ситесь к *кому́/чему́*? Како́е ва́ше отноше́ние к *кому́/чему́*?
attractive симпати́чный
audible слы́шный

auspicious торже́ственный

author а́втор

authority авторите́т

automobile автомоби́ль, (авто)маши́на

autumn о́сень; in — о́сенью

available име́ющиеся; be — име́ются

average сре́дний

aviation авиа́ция

aviator лётчик

avoid об/о/йду́т – обходить, избе́гнуть (избежа́ть) – избега́ют

away from: go —— удали́ться – удаля́ют-ся

awful ужа́сный (very bad); —ly (badly *or* very, extremely) ужа́сно, стра́шно

awkward (situation, etc.) неудо́бный

bachelor's degree сте́пень бакала́вра

back, спина́; за́дний; (*куда́*) наза́д, (*где*) сза́ди; there and — туда́ и обра́тно; go/come —: *see* RETURN; go — to (derive from) восходить к *кому́/чему́*

ball мяч; (dance) бал (на балу́)

bank (shore) бе́рег; (money) ба́нк

banner зна́мя

barely чу́ть, едва́

base обоснова́ть – обосно́вывают

baseball бейсбо́л

bashfulness засте́нчивость

basis осно́ва, основа́ние, обоснова́ние

bathrobe хала́т

bathroom (with bathrub) ва́нная

bathtub ва́нна

be яви́ться – явля́ются, есть, состоя́ть, представля́ют собо́й; *translations* R5.D

bear (give birth to) роди́ть; — in mind име́ют в виду́

bearable сно́сный

beard борода́

beat бьй-ут(ся)

beautiful краси́вый, прекра́сный

because потому́ что, из-за того́ что, оттого́ что R10.B; — of из-за, по *кому́/чему́*

become ста́нут – становиться, (с)де́лают-ся; быть *кому́* к лицу́; becoming к лицу́

bed крова́ть, посте́ль; go to — пойду́т – иду́т спать, ля́гут (ле́чь) – ложи́ться (спать)

bedroom спа́льня

(beef)steak бифште́кс

beer пи́во

beet soup борщ

before до; перед *with nouns* R9 note 1, *with verbs* I.1; за . . . до V.3; (previous) ра́ньше, пре́жде

beforehand зара́нее

begin на́чнут – начина́ют, ста́нут *P only plus inf*; (get at) приступить – приступа́ют к

beginning нача́ло; *adj* нача́льный

behind (*где*) позади́, сза́ди; (*отку́да*) сза́ди; lag — отста́нут – отставать

being (since) бу́дучи (*pres gen of* бы́ть): Being a doctor (since he is a doctor), he knows this disease. Бу́дучи врачо́м, он зна́ет э́ту боле́знь.

belief ве́ра

believe (по)ве́рить, ве́ровать; ду́мают R6 note 17; — in (по)-ве́рить, ве́ровать в *кого́/что*; —г ве́рующий

bell звоно́к

belong принадлежа́ть *кому́/чему́*; (to a group) к *чему́*, входить в соста́в *чего́*

Belorussia Белору́ссия; —n белору́сский; белору́с, белору́с/ка

below внизу́, ни́же; под

beside во́зле, ря́дом с *кем/чём*

besides кро́ме, кро́ме того́ чтобы

beware (of) берёгу́тся *кого́/чего́*

bigger бо́льший

bill счёт

bird пти́ца

birth: give birth to роди́ть – рожда́ют; рожде́ние

black чёрный

blackboard (чёрная) доска́

blood кро́вь; —у крова́вый

blouse блу́зка

blue (light) голубо́й; (dark) си́ний

board доска́

boat ло́дка

body те́ло

Bolshevik большеви́к; Bolshevist большеви́стский

bone кость
boot сапо́г
border грани́ца
bored ску́чно (мне́ ску́чно, ему́ ску́чно);
    boring ску́чный
born: be — роди́ться - рожда́ются
borscht (beet soup) бо́рщ
both о́ба IV.3a; и то́т и друго́й IV.3b; —
    X and Y и X и Y R8 note 3
bother (по)меша́ют
bottle буты́лка
bottom (*где*) внизу́; (*отку́да*) сни́зу; (*куда*)
    вни́з; get to the — of разобра́ться -
    разбира́ются в *чём*
boundary грани́ца
bourgeoisie буржуази́я
box office ка́сса
brackets ско́бки
bread хле́б; a loaf of — хле́б
breakfast за́втрак; (по)за́втракают
breast гру́дь
breath ду́х
bride неве́ста
bridegroom жени́х
bridge мо́ст; (cards) бри́дж
briefcase портфе́ль
bright я́ркий, све́тлый, я́сный; (intelligent)
    у́мный
bring принесу́т - приноси́ть, приведу́т -
    приводи́ть, привезу́т - привози́ть
broad широ́кий
broadcast пе́редать - передава́ть; пере-
    да́ча
brown кори́чневый; (of eyes) ка́рий
brush teeth (вы)чи́стить зу́бы
build (по)стро́ить
building зда́ние; insides of a — (premises)
    помеще́ние; (construction) строи́тель-
    ство
Bulgaria Болга́рия; —n болга́рский;
    болга́рин, болга́рка
bulwark опло́т
bunch: a whole — of (a large number of)
    це́лый ря́д *кого́/чего́*
bureau бюро́; bureaucracy бюрократи́зм
bureaucrat чино́вник, бюрокра́т
burn *tr* жгут (жечь); *intr* горе́ть
burst into tears запла́кать
bus авто́бус

business де́ло, дела́; —man коммерса́нт;
    — trip командиро́вка
busy занято́й; (occupied) за́нятый
but но́, а, да (*stressless*)
but for не бу́дь *кого́/чего́*, е́сли не *кто́/что́*
butter ма́сло
buy купи́ть - покупа́ют
by (amount or degree) VIII.5

cab (taxi) такси́
cabbage soup щи́
calculation счёт
calendar календа́рь
call (по)зва́ть; be —ed называ́ются; — up
    (по)звони́ть R8 note 6, вы́звать - вы-
    зыва́ют; — out *tr* вы́звать(вы́-
    зовут) - вызыва́ют; telephone — зво-
    но́к, вы́зов (по телефо́ну)
calm споко́йный, ти́хий; — down *tr*
    успоко́ить - успока́ивают, *intr*
    успоко́иться - успока́иваются
calque ка́лька
camera фотоаппара́т
camp ла́герь (sociopolitical) *stem stress*;
    (military, boy scout, etc.) *E pl* -я́; con-
    centration — концла́герь
can, мо́гут, бы́ть в состоя́нии *inf* (*esp com-
    mon in negative*); *see also* KNOW HOW
cap ша́пка
capacity объём; in the — of в ка́честве
    кого́/чего́
capital city столи́ца, capital construction
    капита́льное строи́тельство
capitalism капитали́зм; capitalist капи-
    тали́ст; *adj* капиталисти́ческий
captain капита́н
car: *see* AUTOMOBILE; railroad — ваго́н
card: playing — ка́рта; play —s игра́ют в
    ка́рты; post— откры́тка
cardinal numeral коли́чественное числи́-
    тельное
care: take — of (по)забо́титься о *ко́м/чём*;
    I don't — мне всё равно́
career карье́ра
careful осторо́жный, *бе́режный*
careless неосторо́жный, неб*ре́жный*; —ly
    ко́е-ка́к
carry: — to a place (deliver) отнесу́т - от-
    носи́ть V.6; — on (conduct) про-

веду́т – проводи́ть; — out вы́полнить – выполня́ют

case слу́чай; *gr* паде́ж

cashier's office ка́сса

cast (of characters) де́йствующие ли́ца

cat ко́шка

catch пойма́ют – лови́ть

catch cold простуди́ться – простужа́ются

catch sight of уви́деть

category катего́рия

cathedral собо́р

Caucasus Кавка́з (на) .

cause причи́на; де́ло; вы́звать (вы́зовут) – вызыва́ют, обусло́вить – обусло́вивают

caviar икра́

ceiling потоло́к

center центр

central центра́льный, сре́дний

century век, столе́тие

cereal (porridge) ка́ша; —s (grains) зёрна

certain (*sg a* certain) оди́н, не́который, изве́стный, не́кий, не́кто; to a — extent/degree до не́которой/изве́стной сте́пени; (sure) уве́рен(ный), убеждён(ный)

certainly наверняка́, непреме́нно, обяза́тельно

chalk мел

challenge вы́звать (вы́зовут) – вызыва́ют; вы́зов

change измени́ть(ся) – изменя́ют(ся); перейду́т – переходи́ть в *кого́/что́*; — clothes переоде́нут(ся) – переодева́ют(ся)

character хара́ктер; cast of —s де́йствующие ли́ца

characterize характеризова́ть; be —d by характеризова́ться *чем*, отлича́ются *чем*

chatter болтовня́

cheap дешёвый

cheek щека́

cheese сыр

chemical хими́ческий

chemistry хи́мия

chess ша́хматы

chest грудь

chicken цыплёнок (*nom pl* цыпля́та)

chief гла́вный; —ly гла́вным о́бразом

chill, chilly air холодо́к

China Кита́й; Chinese кита́ец, китая́нка; кита́йский

chocolate шокола́д; шокола́дный

choice вы́бор

choose вы́брать (вы́берут) – выбира́ют

Christian христиани́н, -а́не

Christian *adj* христиа́нский

Christianity христиа́нство

Christmas Рождество́; Merry — С Рождество́м; — vacation рожде́ственские кани́кулы

church це́рковь; церко́вный; Church Slavonic церковнославя́нский; Old (Church) Slavonic старославя́нский; Church Slavonicism церковнославяни́зм

cigar сига́ра

cigarette (with holder, Russian style) папиро́са; (without holder) сигаре́та

cinema кино́

circumstances обстано́вка, усло́вия

circumvent об/о/йду́т – обходи́ть

citizen граждани́н, гражда́нка

city *adj* городско́й

civil гражда́нский; — rights гражда́нские права́; — war гражда́нская война́

civilian шта́тский

class (social; school; category in general) класс; —es (school) заня́тия

classical класси́ческий

classroom класс

clause предложе́ние

clean чи́стый; чи́стить, вы́чистить – вычища́ют

clear я́сный

climate кли́мат

close (near) бли́зкий; (contact) те́сный; — friends бли́зкие друзья́; —ly connected те́сно свя́занный

clothes оде́жда, пла́тье; put on — наде́нут – надева́ют *что́*; take off — сни́мут – снима́ют *что́*; change — переоде́нутся – переодева́ются

club клуб

coal у́голь

coat (overcoat) пальто́; (jacket) пиджа́к; take off — разде́нутся – раздева́ются

coexist сосуществовáть; —ence сосуще-
ствовáние

coincide совпадýт – совпадáют; —nce
совпадéние

cold холóдный; холод; common — про-
стýда; head — нáсморк; extreme —
(frost) морóз

collaborate сотрýдничают

collaborator сотрýдник

collar вóрот

colleague коллéга

collect собрáть – собирáют; —ion собрáние

collective коллектúв

collective farm колхóз; collective farmer
колхóзник, —ница

collective numeral úмя числúтельное

college (college-level school) вы́сшая
шкóла; (in USA) коллéдж

colon двоетóчие

color цвéт CL5.5

comb причёсать – причёсывают; — oneself причёсаться – причёсываются

combine соединúть – соединяют

come идýт R4 note 15; — back: see BACK;
— forward (with) вы́ступить – высту-
пáют с кéм/чéм; —. from произой-
дýт – происходить; Where do you
from? Откýда вы рóдом? — on (fall
on a day, etc.) придýтся – приходиться на чтó; — out вы́йдут – выходить;
— up (question, etc.) вознúк(ну)ть –
возникáют

comfortable удóбный, ую́тный

comma запятáя

commander командúр

commercial торгóвый

committee комитéт

common óбщий

commonplace обы́чный

communication свя́зь

communism коммунúзм; communist ком-
мунúст; adj коммунистúческий

comparative сравнúтельный; — degree gr
сравнúтельная стéпень

compare сравнúть – срáвнивают

comparison сравнéние; by —/compared
with по сравнéнию с кéм/чéм

compile состáвить – составля́ют

complement дополнéние

complete пóлный

completely вполнé, совершéнно

complicated слóжный

compose состáвить – составля́ют

composer композúтор

composite составнóй, слóжный

composition состáв; (written) сочинéние

compound слóжный, составнóй

comprise состáвить – составля́ют

comrade товáрищ

conceal скрóют – скрывáют; — self
скрóются – скрывáются

concentrate сосредотóчить – сосредотó-
чивают

concentration camp концлáгерь

concept поня́тие, идéя

conception представлéние, поня́тие; have
no/not the slightest — не имéют ни-
какóго/ни малéйшего представлé-
ния/поня́тия; (origin) зарождéние

concern (have to do with) касáется; as far
as X is —ed что касáются когó/чегó
CL5.7; — self with (по)забóтиться
о кóм/чём; be —ed about беспо-
кóиться о кóм/чём
That isn't your —. Это не вáше дéло.
Это вáс не касáется.

concert концéрт

concise крáткий

conclude заключúть – заключáют

conclusion заключéние; come to a — придýт – приходить к заключéнию

concrete конкрéтный

condition (state) состоя́ние; (term) услó-
вие; —s услóвия (both terms and circumstances); (circumstances)
обстанóвка; make a — обуслóвить –
обуслóвливают; —ed by обуслóвлен-
ный кéм/чéм

conditional услóвный; — mood gr услóвное наклонéние

conduct (lead) (по)ведýт; (carry on/out)
проведýт – проводить, ведýт: — self
(по)ведýт себя́

confess признаю́т – признавáть

confirm подтвердúть – подтверждáют

congratulate поздрáвить – поздравля́ют с
чéм CL5.9

conjecture догада́ются – дога́дываются; дога́дка

conjugate (про)спряга́ют

conjugation спряже́ние

conjunction *gr* сою́з

connect связа́ть – свя́зывают, соедини́ть – соединя́ют

connection свя́зь; in — with в связи́ с *ке́м/ че́м*, по *чему́*

consent согла́сие; согласи́ться – соглаша́ются на *что*

consequence сле́дствие, после́дствие; as a — of всле́дствие *чего́*

consider (weigh) сообрази́ть – сообража́ют; — X (to be) Y VI.2; — self X VI.2; be —ed X VI.2; (examine) рассмотре́ть – рассма́тривают

consideration соображе́ние; take into — при́мут – принима́ют в соображе́ние/во внима́ние

consist: — in состоя́ть в *чём*, заключа́ются в *чём*; — of состоя́ть из *кого́/чего́* VII.3а

consistency после́дова́тельность

consistent после́дова́тельный

consonant согла́сный (зву́к)

constant постоя́нный

constitute соста́вить – составля́ют

constitution конститу́ция

construct (по)стро́ить

construction (building in general) стройтельство; *gr* констру́кция

contain содержа́ть

contemporary совреме́нный; совреме́нник

content(s) содержа́ние

continent контине́нт

continental континента́льный

continually всё вре́мя, постоя́нно

continue продо́лжить(ся) – продолжа́ют(ся)

contrary: on the — напро́тив, наоборо́т

contrast противополо́жность; in — to в противополо́жность *кому́/чему́*, по сравне́нию к *кому́/чему́*

contribution вкла́д; make — to внесу́т – вноси́ть вкла́д во *что́*

convenient удо́бный

conventional усло́вный

conversation разгово́р

converse разгова́ривают

convey вози́ть, (по)везу́т

conviction убежде́ние

convince убеди́ть – убежда́ют, уве́рить – уверя́ют; I'm —d я убеждён/уве́рен

cook (при)гото́вить; по́вар, куха́рка

cool прохла́дный; охлади́ть – охлажда́ют

cooperate оказа́ть – ока́зывают соде́йствие, соде́йствовать

cooperation соде́йствие

cope спра́виться – справля́ются с *ке́м/че́м*

copeck копе́йка

corner у́гол

corporation корпора́ция

correct попра́вить – поправля́ют; — self попра́виться – поправля́ются; *adj* пра́вильный

correction попра́вка

corridor коридо́р

cost сто́ить VII.2; цена́

costume костю́м

cottage (summer) да́ча

couch дива́н

cough ка́шель

council сове́т

counsel сове́т; (по)сове́товать

count счёт; (со)счита́ют

country страна́; —side дере́вня; in the — в дере́вне, за́ городом

course: in the — of III.6c; of — коне́чно (*also concessive meaning*); ведь; — of events хо́д собы́тий; — (meal) блю́до CL1.3; — (school or university) ку́рс; take a — слу́шают ку́рс

courtyard дво́р; court (of law) су́д

cover покро́ют – покрыва́ют

cow коро́ва

co-worker сотру́дник

cramped те́сный

crazy сумасше́дший

cream сли́вки; *adj* сли́вочный

create созда́ть – создава́ть

creation созда́ние; тво́рчество

creative work тво́рчество

Crimea Кры́м

criticism кри́тика, напа́дки

criticize критикова́ть

Croatia(n) Хорва́тия (хорва́тский)

crowded тéсный

crush *fig* (за)/души́ть,

cry (shout) кри́кнуть – крича́ть; (weep) пла́кать; burst out —ing запла́кать

cuisine стол

cultural культу́рный

culture культу́ра

cultured культу́рный

cup ча́шка

cupboard шкаф

cure (вы́)лечить – выле́чивают

curiosity любопы́тство

curious (worthy of curiosity, manifesting curiosity) любопы́тный

current тече́ние; теку́чий, настоя́щего вре́мени

custom: it is the — to при́нято *inf*

customary обы́чный

cutlet котле́та

Cyril Кири́лл

Cyrillic alphabet кири́ллица

czar, czarina: *see* TSAR, TSARINA

Czech че́шский; чех, че́шка

Czechoslovakia Чехослова́кия; —n чехослова́цкий

dacha (summer cottage) да́ча

daily ежедне́вний

damn: *see* чёрт

dance та́нец; танцева́ть

dangerous опа́сный

dark тёмный

darn (mild oath) чёрт CL3.8

dash *gr* тире́

data да́нные

date число́

dative case да́тельный паде́ж

dawn *also fig* рассве́т (на)

day день; (24 hours) су́тки: *see* Appendix B; — after tomorrow послеза́втра; — before yesterday тре́тьего дня; on the next/following — на друго́й/сле́дующий день; the other — на днях; in a few —s на днях; — off выходно́й день

daybreak рассве́т

daydream мечта́; мечта́ют

dead мёртвый

deal: a great — мно́го

dear (expensive; familiar address in letters) дорого́й; (nonfamiliar address in letters) многоуважа́емый

death смерть

decade десятиле́тие

decanter графи́нчик

decay распа́д

deceit обма́н

deceive обманну́ть – обма́нывают

deception обма́н

decide реши́ть – реша́ют

decision реше́ние

declension склоне́ние

decline *gr* (про)склоня́ют; — *tr* отказа́ться – отка́зываются от *кого́/чего́*

deep глубо́кий

defeat победи́ть – побежда́ют; пораже́ние

define определи́ть – определя́ют

definite определённый

definitely обяза́тельно, непреме́нно (*as in* I'll — come, *etc.*)

definition определе́ние

degree сте́пень; *see* BACHELOR'S, DOCTOR'S, MASTER'S; *gr* positive — положи́тельная сте́пень, comparative — сравни́тельная сте́пень, superlative — превосхо́дная сте́пень; (temperature) гра́дус

deliver (provide, supply) доста́вить – доставля́ют; (take to a place) V.6; — a report вы́ступить – выступа́ют с докла́дом, (с)де́лают докла́д

demand (по)тре́бовать; тре́бование

democratic демократи́ческий; Democratic Party Демократи́ческая па́ртия

demonstrative *gr* указа́тельный

denial отрица́ние

dental зубно́й

dentist данти́ст, зубно́й врач

deny отрица́ют; — someone something отказа́ть – отка́зывают *кому́* в *чём*

depart отбы́ть – отбыва́ют; — from (take as point of departure) исходи́ть из *чего́*

department отде́л, отделе́ние; (college) ка́федра, отделе́ние

department store универса́льный магази́н

departure отъе́зд, отбы́тие; take as point of — исходи́ть из *чего́*; point of — исхо́дный пункт

depend on (a condition) зави́сеть от *чего́*;
(rely on) наде́яться на *кого́/что́*
dependable надёжный
depending on (condition) смотря́ по
чему́
deposit вкла́д
derivation происхожде́ние; (of a word)
этимоло́гия
derive from произойду́т – происходить;
(go back to) восходить к *кому́/чему́*
descend сойду́т – сходить, спуститься –
спуска́ються
descendant пото́мок
describe описать – опи́сывают
description описа́ние
designate обозна́чить – обознача́ют
designation обозначе́ние
desire (по)жела́ют; жела́ние
desk (пи́сьменный) сто́л
despite несмотря́ на *кого́/что́*
dessert сла́дкое
detail подро́бность; —ed подро́бный
determine определи́ть – определя́ют,
установить – устана́вливают
determined *gr* определённый
develop разовьй-ут – развива́ют
development разви́тие
deverbative noun отглаго́льное существи́-
тельное
devil дья́вол, чёрт
dial (number) набрать – набира́ют
(но́мер)
dialect диале́кт
dictate (про)диктова́ть
dictation дикто́вка
dictionary слова́рь
die у̌мрут – умира́ют; — down за̌мрут –
замира́ют
differ from отлича́ются от *кого́/чего́ чём*
difference ра́зница; отли́чие
different (other) друго́й; (various) ра́зный;
(distinct) разли́чный, ра́зный
difficult тру́дный; тяжёлый — person
тяжёлый челове́к
difficulty тру́дность; with — с трудо́м;
without — без труда́
diminutive *gr* уменьши́тельный
dine (по)обе́дают
dining room столо́вая

dinner обе́д
direct прямо́й; — *also gr for case, speech,
object*; напра́вить – направля́ют
direction *also fig* направле́ние, сторона́
directions указа́ния
director дире́ктор
dirt гря́зь; —у гря́зный
disappear исче́з(ну)ть – исчеза́ют; —ance
исчезнове́ние
disappoint разочарова́ть – разочаро́вы-
вают; be —ed разочарова́ться –
разочаровываются в *ко́м/чём*;
—ment разочарова́ние
disarm разоружи́ть – разоружа́ют
disarmament разоруже́ние
discourse: *see* SPEECH
discover откро́ют – открыва́ют
discuss обсудить – обсужда́ют; X is being
—ed ре́чь идёт о *ко́м/чём*
discussion обсужде́ние
disease боле́знь, заболева́ние
dish (plate) таре́лка; —es посу́да; wash
—es (вы)мо́ют посу́ду; (food, course)
блю́до
disintegration распа́д
display (manifest) прояви́ть – проявляют,
обнару́жить – обнару́живают; — itself прояви́ться – проявля́ются,
обнару́житься – обнару́живаются;
(exhibit) вы́ставка
displeased недово́льный
disposal расположе́ние; have at one's —
располага́ют *чём*
dispose расположить – располага́ют
disposition расположе́ние
dissatisfied недово́льный
dissertation диссерта́ция
dissolve раствори́ть – растроря́ют
distant далёкий, да́льний
distinguish отличи́ть – отлича́ют; — self
отличи́ться – отлича́ются; be —ed by
отлича́ются *чём*; be —ed from отли-
ча́ются от *кого́/чего́ чём*
disturb (по)меша́ют; (upset) беспоко́ить;
be —ed about беспоко́иться о *ко́м/
чём*
diverse ра́зный, разли́чный, разнообра́з-
ный, многообра́зный; diversity раз-
нообра́зие, многообра́зие

divide (раз)делить – разделяют;
отделить – отделяют
division деление, разделение; (department, section) отделение
Dnepr Днепр
do (с)делают, занимаются *чем* II.7; have
to — with (have business with) имеют
дело с *кем/чем* R9 note 12
doctor (physician) врач, *colloq* доктор;
(possessing degree) доктор; —'s
degree докторская степень
document документ; (literary) памятник
dog собака
dollar доллар
doubt: I — it/whether вряд ли
down: go — сойдут – сходить, спуститься – спускаются; —hill под гору *also*
fig; —stairs (*где*) внизу; (*куда*) вниз
dream (during sleep) сон; видеть сон
(сны); (while awake) мечта; мечтают
dress *tr* оденут – одевают; — self оденут-
ся – одеваются; — up разоденут *P*
only; —self up разоденутся *P only*; —
(woman's) платье
dressing gown халат
drink to CL14
drink (up) (вы)пьй-ут – выпивают R2.A5
drive (convey) (R5 note 7) возить, (по)-
везут; — (car, etc.) управляют *чем*,
водить, (по)ведут
drop in зайдут – заходить, заедут – за-
ежают
dry сухой; — land суша (на)
dryness сухость
due to из-за *кого/чего* благодаря *кому/*
чему, в связи с *чем*, за *чем*
duel дуэль
dull скучный
durable прочный
during III.6

each каждый; — other друг друг-
ear ухо
earliest (furthest back in time) младенчес-
кий
early ранний
earth земля; the Earth Земля; *adj* земной
ease смягчить – смягчают
east, восток; —ern восточный

East Slavic восточнославянский
easy лёгкий
eat есть, кушают CL1.1; eating еда
ecclesiastical духовный, церковный
economics экономика
economy хозяйство, экономика; (thrift)
экономия; *NB* political — полити-
ческая экономия
edge край
editorial передовая статья
educated образованный
education образование; public — народ-
ное просвещение
effect действие; следствие; cause and —
причина и следствие
either . . . or или . . . или R8 note 3
elapse (time) пройдут – проходить, про-
текут – протекают
elder старший
elect выбрать – выбирают; —ions выборы
electric электрический
electricity электричество
element элемент
elementary начальный; — school началь-
ная школа
elevation высота
elevator лифт; — operator лифтёр
eloquence красноречие
else: or — а то, иначе; somebody — другой, кто-нибудь другой; somebody
—'s чужой
embassy посольство
emerge возник(ну)ть – возникают
emergence возникновение
eminent видный, знаменитый
emperor император
employee сотрудник
empress императрица
empty пустой
encircle окружить – окружают
end кончить(ся) – кончают(ся);
окончить – оканчивают; — in *gr*
кончаются на *что*; конец; (of
semester, etc.) окончание; *gr* — stress
наконечное ударение
ending *gr* окончание
endure перенесут – переносить, выдер-
жать – выдерживают

enemy проти́вник

engineer инжене́р

engineering те́хника; — school те́хникум

England Англия; English англи́йский;
Englishman англича́нин, англича́нка

enjoy (success, authority, etc.) по́льзоваться *чём*

enlarge увели́чить – увели́чивают

enormous огро́мный

enough дово́льно; доста́точно, доста́точный; not — недоста́точно, недоста́точный; be — хвати́ть – хвата́ют

enroll *intr* поступи́ть – поступа́ют

enrollment поступле́ние

ensuing (по)сле́дующий

enter (a school, government service) поступи́ть – поступа́ют; (join army or other organization) вступи́ть – вступа́ют

enterprise предприя́тие

entrance вхо́д; поступле́ние, вступле́ние

envelope конве́рт

environment среда́, окруже́ние

epoch эпо́ха

equal ра́вный

equality ра́венство

error оши́бка

especially осо́бенно

essence су́ть; the — of the matter су́ть де́ла; in — по су́ти де́ла

establish установи́ть – устана́вливают

esteem уваже́ние; уважа́ют; —ed уважа́емый

estimate оце́нка; оцени́ть – оце́нивают

et cetera (etc.) и та́к да́лее (и т.д.), и тому́ подо́бное (и т.п.)

eternity ве́чность

etymology этимоло́гия

Europe Евро́па; European европе́йский

evaluate оцени́ть – оце́нивают; evaluation оце́нка; *see also* CL5.4

even да́же; и III.1; — ро́вный; — so всё равно́, всё же

evening *adj* вече́рний; — (party) ве́чер

event собы́тие; course of —s хо́д собы́тий

-ever ни VII; X-ever X уго́дно

every (time unit) еже-; ка́ждый, вся́кий

everywhere везде́, всю́ду, повсю́ду

evil зло́; зло́й

ex- (former) бы́вший

exact то́чный

exactly то́чно; (just) и́менно, ка́к раз; (time) ро́вно

examination экза́мен; take — сдава́ть – держа́ть экза́мен; pass — сдать – вы́держать экза́мен; fail — провали́ться – прова́ливаются на экза́мене

examine (look at city, etc.) осмотре́ть – осма́тривают; — question рассмотре́ть – рассма́тривают вопро́с

example приме́р; for — наприме́р; give — приведу́т – приводить приме́р

exceed превы́сить – превыша́ют

excellent отли́чный, превосхо́дный

except кро́ме, кро́ме того́ что́бы; исключи́ть – исключа́ют

exception исключе́ние; with the — of за исключе́нием *кого́/чего́*

excite (вз)волнова́ть

exclamation point восклица́тельный зна́к

exclude исключи́ть – исключа́ют

exclusion исключе́ние

excuse извини́ть – извиня́ют, прости́ть – проща́ют

exercise упражне́ние

exert influence on оказа́ть – ока́зывают влия́ние на *кого́/что́*

exhibit(ion) вы́ставка

exist существова́ть; —ence существова́ние

exit вы́ход

expect ожида́ют

expel исключи́ть – исключа́ют

expensive дорого́й

experience пережи́вут – пережива́ют; пережива́ние

explain объясни́ть – объясня́ют

express вы́разить – выража́ют; — self вы́разиться – выража́ются

express train ско́рый по́езд

expression выраже́ние

extent протяже́ние; to a certain — до изве́стной/не́которой сте́пени

exterior нару́жность; вне́шний

external вне́шний

extraction: be of X — бы́ть X-ого происхожде́ния

extraordinary чрезвыча́йный

extraordinarily чрезвыча́йно, весьма́

extreme кра́йний; кра́йность; —ly крайне, о́чень

eye глаз; глазно́й; — doctor глазно́й врач, окули́ст; —glasses очки́; —sight зре́ние

face лицо́

fact факт; — that то́, что IV.A; the — is that де́ло в то́м, что; a — which что́ V.10; in — действи́тельно, на са́мом де́ле, и III.1; in actual — на са́мом де́ле

factory фа́брика, заво́д

faculty факульте́т

fail не удаться – не удава́ться *кому что or inf*; — exam провалиться – прова́ливаются на экза́мене; *tr* провалить – прова́ливают

failure неуспе́х; (exam) прова́л

fair (just) справедли́вый; (average) сре́дний; *adv* сре́дне; (exhibition) вы́ставка

faith ве́ра

fall (season) о́сень; in the — о́сенью; — asleep засну́ть – засыпа́ют; — in love влюби́ться – влюбля́ются в кого́/что́; — into thought заду́маются – заду́мываются

fame сла́ва; be —d for сла́виться *че́м*

familiar изве́стный, знако́мый

family семья́; (*broad sense* clan, *plants, animals, etc.*) род

famous знамени́тый; be — for сла́виться *че́м*

far далёкий; by — намно́го; гора́здо; by — not далеко́ не; as/so — as поско́льку, наско́лько; as — as X is concerned что́ каса́ется кого́/чего́

farm: *see* COLLECTIVE FARM

fashion: in one's own — по-сво́ему, на свой лад

fast бы́стрый, ско́рый; run — (clock) спеши́ть

fat то́лстый

fate судьба́

fatherland оте́чество, ро́дина

faucet кран

favor про́сьба; расположе́ние

favorite люби́мый CL5.12

fear страх; боя́ться *кого́/чего́*

fearful стра́шный

feather перо́

feature черта́

feel *tr* (по)чу́вствовать; *intr* (по)чу́вствовать себя́ *adv or adj inst*; — (with fingers, etc.) (по)щу́пают; be felt чу́вствоваться; — like doing X.F (за)хо́чет/ся *кому́*; —ing чу́вство

fellow това́рищ; fellow X това́рищ по *кому́*; — worker това́рищ по рабо́те, сотру́дник

female же́нский

feminine же́нский; — gender же́нский род

festival, festive occasion пра́здник

festive торже́ственный, пра́здничный

few ма́ло, немно́го R4 note 14, немно́ги-R6.A2; a — ма́ло, немно́го; (several) не́сколько R4 note 14, не́скольки-R6.A2, не́которые R6.A2; ко́е-

fiancé жени́х; —e неве́ста

field по́ле; (area) о́бласть: He works in (the — of) physics. Он рабо́тает в о́бласти фи́зики.

fight борьба́; боро́ться

figure out сообрази́ть – сообража́ют, раз/о/бра́ться – разбира́ются в *чём*

fill (glass) for X with Y нальют – налива́ют *кому́ что́/чего́*

film фильм

finally наконе́ц

find найду́т – находи́ть, отыскать – оты́скивают; — out узна́ют – узнава́ть

fine здо́рово; прекра́сный, хоро́ший; (not coarse) ме́лкий

finger па́лец

finish ко́нчить – конча́ют; (a set program) око́нчить – ока́нчивают

fire (general) ого́нь; (conflagration) пожа́р

firm про́чный, твёрдый; фи́рма

first; at — снача́ла, сперва́ IV.7; — of all, — and foremost пре́жде всего́, в пе́рвую о́чередь; in the — place во-пе́рвых; вообще́; for the — time впервы́е, (в) пе́рвый раз

fish ры́ба; — soup уха́

fit под/о/йду́т – подходи́ть

fitting к лицу́; not — не к лицу́

fix (set, determine) назна́чить – назнача́ют, определи́ть – определя́ют

fixed stress постоя́нное ударе́ние

flashy крича́щий

flee бежа́ть

fleet флóт

flier лётчик, лётчица

floor пóл; (story) эта́ж

flourish: May X — Да здра́вствует *ктó/ чтó*

flow льют(ся), тёку́т, протёку́т – протека́ют

flower цветóк CL5.5

fluctuate колеба́ться

fluently (of foreign language) свобóдно

fly *det* лете́ть; *nondet* лета́ют; —er: *see* FLIER

folk нарóд; нарóдный; — song нарóдная пе́сня

follow (по)сле́довать *комý/чемý or* за *кéм/ чéм*; it —s from X из *чегó* вытека́ет – сле́дует

following сле́дующий, после́дующий; the — morning на сле́дующее у́тро; the — day на сле́дующий де́нь

food еда́

fool дура́к; *F* ду́ра

foolish глу́пый

foot ногá; on — пешкóм

football (European —, soccer) футбóл

for (during) III.6; *with time expressions* на R7.A3; на, за, для IV.4; *ethical dative* IV.4; — now покá, покá что; — the time being покá, покá что

forbid запрети́ть – запреща́ют

force си́ла; armed —s вооружённые си́лы

forefather пре́док

forehead лóб

foreign иностра́нный; — country (*гдé*) за грани́цей; (*кудá*) за грани́цу; (*откýда*) из-за грани́цы

foremost передовóй

forever навéки, навсегда́

forgive прости́ть – проща́ют

fork ви́лка

form образова́ть; фóрма *also gr* ви́д; in X — в X-ом ви́де; in the — of X в ви́де *когó/чегó*

formalize (make official) офóрмить – офор-

мля́ют

formant *gr* су́ффикс (словообразова́тельный)

formation образова́ние

former бы́вший; пéрвый VII.5

formerly ра́ньше, пре́жде

forth: and so — и та́к да́лее (и т.д.), и томý подóбное (и т.п.)

fortunately к сча́стью

fortune (good) сча́стье

forward (*гдé*) впереди́; (*кудá*) вперёд

fragment отры́вок

France Фра́нция

frank открове́нный

frankness открове́нность

free свобóдный; —dom свобóда; (set —) освободи́ть – освобожда́ют; — self of/get — (rid) of освободи́ться – освобожда́ются от

freeze *intr* замёрз(ну)ть – замерза́ют

French францу́зский; —man францу́з, францу́женка

frequent ча́стый

frequentative aspect *gr* многокра́тный ви́д

fresh свéжий

fried жа́реный

from X time с *чéго*; — X (time) to Y (time) от *чегó* до *чегó*, с *чегó* по *чтó*

front *adj* пере́дний; (leading) передовóй; military and *fig* фронт; *sub adj* передова́я; in — of перед; — hall пере́дняя

frontier грани́ца

frost морóз

fruit фру́кт(ы); stewed — компóт

fulfill вы́полнить – выполня́ют

full пóлный; *gr* — stem пóлная оснóва

function дéйствовать, иду́т R7 note 12

funny смешнóй

furniture мéбель, обстанóвка

furthermore крóме тогó, к томý же; and, —, (да) и (то) CL5.4; притóм VIII.2

futile напра́сный

future бу́дущий; the — бу́дущее; — tense *gr* бу́дущее врéмя

gain добьй-утся – добива́ются *чегó*

game игра́

gas газ

gasoline бензи́н

gates воро́та

gay весёлый

gender *gr* род; masculine/feminine/neuter
— мужско́й/же́нский/сре́дний род

general о́бщий, всео́бщий; in — вообще́/в
о́бщем IV.7

generalize обобщи́ть – обобща́ют

genitive: — case роди́тельный паде́ж;
partitive — роди́тельный раздели́-
тельный

genius ге́ний; *adj* (of genius) гениа́льный

gentle мя́гкий, не́жный

geography геогра́фия

German неме́цкий; не́мец, не́мка; —ic
герма́нский; —у Герма́ния

gerund дееприча́стие

get получить – получа́ют, доста́нут – до-
става́ть; — accustomed/used to при-
вы́к(ну)ть – привыка́ют к *кому́/чему́*;
— along with обраща́ются с *кем/чем*;
— along without об/о/йду́тся – обхо-
ди́ться без *кого́/чего́*; — at/down to
приступи́ть – приступа́ют; — to
(arrive at) попаду́т – попада́ют; — up
вста́нут – встава́ть

gift (present) пода́рок; (talent, etc.) да́р
(ре́чи); give a — (по)дари́ть *что
кому́*

girl де́вуш/ка; *as form of address* R9 note
10; — friend (*us* of girl) подру́га

give: (hand) по́дать – подава́ть; (assign
task) за́дать – задава́ть; *NB —
assignment* дать – дава́ть зада́ние
(*avoids duplication*); — back о́тдать –
отдава́ть; *see also* RETURN; — gift
(по)дари́ть *что кому́*; — (hand over)
пе́редать – передава́ть; — up *tran* о́т-
дать – отдава́ть; (surrender) сда́ть –
сдава́ть

given: a — X да́нный

glad ра́д *sh f only*, ра́достный; make —
(об)ра́довать; be — of (об)ра́доваться
ся *кому́/чему́*; I'm — he came (of him,
that he came) я ра́д ему́

glance взгля́д; взгляну́ть – взгля́дывают

glass стака́н

glory сла́ва

go: — on произ/о/йду́т – происходи́ть,
име́ют ме́сто, случи́ться – случа́ют-
ся, иду́т, протёкут – протека́ют (of a
process); — on (proceed) Да́льше!;
— over в *что́* (of a sound) перейду́т –
переходи́ть; — to see *motion verb* + к
кому́/чему́ R3 note 9

goal це́ль

god бо́г; my God бо́же мо́й

gold зо́лото

golf го́льф

good-hearted до́брый

good-night споко́йной но́чи

gossip болтовня́

goulash гуля́ш

govern руководи́ть *кем/чем*, пра́вить *кем/
чем*; управля́ют *кем/чем*; — a case
управля́ют падежо́м

government прави́тельство; *adj* прави́тель-
ственный; (state) госуда́рственный

grade (mark in school) отме́тка; (class in
school) кла́сс

gradual постепе́нный

graduate (from) око́нчить – ока́нчивают

graduate course аспиранту́ра

graduate student аспира́нт

grain зёрно; —s (cereals) зёрна

grammar грамма́тика

grammatical граммати́ческий

grand вели́кий; торже́ственный

granddaughter вну́чка

grandson вну́к

grass трава́

gratuities чаевы́е

gray се́рый; (of hair) седо́й

great вели́кий, большо́й, огро́мный;
Great! Здо́рово, Прекра́сно

greatest велича́йший

greatly весьма́

Greece Гре́ция; Greek гре́ческий; гре́к,
греча́нка

green зелёный

greeting приве́т

grief печа́ль, го́ре

grilled жа́реный

grippe гри́пп

ground земля́; (base on) основа́ть – осно́-
вывают, обоснова́ть – обосно́вы-
вают

grounds основа́ние, основа́ния; on the — that на то́м основа́нии, что

group гру́ппа

grow расту́т; — up вы́растут – выраста́ют

growth ро́ст

guard берёгу́т

guess дога́дка; догада́ются – дога́дываются

guest го́сть

guide ги́д

GUM ГУМ *acronym for* Госуда́рственный Универса́льный Магази́н

gun ружьё

hair во́лос(ы)

half пол-, полу- R7 note 6; полови́на; one and a — полтора́

half hour полчаса́

hall (front —) пере́дняя; (auditorium) за́л; (corridor) коридо́р

hand рука́; be on — име́ются; on the one — . . ., on the other — с одно́й стороны́ . . ., с друго́й стороны́; *v* по́дать – подава́ть; — in сдать – сдава́ть; — in application по́дать – подава́ть заявле́ние; — over пере́дать – передава́ть

handbag су́мка

handkerchief (носово́й) плато́к

handle (people or objects) обраща́ются с ке́м/че́м

hang *tr* пове́сить – ве́шают; *intr* висе́ть

happen случи́ться – случа́ются, произо́йду́т – происходи́ть, получи́ться – получа́ются; no matter what (—s) во что́ бы то́ ни ста́ло; it sometimes —s that быва́ет, что

happiness сча́стье

happy счастли́вый; Happy New Year (greeting) С Но́вым го́дом; be/make —: *see* GLAD

harbor по́рт

hard твёрдый; (difficult) тру́дный; (severe, cruel) жесто́кий

hardly едва́ (ли), вря́д ли, чу́ть

harsh ре́зкий

hat шля́па

have име́ют R9 note 12, располага́ют че́м; — to: *see* MUST; — been R3 note 18; — been X-ing R4 note 2

hazel(-colored) ка́рий

head голова́; come into one's — приду́т – приходи́ть кому́ в го́лову, на у́м

health здоро́вье; to one's — за здоро́вье

healthy здоро́вый

heard: be — разда́ться – раздава́ться; can be — слы́шный

heart се́рд/це

heat нагре́ют – нагрева́ют; (hot weather) жара́

height высота́; (a person's growth) ро́ст

heir насле́дник

hell (mild oath) CL3.8

hello здра́вствуйте, приве́т

help по́мощь; помо́гут – помога́ют, оказа́ть – ока́зывают по́мощь

hero геро́й

heroine герои́ня

herring селёдка

hesitate колеба́ться

hide скро́ют – скрыва́ют; — self скро́ются – скрыва́ются

high высо́кий; —est высоча́йший

highly весьма́

hill гора́

hinder (по)меша́ют

history исто́рия

hockey хокке́й

hold держа́ть; — fast удержа́ть – уде́рживают; — out вы́держать – выде́рживают

holiday пра́здник; —s отпуск, (from school or college); кани́кулы *adj* пра́здничный

homework дома́шнее зада́ние

honest че́ст/ный

hope наде́жда; наде́яться

horrible стра́шный, ужа́сный

horribly (very much) ужа́сно

hors d'œuvres заку́ски; eat — закуси́ть – заку́сывают

horse ло́шадь; —back верхо́м

host хозя́ин; —ess хозя́йка

hot горя́чий, жа́ркий; — water горя́чая вода́; — weather жа́ркая пого́да, жара́

hotel гости́ница; — room (suite) но́мер

hourly ежеча́сно

house *v* помести́ть – помеща́ют (*где́*)

however одна́ко, всё-таки, впро́чем, зато́, тём не ме́нее
huge огро́мный
human челове́ческий
human being челове́к
humanity (mankind) челове́чество
humor ю́мор
humorous смешно́й
hundred со́тня; —s со́тни
Hungary Ве́нгрия; Hungarian венге́рский
hungry голо́дный
hurry (по)спеши́ть
hurt боле́ть; begin to — заболе́ть – заболева́ют CL3.2; it —s бо́льно
hushing consonant gr шипя́щий согла́сный
hydrogen водоро́д; adj водоро́дный
hymn (anthem) ги́мн; (church) церко́вный ги́мн
hyphen дефи́с

ice лёд
ice cream моро́женое; chocolate — шокола́дное мороженое; vanilla — сли́вочное мороженое
idea иде́я, мы́сль; (conception) представле́ние, поня́тие; he has no — of о́н не име́ет никако́го представле́ния/поня́тия о
identical одина́ковый
idiot идио́т
i.e. (that is) т.е. (то́ есть)
if R3.C; (whether) ли; (condition) е́сли; —... not (n't) (unless) е́сли не
ill, —ness: see SICK, —NESS
image о́браз
imagine предста́вить – представля́ют (себе́); Imagine! Предста́вь(те) себе́!
immediately сейча́с (же), сра́зу, то́тчас (же)
immense огро́мный
immortal бессме́ртный
immortality бессме́ртие
imperative mood gr повели́тельное наклоне́ние
imperfective: — aspect gr несоверше́нный ви́д; — derivation образова́ние глаго́лов несоверше́нного ви́да

imperialism империали́зм; imperialist империали́ст; adj империалисти́ческий
impersonal construction gr безли́чная констру́кция
importance ва́жность, значе́ние
important ва́жный
impossible невозмо́жный, нельзя́
improve улу́чшить – улучша́ют
in (ending in X, stem in X, etc.) на что́ (оконча́ние на что́, осно́ва на что́ и т.д.)
inasmuch as поско́льку
incident слу́чай
include включи́ть – включа́ют (в себе́)
including в том числе́ и, включа́я
incompatible несовмести́мый
inconvenient неудо́бный
incorrect непра́вильный
increase ро́ст; увели́чить – увели́чивают, умно́жить – умножа́ют
indeclinable gr несклоня́емый
indeed действи́тельно, на са́мом де́ле, в са́мом де́ле
indefinite неопределённый
indicate указа́ть – ука́зывают
indicative mood gr изъяви́тельное наклоне́ние
indignant: make — возмути́ть – возмуща́ют; be — возмути́ться – возмуща́ются; I am — я возмущён
indignation возмуще́ние
indirect ко́свенный also gr; — speech ко́свенная ре́чь; — object ко́свенное дополне́ние
indispensable необходи́мый
individual отде́льный, индивидуа́льный
industrial промы́шленный
industrious приле́жный
industry промы́шленность
inexpensive дешёвый
infantile младе́нческий
infinitive gr инфинити́в
inflection gr фле́ксия
influence влия́ние; оказа́ть – ока́зывают влия́ние на кого́/что́; (по)де́йствовать на кого́/что́
initial нача́льный, первонача́льный
inserted vowel бе́глый гла́сный

inside *adj* вну́тренний; — (of) внутри́ *adv or prep* кого́/чего́

insist настоя́ть – наста́ивают на *чём*

inspect осмотре́ть – осма́тривают

instance слу́чай; for — наприме́р

instead (of) вме́сто кого́/чего́; вме́сто того́ чтобы

institute институ́т

instructions указа́ния

instrumental case твори́тельный паде́ж

insufficient недоста́точный

insult оби́деть – обижа́ют; get/be —ed оби́деться – обижа́ются

intellect у́м

intelligence (military or government) разве́дка; (mental) у́м

intelligent у́мный

intend ду́мают CL.42; собра́ться – собира́ются, быть наме́рен(ным); (propose) предполага́ют

intensify уси́лить – уси́ливают

interest (in) интере́с (к *кому́/чему́*); *v tr* интересова́ть; (arouse someone's —) заинтересова́ть; be —ed in интересова́ться *кём/чём*; become —ed in заинтересова́ться *кём/чём*

interesting интере́сный

interior *adj* вну́тренний

interjection *gr* междоме́тие

internal вну́тренний

international междунаро́дный

interpret (as) воспри́мут – восприни́ма́ют

interrogation допро́с (на)

interrogative *gr* вопроси́тельный

Intourist (Soviet bureau for foreign travel) Интури́ст

introduce введу́т – вводить; (people to one another) предста́вить – представля́ют *кого́ кому́*

introduction введе́ние

introductory вступи́тельный

investigate раз/о/бра́ться – разбира́ются в *ко́м/чём*

investment вкла́д

invincible непобеди́мый CL5.11

invite пригласи́ть – приглаша́ют (*куда́*)

irregular *gr* непра́вильный

island о́стров (на)

issue (periodical) но́мер

it: *translations* R3.E

Italian италья́нский; италья́нец, италья́нка; Italy Ита́лия

jacket пиджа́к

Japan Япо́ния; —ese япо́нский; япо́нец, япо́нка

join соедини́ть – соединя́ют, сплоти́ть – спла́чивают; (*куда́*) поступи́ть – поступа́ют, вступи́ть – вступа́ют

jolly весёлый

jot *gr* "*j*" йо́т

journal журна́л; —ism журнали́стика; —ist журнали́ст, журнали́стка

journey пое́здка

joy ра́дость

joyous ра́достный

judge судья́

jump in впры́гнуть – впры́гивают

junior мла́дший

just R6 note 2; ка́к ра́з, и́менно, то́лько; *with past tense of verbs* то́лько что: He — came. Он то́лько что пришёл. *Cf.* He came — now. Он то́лько тепе́рь пришёл. Yes, that's — it. Да, и́менно.

just *adj* справедли́вый

keep сохрани́ть – сохраня́ют; (maintain) держа́ть; — X-ing всё, всё ещё, всё вре́мя; *verb* X R4 note 7; — in mind име́ют в виду́

kerchief плато́к

key клю́ч

kilogram килогра́мм

kilometer киломе́тр

kind до́брый; (type) ро́д; вид; all —s of вся́кого ро́да (*us precedes noun*)

kissel кисе́ль

kitchen ку́хня

knee коле́но

knife но́ж

know зна́ют, разбира́ются в *чём*; — how уме́ют R3 note 17

knowledge зна́ние, зна́ния

known изве́стный, знако́мый

kopeck копе́йка

Kremlin Кре́мль

labial consonant *gr* губнóй соглáсный
labor трýд; *adj* рабóчий
laboratory лаборатóрия
ladder лéстница
ladies' man волокúта
lady дáма
lag behind отстáнут – отставáть
lake óзеро
lamp лáмпа
land земля́, странá, крáй
land in попадýт – попадáют (*кудá*)
landlord хозя́ин
language язы́к; *adj* языковóй
last послéдний, прóшлый; (week, etc.) R7
    note 6; at — наконéц
late пóздний, пóздно; be — опоздáют –
    опáздывают
later (on) потóм
Latin латúнский; — (Roman) alphabet
    латúница
latter послéдний VII.5
laugh смея́ться; — at смея́ться над *кéм/
    чéм*; begin to — засмея́ться
laughter смéх
lavatory убóрная
law (a law or law in general) закóн; (as a
    science) прáво
law student юрúст
lawyer адвокáт, юрúст
lay (foundation, etc.) заложúть – заклáды-
    вают
layer слóй
lazy ленúвый
lead (direct) вёдýт, руководúть *кéм/чéм*
leader руководúтель, (of the people) вóждь
leading ведýющий, передовóй
leak протёкýт – протекáют
learn (teach/study) II.7
learnèd учёный
least малéйший; not the — не малéйшего;
    without the — без малéйшего; at —
    по крáйней мéре; хотя́ бы, хоть
leave *tr* остáвить – оставля́ют R4 note 16;
    intr y- *motion verb*
lecture лéкция
left лéвый; to the — налéво; at the —
    слéва, налéво
less мéньший
lesson урóк IV.5

let пýсть, пускáй; (allow) дать – давáть
    R 7 note 9
letter письмó; (of alphabet) бýква
level ýровень; on a — with наря́дý с *кéм/
    чéм*
lexical лексúческий; lexicon лéксика
liaison свя́зь
liberate освободúть – освобождáют
library библиотéка
lie R8.B
lieutenant лейтенáнт
life: way of — óбраз жúзни
lift пóднимут – поднимáют
light (weight) лёгкий; (shade, color) свéт-
    лый, я́сный; свéт
likable симпатúчный
like (similar to) похóжий на *когó/чтó*;
    any X you — любóй, *ктó/чтó*
    угóдно; (по)нрáвиться *комý*, любúть
    R4 note 13; I'd — я бы хотéл R3 note
    12; — it when (that) CL4.4
likewise тáкже
limit *tr* огранúчить – огранúчивают; —
    self to, be —d to огранúчиться –
    огранúчиваются *кéм/чéм*
line óчередь; get in — стáнут – становúть-
    ся в óчередь; stand in — стоя́ть в
    óчереди; general — (party, etc.) лú-
    ния; — (which one draws) чертá; —
    (on a page) стрóчка, строкá
linen бельё
linguistic языковóй, лингвистúческий
linguistics языковéдение, языкознáние,
    лингвúстика
link свя́зь
lip губá; *adj* (labial) губнóй
liqueur ликёр
liquid *adj* жúдкий; *n* жúдкость
literary литератýрный
literature литератýра
little мáло, немнóго (немнóжко); (some-
    what) нéсколько, немнóго, немнóжко
    R4 note 14; a — X-er по + *comp*
    R5.A5
live: long — X здрáвствует *ктó/чтó*; *adj*
    —/—ly живóй; — through прóживут –
    проживáют; (experience) пéреживут –
    переживáют
living room гостúная

living space жилпло́щадь
living standard жи́зненный у́ровень
loan translation *gr* ка́лька
local ме́стный
locate *tr* (find) найду́т – находи́ть; (place,
    house) помести́ть – помеща́ют;
    (place) расположи́ть – располага́ют;
    be —d находи́ться
location расположе́ние, местонахожде́ние
locative case ме́стный паде́ж
long (measure) дли́нный; (time) дли́нный,
    до́лгий; for a — time до́лго, давно́;
    — ago давно́; not — ago неда́вно; —
    before задо́лго до *чего́*; so — пока́
longer длинне́е, до́льше; по — уже́ не,
    бо́льше не R3 note 18
long-nosed длиннonóсый
look взгля́д; (по)смотре́ть; — at (по)-
    смотре́ть R8 note 5; (glance) взгля́д-
    нуть – взгля́дывают; (inspect, — at
    sights) осмотре́ть – осма́тривают; —
    around (— at sights; get bearings)
    осмотре́ться – осма́триваются; —
    for иска́ть; — up разыска́ть – разы́-
    скивают; — after смотре́ть за *кем/
    чем*
lose (по)теря́ют; (game, war) проигра́ют –
    прои́грывают
loss поте́ря
loud гро́мкий; (flashy) крича́щий
love любо́вь; люби́ть; fall in — влюби́ть-
    ся – влюбля́ются в *кого́/что́*; —
    affair связь
low ни́зкий
lower ни́зший, ни́жний; спусти́ть – спу-
    ска́ют
luck сча́стье; have —/be —y (по)везёт/
    (по)везло́ *кому́/чему́*
lump кусо́к
lunar лу́нный
lunch (второ́й) за́втрак; (по)за́втракают
luxury ро́скошь

Macedonia Македо́ния; —n македо́нский
machine маши́на
mad сумасше́дший; go — с/о/йду́т –
    сходи́ть с ума́
magazine журна́л
magnificent прекра́сный, превосхо́дный

mail по́чта; by — по по́чте
main гла́вный; —ly гла́вным о́бразом
maintain поддержа́ть – подде́рживают
maintenance поддержа́ние
major *n* майо́р; *adj* гла́вный
majority большинство́
makeup (composition) соста́в
make up *v* входи́ть в соста́в *кого́/чего́*
male мужско́й
malicious злой
man (human being) челове́к; young — R9
    note 10; (*vs.* woman) мужчи́на; —'s
    мужско́й
manifest прояви́ть – проявля́ют, обнару́-
    жить – обнару́живают; — self про-
    яви́ться – проявля́ются, обнару́жить-
    ся – обнару́живаются
manifestation проявле́ние
mankind челове́чество
manner о́браз; in an X — (*with various adj*)
    X-ым о́бразом
manuscript ру́копись
many мно́го R4 note 14; мно́ги- R6.A2
map ка́рта
march марширова́ть
maritime морско́й
mark знак; (grade in school) отме́тка; *gr*
    question — вопроси́тельный знак;
    exclamation — восклица́тельный знак
marketplace пло́щадь
marriage жени́тьба
marry R5 note 9; (of a man) жени́ться *P
    and I* на *ко́м*; (of a woman) вы́йдут –
    выходи́ть за́муж за *кого́*; married (of
    a man) жена́т(ый); married (of a
    woman) за́мужем
Marxism маркси́зм; —ist маркси́ст; *adj*
    маркси́стский
masculine (male) мужско́й; — gender
    мужско́й род
mass ма́сса; —es ма́ссы
master господи́н, хозя́ин; be — of вла-
    де́ют *кем/чем*; —'s degree маги́стер-
    ская сте́пень
match (for lighting) спи́чка
-mate това́рищ по *чему́*
material материа́л (*pl* материа́лы)
mathematics матема́тика
matter де́ло; on a certain — по одному́

де́лу; on business —s по дела́м; for that — (да) и (то́); no — what (happens) во что́ бы то́ ни ста́ло VII, p. 227 What's the —? (What's going on?) В чём де́ло?
It doesn't —. (Это) всё равно́.
What's the — with him/you? Что́ с ним/ва́ми?
What's the — with you! (strong) Что́ вы!
For that — CL5.4
no — what kind VII, p. 227
mausoleum мавзоле́й
may мо́жно, мо́жет бы́ть, возмо́жно
maybe мо́жет быть
meal еда́
mean зна́чить, означа́ют; this —s that (thus, in other words) зна́чит *paren*; —ing значе́ние
means сре́дство (*pl* сре́дства); live beyond one's — живут не по сре́дствам; by — of путём *чего́*
meanwhile ме́жду те́м
measure ме́ра, мероприя́тие; take —(s) при́мут – принима́ют ме́ру (ме́ры); — off отме́рить – отме́ривают
meat мя́со; *adj* мясно́й; — course жарко́е
mechanic меха́ник
medicine (science) медици́на; (remedy) лека́рство
mediocre сре́дний
medium среда́
meet встре́тить – встреча́ют; *intr* встре́титься – встреча́ются с *кем*
meeting встре́ча; (gathering) собра́ние
member член
mental у́мственный, психи́ческий
mention: not to — не говори́ть уже́ о *ком/ чём* (не говоря́ уже́ о *ком/чём*)
menu меню́
merchant купе́ц, коммерса́нт
Merry Christmas (greeting) С Рождество́м
metal мета́лл; *adj* металли́ческий
method ме́тод
Methodius Мефо́дий
middle середи́на; *adj* сре́дний
migrate пересели́ться – переселя́ются
migration переселе́ние

mild мя́гкий; —ness мя́гкость
mile ми́ля
milieu среда́
military вое́нный
milk молоко́; *adj* моло́чный
million миллио́н
mind ум; keep in — име́ют в виду́ R9 note 12
mineral минера́л; *adj* минера́льный
minus ми́нус
minute мину́та
miss (omit, skip) пропусти́ть – пропуска́ют, не хвата́ет
mistake оши́бка; be —n ошиби́ться – ошиба́ются; —nly оши́бочно
mistress (of a household, etc.) хозя́йка
mobile (vowel) бе́глый; (stress) подвижно́е (ударе́ние)
modal мода́льный; mode: *see* MOOD
modern совреме́нный
modify определи́ть – определя́ют
mollify смягчи́ть – смягча́ют
monopolistic монополисти́ческий
monosyllabic односло́жный
month ме́сяц; —ly ежеме́сячный
monument (also literary) па́мятник
mood *gr* наклоне́ние; *see* INDICATIVE, IMPERATIVE, SUBJUNCTIVE, CONDITIONAL
moon луна́; *adj* лу́нный
more (in addition to) ещё R6 note 3; *comp* бо́льше; the — so as те́м бо́лее, что; — than that бо́лее того́; — than once не ра́з
moreover кро́ме того́, к тому́ же, прито́м, ма́ло того́
morning *adj* у́тренний
morpheme морфе́ма
morphology морфоло́гия
morphophoneme морфофоне́ма
Moscow *adj* моско́вский; near — *adj* подмоско́вный
most (majority) большинство́
motherland ро́дина
motion движе́ние, ход; *gr* — verb глаго́л движе́ния
mountain гора́
mouth рот (*but adj* oral = у́стный)
movable подви́жный; *gr* — stress подвижно́е ударе́ние

move дви́гнуть – дви́гают *or* дви́гать;
intr дви́гнуться – дви́гаются
(дви́гаться);   — hand/leg дви́гнуть-
ся – дви́гаются/дви́гаться   руко́й/
ного́й;   — (to a new location) пере-
е́дут – переезжа́ют, пересели́ть(ся) –
переселя́ют(ся)
movie house кинотеа́тр; *colloq* кино́
movies (the industry in general) кино́; let's
go to the — поидём в кино́
much мно́го;   — X-er гора́здо R5.A8,
куда́;   — less (to say nothing of) не го-
вори́ть о *ко́м/чём* (не говоря́ уже́ о
ко́м/чём); о́чень R4 note 3
multiply (by) умно́жить – умножа́ют (на
что́)
municipal городско́й
Muscovite *adj* моско́вский
museum музе́й
mushroom гри́б; *adj* грибно́й
music му́зыка
musician музыка́нт, музыка́нтша
must R6.C
mutation *gr* перехо́д

name (general) и́мя, назва́ние; first — и́мя;
(patronymic) о́тчество; last — фами́-
лия; *v* назва́ть – называ́ют *кого́/что́
кем/чём*
What's your —? Ка́к ва́с зову́т?
My — is . . . Меня́ зову́т *кем or colloq
кто́.*
namely и́менно
narrate рассказа́ть – расска́зывают
narrow у́зкий, те́сный
nation страна́, на́ция
national наро́дный; (pertaining to nation
or nationality) национа́льный
nationality национа́льность
native родно́й; be a — of бы́ть ро́дом (*откуда*);   — land ро́дина
natural есте́ственный
nature приро́да; хара́ктер; by — от при-
ро́ды, по приро́де
naval морско́й, военно-морско́й
navy военно-морско́й фло́т
near бли́зкий; о́коло; под *чём* R8 note 15
necessary ну́жный, необходи́мый
necktie га́лстук

negative *also gr* отрица́тельный
negotiations перегово́ры
neighbor сосе́д, сосе́дка
neither ни то́т ни друго́й, о́ба . . . не IV.3;
  — . . . nor . . . ни . . . ни . . . R8 note
3
nephew племя́нник
nest (*also gr* word nest) гнездо́
nettle крапи́ва
neuter gender сре́дний ро́д
neutral нейтра́льный
nevertheless те́м не ме́нее, всё-таки, одна́-
ко, всё-же, ме́жду те́м VIII.1
New Year: Happy — — С Но́вым го́дом
news но́вости; item of — но́вость
newspaper газе́та
next сле́дующий; бу́дущий (week, etc.)
R7.A6; Next! Сле́дующий!;   — to
о́коло *кого́/чего́*, во́зле *кого́/чего́*,
по́дле *кого́/чего́*, ря́дом с *кого́/чего́*
nice любе́зный, ми́лый
niece племя́нница
night: good-— споко́йной но́чи; *adj* ноч-
но́й;   — slippers ночны́е ту́фли
no X at all, none никако́й, ни оди́н
noise шу́м; noisy шу́мный
nominative case имени́тельный паде́ж
nonbeliever неве́рующий
nondetermined aspect *gr* неопределённый
ви́д
none, no X at all никако́й, ни оди́н
nonsense вздо́р
nonsyllabic неслогово́й
norm но́рма
north се́вер; —ern се́верный; —east
северо-восто́к; —eastern се́веро-во-
сто́чный; —west северо-за́пад;
  —western се́веро-за́падный
nose но́с
not: — at all во́все не, вообще́ не, совсе́м
не, ника́к, ниско́лько; — one (not a
single) ни оди́н; — that: it's — that
CL5.1
notable ви́дный; be — for отлича́ются
чём
note заме́тка, отме́тка, запи́ска; make —s
(с)де́лают заме́тки; leave a — (for)
оста́вить – оставля́ют запи́ску *кому́*
notebook тетра́дь, тетра́дка

nothing: to say — of не говоря́ уже́ о ко́м/
чём, уже́ не говоря́ о ко́м/чём V.2
notice заме́тить – замеча́ют; things
worthy of — (sights, etc.) достоприме-
ча́тельности
noticeable заме́тный
notion поня́тие, представле́ние, иде́я
noun и́мя существи́тельное; deverbative
— отглаго́льное существи́тельное
novel рома́н; —ette по́весть
now . . . , now . . . то . . . то . . . ; ну́
now that ра́з
number (general) число́, коли́чество; (issue
of periodical) но́мер; a great — of
большо́е коли́чество кого́/чего́; quite
a — of це́лый ря́д кого́/чего́; a — of
ря́д кого́/чего́
numeral gr и́мя числи́тельное: see
CARDINAL, ORDINAL, COLLECTIVE
numerous многочи́сленный
nurse медици́нская сестра́, медсестра́,
сестра́

obey (по)слу́шаются кого́/чего́
object предме́т; (aim) це́ль; gr дополне́-
ние: see DIRECT, INDIRECT
obligatory обяза́тельный
oblique case gr ко́свенный паде́ж
observation наблюде́ние
observe наблюда́ют
obstruent consonant gr шу́мный согла́с-
ный
obtain получи́ть – получа́ют, доста́нут –
достава́ть
obvious ви́дно
occasion слу́чай; have — to придётся –
прихо́дится кому́ inf X7
occupation заня́тие
occupy за́ймут – занима́ют; — self with
займу́тся (past tense E) – занима́ются
ке́м/че́м II.7
ocean океа́н
October adj октя́брьский
offend оби́деть – обижа́ют; be/get —ed
оби́деть – обижа́ются
offensive adj проти́вный
office конто́ра, бюро́; (study) кабине́т
officer офице́р
official чино́вник; make —, write up —ly

офо́рмить – оформля́ют
often ча́сто
oh! ах!
oil ма́сло; (petroleum) нефть
old (ancient) дре́вний; — man стари́к; —
woman стару́ха; Old Church Slavonic
старославя́нский
omit пропусти́ть – пропуска́ют
once (one time) (оди́н) ра́з; (in the past)
не́когда; — upon a time одна́жды;
(now that) ра́з; at — сейча́с (же), сра́зу
one (impersonal) R4 note 18
one and a half полтора́
one another друг дру́г-
oneself: say to — про себя́ V.8
only то́лько, лишь; всего́; the — еди́нст-
венный
opera о́пера
operate де́йствовать
opinion мне́ние, взгля́д
opportunity возмо́жность, слу́чай
opposed противополо́жный
opposite n противополо́жность; adj про-
тивополо́жный, проти́вный; adv
(across the street; on the contrary) на-
про́тив
opposition противоде́йствие; offer — ока-
за́ть – ока́зывают противоде́йствие
кому́/чему́; in — to (in contrast to, unlike) в противополо́жность кому́/
чему́
oppress fig души́ть
oral у́стный
or else а то́, и́на́че
order поря́док; gr word — поря́док слов;
in —, all right в поря́дке; put in —
приведу́т – приводи́ть в поря́док; in
— to (для того́, зате́м, с те́м) чтобы
IX.A, R7.C; v (a meal, room) зака-
за́ть – зака́зывают; (command) при-
каза́ть – прика́зывают
ordinal numeral поря́дковое числи́тельное
ordinary обыкнове́нный, обы́чный; out of
the — чрезвыча́йный
organization организа́ция
organize организова́ть – организо́вывают
or организова́ть P, I
origin происхожде́ние, возникнове́ние;
(conception) зарожде́ние

original (very first) первонача́льный;
(unique, not copied) оригина́льный
originate (arise from) возни́к(ну)ть – возника́ют
orthography орфогра́фия, правописа́ние
oscillate колеба́ться
other друго́й, ино́й, остально́й; each — друг дру́г-
otherwise а то́, и́на́че, в противном слу́чае; (in another way) по-друго́му, по-ино́му, и́на́че
ought R6.C
outdoors (outside) на дворе́
outside на дворе́; *prep* — of вне́ *кого́/чего́*; *adj* вне́шний
over: spread — об/о/иду́т – обходить, распространи́ть(ся) – распространя́ют(ся)
overcoat пальто́
overcome одоле́ют – одолева́ют, преодоле́ют – преодолева́ют
overfulfill перевы́полнить – перевыполня́ют
oversleep проспа́ть – просыпа́ют
own сво́й, со́бственный; in one's — way/fashion по-сво́ему
oxygen кислоро́д; *adj* кислоро́дный

package паке́т
page страни́ца
pain *v* боле́ть; begin to —/hurt заболе́ть – заболева́ют CL3.2
painful бо́льно *кому́/чему́*; *fig* больно́й; — question больно́й вопро́с
paint (по)кра́сить; —er (artist) худо́жник, худо́жника, живопи́сец; —ing карти́на; жи́вопись
pair па́ра
paired consonant *gr* па́рный согла́сный
palatal *gr* палата́льный согла́сный; —ization палатализа́ция, смягче́ние; —ize палатализова́ть, смягчи́ть – смягча́ют
pale бле́дный; — faced бледноли́цый
pants (trousers) брю́ки *pl only*
paper бума́га; докуме́нт; (newspaper) газе́та
parade пара́д; *adj* пара́дный
paradigm *gr* паради́гма

parentheses ско́бки; in — в ско́бках
parenthetic: — word *gr* вво́дное сло́во; — clause вво́дное предложе́ние
parents роди́тели
park па́рк
part ча́сть; *gr* — of speech ча́сть ре́чи; for the most — бо́льшей ча́стью; on the — of со стороны́ *кого́/чего́*; on my — с мое́й стороны́; take — in при́мут – принима́ют уча́стие в *чём*; in — ча́стью
partial части́чный
participate (in) при́мут – принима́ют уча́стие в *чём*
participation уча́стие
participle *gr* прича́стие; passive — прича́стие страда́тельного зало́га; active — прича́стие действи́тельного зало́га
particle *also gr* части́ца
particular осо́бенный
particularly осо́бенно
partitive genitive *gr* роди́тельный, раздели́тельный
partly отча́сти, ча́стью
party (political) па́ртия; *adj* парти́йный; — spirit/membership парти́йность; evening — ве́чер
pass (go through or by) ми́мо *кого́/чего́*; про- *motion verbs*; (time) проведу́т – проводить вре́мя (*or time unit*); —/ elapse (of time) пройду́т – проходить, протёку́т – протека́ют; (hand over, transmit) пе́редать – передава́ть; (exam) сдать/вы́держать экза́мен
passage (in a book, etc.) отры́вок
passenger пассажи́р
passion стра́сть; —ate стра́стный
passive voice *gr* страда́тельный зало́г
past *adj* про́шлый; *n* про́шлое; — tense *gr* проше́дшее вре́мя
path пу́ть
patronymic о́тчество
peace (*vs.* war) ми́р; (rest) поко́й
peaceful ми́рный; споко́йный
people лю́ди, наро́д; а — наро́д; many — (a crowd) мно́го наро́ду; —'s наро́дный
per (time unit) во *что́* R7.A2; (person or object) на *кого́/что́*

percent проце́нт

perceive воспри́мут – воспринима́ют

perception восприя́тие

perfect соверше́нный

perfective aspect *gr* соверше́нный ви́д

perform (publicly) вы́ступить – выступа́ют с *чём*; — a song вы́ступить – выступа́ют с пе́сней; —ance представле́ние, выступле́ние

perhaps мо́жет быть, пожа́луй, возмо́жно

period пери́од; (point) то́чка

periodical журна́л

permit позво́лить – позволя́ют

person челове́к R9 note 10; *us* F осо́ба; лицо́ *also gr*; first/second/third — пе́рвое/второ́е/тре́тье лицо́

personal *also gr* ли́чный

persuade уговори́ть – угова́ривают

phenomenon явле́ние

phoneme *gr* фоне́ма

phonetics *gr* фоне́тика

phonology *gr* фоноло́гия

photograph сни́мут – снима́ют, фотографи́ровать; сни́мок, фотогра́фия

physical физи́ческий

physician вра́ч, *colloq* до́ктор

physicist фи́зик

physics фи́зика; *adj* физи́ческий

piano роя́ль, пиани́но

pick up за- *motion verb* за *ке́м/че́м* R 4 note 4

pick out вы́брать – выбира́ют

picture карти́на (*colloq* movie)

pie пиро́г, пирожо́к

piece кусо́к; (of music) пье́са

pig свинья́; *adj* свино́й

pipe (metal and smoking) тру́бка

pity сожале́ние; it's a — жа́ль

placard плака́т

place ме́сто; take — произо́/йду́т – происходи́ть, случи́ться – случа́ются, протеку́т – протека́ют, состоя́ться *P only*; име́ют ме́сто R9 note 12; in the X — VIII.6; in the first — во-пе́рвых; вообще́; *v* помести́ть – помеща́ют (*где́*), положи́ть – кла́дут (*куда́*) R8.B; (по)ста́вить

plan пла́н

plan to ду́мают CL4.2; собра́ться – собира́ться

plant (factory) заво́д

plate (dish) таре́лка

play (с)игра́ют (сыгра́ют); — a sport or game (с)игра́ют (сыгра́ют) во *что́*; — an instrument (с)игра́ют (сыгра́ют) на *чём* R10 note 6; — role (с)игра́ют (сыгра́ют) ро́ль; stage — пье́са

playing card ка́рта

playwright драмату́рг

pleasant прия́тный

please (по)нра́виться *кому́/чему́*; —/if you — пожа́луйста, бу́дьте добры́, бу́дьте любе́зны

pleasure удово́льствие; give — доста́вить – доставля́ют удово́льствие *кому́/чему́*; with — с удово́льствием

pleophonic полногла́сный

pleophony *gr* полногла́сие

plump по́лный

plural number *gr* мно́жественное число́

plus плю́с

pocket карма́н

pocketbook (handbag) су́мка

poem стихотворе́ние; long (epic) — поэ́ма

poet поэ́т

point то́чка, пу́нкт; exclamation — восклица́тельный зна́к; to the — кста́ти; — of view то́чка зре́ния; from the — of view of с то́чки зре́ния *кого́/чего́*; *v* показа́ть – пока́зывают; — out указа́ть – ука́зывают

Poland По́льша; Pole поля́к, по́лька; Polish по́льский

police мили́ция; policeman милиционе́р

policy, policies поли́тика

polite любе́з/ный, ве́жливый, культу́рный

politics поли́тика

ponder заду́маются – заду́мываются

poor (*vs.* rich; worthy of pity) бе́дный; (bad quality) плохо́й, нехоро́ший

popular популя́рный; (of the people) наро́дный

population населе́ние

porridge ка́ша

port по́рт

portrait портре́т

position положе́ние, пози́ция; be in a — to бы́ть в состоя́нии *inf*
positive *also gr* положи́тельный; — degree *gr* положи́тельная сте́пень
possess име́ют, владе́ют *ке́м/че́м*, облада́ют *ке́м/че́м*
possessive *gr* притяжа́тельный
possibility возмо́жность
possible возмо́жный; возмо́жно; as X as — ка́к мо́жно *comp* X R5.A4
postcard откры́тка
post office по́чта
poster плака́т
pour лblй-ут(ся); — (into someone's glass) нальй-ут – налива́ют *кому́ что́/чего́* (of liquid)
power вла́сть, си́ла; be in — бы́ть у вла́сти; come to — приду́т – приходи́ть к вла́сти
powerful си́льный, мо́щный
practical практи́ческий
practice пра́ктика; in -— на пра́ктике
praise: be —d for сла́виться *чем*
prearranged усло́вный
precisely то́чный; и́менно, ка́к ра́з; more — верне́е, точне́е R3 note 14
prefer предпочту́т (-че́сть) – предпочита́ют *кого́/что́ кому́/чему́*
prefix *gr* пре́фикс, приста́вка
prejudice предрассу́док
preliminary предвари́тельный
premier *n* премье́р
premises помеще́ние
preparatory подготови́тельный, предвари́тельный
prepare пригото́вить – приготовля́ют *or* (при)гото́вить; пригото́виться – приготовля́ются *or* (при)гото́виться *intr*; —d гото́вый к *чему́*, на что
preposition *gr* предло́г
prepositional case предло́жный паде́ж
presence прису́тствие; in the — of при *ко́м/чём* R9 note 4
present: be — прису́тствовать; (this, given) настоя́щий; in this/the — article в настоя́щей статье́; at this/the — time в настоя́щее вре́мя; — tense *gr* настоя́щее вре́мя
present предста́вить – представля́ют;

(give a gift) (по)дари́ть *кому́/чему́*; —ation представле́ние
preserve сохрани́ть – сохраня́ют
president президе́нт
presidium прези́диум
press пожму́т – пожима́ют *or* (по)жму́т, дави́ть; (newspapers, etc.) печа́ть
pressure *also fig* давле́ние
pretty краси́вый, хоро́шенький; дово́льно R5 note 13
prevent (по)меша́ют *кому́/чему́*
previous пре́жний
previously пре́жде R9 note 1
price цена́
primarily в пе́рвую о́чередь, пре́жде всего́, гла́вным о́бразом
primary первонача́льный, основно́й
print (на)печа́тают; appear in —, be published (на)печа́таются
prison тюрьма́; put into — посади́ть – сажа́ют в тюрьму́
private ча́стный
probable вероя́тный
probably вероя́тно, наве́рно, должно́ бы́ть
problem пробле́ма, вопро́с; (task, *also* problem, *as in mathematics*, etc.) зада́ча
proceed протёку́т – протека́ют; Proceed! Да́льше! R10 note 3
process проце́сс
produce произведу́т – производи́ть
production произво́дство
profession профе́ссия
professor профе́ссор; Russian — R3 note 6
program програ́мма
progress прогре́сс, успе́хи; make — (с)де́лают успе́хи
proletarian *n* пролета́рий; *adj* пролета́рский
promise обеща́ют *P and I or* (по)обеща́ют; *n* обеща́ние
pronoun местоиме́ние: *see* POSSESSIVE, REFLEXIVE, PERSONAL, DEMONSTRATIVE, INTERROGATIVE, RELATIVE
pronounce произнесу́т – произноси́ть
pronunciation (language) произноше́ние; (utterance (of a toast, etc.)) произнесе́ние

propaganda пропага́нда

proper name *gr* и́мя со́бственное

properly ка́к сле́дует; — speaking со́бственно говоря́

propose (suggest) предложи́ть – предлага́ют; (intend) предполага́ют

proprietor хозя́ин

prosper здра́вствовать

protagonist (гла́вный) геро́й

proto- пра-

protolanguage праязы́к

prove доказа́ть – дока́зывают; — able to суме́ют; — to be оказа́ться – ока́зываются *кем/чем*

proverb посло́вица I.7

provide доста́вить – доставля́ют

provoke (call out, cause) вы́звать (вы́зовут) – вызыва́ют; (cause) обусло́вить – обусло́вливают

psychological психи́ческий, психологи́ческий

public пу́блика

pulse пу́льс

punctuation: marks of — зна́ки препина́ния

pupil (through high school) учени́к, учени́ца

pure чи́стый

purpose це́ль

purse кошелёк

put: — on (article of clothing, glasses, etc.) наде́нут – надева́ют; (clothes, get dressed) оде́нутся – одева́ются; — together соста́вить – составля́ют; — up (house) помести́ть – помеща́ют

qualitative *also gr* ка́чественный; — analysis ка́чественный ана́лиз; — adjective ка́чественное прилага́тельное

quality ка́чество

quantitative *also gr* коли́чественный; — adjective коли́чественное прилага́тельное

quantity коли́чество, число́

quarrel (по)ссо́риться

quarter че́тверть

question (query and problem) вопро́с; ask a — зада́ть – задава́ть вопро́с *кому́/чему́*, спроси́ть – спра́шивают *кого́* о

чём or чтó у *кого́*

quick бы́стрый, ско́рый

quiet ти́хий, споко́йный; — down успоко́ить – успока́ивают; — self down успоко́иться – успока́иваются

quite совсе́м, весьма́, во́все; (rather) дово́льно

radio ра́дио; on the — по ра́дио; — (set) радиоаппара́т

railroad желе́зная доро́га

rain до́ждь; it's —ing до́ждь идёт

raise по́днимут – поднима́ют, повы́сить – повыша́ют

rare ре́дкий

rather R5 note 13; дово́льно; скоре́е R5.A9; точне́е, верне́е R3 note 14

reaction реа́кция

ready гото́вый

real действи́тельный, настоя́щий; —ly действи́тельно, на/в са́мом де́ле, по-настоя́щему; у́ж; really? (*or within a question expressing surprise or disbelief*) ра́зве, неуже́ли R10 note 9

rearm вооружи́ть(ся) – вооружа́ют(ся); —ament вооруже́ние

reason причи́на; (grounds) основа́ние, основа́ния; for some — почему́-то; *v* сообрази́ть – сообража́ют

rebel восста́нут – восстава́ть; —lion восста́ние

receive при́мут – принима́ют; (get) получи́ть – получа́ют, при́мут – принима́ют

receiver: telephone — телефо́нная тру́бка

recently неда́вно, в после́днее вре́мя

reciprocal *also gr* взаи́мный

reckon with (по)счита́ются с *кем/чем*

recognize (a fact, country, etc.) признаю́т – признава́ть; (as familiar, etc.) узнаю́т – узнава́ть

reconcile примири́ть – примиря́ют; become —d примири́ться – примиря́ются

reconstruct (a language) установи́ть – устана́вливают

recover (from illness) попра́виться – поправля́ются

red tape волоки́та

reflexive *gr* возвра́тный

refreshments заку́ски

refuse *tr* отказа́ть – отка́зывают *кому́/чему́* в *чём*; *intr* — to отказа́ться – отка́зываются *inf or* от *чего́*

regard: — as (consider as) рассма́тривают ка́к *кого́/что́*, сочту́т(счесть) – счита́ют *кем/чём or* ка́к *кого́/что́*; in this —, with — to, etc. II.5b

regards приве́т; give — переда́ть – передава́ть приве́т

region райо́н, кра́й, о́бласть

register офо́рмить – оформля́ют

regret (по)жале́ют; сожале́ние

regulation (rule) пра́вило

relate отнесу́т – относи́ть IV.6

related ро́дственный, свя́занный; closely — (of things) те́сно свя́занные

relation(ship) отноше́ние IV.6; in relation to (with respect to) относи́тельно IV.6

relative относи́тельный; (arbitrary) усло́вный; *gr* относи́тельный; *n* ро́дственник, родны́е *pl only*

reliable надёжный

religion рели́гия

religious религио́зный

remain оста́нутся – остава́ться R7 note 3; —ing остально́й

remark заме́тить – замеча́ют; замеча́ние, наблюде́ние; —able замеча́тельный

remedy лека́рство

remove удали́ть – удаля́ют

render aid/cooperation оказа́ть – ока́зывают по́мощь/соде́йствие

rendezvous свида́ние

renounce отказа́ться – отка́зываются от *чего́*

rent сни́мут – снима́ют

repair попра́вить – поправля́ют; ремо́нт; —ed в ремо́нте

repeat повтори́ть – повторя́ют

replace замени́ть – заменя́ют

report докла́д

represent предста́вить – представля́ют; —ation представле́ние; —ative представи́тель

republic респу́блика; —an респу̃лика́нский; Republican Party Республика́нская па́ртия

repulsive проти́вный

request про́сьба; (по)проси́ть R3.F

require (по)тре́бовать *кого́/чего́ or* чтобы; —ment тре́бование

resemble бы́ть похо́ж(им) на *кого́/что́*, подо́б/е/н(-ным) *кому́/чему́*

reserve заказа́ть – зака́зывают; (official priority, etc.) (за)брони́ровать

resonant consonant *gr* соно́рный согла́сный

resound разда́ться – раздава́ться

respect уваже́ние; уважа́ют; —ed уважа́емый

rest о́тдых, поко́й; отдохну́ть – отдыха́ют; get a good — вы́спаться – высыпа́ются; the — остально́й

restaurant рестора́н; столо́вая

restrain удержа́ть – уде́рживают; — self from удержа́ться – уде́рживаются от *чего́*

restrict *tr* ограни́чить – ограни́чивают; — self to/be —ed to ограни́читься – ограни́чиваются *кем/чём*

result результа́т; as a — of в результа́те *чего́*; with the — that та́к что

retain удержа́ть – уде́рживают

return *tr* возврати́ть – возвраща́ют; вер̆ну́ть *P only*; *intr* возврати́ться – возвраща́ются; вер̆ну́ться *P only adj* обра́тный; — trip туда́ и обра́тно

reveal обнару́жить – обнару́живают; —self обнару́житься – обнару́живаются

reverse *adj* обра́тный

revolt восста́нут – восстава́ть; восста́ние

revolution револю́ция; —ary революцио́нный

rich бога́тый

ride е́здить, ката́ются на *чём*

right (*vs.* wrong) пра́вый; he's — о́н пра́в; (*vs.* left: *no sh f*) пра́вый; not the — (one) не то́т R5 note 11; not the — way не та́к; *n* пра́во; have the — име́ют пра́во R9 note 12

ring (*also* call on the telephone) (по)звони́ть

rise (go up) подни́мутся (*past tense E*) – поднима́ются; *n* подъём; (stand up in revolt) восста́нут – восстава́ть

river река́
road доро́га, пу́ть
roast beef ро́стбиф
roasted жа́реный
robust кре́пкий
rocket раке́та
role ро́ль; play — (с)игра́ют (сыгра́ют) ро́ль
Roman ри́мский
Romania: *see* RUMANIA
room (space) ме́сто; hotel — но́мер; —s: *names of* V.9; —mate това́рищ по ко́мнате
root ко́рень *also gr*
round кру́глый
rubbish вздо́р
ruble ру́бль
rule пра́вило; руководи́ть *ке́м/че́м*, пра́вить *ке́м/че́м*, управля́ют *ке́м/ че́м*; as a — ка́к пра́вило
Rumania Румы́ния; —n румы́нский
run (function) иду́т; (of trains, etc.) иду́т, ходи́ть R7 note 12; — over перее́дут – переезжа́ют
rural се́льский, дереве́нский
Russia Росси́я; older — Ру́сь
rust-colored (rusty) ржа́вый
rustle шо́рох

sad гру́стный, печа́льный
sailor матро́с
sake: for the — of *кого́/чего́* ра́ди
salt со́ль
same то́т же (са́мый), оди́н и то́т же, одина́ковый; *see also* R5 note 10; all the — (nevertheless) всё же
samovar самова́р
satisfied (with) дово́льный
satisfy удовлетвори́ть – удовлетворя́ют *кого́/что́ or кому́/чему́*
sausage колбаса́
save берёгу́т
saying погово́рка I.7
scarcely едва́ ли, вря́д ли, чу́ть
scared: be — стра́шно *кому́/чему́*
schnitzel шни́цель
scholar (pupil) учени́к, учени́ца; (general) учёный
school *adj* уче́бный; — year уче́бный го́д;

—mate това́рищ по шко́ле
science нау́ка
scientist учёный
scissors но́жницы
sea мо́ре; *adj* морско́й
search for иска́ть
seat посади́ть – сажа́ют
second секу́нда
secretary секрета́рь, секрета́рша
secrete вы́делить – выделя́ют
section отделе́ние
security безопа́сность
see: R8 note 4; look R4 note 10; *see also* GO TO SEE; See you soon. До ско́рого свида́ния.
seem (по)каза́ться
seething кипу́чий
seldom ре́дко
select вы́брать – выбира́ют
sell прода́ть – продава́ть
semantic семанти́ческий
semester семе́стр
semicolon то́чка с запято́й
send (по)сла́ть *or* посла́ть(пошлю́т) – посыла́ют; — off отпра́вить – отправля́ют
senior ста́рший
sentence фра́за, предложе́ние
separate отде́льный; *v* отдели́ть – отделя́ют
sequence поря́док; *gr* tense — после́довательность времён
Serb се́рб, се́рб/ка
Serbia Се́рбия; —n се́рбский
Serbo-Croatian сербохорва́тский
serious серьёзный
serve служи́ть *кому́/чему́*; (food and in sports) пода́ть – подава́ть; (people, public) обслужи́ть – обслу́живают
service слу́жба, обслу́живание, услу́га(и); пода́ча
session: school — заня́тия
set (stand) R8.B; — out (start out) отпра́виться – отправля́ются, по- *motion verb with inceptive meaning* R4.A2
settle насели́ть – населя́ют; get —d устро́иться – устра́иваются
several R6.A2
severe стро́гий

shake (по)колебáть; — hand(s) (по)жмý рýку *комý*

shallow мéлкий

shape óбраз

share делить, разделить – разделя́ют

sharp (keen: of knife, mind) óстрый; (harsh, abrupt: of pain, sound, criticism) рéзкий; (time) рóвно; —ness (harshness, abruptness) рéзкость

shave (по)брéют(брить); — self (по)-брéют(брить)ся

shelf пóлка

shift (change) смéна

shifting stress *gr* подви́жнóе ударéние

shirt рубáшка

shoes (men's, with laces) боти́нки; (loafers without laces) тýфли

shore бéрег

short корóткий, крáткий; (of a person) ни́зкого рóста

should: *see* OUGHT

shoulder плечó

shout крик; кри́кнуть – кричáть

show показáть – покáзывают; (manifest, display) прояви́ть – проявля́ют, обнарýжить – обнарýживают

Siberia Сиби́рь

sick больнóй; — person больнóй; be — болéют; get — заболéют – заболевáют; (to hurt, pain) заболéть – заболевáют CL3.2; —ness болéзнь, заболевáние

side сторонá

sidewalk тротуáр

sight (eyesight) зрéние; — (of a city, etc.) достопримечáтельности; catch — of уви́деть

sign знак; significance значéние

signify знáчить, означáют

silent: be — молчáть; fall — замолчáть

silently мóлча

silver серебрó

similar (to) похóж(ий) на *когó/чтó*, подóбный *комý/чемý*

simple простóй

simultaneously with наряду́ с *кéм/чéм*

sin грех

since (time) с *тогó*; с тéх пор как; (causal) тáк как, поскóльку R9 note 3; ráз

IX.B7

sing (с)поют(пéть)

singular number *gr* еди́нственное числó

sit R9 note 7; — down R8.B; — down at table R9 note 7; — for a certain period просидéть – проси́живают

situation положéние, состоя́ние, обстанóвка

size нóмер

sja verbs глагóлы на-ся

ski лы́жа; *v* ходить/катáются на лы́жах

skirt ю́бка

sky нéбо; —scraper небоскрёб

Slav славяни́н (*pl* -я́не), славя́нка

Slavic (Slavonic) славя́нский

sleep: go to — идýт спать, ля́гут (лéчь) – ложи́ться спать; — oneself out вы́спаться – высыпáются; *n* с/ó/н

slightest: not the —: *see* LEAST

slightly немнóго, немнóжко

Slovakia Словáкия; Slovak словáцкий; словáк, словáч/ка

Slovenia Словéния; —n словéнский; словéн/е/ц, словéн/ка

slow мéдленный, ти́хий; run — (clock) отстáнут – отстⁿвáть

smear on намáзать – намáзывают

smile улы́бка; улыбнýться – улыбáются

smoke курить

snack закýска; have a — закуси́ть – закýсывают *чéм*

snow снéг; it's —ing снéг идёт

so: isn't it —? не прáвда ли? не тáк ли?; — much стóлько; — much the X for тéм *comp* X для

so-called тáк назывáемый

so-so тáк себé, срéдне

so that R7.C; (in order that) (для тогó, затéм, с тéм) чтóбы; (with the result that) тáк что

soccer футбóл

social общéственный

socialism социали́зм; socialist социали́ст; *adj* социалисти́ческий

society óбщество

sofa дивáн

soft (substances) мя́гкий; (sounds) ти́хий

soften (*also of consonants*) смягчи́ть(ся) – смягчáют(ся); —ing (*also of conson-*

ants) смягче́ние
soil по́чва
soldier солда́т
sole (only) еди́нственный
solemn торже́ственный
solid про́чный, кре́пкий
solve реши́ть – реша́ют
some не́сколько, нескольки-, не́которые, каки́е-нибудь; — . . ., others одни́ . . ., други́е
somebody кто́-то, кто́-нибудь, не́кто, не́кий
somehow ка́к-то
something что́-то, что́-нибудь, не́что, ко́е-что
sometimes иногда́
somewhat не́сколько, дово́льно
sonant: *see* RESONANT
song пе́сня; folk — наро́дная пе́сня
soon ско́ро (-ый); —er (rather) скоре́е R5.A9
sorrow печа́ль
sorry: be — for X жа́ль *кому́ кого́/что́*; be — that (по)жале́ют, что
sort ро́д, ти́п, вид
soul душа́
sound *also gr* зву́к; (noise) шу́м
soup су́п; beet — бо́рщ; cabbage — щи́; fish — уха́
sour ки́слый
source исто́чник
south юг; —ern ю́жный; —east юго-восто́к; —eastern юго-восто́чный; —west юго-за́пад; —western юго-за́падный
South Slavic южнославя́нский
Soviet *adj* сове́тский; — Union Сове́тский Сою́з
space: living — жилпло́щадь
Spain Испа́ния; Spaniard испа́нец, испа́нка; Spanish испа́нский
sparrow вороб/е́/й
speak: begin to — заговори́ть
special осо́бенный, осо́бый
specialist специали́ст
specific определённый
specify определи́ть – определя́ют
spectacle (spectator event) спекта́кль
speech (*also gr*: *see* DIRECT, INDIRECT) ре́чь;

make a — вы́ступить – выступа́ют с ре́чью
speed ско́рость
spelling system орфогра́фия, правописа́ние
spend (time) проведу́т – проводить, проживу́т – прожива́ют
spirit ду́х; out of —s не в ду́хе; —ual духо́вный
spite: in — of несмотря́ на *кого́/что́*; при R9 note 4
splendid замеча́тельный, прекра́сный
spoon ло́жка
sport(s) спо́рт; play —s занима́ются спо́ртом
spread распространи́ть(ся) – распространя́ют(ся); — on нама́зать – нама́зывают; — over распространи́ть(ся) – распространя́ют(ся)
spring (season) весна́; (source of water) клю́ч, исто́чник
square (city, etc.) пло́щадь
squeeze (по)жму́т – пожима́ют
stable про́чный
staff соста́в
stage (of development, etc.) эта́п; — play пье́са
stairs (stairway) ле́стница
stand R8.B; — up R8.B; — up from table R9 note 7
standard (banner) зна́мя; (level) у́ровень; living — жи́зненный у́ровень; (norm) но́рма
standstill: come to a — (noise, activity) за́мрут – замира́ют
star звезда́
start на́чнут – начина́ют, ста́нут R8.B
state госуда́рство; (territorial unit as of United States) шта́т I.5; *adj* госуда́рственный
station ста́нция (на)
stay оста́нуться – остава́ться R7 note 3
steak: *see* BEEFSTEAK
stem *gr* осно́ва; full — по́лная осно́ва
step: — away от/о/йду́т; — away from отступи́ть – отступа́ют; — forward (out) вы́ступить – выступа́ют
stern стро́гий

still ещё; пока́ (ещё), пока́ что; — X-ing
всё (ещё), всё вре́мя; (nevertheless) всё
равно́, всё же R5 note 6; *adj* ти́хий
stipulate обусло́вить – обусло́вливают
stomach желу́док
stop V.1; (come to a standstill): *see* STAND-
STILL
store магази́н; department — универса́ль-
ный магази́н
story расска́з; исто́рия; (floor) эта́ж
stout по́лный
straight прямо́й
strange стра́нный
strangle (за)души́ть
stream тече́ние
street у́лица
streetcar трамва́й
strength си́ла
strengthen уси́лить – уси́ливают
stress *gr* ударе́ние; — falls on ударе́ние
па́дает на *что́*
stressed ударя́емый, уда́рный
strict стро́гий
strictly speaking со́бственно говоря́
strike (hit) уда́рить – ударя́ют; (*vs.* miss;
hit home, etc.) попаду́т – попада́ют;
(*fig* amaze) порази́ть – поража́ют; (of
workers) бастова́ть; go on — заба-
стова́ть, *n* забасто́вка; —r бастую́-
щий
stroll гуля́ют
strong си́льный, кре́пкий
stronghold опло́т
structure структу́ра
struggle боро́ться; борьба́
student (college or above) студе́нт, сту-
де́нтка; (precollege) учени́к, учени́ца
studies учёба; (classes) заня́тия
study (teach/learn) II.7; *n* кабине́т
stupid глу́пый
subject те́ма; on the — of II.6; *gr* под-
лежа́щее
subjunctive mood сослага́тельное накло-
не́ние
subsequent дальне́йший; —ly впосле́д-
ствии, в дальне́йшем
substance вещество́
substantiate подтверди́ть – подтвержда́ют
subway метро́

succeed удаться – удава́ться *кому́/чему́*;
(prove able to) суме́ют VI.5
success успе́х; —ful успе́шный
successor пото́м/о/к
such тако́й, подо́бный, тако́го ро́да; as —
ка́к таково́й; — and — а тако́й-то
suddenly вдруг
suffer (по)страда́ют
sufficient доста́точно, доста́точный; be —
хвати́ть – хвата́ет *кого́/чего́*
suffix су́ффикс
sugar са́хар
suit под/о/йду́т – подходи́ть *кому́/чему́*;
(к) (clothing) костю́м
suitcase чемода́н
suite (hotel, etc.) но́мер
summer ле́то; in — ле́том
summit верши́на
summon вы́звать – вызыва́ют
sun со́лнце
superficial пове́рхностный
superlative *also gr* превосхо́дный; —
degree превосхо́дная сте́пень
supervise наблюда́ют за *ке́м/че́м*
supper у́жин; eat — (по)у́жинают
supply доста́вить – доставля́ют
support поддержа́ть – подде́рживают;
подде́ржка
suppose предположи́ть – предполага́ют;
let's — предполо́жим, допу́стим; —d
to R6.C
supreme верхо́вный
sure: I'm — я уве́рен/убеждён; to be —
пра́вда; *adversative meaning* VI.3
surely наверняка́; ведь
surface пове́рхность
surname фами́лия
surprise удиви́ть – удивля́ют; be —d уди-
ви́ться – удивля́ются *n* удивле́ние
surrender сдать(ся) – сдава́ть(ся), о́тдать-
(ся) – отдава́ть(ся)
surround окружи́ть – окружа́ют
survive переживу́т – пережива́ют
sustain вы́держать – выде́рживают
sweet сла́дкий; (of a person) ми́лый
swim плыву́т; *nondet* пла́вают
switch: — off вы́ключить – выключа́ют
— on включи́ть – включа́ют
syllabic *gr* слогово́й

syllable слóг
symbol знáк
sympathy учáстие
symphony симфóния
syntactic синтаксúческий
syntax сúнтаксис
system систéма, порядок, стрóй

table *also* (cuisine) стóл
take (deliver to a place) V.6; — exam сдавáть/держáть экзáмен; — for прúмут – принимáют за *когó/чтó*; — off (article of clothing) снúмут – снимáют; — clothes off раздéнуться – раздевáются; — measures прúмут – принимáют мéры; — part in прúмут – принимáют учáстие в *чём*; — photograph of снúмут – снимáют *когó/чтó*; — place: *see* PLACE; — up (occupy) зáймут – занимáют; (occupy self with) займýтся (*past tense E*) – занимáются *кéм/чём*
tale пóвесть, расскáз
talent талáнт; —ed талáнтливый
talk говорúть; (converse) разговáривают; — about: X is being —ed about рéчь идёт о *кóм/чём*; — over обсудúть – обсуждáют; —s (negotiations) переговóры (на)
tall высóкий, высóкого рóста
tank (military) тáнк
tape: red — волокúта
task (problem) задáча; (assignment) задáние
taste вкýс
tasty вкýсный
taxi таксú
teach (study/learn) II.7, R5 note 4; —er учúтель
technical school тéхникум
technique(s) тéхника
technology тéхника, технолóгия
telegram телегрáмма
telegraph телеграфúровать
telephone телефóн; (по)звонúть (по телефóну) R8 note 6; *adj* телефóнный; — receiver трýбка
tell сказáть – говорúть; (recount) рассказáть – расскáзывают R7 note 10

temperature температýра
temple хрáм
temporary врéменный
tender нéжный
tennis тéннис
tense *gr* врéмя; — sequence послéдовательность времён
terrestrial земнóй
terrible стрáшный, ужáсный
terribly (very bad; very much) ужáсно
territory крáй
textbook учéбник
thank God слáва бóгу
thanks to благодаря *комý/чемý*
that этот, тóт; такóй VIII.7
that is тó есть, т.е.
the X-er, the Y-er чéм *comp*, тéм *comp*
theater теáтр
theme тéма
then R7.A5; тогдá, затéм, потóм; в это/тó врéмя, знáчит
therefore поэтому
thermometer термóметр
thesis (dissertation) диссертáция
they *imps 3 pl* R8 note 8
thick тóлстый
thin тóнкий, худóй
thing вéщь
think (по)дýмают; дýмают CL4.2
third трéт/и/й: *see* R6 note 6
this этот, такóй VIII.7
though: *see* HOWEVER, ALTHOUGH
thought мысль; fall into — задýмаются – задýмываются
thoughtful внимáтельный
thrive здрáвствовать
throat гóрло
throw брóсить – бросáют
thus тáк, итáк, такúм óбразом, знáчит
ticket билéт
tie (together) связáть – связывают
tie (necktie) гáлстук; связь
time врéмя; порá R9 note 8; (a single, many, etc.) рáз; in/on — вóвремя; have — to успéют – успевáют; be on — for, make, успéют – успевáют на *чтó or* к *чемý*; in the — of при; for the first — впервые, (в) пéрвый рáз; at one — нéкогда; at this (the present)

— в настоя́щее вре́мя; this — на э́тот раз CL4.3; for the — being пока́; have a good — (go out) гуля́ют; in one's — в своё вре́мя; it is — to R9 note 8 What — is it? Ско́лько вре́мени? Кото́рый (сейча́с) час? R6.3
At what —...? Во ско́лько (часо́в) ...? В кото́ром часу́...? R6.3

tip (де́ньги) на чай; дать – дава́ть на чай

tire of уста́нут – уставать inf or от кого́/чего́

tired уста́лый; be/get — уста́нут – уставать; —ness уста́лость

to oneself про себя́ V.8

to (in order to) (для того́) чтобы R7.C, IX.A

toast (while drinking) тост

toe па́лец (на ноге́)

together вме́сте; put — соста́вить – составля́ют

toil труди́ться

toiler трудя́щийся

toilet туале́т; (room with —) убо́рная sub adj; (washing, combing, dressing, etc.) туале́т

tolerable сно́сный

tone тон

too то́же, та́кже; и III.1

tooth зуб

top верши́на; from the — све́рху

topic те́ма

torment му́чить; — self му́читься

total: in —, a — of всего́

tourist тури́ст

tower ба́шня

trace след

tractor тра́ктор

trade торго́вля; adj торго́вый

trait черта́

transcription транскри́пция

transfer переведу́т – переводи́ть

translate переведу́т – переводи́ть с чего́ на что́; translation перево́д; translator перево́дчик

transliteration транслитера́ция

transmit переда́ть – передава́ть

transport(ation) тра́нспорт

travel е́здить

treat (attempt to cure) лечи́ть; be —ed лечи́ться; (people and things) обраща́ются с кем/чем

tree де́рево

trick обма́нуть – обма́нывают

trip пое́здка; business/official — командиро́вка

troika тро́й/ка

trolleybus тролле́йбус

trouble труд; with — с трудо́м; without — без труда́

trousers брю́ки

true: (it is) — (concessive sense) пра́вда VI.3

truncate gr усеку́т – усека́ют

truncation gr усече́ние

truth пра́вда

try X.8; use of aspect to convey trying R2.A4

tsar царь; —ina цари́ца

tube тру́бка

turkey (hen) инде́йка

turn intr поверну́ть – повора́чивают; — attention to обрати́ть – обраща́ют внима́ние на кого́/что́; — to (address self to) обрати́ться – обраща́ются к кому́/чему́; — off вы́ключить – выключа́ют; — on включи́ть – включа́ют; — out вы́йдут – выходи́ть; — out to be оказа́ться – ока́зываются кем/чем; n о́чередь; in one's (its) — в свою́ о́чередь

twice два ра́за

type тип, род

typewriter (пи́шущая) маши́нка

typical типи́чный

Ukraine Украи́на; Ukrainian украи́нский

uncle дя́дя

uncomfortable неудо́бный

uncultured некульту́рный

under (during reign, tenure, etc.) при ком/чём R9 note 4; from — из-под кого́/чего́

understand (apprehend, interpret) воспри́мут – воспринима́ют

undertake предпри́мут – предпринима́ют

undertaking предприя́тие

underwear ни́жнее бельё

undress разде́нут – раздева́ют; get —ed разде́нутся – раздева́ются

unfortunately к сожале́нию

unhappy несча́стный

unified еди́ный

union сою́з

unit (military) часть

unite соедини́ть – соединя́ют; —d соединённый, еди́ный; United States (of America) Соединённые Шта́ты (Аме́рики)

unity еди́нство

universal универса́льный

university университе́т

unknown неизве́ст/ный, незнако́мый; the — неизве́стное

unless е́сли . . . не III.5

unlike X в противополо́жность кому́/чему́

unnecessary нену́жный

unpaired consonant непа́рный согла́сный

unpleasant неприя́тный

unspecific неопределённый

unstressed неударя́емый, безуда́рный

unsuccessful неуспе́шный

until пока́ . . . не (with verb) I.2; до чего́ (with noun); not — то́лько I.2, R9 note 5

unvoiced consonant глухо́й согла́сный

up: go — поднимутся (past tense E) – поднима́ются

uphill в го́ру also fig

upset беспоко́ить; be/become — беспоко́иться о ком/чём

upstairs (куда́) наве́рх; (где́) наверху́

Urals Ура́л (на)

USA США

usage употребле́ние; use VIII.9

used: get — to привы́к(ну)ть – привыка́ют

USSR СССР

usual обы́чный, обыкнове́нный

vacation кани́кулы; о́тпуск R10 note 4

vain напра́сный; in — напра́сно

valid действи́тельный

valley доли́на

vanilla ice cream сли́вочное моро́женое

variant вариа́нт

varied разнообра́зный, многообра́зный, разли́чный

various ра́зный, разли́чный

vary колеба́ться

vast огро́мный

vegetables о́вощи

velar consonant веля́рный согла́сный

verb глаго́л; sja verb глаго́л на -ся; reflexive — возвра́тный глаго́л; reciprocal — взаи́мный глаго́л; (in)transitive — (не)перехо́дный глаго́л

verbal глаго́льный; (from a verb, deverbative) отглаго́льный

versed: be — in разбира́ются в чём

very: the — са́мый

via че́рез что́ R4 note 20

victory побе́да

view (opinion) взгля́д; (scenery) ви́д; in — of ввиду́ чего́; point of — то́чка зре́ния; from the point of — of с то́чки зре́ния чего́

village дере́вня, село́; дереве́нский, се́льский

violin скри́пка

visible ви́дный

vision (eyesight) зре́ние

visit посети́ть – посеща́ют; motion verb в го́сти, быть в гостя́х; побыва́ют (где́); freq ходи́ть к кому́/чему́, быва́ют у кого́ R5.D2

vodka во́дка

voice го́лос; gr зало́г: see ACTIVE, PASSIVE

voiced consonant зво́нкий согла́сный

Volga Во́лга

volume объём

vowel гла́сный (зву́к); — shift перегласо́вка; — alternation чередова́ние гла́сных

wait: — for (подо)жда́ть; — on обслужи́ть – обслу́живают

waiter официа́нт

waitress официа́нтка

wake (up) tr (раз)буди́ть; intr просну́ться – просыпа́ются

wall стена́

war война́; adj вое́нный

wardrobe шкаф

warm тёплый

wash (вы́)мо́ют – вымыва́ют; — self (вы́)мо́ются – вымыва́ются; — face and hands умо́ются – умыва́ются; — against (of sea, etc.) омо́ют – омыва́ют; — dishes (вы́)мо́ют посу́ду

watch (observe, — over) наблюда́ют за ке́м/че́м; — out for берегу́тся кого́/чего́

wave волна́

way пу́ть; by the — кста́ти; in one's own — по-сво́ему; in X — X-ым о́бразом; in that — таки́м о́бразом; on the — по пути́ (куда́) R10 note 2; in its — своего́ ро́да; by — of через что R4 note 20; — out also fig вы́ход

weak сла́бый

wear носи́ть
She's —ing X today. На не́й сего́дня X.

weather пого́да

wedding сва́дьба

week неде́ля; —ly еженеде́льный

weigh (consider) сообрази́ть – сообража́ют

welcome приве́тствовать
Welcome! Добро́ пожа́ловать (куда́). You're —. (Don't mention it.) Не́ за что. Не сто́ит (благода́рности). На здоро́вье.

well здоро́вый; get — попра́виться – поправля́ются; be — (thrive) здра́вствовать; Well, ... Ну́, ... as — III.1

well-known изве́стный

were not: if it weren't for, were it not for е́сли не что́/кто́, не бу́дь кого́/чего́

west за́пад; —ern за́падный

West Slavic западнославя́нский

what's the matter В чём де́ло? Ну, что?; (with you, him, etc.) Что с ва́ми, с ни́м?; (surprise or reproach) Что вы́!; what is что тако́е R5 note 3

wheel колесо́

whereas VIII.1; ме́жду те́м как, тогда́ как, в то́ вре́мя как

which (a fact —) что V.10

while когда́, пока́; concessive VIII.1

white бе́лый

who is X кто тако́й R5 note 3

whole ве́сь, це́лый

whose ч/е/й; declension R6 note 6; usage R4 note 21

why почему́, заче́м, отчего́, к чему́; ведь

wide широ́кий

will во́ля

wind ве́тер

wind up (arrive at) попаду́т – попада́ют

wine вино́

winter зима́; in — зимо́й

wish (desire) (по)жела́ют; жела́ние; —es (greetings) пожела́ния; (congratulations, etc.) поздра́вить – поздравля́ют; поздравле́ние

wit у́м

without без кого́/чего́; get along — об/о/-йду́тся – обходи́ться без кого́/чего́; — X-ing, having X-ed R9.D, II.3

woe го́ре

woman же́нщина; old — стару́ха

wonder чу́до; —ful чу́дный

woods ле́с

word-formation словообразова́ние

word order поря́док сло́в

work рабо́та, тру́д; creative — тво́рчество; — of art произведе́ние иску́сства; v рабо́тают; — on (над ке́м/че́м), труди́ться; (run, function) иду́т R7 note 12; (study) занима́ются

worker n and sub adj рабо́чий; (more abstract, toiler) трудя́щийся; (employee, co-worker) сотру́дник

world ми́р, све́т; adj мирово́й

worry беспоко́ить; intr беспоко́иться о ко́м/чём

worst: if — comes to — в кра́йнем слу́чае

worth сто́ить VII.2

would: various translations p. 62

write: — down записа́ть – запи́сывают; — up (make official) офо́рмить – оформля́ют

writing (written language) пи́сьменность; adj пи́сьменный

wrong непра́вый; (incorrect) непра́вильный; не то́, не то́т, не та́к R5 note 11

X икс

Yalta Ялта
yard двóр
year год
yellow жёлтый

yesterday: day before — трéтьего дня́
youth ю́ноша; (as a group) молодёжь
Yugoslavia Югослáвия; Yugoslav юго-
    слáв, югослáвка; *adj* югослáвский

zero нýль; *adj* нулевóй

INDEX

All Russian and English words of grammatical or special lexical interest are listed with references in the General Vocabulary. This subject index gives only a few English words, mostly lexical items, plus a handful of Russian words, alphabetized according to the English letters that would transliterate them, which identify lesson topics or certain smaller points. In addition to general and specific subject headings, the index contains a few definitions, given after colons, usually without page references.

-*á*, nouns in stressed, 104

Abbreviations, list of, inside covers and 24–25
  used as independent words (secondary stress), 153

"About," words meaning, 165–166, 189–190
  with по plus dative, 164

Abstract meaning, adjectives in neuter singular form expressing, 144
  of motion verbs, 75–76, 82 n17

Accusative, vs. genitive as object of negated verb, 152 n2

plural, instead of genitive with animates, 260
of time, 113

Address, direct, 89–90, 141 n10

Adjectives, comparison of, 84–88
  compound ("part of body"), 300
  pertaining to a science or discipline, 163–164
  from (and vs.) participles, 131–132, 277, 312–313
  act like past passive participles, 137–138, 146 n8, 305 больно́й